Culture
and Values

Reproduced on the cover and title page:

Bernardo Bellotto. *Capriccio Romano*. 1742–1747. Oil on canvas,
117 × 132 cm. National Gallery, Parma.
(Cover: detail; Title Page: entire work.)

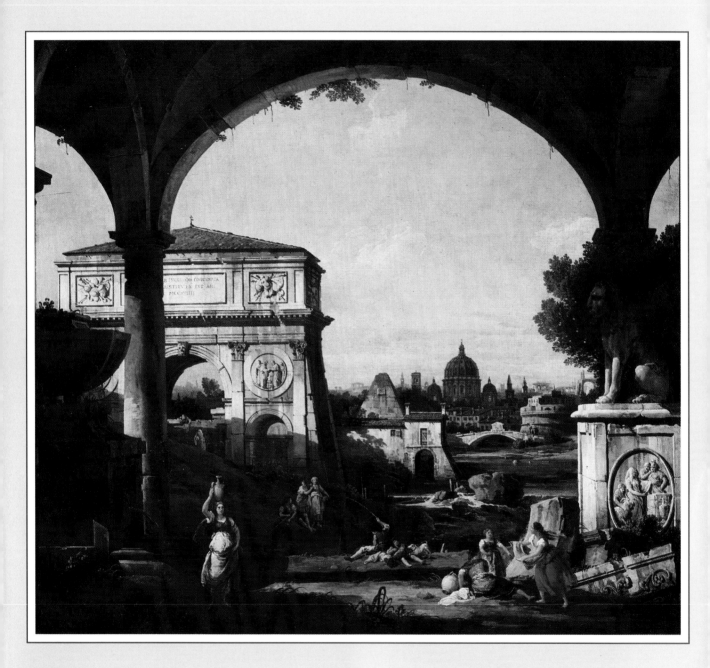

Holt, Rinehart and Winston

Fort Worth   Chicago   San Francisco   Philadelphia   Montreal
Toronto   London   Sydney   Tokyo

Culture and Values

A SURVEY OF THE WESTERN HUMANITIES

VOLUME I

Lawrence S. Cunningham
University of Notre Dame

John J. Reich

SECOND EDITION

Publisher   Charlyce Jones Owen
Acquisitions Editor   Janet Wilhite
Picture Research   Elsa Peterson
Project Management   York Production Services
Production/Manufacturing Coordinator   Kathleen Ferguson
Cover Design   David Harper
Composition/Color Separations   York Graphic Services
Printing and Binding   R. R. Donnelley & Sons

Library of Congress Cataloging-in-Publication Data

Cunningham, Lawrence.
    Culture and values : a survey of the Western humanities/Lawrence
Cunningham, John Reich.—2nd ed.
        p.   cm.
    Includes bibliographical references.
    ISBN 0-03-026589-4 (v. 1).—ISBN 0-03-026592-4 (v. 2)
    1. Civilization, Occidental.   2. Europe—Intellectual life.
I. Reich, John.   II. Title.
CB245.C86   1990
909'.09821—dc20   89-19989
                                                         CIP

ISBN: 0-03-026589-4

Address Editorial Correspondence to: 301 Commerce Street, Suite 3700, Fort Worth, TX 76102

Address Orders to: 6277 Sea Harbor Drive, Orlando, FL 32887
                1-800-782-4479, or 1-800-433-0001 (in Florida)

Printed in the United States of America

0 1 2 3   0 3 9   9 8 7 6 5 4 3 2 1

Holt, Rinehart and Winston, Inc.
The Dryden Press
Saunders College Publishing

Literary acknowledgments appear on page 416.
Photographic credits appear on pages 417–418.

Preface

In the first edition of this book we set out our aim: to create a readable and reliable textbook for college and university students in the integrated humanities that would satisfy the needs of the students and the standards of their instructors. We hoped to describe the most important landmarks of Western civilization's cultural heritage as enthusiastically as we could so that students would learn to love and appreciate them as we did when we first studied them ourselves.

We trust that our basic philosophy in preparing this book still shows forth in this new edition. We are still convinced of the need to use a historical approach to the humanities. We still believe that the text should focus fundamentally on the Western tradition, even if we try and remind ourselves that culture is not so neatly packaged. We are unapologetic about our focus on high culture—since that is the heritage which has shaped our civilization, for better or worse. Finally, we have held to our principle of selectivity both because we did not want this book to look like a catalogue and because we feel that fewer things understood well can stand as a springboard for broader understanding. Behind all of these convictions is our strong conviction that any textbook should be the first word and not the final one. We trust in the teacher to explain what we have left unexplained and to speak where we have been silent.

In the nearly ten-year period since the first edition appeared we have enjoyed the contact with students and teachers who have used the books and given us their reactions, generous in their praise and pointed in their criticisms, as they have tried to make our book their own. In that period, as we have predicted in the first preface, we also became aware that deficiencies, omissions, errors of fact, and unsubtle judgments would be found. And so they were. We are grateful for those criticisms just as we were chagrined by our mistakes. We trust that this new edition will respond to those criticisms and suggestions. We have taken them seriously and have tried to be responsive to them.

The decision to do a second edition of the book was made in late 1987 after the entire work was reviewed both by users and those who had no previous acquaintance with it. Their criticisms, our own discussions, and consultations with the Holt editors form the critical background for this second edition. *Culture and Values* is still here, but some significant changes and additions have been made.

In the first place, we have completely rewritten the chapter on the biblical tradition and placed it in a different part of the book to provide a better sense of chronological continuity. Secondly, we have added some boxed features to highlight different areas of cultural importance that we could not adequately treat in the text itself. *The Arts and Invention* talks about technological advances which help the student understand the arts better. Each chapter also has a box relating the contact of the West with other parts of the world; this addition is headed *East Meets West*. In order to personalize the chapters we also have a box entitled *Contemporary Voices* that provides some contact with a "living voice" of the period.

There have also been some editorial shifts in the chapters. In the first edition the primary readings were integrated into the running text. In this edition they are all at the ends of the chapters. We have also redone the end matter of each chapter with updated bibliographies, a pronunciation guide, and some exercises for further student reflection and discussion. We have also greatly expanded the glossary of terms in this edition. These changes were all done in response to the pedagogical needs expressed by our reviewers. It is for that same reason that we rearranged some of the sections in the individual chapters to make matters easier for those who use a team teaching approach in the classroom.

Some sections of the chapters were rewritten for greater clarity. We have also added more material on music, in response to a number of requests. Some readings were changed to provide longer selections or more representative ones. We felt that some of the earlier readings were too short and there were too many of them.

With the addition of so much new material it was necessary to cut the manuscript lest it should end up unmanageably bulky. With a heavy heart we reduced the interludes because instructors told us that they loved to read them but had not the time to present them in class. We have retained some of them because we think they provide a model for students to consider when they work in an interdisciplinary fashion. Likewise, we have cut the final epilogue to the book. Those cuts have been modest ones and we hope that they have not been in places which reflect favorites among our users; we hope, similarly, that the additions will be adequate compensation for those omissions.

We are now left with the happy task of expressing our gratitude to those who have helped us in preparing this second edition.

Jan Widmayer
Boise State University, Boise, ID

Dr. Charline Burton
Central State University, Edmond, OK

Jim Axley
Rose State College, Norman, OK

Donald Andrews
Valencia Community College, Orlando, FL

Janice Allen
Seminole Community College, Sanfore, FL

Timothy Ulman
Palomar College, San Marcos, CA

Kenneth Simonsen
College of Lake County, Wildwood, IL

In addition, the helpful comments given by reviewers of the first edition were most appreciated. Our thanks go to:

Margaret Flansburg
Central State University, Edmond, OK

Anna C. Blackman
Brevard Community College, Melbourne, FL

Karl Schleunes
University of North Carolina at Greensboro, NC

Paul Turpen
Eastern New Mexico University, Portales, NM

Dorothy Corsberg
Northeastern Jr. College, Sterling, CO

David McKillop
Grove City College, Grove City, PA

Sylvia White
Florida Jr. College Kent, Jacksonville, FL

Alma Williams
Savannah State College, Savannah, GA

Julia Walther
Grambling University, Rustin, LA

Arthur Chiasson
Suffolk University, Boston, MA

Barbara Kramer
Santa Fe Community College, Gainesville, FL

Charles Davis
Boise State University, Boise ID

This book began—as did the first stages of the revisions—while we served on the faculty of the Florida State University. We wish to thank the faculty and staff of the Department of Classics and the Department of Religion as well as the Program in Humanities and The Florida State University Study Center in Florence, Italy, for their assistance and their many kindnesses. Lawrence S. Cunningham is now with the Department of Theology at the University of Notre Dame. He is grateful to that department and its chair, Richard McBrien, for unfailing support and collegial atmosphere within which it is possible to write and think.

The staff at Holt, Rinehart and Winston exemplified professionalism and meticulous care in the production of this edition. We would like to single out Karen Dubno, who dealt with two not infrequently recalcitrant authors with a wholesome blend of determination and kindness. If this book deserves any praise at all, a large measure of it must be directed to Karen. Special thanks go to Mary Jo Gregory of York Production Services and Kathy Ferguson of Holt who effectively managed the intricate design and production; Elsa Peterson, for her dedication to the massive task of picture research; Buddy Barkalow, for his expertise in informational processing; Mary Pat Sitlington, for her many creative ideas, so important to the marketing of this book; and to our current editor, Janet Wilhite, who managed to move the office from New York to Fort Worth, and keep the book on schedule and on target.

Finally, we are grateful to all of the teachers and students who have used *Culture and Values* over the years. In a very basic sense, this book is theirs.

LSC
JJR

Contents

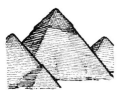

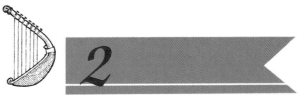

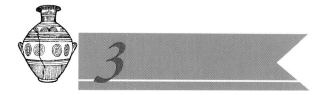

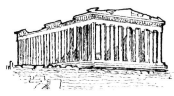

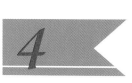

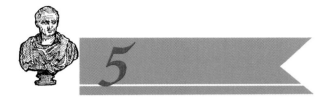

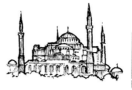

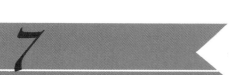 7

 8

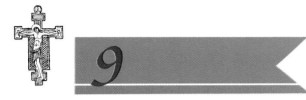

THE ARTS:
AN INTRODUCTION

One way to see the arts as a whole is to consider a widespread mutual experience: a church or synagogue service. Such a gathering is a celebration of written literature done, at least in part, in music in an architectural setting decorated to reflect the religious sensibilities of the community. A church service makes use of visual arts, literature, and music. While the service acts as an integrator of the arts, considered separately, each art has its own peculiar characteristics that give it shape.

Music is primarily a temporal art, which is to say that there is music when there is someone to play the instruments and sing the songs. When the performance is over, the music stops.

The visual arts and *architecture* are spatial arts that have permanence. When a religious service is over people may still come into the building to admire its architecture or marvel at its paintings or sculptures or look at the decorative details of the building.

Literature has a permanent quality in that it is recorded in books, although some literature is meant not to be read but to be heard. Shakespeare did not write plays for people to read but for audiences to see and hear performed. Books nonetheless have permanence in the sense that they can be read not only in a specific context but also at one's pleasure. Thus, to continue the religious-service example, one can read the psalms for their poetry or for devotion apart from their communal use in worship.

What we have said about the religious service applies equally to anything from a rock concert to grand opera: artworks can be seen as an integrated whole. Likewise, we can consider these arts separately. After all, people paint paintings, compose music, or write poetry to be enjoyed as discrete experiences. At other times, of course, two arts may be joined when there was no original intention to do so, as when a composer sets a poem to music or an artist finds inspiration in a literary text or, to use a more complex example, when a ballet is inspired by a literary text and is danced against the background of sets created by an artist to enhance both the dance and the text that inspired it.

However we view the arts, either separately or as integrated, one thing is clear: they are the product of human invention and human genius. When we speak of *culture* we are not talking about something strange or "highbrow"; we are talking about something that derives from human invention. A jungle is a product of nature, but a garden is a product of culture: human ingenuity has modified the vegetative world.

In this book we discuss some of the works of human culture that have endured over the centuries. We often refer to these works as *masterpieces,* but what does the term mean? The issue is complicated because taste and attitudes change over the centuries. Two hundred years ago the medieval cathedral was not appreciated; it was called Gothic because it was considered barbarian. Today we call such a building a masterpiece. Very roughly we can say that a masterpiece of art is any work that carries with it a surplus of meaning.

Having "surplus of meaning" means that a certain work not only reflects technical and imaginative skill but that its very existence also sums up the best of a certain age, which spills over as a source of inspiration for further ages. As one reads through the history of the Western humanistic achievement it is clear that certain products of human genius are looked to by subsequent generations as a source of inspiration; they have a "surplus of meaning." Thus the Roman achievement in architecture with the dome of the Pantheon both symbolized their skill in architecture and became a reference point for every major dome built in the West since. The dome of the Pantheon finds echoes in 6th-century Constantinople (Hagia Sophia); in 15th-century Florence (the Duomo); in 16th-century Rome (St. Peter's); and in 18th-century Washington, D.C. (the Capitol building).

The notion of "surplus of meaning" provides us with a clue as to how to study the humanistic tradition and its achievements. Admittedly simplifying, we can say that such a study has two steps that we have tried to synthesize into a whole in this book:

1. **The work in itself.** At this level we are asking the question of fact and raising the issue of observation: What is the work and how is it achieved? This question includes not only the basic information about, say, what kind of visual art this is (sculpture, painting, mosaic) or what its formal elements are (Is it geometric in style? bright in color? very linear? and so on) but also questions of its function: Is this work homage to politics? for a private patron? for a church? We look at artworks, then, to ask questions about both their form and their function.

This is an important point. We may look at a painting or sculpture in a museum with great pleasure, but that pleasure would be all the more enhanced were we to see that work in its proper setting rather than as an object on display. To ask about form and function, in short, is to ask equally about context. When reading certain literary works (such as the *Iliad* or the *Song of Roland*) we should read them aloud since, in their original form, they were written to be recited, not read silently on a page.

2. **The work in relation to history.** The human achievements of our common past tell us much about earlier cultures both in their differences and in their similarities. A study of the tragic plays that have survived from ancient Athens gives us a glimpse into Athenians' problems, preoccupations, and aspirations as filtered through the words of Sophocles or Euripides. From such a study we learn both about the culture of Athens and something about how the human spirit has faced the perennial issues of justice, loyalty, and duty. In that sense we are in dialogue with our ancestors across the ages. In the study of ancient culture we see the roots of our own.

To carry out such a project requires willingness really to look at art and closely read literature with an eye equally to the aspect of form/function and to the past and the present. Music, however, requires a special treatment because it is the most abstract of arts (How do we speak about that which is meant not to be seen but to be heard?) and the most temporal. For that reason a somewhat more extended guide to music appears below.

How to Look at Art

Anyone who thumbs through a standard history of art can be overwhelmed by the complexity of what is discussed. We find everything from paintings on the walls of caves and huge sculptures carved into the faces of mountains to tiny pieces of jewelry or miniature paintings. All of these are art because they were made by the human hand in an attempt to express human ideas and/or emotions. Our response to such objects depends a good deal on our own education and cultural biases. We may find some modern art ugly or stupid or bewildering. We may think of all art as highbrow or elitist despite the fact that we like certain movies (film is an art) enough to see them over and over.

Our lives are so bound up with art that we often fail to recognize how much we are shaped by it. We are bombarded with examples of graphic art (television commercials, magazine ads, record-album jackets, displays in stores) every day; we use art to make statements about who we are and what we value in the way we decorate our rooms and in the style of our dress. In all of these ways we manipulate artistic symbols to make statements about what we believe in, what we stand for, and how we want others to see us.

The history of art is nothing more than the record of how people have used their minds and imaginations to symbolize who they are and what they value. If a certain age spends enormous amounts of money to build and decorate churches (as in 12th-century France) and another spends the same kind of money on palaces (like 18th-century France) we learn about what each age values the most.

The very complexity of human art makes it difficult to interpret. That difficulty increases when we are looking at art from a much different culture and/or a far different age. We may admire the massiveness of Egyptian architecture but find it hard to appreciate why such energies were used for the cult of the dead. When confronted with the art of another age (or even our own art, for that matter) a number of questions we can ask of ourselves and of the art may lead us to greater understanding.

For what was this piece of art made? This is essentially a question of *context*. Most of the religious paintings in our museums were originally meant to be seen in churches in very specific settings. To imagine them in their original setting helps us to understand that they had a devotional purpose that is lost when they are seen on a museum wall. To ask about the original setting, then, helps us to ask further whether the painting is in fact devotional or meant as a teaching tool or to serve some other purpose.

Setting is crucial. A frescoed wall on a public building is meant to be seen by many people while a fresco on the wall of an aristocratic home is meant for a much smaller, more elite, class of viewer. A sculpture designed for a wall niche is going to have a shape different than one designed to be seen by walking around it. Similarly, art made under official sponsorship of an authoritarian government must be read in a far different manner than art produced by underground artists who have no standing with the government. Finally, art may be purely decorative or it may have a didactic purpose, but (and here is a paradox) purely decorative art may teach us while didactic art may end up being purely decorative.

What, if anything, does this piece of art hope to communicate? This question is one of *intellectual* or *emotional* context. Funeral sculpture may reflect the grief of the survivors or a desire to commemorate the achievements of the deceased or to affirm what the survivors believe about life after death or a combination of these purposes. If we think of art as a variety of speech we can then inquire of any artwork: What is it saying?

An artist may strive for an ideal ("I want to paint the most beautiful woman in the world" or "I wish my painting to be taken for reality itself" or "I wish to move people to love or hate or sorrow by my sculpture") or to illustrate the power of an idea or (as is the case with most primitive art) to "capture" the power of the spirit world for religious and/or magical purposes.

An artist may well produce a work simply to demonstrate inventiveness or to expand the boundaries of what art means. The story is told of Pablo Picasso's reply to a woman who said that her ten-year-old child could paint better than he. Picasso replied, "Congratulations, Madame. Your child is a genius." We know that before he was a teenager Picasso could draw and paint with photographic accuracy. He said that during his long life he tried to learn how to paint with the fresh eye and spontaneous simplicity of a child.

How was this piece of art made? This question inquires into both the materials and the skills the artist employs to turn materials into art. Throughout this book we will speak of different artistic techniques, like bronze casting or etching or panel painting; here we make a more general point. To learn to appreciate the *craft* of the artist is a first step toward enjoying art for its worth as art—to developing an "eye" for art. This requires *looking* at the object as a crafted object. Thus, for example, a close examination of Michelangelo's *Pietà* shows the pure smooth beauty of marble while his *Slaves* demonstrate the roughness of stone and the sculptor's effort to carve meaning from hard material. We might stand back to admire a painting as a whole, but then to look closely at one portion of it teaches us the subtle manipulation of color and line that creates the overall effect.

What is the composition of this artwork? This question addresses how the artist "composes" the work. Much Renaissance painting uses a pyramidal construction so that the most important figure is at the apex of the pyramid and lesser figures form the base. Some paintings presume something happening outside the picture itself (such as an unseen source of light); a cubist painting tries to render simultaneous views of an object. At other times an artist may enhance the composition by the manipulation of color with a movement from light to dark or a stark contrast between dark and light, as in the *chiaroscuro* of Baroque painting. In all these cases the artists intend to do something more than merely "depict" a scene; they appeal to our imaginative and intellectual powers as we enter into the picture or engage the sculpture or look at their film.

Composition, obviously, is not restricted to painting. Filmmakers compose with close-ups or tracking shots just as sculptors carve for frontal or side views of an object. Since all these techniques are designed to make us see in a particular manner, only by thinking about composition do we begin to reflect on what the artist has done. If we do not think about composition, we tend to take an artwork at "face value" and, as a consequence, are not training our "eye."

What elements should we notice about a work of art? The answer to this question is a summary of what we have stated above. Without pretending to exclusivity, we should judge art on the basis of the following three aspects:

Formal elements. What kind of artwork is it? What materials are employed? What is its composition in terms of structure? In terms of pure form, how does this particular work look when compared to a similar work of the same or another artist?

Symbolic elements. What is this artwork attempting to "say"? Is its purpose didactic, propagandistic, to give pleasure, or what? How well do the formal elements contribute to the symbolic statement being attempted in the work of art?

Social elements. What is the context of this work of art? Who is paying for it and why? Whose purposes does it serve? At this level many different philosophies come into play. A Marxist critic might judge a work in terms of its sense of class or economic aspects, while a feminist might inquire whether it affirms women or acts as an agent of subjugation and/or exploitation.

It is possible to restrict oneself to formal criticism of an artwork (Is this well done in terms of craft and composition?), but such an approach does not do full justice to what the artist is trying to do. Conversely, to judge every work purely in terms of social theory excludes the notion of an artistic work and, as a consequence, reduces art to politics or philosophy. For a fuller appreciation of art, then, all the elements mentioned above need to come into play.

How to Listen to Music

The sections of this book devoted to music are designed for readers who have no special training in musical theory and practice. Response to significant works of music, after all, should require no more specialized knowledge than the ability to respond to *Oedipus Rex,* say, or a Byzantine mosaic. Indeed, many millions of people buy recorded music in one form or another, or enjoy listening to it on the radio, without the slightest knowledge of how the music is constructed or performed.

The gap between the simple pleasure of the listener and the complex skills of composer and performer often prevents the development of a more serious grasp of music history and its relation to the other arts. The aim of this section is to help bridge that gap without trying to provide too much technical information. After a brief survey of music's role in Western culture we shall look at the "language" used to discuss musical works.

Music in Western Culture

The origins of music are unknown, and neither the excavations of ancient instruments or depictions of performers nor the evidence from modern primitive societies gives any impression of its early stages. Presumably, like the early cave paintings, it served some kind of magical or ritual purpose. This is borne out by the fact that music still forms a vital part of most religious ceremonies today, from the hymns sung in Christian churches or the solo singing of the cantor in an Orthodox Jewish synagogue to the elaborate musical rituals performed in Buddhist or Shinto temples in Japan. The Old Testament makes many references to the power of music, most notably in the famous story of the battle of Jericho, and it is clear that by historical times music played an important role in Jewish life, both sacred and secular.

By the time of the Greeks, the first major Western culture to develop, music had become as much a science as an art. It retained its importance for religious rituals; in fact, according to Greek mythology the gods themselves invented it. At the same time the theoretical relationships between the various musical pitches attracted the attention of philosophers such as Pythagoras (c. 550 B.C.), who described the underlying unity of the universe as the "harmony of the spheres." Later 4th-century-B.C. thinkers like Plato and Aristotle emphasized music's power to affect human feeling and behavior. Thus for the Greeks music represented a religious, intellectual, and moral force. Once again, music is still used in our own world to affect people's feelings, whether it be the stirring sound of a march, a solemn funeral dirge, or the eroticism of much modern "pop" music (of which Plato would thoroughly have disapproved).

Virtually all the music—and art, for that matter—to have survived from the Middle Ages is religious. Popular secular music certainly existed, but since no real system of notation was invented before the 11th century, it has disappeared without trace. The ceremonies of both the Western and the Eastern (Byzantine) church centered around the chanting of a single musical line, a kind of music that is called *monophonic* (from the Greek "single voice"). Around the time musical notation was devised, composers began to become interested in the possibilities of notes sounding simultaneously—what we would think of as harmony. Music involving several separate lines sounding together (as in a modern string quartet or a jazz group) became popular only in the 14th century. This gradual introduction of *polyphony* ("many voices") is perhaps the single most important development in the history of music, since composers began to think not only horizontally (that is, melodically) but also vertically, or harmonically. In the process the possibilities of musical expression were immeasurably enriched.

The Experience of Listening

"What music expresses is eternal, infinite, and ideal. It does *not* express the passion, love, or longing of this or that individual in this or that situation, but passion, love, or longing in itself; and this it presents in that unlimited variety of motivations which is the exclusive and particular characteristic of music, foreign and inexpressible in any other language" (Richard Wagner). With these words one of the greatest of all composers described the power of music to express universal emotions. Yet for those unaccustomed to serious listening, it is precisely this breadth of experience that is difficult to identify with. We can understand a joyful or tragic situation. Joy and tragedy themselves, though, are more difficult to comprehend.

There are a number of ways by which the experience of listening can become more rewarding and more enjoyable. Not all of them will work for everyone, but over the course of time they have proved helpful for many newcomers to the satisfactions of music.

1. *Before listening* to the piece you have selected, ask yourself some questions:

What is the historical context of the music? For whom was it composed—for a general or for an elite audience?

Did the composer have a specific assignment? If the work was intended for performance in church, for example, it should sound very different from a set of dances. Sometimes the location of the performance affected the sound of the music: composers of masses to be sung in Gothic cathedrals used the buildings' acoustical properties to emphasize the resonant qualities of their works.

With what forces is the music to be performed? Do they correspond to those intended by the composer? Performers of medieval music, in particular, often have to reconstruct much that is missing or uncertain. Even in the case of later traditions, the original sounds can sometimes be only approximated. The superstars of the 18th-century world of opera were the *castrati,* male singers who had been castrated in their youth and whose voices had therefore never broken; contemporaries described the sounds they produced as incomparably brilliant and flexible. The custom, which seems to us so barbaric, was abandoned in the 19th century, and even the most fanatic musicologist must settle for a substitute today. The case is an extreme one, but it points the moral that even with the best of intentions, modern performers cannot always reproduce the original sounds.

Does the work have a text? If so, read it through before you listen to the music; it is easiest to concentrate on one thing at a time. In the case of a translation, does the version you are using capture the spirit of the original? Translators sometimes take a simple, popular lyric and make it sound archaic and obscure in order to convey the sense of "old" music. If the words do not make much sense to you, probably they would seem equally incomprehensible to the composer. Music, of all the arts, is concerned with direct communication.

Is the piece divided into sections? If so, why? Is their relationship determined by purely musical considerations—the structure of the piece—or by external factors, the words of a song, for example, or the parts of a Mass?

Finally, given all the above, what do you expect the music to sound like? Your preliminary thinking should have prepared you for the kind of musical experience in store for you. If it has not, go back and reconsider some of the points above.

2. *While you are listening* to the music:

Concentrate as completely as you can. It is virtually impossible to gain much from music written in an unfamiliar idiom unless you give it your full attention. Read record-sleeve notes or other written information before you begin to listen, as you ask yourself the questions above, not *while* the music is playing. If there is a text, keep an eye on it but do not let it distract you from the music.

Concentrating is not always easy, particularly if you are mainly used to listening to music as a background, but there are some ways in which you can help your own concentration. To avoid visual distraction, fix your eyes on some detail near you—a mark on the wall, a design in someone's dress, the cover of a book. At first this will seem artificial, but after a while your attention should be taken by the music. If you feel your concentration fading, do *not* pick up a magazine or gaze around; consciously force your attention back to the music and try to analyze what you are hearing. Does it correspond to your expectations? How is the composer trying to achieve an effect? By variety of instrumental color? Are any of the ideas, or tunes, repeated?

Unlike literature or the visual arts, music occurs in the dimension of time. When you are reading, you can turn backward to check a reference or remind yourself of a character's identity. In looking at a painting, you can move from a detail to an overall view as often as you want. In music, the speed of your attention is controlled by the composer. Once you lose the thread of the discourse, you cannot regain it by going back; you must try to pick up again and follow the music as it continues—and that requires your renewed attention.

On the other hand, in these times of easy access to recordings, the same pieces can be listened to repeatedly. Even the most experienced musicians cannot grasp some works fully without several hearings. Indeed, one of the features that distinguishes "art" music from more "popular" works is its capacity to yield increasing rewards. On a first hearing, therefore, try to grasp the general mood and structure and note features to listen for the next time you hear the piece. Do not be discouraged if the idiom seems strange or remote, and be prepared to become familiar with a few works from each period you are studying.

As you become accustomed to serious listening, you will notice certain patterns used by composers to give form to their works. They vary according to the styles of the day, and throughout this book there are descriptions of each period's musical characteristics. In responding to the general feeling the music expresses, therefore, you should try to note the specific features that identify the time of its composition.

3. *After you have heard the piece,* ask yourself these questions:

Which characteristics of the music indicated the period of its composition? Were they due to the forces employed (voices and/or instruments)?

How was the piece constructed? Did the composer make use of repetition? Was there a change of mood and, if so, did the original mood return at the end?

What kind of melody was used? Was it continuous or did it divide into a series of shorter phrases?

If a text was involved, how did the music relate to the words? Were they audible? Did the composer intend them to be? If not, why not?

Were there aspects of the music that reminded you of the literature and visual arts of the same period? In what kind of buildings can you imagine it being performed? What does it tell you about the society for which it was written?

Finally, ask yourself the most difficult question of all: What did the music express? Richard Wagner described the meaning of music as "foreign and inexpressible in any other language." There is no dictionary of musical meaning, and listeners must interpret for themselves what they hear. We all understand the general significance of words like *contentment* or *despair,* but music can distinguish between a million shades of each.

Concepts in Music

There is a natural tendency in talking about the arts to use terms from one art form in describing another. Thus most people would know what to expect from a "colorful" story or a painting in "quiet" shades of blue. This metaphorical use of language helps describe characteristics that are otherwise often very difficult to isolate, but some care is required to remain within the general bounds of comprehension.

Line. In music, *line* generally means the progression in time of a series of notes: the melody. A melody in music is a succession of tones related to one another to form a complete musical thought. Melodies vary in length and in shape and may be made up of several smaller parts. They may move quickly or slowly, smoothly or with strongly accented (stressed) notes. Some melodies are carefully balanced and proportional, others are irregular and asymmetrical. A melodic line dictates the basic character of a piece of music, just as lines do in a painting or the plot line does for a story or play.

Texture. The degree to which a piece of music has a thick or thin *texture* depends on the number of voices and/or instruments involved. Thus the monophonic music of the Middle Ages, with its single voice, has the thinnest texture possible. At the opposite extreme is a 19th-century opera, where half a dozen soloists, chorus, and a large orchestra were sometimes combined. Needless to say, thickness and thinness of texture are neither good nor bad in themselves, merely simple terms of description.

Composers control the shifting texture of their works in several ways. The number of lines heard simultaneously can be increased or reduced—a full orchestral climax followed by a single flute, for example. The most important factor in the texture of the sound, however, is the number of combined independent melodic lines; this playing (or singing) together of two or more separate melodies is called *counterpoint*. Another factor influencing musical texture is the vertical arrangement of the notes: six notes played close together low in the scale will sound thicker than six notes more widely distributed.

Color. The color, or *timbre*, of a piece of music is determined by the means employed. Gregorian chant is monochrome, having only one line. The modern symphony orchestra has a vast range to draw upon, from the bright sound of the oboe or the trumpet to the dark, mellow sound of the cello or French horn. Some composers have been more interested than others in exploiting the range of color instrumental combinations can produce; not surprisingly, Romantic music provides some of the most colorful examples.

Medium. The *medium* is the method of performance. Pieces can be written for solo piano, string quartet, symphony orchestra, or any other combination the composer chooses. A prime factor will be the importance of color in the work. Another is the length and seriousness of the musical material. It is difficult, although not impossible, for a piece written for solo violin to sustain the listener's interest for half an hour. Still another is the practicality of performance. Pieces using large or unusual combinations of instruments stand less chance of being frequently programmed. In the 19th century composers often chose a medium that allowed performance in the home, thus creating a vast piano literature.

Form. *Form* is the outward, visible (or hearable) shape of a work as opposed to its substance (medium) or color. This structure can be created in a number of ways. Baroque composers worked according to the principle of unity in variety. In most Baroque movements the principal melodic idea continually recurs in the music, and the general texture remains consistent. The formal basis of much classical music is contrast, where two or more melodies of differing character (hard and soft, or brilliant and sentimental) are first laid out separately, then developed and combined, then separated again. The Romantics often pushed the notion of contrasts to extremes, although retaining the basic notions of classical form. Certain types of work dictate their own form. A composer writing a requiem mass is clearly less free to experiment with formal variation than one writing a piece for symphony orchestra. The words of a song strongly suggest the structure of the music, even if they do not impose it. Indeed, so pronounced was the Baroque sense of unity that the sung arias in Baroque operas inevitably conclude with a repetition of the words and music of the beginning, even if the character's mood or emotion has changed.

Thus music, like the other arts, involves the general concepts described above. A firm grasp of them is essential to an understanding of how the various arts have changed and developed over the centuries and how the changes are reflected in similarities—or differences—between art forms. The concept of the humanities implies that the arts did not grow and change in isolation from one another or from the world around. As this book shows, they are integrated both among themselves and with the general developments of Western thought and history.

How to Read Literature

"Reading literature" conjures up visions of someone sitting in an armchair with glasses on and nose buried in a thick volume—say, Tolstoy's *War and Peace*. The plain truth is that a fair amount of the literature found in this book was never meant to be read that way at all. Once that fact is recognized, reading becomes an exercise in which different methods can serve as a great aid for both pleasure and understanding. That becomes clear when we consider various literary forms and ask ourselves how their authors originally meant them to be encountered. Let us consider some of the forms that will be studied in this volume to make the point more specifically:

Dramatic literature. This is the most obvious genre of literature that calls for something more than reading the text quietly. Plays—ancient, medieval, Elizabethan, or modern—are meant to be acted, with living voices interpreting what the playwright wrote in the script. What seems to be strange and stilted language as we first encounter Shakespeare becomes powerful and beautiful when we hear his words spoken by someone who knows and loves language.

A further point: Until relatively recent times most dramas were played on stages nearly bare of scenery and, obviously, extremely limited in terms of lighting, theatrical devices, and the like. As a consequence, earlier texts contain a great deal of description that in the modern theater (and, even more, in a film) can be supplied by current technology. Where Shakespeare has a character say "But look, the morn in russet mantle clad / Walks o'er the dew of yon high eastward hill," a modern writer might simply instruct the lighting manager to make the sun come up.

Dramatic literature must be approached with a sense of its oral aspect as well as an awareness that the language reflects the intention of the author to have the words acted out. Dramatic language is meant to be *heard* and *seen*.

Epic. Like drama, epics have a strong oral background. It is a commonplace to note that before Homer's *Iliad* took its present form it was memorized and recited by a professional class of bards. Similarly, the *Song of Roland* was probably heard by many people and read by relatively few in the formative decades of its composition. Even epics that are more consciously literary echo the oral background of the epic; Vergil begins his elegant *Aeneid* with the words "Arms and the man I sing" not "Of Arms and the man I write."

The practical conclusion to be drawn from this is that these long poetic tales take on a greater power when they are read aloud with sensitivity to their cadence.

Poetry. Under this general heading we have a very complicated subject. To approach poetry with intelligence we need to inquire about the kind of poetry with which we are dealing. The lyrics of songs are poems, but they are better heard sung than read in a book. On the other hand, certain kinds of poems are so arranged on a page that not to see them in print is to miss a good deal of their power or charm. Furthermore, some poems are meant for the individual reader while others are public pieces meant for the group. There is, for example, a vast difference between a love sonnet and a biblical psalm. Both are examples of poetry, but the former expresses a private emotion while the latter most likely gets its full energy from use in worship: we can imagine a congregation singing a psalm but not the same congregation reciting one of Petrarch's sonnets to Laura.

In poetry, then, context is all. Our appreciation of a poem is enhanced once we have discovered where the poem belongs: with music? on a page? for an aristocratic circle of intellectuals? as part of a national or ethnic or religious heritage? as propaganda or protest or to express deep emotions?

At base, however, poetry is the refined use of language. The poet is the maker of words. Our greatest appreciation of a poem comes when we say to ourselves that this could not be said better. An authentic poem cannot be edited or paraphrased or glossed. Poetic language, even in long poems, is economical. One can understand that by simple experiment: take one of Dante's portraits in the *Divine Comedy* and try to do a better job of description in fewer words. The genius of Dante (or Chaucer in the *Prologue* to *The Canterbury Tales*) is his ability to sketch out a fully formed person in a few stanzas.

Prose. God created humans, the writer Elie Wiesel once remarked, because he loves a good story. Narrative is as old as human history. The stories that stand behind the *Decameron* and *The Canterbury Tales* have been shown to have existed not only for centuries but in widely different cultural milieus. Stories are told to draw out moral examples or to instruct or warn, but, by and large, stories are told because we enjoy hearing them. We read novels in order to enter into a new world and suspend the workaday world we live in, just as we watch films for the same purpose. The difference between a story and a film is that one can linger over a story, but in a film there is no "second look."

Some prose obviously is not fictional. It can be autobiographical like Augustine's *Confessions* or it may be a philosophical essay like Jean-Paul Sartre's attempt to explain what he means by existentialism. How do we approach that kind of writing? First, with a willingness to listen to what is being said. Second, with a readiness to judge: Does this passage ring true? What objections might I make to it? and so on. Third, with an openness that says, in effect, there is something to be learned here.

A final point has to do with attitude. We live in an age in which much of what we know comes to us in very brief "sound bites" via television and much of what we read comes to us in the disposable form of newspapers and magazines and inexpensive paperbacks. To read—*really* to read—requires that we discipline ourselves to cultivate a more leisurely approach to that art. There is merit in speed-reading the morning sports page; there is no merit in doing the same with a poem or a short story. It may take time to learn to slow down and read at a leisurely pace (leisure is the basis of culture, says Aristotle), but if we learn to do so we have taught ourselves a skill that will enrich us all our lives.

PREHISTORY

EGYPT

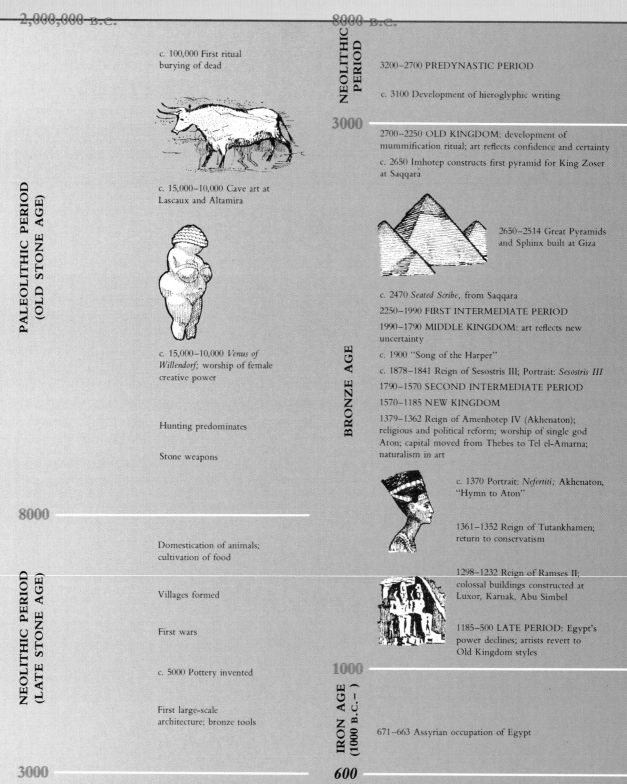

2,000,000 B.C.   8000 B.C.

NEOLITHIC PERIOD

PALEOLITHIC PERIOD (OLD STONE AGE)

NEOLITHIC PERIOD (LATE STONE AGE)

BRONZE AGE

IRON AGE (1000 B.C.–)

c. 100,000 First ritual burying of dead

3200–2700 PREDYNASTIC PERIOD

c. 3100 Development of hieroglyphic writing

3000

c. 15,000–10,000 Cave art at Lascaux and Altamira

2700–2250 OLD KINGDOM: development of mummification ritual; art reflects confidence and certainty

c. 2650 Imhotep constructs first pyramid for King Zoser at Saqqara

2650–2514 Great Pyramids and Sphinx built at Giza

c. 15,000–10,000 *Venus of Willendorf;* worship of female creative power

c. 2470 *Seated Scribe,* from Saqqara

2250–1990 FIRST INTERMEDIATE PERIOD

1990–1790 MIDDLE KINGDOM: art reflects new uncertainty

c. 1900 "Song of the Harper"

c. 1878–1841 Reign of Sesostris III; Portrait: *Sesostris III*

1790–1570 SECOND INTERMEDIATE PERIOD

1570–1185 NEW KINGDOM

Hunting predominates

1379–1362 Reign of Amenhotep IV (Akhenaton); religious and political reform; worship of single god Aton; capital moved from Thebes to Tel el-Amarna; naturalism in art

Stone weapons

c. 1370 Portrait: *Nefertiti;* Akhenaton, "Hymn to Aton"

8000

1361–1352 Reign of Tutankhamen; return to conservatism

Domestication of animals; cultivation of food

1298–1232 Reign of Ramses II; colossal buildings constructed at Luxor, Karnak, Abu Simbel

Villages formed

1185–500 LATE PERIOD: Egypt's power declines; artists revert to Old Kingdom styles

First wars

c. 5000 Pottery invented

1000

First large-scale architecture; bronze tools

671–663 Assyrian occupation of Egypt

3000   600

Most dates are approximate

MESOPOTAMIA   AEGEAN WORLD

1

The Beginnings of Civilization

c. 6000 Introduction of new agricultural techniques from the East

3500–2350 SUMERIAN PERIOD: development of pictographic writing; construction of first ziggurats; cult of mother goddess

c. 3000 *Lady of Warka*

2800–2000 Early Minoan Period on Crete; growth of Cycladic culture

c. 2700 Reign of Gilgamesh

c. 2500 Cycladic idol

c. 2600–2400 *Ram in a Thicket,* from Royal Cemetery at Ur

2350–2150 AKKADIAN PERIOD: rule of Sargon and descendants; ended by invasion of Gutians from Iran

2000–1600 Middle Minoan Period on Crete; construction of palace complexes; development of linear writing

2330–2320 *Head of Akkadian king,* probably Sargon

c. 2300 *Stele of Naram-Sin*

2150–1900 NEO-SUMERIAN PERIOD

c. 1700 Knossos Palace destroyed by earthquake and rebuilt on grander scale; *Wasp Pendant,* from Mallia

2100–2000 Construction of ziggurat at Ur

1600–1400 Late Minoan Period on Crete

c. 2100 Gudea, governor of Lagash

c. 1600 First Mycenaean palace constructed; Royal Grave Circle at Mycenae

c. 2000 Earliest version of *The Epic of Gilgamesh*

c. 1600 *Snake Goddess,* from Knossos

1900–1600 BABYLONIAN PERIOD

1792–1750 *The Law Code of Hammurabi*

c. 1550 Gold death mask, from Mycenae

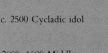

c. 1760 *Stele of Hammurabi*

1500 Frescoes from House Delta, Thera

1400 Fall of Knossos and decline of Minoan civilization

1400–1200 Mycenaean empire flourishes

1250 Mycenaean war against Troy

1600–1150 KASSITE PERIOD

100 Final collapse of Mycenaean power

1150–612 ASSYRIAN PERIOD

1100–1000 DARK AGE

883–859 Reign of Assurnasirpal II; palace at Nimrud

1000–750 HEROIC AGE

c. 900–700 Evolution of Homeric epics *Iliad* and *Odyssey*

668–626 Reign of Assurbanipal; palace at Nineveh

750–600 AGE OF COLONIZATION

612 Fall of Nineveh

The basic advances that made possible the growth of Western civilization were first achieved by the earlier civilizations of the ancient Middle East.

These ancient peoples were the first who systematically produced food, mined and processed metals, organized themselves into cities, and devised legal and moral codes of behavior, together with systems of government and religion. In all these areas they had a profound influence on later peoples. At the same time they produced a major artistic tradition which, quite apart from its high intrinsic interest, was to have a number of effects on the development of Western art.

To discover the origins of Western civilization, therefore, we must look at cultures that at first seem remote in both time and place. Yet these peoples produced the achievements described in this chapter—achievements that form the background to the history of our own culture.

The Earliest People and Their Art

Even the earliest civilizations appeared relatively late in human history, at the beginning of the period known as the Neolithic or Late Stone Age (c. 8000 B.C.). The process of human evolution is long and confusing, and many aspects of it remain uncertain. Our first ancestors probably appeared between a million and half a million years ago, in the Paleolithic period or Old Stone Age. For most of the succeeding millennia, people were dominated by the physical forces of geography and climate, able to keep themselves alive only by a persistent search for food and shelter. Those who chose the wrong places or the wrong methods did not survive, while others were preserved by their instincts or good fortune.

Primitive conditions hardly encouraged the growth of civilization, yet there is some evidence of a kind of intellectual development. Archaeological evidence has shown that about one hundred thousand years ago the ancestors of *Homo sapiens* belonging to the type known as Neanderthal people were the first to bury their dead carefully and place funerary offerings in the graves—the earliest indication of the existence of religious beliefs.

Toward the end of the Paleolithic period, around 15,000 B.C., there was a major breakthrough. The human desire for self-expression resulted in the invention of visual art. The cave paintings of Lascaux and Altamira and statuettes like the *Venus of Wil-*

1.1 Hall of Bulls, left wall, Lascaux (Dordogne), France. c. 15,000–10,000 B.C. Paintings like these were not intended to be decorations, since they are not in the inhabited parts of the caves but in the dark inner recesses. They probably had magical significance for their creators, who may have believed that gaining control of an animal in a painting would help to defeat it in the hunt.

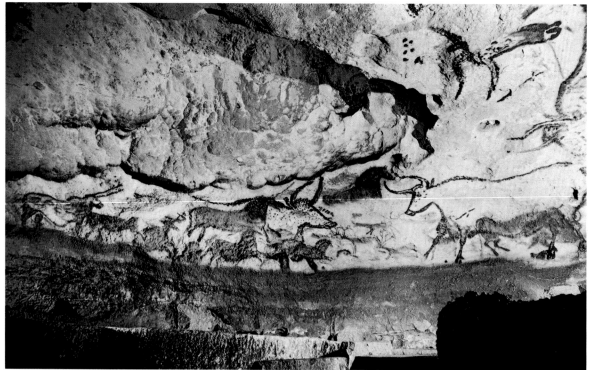

lendorf are among the earliest products of the human creative urge. Although the art of this remote age would be valuable for its historical significance alone, many of the paintings and statues can stand as masterpieces in their own right. The lines are concentrated but immensely expressive. In some cases artists used the surface on which they were painting to create an added sense of realism—a bulge on a cave wall suggested the hump of a bull [1.1]. The combination of naturalistic observation and abstraction can only be described as sophisticated, and since their discovery in our own century the paintings have served as a powerful inspiration to modern eyes.

The choice of subjects tells us something about the world view of Paleolithic people. The earliest cave paintings show animals and hunting, which played a vital part in providing food and clothing. More significant, perhaps, is the fact that all the oldest known statuettes of human figures represent women, who are shown with their sexual characteristics emphasized or enlarged [1.2]. The Paleolithic world perhaps saw woman's practical role—the source of birth and life—as symbolic of a more profound feminine force that underlay the masculine world of the hunt. Worship of female creative power was also to play an important part in the religion of the ancient Middle East and of Bronze Age Greece. Even though the Greeks of a later period emphasized other aspects of human power, reverence for a mother goddess or Earth Mother was to live on.

The Neolithic period (c. 8000 B.C.) represents in all aspects a major break with the past. After a million years of hunting, ways to domesticate animals and cultivate food were discovered. People began to gather together in villages where they could lead a settled existence. The development of improved farming techniques made it possible for a community to accumulate stores of grain and thereby become less dependent for their survival on a good harvest each year. But these stores provided a motive for raids by neighboring communities. Thus war, for the first time in human history, became profitable. Other more constructive changes followed at a rapid pace. Pottery was invented around 5000 B.C. and not long afterward metal began to replace stone as the principal material for tools and weapons. The first metal used was copper, but it was soon discovered that an alloy of copper and tin would produce a much stronger metal, bronze. The use of bronze became widespread, giving its name to the Bronze Age, which lasted from around 3000 B.C. to the introduction of iron around 1000 B.C.

At the beginning of the Bronze Age, large-scale architecture began to appear. The fortified settlements that had been established in Egypt and Mesopotamia now were able to develop those aspects of

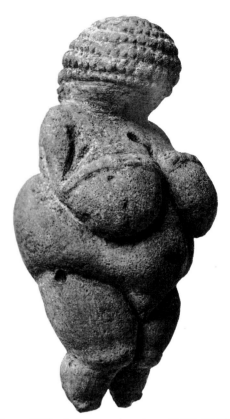

1.2 *Venus of Willendorf.* Lower Austria, c. 30,000–25,000 B.C. Limestone, height 4⅜″ (11 cm). Natural History Museum, Vienna. This tiny statuette is one of a series of female figurines from the Upper Paleolithic period that are known as Venus figures. The statuette, which has no facial features, is evidently a fertility symbol.

existence which entitle them to be called the first true civilizations.

Egypt and Mesopotamia have much in common. Their climates are similar and both are dominated by great rivers, Egypt by the Nile and Mesopotamia by the Tigris and Euphrates (see map on p. 14). Yet each was to develop its own distinct culture and make its own contribution to the history of civilization. Egypt is discussed first in the following account, but both areas developed over the same general time span.

Ancient Egypt

One major determinant in the development of ancient Egyptian culture was geography. In total area, ancient Egypt was only a little larger than the State of Maryland. At the delta of the Nile was Lower Egypt, broad and flat, within easy reach of neighboring parts of the Mediterranean. Upper Egypt, more isolated

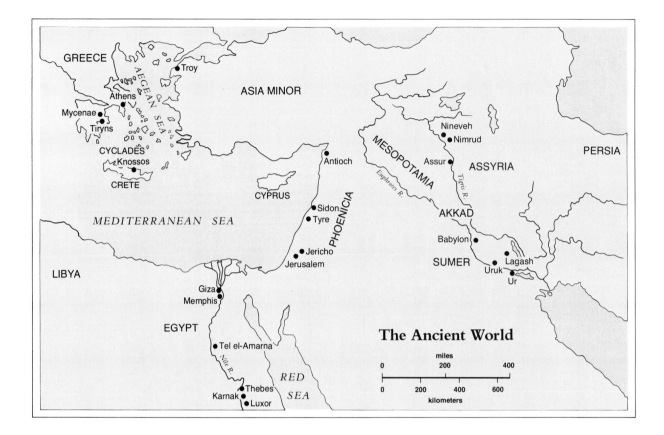

The Ancient World

from foreign contacts, consisted of a long narrow strip of fertile soil, hemmed in by high cliffs and desert, running on either side of the Nile for most of its 1250 miles (2000 kilometers). Since rainfall was very sparse along the Nile, agriculture depended on the yearly flooding of the river.

The immensely long span of Egyptian history was divided into 31 dynasties by an Egyptian priest, Manetho, who wrote a *History of Egypt* in Greek around 280 B.C. Modern scholars still follow his system, putting the dynasties into four groups and calling the period that preceded them the Predynastic. The four main divisions, with their approximate dates, are: the Old Kingdom, c. 2700 B.C.; the Middle Kingdom, c. 1990 B.C.; the New Kingdom, c. 1570 B.C.; and the Late Period, c. 1185 B.C. until Egypt was absorbed into the Persian empire around 500 B.C. The periods were separated from one another by intermediate times of disturbances and confusion.

In spite of its long history, the most striking feature of Egyptian culture is its unity and consistency. Nothing is in stronger contrast to the process of dynamic change initiated by the Greeks and still characteristic of our own culture than the relative absence of change of Egyptian art, religion, language, and polit-

ical structure over thousands of years. Naturally, even the Egyptians were subject to outside influences, and events at home and abroad affected their world view. It is possible to trace a mood of increasing pessimism from the vital, life-affirming spirit of the Old Kingdom to the New Kingdom vision of death as an escape from the grim realities of life. Nevertheless, the Egyptians maintained a strong resistance to change. Their art, in particular, remained conservative and rooted in the past.

In a land where regional independence already existed in the natural separation of Upper from Lower Egypt, national unity was maintained by a strong central government firmly controlled by a single ruler, the pharaoh. He was regarded as a living god, the equal of any other deity. He had absolute power, although the execution of his orders depended on a large official bureaucracy whose influence tended to increase in time.

Beneath the pharaoh were the priests, who saw as their responsibility the preservation of traditional religious beliefs. One of the most fundamental of these was the concept of divine kingship involving the pharaoh himself, a belief that reflected the Egyptian view of creation. The first great god of Egyptian religion, the sun god Aton-Ra, had created the world by

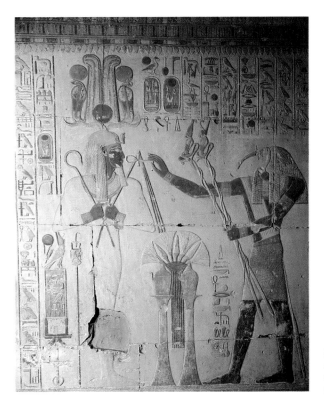

1.3 Painted relief from the funerary temple of Sethos I at Abydos. c. 1300 B.C. Sethos in the guise of the god Osiris, standing at left, is conversing with Thoth, the ibis-headed god of writing.

imposing order on the primeval chaos of the universe; in the same way, the pharaoh ordered and controlled the visible world.

The most striking aspect of Egyptian religious thought, however, is its obsession with immortality and the possibilities of life after death. All Egyptians, not only the ruling class, were offered the hope of survival in the next world as a reward for a good life in a form that was thought of in literal, physical terms. Elaborate funeral rituals at which the dead would be judged and passed as worthy to move on to the afterlife began to develop. The god who presided over these ceremonies was Osiris [1.3]. The worship of Osiris, his wife Isis, and their son, the falcon god Horus, which came in time to symbolize a sense of spiritual afterlife, as opposed to simple material survival, represented the mystical side of Egyptian religion. Osiris himself, according to the myth, had been killed and then reborn, providing a divine parallel to the annual rebirth of the land caused by the flooding Nile.

At the same time the Egyptians worshiped a host of other deities, subdeities, and nature spirits whose names were often confused and sometimes interchangeable. These gods, responsible for all aspects of existence, inspired mythology and ritual that affected the daily life of every Egyptian. They included Hathor, the goddess of beauty and love, often represented as a cow; Bes, the god of war; and Hapi,

the god of the Nile. A number of animals, like the jackal and the cat, also had special sacred significance (Table 1.1).

Traditional Egyptian religion involved, then, a bewildering confusion of figures whose rights and privileges were jealously guarded by their priests. One of the ways to worship them was to give them visible form in works of art—a principal function of Egyptian artists. In addition to producing images of deities, artists were required to provide temples and shrines where they could be honored. Even the buildings that commemorated the names and deeds of real people served religious purposes. Thus the same central authority that controlled religion affected the development of the arts. The pharaoh's court laid down the standards applied throughout Egypt. Individual artists had little opportunity to exercise their own ingenuity by deviating from them.

The Old and Middle Kingdoms

The huge scale of many Egyptian works of art is at least in part the result of the easy availability of stone, the most frequently used material from the early Old Kingdom to the Late Period. In the Third Dynasty, the architect Imhotep used stone to construct the earliest pyramid as a tomb for his master, the pharaoh Zoser. This began the tradition of building massive

TABLE 1.1	Principal Egyptian Deities	
Aton-Ra	Sun God	Creator of Heaven and Earth
Osiris	King of the Underworld	Judge of the Dead
Isis	Sister and Wife of Osiris	Mourner of the Dead
Horus	Son of Isis and Osiris	God of the Morning Sun
Chensu	Moon God	Human-headed with crescent moon
Ptah	Father of the Gods	Created humans
Thoth	Ibis (bird) God	The Scribe of the Gods
Set	Brother of Osiris	Personification of Evil
Anubis	Jackal God	God of the Dead
Hapi	God of the Nile	Fertility God
Hathor	Cow Goddess	Sky Goddess
Seker	Hawk God	God of the Night Sun

funerary monuments that would serve to guarantee immortality for their occupants. At the same time, the practice of mummification developed. The body was embalmed to maintain its physical form, since Egyptian religious belief held that preservation of the body was necessary for the survival of the soul. Im-

hotep himself, the first architect known to history, was in later ages regarded as the epitome of wisdom and was deified.

The great age of the pyramid came in the Fourth Dynasty with the construction of the three colossal pyramids at Giza for the pharaohs Cheops, Chefren,

1.4 Sphinx at Giza. c. 2540–2514 B.C. Limestone, length 240′ (73.2 m), height 65′ (19.83 m). The lion's body symbolizes immortality. The pharaohs were often buried in lion skins. About 500 yards (457 meters) away is the Pyramid of Chefren.

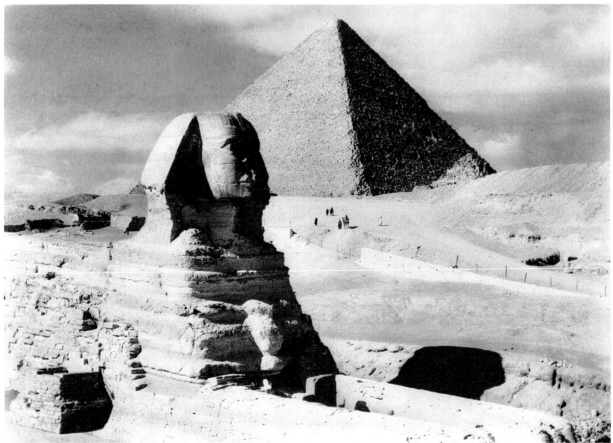

and Mycerinus [1.4]. In size and abstract simplicity, these structures show Egyptian skill in design and engineering on a massive scale—an achievement made possible only by slave labor. The pyramids and almost all other Egyptian works of art perpetuate the memories of members of the upper classes, but their life style would not have been possible without slaves. There were also many poor Egyptians who were farmers. We still know little about the farmers and slaves.

The construction of the pyramids was an elaborate and complex affair. Stone quarried on the spot formed the core of each structure, but the fine limestone blocks used for facing came from across the Nile. These were quarried in the dry season; then when the floods came they were ferried across the river, cut into shape, and dragged into place. At the center of each pyramid was a chamber in which was placed the mummified body of the pharaoh, surrounded by the treasures that were to follow him into the next life. These massive constructions the pharaohs planned as their resting places for eternity and as monuments that would perpetuate their names. Their success was partial. Four and a half thousand years later, their names are remembered—their pyramids, still dominating the flat landscape, symbolize the enduring character of ancient Egypt. As shelters for their occupants and their treasures, however, the pyramids were vulnerable. The very size of the pyramids drew attention to the riches hidden within them, and robbers were quick to tunnel through and plunder them, sometimes only shortly after the burial chamber had been sealed.

Chefren, who commissioned the second of the three pyramids at Giza, was also responsible for perhaps the most famous of all Egyptian images, the colossal Sphinx [1.4], a guardian for his tomb. The aloof tranquility of the human face, perhaps a portrait of the pharaoh, set on a lion's body made an especially strong impression fifteen hundred years later on the Classical Greeks, who saw it as a divine symbol of the mysterious and enigmatic. Greek art makes frequent use of the sphinx as a motif, and it also appears in Greek mythology, most typically in the story of how Oedipus solved its riddle and thereby saved the Greek city of Thebes from disaster.

The appearance of Chefren himself is preserved for us in a number of statues that are typical of Old Kingdom art [1.5]. The sculptor's approach to anatomy and drapery is realistic, and details are shown with great precision. But the features of the pharaoh are idealized; it is a portrait not of an individual but of the concept of divine power, power symbolized by the falcon god Horus perched behind the pharaoh's head. The calmness, even indifference, of the expression is particularly striking.

The art of the Old Kingdom reflects a mood of confidence and certainty that was brought to an abrupt end around 2200 B.C. by a period of violent disturbance. Divisions between the regions began to strengthen the power of local governors. By the time of the Middle Kingdom, it was no longer possible for pharaoh, priests, or nobles to face the future with complete trust in divine providence. Middle Kingdom art reflects this new uncertainty in two ways. On the one hand, the Old Kingdom came to represent a kind of Golden Age; artists tried to recapture its lofty serenity in their own works. At the same time, the more troubled spirit of the new period is reflected in the massive weight and somber expressions of some of the official portraits. The furrowed brow and grim look of Sesostris III convey the impression that to be a Middle Kingdom pharaoh was hardly a very relaxing occupation [1.6].

1.5 *Chefren*. Giza, c. 2560 B.C. Dark green diorite, height 5′ (1.52 m). Egyptian Museum, Cairo.

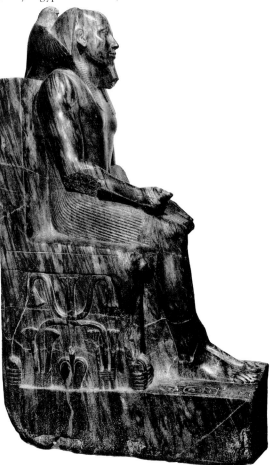

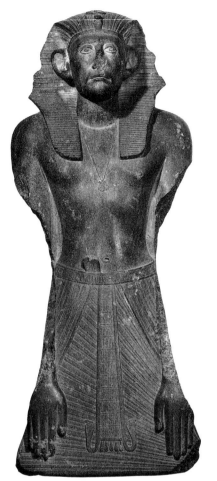

1.6 *Sesostris III.* c. 1878–1841 B.C. Black granite, height 4'10½" (1.5 m). Egyptian Museum, Cairo.

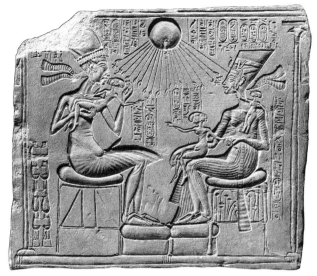

1.7 *Akhenaton, Nefertiti, and Three of Their Children.* Amarna, c. 1370–1350 B.C. Limestone relief, height 17" (43 cm). Egyptian Museum, State Museums, West Berlin. The naturalism of this relief, verging on sentimentality, is typical of late Amarna art.

1.8 *Queen Nefertiti.* Tel el-Amarna. c. 1370 B.C. Painted limestone, height 20" (51 cm). State Museums, West Berlin. Though the portrait is not exaggerated, it is idealized.

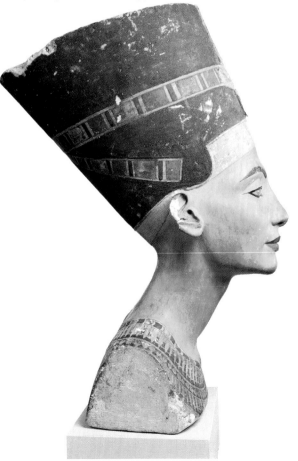

The New Kingdom

In spite of increasing contacts with foreign cultures, New Kingdom artists continued basically to work within age-old traditions. Like virtually all artists in the ancient world they depicted the idea of what they wanted to show rather than its actual appearance; an eye in a profile carving, for example, would be depicted as if seen from the front. This approach is often called "conceptual," as opposed to the "descriptive" style the Greeks were to develop. In the Eighteenth Dynasty, however, there was a remarkable change. The pharaoh Amenhotep IV, who ruled from 1379 to 1362 B.C., single-handedly attempted a total reform of Egyptian religious and political life. He replaced the numberless deities of traditional religion with a single one, the sun god Aton, and changed his own name to Akhenaton, or "the servant of Aton." In order to make these revolutionary moves more effective and to escape the influence of the priests at the royal court of Thebes, he transferred the capital to a new location, known today as Tel el-Amarna.

Here a new kind of art developed. The weight and idealism of the traditional conceptual style gave way to a new lightness and naturalism. For the first time physical characteristics are depicted in detail, and scenes are relaxed and even humorous. A stone relief showing the royal couple and three of their children sitting quietly under the rays of the sun disc is an astonishing departure from the dignified style of the preceding thousand years [1.7]. Queen Nefertiti herself is the subject of perhaps the most famous of all Egyptian portraits [1.8], a sculpture that shows none of the exaggeration to which Amarna art is sometimes prone, but a grace and elegance very different from earlier official portraits.

All these artistic changes were, of course, the result of Akhenaton's sweeping and revolutionary reli-

gious reforms. They did not last long. Akhenaton's belief in a single god who ruled the universe was threatening to the priests, who had a vested interest in preserving the old polytheistic traditions. Not surprisingly, Akhenaton's successors branded him a heretic and fanatic and cut his name out of all the monuments that survived him.

The reaction against Akhenaton's religious policy and the Amarna style was almost immediate. His successor, Tutankhamen, however, is remembered not for leading the opposition—or indeed for any event in his short life. He owes his fame to the treasures found intact in his unrobbed tomb. These sumptuous gold objects, enriched with ivory and precious stones, still show something of the liveliness of Amarna art, but a return to conservatism is beginning; in fact by the Nineteenth and Twentieth Dynasties Akhenaton had been completely forgotten.

In any case, it is not so much for what they reveal about the trends in art that the treasures of Tutankha-

1.9 The first view of the treasures of Tutankhamen: This is what Howard Carter saw when he opened the doorway of the antechamber of the tomb of Tutankhamen on November 26, 1922. The objects include three gilt couches in the form of animals and, at the right in back, the pharaoh's golden throne. The tomb itself was opened three months later.

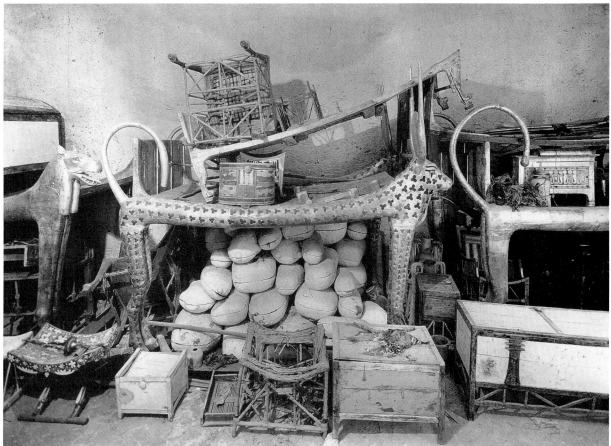

men are significant. The discovery of the tomb is important for a different reason. Our knowledge of the cultures of the ancient world is constantly being revised by the work of archaeologists; many of their finds are minor, but some are major and spectacular. In the case of excavations such as the tomb of Tutankhamen, the process of uncovering the past sometimes becomes as exciting and significant as what is discovered. The long search conducted by Howard Carter in the Valley of the Kings that culminated in the opening of the inner chamber of the sealed tomb of Tutankhamen on February 17, 1923, and the discovery of the intact sarcophagus of the king has become part of history [1.9].

The excavations of Knossos and Mycenae, discussed later in this chapter, and the discovery of Pompeii (Chapter 4) are also major turning points in the growth of our knowledge of the past. But sensational finds like these are exceptions. Understanding the cultural achievements of past civilizations involves a slow and painstaking series of minor discoveries, each of which adds to the knowledge that thus must be constantly revised and reinterpreted.

By the end of the New Kingdom the taste for monumental building had returned. The temples constructed during the reign of Ramses II (1298–1232 B.C.) at Luxor, Karnak, and Abu Simbel are probably the most colossal of all Egyptian constructions [1.10]. Within a century, however, internal dissensions and foreign events had produced a sharp decline in Egypt's power. Throughout the Late Period, artists reverted again to the styles of earlier periods. Tombs were once again constructed in the shape of pyramids, as they had been in the Old Kingdom, and sculptors tried to recapture the realism and sense of volume of Old and Middle Kingdom art. Even direct contacts with the Assyrians, Persians, and Greeks—during the period between the Assyrian

1.10   Temple of Ramses II at Abu Simbel, c. 1257 B.C. Height of statues about 60′ (18.3 m). These four huge statues, erected in commemoration of Ramses' military victories, are all of the pharaoh himself. Between and near the feet are small statues of Ramses' mother, wife, and children. Below are statues of the pharaoh as the god Osiris and the falcon god Horus, to whom the temple was dedicated.

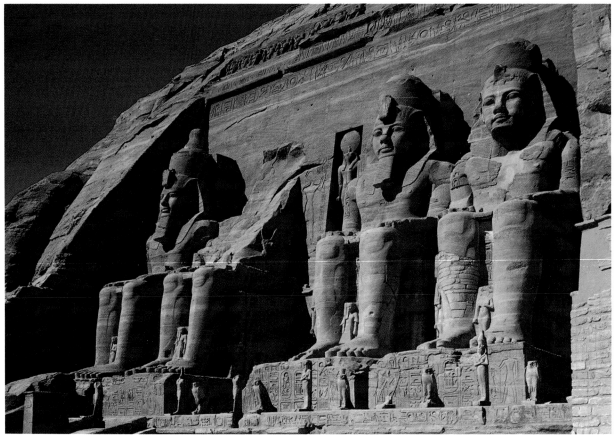

occupation of 671–633 B.C. and Alexander's conquest of Egypt in 331 B.C.—produced little effect on
late Egyptian art. To the end of their history, the
Egyptians remained faithful to their three-thousand-
year-old tradition. Probably no other culture in
human history has ever demonstrated so strong a
conservatism and determination to preserve its separate traditions.

The Cultures of Mesopotamia

The unity so characteristic of ancient Egyptian culture has no parallel in the history of ancient Mesopotamia. A succession of different peoples, each with
their own language, religion, and customs, produced
a wide variety of achievements. This makes it far

more difficult to generalize about Mesopotamian culture than about ancient Egyptian. The picture is further complicated by the presence of a series of related
peoples on the periphery of the Mesopotamian territory. The Hittites, the Syrians, and the peoples of
early Iran all had periods of prosperity and artistic
greatness, although in general they were overshad-
owed by the more powerful nations of Mesopotamia
and Egypt. A description of their achievements
would be beyond the scope of this book.

Sumer

The history of Mesopotamia can be divided into two
major periods, the Sumerian (c. 3500–2350 B.C.) and
the Semitic (c. 2350–612 B.C., when Nineveh fell).
The earliest Sumerian communities were agricultural
settlements on the land between the Tigris and Eu-

phrates rivers. Unlike Upper Egypt, the land here is flat, and so dikes and canals were needed to prevent flooding during the rainy season and to provide water during the rest of the year. When the early settlers found that they had to undertake these large-scale construction projects in order to improve their agriculture, they began to merge their small villages to form towns.

By far the most important event of this stage in the development of Sumerian culture was the invention of the first system of writing, known as cuneiform [1.11]. The ability to write made it possible to

1.11 *Top:* Picture writing: Copy of a limestone tablet from Kish. c. 3200 B.C. Ashmolean Museum, Oxford; original in Baghdad Museum. *Center:* Hieroglyphics: detail of a pillar of a festival building of Sesostris I, Karnak. c. 1940 B.C. Egyptian Museum, Cairo. *Bottom:* Cuneiform: detail of the *Stele of Hammurabi* (see figure 1.17). c. 1760 B.C. The limestone tablet is the oldest known example of picture writing. Among the signs are several representing parts of the human body, including a head, hand, and foot. This writing system later developed into cuneiform. The Egyptians, however, continued to use hieroglyphics throughout their history.

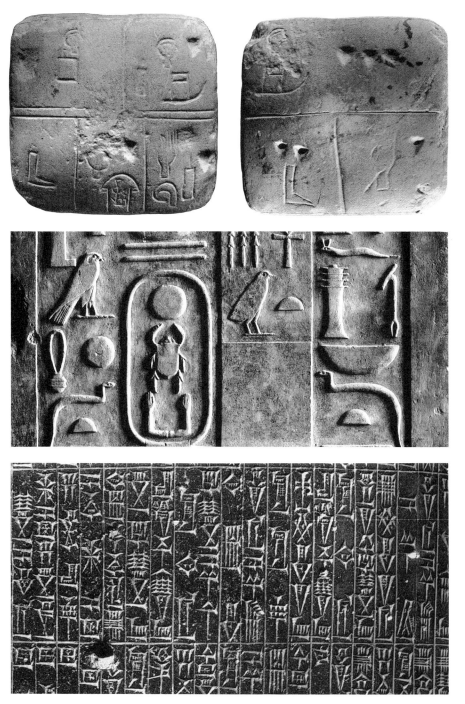

THE ARTS AND INVENTION: *The Invention of Writing*

The earliest known writing system was invented by the people of Uruk (now Warka), one of the first great Mesopotamian cities, around the middle of the fourth millennium B.C. It consisted of a series of simplified picture signs that represented the objects they showed and, in addition, related ideas. Thus a leg could mean either a leg itself or the concept of walking. The signs were drawn on soft clay tablets that were then baked. The Egyptian hieroglyphic system of writing, which was probably derived from this method, retained throughout its history the use of recognizable pictures.

The Sumerian pictorial signs, however, evolved into a series of wedge-shaped marks that were pressed in clay with a split reed. The cuneiform system (*cuneus* is the Latin word for "wedge") had the advantage of being quick and economical. Furthermore, the clay tablets were easy to store; excavation of the palace archives at great cities such as Ur has revealed thousands of documents, some of them inventories of goods, others copies of letters sent to the rulers of other cities. Mesopotamian bureaucrats evidently had the same passion as their modern counterparts for accumulating their clay equivalents of paperwork.

Cuneiform script was picked up and widely used throughout the ancient New East; Akkadians, Hittites, and others employed it to write their own languages. With the gradual decline of Mesopotamian civilization in the first millennium B.C. it gradually dropped out of use, to be rediscovered and deciphered in the mid-19th century.

It is impossible to overestimate the significance of the invention of writing for the development of all world civilizations. The early scribes may have devised their system to keep track of financial and other transactions, but nearly every aspect of human life as we now live it would be unimaginable without the written word in some form or another—whether on the page of a book or on a computer screen. By permitting the accumulation and preservation of knowledge, the scribes of Uruk made civilization possible, and with it the art of literature.

---

trade and to administer on a wider scale, and with the increasing economic strength this more highly organized society brought, a number of powerful cities began to develop.

The central focus of life in these larger communities was the temple, the dwelling place of the particular god who watched over the town. Religion, in fact, played a central part in all aspects of Sumerian culture. The gods themselves were manifest in natural phenomena, sky and earth, sun and moon, lightning and storm. The chief religious holidays were closely linked to the passage of the seasons. The most important annual event was the New Year, the crucial moment when the blazing heat of the previous summer and the cold of winter gave way to the possibility of a fertile spring. The fertility of the earth was symbolized by the Great Mother and the sterility of the winter by the death of her partner, Tammuz. Each year his disappearance was mourned at the beginning of the New Year festival. When his resurrection was celebrated at the end of the festival, hope for the season to come was expressed by the renewal of the sacred marriage of god and goddess.

As in the Paleolithic period, the importance of female creative power is reflected in Sumerian art. Among its finest achievements is the so-called *Lady of Warka* [1.12], a female head from the city of Uruk. It is not clear whether the head is of a divine or mortal figure. The face shows an altogether exceptional nobility and sensitivity.

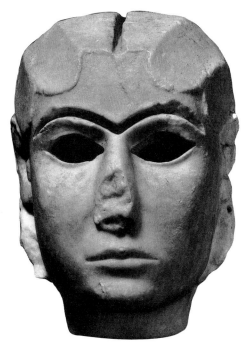

1.12 *Lady of Warka*. Uruk, c. 3000 B.C. White marble, height 7⅞″ (20 cm). Iraq Museum, Baghdad. Originally the hair was probably gold leaf and the eyes and eyebrows were colored inlays.

The governing power in cities like Uruk was in the hands of the priests, who controlled and administered both religious and economic affairs. The ruler himself served as the representative on earth of the god of the city but, unlike the pharaoh, was never thought of as divine and never became the center of a cult. His purpose was to watch over his people's interests by building better temples and digging more canals rather than acquiring personal wealth or power. Over the centuries rulers began to detach themselves increasingly from the control of the priests, but the immense prestige of the temples assured the religious leaders a lasting power.

The most famous of all Sumerian rulers was Gilgamesh, who ruled at Uruk about 2700 B.C. Around his name grew up a series of legends that developed into one of the first great masterpieces of poetic expression. *The Epic of Gilgamesh* begins with the adventures of Gilgamesh and his warrior friend Enkidu. Gilgamesh himself is courted by the queen of heaven, the goddess Ishtar. He rejects her advances and later kills a bull sent against him as a punishment.

In revenge, the gods kill Enkidu; his death marks the turning point of the poem's mood. With the awareness of death's reality even for the bravest, Gilgamesh now sets out to seek the meaning of life. Toward the end of his journey he meets Utnapishtim, the only person to whom the gods have given everlasting life; from him Gilgamesh seeks the secrets of immortality. Utnapishtim, in the course of their conversation, tells him the story of the flood as it was known in Babylonia. By the end of the epic, Gilgamesh fails to achieve immortality and returns home to die.

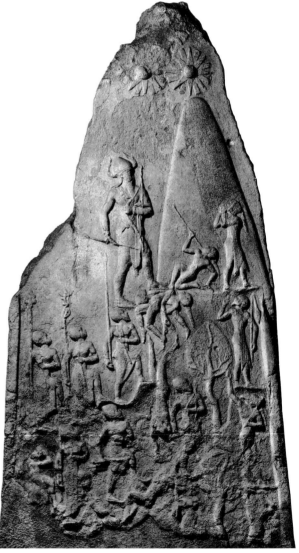

1.14 *Stele of Naram-Sin,* from Susa, Iran. Akkadian, c. 2300 B.C. Red sandstone, height 6'6" (2 m). Louvre, Paris. The king, wearing a horned crown, stands beneath symbols of the gods. The diagonal composition is well suited to the triangular shape of the stele.

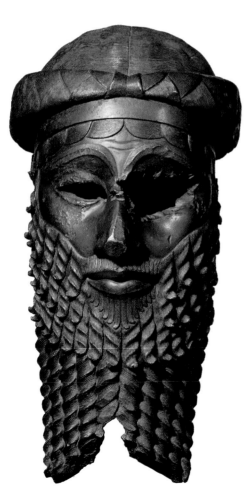

1.13 Head of a king (Sargon?), from Nineveh. Akkadian, c. 2330 B.C. Bronze, height 14¼" (37 cm). Iraq Museum, Baghdad. Originally, the eyes were probably precious stones.

Originally composed in Sumerian c. 2000 B.C., the epic was eventually written down on clay tablets in their own languages by Babylonians, Hittites, and others. The poem was widely known. The story of the flood, recorded in tablet eleven, bears a striking resemblance to that of the biblical story in Genesis, except for the tone. The God of the Hebrews acts out of moral disapproval, while the divinities in the epic were disturbed in their sleep by noisy mortals.

The Epic of Gilgamesh is a profoundly pessimistic work. Unlike the ancient Egyptians, the Mesopotamians saw life as a continual struggle whose only alternative was the bleak darkness of death. Dying Egyptians—if they were righteous—could expect a happy existence in the next life, but for the Mesopotamian there was only the dim prospect of eternal gloom.

The story of Gilgamesh rises to a supreme level in the section that describes the last stages of his journey. Then the epic touches on universal questions: Is all human achievement futile in the face of death? Is there a purpose in human existence? If so, how can it be discovered? The quest of Gilgamesh is the basic human search.

Only at the end of Gilgamesh's journey do we sense that the purpose of the journey may have been the journey itself and that what was important was to have asked the questions. Weary as he was on his return he was wiser than when he left, and in leaving us an account of his experiences, "engraved on a

1.15 Ziggurat at Ur. Neo-Sumerian, c. 2100–2000 B.C. Mudbrick faced with baked brick laid in bitumen. The drawing shows the probable original appearance. The photograph shows the ziggurat now, partially restored. The Akkadian word *ziggurat* means "pinnacle" or "mountain top"—a place where the gods were thought to reveal themselves. These plains dwellers made artificial mountains surmounted by shrines.

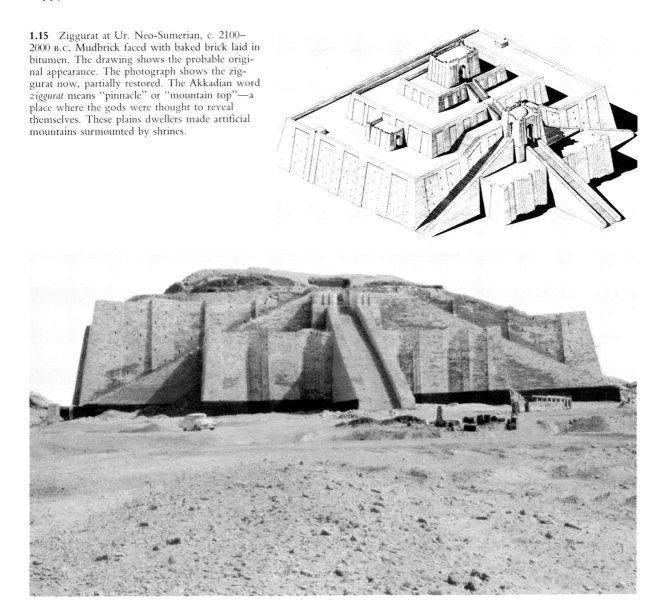

stone," he communicates them to us, a powerful and moving illustration of the power of the written word.

Akkadian and Babylonian Culture

In the years from 2350 to 2150 B.C. the whole of Mesopotamia fell under the control of the Semitic king Sargon and his descendants. The art of this Akkadian period (named for Sargon's capital city, Akkad) shows a continuation of the trends of the Sumerian age, although total submission to the gods is replaced by a more positive attitude to human achievement. A bronze head from Nineveh [1.13], perhaps a portrait of Sargon himself, expresses a pride and self-confidence that recur in other works of

1.16 *Gudea.* c. 2100 B.C. Diorite, height 41″ (105 cm). Louvre, Paris. Gudea is shown in an attitude of devotion, hands tightly clasped, as he stands before the gods.

1.17 *Stele of Hammurabi.* c. 1760 B.C. Basalt, height 7′3¾″ (2.25 m). Louvre, Paris. The sun god is dictating the law to the king, who is listening reverently. They are shown on a mountain, indicated by the irregular ridges beneath the god's feet. Below is *The Law Code of Hammurabi,* carved in cuneiform.

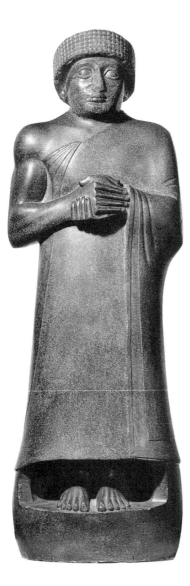

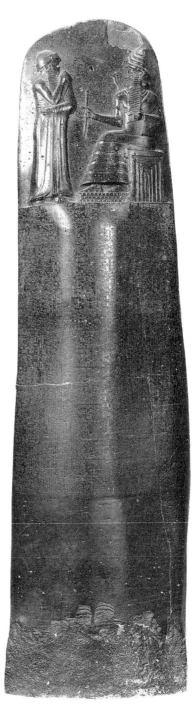

the period like the famous *Stele of Naram-Sin* (*stele:* sculpted stone slab), showing a later Akkadian king standing on the bodies of his enemies [1.14].

When Akkadian rule was brought to an abrupt and violent end by the invasion of the Gutians from Iran, the cities of Mesopotamia reverted to earlier ways. As in the early Sumerian period, the chief buildings constructed were large brick platforms with superimposed terraces, known as *ziggurats*. These clearly had religious significance; the one built at Ur around 2100 B.C. [1.15] had huge staircases that led to a shrine at the top. The same return to traditional beliefs is illustrated by the religious inscriptions on the bases of the many surviving statues of Gudea, the governor of the city of Lagash around 2100 B.C., as well as by his humble attitude [1.16].

By around 1800 B.C., Mesopotamia had once again been unified, this time under the Babylonians. Their most famous king, Hammurabi, was the author of a law code that was one of the earliest attempts to achieve social justice by legislation—a major development in the growth of civilization. The laws were carved on a stele, with Hammurabi himself shown at the top in the presence of the sun god Shamash [1.17]. Many of the law code's provisions deal with the relationship between husbands, wives, and other family members. They often show a surprisingly enlightened attitude toward equal rights in the 18th century B.C.—almost four thousand years ago—as the following extracts show:

from THE LAW CODE OF HAMMURABI

131. If a man accuse his wife and she have not been taken in lying with another man, she shall take an oath in the name of god and she shall return to her house.

142. If a woman hate her husband and say, "Thou shalt not have me," her past shall be inquired into for any deficiency of hers; and if she have been careful and be without past sin and her husband have been going out and greatly belittling her, that woman has no blame. She shall take her dowry and go to her father's house.

145. If a man take a wife and she do not present him with children, and he set his face to take a concubine, that man may take a concubine and bring her into his house. That concubine shall not take precedence of his wife.

162. If a man take a wife and she bear him children and that woman die, her father may not lay claim to her dowry. Her dowry belongs to her children.

The Assyrians

By 1550 B.C. Babylon had been taken over by the Kassites, a formerly nomadic people who had occupied Babylonia and settled there, but they too would fall in turn under the domination of the Assyrians, who evolved the last great culture of ancient Mesopotamia. The peak of Assyrian power was between 1000 and 612 B.C.—the time when Greek civilization was developing, as described in Chapter 2. But Assyrian achievements are the culmination of the culture of ancient Mesopotamia.

A huge palace constructed at Nimrud during the reign of Assurnasirpal II (883–859 B.C.) was decorated with an elaborately carved series of relief slabs. The subjects are often religious, but a number of slabs that show the king on hunting expeditions have a vigor and freedom that are unusual in Mesopotamian art. The palaces of later Assyrian kings were decorated with similar reliefs. At Nineveh the palace of Assurbanipal (668–626 B.C.) was filled with scenes of war appropriate to an age of increasing turmoil. The representations of dead and dying soldiers on the battlefields are generally conventional, if highly elaborate. But again the hunting scenes are different— they show a genuine and moving identification with the suffering animals [1.18].

With the fall of Nineveh in 612 B.C. Assyrian domination ended. The Assyrian empire fell into the hands of two nomadic tribes, first the Medes and then the Persians; the great age of Mesopotamia was over. Lacking the unifying elements provided in Egypt by the pharaoh and a national religion, the peoples of Mesopotamia perhaps never equaled Egyptian achievements in the arts. However, they formed ordered societies within independent city-states that anticipated the city-states of the Greeks. They also evolved a comparatively enlightened view of human relationships, as shown by *The Law Code of Hammurabi*.

Aegean Culture in the Bronze Age

Neither the Egyptians of the Old Kingdom nor the Sumerians seem to have shown any interest in their contemporaries living to the west of them, and with good reason. In Greece and the islands of the Aegean Sea, though the arrival of immigrants from farther east in the early Neolithic period (c. 6000 B.C.) had brought new agricultural techniques, in general life continued there for the next three thousand years almost completely untouched by the rise of organized cultures elsewhere.

Yet, beginning in the early Bronze Age, there developed in the area around the Aegean Sea a level of civilization as brilliant and sophisticated as any other in Europe or western Asia. (The same period saw the appearance of a similarly urban culture in the Indus valley on the Indian subcontinent.) Then around 1100 B.C., after almost two thousand years of exis-

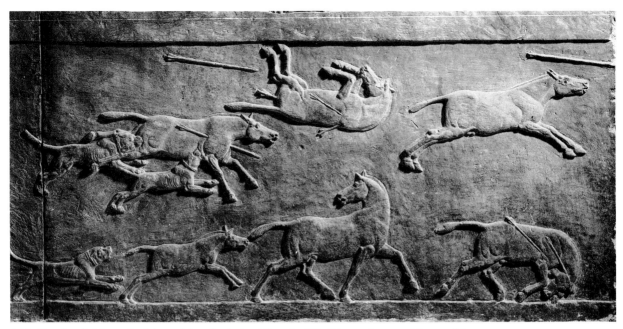

1.18 Detail, relief from the Palace of Assurbanipal at Nineveh, 668–626 B.C. Gypsum slab carved in low relief, height 19″ (50 cm). British Museum, London (reproduced by courtesy of the Trustees). Wild asses are being hunted by mastiffs. The mare below turns in her flight to look back for her foal.

tence, this Bronze Age Agean civilization disappeared as dramatically as it had arisen. The rediscovery in the 20th century of these peoples, the Minoans of Crete and the Mycenaeans of mainland Greece, is perhaps the most splendid achievement in the history of archaeology in the Mediterranean—and one that has opened up vast new perspectives in the study of the later Greeks.

What connection is there between Greek culture and the magnificent civilization of the Bronze Age? Did much of later Greek religion, thought, and art have its origins in this earlier period, even though the Greeks themselves seemed to know nothing about it? Or was the culture of the Minoans and Mycenaeans an isolated phenomenon, destroyed utterly near the end of the Bronze Age, lost until it was found again in our own time? The Aegean culture is important not only for the possible light it throws on later times. Its existence also shows that the ancient world could reach beyond the monumentality and earnestness of the Egyptians and Mesopotamians, that it could attain a way of life that valued grace, beauty, and comfort—a life that could truly be called civilized.

Cycladic Art

During most of the Bronze Age the major centers of Aegean culture were on Crete or the mainland, but in the early phase there were settlements on a group of islands of the central Aegean, the Cyclades. Little is known about these Cycladic people. They used bronze tools. They also produced pottery which, though less finely made than that produced elsewhere in the Acgean at the time, sometimes shows remarkable imagination and even humor [1.19]. The chief claim to fame of Cycladic art—a considerable one—lies in the marble statues, or idols, that were produced in large quantities and in many cases buried with the dead. The statues range in height from a few inches to almost life-size; the average is about a foot (30.5 centimeters) high. Most of the figures are female; the most common type shows a naked woman standing or, more probably, lying, with her arms folded and head tilted back [1.20]. The face is indicated only by a central ridge for the nose. The simplicity of the form and the fine working of the marble—stone of superb quality—often produce an effect of great beauty.

The purpose of the Cycladic idols remains uncertain. The fact that most of them have been found in graves suggests that they had a religious function in the funeral ritual. The overwhelming preponderance of female figures seems to indicate that they were in some way connected with the cult of the mother goddess, which was common in Mesopotamia and which dominated Aegean Bronze Age religion. Whether the figures actually represent goddesses remains uncertain.

We now know that the period of the production of

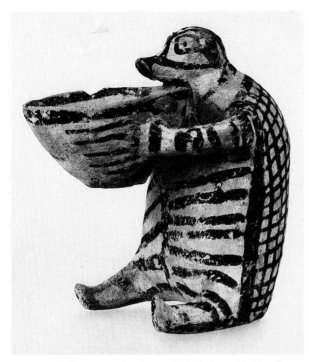

1.19 Cycladic vase in the shape of a hedgehog drinking from a bowl. Syros, c. 2500–2200 B.C. Painted clay, height 4¼″ (11 cm). National Archaeological Museum, Athens.

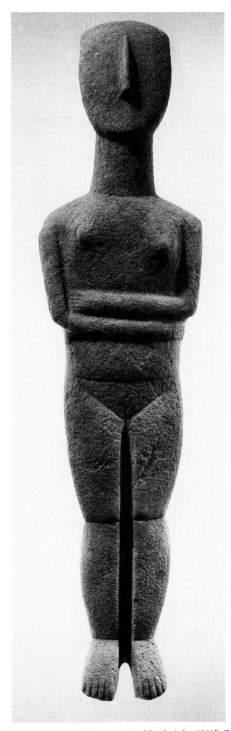

the Cycladic idols was one of increasing development on Crete. Yet for the classical Greeks of the 5th century B.C. Crete was chiefly famous as the home of the legendary King Minos, who ruled at Knossos. Here, according to myth, was a Labyrinth that housed the Minotaur, a monstrous creature, half man and half bull, the product of the union of Minos' wife Pasiphae with a bull. Minos exacted from Athens a regular tribute of seven boys and seven girls who were sent to be devoured by the Minotaur. According to the myths, after this had been going on for some time, the Athenian hero Theseus volunteered to stop the grisly tribute. He went to Knossos with the new group of intended victims and, with the help of the king's daughter Ariadne (who had fallen in love with him) killed the Minotaur in its lair in the middle of the Labyrinth. He then escaped with Ariadne and the Athenian boys and girls. Theseus later abandoned Ariadne on the island of Naxos, but the god Dionysus discovered her there and comforted her. The story had many more details, and other myths describe other events. The important point is that the later Greeks had a mythological picture of Knossos as a prosperous and thriving community

1.20 Cycladic idol. c. 2500 B.C. Marble, height 19¾″ (50 cm). British Museum, London (reproduced by courtesy of the Trustees).

The Indus Valley People

In the 1920s another ancient civilization was first discovered, that of the Indus valley, in what is now Pakistan. Like the Minoans, the Indus valley people must have had myths involving bulls, since the bull appears frequently on their carved seal stones. There is no direct evidence of contact between the two cultures, but we do know that the Indus valley people traded with the Akkadians in the time of Sargon, a period during which the Minoans were active in the eastern Mediterranean.

Originally founded around 3000 B.C., the two principal centers of Indus culture, Harappa and Mohenjo-daro, became large-scale flourishing cities. They were built of baked bricks and had elaborate drainage systems. At Mohenjo-daro a great bath, an assembly hall, and other monumental public buildings have been excavated. Farming seems to have been the principal occupation; wheat, barley, and rice were grown, and the Indus valley culture were the first people known to cultivate cotton.

A standardized writing system that makes use of picture-signs and has not been deciphered was widely used throughout Indus territory. The Indus people were not great metalworkers; the finest of their surviving statues are of stone [1.21]. Pottery was mass-produced and its general distribution as well as a standard system of weights and measures suggest a powerfully centralized state.

Like that of the Minoans, the collapse of the Indus civilization is still not fully understood. By around 1700 B.C. most of the Indus valley centers were in decline, in part due to a series of disastrous floods of the river. Another factor was probably overexploitation of the land; huge amounts of wood and other vegetation must have been used to stoke the fires that baked the bricks of which the cities were constructed. The final blow was the invasion of a new people, the Aryans,

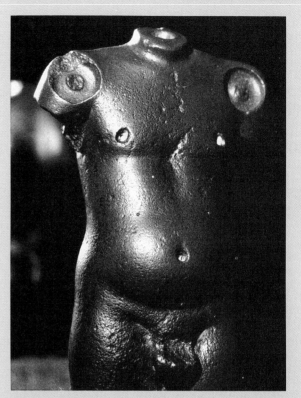

1.21 Torso of a man from Mohenjo-daro. 3rd millennium B.C. Red stone. National Museum, New Delhi.

who moved southeast into India at the end of the second millennium B.C.

Thus, like the Minoans, the Indus valley people were forgotten for some three thousand years before being rediscovered by modern archaeologists. We now know that Indus culture represents one of the high points in the development of civilization in the Orient.

ruled by a powerful and ruthless king from his palace. Nor was Knossos the only center mentioned in Greek stories of Crete. In the *Odyssey* Homer even refers to "Crete of a hundred cities."

These, however, were legends. By the time of Classical Greece no evidence whatever for the existence of the Palace of Minos or the other cities could be seen. It is not surprising that the Greeks themselves showed no inclination to try to find any hidden traces. Archaeology, after all, is a relatively modern pursuit, and there is little indication of any serious enthusiasm in Classical antiquity for the material remains of the past. Later ages continued to accept the Greeks' own judgment. For many centuries the story of Minos and the Labyrinth was thought to be a good tale with no foundation in fact.

The Excavation of Knossos

By the end of the 19th century, however, things had changed. Heinrich Schliemann had proved that the stories of the war against Troy and the Mycenaeans who had waged it were far from mere legends (see page 34). Was it possible that the mythical palace of King Minos at Knossos also really existed?

In 1894 the English archaeologist Arthur Evans first went to Crete to see if he could discover something of its history in the Bronze Age. At Knossos he found evidence of ancient remains, some of them already uncovered by amateur enthusiasts. He returned in 1899 and again in 1900, this time with a permit to excavate. On March 23, 1900, serious work began at Knossos, and within days it became apparent that the finds represented a civilization even older than that of the Mycenaeans. The quantity was staggering: pottery, frescoes, inscribed tablets, and, on April 13, a room with elaborate paintings and a raised seat with high back—the throne room of King Minos. Evans' discoveries at Knossos (and finds later made elsewhere on Crete by other archaeologists) did much to confirm legendary accounts of Cretan prosperity and power. Yet these discoveries did far more than merely give a true historical background to the myth of the Minotaur.

Evans had in fact found an entire civilization, which he called Minoan after the legendary king. Evans himself is said to have once remarked modestly "Any success as an archaeologist I owe to two things: very short sight, so I look at everything closely, and being slow on the uptake, so I never leap to conclusions." Actually, the magnitude of his achievement can scarcely be exaggerated. All study of the Minoans has been strongly influenced by his initial classification of the finds, especially the pottery. Evans divided the history of the Bronze Age in Crete into three main periods—Early Minoan, Middle Minoan, and Late Minoan—and further subdivided each of these into three. The precise dates of

each period can be disputed, but all the excavations of the years following Evans have confirmed his initial description of the main sequence of events.

Life and Art in the Minoan Palaces

The Early Minoan period was one of increasing growth. Small towns began to appear in the south and east of Crete, and the first contacts were established with Egypt and Mesopotamia. Around 2000 B.C., however, came the first major development in Minoan civilization, marking the beginning of the Middle Minoan period. The earlier scattered towns were abandoned and large urban centers evolved. These are generally called palaces, although their function was far more than just to provide homes for ruling families.

The best known of these centers is Knossos (other important ones have been excavated at Phaistos, Mallia, and Zakro). The main palace building, constructed around an open rectangular courtyard, contained rooms for banquets, public receptions, religious ceremonies, and administrative work. In addition, there were living quarters for the royal family and working areas for slaves and craftsmen

1.22 Plan of the Palace of Minos at Knossos. c. 1600–1400 B.C. Each Cretan palace had a central court oriented north–south, state apartments to the west, and royal living apartments to the east.

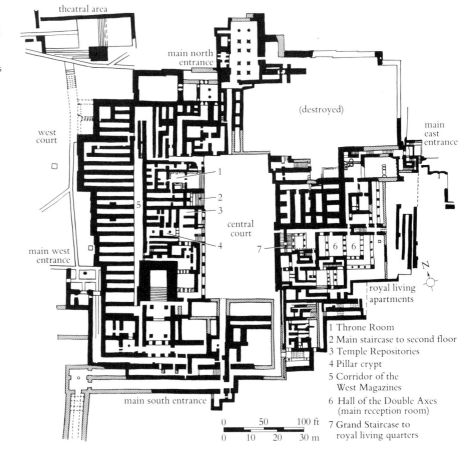

theatral area

main north entrance

(destroyed)

west court

main east entrance

central court

main west entrance

7

6 6

royal living apartments

main south entrance

1 Throne Room
2 Main staircase to second floor
3 Temple Repositories
4 Pillar crypt
5 Corridor of the West Magazines
6 Hall of the Double Axes (main reception room)
7 Grand Staircase to royal living quarters

0   50   100 ft
0 10 20 30 m

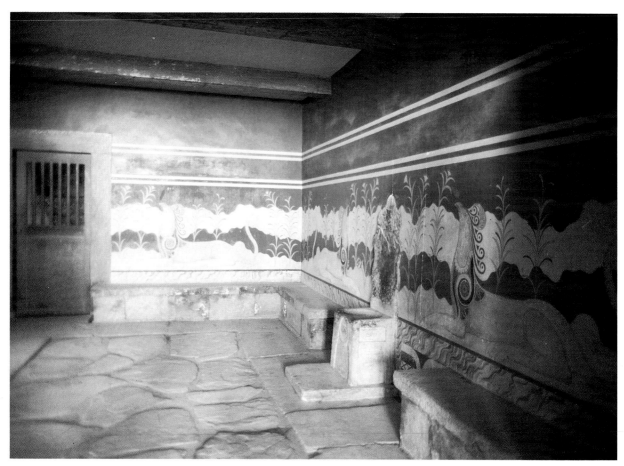

1.23 Throne Room, Palace of Minos at Knossos. The room was reconstructed about 1450 B.C., shortly before the final destruction of the palace. The frescoes around the throne show sacred flowers and griffins—mythological beasts with lion bodies and bird heads.

[1.22, 1.23]. Around the palace were the private houses of the aristocrats and chief religious leaders. The technical sophistication of these great centers was remarkable. There were elaborate drainage systems, and the palaces were designed and constructed to remain cool in summer and be heated easily in winter.

Middle Minoan art shows great liveliness and color. The brilliantly painted pottery, superb jewelry such as the famous *Wasp Pendant* from Mallia [1.24], and the many exquisitely carved seal stones all attest to the Minoans' love of beauty and artistic skill. Unlike their contemporaries in Egypt and Mesopotamia, the Minoans showed little interest in monumental art. Their greatest works are on a small, even

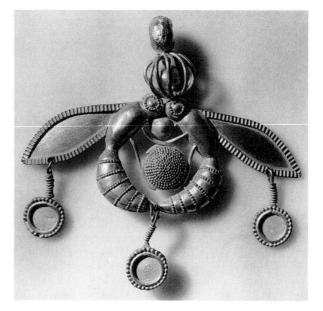

1.24 *Wasp Pendant,* from Mallia. c. 1700 B.C. Gold, width 1⅞″ (5 cm). Archaeological Museum, Heraklion. This enlarged view shows the exquisite craftsmanship, using the techniques of granulation and wire-working. Two wasps (or perhaps hornets) are curved around a honeycomb.

miniature, scale. At the same time, they invented a writing system of hieroglyphic signs that was used in the archives of the palace for administrative purposes.

Toward the end of the Middle Minoan period (c. 1700 B.C.) the palaces were destroyed, probably by an earthquake, then rebuilt on an even grander scale. There was further reconstruction about a century later, perhaps because of another earthquake. These palaces of the Late Minoan period represent the high point of Minoan culture. The wall paintings of this period are among the greatest treasures of all. Their spontaneity and freedom create a mood very different from Egyptian and Mesopotamian art, and they show a love of nature expressed with brilliant colors and vivid observation. Most of the best examples of these later paintings are from Knossos, but some particularly enchanting scenes have been found in the recent excavation of a Minoan colony on the island of Thera [1.25].

Although the rulers of the palaces seem to have been male, the central figure of Minoan religion was a mother goddess who was connected with fertility. She seems to have taken on different forms, or rather the function of female divinity was divided among several separate deities. Sometimes when she is shown flanked by animals, the Mistress of the Beasts, she seems to be the ancestor of the Greek goddess Artemis. Other depictions show goddesses of vegetation. The most famous Minoan figurine is the so-called *Snake Goddess* [1.26].

Throughout the last great age of the palaces, the influence of Minoan artistic styles began to spread to the mainland. But Minoan political and military power was on the wane, and Knossos seems to have been invaded and occupied by mainlanders around 1450 B.C. Shortly afterward, both at Knossos and elsewhere, there is evidence of widespread destruction. By 1400 B.C., Minoan culture had come to an abrupt end. The causes are mysterious and have been much argued; we shall probably never know exactly what happened. The eruption of a volcano on Thera a century earlier, about 1500 B.C., may have played some part in changing the balance of power in the Aegean. In any case, there is no doubt that throughout the last period of the palaces a new power was growing, the Mycenaeans. These people may well have played a part in the destruction of Knossos.

Schliemann and the Discovery of Mycenae

The Mycenaeans, the people of mainland Greece in the Bronze Age, are named after the largest of their settlements, Mycenae. Most of the Mycenaean centers were in the southern part of Greece known as the Peloponnesus, although there were also some settlements farther north, of which the two most important were Athens and Thebes. Like the Minoans, the Mycenaeans were familiar from Greek myths long before their material remains were excavated. They

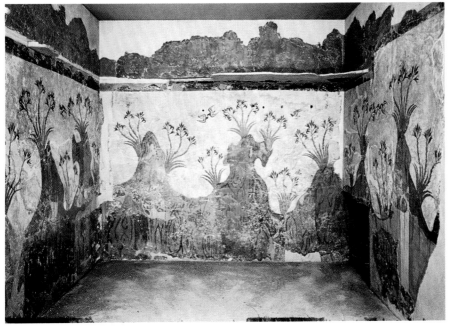

1.25 Room with landscape frescoes, House Delta, Thera. Minoan, c. 1500 B.C. National Archaeological Museum, Athens. A springtime scene—bright flowers and soaring birds—covers three sides of a small room.

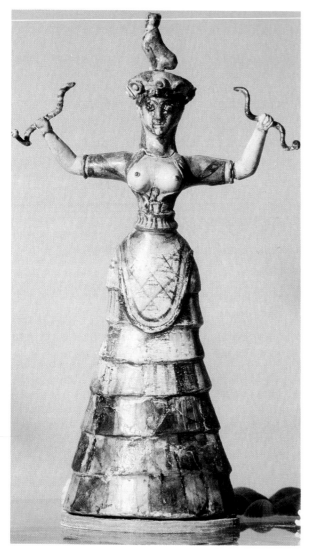

Troy and prove the poet right. Excavation has always been expensive, and Schliemann therefore decided to make his fortune in business, retire early, and devote his profits to the pursuit of his goal. By 1863, this remarkable man had accumulated a considerable amount of money from trading in, among other things, tea and was ready to devote himself to his second career. After a period of study and travel, in 1870 he finally began excavations on the site where he had decided the remains of Homer's Troy lay buried beneath the Roman city of Ilium. By 1873 he had found not only walls and the gate of the city but quantities of gold, silver, and bronze objects.

Inspired by the success of his Trojan campaign, Schliemann moved on to the second part of his task: to discover the Mycenaeans who had made war on Troy. In 1876 he began to excavate within the walls of Mycenae itself, and there he almost immediately came upon the Royal Grave Circle with its stupendous quantities of gold treasures [1.27]. Homer had described Mycenae as "rich in gold," and Schliemann was always convinced that the royal family whose graves he had unearthed was that of Agamemnon, leader of the Mycenaean expedition against Troy. We now know that the finds date to an even earlier period, and later excavations both at Mycenae and at other mainland sites have provided a much more exact picture of Mycenaean history. This does not diminish Schliemann's achievement. However unsci-

1.26 *Snake Goddess,* from the Temple Repository at Knossos. c. 1600 B.C. Faience, height 11½″ (30 cm). Archaeological Museum, Heraklion. The bare breasts are typical for Minoan court ladies, but the apron indicates a religious function. The figure probably represents a priestess serving the goddess, not the goddess herself.

were famous in legend mainly for launching an expedition against Troy, across the Aegean Sea. The Trojan War (c. 1250 B.C.) and its aftermath provided the material for many later Greek works, most notably the *Iliad* and the *Odyssey,* the two great epic poems of Homer, but for a long time it was believed that the war and even the very existence of Troy were myths.

Heinrich Schliemann dedicated his life and work to proving that the legends were founded on reality. Schliemann, born in Germany in 1822, was introduced to the Homeric poems as a child by his father and was overwhelmed by their incomparable vividness. He became determined to discover Homer's

1.27 "Mask of Agamemnon," from Shaft Grave V, Mycenae. c. 1550 B.C. Beaten gold, height 10⅛″ (26 cm). National Archaeological Museum, Athens. This death mask is actually a portrait of a Mycenaean ruler of three centuries earlier than Agamemnon.

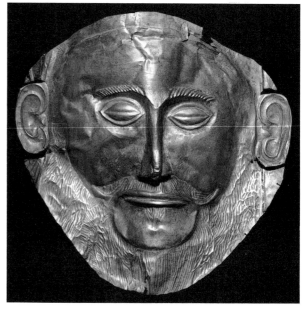

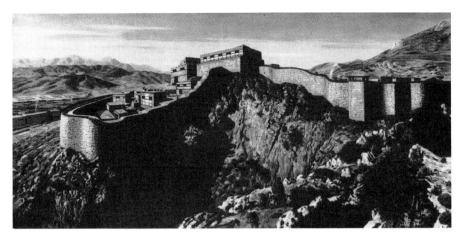

1.28 Reconstruction of the Citadel of Mycenae as it would have looked around 1300 B.C. The very thick walls are visible. The palace has a commanding position at the summit.

entific his methods, he had proved the existence of a civilization in Bronze Age Greece that surpassed in splendor even the legends; he had opened a new era in the study of the past.

Mycenaean Art and Architecture

Like the Minoans, the Mycenaeans centered their life around great palace complexes. In Mycenae itself, the palace probably was first built around 1600 B.C., and the graves found by Schliemann date to shortly thereafter. Until the fall of Knossos in 1400 B.C., the Mycenaeans were strongly under the influence of Minoan culture, but with the end of Minoan power they became the natural leaders in the Aegean area. From 1400 to 1200 B.C., Mycenaean traders traveled throughout the Mediterranean, from Egypt and the Near East as far west as Italy. The Mycenaean empire grew in power and prosperity. Toward the end of this period, around 1250 B.C., the successful expedition was launched against Troy, perhaps for reasons of trade rivalry. A short time later, around 1200 B.C., the Mycenaean empire itself fell, its major centers destroyed and most of them abandoned. Invasion by enemies, internal strife, and natural causes have all been suggested, but the fall of the Mycenaeans still remains mysterious.

Their collapse is made even more incomprehensible by the massive fortifications that protected most of the palaces. At Mycenae itself, the walls are 15 feet (4.6 meters) thick and probably were 50 feet (15.3 meters) high. As in the case of other Mycenaean centers, the actual location was chosen for its defensibility [1.28]. The somber character of these fortress-palaces is reflected in the general tone of Mycenaean civilization. Unlike the relaxed culture of the Minoans, Mycenaean culture as reflected in its art was preoccupied with death and war. It is no coincidence that many of the richest finds have come from

tombs. Like the Minoans, the Mycenaeans decorated their palaces with frescoes, although the Mycenaean paintings are more solemn and dignified than their Minoan counterparts.

The disaster of 1200 B.C. brought a violent end to the Mycenaeans' political and economic domination of the Mediterranean, but their culture lingered on for another hundred years. A few of the palaces were inhabited again, and some Mycenaeans fled eastward, where they settled on the islands of Rhodes and Cyprus. By 1100 B.C., however, renewed violence had extinguished the last traces of Bronze Age culture in Greece. A century later, after a period our lack of information forces us to call the Dark Age, the story of Western culture truly begins with the dawning of the Iron Age.

Before leaving the rich achievements of the Bronze Age world, both in Greece and farther afield, it is worth asking how much survived to be handed down to our own civilization. For the Greeks themselves, the Iron Age brought a new beginning in most material respects. At the same time, however, there are links with the earlier era in less tangible areas. In particular, although Greek religion never placed as strong an emphasis on worship of the mother goddess as the Bronze Age did, she remained a potent force in traditional beliefs. Behind the official reverence for Zeus, father of the gods and mortals, there lay a profound respect for goddesses like Hera, patroness of the family, Artemis, Mistress of the Beasts and goddess of childbirth, and Demeter, the goddess of fertility and agriculture. The continued worship of these goddesses, which was to last under different guises for centuries, represents a reverence for female creative power that is one of the oldest legacies from the period before our culture began—we saw it as far back as the Paleolithic period—and perhaps one of the most significant.

As for Egypt and Mesopotamia, much of their impact on later culture was secondhand. In the course of their growth and development, the Greeks were brought into contact with the later Egypt and Mesopotamia of their own times, and Greek art and architecture were decisively influenced by them. Although the Greeks retained their artistic independence, the style they developed under the inspiration of eastern models has conditioned the entire history of Western art. The cultures of ancient Egypt and the Middle East had very little direct influence on the formation of our civilization, partly because Greek culture had a vitality that was by this time lacking in the older peoples and at least partly because of historical accident. Egypt and Assyria, powerful though they were, fell to the Persians, while Greece managed not only to survive but even to inflict an ignominious defeat on its Persian invaders.

Yet even if ancient Egypt and Mesopotamia lie outside the mainstream of our cultural tradition, they continue to exert a powerful influence on the Western imagination, as the Tutankhamen exhibitions and their accompanying "Tut mania" showed in the 1970s. In part their fascination lies in their exoticism and in the excitement of their rediscovery in our own day. The pharaoh who can curse his excavator from beyond the grave is certainly a dramatic, if fictional, representative of his age. At the same time, the artistic achievements of those distant times need no historical justification. Created in a world very remote from our own, they serve as a reminder of the innate human urge to give expression to the eternal problems of existence.

Summary

The early civilizations of the ancient Middle East laid the basis for the development of Western culture. In Egypt and Mesopotamia, in the period around 3000 B.C., the simple farming communities of the earlier Neolithic (New Stone) Age were replaced by cities, the product of agricultural discoveries that provided the food supply for relatively large numbers of people to live together.

Many of the characteristics of urban life developed during the following centuries: large-scale buildings, trade and commerce, systems of government and religion. The people of the Mesopotamian city of Uruk invented the earliest known writing system in the world.

Egyptian society was dominated by a strong central monarchy, with the pharaoh (the Egyptian king) presiding over a large bureaucracy that administered the affairs of state. Egyptian religious life was controlled by the priests, who sought to maintain old traditions, and Egyptian art generally reflected the policy of state control. Periods of political uncertainty were reflected in contemporary art. The confidence and stability of Old Kingdom sculpture, for example, disappeared in the unsettled conditions of the Middle Kingdom.

In the reign of the New Kingdom pharaoh Amenhotep IV, better known as Akhenaton (1379–1362 B.C.), there was a change: the numberless deities of Egyptian religion were replaced by a single sun god, and Egyptian art became naturalistic for the first time in its history. Akhenaton's successors, however, restored the traditional system of deities and the artistic conventions of former times.

The chief characteristic of Egyptian religious thought was the belief in survival after death for those who had led a good life. Elaborate funeral rituals were devised, in which the god Osiris, Judge of the Dead, was invoked. From early in Egyptian history monumental tombs were constructed for the ruling classes, the most famous of which are the Great Pyramids at Giza.

Mesopotamian culture lacked the unity of Egyptian life: a series of different peoples had their own languages, religions, and customs. The Sumerians, the earliest, lived in cities dominated by great temples built on artificial platforms. The temple priests administered both religious and economic affairs, sharing their duties with local civic rulers. Unlike the Egyptian pharaohs, who were thought of as gods, Sumerian rulers never became the focus of a cult. They represented their city's god and served the interests of their people by overseeing government projects. Among the earliest of Sumerian kings was Gilgamesh, whose legendary deeds are described in the epic poem that bears his name.

Mesopotamia was ruled by the Akkadians, a Semitic people, from 2350 to 2150 B.C. Their kingdom was invaded and destroyed, and in a brief period of Neo-Sumerian revival the principal religious monument at Ur, the Ziggurat, was built. Around 1800 B.C. Mesopotamia was reunified by the Babylonians, whose most famous king, Hammurabi, was the author of an important law code.

The last people to rule Mesopotamia were the Assyrians, the peak of whose power was between 1000 B.C. and 612 B.C., the year in which their capital Nineveh was sacked by the Persians. Successive royal palaces, first at Nimrud and then at Nineveh, were decorated with massive stone relief carvings that showed aspects of life at court (royal processions, hunting scenes) with considerable realism.

The first urban culture in the West, known as Minoan, developed on the Mediterranean island of Crete. Around 2000 B.C. large towns were constructed; these served as centers for the ruling families and the chief religious leaders. The largest Minoan community, Knossos, was destroyed several times by earthquakes and each time was rebuilt on a grander scale. Like the other Minoan palaces, Knossos was decorated with vivid wall paintings depicting religious ceremonies and scenes from daily life. Many examples have been found of the elaborate jewelry worn by figures in the paintings; one of the richest is the gold Wasp Pendant from Mallia.

Around 1400 B.C. Knossos was abandoned for reasons that remain mysterious, and power passed to mainland Greece, where a people called the Mycenaeans had appeared by 1600 B.C. Most of our information about the Mycenaeans comes from their tombs. The earliest ones, at Mycenae itself, were dug into the ground within a circular enclosure; vast quantities of gold treasure, including death masks, jewelry, and weapons were buried with the bodies of the dead. The Mycenaeans traded widely in the Mediterranean area, and around 1250 B.C. they sacked the city of Troy, an economic rival. Shortly after, however, their own cities were destroyed. Within a century Mycenaean culture had vanished, although it was to have important influence upon later Greek civilization.

Pronunciation Guide

Akhenaton: Ak-en-AH-tun
Akkadian: Ak-AY-di-un
Amarna: Am-AR-nuh
Assurbanipal: As-er-BAN-i-pal
Assurnasirpal: A-ser-na-SEER-pal
Chefren: KEF-ren
Cheops: CHOPS
Cuneiform: CUE-ni-form
Cyclades: SIK-la-dees
Euphrates: You-FRAY-tees
Gilgamesh: GIL-gum-esh
Hammurabi: Ham-oo-RA-bee
Hieroglyph: HIGH-ro-glif
Knossos: KNO-sos
Lascaux: Lasc-OWE
Mallia: MAR-lia
Mesopotamia: Mes-o-pot-AIM-i-a
Minos: MY-nos
Mycenae: My-SEEN-ee
Nefertiti: Nef-er-TEE-TEE
Phaistos: FES-tos
Pharaoh: FARE-owe
Schliemann: SHLEE-man
Stele: STAY-lay
Sumerian: Soo-MEE-ri-an
Tutankhamen: Tut-an-KA-mun
Uruk: Oo-ROOK
Willendorf: VIL-en-dorf
Zakro: ZAK-roe
Ziggurat: ZIG-oo-rat

Exercises

1. Compare the religious beliefs of the Egyptians and the Mesopotamians. What do their differences tell us about the cultures involved?
2. How did the development of Egyptian society affect their art? What were the principal subjects depicted by Egyptian artists?
3. What evidence is there for the role of women in the cultures discussed in this chapter?
4. What information do the excavations at the Palace of Knossos provide about Minoan daily life?
5. If you could return in time to visit one of the peoples described in the chapter, which would you choose?

Further Reading

Aldred, C. *The Egyptians*. New York: Praeger, 1961. A short but comprehensive account of Egyptian culture by one of the leading Egyptologists of the century.

Childe, V. Gordon. *What Happened in History*. Baltimore: Penguin, 1942. One of the most important books on the early development of civilization. The author's account is strongly influenced by his political views but is fundamental to an understanding of modern research on early Mesopotamia.

Frankfort, H. *The Art and Architecture of the Ancient Orient*. Baltimore: Penguin, 1970. The best single-volume guide to its subject. Technical in places but written with immense breadth of knowledge and fully illustrated.

———, et al. *Before Philosophy*. Baltimore: Penguin, 1949. Subtitled "The Intellectual Adventure of Ancient Man," this book discusses Egyptian and Mesopotamian views on life, death, the function of the state, and the nature of the world. Not easy to read, but well worth the effort.

Hood, S. *The Arts in Prehistoric Greece*. Baltimore: Penguin, 1978. An up-to-date introduction to Minoan and Mycenaean art. The author, who has himself dug both in Crete and at Mycenae, includes evidence from the most recent excavations.

Johnson, R. *The Civilization of Ancient Egypt*. London: Thames and Hudson, 1978. A good, well-balanced account that gives a general picture of Egyptian art and society.

Marinatos, S., and M. Hirmer. *Crete and Mycenae*. New York: Abrams, 1960. Chiefly valuable for its pictures, although Marinatos' commentary is authoritative and informative.

Roux, G. *Ancient Iraq,* 2nd ed. Baltimore: Penguin, 1980. A history of the ancient Near East from the Paleolithic period to Roman times.

Seton Lloyd, H. *Archaeology of Mesopotamia*. London: Methuen, 1978. An authoritative survey of recent archaeological discoveries in Mesopotamia and their significance for our knowledge of the cultures involved.

Smith, W. S., revised by W. K. Simpson. *The Art and Architecture of Ancient Egypt,* 2nd ed. Baltimore: Penguin, 1981. A thorough survey of all aspects of Egyptian art, with numerous photographs and diagrams.

Warren, P. *The Aegean Civilizations*. Oxford: Elsevier-Phaidon, 1975. A good general account of Bronze Age Aegean culture, especially well illustrated. The author includes an interesting account of his own excavations in Crete.

Willetts, R. F. *The Civilization of Ancient Crete*. London: Methuen, 1977. Deals with the Minoans and their successors on Crete and concludes with a section on Crete in the 20th century.

Reading Selections

from THE EPIC OF GILGAMESH

The following extracts are from *The Epic of Gilgamesh,* which describes the exploits of the Sumerian ruler Gilgamesh and his friend Enkidu. In the course of the poem Enkidu dies of an illness sent by the gods and Gilgamesh goes on a journey in search of the meaning of existence. Toward the end he meets Utnapishtim, the only mortal to whom the gods have given eternal life, and tries to learn from him the secret of immortality. The futility of his quest is expressed by his inability even to stay awake.

The Flood

With the first light of dawn a black cloud came from the horizon; it thundered within where Adad, lord of the storm, was riding. In front over hill and plain Shullat and Hanish, heralds of the storm, led on. Then the gods of the abyss rose up; Nergal pulled out the dams of the nether waters, Ninurta the war-lord threw down the dykes, and the seven judges of hell, the Annunaki, raised their torches, lighting the land with their livid flame. A stupor of despair went up to heaven when the god of the storm turned daylight to darkness, when he smashed the land like a cup. One whole day the tempest raged gathering fury as it went, it poured over the people like the tides of battle; a man could not see his brother nor the people be seen from heaven. Even the gods were terrified at the flood, they fled to the highest heaven, the firmament of Anu; they crouched against the walls, cowering like curs. Then Ishtar the sweet-voiced Queen of Heaven cried out like a woman in travail: "Alas the days of old are turned to dust because I commanded evil; why did I command this evil in the council of all the gods? I commanded wars to destroy the people, but are they not my people, for I brought them forth? Now like the spawn of fish they float in the ocean." The great gods of heaven and of hell wept, they covered their mouths.

The Afterlife

Enkidu slept alone in his sickness and he poured out his heart to Gilgamesh, "Last night I dreamed again, my friend. The heavens moaned and the earth replied; I stood alone before an awful being; his face was sombre like the black bird of the storm. He fell upon me with the talons of an eagle and he held me fast, pinioned with his claw, till I smothered; then he transformed me so that my arms became wings covered with feathers. He turned his stare towards me, and he led me away to the palace of Irkalla, the Queen of Darkness, to the house from which none who enters ever returns, down the road from which there is no coming back.

"There is the house whose people sit in darkness; dust is their food and clay their meat. They are clothed like birds with wings for covering, they see no light, they sit in darkness. I entered the house of dust and I saw the kings of the earth, their crowns put away for ever; rulers and princes, all those who once wore kingly crowns and ruled the world in the days of old. They who had stood in the place of the gods, like Anu and Enlil, stood now like servants to fetch baked meats in the house of dust, to carry cooked meat and cold water from the water-skin. In the house of dust which I entered were high-priests and acolytes, priests of the incantation and of ecstasy; there were servers of the temple, and there was Etana, that king of Kish whom the eagle carried to heaven in the days of old. I saw also Samuqan, god of cattle, and there was Ereshkigal the Queen of the Underworld; and Belit-Sheri squatted in front of her, she who is recorder of the gods and keeps the book of death. She held a tablet from which she read. She raised her head, she saw me and spoke: 'Who has brought this one here?' Then I awoke like a man drained of blood who wanders alone in a waste of rushes; like one whom the bailiff has seized and his heart pounds with terror. O my brother, let some great prince, some other, come when I am dead, or let some god stand at your gate, let him obliterate my name and write his own instead."

The Return of Gilgamesh

Utnapishtim said, "As for you, Gilgamesh, who will assemble the gods for your sake, so that you may find that life for which you are searching? But if you wish, come and put it to the test: only prevail against sleep for six days and seven nights." But while Gilgamesh sat there resting on his haunches, a mist of sleep like soft wool teased from the fleece drifted over him, and Utnapishtim said to his wife, "Look at him now, the strong man who would have everlasting life, even now the mists of sleep are drifting over him." His wife replied, "Touch the man to wake him, so that he may return to his own land in peace, going back through the gate by which he came." Utnapishtim said to his wife, "All men are deceivers, even you he will attempt to deceive; therefore bake loaves of bread, each day one loaf, and put it beside his head; and make a mark on the wall to number the days he has slept."

So she baked loaves of bread, each day one loaf, and put it beside his head, and she marked on the wall the days that he slept; and there came a day when the first loaf was hard, the second loaf was like leather, the third loaf was soggy, the crust of the fourth had mould, the fifth was mildewed, the sixth was fresh, and the seventh was still on the embers. Then Utnapishtim touched him and he woke. Gilgamesh said to Utnapishtim the Faraway, "I hardly slept when you touched and roused me." But Utnapishtim said, "Count these loaves and learn how many days you slept, for your first is hard, your second is like leather, your third is soggy, the crust of your fourth has mould, your fifth is mildewed, your sixth is fresh, and your seventh was still over the glowing embers when I touched and woke you." Gilgamesh said, "What shall I do, O Utnapishtim, where shall I go? Already the thief in the night has hold of my limbs, death inhabits my room; wherever my foot rests, there I find death."

Then Utnapishtim spoke to Urshanabi the ferryman: "Woe to you Urshanabi, now and for ever more you have become hateful to this harbourage; it is not for you, nor for you are the crossings of this sea. Go now, banished from the shore. But this man before whom you walked, bringing him here, whose body is covered with foulness and the grace of whose limbs has been spoiled by wild skins, take him to the washing-place. There he shall wash his long hair clean as snow in the water, he shall throw off his skins and let the sea carry them away, and the beauty of his body shall be shown, the fillet on his forehead shall be renewed, and he shall be given clothes to cover his nakedness. Till he reaches his own city and his journey is accomplished, these clothes will show no sign of age, they will wear like a new garment." So Urshanabi took Gilgamesh and led him to the washing-place, he washed his long hair as clean as snow in the water, he threw off his skins, which the sea carried away, and showed the beauty of his body. He renewed the fillet on his forehead, and to cover his nakedness gave him clothes which would show no sign of age, but would wear like a new garment till he reached his own city, and his journey was accomplished.

Then Gilgamesh and Urshanabi launched the boat on to the water and boarded it, and they made ready to sail away; but the wife of Utnapishtim the Faraway said to him, "Gilgamesh came here wearied out, he is worn out; what will you give him to carry him back to his own country?" So Utnapishtim spoke, and Gilgamesh took a pole and brought the boat in to the bank. "Gilgamesh, you came here, a man wearied out, you have worn yourself out; what shall I give you to carry you back to your own country? Gilgamesh, I shall reveal a secret thing, it is a mystery of the gods that I am telling you. There is a plant that grows under the water, it has a prickle like a thorn, like a rose; it will wound your hands, but if you suc-

ceed in taking it, then your hands will hold that which restores his lost youth to a man."

When Gilgamesh heard this he opened the sluices so that a sweet-water current might carry him out to the deepest channel; he tied heavy stones to his feet and they dragged him down to the water-bed. There he saw the plant growing; although it pricked him he took it in his hands; then he cut the heavy stones from his feet, and the sea carried him and threw him on to the shore. Gilgamesh said to Urshanabi the ferryman, "Come here, and see this marvellous plant. By its virtue a man may win back all his former strength. I will take it to Uruk of the strong walls; there I will give it to the old men to eat. Its name shall be 'The Old Men Are Young Again'; and at last I shall eat it myself and have back all my lost youth." So Gilgamesh returned by the gate through which he had come, Gilgamesh and Urshanabi went together. They travelled their twenty leagues and then they broke their fast; after thirty leagues they stopped for the night.

Gilgamesh saw a well of cool water and he went down and bathed; but deep in the pool there was lying a serpent, and the serpent sensed the sweetness of the flower. It rose out of the water and snatched it away, and immediately it sloughed its skin and returned to the well. Then Gilgamesh sat down and wept, the tears ran down his face, and he took the hand of Urshanabi; "O Urshanabi, was it for this that I toiled with my hands, is it for this I have wrung out my heart's blood? For myself I have gained nothing; not I, but the beast of the earth has joy of it now. Already the stream has carried it twenty leagues back to the channels where I found it. I found a sign and now I have lost it. Let us leave the boat on the bank and go."

After twenty leagues they broke their fast, after thirty leagues they stopped for the night; in three days they had walked as much as a journey of a month and fifteen days. When the journey was accomplished they arrived at Uruk, the strong-walled city. Gilgamesh spoke to him, to Urshanabi the ferryman, "Urshanabi, climb up on to the wall of Uruk, inspect its foundation terrace, and examine well the brickwork; see if it is not of burnt bricks; and did not the seven wise men lay these foundations? One third of the whole is city, one third is garden, and one third is field, with the precinct of the goddess Ishtar. These parts and the precinct are all Uruk."

This too was the work of Gilgamesh, the king, who knew the countries of the world. He was wise, he saw mysteries and knew secret things, he brought us a tale of the days before the flood. He went a long journey, was weary, worn out with labour, and returning engraved on a stone the whole story.

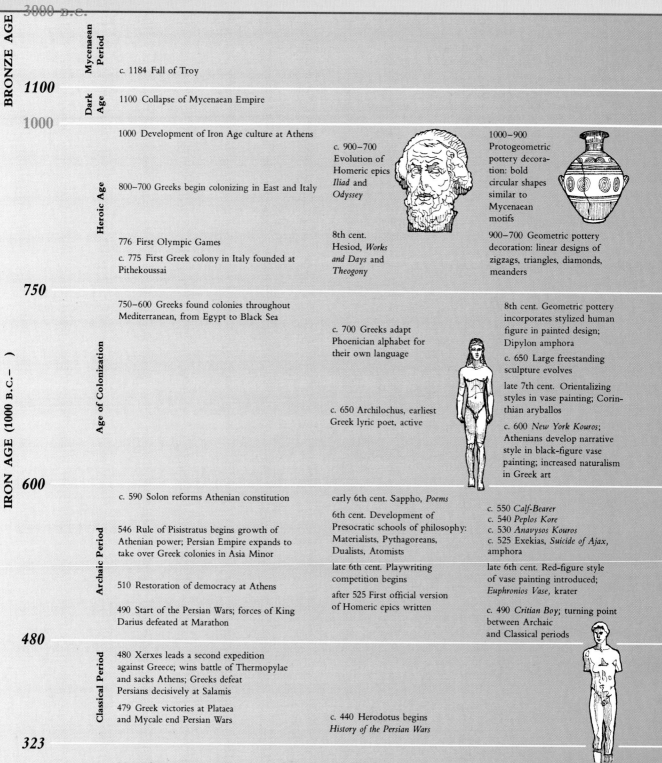

		GENERAL EVENTS	LITERATURE & PHILOSOPHY	ART

BRONZE AGE

3000 B.C.

Mycenaean Period

c. 1184 Fall of Troy

1100

Dark Age

1100 Collapse of Mycenaean Empire

1000

1000 Development of Iron Age culture at Athens

Heroic Age

800–700 Greeks begin colonizing in East and Italy

776 First Olympic Games

c. 775 First Greek colony in Italy founded at Pithekoussai

c. 900–700 Evolution of Homeric epics *Iliad* and *Odyssey*

8th cent. Hesiod, *Works and Days* and *Theogony*

1000–900 Protogeometric pottery decoration: bold circular shapes similar to Mycenaean motifs

900–700 Geometric pottery decoration: linear designs of zigzags, triangles, diamonds, meanders

750

IRON AGE (1000 B.C. –)

Age of Colonization

750–600 Greeks found colonies throughout Mediterranean, from Egypt to Black Sea

c. 700 Greeks adapt Phoenician alphabet for their own language

c. 650 Archilochus, earliest Greek lyric poet, active

8th cent. Geometric pottery incorporates stylized human figure in painted design; Dipylon amphora

c. 650 Large freestanding sculpture evolves

late 7th cent. Orientalizing styles in vase painting; Corinthian aryballos

c. 600 *New York Kouros*; Athenians develop narrative style in black-figure vase painting; increased naturalism in Greek art

600

Archaic Period

c. 590 Solon reforms Athenian constitution

546 Rule of Pisistratus begins growth of Athenian power; Persian Empire expands to take over Greek colonies in Asia Minor

510 Restoration of democracy at Athens

490 Start of the Persian Wars; forces of King Darius defeated at Marathon

early 6th cent. Sappho, *Poems*

6th cent. Development of Presocratic schools of philosophy: Materialists, Pythagoreans, Dualists, Atomists

late 6th cent. Playwriting competition begins

after 525 First official version of Homeric epics written

c. 550 *Calf-Bearer*
c. 540 *Peplos Kore*
c. 530 *Anavysos Kouros*
c. 525 Exekias, *Suicide of Ajax*, amphora

late 6th cent. Red-figure style of vase painting introduced; *Euphronios Vase*, krater

c. 490 *Critian Boy*; turning point between Archaic and Classical periods

480

Classical Period

480 Xerxes leads a second expedition against Greece; wins battle of Thermopylae and sacks Athens; Greeks defeat Persians decisively at Salamis

479 Greek victories at Plataea and Mycale end Persian Wars

c. 440 Herodotus begins *History of the Persian Wars*

323

Many dates are approximate

2

Early Greece

Early music primarily vocal with instrumental accompaniment; use of flute and simple lyre popular

7th cent. Development of aulos (double flute), used to accompany songs

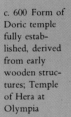

c. 600 Form of Doric temple fully established, derived from early wooden structures; Temple of Hera at Olympia

c. 675 Terpander of Lesbos introduces cithara

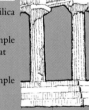

c. 550 Basilica at Paestum

c. 540 Temple of Apollo at Corinth

c. 500 Temple of Aphaia, Aegina

586 Sacadas of Argos composes first known purely instrumental work for performance on aulos at Pythian Games in Delphi

c. 550 Pythagoras discovers numerical relationship of music harmonies and our modern musical scale

5th cent. First widespread use of Ionic order

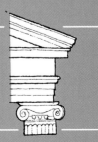

late 5th cent. Earliest surviving fragment of Greek music

One of the major turning points of history is the period around 1000 B.C., the change from the Bronze Age to the Iron Age throughout the Mediterranean area. In the following centuries a culture developed in a small corner of southeastern Europe, Greece, which was to form the foundation of Western civilization. By the 5th century B.C. this culture had produced one of the greatest eras of human achievement.

In certain basic ways, of course, there was some continuity between the Bronze Age and the Iron Age. For example, Athens, which in the 5th century B.C. became the intellectual center of Classical Greece, had been a Mycenaean city long before the Iron Age began. In most significant respects, however, the Iron Age Greeks had to discover for themselves almost all the cultural skills associated with civilization—the visual arts, architecture, literature, philosophy, even the art of writing. The Mycenaeans had known how to write and build and create art. However, their abrupt and violent end around 1100 B.C. was followed by a century of disturbance and confusion that cut off the Bronze Age from the new world of the Iron Age. To follow the first attempts of these Iron Age people to develop an artistic style, organize their societies, and question the nature of the universe is to witness the birth of Western culture.

The history of early Greece falls naturally into three periods, each marked by its own distinctive artistic achievement. During the first three hundred years or so of the Iron Age, development was slow and the Greeks had only limited contact with other Mediterranean peoples. During this period the first great works of literature were created—the epic

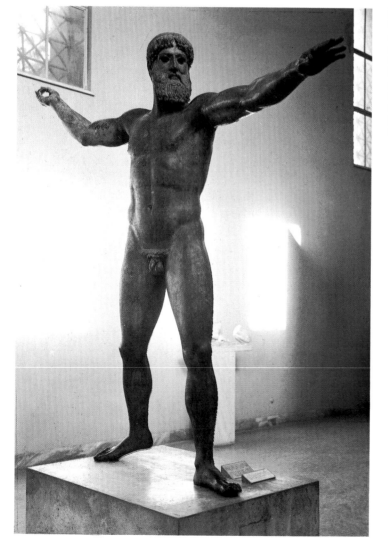

2.1 *Zeus (Poseidon?)*. c. 465 B.C. Bronze, height 6′10″ (2.08 m). National Archaeological Museum, Athens. Whether this striding god is Zeus or Poseidon, god of the sea, the combination of majestic dignity and physical strength reflects the Greeks' view of their gods as superior beings with definitely human attributes. This statue, found in the sea off Cape Artemisium, comes from the end of the period of this chapter; it may have been intended to commemorate the Greek victory over the Persians.

poems known as the *Iliad* and the *Odyssey*. Because these works treat heroic themes, the early Iron Age in Greece is sometimes known as the Heroic Age.

By the beginning of the 8th century B.C. Greek travelers and merchants had already begun to explore the lands to the east and west. In the next 150 years (c. 750–600 B.C.), called the Age of Colonization, many new ideas and artistic styles were brought to Greece. These foreign influences were finally absorbed in the third era of early Greece known as the Archaic period (c. 600–480 B.C.). This period, the culmination of the first five hundred years of Greek history, paved the way for the Classical period, discussed in Chapter 3. The Greeks' relationship to the world around them took a decisive turn at the very end of the Archaic period with their victory over the Persians in the wars that lasted from 490 to 479 B.C. The events of the Persian Wars thus end this chapter.

Homer and the Heroic Age

During the Mycenaean period most of Greece had been united under a single influence. When the Mycenaeans fell, however, Greece split up into a series of independent regions that corresponded to the geographically separated areas created by the mountain ranges and high hills that crisscross the terrain. Within each of these geographically discrete areas there developed an urban center that controlled the surrounding countryside. Thus Athens became the dominating force in the geographical region known as Attica; Thebes controlled Boeotia; Sparta controlled Laconia, and so on (see map, page 44). A central urban community of this kind was called by the Greeks of a later period a *polis,* a term generally translated as "city-state."

The polis served as focal point for all political, religious, social, and artistic activities within its region. Its citizens felt toward their own individual city a loyalty that was far stronger than any generalized sense of community with their fellow Greeks over the mountains. Each of the leading cities developed its own artistic style, which led to fierce competition and in time bitter and destructive rivalries. The polis was, therefore, both the glory and the ruin of Greek civilization, producing on the one hand an unequaled concentration of intellectual and cultural development, on the other a tendency to internal squabbling at the least provocation.

The fragmentation of social and cultural life had a marked effect on the development of Greek mythology and religion. Religion played an important part in Greek life, as Greek art and literature demonstrate, but it was very different in nature from the other systems of belief that influenced our culture, Judaism and Christianity. For one thing, Greek mythology offers no central body of information or teaching corresponding to the Old or New Testaments. Often there are varying versions of the same basic story; even when these versions do not actually contradict one another, they often are difficult to reconcile. For another thing, the very characters of the Greek gods and goddesses often seem confused and self-contradictory. For example, Zeus, President of the Immortals and Father of gods and humans, generally represented the concept of an objective moral code to which both gods and mortals were expected to conform; Zeus imposed justice and supervised the punishment of wrongdoers [2.1]. Yet this same majestic ruler was also involved in many love affairs and seductions, in the course of which his behavior was often undignified and even comical. How could the Greeks have believed in a champion of morality whose own moral standards were so lax?

The answer lies in the fact that Greek myth and religion of later times consist of a mass of folk tales, primitive customs, and traditional rituals that grew up during the Heroic Age and were never developed into a single unified system. Individual cities had their own mythological traditions, some of them going back to the Bronze Age, others gradually developing under the influence of neighboring peoples. Poets and artists felt free to choose the versions that appealed to their own tastes or helped them to express their ideas. Later Greeks, it is true, tried to organize all these conflicting beliefs into something resembling order. Father Zeus ruled from Mount Olympus, where he was surrounded by the other principal Olympian deities. His wife Hera was the goddess of marriage and the protectress of the family. His daughter Athena symbolized intelligence and understanding. Aphrodite was the goddess of love, Ares, her lover, the god of war, and so on. But the range and variety of the Greek imagination defied this kind of categorization. The Greeks loved a good story, and so tales that did not fit the ordered scheme continued to circulate.

These contradictions were, of course, perfectly apparent to the Greeks themselves, but they used their religion to illuminate their own lives, rather than to give them divine guidance. One of the clearest examples is the contrast that Greek poets drew between the powers of Apollo and Dionysus, two of the most important of their gods. Apollo represented logic and order, the power of the mind; Dionysus was the god of the emotions, whose influence, if excessive, could lead to violence and disorder. By worshiping both these forces, the Greeks were acknowledging their obvious dual existence in human nature and trying to strike a prudent balance between them.

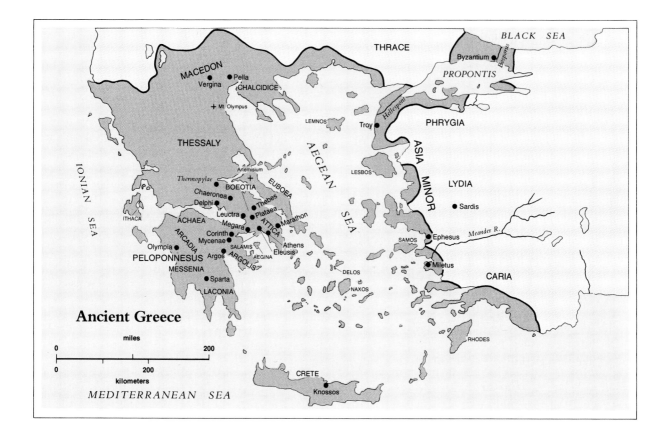

Ancient Greece

The Greek deities served many purposes, therefore, but these purposes were very different from those of the other Western religions. No Greek god, not even Zeus, represents supreme good. At the other end of the moral scale, there is no Greek figure of supreme evil corresponding to the Christian concept of Satan. The Greeks turned to their deities for explanations of both natural phenomena and psychological characteristics they recognized in themselves. At the same time they used their gods and goddesses as yet another way of enhancing the glory of their individual city-states, as in the case of the cult of Athena at Athens. Problems of human morality required human, rather than divine, solutions. The Greeks turned to art and literature, rather than prayer, as a means of trying to discover them (Table 2.1).

At the beginning of Greek history stand two epic poems which even the quarrelsome Greeks themselves saw as national, indeed universal, in their significance. The *Iliad* and the *Odyssey* have, from the time of the Greeks, been held in the highest esteem. Homer, their accepted author, is generally regarded as not only the first figure in the Western literary tradition but also one of the greatest. Yet even though Homer's genius is beyond doubt, little else

about him is clear. In fact, the many problems and theories connected with the Homeric epics and their creator are generally summed up under the label "the Homeric Question."

The ancient Greeks themselves were not sure who had composed the *Iliad* and the *Odyssey*, when and where the author had lived, or even if one person was

TABLE 2.1	The Principal Greek Deities
Zeus	Father of Gods and Men
Hera	Wife of Zeus, Queen of Heaven
Poseidon	Brother of Zeus, God of the Sea
Hephaestus	Son of Zeus and Hera, God of Fire
Ares	God of War
Apollo	God of the Sun, Music, the Intellect
Artemis	Goddess of Chastity and the Moon
Demeter	Earth Mother, Goddess of Fertility
Aphrodite	Goddess of Beauty, Love, and Marriage
Athena	Goddess of Wisdom
Hermes	Messenger of the Gods, God of Cleverness
Dionysus	God of Wine and the Emotions

responsible for both of them. In general, tradition ascribed the epics to a blind poet called Homer; almost every city worthy of the name claimed to be his birthplace. Theories about when he had lived ranged from the time of the Trojan War, around 1250 B.C., to 500 years later.

The problem of who Homer was, and even whether he existed at all, continues to vex scholars to this day. In any case most experts would probably now agree that the creation of the *Iliad* and the *Odyssey* was a highly complex affair. Each of the epics basically consists of a number of shorter folk tales that were combined, gradually evolving over a century or more into the works as we now know them. The first crystallization of these popular stories had probably occurred by around 800 B.C., but the poems were still not in their final form. The first written official version of each epic was probably not made before the late 6th century B.C. The edition of the poems used by modern scholars was made by a scribe working at Alexandria in the 2nd century B.C.

Where, then, in this long development must we place Homer? He may perhaps have been the man who first began to combine the separate tales into a single whole; or perhaps he was the man who sometime after 800 B.C. imposed an artistic unity on the mass of remembered folk stories he had inherited. The differences between the *Iliad* and the *Odyssey* have suggested to a number of commentators that a different "Homer" may have been responsible for the creation or development of each work, but here we are in the realm of speculation. Perhaps after all it would be best to follow the ancient Greeks themselves, contenting ourselves with the belief that at some stage in the evolution of the poems they were filtered through the imagination of the first great genius of the Western literary tradition, without being too specific about which stage it was.

Both works show evidence of their long evolution by word of mouth. All the chief characters are given standardized descriptive adjectives as "epithets," that are repeated whenever they appear: Achilles is "swift-footed" and Odysseus "cunning." Phrases, lines, and entire sections are often repeated.

Furthermore, the heroic world of warfare is made more accessible to the poem's audience by the use of elaborate similes, which compare aspects of the story to everyday life in the early Iron Age—the massing of the Greek forces, for example, is likened to a swarm of flies buzzing around pails of milk.

Although the two poems are clearly the result of a single tradition, they are very different in spirit. The *Iliad* is somber, taut, direct. The concentration of its theme makes it easier to understand, and certainly easier to explain, than the more digressive and light-hearted *Odyssey*. But the *Odyssey* is certainly not a lesser work; if anything, its range and breadth of humanity are even greater, and its design is more elaborate.

The action of the *Iliad* takes place during the final year of the Greeks' siege of Troy, or Ilium. Its subject is only indirectly concerned with the Trojan War, however, and the poem ends before the episode of the wooden horse and the fall of the city. Its principal theme is stated in the opening lines of Book I, which establish the tragic mood of the work. Here the poet invokes the goddess of poetic inspiration: "Sing, goddess, of the anger of Peleus' son Achilles, which disastrously inflicted countless sufferings on the Greeks, sending the strong souls of many heroes to Hades and leaving their bodies to be devoured by dogs and all birds. . . . "

The subject of the *Iliad,* then, is the anger of Achilles and its consequences. Its message is a direct one: We must be prepared to answer for the results of our own actions and realize that when we act wrongly we will cause suffering both for ourselves and, perhaps more important, for those we love. Although the setting of the *Iliad* is heroic, even mythic, the theme of human responsibility is universal. This relevance to our own experience is underlined by the realism in the scenes of battles and death, which are characteristic of epic literature's interest in heroic warfare.

The story of Achilles' disastrous mistake is told in a basically simple and direct narrative. It begins with a quarrel between Agamemnon, commander-in-chief of the Greek forces, and Achilles, his powerful ally, who resents Agamemnon's overbearing assertion of authority. After a public argument, Achilles decides to punish Agamemnon by withdrawing his military support and retiring to his tent, in the hope that without his aid the Greeks will be unable to overcome the Trojans. In the battles that follow he is proved correct; the Trojans inflict a series of defeats on the Greeks, killing many of their leading warriors.

Agamemnon eventually (Book IX) admits that he behaved too high-handedly and offers Achilles, through intermediaries, not only a handsome apology but a generous financial inducement to return to the fighting and save the Greek cause. Achilles, however, rejects this attempt to make amends and stubbornly nurses his anger as the fighting resumes and Greek casualties mount. Then his dearest friend Patroclus is killed by the Trojan leader Hector, son of their king (Book XVI). Only now does Achilles return to battle, his former anger against Agamemnon now turned against the Trojans in general and Hector in particular.

After killing Hector in single combat (Book XXII), Achilles maltreats Hector's corpse in order to relieve his own sense of guilt at having permitted Patroclus' death. Finally, Priam, the old king of

Troy, steals into the Greek camp by night to beg for the return of his son's body (Book XXIV). In this encounter with Priam, Achilles at last recognizes and accepts the tragic nature of life and the inevitability of death. His anger melts and he hands over the body of his dead enemy. The *Iliad* ends with the funeral rites of Hector, "tamer of horses."

As is clear even from this brief summary, there is a direct relationship between human actions and their consequences. The gods appear in the *Iliad* and frequently play a part in the action, but at no time can divine intervention save Achilles from paying the price for his unreasonable anger. Furthermore, Achilles' crime is committed not against a divine code of ethics but against human standards of behavior. All his companions, including Patroclus, realize that he is behaving unreasonably.

From its earliest beginnings, therefore, the Greek view of morality is in strong contrast to the Judeo-Christian tradition. At the center of the Homeric universe is not God but human beings, who are at least partly in control of their own destiny. If they cannot choose the time when they die, they can at least choose how they live. The standards by which human life will be judged are those established by one's fellow humans. In the *Iliad* the gods serve as divine "umpires." They watch the action and comment on it and at times enforce the rules, but they do not affect the course of history. Humans do not always, however, fully realize the consequences of their behavior. In fact, they often prefer to believe that things happen "according to the will of the gods" rather than because of their own actions. Yet the gods themselves claim no such power. In a remarkable passage at the beginning of Book I of the *Odyssey* we see the world for a moment through the eyes of Zeus as he sits at dinner on Mount Olympus:

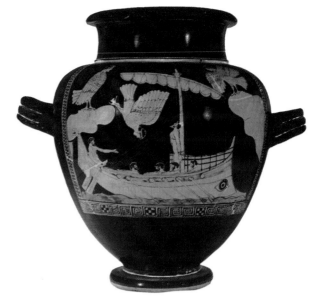

2.2 Siren Painter. *Odysseus and the Sirens,* detail of red-figure vase. c. 475 B.C. Terra cotta, height of vase 13⅞" (35 cm). British Museum, London (reproduced by courtesy of the Trustees). Odysseus is tied to the mast of his ship, at his own order, so he can resist the call of the Sirens' song. He has ordered his men to put wax in their ears.

"How foolish men are! How unjustly they blame the gods! It is their lot to suffer, but because of their own folly they bring upon themselves sufferings over and above what is fated for them. And then they blame the gods." These are hardly words we can imagine coming from the God of the Old Testament.

The principal theme of the *Odyssey* is the return home of the Greek hero Odysseus from the war against Troy. Odysseus' journey, which takes ten years, is filled with adventures involving one-eyed giants, monsters of various kinds, a seductive enchantress, a romantic young girl, a floating island, a trip to the underworld, and many other fairy-tale ele-

---

CONTEMPORARY VOICES
Daily Life in the World of Homer

From the description of scenes on the shield of Achilles:

Next he showed two beautiful cities full of people. In one of them weddings and banquets were afoot. They were bringing the brides through the streets from their homes, to the loud music of the wedding-hymn and the light of blazing torches. Youths accompanied by flute and lyre were whirling in the dance, and the women had come to the doors of their houses to enjoy the show. But the men had flocked to the meeting-place, where a case had come up between two litigants, about the payment of compensation for a man who had been killed. The defendant claimed the right to pay in full and was announcing his intention to the people; but the other contested his claim and refused all compensation. Both parties insisted that the issue should be settled by a referee; and both were cheered by their supporters in the crowd, whom the heralds were attempting to silence. The Elders sat on the sacred bench, a semicircle of polished stone; and each, as he received the speaker's rod from the clear-voiced heralds, came forward in his turn to give his judgment staff in hand. Two talents of gold were displayed in the centre: they were the fee for the Elder whose exposition of the law should prove the best.

Homer, *Iliad,* trans. E. V. Rieu (Baltimore: Penguin, 1950), Book XVIII, p. 349

ments [2.2]. Into this main narrative is woven a description of the wanderings of Odysseus' son, Telemachus, who, searching for his missing father, visits many of the other Greek leaders who have returned safely from Troy.

In the last half of the poem Odysseus finally returns home in disguise. Without revealing his identity to his ever-faithful wife Penelope, he kills the suitors who have been pestering her for ten years to declare her husband dead and remarry. Homer keeps us waiting almost to the very end for the grand recognition scene between husband and wife. All ends happily, with Penelope, Odysseus, and his aged father Laertes peacefully reunited.

It is worth examining the Homeric world at some length, because the *Iliad* and the *Odyssey* formed the basis of education and culture throughout the Greek and Roman world; children learned the two poems by heart at school. Ideas changed and developed, but reverence for Homer remained constant.

The Visual Arts in Early Greece

Geometric Art

Our impressions of the first three hundred years of Greek art (1000–700 B.C.) are based largely on painted pottery, hardly a major art form even in later times, for little else has survived. Of architecture there is almost no trace. Although small bronze and ivory statuettes and relief plaques were being made from the 9th century B.C. on, the earliest surviving large stone sculptures date to the mid-7th century B.C.

Painted vases, therefore, are our major source of information about artistic developments. It comes as something of a surprise to find that Homer's contemporaries decorated their pots with abstract geometric designs, with no attempt at the qualities most typical of their literature, vividness and realism. This style has given its name to the two subdivisions of the period, the Protogeometric (1000–900 B.C.) and the Geometric (900–700 B.C.).

For the first hundred years, artists decorated their vases with simple, bold designs consisting mainly of concentric circles and semicircles [2.3]. In some ways this period represents a transition from the end of the Mycenaean age, but the memory of Mycenaean motifs soon gave way to a new style. If Protogeometric pottery seems a long way from Greek art of later centuries, it does show qualities of clarity and order that reappear later, although in a very different context.

In the Geometric pottery of the following two centuries (900–700 B.C.) the use of abstract design continued, but the emphasis changed. Circles and

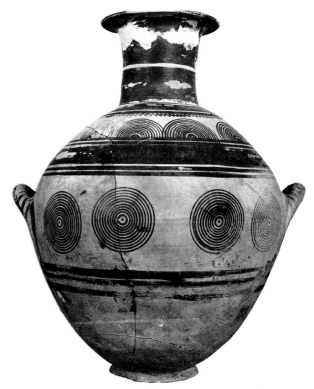

2.3 Protogeometric amphora. c. 950 B.C. Height 21¾″ (56 cm). Kerameikos Museum, Athens. The circles and semicircles typical of this style were drawn with a compass.

semicircles were replaced by linear designs, zigzags, triangles, diamonds, and above all the *meander* (a maze pattern). The size of the pots increased and their shape became increasingly distorted to accommodate more and more bands of geometric design [2.4].

There is something strangely obsessive about many of these vessels—a sense of artists searching for a subject, meanwhile working out over and over the implications of mathematical formulas. Once again we seem a long way from the achievements of later Greek artists, with their emphasis on realism, yet precise mathematical relationships lie behind the design of much of the greatest Greek art. The Geometric period is best thought of not as a temporary aberration, a wrong track that was abandoned, but as an expression of the obsession with order and balance so characteristic of Greek culture in general.

By the 8th century B.C., artists had begun to find their way toward the principal subject of later Greek art, the human form. Thus human and animal figures begin to appear among the meanders and zigzags. This is a moment of such importance in the history of Western art that we should not take it for granted. We have been so conditioned by the art of the ancient Greeks that from the late Geometric period until our

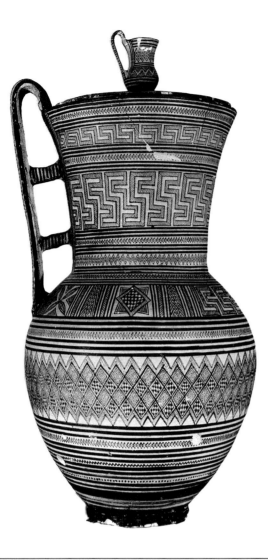

2.4 Geometric pitcher. c. 800 B.C. Height 31¼″ (80 cm). National Archaeological Museum, Athens. The bands of decoration cover the entire surface. The lid has a handle in the form of a miniature pitcher, and it too is covered with geometric designs.

own time Western art has been primarily concerned with the depiction of human beings. Landscapes are a popular subject, it is true, and in our own century art has become abstract again. Yet most paintings and sculptures deal with the human form, treated in a more or less realistic way.

This realism may seem so obvious as to be hardly worth stating, but it must be remembered that the art of peoples who were not influenced by the Greeks is very different. Islamic art, for example, deals almost exclusively in abstract design. Indian sculptors depicted their gods and heroes in human form, but they certainly did not treat them realistically. The Hindu god Shiva, for example, is often shown with many arms. It is a tribute to the Greeks' overwhelming influence on our culture that, from the Roman period to the 20th century, artists have accepted the Greeks' decision to make the realistic treatment of the human form the central focus of art, whether the forms were those of mortal people or divine gods and goddesses.

The Greeks themselves did not achieve this naturalism overnight. The first depictions of human beings, which appear on Geometric vases shortly after 800 B.C., are highly stylized. They are painted in silhouette, and a single figure often combines front and side views, the head and legs being shown in profile while the upper half of the body is seen from the front. Clearly these are abstractions of men and

THE ARTS AND INVENTION: *The Potter's Wheel*

The high quality of the Greeks' pottery owes much to their use of a wheel in its manufacture. A potter's wheel rotates horizontally at high speed to help the potter shape the clay into symmetrical vessels whose walls are of uniform thickness. The driving mechanism varies but it is often run by pedals operated by the feet.

Although a fast potter's wheel was already in use by the early Sumerian period, around 3400 B.C., the technique spread slowly. The first people in Europe to produce wheel-made pottery were the Minoans, who were followed by the Mycenaeans. The Greeks' use of the wheel from their earliest times is a legacy from their Bronze Age predecessors. Some of the peoples of northern Europe, including Britain, made pottery without a wheel as late as the first century B.C., and its use was never discovered in America; it was introduced there by the followers of Columbus.

One of the advantages of wheel-made production was that large quantities of high-quality vessels could be produced quickly and efficiently. This, in turn, led to the development of more efficient kilns, the chambers that were built to contain the pottery while it was being baked. The earliest kilns were simple clay structures with a fire in the base and the pottery above, placed on bars. The obvious drawback to these, however, was that they had to be demolished each time to remove the fired pottery. By the time of the Greeks permanent kilns were in use. The fire lay to one side of the chamber and the heat was conducted either from below or from above by a "draft" or a "down-draft" tunnel. The mass-production of pots these technological innovations made possible was to have important consequences for the political and economic development of Corinth and Athens.

women, rather than literal depictions, although the artists do sometimes try to distinguish between the sexes by adding small projections below the armpits to represent female breasts.

A number of the vases decorated with stick figures of this kind are of immense size. One of them, the *Dipylon Amphora,* is almost 5 feet (1.24 meters) tall [2.5]. These vases were set up over tombs to serve as grave markers; they had holes in their bases so that offerings poured into them could seep down to the dead below. The scenes on them frequently show the funeral ceremony. Others show processions of warriors, both on foot and in chariots.

2.5 *Dipylon Amphora.* c. 750 B.C. Height 4′11″ (1.24 m). National Archaeological Museum, Athens. This immense vase originally was a grave marker. The main band, between the handles, shows the lying-in-state of the dead man on whose grave the vase stood; on both sides of the bier are mourners tearing their hair in grief. Note the two bands of animals, deer and running goats, in the upper part of the vase.

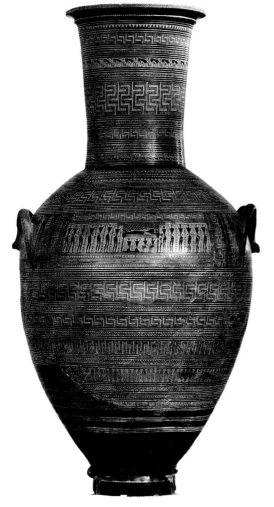

The Age of Colonization: Vase Painting at Corinth and Athens

Throughout the period of Homer and Geometric art, individual city-states were ruled by small groups of aristocrats who concentrated wealth and power in their own hands. Presumably, it is their graves that were marked with great amphoras like the *Dipylon* vase. By the 8th century B.C., however, two developments had occurred. First, two centuries of peace had allowed the individual city-states to become quite prosperous. Second, the continuing rule of a small hereditary aristocracy left a growing urban population increasingly frustrated. Both the accumulation of wealth and the problem of overpopulation produced a single result, colonization.

Throughout the 8th and 7th centuries, enterprising Greeks went abroad either to make their fortunes or to increase them. To the west, Italy and Sicily were colonized and Greek cities established there. Some of these, like Syracuse in Sicily or Sybaris in southern Italy, became even richer and more powerful than the mother cities from which the colonizers had come. Unfortunately if inevitably, the settlers took with them not only the culture of their *polis* but their intercity rivalries, often with disastrous results. To the south and east, cities were also established in Egypt and on the Black Sea.

The most significant wave of colonization was that which moved eastward to the coast of Asia Minor, in some cases back to territory that had been inhabited by the Mycenaeans centuries earlier. From here the colonizers established trade contacts with peoples in the ancient Near East, including the Phoenicians and the Persians. Within Greece itself the effect on art and life of this expansion to the east was immense. After almost three hundred years of cultural isolation, in a land cut off from its neighbors by mountains and sea, the Greeks were brought face to face with the immensely rich and sophisticated cultures of the ancient Near East. Oriental ideas and artistic styles were seen by the colonizers and carried home by the traders. A growing quantity of eastern artifacts, ivories, jewelry, and metalwork was sent back to the mother cities and even to the Greek cities of Italy. So great was the impact of Near Eastern art on the Greeks from the late 8th century to around 600 B.C. that this period and its style are generally known by the name *Orientalizing.*

Different Greek cities reacted to Oriental influences in different ways, although all were strongly influenced. In particular, the growing hostility between the two richest city-states, Athens and Corinth, which two centuries later led to the Peloponnesian War and the fall of Athens, seems already symbolized in the strong differences between their

Orientalizing pottery. The Corinthian artists developed a miniature style that made use of a wide variety of eastern motifs—sphinxes, winged human figures, floral designs—all of them arranged in bands covering almost the entire surface of the vase. Individual figures were depicted in the so-called *black-figure technique.* They were first painted in silhouette, in black, and details were then etched in by scratching lines with a fine point. White, yellow, and purple were often used to highlight details, producing a bold and striking effect. After the monotony of Geometric pottery the variety of subject and range of color come as a welcome change.

The small size of the pots made them ideal for export. Corinthian vases have in fact been discovered not only throughout Greece but also in Italy, Egypt, and the Near East. Clearly, any self-respecting woman of the 7th century B.C. wanted an elegant little Corinthian flask [2.6] for her perfume, oil, or make-up. The vases are well made, the figures lively, and the style instantly recognizable as Corinthian—an important factor for commercial success. Corinth's notable political and economic strength throughout the 7th and early 6th centuries B.C. was, in fact, built on the sale of these little pots and their contents.

In Athens, potters were slower to throw off the effects of the Geometric period and less able to de-velop an all-purpose style like the Corinthian. The vases remain large and the attempts to depict humans and animals, using a combination of the black-figure technique and freehand drawing, are often clumsy. The achievements of later Athenian art are nonetheless clearly foreshadowed in the vitality of the figures

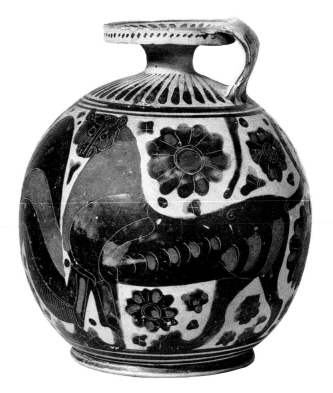

2.6   Aryballos. Middle Corinthian, c. 625 B.C. State Museums, West Berlin. This little flask held perfumed oil. The black-figure technique and the very Eastern-looking panther are characteristic of the Orientalizing style. Also characteristic are the flowerlike decorations, which are blobs of paint scored with lines. The musculature and features of the panther are also the result of scoring.

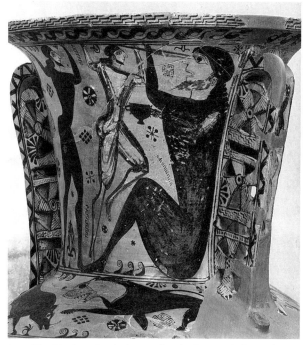

2.7 *The Blinding of Polyphemus,* detail of proto-Attic amphora. c. 650 B.C. Height of frieze 17″ (43 cm). Museum, Eleusis. The technique is crude, but the artist shows imagination and even humor in depicting an episode from the *Odyssey.* At the center is Odysseus himself, guiding a sharpened, heated pole into the single eye of Polyphemus, the Cyclops, seated drunkenly at the right—note the wine cup in his hand.

and the constant desire of the artists to illustrate events from mythology [2.7] or daily life rather than simply to decorate a surface in the Corinthian manner.

By 600 B.C. the narrative style had become established at Athens, and the full-scale use of the black-figure technique permitted the designer greater artistic control. As Athens began to take over an increasing share of the market for painted vases and their contents, Corinth's position declined, and the trade rivalry that later had devastating results began to develop.

The Beginnings of Greek Sculpture

The influence of Near Eastern and Egyptian models on Greek sculpture is more consistent and easier to trace than on pottery. The first Greek settlers in Egypt were given land around the mid-7th century B.C. by the Egyptian pharaoh Psammetichos I. It is surely no coincidence that the earliest Greek stone sculptures, which date from about the same period, markedly resemble Egyptian cult statues and were placed in similarly grandiose temples. (The earliest

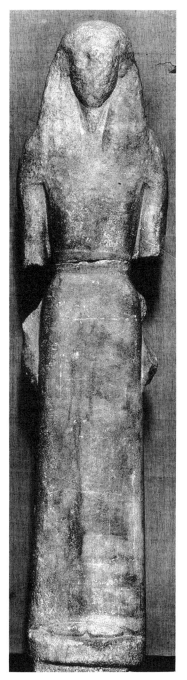

2.8 *Kore* from Delos, dedicated by Nikandre. c. 650 B.C. Marble. National Archaeological Museum, Athens. Unlike the *kouros,* the figure is completely clothed, though both have the same rigid stance, arms by sides, and wiglike hair.

surviving temple, that of Hera at Olympia, dates at least in part to this period.) These stone figures consist of a small number of types repeated over and over. The most popular were the standing female, or *kore,* clad in drapery [2.8], and the standing male, or

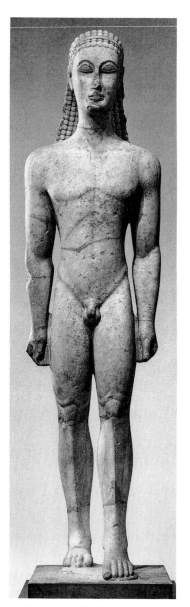

2.9 *Kouros.* c. 615 B.C. Marble, height 6'1½" (1.87 m). Metropolitan Museum of Art, New York (Fletcher Fund, 1932).

stage. After the slow and cautious progress of the Geometric period, the entire character of painting and sculpture had changed, and within the century following 700 B.C. Greek artists had abandoned abstract design for increasing realism. At this point in their development the Greek spirit of independence and inquiry asserted itself. Instead of following their eastern counterparts and repeating the same models and conventions for centuries, Greek painters and sculptors allowed their curiosity to lead them in a new direction, one that changed the history of art. The early stone figures and painted silhouettes had represented human beings, but only in a schematic, stylized form. Beginning in the Archaic period artists used their work to try to answer such questions as What do human beings really look like? How do perspective and foreshortening work? What in fact is the true nature of appearance? For the first time in history they began to reproduce the human form in a way true to nature rather than merely echoing the achievements of their predecessors.

Sculpture and Painting in the Archaic Period

It is tempting to see the works of art and literature of the Archaic period (600–480 B.C.) as steps on the road that leads to the artistic and intellectual achievement in the Classical Age of the 5th and 4th centuries B.C. rather than to appreciate them for their own qualities. This would be to underestimate seriously the vitality of one of the most creative periods in the development of our culture. In some ways, in fact, the spirit of adventure, of striving toward new forms and new ideas, makes the Archaic achievement more exciting, if less perfected, than that of the Classical period. It is better to travel hopefully than to arrive, as Robert Louis Stevenson put it.

The change in Archaic art is a reflection of similar social developments. The hereditary aristocrats were being replaced as rulers by a new class of rich merchant traders who had made their fortunes in the economic expansion and who won power by playing on the discontent of the oppressed lower classes. These new rulers were called "tyrants"—although the word had none of the unfavorable sense that it now has. Many of them, in fact, were patrons of the arts. The most famous of them all was Pisistratus, who ruled Athens from 546–528 B.C. Clearly, revolutions like those that brought him and his fellow tyrants to power were likely to produce revolutionary changes in the arts.

In sculpture there was an astounding progress from the formalized *kouroi* of the early Archaic period, with their flat planes and rigid stances, to the fully rounded figures of the late 6th century, toward

kouros, always shown nude [2.9]. This nudity already marks a break with the Egyptian tradition in which figures wore loincloths and foreshadows the heroic male nudity of Classical Greek art. The stance of the *kouros* figures, however, was firmly based on Egyptian models. One foot (usually the left) is forward, the arms are by the sides, and the hands are clenched. The elaborate wiglike hair is also Egyptian in inspiration.

By 600 B.C., only a few years after the first appearance of these statues, Greek art had reached a critical

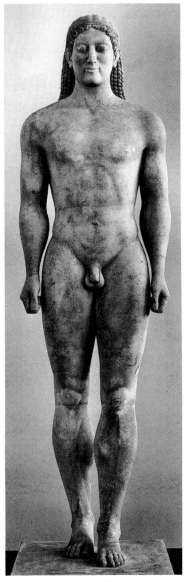

2.10 *Kouros* from Anavysos. c. 530 B.C. Marble, height 6'4"
(1.93 m). National Archaeological Museum, Athens. Note the
realism of the muscles and the new sense of power. According
to an inscription on the base, this was the funerary monument
to a young man, Kroisos, who had died heroically in battle.

the end of the period. Statues like the *Anavysos
Kouros* [2.10] show a careful study of the human anatomy. The conventions remain the same, but the statues have a new life and vigor.

Although most of the male figures are shown in
the traditional stance, there are a few important exceptions. The finest is perhaps the famous *Calf-
Bearer* [2.11] from the Athenian Acropolis (the hill
that dominated the center of ancient Athens). The
essential unity between man and beast is conveyed

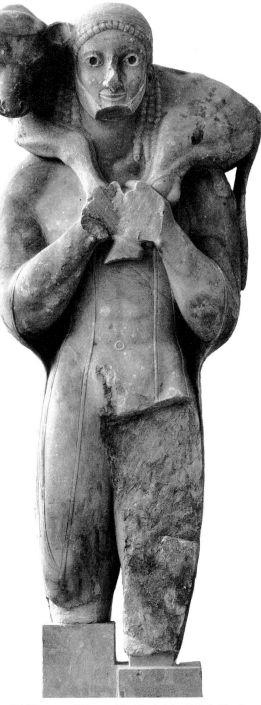

2.11 *Calf-Bearer*. c. 550 B.C. Marble, height 5'5" (1.65 m).
Acropolis Museum, Athens. The archaic smile is softened in
this figure. Realism appears in the displacement of the man's
hair by the animal's legs and in the amazingly lifelike
expression of the calf.

THE VISUAL ARTS IN EARLY GREECE **53**

simply but with great feeling by the diagonals formed by the man's hands and the calf's legs and by the alignment of the two heads.

The finest female figures of the period also come from the Acropolis. The Persians broke them when they sacked Athens in 480 B.C., and then the Athenians buried them when they returned to their city the next year after defeating the Persians. Rediscovered by modern excavators, the statues are among the most impressive of Archaic masterpieces. They show

2.12 *Peplos Kore.* c. 540 B.C. Marble, height 4′ (1.21 m). Acropolis Museum, Athens. The statue is identified by the woolen peplos or mantle the woman is wearing over her dress. The missing left arm was extended. The Greeks painted important parts of their stone statues; traces of paint show here.

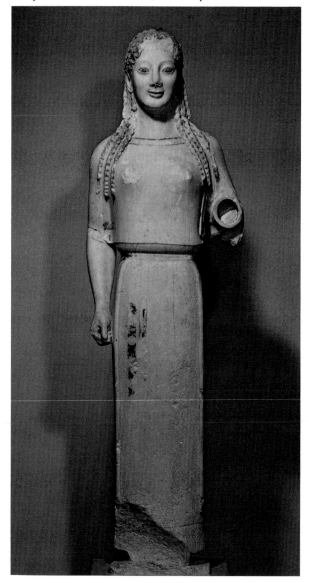

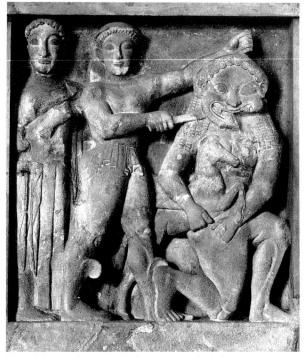

2.13 Metope showing the decapitation of Medusa. Selinus, c. 540 B.C. Archaeological Museum, Palermo. Medusa was a gorgon whose look turned anyone to stone. Perseus is cutting off Medusa's head with the encouragement of Athena, who stands at left. The gorgon's son Pegasus, the winged horse, leaps up at her side. Medusa is shown in the conventional pose indicating rapid motion.

a gradual but sure development from the earliest *korai* to the richness and variety of the work of the late 6th century, with its emphasis on elaborate drapery and delicate details [2.12].

In addition to these freestanding figures, two other kinds of sculpture now appeared: large-scale statues made to decorate temples and carved stone slabs. In both cases sculptors used the technique of *relief* carving: figures do not stand freely, visible from all angles, but are carved into a block of stone, part of which is left as background. In *high relief* the figures project from the background so much as to seem almost three-dimensional. In *low relief* the carving preserves the flat surface of the stone. Although the technique is generally used for stone, it can also be applied to metalwork. Temple sculpture, or as it is often called, architectural sculpture, was frequently in high relief, as in the depiction of the decapitation of Medusa from Selinus [2.13]. Individual carved stone slabs are generally in low relief. Most that have survived were used as grave markers. The workmanship is often of a remarkable subtlety, as on the grave stele, or gravestone, of Aristion [2.14].

The range of Archaic sculpture is great, and the best pieces communicate something of the excitement of their makers in solving new problems. Almost all of them, however, have in common one feature that often disturbs the modern viewer—the

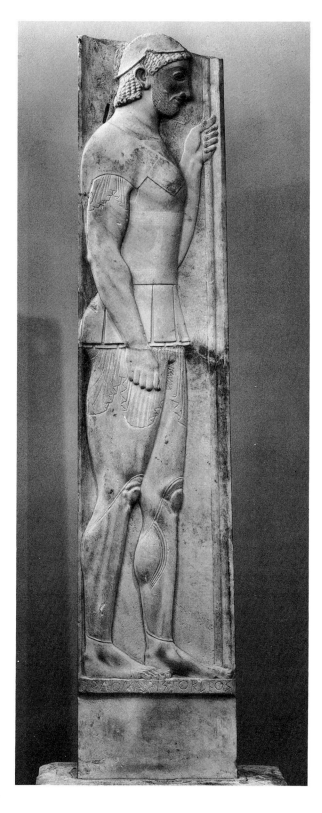

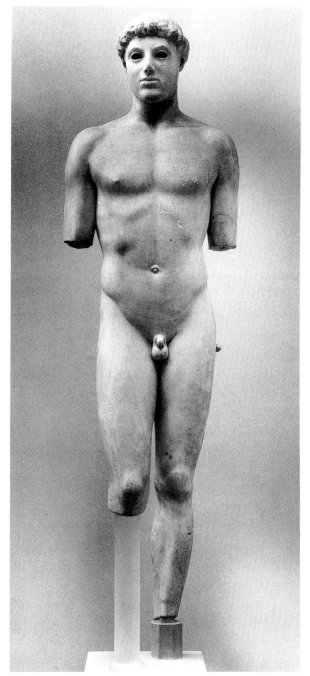

2.14 Aristokles. *Stele of Aristion*. c. 510 B.C. Height without base 8′ (2.44 m). National Archaeological Museum, Athens. The leather jacket contrasts with the soft folds of the undershirt.

2.15 *Critian Boy*. c. 490 B.C. Marble, height 34″ (86 cm). Acropolis Museum, Athens. The archaic smile has been superseded by a more natural expression.

famous "archaic smile." This facial expression, which to our eyes may seem more like a grimace, has been explained in a number of ways. Some believe that it is merely the result of technical inexperience on the part of the sculptors. Others see it as a reflection of the Archaic Greeks' sense of certainty and optimism in facing a world that they seemed increasingly able to control. Whatever its cause, by the end of the 6th century B.C., and with the increasing threat posed by the Persians, the archaic smile had begun to fade. It was replaced by the more somber expression of works like the *Critian Boy* [2.15]. This statue marks a literal "turning point" between the late Archaic world and the early Classical period. For the first time in ancient art the figure is no longer looking or walking straight ahead. The head and the upper part of the body turn slightly; as they do so, the weight shifts from one leg to the other and the hips move. Having solved the problem of representing a standing figure in a realistic way, the sculptor has tackled a new and even more complex problem—showing a figure in motion. The consequences of this accomplishment were explored to the full in the Classical period.

By the mid-6th century B.C. the art of vase painting had also made great progress. Works like those of Exekias, perhaps the greatest of black-figure painters, combine superb draftsmanship and immense power of expression [2.16]. For so restricted a medium, vase painting shows a surprising range. If Exekias' style is serious, somber, sometimes even

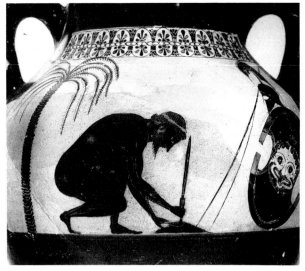

2.16 Exekias. *The Suicide of Ajax*. c. 525 B.C. Black-figure vase, height 21¼″ (54 cm). Musée des Beaux-Arts, Boulogne. Ajax buries his sword in the ground so that he can throw himself on to it. The pathos of the warrior's last moments is emphasized by the empty space around him, the weeping tree, and his now useless shield and helmet.

grim, the style of his contemporary the Amasis painter is relaxed, humorous, and charming.

The end of the 6th century B.C. marks a major development in vase painting with the introduction of the new *red-figure style*. Instead of painting the figures in black silhouette against the red clay of the vase and then etching out the details, the artist paints the background black and leaves the figures in the red color of the clay. Details are now filled in with the brush, allowing much greater variation in fineness or

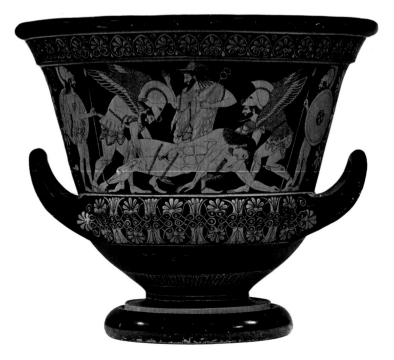

2.17 Euphronios, painter; Euxitheos, potter. Red-figure calyx krater. c. 515 B.C. Terra cotta, height of vase 18″ (46 cm), diameter 21¾″ (55 cm). Metropolitan Museum of Art, New York (bequest of Joseph H. Durkee, gift of Darius Ogden Mills, and gift of C. Ruxton Love, by exchange, 1972). This masterpiece of red-figure vase painting, generally known as the *Euphronios Vase,* shows the moment when Sarpedon falls in battle during the Trojan War. As his body stiffens in agony, his wounds streaming blood, the twin gods Death (on the right) and Sleep come to his aid. The god Hermes, who leads the souls of the dead to Hades, stands sympathetically behind.

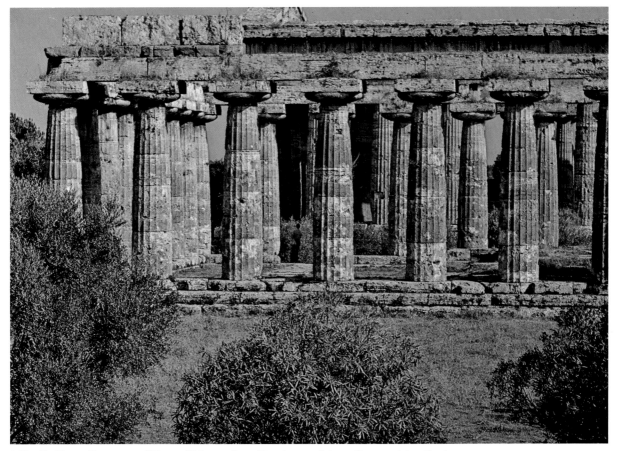

2.18 Basilica at Paestum. c. 550 B.C. This temple to Hera is one of the earliest surviving Greek temples. The bulging columns and spreading capitals are typical of Doric architecture in the Archaic period. (Visible through the columns and above the entablature are columns and part of the pediment of a second temple of Hera beyond, built a century later.)

thickness of line. The increased subtlety made possible by this style was used to develop new techniques of foreshortening, perspective, and three-dimensionality.

Although some artists continued to produce black-figure works, by the end of the Archaic period around 525 B.C. almost all had turned to the new style. The last Archaic vase painters are among the greatest red-figure artists. Works like the *Euphronios Vase* [2.17] have a solidity and monumentality that altogether transcend the usual limitations of the medium.

Architecture:
The Doric and Ionic Orders

In architecture, the Archaic period was marked by the construction of a number of major temples in the Doric style or order. This order seems to have been firmly established by 600 B.C., though none of the earlier examples of the evolving style have survived. Important Doric temples include the Temple of Hera at Olympia, the Temple of Apollo at Corinth, and

the earliest of the three Doric temples at Paestum, often called the Basilica (meeting hall), though it is now known to have been dedicated to the goddess Hera [2.18]. The Ionic style of temple architecture, which was widely used in Classical Greece, did not become fully established until later. In the Archaic period, Ionic buildings were constructed at such sites as Samos and Ephesus, but most Ionic temples date to the 5th century B.C. and later. For the sake of convenience both the Doric and Ionic orders [2.19] are described here. A later order, the Corinthian, is principally of interest for its popularity with Roman architects and is discussed in that context in Chapter 4.

The Doric order is the simpler and the grander of the two. Some of its characteristics seem directly derived from construction methods used in earlier wooden buildings, and its dignity is perhaps in part related to the length of its history. Doric columns have no base but rise directly from the floor of a building. They taper toward the top and have twenty flutes, or vertical grooves. The *capital,* which forms the head of each column, consists of two sections, a spreading convex disc (the *echinus*) and, above, a square block (the *abacus*). The upper part of the tem-

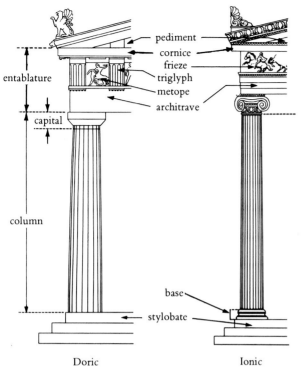

2.19 The Doric and Ionic orders.

ple, or *entablature,* is divided into three sections. The lowest, the *architrave,* is a plain band of rectangular blocks, above which is the *frieze,* consisting of alternating *triglyphs* and *metopes.* The triglyphs are divided by grooves into three vertical bands. The metope panels are sometimes plain, sometimes decorated with sculpture or painting. The building is crowned by a *cornice,* or projecting upper part, consisting of a horizontal section and two slanting sections meeting at a peak. The long extended triangle thus formed is the *pediment,* often filled with sculptural decoration.

In contrast, the Ionic order is more graceful and more elaborate in architectural details. Ionic columns rise from a tiered base and have 24 flutes. These flutes do not meet at a sharp angle as Doric flutes do but are separated by narrow vertical bands. The capitals consist of a pair of spirals, or *volutes.* The architrave is not flat as in the Doric order but composed of three projecting bands. In place of the Doric triglyphs and metopes is a continuous band often decorated with a running frieze of sculpture.

The two orders produced different effects. The Doric order suggested simple dignity; the absence of decorative detail drew attention to the weight and massiveness of the Doric temple itself. Ionic temples, on the other hand, conveyed a sense of lightness and delicacy by means of ornate decorations and fanciful carving. The surface of an Ionic temple is as important as its structural design.

Music and Dance in Early Greece

In comparison with the visual arts, the history of Greek music is highly problematic. The very small quantity of evidence is as confusing as it is helpful. Although the frequent references to musical performance make it clear that music played a vital role in all aspects of Greek life, less than a dozen fragments of actual Greek music have survived; the earliest of these dates from the late 5th century B.C. Unfortunately, the problem of understanding the system of notation makes authentic performance of these fragments impossible.

Our inability to re-create even the examples we have is particularly frustrating because from the earliest times music was renowned for its emotional and spiritual power. For the Greeks music was of divine origin; the gods themselves had invented musical instruments: Hermes or Apollo the lyre, Athena the flute, and so on. Many of the earliest myths told of the powerful effect of music. Orpheus could move trees and rocks and tame wild beasts by his song; the lyre-playing of Amphion brought stones to life. Nor was music-making reserved for professional performers or women, as so often in later centuries. When, in Book IX of the *Iliad,* Agamemnon's ambassadors arrive at the tent of Achilles they find the great hero playing a lyre, "clear-sounding, splendid and carefully wrought," and entertaining himself by singing "of men's fame." How one would like to have heard that song.

The Greek belief that music could profoundly affect human behavior meant that it played an important part in both public and private life and was especially important in a religious context. Greek musical theory was later summarized by the two great philosophers of the fourth century B.C., Plato and Aristotle, both of whom discuss the doctrine of *ethos* and give music an important place in their writings. An understanding of doctrines of musical theory was also considered fundamental to a good general education.

Greek music was built up of a series of distinct modes, or scale types, each of which had its own name (see page 83). According to the doctrine of *ethos,* the characteristic, or *ethos,* of each mode was so powerful that it gave music written in it the ability to affect human behavior in a specific way. Thus the Dorian mode expressed firm, powerful, even warlike feelings, while the Phrygian mode produced passionate, sensual emotions. This identification of specific note patterns with individual human reactions seems to reach back to the dawn of Greek music history. The legendary founder of Greek music was Olympus, who was believed by the Greeks to have come from Asia Minor; it is surely no coincidence that two of the modes—the Phrygian and the Lydian—bear names of places in Asia Minor.

The first figure in music about whose existence we can be relatively certain was Terpander, who came from the island of Lesbos. Around 675 B.C. he used the *kithara,* an elaborate seven-string lyre, to accompany vocal music on ceremonial occasions. The simple lyre, relatively small and easy to hold, had a sounding box made of a whole tortoise shell and sides formed of goat horns or curved pieces of wood. On the other hand, the kithara had a much larger sounding box made of wood, metal, or even ivory and broad, hollow sides, to give greater resonance to the sound. The player had to stand while performing on it; the instrument had straps to support it, leaving the player's hands free [2.20].

Another musical instrument developed about this time was the *aulos,* a double-reed instrument similar to the modern oboe [2.21], which according to the traditional account had first been brought into Greece by Olympus. Like the kithara and lyre, the aulos was generally used to accompany songs.

The little evidence we have suggests that early Greek music was primarily vocal—the instruments were used mainly to accompany the singers. The breakthrough into purely instrumental music seems to have come at the beginning of the Archaic period. We know that in 586 B.C. Sacadas of Argos composed a work to be played on the aulos for the Pythian Games at Delphi—a piece that remained well known and popular for centuries. Also, its character confirms the Greek love of narrative, for it described in music Apollo's fight with the dragon that the Pythian Games commemorated. The information is tantalizing indeed, since this first piece of "program music," the remote ancestor of Richard Strauss' *Till Eulenspiegel* and *Don Quixote,* must have been highly effective for its appeal to have lasted so long.

We know little more of the music of the Archaic period than these odd facts. The lyrics of some of the

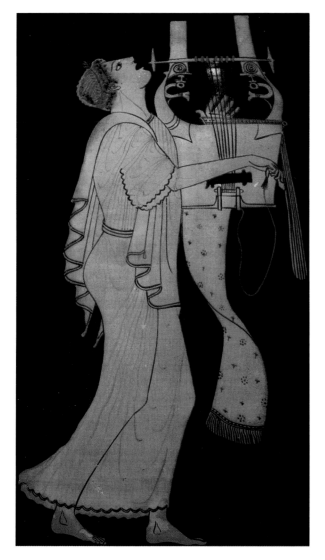

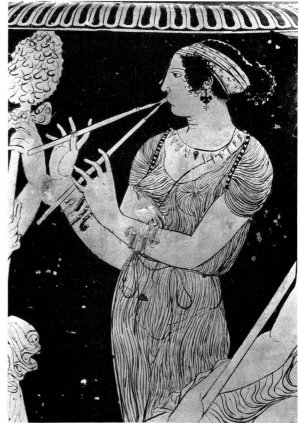

2.20 Berlin Painter. Detail of red-figure amphora. Nola, c. 490 B.C. Terra cotta, height of vase 16⅜″ (42 cm). Metropolitan Museum of Art, New York (Fletcher Fund, 1956). This vase gives a good idea of the Greeks' enthusiasm for music in general and the cithara in particular. The young musician is singing to his own accompaniment.

2.21 Karneia Painter. Detail of red-figure krater. Ceglie del Campo, c. 410 B.C. Terra cotta. Museo Nazionale, Taranto. A young woman plays the aulos for the god Dionysus. The flowing lines of the dress accentuate her figure. The necklace and bracelets are in low relief.

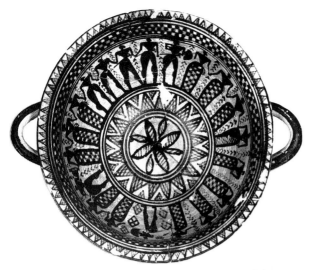

2.22 Geometric bowl showing dancing. c. 740 B.C. Diameter 6¼″ (16 cm). National Archaeological Museum, Athens. The dancers include both women and men, three playing lyres.

Early Greek Literature and Philosophy

Our knowledge of literary developments between the time of Homer and the Archaic period is very limited. An exception is Hesiod, who probably lived shortly before 700 B.C. He is the author of a poetic account of the origins of the world called the *Theogony* and a rather more down-to-earth work, the *Works and Days,* which mainly concerned the disadvantages in being a poor, oppressed (and depressed) farmer in Boeotia, where the climate is "severe in winter, stuffy in summer, good at no time of year." In the Archaic period, however, the same burst of creative energy that revolutionized the visual arts produced a wave of new poets. The medium they chose was lyric verse.

Lyric Poetry

The emergence of lyric poetry was, like developments in the other arts, a sign of the times. The heroic verse of Homer was intended for the ruling class of an aristocratic society, who had the leisure and the inclination to hear of the great and not so great deeds of great men and who were interested in the problems of mighty leaders like Agamemnon and Achilles. Lyric verse is concerned above all else with the poet's own feelings, emotions, and opinions. The writers of the 6th century B.C. do not hesitate to tell us what they themselves feel about life, death, love, drinking too much wine, or anything else that crosses their minds. Heroes and the glories of battle are no longer the ideal.

Above all other Greek lyric poets, Sappho has captured the hearts and minds of the following ages. She is the first woman to leave a literary record that reflects her own personal experiences. Her poems have survived only in fragmentary form, and the details of her life remain confused and much disputed. We must be grateful, then, for what we have and not try to overinterpret it.

Sappho was born around 612 B.C. on the island of Lesbos, where she spent most of her life. She seems to have been able to combine the roles of wife and mother with those of poet and teacher; within her own lifetime she was widely respected for her works and surrounded by a group of younger women who presumably came to Lesbos to finish their education, in much the same way that Americans used to go to Paris for a final cultural polish.

The affection between Sappho and her pupils was deep and sincere and is constantly reflected in her poems. The nature of this affection has been debated for centuries. The plain fact is that apart from her

songs have survived, including some of the choral odes performed in honor of various gods. Apollo and his sister Artemis were thanked for delivery from misfortune by the singing of a *paean,* or solemn invocation to the gods, while the *dithyramb,* or choral hymn to Dionysus, was sung in his honor at public ceremonies.

Also closely tied to music was dance, which also played a significant part in the development of drama. We know both more and less about the early stages of Greek dance than we do about music. On the one hand, we have from as early as the late Geometric period actual depictions of dances in progress [2.22], whereas the sound of music of the same period is entirely lost to us. On the other hand, in the Classical period the function of dance remained religious and social, whereas a vast literature on music theory developed, with philosophical implications that became explicit in the writings of Plato and Aristotle; through this literature some information on early music has been preserved.

What we do know about dancing and individual dances suggests that here, as in music and visual arts, telling a story was important. One famous dance was called the *geranos,* from the word for "crane." The dancers apparently made movements reminiscent of the bird, but the steps of the dance had a more specific meaning. According to tradition, it was first performed by Theseus outside the Labyrinth with the boys and girls he had saved by killing the Minotaur (see pages 29–30). The intricate patterns of the dance were supposed to represent the Labyrinth itself. Having accomplished two dangerous feats—killing the Minotaur and finding his way out of the Labyrinth—Theseus stayed around long enough to lead a complicated performance. Dancing was obviously of great importance to the Greeks.

poetry we know almost nothing about Sappho herself. Even her appearance is debatable; she is described by one ancient authority as "beautiful day" and by another as short, dark, and ugly. Her fellow poet Alcaeus calls her "violet-haired, pure, and honey-smiling." Thus those who read Sappho must decide for themselves what the passion of the poems expresses, for passionate they certainly are.

Perhaps Sappho's greatest quality lies in her ability to probe the depths of her own responses and by describing them to understand them. Just as contemporary sculptors and painters sought to understand the workings of their own bodies by depicting them, so Sappho revealed both to herself and to us the workings of her emotions.

The First Philosophers: The Presocratics

The century that saw the expression of the intimate self-revelations of lyric poetry was marked by the development of rational philosophy, which challenged the traditional religious ideas of Homer and Hesiod and scoffed at gods who took human form. If horses and cows had hands and could draw, they would draw gods looking like horses and cows, wrote Xenophanes of Colophon in the second half of the 6th century B.C. Other thinkers began to debate the nature of the universe and try to account for the diversity of the natural world with as few as possible fundamental principles.

There developed a wide variety of schools of thought originated by philosophers generally described by the somewhat confusing label *Presocratics.* The label is accurate in that they all lived and died before the time of Socrates (469–399 B.C.), who, together with his pupil Plato (c. 427–347 B.C.), is the greatest name in Greek philosophy. On the other hand, these 6th-century philosophers had little in common except the time when they lived. Thus it is important to remember that the term "Presocratic" does not describe any single philosophical system. The various schools were united principally by their use of logic and theoretical reasoning to solve practical questions about the world and human existence.

The earliest school to develop was that of the *Materialists,* who sought to explain all phenomena in terms of one or more elements. Thales of Miletus (c. 585 B.C.), for example, thought that water underlay the changing world of nature. Later, Empedocles of Acragas (c. 495 B.C.) introduced four elements—fire, earth, air, water. The various combinations (through love) and separations (through strife and war) of these elements in a cyclical pattern explained how creatures as well as nations were born, grew, decayed, and died. Anaxagoras of Clazomenae (c. 500 B.C.) postulated an infinite number of small particles, which, however small they might be, always contained not only a dominant substance (for example, bone or water) but also stray bits of other substances in lesser quantities. Unity in nature, he claimed, came from the force of Reason.

The Presocratic philosopher who had the greatest influence on later times was Pythagoras of Samos (c. 550 B.C.). He left his home city for political reasons and settled in southern Italy, where he founded a school of his own. He required his followers to lead pure and devout lives, uniting together to uphold morals and chastity, as well as order and harmony, for the common good. These apparently noble principles did nothing to win him favor from the people among whom he had settled; according to one account he and three hundred of his followers were killed.

It is difficult to know which of the principles of *Pythagoreanism* can be directly attributed to Pythagoras himself and which were added later by his disciples. His chief religious doctrines seem to have been belief in the transmigration of souls and the kinship of all living things, teachings that led to the development of a religious cult that bore his name. In science, his chief contribution was in mathematics. He discovered the numerical relationship of musical harmonies. Our modern musical scale, consisting of an *octave* (a span of eight tones) divided into its constituent parts, derives ultimately from his researches. Inspired by this discovery, Pythagoras went on to claim that mathematical relationships represented the underlying principle of the universe and of morality, the so-called "harmony of the spheres." He is chiefly remembered today for a much less cosmic discovery, the geometrical theorem that bears his name.

In contrast to Pythagoras' belief in universal harmony, the *Dualists* claimed that there existed two separate universes, the world around us, subject to constant change, and another ideal world, perfect and unchanging, which could only be realized through the intellect. The chief proponent of this school was Heraclitus of Ephesus (c. 500 B.C.), who summed up the unpredictable, and therefore unknowable, quality of Nature in the well-known saying "It is not possible to step twice into the same river." But if the universe were too changeable to be known directly, knowledge of the Reason by which the world works was still open to the philosopher. Similarly, Parmedides of Elea (c. 510 B.C.) went so far as to claim that all change, motion, and what we commonly call nature were but a sham and delusion, whereas true reality was all perfect, unchanging, and spherical in shape. His younger pupil, Zeno (c. 490 B.C.), presented a number of difficult paradoxes in support of their doctrines. These paradoxes were later discussed by Plato and Aristotle.

The last and perhaps the greatest school of Presocratic philosophy was that of the *Atomists,* led by Leucippus and Democritus (c. 460 B.C.), who believed that the ultimate, unchangeable reality consisted of atoms (small "indivisible" particles not obvious to the naked eye) and the void (nothingness). Atomism survived into Roman times in the later philosophy of Epicureanism and into the 19th century in the early Atomic Theory of John Dalton. Even in our own times, the great physicist Werner Heisenberg (1901–1976), who astonished the world of science with his discoveries in quantum mechanics, derived his initial inspiration from the Greek Atomists.

Herodotus, The First Greek Historian

At the beginning of the 5th century B.C. the Greeks had to face the greatest threat in their history. Their success in meeting the challenge precipitated a decisive break with the world of Archaic culture. In 499 B.C. the Greek cities of Asia Minor, with Athenian support, rebelled against their Persian rulers. The Persian king, Darius, succeeded in checking this revolt; he then resolved to lead a punitive expedition against the mainland Greek cities that had sent help to the eastern cities. In 490 B.C. he took a massive army to Greece; to everyone's surprise, the Persians were defeated by the Athenians at the Battle of Marathon. After Darius' death in 486 B.C., his son Xerxes launched an even more grandiose expedition in 480 B.C. Xerxes defeated the Spartans at Thermophylae and then attacked and sacked Athens itself. While the city was falling, the Athenians took to their ships, obeying an oracle that enjoined them to "trust to their wooden walls." Eventually they inflicted a crushing defeat on the Persian navy at nearby Salamis. In 479 B.C., after being conquered on land and sea, at Plataea and Mycale, the Persians returned home, completely beaten.

The great historian Herodotus (484–420 B.C.) has left us, in the nine books of his *History of the Persian Wars,* a detailed account of the closing years of the Archaic period. He also, however, has two other claims on our attention. He is the first writer in the Western tradition to devote himself to historical writing rather than epic or lyric poetry, a fact that has earned him the title Father of History. At the same time he is one of the greatest storytellers, always sustaining the reader's interest, in both the main line of his narrative and the frequent and entertaining digressions. One of these, the tale of Rhampsinitus and the thief, has been described as the first detective story in Western literature.

Herodotus was not a scientific historian in our terms—he had definite weaknesses. He never really understood the finer points of military strategy. He almost always interpreted events in terms of personalities, showing little interest in underlying political or economic causes. His strengths, however, were many. Although his subject involved conflict between Greeks and foreigners, he remained remarkably impartial and free from national prejudice. His natural curiosity about the world around him and about his fellow human beings was buttressed by acute powers of observation. Above all, he recorded as much information as possible, even when versions conflicted. He also tried to provide a reasonable evaluation of the reliability of his sources so later readers could form their own opinions.

Herodotus' analysis of the Greek victory was based on a serious philosophical, indeed theological, belief—that the Persians were defeated because they were morally in the wrong. Their moral fault was *hubris,* excessive ambition; thus the Greeks' victory was at the same time an example of right over might and a demonstration that the gods themselves would guarantee the triumph of justice.

Modern readers, however, less influenced by Herodotus' religious beliefs, will be more inclined to draw a political message from the Persian defeat. The Greeks were successful at least partly because for once they had managed to unite in the face of a common enemy. Their victories inaugurated the greatest period in Greek history, the Classical Age.

Summary

Shortly after 1000 B.C. Greek civilization began to develop. From the beginning, the Greek world was divided into separate city-states among which fierce rivalries would grow. For the first two centuries the Greeks had little contact with other peoples, but around 800 B.C. Greek travelers and merchants began to explore throughout the Mediterranean. The visual arts during these early centuries are principally represented by pottery decorated with geometric designs. The period also saw the creation of two of the greatest masterpieces of Western literature, the *Iliad* and the *Odyssey.*

During the Age of Colonization (c. 750–600 B.C.) the Greeks came in contact with a wide range of foreign peoples. The ancient Near East, in particular, played a large part in influencing the development of Greek art and architecture. The decoration of pottery became Orientalizing in style, while large freestanding sculpture based on Egyptian models began to evolve. Important Greek colonies began to develop in southern Italy and Sicily.

The period from 600 B.C. to 480 B.C., known as the Archaic Age, was marked by political and cultural change. A new literary form, lyric poetry, became popular; one of its leading practitioners was the poetess Sappho. The so-called Presocratics began to develop a wide range of philosophical schools. Sculpture and vase painting both became increasingly naturalistic. The aristocratic rulers of earlier times were supplanted by "tyrants," rich merchant traders who depended on the support of the lower classes. In Athens, Solon's reform of the constitution introduced a form of democracy, which was overthrown by the tyrant Pisistratus in 546 B.C..

Democratic government was restored at Athens in 510 B.C., and shortly thereafter the Greeks became embroiled with the mighty Persian empire to their east. In 499 B.C. the Greek cities of western Asia, established more than a century earlier, rebelled against their Persian rulers; the Athenians sent help. The Persians crushed the revolt, and in 490 B.C. the Persian king, Darius, led an expedition against the Greeks to punish them for their interference.

Against all odds, the Persians were defeated at the Battle of Marathon. Darius, humiliated, was forced to withdraw, but ten years later Xerxes, his son, mounted an even more grandiose campaign to restore Persian honor. In 480 B.C. he invaded Greece, defeated Spartan troops at Thermopylae, and sacked Athens. The Athenians took to their ships, however, and destroyed the Persian navy at the Battle of Salamis.

The following year combined Greek forces defeated Xerxes' army on land, and the Persians returned home in defeat. Faced by the greatest threat in their history, the Greeks had managed to present a united front. Their victories set the scene for the Classical Age of Greek culture. A detailed account of the Greeks' success can be found in the *History of the Persian Wars* written by Herodotus, the first Greek historian and the earliest significant prose writer in Western literature.

Pronounciation Guide

Achilles: A-KILL-ees
Agamemnon: A-ga-MEM-non
Amphora: AM-fo-ra
Aphrodite: Af-ro-DIE-tee
Boeotia: Bee-OWE-sha
Dionysus: Di-on-ICE-us
Darius: Dar-I-us
Dithyramb: DITH-ee-ram
Euphronius: You-FRO-ni-us
Hera: HERE-a
Herodotus: Her-ODD-ot-us
Kore: KO-ray
Laconia: La-CONE-ee-a
Metope: MET-owe-pe
Paestum: PIE-stum
Peloponnesian: Pel-op-on-EASE-i-an
Phoenician: Fun-EESH-i-an
Priam: PRY-am
Sappho: SAF-owe
Stele: STAY-lay
Thales: THAY-lees
Thermopylae: Ther-MOP-u-lee

Triglyph: TRIG-lif
Xerxes: ZER-ksees

Exercises

1. What are the main features of the Homeric world view? What effect do they have on the style of the Homeric epics?
2. Describe the development of Greek sculpture from the mid-7th century to the end of the Archaic period.
3. What evidence has survived as to the nature of Greek music? What does it tell us about the Greeks' attitude to music?
4. Discuss the principal schools of Presocratic philosophy.
5. What are the chief differences between the Doric and Ionic orders of architecture?

Further Reading

Boardman, J. *The Greek Overseas*. Baltimore: Penguin, 1973. A vivid and informative account of the development and effects of Greek colonization.

Bury, J. B., and R. Meiggs. *A History of Greece to the Death of Alexander the Great*. 4th ed. New York: St. Martin's, 1975. The best single-volume history of ancient Greece.

Coldstream, J. N. *Geometric Greece*. London: Methuen, 1977. A technical but readable account of all aspects of life in Geometric Greece.

Cook, R. M. *Greek Art*. Baltimore: Penguin, 1976. The best single-volume survey of all the visual arts in Greece, this book places them in their historical context.

Hooker, J. T. *The Ancient Spartans*. London: Methuen, 1980. A detailed study of a still relatively neglected subject that collects and interprets recent discoveries.

Johnston, A. *The Emergence of Greece*. Oxford: Elsevier-Phaidon, 1976. Primarily an up-to-date account of the archaeology of early Greece, the book also gives an excellent synthesis of history and art.

Luce, J. V. *Homer and the Heroic Age*. New York: Harper, 1975. A masterly account of the historical background of the Homeric epics, although the author's view that Homer's world chiefly reflects that of the Mycenaeans is by no means universally shared.

Schups, K. *Economic Rights of Women in Ancient Greece*. Edinburgh: Edinburgh University Press, 1979. By using modern research techniques to analyze a wide range of material, this book significantly enlarges our view of Greek society.

Snodgrass, A. *Archaic Greece*. Berkeley: University of California Press, 1980. An important survey of the historical and archaeological evidence for a rich and complex period.

Vermeule, E. *Aspects of Death in Early Greek Art and Poetry*. Berkeley: University of California Press, 1981. In a sensitively written study, the author uses the visual arts and poetry to deal with themes that are, by their nature, difficult to pin down.

Reading Selections

Homer
from ILIAD, Book XXIV

This extract from Book XXIV of the Iliad *comprises the last great episode in the work, the confrontation between Priam, king of Troy, and the Greek hero Achilles over the body of Priam's son Hector. Throughout the long scene Homer maintains the heroic dignity of his characters while allowing us to identify with them as human beings. After the pathos of Priam's appeal, Achilles' immediate reaction is as perfectly appropriate as it is unexpected. His own changing moods, veering from philosophical resignation to sudden anger to tenderness, seem to run the gamut of emotional response. How typical it is, too, of a Homeric hero to be practical enough after such an intense encounter to think of dinner and supervise its serving.*

[Priam] made straight for the dwelling
where Achilleus the beloved of Zeus was sitting.
    He found him
inside, and his companions were sitting apart, as
    two only,
Automedon the hero and Alkimos, scion of Ares,
were busy beside him. He had just now got
    through with his dinner,
with eating and drinking, and the table still stood
    by. Tall Priam
came in unseen by the other men and stood close
    beside him
and caught the knees of Achilleus in his arms, and
    kissed the hands
that were dangerous and manslaughtering and had
    killed so many
of his sons. As when dense disaster closes on one
    who has murdered   480
a man in his own land, and he comes to the
    country of others,
to a man of substance, and wonder seizes on those
    who behold him,
so Achilleus wondered as he looked on Priam, a
    godlike
man, and the rest of them wondered also, and
    looked at each other.
But now Priam spoke to him in the words of a
    suppliant:
"Achilleus like the gods, remember your father,
    one who
is of years like mine, and on the door-sill of
    sorrowful old age.
And they who dwell nearby encompass him and
    afflict him,
nor is there any to defend him against the wrath,
    the destruction.

Yet surely he, when he hears of you and that you
    are still living,   490
is gladdened within his heart and all his days he is
    hopeful
that he will see his beloved son come home from
    the Troad.
But for me, my destiny was evil. I have had the
    noblest
of sons in Troy, but I say not one of them is left
    to me.
Fifty were my sons, when the sons of the Achaians
    came here.
Nineteen were born to me from the womb of a
    single mother,
and other women bore the rest in my palace; and
    of these
violent Ares broke the strength in the knees of
    most of them,
but one was left me who guarded my city and
    people, that one
you killed a few days since as he fought in defence
    of his country,   500
Hektor; for whose sake I come now to the ships
    of the Achaians
to win him back from you, and I bring you gifts
    beyond number.
Honour then the gods, Achilleus, and take pity
    upon me
remembering your father, yet I am still more
    pitiful;
I have gone through what no other mortal on
    earth has gone through;
I put my lips to the hands of the man who has
    killed my children."

So he spoke, and stirred in the other a passion of
    grieving
for his own father. He took the old man's hand
    and pushed him
gently away, and the two remembered, as Priam
    sat huddled
at the feet of Achilleus and wept close for
    manslaughtering Hektor   510
and Achilleus wept now for his own father, now
    again
for Patroklos. The sound of their mourning moved
    in the house. Then
when great Achilleus had taken full satisfaction in
    sorrow
and the passion for it had gone from his mind and
    body, thereafter
he rose from his chair, and took the old man by
    the hand, and set him
on his feet again, in pity for the grey head and the
    grey beard,

and spoke to him and addressed him in winged words: "Ah, unlucky,
surely you have had much evil to endure in your spirit.
How could you dare to come alone to the ships of the Achaians
and before my eyes, when I am one who have killed in such numbers   520
such brave sons of yours? The heart in you is iron. Come, then,
and sit down upon this chair, and you and I will even let
our sorrows lie still in the heart for all our grieving. There is not
any advantage to be won from grim lamentation.
Such is the way the gods spun life for unfortunate mortals,
that we live in unhappiness, but the gods themselves have no sorrows.
There are two urns that stand on the door-sill of Zeus. They are unlike
for the gifts they bestow: an urn of evils, an urn of blessings.
If Zeus who delights in thunder mingles these and bestows them
on man, he shifts, and moves now in evil, again in good fortune,   530
But when Zeus bestows from the urn of sorrows, he makes a failure
of man, and the evil hunger drives him over the shining
earth, and he wanders respected neither of gods nor mortals.
Such were the shining gifts given by the gods to Peleus
from his birth, who outshone all men beside for his riches
and pride of possession, and was lord over the Myrmidons. Thereto
the gods bestowed an immortal wife on him, who was mortal.
But even on him the god piled evil also. There was not
any generation of strong sons born to him in his great house
but a single all-untimely child he had, and I give him   540
no care as he grows old, since far from the land of my fathers
I sit here in Troy, and bring nothing but sorrow to you and your children.
And you, old sir, we are told you prospered once; for as much
as Lesbos, Makar's hold, confines to the north above it

and Phrygia from the north confines, and enormous Hellespont,
of these, old sir, you were lord once in your wealth and your children.
But now the Uranian gods brought us, an affliction upon you,
forever there is fighting about your city, and men killed.
But bear up, nor mourn endlessly in your heart, for there is not
anything to be gained from grief for your son; you will never   550
bring him back; sooner you must go through yet another sorrow."

In answer to him again spoke aged Priam the godlike:
"Do not, beloved of Zeus, make me sit on a chair while Hektor
lies yet forlorn among the shelters; rather with all speed
give him back, so my eyes may behold him, and accept the ransom
we bring you, which is great. You may have joy of it, and go back
to the land of your own fathers, since once you have permitted me
to go on living myself and continue to look on the sunlight."

Then looking darkly at him spoke swift-footed Achilleus:
"No longer stir me up, old sir. I myself am minded   560
to give Hektor back to you. A messenger came to me from Zeus,
my mother, she who bore me, the daughter of the sea's ancient.
I know you, Priam, in my heart, and it does not escape me
that some god led you to the running ships of the Achaians.
For no mortal would dare come to our encampment, not even
one strong in youth. He could not get by the pickets, he could not
lightly unbar the bolt that secures our gateway. Therefore
you must not further make my spirit move in my sorrows,
for fear, old sir, I might not let you alone in my shelter,
suppliant as you are; and be guilty before the god's orders."   570

He spoke, and the old man was frightened and
    did as he told him.
The son of Peleus bounded to the door of the
    house like a lion,
nor went alone, but the two henchmen followed
    attending,
the hero Automedon and Alkimos, those whom
    Achilleus
honoured beyond all companions after Patroklos
    dead. These two
now set free from under the yoke the mules and
    the horses,
and led inside the herald, the old king's crier, and
    gave him
a chair to sit in, then from the smooth-polished
    mule wagon
lifted out the innumerable spoils for the head of
    Hektor.
but left inside it two great cloaks and a finespun
    tunic   580
to shroud the corpse in when they carried him
    home. Then Achilleus
called out to his serving-maids to wash the body
    and anoint it
all over; but take it first aside, since otherwise
    Priam
might see his son and in the heart's sorrow not
    hold in his anger
at the sight, and the deep heart in Achilleus be
    shaken to anger;
that he might not kill Priam and be guilty before
    the god's orders.
Then when the serving-maids had washed the
    corpse and anointed it
with olive oil, they threw a fair great cloak and a
    tunic
about him, and Achilleus himself lifted him and
    laid him
on a litter, and his friends helped him lift it to the
    smooth-polished   590
mule wagon. He groaned then, and called by name
    on his beloved companion:
"Be not angry with me, Patroklos, if you
    discover,
though you be in the house of Hades, that I gave
    back great Hektor
to his loved father, for the ransom he gave me was
    not unworthy.
I will give you your share of the spoils, as much
    as is fitting."
So spoke great Achilleus and went back into the
    shelter
and sat down on the elaborate couch from which
    he had risen,
against the inward wall, and now spoke his word
    to Priam:

"Your son is given back to you, aged sir, as you
    asked it.
He lies on a bier. When dawn shows you yourself
    shall see him   600
as you take him away. Now you and I must
    remember our supper.
For even Niobe, she of the lovely tresses,
    remembered
to eat, whose twelve children were destroyed in
    her palace,
six daughters, and six sons in the pride of their
    youth, whom Apollo
killed with arrows from his silver bow, being
    angered
with Niobe, and shaft-showering Artemis killed
    the daughters;
because Niobe likened herself to Leto of the fair
    colouring
and said Leto had borne only two, she herself had
    borne many;
but the two, though they were only two,
    destroyed all those others.
Nine days long they lay in their blood, nor was
    there anyone   610
to bury them, for the son of Kronos made stones
    out of
the people; but on the tenth day the Uranian gods
    buried them.
But she remembered to eat when she was worn
    out with weeping.
And now somewhere among the rocks, in the
    lonely mountains,
in Sipylos, where they say is the resting place of
    the goddesses
who are nymphs, and dance beside the waters of
    Acheloios,
there, stone still, she broods on the sorrows that
    the gods gave her.
Come then, we also, aged magnificent sir, must
    remember
to eat, and afterwards you may take your beloved
    son back
to Ilion, and mourn for him; and he will be much
    lamented."   620

So spoke fleet Achilleus and sprang to his feet
    and slaughtered
a gleaming sheep, and his friends skinned it and
    butchered it fairly,
and cut up the meat expertly into small pieces, and
    spitted them,
and roasted all carefully and took off the pieces.
Automedon took the bread and set it out on the
    table
in fair baskets, while Achilleus served the meats.
    And thereon

they put their hands to the good things that lay
  ready before them.
But when they had put aside their desire for eating
  and drinking,
Priam, son of Dardanos, gazed upon Achilleus,
  wondering
at his size and beauty, for he seemed like an
  outright vision   630
of gods. Achilleus in turn gazed on Dardanian
  Priam
and wondered, as he saw his brave looks and
  listened to him talking.
But when they had taken their fill of gazing one
  on the other,
first of the two to speak was the aged man, Priam
  the godlike:
"Give me, beloved of Zeus, a place to sleep
  presently, so that
we may even go to bed and take the pleasure of
  sweet sleep.
For my eyes have not closed underneath my lids
  since that time
when my son lost his life beneath your hands, but
  always
I have been grieving and brooding over my
  numberless sorrows
and wallowed in the muck about my courtyard's
  enclosure.   640
Now I have tasted food again and have let the
  gleaming
wine go down my throat. Before, I had tasted
  nothing."

He spoke, and Achilleus ordered his serving-
  maids and companions
to make a bed in the porch's shelter and to lay
  upon it
fine underbedding of purple, and spread blankets
  above it
and fleecy robes to be an over-all covering. The
  maid-servants
went forth from the main house, and in their
  hands held torches.
and set to work, and presently had two beds
  made. Achilleus
of the swift feet now looked at Priam and said,
  sarcastic:
"Sleep outside, aged sire and good friend, for fear
  some Achaian   650
might come in here on a matter of counsel, since
  they keep coming
and sitting by me and making plans; as they are
  supposed to.
But if one of these come through the fleeting black
  night should notice you,

he would go straight and tell Agamemnon,
  shepherd of the people,
and there would be delay in the ransoming of the
  body.
But come, tell me this and count off for me exactly
how many days you intend for the burial of great
  Hektor.
Tell me, so I myself shall stay still and hold back
  the people."

In answer to him again spoke aged Priam the
  godlike:
"If you are willing that we accomplish a complete
  funeral   660
for great Hektor, this, Achilleus, is what you could
  do and give
me pleasure. For you know surely how we are
  penned in our city,
and wood is far to bring in from the hills, and the
  Trojans are frightened
badly. Nine days we would keep him in our palace
  and mourn him,
and bury him on the tenth day, and the people
  feast by him,
and on the eleventh day we would make the
  grave-barrow for him,
and on the twelfth day fight again; if so we must
  do."

Then in turn swift-footed brilliant Achilleus
  answered him:
"Then all this, aged Priam, shall be done as you
  ask it.
I will hold off our attack for as much time as you
  bid me."   670

So he spoke, and took the aged king by the
  right hand
at the wrist, so that his heart might have no fear.
  Then these two,
Priam and the herald who were both men of close
  counsel,
slept in the place outside the house, in the porch's
  shelter;
but Achilleus slept in the inward corner of the
  strong-built shelter,
and at his side lay Briseis of the fair colouring.

Sappho
from Selected Poems

*The chief subject of Sappho's poetry is love, but her work
also gives voice to the contrasting but equally painful agonies of loneliness and of passionate commitment. Perhaps
her greatest quality is her ability to probe the depths of her
own responses and by describing them to understand them.*

Poems such as these reveal a reluctant resignation that comes only from profound self-understanding.

ALONE

The moon and Pleiades
are set. Midnight,
and time spins away.
I lie in bed, alone.

SEIZURE

To me he seems like a god
as he sits facing you and
hears you near as you speak
softly and laugh

in a sweet echo that jolts
the heart in my ribs. For now
as I look at you my voice
is empty and

can say nothing as my tongue
cracks and slender fire is quick
under my skin. My eyes are dead
to light, my ears

pound, and sweat pours over me.
I convulse, paler than grass,
and feel my mind slip as I
go close to death.

TO EROS

From all the offspring
of the earth and heaven
love is the most precious.

THE VIRGIN

Like a sweet apple reddening on the high
tip of the topmost branch and forgotten
by the pickers—no, beyond their reach.
Like a hyacinth crushed in the mountains
by shepherds; lying trampled on the earth
yet blooming purple.

AGE AND LIGHT

Here are fine gifts, children,
O friend, singer on the clear tortoise lyre,

all my flesh is wrinkled with age,
my black hair has faded to white,

my legs can no longer carry me,
once nimble as a fawn's,

but what can I do?
It cannot be undone,

No more than can pink-armed Dawn
not end in darkness on earth,

or keep her love for Tithonos,
who must waste away;

yet I love refinement, and beauty and light
are for me the same as desire for the sun.

Herodotus
from HISTORY OF THE PERSIAN WARS, Book VIII

In Book VIII of his History *Herodotus describes Xerxes' invasion of Greece in 480* B.C. *In the course of their journey southward toward Athens, the Persian troops arrive at the narrow mountain pass of Thermopylae in central Greece. There a small band of Greek soldiers blocks the road and threatens to hold up the entire Persian army. In his justly famous account of the battle Herodotus summons up a world of meaning by carefully chosen details—the Spartan soldiers preparing for battle by combing their hair, for example. As the fighting intensifies, so does the tension of the account. With simplicity and dignity Herodotus leads us to the final desperate struggle over the body of the dead Greek commander, one of the first great prose passages in Western literature.*

The Persian army was now close to the pass, and the Greeks, suddenly doubting their power to resist, held a conference to consider the advisability of retreat. It was proposed by the Peloponnesians generally that the army should fall back upon the Peloponnese and hold the Isthmus; but when the Phocians and Locrians expressed their indignation at this suggestion, Leonidas gave his voice for staying where they were and sending, at the same time, an appeal for reinforcements to the various states of the confederacy, as their numbers were inadequate to cope with the Persians.

During the conference Xerxes sent a man on horseback to ascertain the strength of the Greek force and to observe what the troops were doing. He had heard before he left Thessaly that a small force was concentrated here, led by the Lacedaemonians under Leonidas of the house of Heracles. The Persian rider approached the camp and took a thorough survey of all he could see—which was not, however, the whole Greek army; for the men on the further side of the wall which, after its reconstruction, was now guarded, were out of sight. He did, none the less, carefully observe the troops who were stationed on the outside of the wall. At that moment these happened to be the Spartans, and some of them were stripped for exercise, while others were combing their hair. The Persian spy watched them in astonishment; nevertheless he made sure of their numbers, and of everything else he needed to know, as accurately as he could, and then rode quietly off. No one attempted to catch him, or took the least notice of him.

Back in his own camp he told Xerxes what he had seen. Xerxes was bewildered; the truth, namely that the Spartans were preparing themselves to kill and to be killed according to their strength, was beyond his comprehension, and what they were doing seemed to him merely absurd. Accordingly he sent for Demaratus, the son of Ariston, who had come with the army, and questioned him about the spy's report, in the hope of finding out what the unaccountable behaviour of the Spartans might mean. "Once before," Demaratus said, "when we began our march against Greece, you heard me speak of these men. I told you then how I saw this enterprise would turn out, and you laughed at me. I strive for nothing, my lord, more earnestly than to observe the truth in your presence; so hear me once more. These men have come to fight us for possession of the pass, and for that struggle they are preparing. It is the common practice of the Spartans to pay careful attention to their hair when they are about to risk their lives. But I assure you that if you can defeat these men and the rest of the Spartans who are still at home, there is no other people in the world who will dare to stand firm or lift a hand against you. You have now to deal with the finest kingdom in Greece, and with the bravest men."

Xerxes, unable to believe what Demaratus said, asked further how it was possible that so small a force could fight with his army. "My lord," Demaratus replied, "treat me as a liar, if what I have foretold does not take place." But still Xerxes was unconvinced.

For four days Xerxes waited, in constant expectation that the Greeks would make good their escape; then, on the fifth, when still they had made no move and their continued presence seemed mere impudent and reckless folly, he was seized with rage and sent forward the Medes and Cissians with orders to take them alive and bring them into his presence. The Medes charged, and in the struggle which ensued many fell; but others took their places, and in spite of terrible losses refused to be beaten off. They made it plain enough to anyone, and not least to the king himself, that he had in his army many men, indeed, but few soldiers. All day the battle continued; the Medes, after their rough handling, were at length withdrawn and their place was taken by Hydarnes and his picked Persian troops—the King's Immortals—who advanced to the attack in full confidence of bringing the business to a quick and easy end. But, once engaged, they were no more successful than the Medes had been; all went as before, the two armies fighting in a confined space, the Persians using shorter spears than the Greeks and having no advantage from their numbers.

On the Spartan side it was a memorable fight; they were men who understood war pitted against an inexperienced enemy, and amongst the feints they employed was to turn their backs in a body and pretend to be retreating in confusion, whereupon the enemy would come on with a great clatter and roar, supposing the battle won; but the Spartans, just as the Persians were on them, would wheel and face them and inflict in the new struggle innumerable casualties. The Spartans had their losses too, but not many. At last the Persians, finding that their assaults upon the pass, whether by divisions or by any other way they could think of, were all useless, broke off the engagement and withdrew. Xerxes was watching the battle from where he sat; and it is said that in the course of the attacks three times, in terror for his army, he leapt to his feet.

Next day the fighting began again, but with no better success for the Persians, who renewed their onslaught in the hope that the Greeks, being so few in number, might be badly enough disabled by wounds to prevent further resistance. But the Greeks never slackened; their troops were ordered in divisions corresponding to the states from which they came, and each division took its turn in the line except the Phocian, which had been posted to guard the track over the mountains. So when the Persians found that things were no better for them than on the previous day, they once more withdrew.

How to deal with the situation Xerxes had no idea; but while he was still wondering what his next move should be, a man from Malis got himself admitted to his presence. This was Ephialtes, the son of Eurydemus, and he had come, in hope of a rich reward, to tell the king about the track which led over the hills to Thermopylae—and the information he gave was to prove the death of the Greeks who held the pass.

Later on, Ephialtes, in fear of the Spartans, fled to Thessaly, and during his exile there a price was put upon his head at an assembly of the Amphictyons at Pylae. Some time afterwards he returned to Anticyra, where he was killed by Athenades of Trachis. In point of fact, Athenades killed him not for his treachery but for another reason, which I will explain further on; but the Spartans honoured him none the less on that account. According to another story, which I do not at all believe, it was Onetes, the son of Phanagoras, a native of Carystus, and Corydallus of Anticyra who spoke to Xerxes and showed the Persians the way round by the mountain track; but one may judge which account is the true one, first by the fact that the Amphictyons, who must surely have known everything about it, set a price not upon Onetes and Corydallus but upon Ephialtes of Trachis, and, secondly, by the fact that there is no doubt that the accusation of treachery was the reason for Ephialtes' flight. Certainly Onetes, even though he was not a native of Malis, might have known about the track, if he had spent much time in the neighbourhood—but it was Ephialtes, and no one else, who showed the Persians the way, and I leave his name on record as the guilty one.

Xerxes found Ephialtes' offer most satisfactory. He was delighted with it, and promptly gave orders to Hydarnes to carry out the movement with the troops under his command. They left camp about the time the lamps are lit.

The track was originally discovered by the Malians of the neighbourhood; they afterwards used it to help the Thessalians, taking them over it to attack Phocis at the time when the Phocians were protected from invasion by the wall which they had built across the pass. That was a long time ago, and no good ever came of it since. The track begins at the Asopus, the stream which flows through the narrow gorge, and, running along the ridge of the mountain—which, like the track itself, is called Anopaea—ends at Alpenus, the first Locrian settlement as one comes from Malis, near the rock known as Black-Buttocks' Stone and the seats of the Cercopes. Just here is the narrowest part of the pass.

This then, was the mountain track which the Persians took, after crossing the Asopus. They marched throughout the night, with the mountains of Oeta on their right hand and those of Trachis on their left. By early dawn they were at the summit of the ridge, near the spot where the Phocians, as I mentioned before, stood on guard with a thousand men, to watch the track and protect their country. The Phocians were ready enough to undertake this service, and had, indeed, volunteered for it to Leonidas, knowing that the pass at Thermopylae was held as I have already described.

The ascent of the Persians had been concealed by the oak-woods which cover this part of the mountain range, and it was only when they reached the top that the Phocians became aware of their approach; for there was not a breath of wind, and the marching feet made a loud swishing and rustling in the fallen leaves. Leaping to their feet, the Phocians were in the act of arming themselves when the enemy was upon them. The Persians were surprised at the sight of troops preparing to resist; they had not expected any opposition—yet here was a body of men barring their way. Hydarnes asked Ephialtes who they were, for his first uncomfortable thought was that they might be Spartans; but on learning the truth he prepared to engage them. The Persian arrows flew thick and fast, and the Phocians, supposing themselves to be the main object of the attack, hurriedly withdrew to the highest point of the mountain, where they made ready to face destruction. The Persians, however, with Ephialtes and Hydarnes paid no further attention to them, but passed on along the descending track with all possible speed.

The Greeks at Thermopylae had their first warning of the death that was coming with the dawn from the seer Megistias, who read their doom in the victims of sacrifice; deserters, too, had begun to come in during the night with news of the Persian movement to take them in the rear, and, just as day was breaking, the look-out men had come running from the hills. At once a conference was held, and opinions were divided, some urging that they must on no account abandon their post, others taking the opposite view. The result was that the army split; some dispersed, the men returning to their various homes, and others made ready to stand by Leonidas.

There is another account which says that Leonidas himself dismissed a part of his force, to spare their lives, but thought it unbecoming for the Spartans under his command to desert the post which they had originally come to guard. I myself am inclined to think that he dismissed them when he realized that they had no heart for the fight and were unwilling to take their share of the danger; at the same time honour forbade that he himself should go. And indeed by remaining at his post he left a great name behind him, and Sparta did not lose her prosperity, as might otherwise have happened; for right at the outset of the war the Spartans had been told by the oracle, when they asked for advice, that either their city must be laid waste by the foreigner or one of their kings be killed. The prophecy was in hexameter verse and ran as follows:

> Hear your fate, O dwellers in Sparta of the wide spaces;
> Either your famed, great town must be sacked by Perseus' sons.
> Or, if that be not, the whole land of Lacedaemon
> Shall mourn the death of a king of the house of Heracles,
> For not the strength of lions or of bulls shall hold him,
> Strength against strength; for he has the power of Zeus,
> And will not be checked till one of these two he has consumed.

I believe it was the thought of this oracle, combined with his wish to lay up for the Spartans a treasure of fame in which no other city should share, that made Leonidas dismiss those troops; I do not think that they deserted, or went off without orders, because of a difference of opinion. Moreover, I am strongly supported in this view by the case of Megistias, the seer from Acarnania who foretold the coming doom by his inspection of the sacrificial victims:

this man—he was said to be descended from Melampus—was with the army, and quite plainly received orders from Leonidas to quit Thermopylae, to save him from sharing the army's fate. But he refused to go, sending away instead an only son of his, who was serving with the forces.

Thus it was that the confederate troops, by Leonidas' orders, abandoned their posts and left the pass, all except the Thespians and the Thebans who remained with the Spartans. The Thebans were detained by Leonidas as hostages very much against their will—unlike the loyal Thespians, who refused to desert Leonidas and his men, but stayed, and died with them. They were under the command of Demophilus the son of Diadromes.

In the morning Xerxes poured a libation to the rising sun, and then waited till about the time of the filling of the market-place, when he began to move forward. This was according to Ephialtes' instructions, for the way down from the ridge is much shorter and more direct than the long and circuitous ascent. As the Persian army advanced to the assault, the Greeks under Leonidas, knowing that the fight would be their last, pressed forward into the wider part of the pass much further than they had done before; in the previous days' fighting they had been holding the wall and making sorties from behind it into the narrow neck, but now they left the confined space and battle was joined on more open ground. Many of the invaders fell; behind them the company commanders plied their whips, driving the men remorselessly on. Many fell into the sea and were drowned, and still more were trampled to death by their friends. No one could count the number of the dead. The Greeks, who knew that the enemy were on their way round by the mountain track and that death was inevitable, fought with reckless desperation, exerting every ounce of strength that was in them against the invader. By this time most of their spears were broken, and they were killing Persians with their swords.

In the course of that fight Leonidas fell, having fought like a man indeed. Many distinguished Spartans were killed at his side—their names, like the names of all the three hundred, I have made myself acquainted with, because they deserve to be remembered. Amongst the Persian dead, too, were many men of high distinction—for instance, two brothers of Xerxes, Habrocomes and Hyperanthes, both of them sons of Darius by Artanes' daughter Phratagune.

There was a bitter struggle over the body of Leonidas; four times the Greeks drove the enemy off, and at last by their valour succeeded in dragging it away. So it went on, until the fresh troops with Ephialtes were close at hand; and then, when the Greeks knew that they had come, the character of the fighting changed. They withdrew again into the narrow neck of the pass, behind the walls, and took up a position in a single compact body—all except the Thebans—on the little hill at the entrance to the pass, where the stone lion in memory of Leonidas stands to-day. Here they resisted to the last, with their swords, if they had them, and, if not, with their hands and teeth, until the Persians, coming on from the front over the ruins of the wall and closing in from behind, finally overwhelmed them.

Of all the Spartans and Thespians who fought so valiantly on that day, the most signal proof of courage was given by the Spartan Dieneces. It is said that before the battle he was told by a native of Trachis that, when the Persians shot their arrows, there were so many of them that they hid the sun. Dieneces, however, quite unmoved by the thought of the terrible strength of the Persian army, merely remarked: "This is pleasant news that the stranger from Trachis brings us: for if the Persians hide the sun, we shall have our battle in the shade." He is said to have left on record other sayings, too, of a similar kind, by which he will be remembered. After Dieneces the greatest distinction was won by the two Spartan brothers, Alpheus and Maron, the sons of Orsiphantus; and of the Thespians the man to gain the highest glory was a certain Dithyrambus, the son of Harmatides.

The dead were buried where they fell, and with them the men who had been killed before those dismissed by Leonidas left the pass. Over them is this inscription, in honour of the whole force:

> Four thousand here from Pelops' land
> Against three million once did stand.

The Spartans have a special epitaph; it runs:

> Go tell the Spartans, you who read:
> We took their orders, and are dead.

For the seer Megistias there is the following:

> I was Megistias once, who died
> When the Mede passed Spercheius' tide.
> I knew death near, yet would not save
> Myself, but share the Spartans' grave.

	GENERAL EVENTS	LITERATURE & PHILOSOPHY	ART

500 B.C.

c. 490 *Critian Boy;* turning point between Archaic and Classical Periods

480

478 Formation of Delian League; beginning of Athenian empire

480–323 First naturalistic sculpture and painting appear

c. 460 Sculptures at Temple of Zeus, Olympia

461 Pericles comes to prominence at Athens

458 Aeschylus, *Oresteia* trilogy wins first prize in drama festival of Dionysus

454 Treasury of Delian League moved to Athens

450

Golden Age

443–430 Pericles in full control of Athens

441 Sophocles, *Antigone*

c. 450 Myron, *Discus Thrower*

432 Peloponnesian War begins

429 Pericles dies of plague that devastates Athens

c. 429 Sophocles, *Oedipus the King*

421 Peace of Nicias

c. 421 Euripides, *The Suppliant Women*

c. 440 Polyclitus, *Doryphorus,* treatise *The Canon*

413 Renewed outbreak of Peloponnesian War

c. 420–c. 399 Thucydides, *History of Peloponnesian War*

432 Phidias completes Parthenon sculptures

414 Aristophanes, *The Birds*

411 Aristophanes, *Lysistrata*

late 5th cent. Funerary relief sculpture and white-ground vase painting; lekythos, *Warrior Seated at His Tomb*

404

404 Fall of Athens and victory of Sparta

404–403 Rule of Thirty Tyrants

399 Trial and execution of Socrates

387 King's Peace signed

before 387 Plato, *Republic*

c. 350 Scopas, *Pothos*

371–362 Ascendancy of Thebes

387 Plato founds Academy

359–336 Philip II, king of Macedon

c. 385 Xenophon chronicles teachings of Socrates

c. 350 Frescoes, Royal Cemetery at Vergina

338 Macedonians defeat Greeks at Battle of Chaeronea

c. 347–c. 399 Aristotle, *Politics, Metaphysics*

c. 340 Praxiteles, *Hermes with Infant Dionysus*

336–323 Alexander the Great, king of Macedon

335 Aristotle founds Lyceum

331 City of Alexandria founded

c. 325 Lysippus, *Apoxymenos*

323

323–281 Wars of Alexander's successors

323–146 Development of realistic portraiture

262 Pergamum becomes independent kingdom

197–156 Eumenes II, king of Pergamum

146 Romans sack Corinth; Greece becomes Roman province

c. 150 *Laocoön;* mosaic, House of Masks, Delos

146

CLASSICAL PERIOD · Late Classical Period · HELLENISTIC PERIOD

3

Classical Greece and The Hellenistic Period

470–456 Libon of Elis, Temple of Zeus at Olympia

c. 500–425 Music serves as accompaniment in dramatic performances

449 Pericles commissions work on Acropolis

447–438 Ictinus and Callicrates, Parthenon

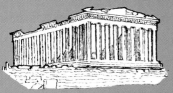

437–432 Mnesicles, Propylaea

c. 427–424 Callicrates, Temple of Athena Nike

421–406 Erechtheum

c. 400 Music dominates dramatic performances

356 Temple of Artemis at Ephesus destroyed by fire and rebuilt

4th cent. Instrumental music becomes popular

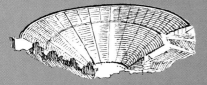

c. 350 Theater at Epidaurus

323–146 *Tholos* and other new building forms appear

279 Lighthouse at Alexandria

c. 180–160 Menocrates of Rhodes, Pergamum Altar

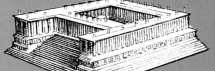

late 2nd cent. Earliest surviving Greek music

The victories in the Persian Wars produced a new spirit of optimism and unity in Greece. Divine forces, it appeared, had guaranteed the triumph of right over wrong. There seemed to be no limit to the possibilities of human development. The achievements of the Classical period, which lasted from 479 B.C. to the death of Alexander the Great in 323 B.C., do much to justify the Greeks' proud self-confidence. They certainly represent a level of civilization that has rarely, if ever, been reached since—a level that has been a continuing inspiration to our culture.

Classical civilization reached its high point in Athens during the last half of the 5th century B.C., a time of unparalleled richness in artistic and intellectual achievement that is often called the Golden Age of Greece. To some extent, the importance of the great figures who dominated this period lies in the fact that they were the first in their fields. There are, in fact, few areas of human thought in which the 5th century Greeks were not pioneers. In subjects as diverse as drama and historiography, town planning and medicine, painting and sculpture, mathematics and government, they laid the foundations of later achievements. Even more astonishing, often they were not merely the first in their fields but also among the greatest of all time. Greek tragedies, for example, are still read and performed today because they give experiences that are as intense emotionally and intellectually as anything in the Western dramatic tradition.

In the Late Classical period, from 404 to 323 B.C., artists and writers continued to explore ideas and styles first outlined in the century before, though in different ways. Greek cultural life was no longer dominated by Athens; a single center no longer governed artistic developments. This 4th-century period was therefore one of greater variety, with individual artists following their own personal visions. The greatest of all Late Classical contributions to our cultural tradition was in the field of philosophy. The works of Plato and Aristotle became the basis of Western thought for the next two thousand years.

Even after the death of Alexander the Great in 323 B.C. and the end of the Classical Age, the Hellenistic period that followed was characterized by an artistic vitality that ultimately drew its inspiration from Classical achievements. Only when Greece was conquered by the Romans in the late 2nd century B.C. did Greek culture cease to have an independent existence.

The Classical Ideal

Although the Roman conquest of Greece ended the glories of the Classical Age, in a way it also perpetu-ated them by contributing to the melding of Greek culture into the Western humanistic tradition. It was not the Greeks themselves but their conquerors who spread Greek ideas throughout the ancient world— and thus down in time to our own day. These conquerors were first the Macedonians and then, above all, the Romans, possessors of practical skills that they used to construct a world sufficiently at peace for ideas to have a place in it. The Greeks did not live in such tranquility; we must always remember that the Athenians of the Golden Age existed not in an environment of calm contemplation but in a world of tension and violence. Their tragic inability to put into practice their own noble ideals and live in peace with other Greeks—the darker side of their genius— proved fatal to their independence; it led to war with the rest of Greece in 431 B.C. and to the fall of Athens in 404 B.C. In this context, the Greek search for order takes on an added significance.

It was the belief that the quest for reason and order could succeed that gave a unifying ideal to the immense and varied output of the Classical Age. The central principle of this Classical Ideal was that existence can be ordered and controlled, that human ability can triumph over the apparent chaos of the natural world and create a balanced society. In order to achieve this equilibrium, individual human beings should try to stay within what seem to be reasonable limits, for those who do not are guilty of hubris, excessive pride—the same hubris of which the Persian leader Xerxes was guilty and for which he paid the price (see page 62). The aim of life should be a perfect balance: everything in due proportion and nothing in excess. "Nothing too much" was one of the most famous Greek proverbs.

The emphasis that the Classical Greeks placed on order affected their spiritual attitudes. Individuals can achieve order, they believed, by understanding why people act as they do and, above all, by understanding the motives for their *own* actions. Thus confidence in the power of both human reason and human self-knowledge was as important as belief in the gods. The greatest of all Greek temples of the Classical Age, the Parthenon, which crowned the Athenian Acropolis [3.1], was planned not so much to honor the goddess Athena as to glorify Athens and thus human achievement. Even in their darkest days the Classical Greeks never lost sight of the magnitude of human capability and, perhaps even more important, human potential—a vision that has returned over the centuries to inspire later generations and has certainly not lost its relevance in our own times.

The political and cultural center of Greece during the first half of the Classical period was Athens. Here, by the end of the Persian Wars in 479 B.C., the Athenians had emerged as the most powerful people

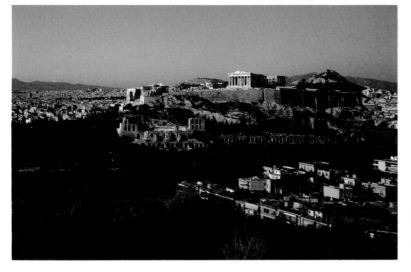

3.1 The Acropolis, Athens, from the northwest. The Parthenon, temple to Athena, is at the highest point. Below it spreads the monumental gateway, the Propylaea. Far left is the Erechtheum.

in the Greek world. For one thing, their role in the defeat of the Persians had been a decisive one. For another, their democratic system of government, first established in the late 6th century B.C., was proving to be both effective and stable. All male Athenian citizens were not only entitled but were required to participate in the running of the state, either as members of the General Assembly, the *ecclesia,* with its directing council, the *boulé,* or by holding individual magistracies. They were also eligible to serve on juries.

Under Athenian leadership in the years following the wars a defensive organization of Greek city-states was formed to guard against any future attack from outside. The money collected from the participating members was kept in a treasury on the island of Delos, sacred to Apollo and politically neutral. This organization became known as the Delian League.

Within a short time a number of other important city-states, including Thebes, Sparta, and Athens' old trade rival Corinth, began to suspect that the League was serving not so much to protect all of Greece as to strengthen Athenian power. They believed the Athenians were turning an association of free and independent states into an empire of subject peoples. Their suspicions were confirmed when in 454 B.C. the funds of the League were transferred from Delos to Athens and some of the money was used to pay for Athenian building projects, including the Parthenon. The spirit of Greek unity was starting to dissolve; the Greek world was beginning to divide into two opposing sides: on the one hand Athens and her allies (the cities that remained in the League) and, on the other, the rest of Greece. Conflict was inevitable. The Spartans were finally persuaded to lead an alliance against Athens to check her "imperialistic designs." This war, called the Peloponnesian War after the homeland of the Spartans and their supporters, began in 431 B.C. and was dragged on until 404 B.C.

Our understanding of the Peloponnesian War and its significance owes much to the account by the great historian Thucydides, who himself lived through its calamitous events. Born around 460 B.C., Thucydides played an active part in Athenian politics in the years before the war. In 424 B.C. he was elected general and put in charge of defending the city of Amphipolis in northern Greece. When the city fell to Spartan troops, Thucydides was condemned in his absence and sentenced to exile. He did not return to Athens until 404 B.C.

Thucydides intended his *History of the Peloponnesian War* to describe the entire course of the war up to 404 B.C., but he died before completing it; the narrative breaks off at the end of 411 B.C. The work is extremely valuable for its detailed description of events, for although its author was an Athenian he managed to be both accurate and impartial. At the same time, however, Thucydides tried to write more than simply an account of a local war. The *History* was an attempt to analyze human motives and reactions so that future generations would understand how and why the conflict occurred and, in turn, understand themselves. The work was not meant to entertain by providing digressions and anecdotes but to search out the truth and use it to demonstrate universal principles of human behavior. This emphasis on reason makes Thucydides' work typical of the Classical period.

The hero of Thucydides' account of the years immediately preceding the war is Pericles, the leader whose name symbolizes the achievements of the Athenian Golden Age [3.2]. An aristocrat by birth, Pericles began his political career in the aftermath of the transfer of the Delian League's funds to Athens. By 443 B.C. he had unofficially assumed the leadership of the Athenian democracy, although he continued democratically to run for reelection every year. Under his guidance the few remaining years of peace were devoted to making visible the glory of Athens

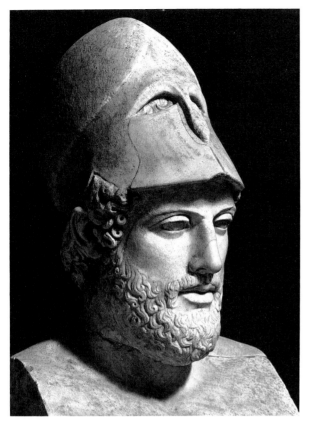

3.2 Kresilas. *Pericles.* Roman copy after original of c. 440 B.C. Marble. Vatican Museum, Rome. Pericles is wearing a helmet, pushed up over his forehead, because his official rank while leader of Athens was that of general.

TABLE 3.1 Athens in the Age of Pericles (ruled 443–429 B.C.)	
Area of the city	7 square miles
Population of the city	100,000–125,000
Population of the region (Attica)	200,000–250,000
Political institution	General Assembly, Council of 500, Ten Generals
Economy	Maritime trade; Crafts (textiles, pottery); Farming (olives, grapes, wheat)
Cultural life	History (Thucydides); Drama (Aeschylus, Sophocles, Euripides, Aristophanes); Philosophy (Socrates); Architecture (Ictinus, Callicrates, Mnesicles); Sculpture (Phidias)
Principal buildings	Parthenon, Propylea (the Erechtheum, the other major building on the Athenian Acropolis, was not begun in Pericles' lifetime)

by constructing on the Acropolis the majestic buildings that still, though in ruins, evoke the grandeur of Periclean Athens (Table 3.1).

Had Pericles continued to lead Athens during the war itself, the final outcome might have been different, but in 430 B.C. the city was ravaged by disease, perhaps bubonic plague, and in 429 B.C. Pericles died. No successor could be found who was capable of winning the respect and support of the majority of his fellow citizens. The war continued indecisively until 421 B.C., when an uneasy peace was signed. Shortly thereafter the Athenians made an ill-advised attempt to replenish their treasury by organizing an unprovoked attack on the wealthy Greek cities of Sicily. The expedition proved a total disaster; thousands of Athenians were killed or taken prisoner. When the war began again in 411 B.C. the Athenian forces were fatally weakened. The end came in 404 B.C. After a siege that left many people dying in the streets, Athens surrendered unconditionally to the Spartans and their allies.

Drama and Philosophy in Classical Greece

The Drama Festivals of Dionysus

The tumultuous years of the 5th century B.C., passing from the spirit of euphoria that followed the ending of the Persian Wars to the mood of doubt and self-questioning of 404 B.C., may seem unlikely to have produced the kind of intellectual concentration characteristic of Classical Greek drama. Yet it was, in fact, in the plays written specifically for performance in the theater of Dionysus at Athens in these years that Classical literature reached its most elevated heights. The tragedies of the three great masters, Aeschylus, Sophocles, and Euripides, not only illustrate the development of contemporary thought but also contain some of the most memorable scenes in the history of the theater.

Tragic drama was not itself an invention of the 5th century B.C. It had evolved over the preceding century from choral hymns sung in honor of the god Dionysus, and the religious character of its origins was still present in its fully developed form. The plays that have survived from the Classical period at Athens were all written for performance at one of the two annual festivals sacred to Dionysus before an audience consisting of the entire population of the city. To go to the theater was to take part in a religious ritual; the theaters themselves were regarded as sacred ground [3.3].

Each of the authors of the works given each year normally submitted four plays to be performed con-

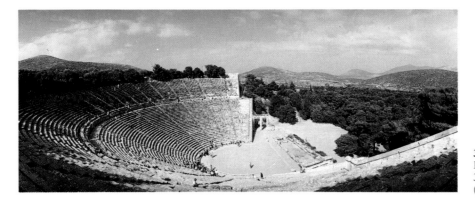

3.3 Polyclitus. Theater, Epidaurus. c. 350 B.C. Diameter 373′ (113.69 m), orchestra 66′ (20.12 m) across.

secutively on a single day—three tragedies, or a "trilogy," and a more light-hearted play called a *satyr* play (a satyr was a mythological figure: a man with an animal's ears and tail). The "trilogies" sometimes narrated parts of a single story, although often the three works were based on different stories with a common theme. At the end of each festival the plays were judged and a prize awarded to the winning author.

The dramas were religious not only in time and place but also in nature. The plots, generally drawn from mythology, often dealt with the relationship between the human and the divine. To achieve an appropriate seriousness, the style of performance was lofty and dignified. The actors, who in a sense served as priests of Dionysus, wore masks, elaborate costumes, and raised shoes.

The chorus, whose sacred dithyrambic hymn had been the original starting point in the development of tragedy, retained an important function throughout the 5th century B.C. In some plays, generally the earlier ones, the chorus forms a group centrally involved in the action, as in Aeschylus' *Suppliants* and *Eumenides.* More often, as in Sophocles' *Oedipus the King* or *Antigone,* the chorus represents the point of view of the spectator, rather than that of the characters participating directly in the events on stage; in these plays the chorus reduces to more human terms the intense emotions of the principals and comments on them. Even in the time of Euripides, when dramatic confrontation became more important than extended poetic or philosophical expression, the chorus still retained one important function, that of punctuating the action and dividing it into separate episodes by singing lyric odes whose subject was sometimes only indirectly related to the action of the play.

These aspects of Classical tragedy are a reminder that the surviving texts of the plays represent only a small part of the total experience of the original performances. The words—or at least some of them—have survived; but the music to which the words were sung and which accompanied much of the action, the elaborate choreography to which the chorus moved, indeed the whole grandiose spectacle per-

formed out-of-doors in theaters located in sites of extreme natural beauty before an audience of thousands—all of this can only be recaptured in the imagination. It is perhaps relevant to remember that when, almost two thousand years later, around A.D. 1600, a small group of Florentine intellectuals decided to revive the art of Classical drama, they succeeded instead in inventing opera. Similarly, in the 19th century the German composer Richard Wagner was inspired by Greek tragedy to devise his concept of a *Gesamtkunstwerk* (literally "total work of art"), a work of art that combined all the arts into one; he illustrated this concept by writing his dramatic operas.

The Athenian Tragic Dramatists

Even if some elements of the surviving Greek dramas are lost, we do have the words. The differing world views of the authors of these works vividly illustrate the changing fate of 5th-century-B.C. Athens. The earliest of the playwrights, Aeschylus (525–456 B.C.), died before the lofty aspirations of the early years of the Classical period could be shaken by contemporary events. His work shows a deep awareness of human weakness and the dangers of power (he had himself fought at the Battle of Marathon in 490 B.C.), but he retains an enduring belief that in the end right will triumph. In Aeschylus' plays the process of being able to recognize what is right is painful: One must suffer to learn one's errors; yet the process is inevitable, controlled by a divine force of justice personified under the name of Zeus.

The essential optimism of Aeschylus' philosophy must be kept in mind because the actual course of the events he describes is often violent and bloody. Perhaps his most impressive plays are the three that form the *Oresteia* trilogy. This trilogy, the only complete one that has survived, won first prize in the festival of 458 B.C. at Athens. The subject of the trilogy is nothing less than the growth of civilization, represented by the gradual transition from a primitive law of "vendetta" and blood for blood to the rational society of civilized human beings.

The first of the three plays, *Agamemnon,* presents

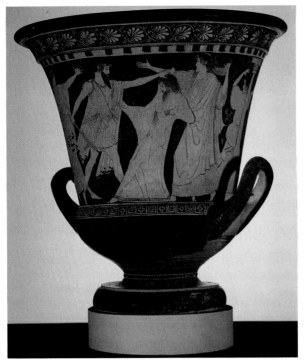

3.4 Dokimasia Painter. *The Murder of Agamemnon,* detail of red-figure krater. Attic, c. 470–465 B.C. Terra cotta. Museum of Fine Arts, Boston (William Francis Warden Fund). Aegisthus strikes the blow in this version of the story, with Clytemnestra standing behind him grasping an axe. Agamemnon, killed as he was about to take a bath, is wearing only a light robe.

the first of these systems in operation. King Agamemnon returns to his homeland, Argos, after leading the Greeks to victory at Troy. Ten years earlier, on the way to Troy, he had been forced to choose either to abandon the campaign because of unfavorable tides or to obtain an easy passage by sacrificing his daughter Iphigenia. (The situation may seem contrived, but it clearly symbolizes a conflict between public and personal responsibilities.) After considerable hesitation and self-doubt he had chosen to sacrifice his daughter. On his return home at the end of the Trojan War, he pays the price for her death by being murdered by his wife Clytemnestra [3.4]. Her ostensible motive is vengeance for Iphigenia's death, but an equally powerful, if less noble, one is her desire to replace Agamemnon both as husband and king by her lover Aegisthus. Thus Aeschylus shows us that even the "law of the jungle" is not always as simple as it may seem, while at the same time the punishment of one crime creates in its turn another crime to be punished. If Agamemnon's murder of his daughter merits vengeance, then so does Clytemnestra's murder of her husband. Violence breeds violence.

The second play, *The Libation Bearers,* shows us the effects of the operation of this principle on Aga-

memnon and Clytemnestra's son, Orestes. After spending years in exile Orestes returns to Argos to avenge his father's death by killing his mother. Although a further murder can accomplish nothing except the transfer of blood guilt to Orestes himself, the primitive law of "vendetta" requires him to act. With the encouragement of his sister Electra, he kills Clytemnestra. His punishment follows immediately. He is driven mad by the Furies, the implacable goddesses of vengeance, who hound him from his home.

The Furies themselves give their name to the third play, in which they are tactfully called *The Eumenides,* or "the kindly ones." In his resolution of the tragedy of Orestes and his family, Aeschylus makes it clear that violence can only be brought to an end by the power of reason and persuasion. After a period of tormented wandering, Orestes comes finally to Athens where he stands trial for the murder of his mother before a jury of Athenians, presided over by Athena herself. The Furies insist on his condemnation on the principle of blood for blood, but Orestes is defended by Apollo, the god of reason, and finally acquitted by his fellow human beings. Thus the long series of murders is brought to an end, and the apparently inevitable violence and despair of the earlier plays is finally dispelled by the power of persuasion and human reason, which—admittedly with the help of Athena and Apollo—have managed to bring civilization and order out of primeval chaos.

In spite of all of the horror of the earlier plays, therefore, the *Oresteia* ends on a positive note. Aeschylus affirms his belief that progress can be achieved by reason and order. This gradual transition from darkness to light is handled throughout the three plays with unfailing skill. Aeschylus matches the grandeur of his conception with majestic language. His rugged style makes him sometimes difficult to understand, but all the verbal effects are used to dramatic purpose. The piling up of images and complexity of expression produce an emotional tension that has never been surpassed.

The life of Sophocles (496–406 B.C.) spanned both the glories and the disasters of the 5th century B.C. Of the three great tragic poets, Sophocles was the most prosperous and successful; he was a personal friend of Pericles. He is said to have written 123 plays, but only seven have survived, all of them from the end of his career. They all express a much less positive vision of life than that of Aeschylus. His philosophy is not easy to extract from his work, since he is more concerned with exploring and developing the individual characters in his dramas than with expounding a point of view; in general, he seems to combine an awareness of the tragic consequences of individual mistakes with a belief in the collective ability and dignity of the human race.

The consequences of human error are vividly depicted in his play *Antigone,* first performed around 440 B.C. Thebes has been attacked by forces under the leadership of Polynices; the attack is beaten off and Polynices killed. In the aftermath Creon, king of Thebes, declares the dead warrior a traitor and forbids anyone to bury him on pain of death. Antigone, Polynices' sister, disobeys, claiming that her religious and family obligations override those to the state. Creon angrily condemns her to death. He subsequently relents, but too late: Antigone, his son (betrothed to Antigone), and his wife have all committed suicide. Creon's stubbornness and bad judgment thus bring tragedy for him as well as for Antigone.

Paradoxically, however, the choice between good and evil is never clear or easy and is sometimes impossible. More than any of his contemporaries, Sophocles emphasizes how much lies outside our own control, in the hands of destiny or the gods. His insistence that we respect and revere the forces that we cannot see or understand makes him the most traditionally religious of the tragedians. These ambiguities appear in his best-known play, *Oedipus the King,* which has stood ever since Classical times as a symbol of Greek tragic drama [3.5]. A century after it was first performed around 429 B.C., Aristotle used it as his model when, in the *Poetics,* he discussed the nature of tragedy. Its unities of time, place, and action, the inexorable drive of the story with its inevitable yet profoundly tragic conclusion, the beauty of its poetry—all these have made *Oedipus the King* a true classic, in all senses. Its impact has lasted down to our own times; it had a notable effect on the ideas of Sigmund Freud. Yet in spite of the universal admiration the play has excited, its message is far from clear.

The story concerns Oedipus, doomed even before his birth to kill his father and marry his mother, his attempts to avoid fate, and his final discovery that he has failed. If the play seems, in part, to be saying that we cannot avoid our destiny, it leaves unanswered the question of whether we deserve that destiny or not. Certainly Oedipus does not choose deliberately to kill his father and marry his mother, even though unknowingly everything he does leads to this end. Then why does he deserve to suffer for his actions?

One of the traditional answers to this question can be found in Aristotle's analysis of tragedy in the *Poetics.* Referring particularly to *Oedipus,* Aristotle makes the point that the downfall of a tragic figure is generally the result of a flaw (the Greek word is *hamartia*) in his character. Thus Oedipus' pride and stubbornness in insisting on discovering who he is and the anger he shows in the process bring about the final disastrous revelation. In this way the flaws, or weaknesses, in his character overcome his good points and destroy him.

As a description of Oedipus' behavior, this explanation is convincing enough, but it fails to provide a satisfactory account of the original causes of his condition. Perhaps the message of the play is, in fact, that there are some aspects of existence beyond our understanding, aspects that operate by principles outside our range of experience. If this is so, and many literary critics would deny it, Sophocles seems to be describing the final helplessness of humanity in the face of forces that we cannot control and warning against too great a belief in self-reliance.

The significance for the Athenians themselves of Oedipus' fall from greatness emerges in full force in the work of Euripides (c. 484–406 B.C.). Although only a little younger than Sophocles, Euripides expresses all the weariness and disillusion of the war-torn years at the end of the 5th century B.C. Of all the tragedians he is perhaps the closest to our own time, with his concern for realism and his determination to expose social, political, and religious injustices.

Although Euripides admits the existence of irrational forces in the universe that can be personified in the form of gods and goddesses, he certainly does not regard them as worthy of respect and worship. This skepticism won him the charge of impiety. His plays show characters frequently pushed to the limits of endurance; their reactions show a new concern for psychological truth. In particular, Euripides exhibits a profound sympathy and understanding for the problems of women who live in a society dominated by men. Characters like Medea and Phaedra chal-

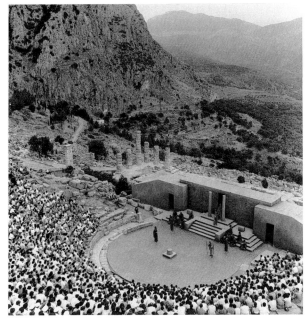

3.5 A modern performance of *Oedipus the King* in the ancient theater at Delphi. 1951. The columns in the background are the ruins of the Temple of Apollo.

lenged many of the basic premises of contemporary Athenian society.

Euripides' deepest hatred is reserved for war and its senseless misery. Like the other dramatists he draws the subject matter of his plays from traditional myths, but the lines delivered by the actors must have sounded in their hearer's ears with a terrible relevance. *The Suppliant Women* was probably written in 421 B.C., when ten years of indecisive fighting had produced nothing but an uneasy truce. Its subject is the recovery by Theseus, ruler of Athens, of the bodies of seven chiefs killed fighting at Thebes in order to return them to their families for burial. He yields to their mothers—the women of the title—who beg him to recover the corpses. The audience would have little need to be reminded of the grief of wives and mothers or of the kind of political processes that produced years of futile fighting.

If Aeschylus' belief in human progress is more noble, Euripides is certainly more realistic. Although unpopular in his own time, he later became the most widely read of the three tragedians. As a result, more of his plays have been preserved (nineteen in all), works with a wide range of emotional expression. They extend from romantic comedies like *Helen* and *Iphigenia in Taurus* to the profoundly disturbing *Bacchae,* his last completed play, in which Euripides the rationalist explores the inadequacy of reason as the sole approach to life. In this acknowledgement of the power of emotion to overwhelm the order and balance so typical of the Classical ideal, he is most clearly speaking for his time.

Aristophanes and Greek Comedy

Euripides was not, of course, the only Athenian to realize the futility of war. The plays of Aristophanes (c. 450–385 B.C.), the greatest comic poet of 5th-century-B.C. Athens, deal with the same theme. His work combines political satire with a strong vein of fantasy.

In *The Birds,* produced in 414 B.C., two Athenians decide to leave home and find a better place to live. They join forces with the birds and build a new city in midair called Cloudcuckooland, which cuts off contact between gods and humans by blocking the path of the steam rising from sacrifices. The gods are forced to come to terms with the new city and Zeus hands over his scepter of authority to the birds.

This is simple escapism, but *Lysistrata,* written a few years later, in 411 B.C., deals with the problem of how to prevent war in a more practical fashion. In the course of the play the main protagonist, Lysistrata, persuades her fellow women of Athens to refuse to make love with their husbands until peace is negotiated. At the same time her followers seize the Acropolis. The men, teased and frustrated, finally give in and envoys are summoned from Sparta. The play ends with the Athenians and Spartans dancing together for joy at the new peace.

With the end of the Peloponnesian War in 404 B.C. and the fall of Athenian democracy, both art and political life were to be affected by an atmosphere of considerable confusion. Though Athens had been removed as the dominating force in Greece, there was no successor among her rivals. The vacuum was not filled until the mid-4th century with the appearance on the scene of Philip of Macedon. Earlier, a disastrous series of skirmishes between Sparta, Thebes, Athens, Corinth, and Argos had been temporarily suspended by the intervention of the Great King of the Persians himself, and the so-called King's Peace was signed in 387 B.C. But after a brief respite, the Thebans decisively defeated the Spartan forces at Leuctra in 371 B.C. and remained for a few years the leading force in Greek political life.

With the accession of Philip in Macedon in 359 B.C., however, the balance of power in Greece began to change. The hitherto backward northern kingdom of Macedon began to exert a new unifying influence, despite opposition in Thebes and in Athens, where the great Athenian orator Demosthenes led the resistance. In 338 B.C., at the Battle of Chaeronea (see map, page 44), Philip defeated Athenian and Theban forces and unified all the cities of Greece, with the exception of Sparta, in an alliance known as the League of Corinth.

Even before his assassination in 336 B.C., Philip had developed schemes for enlarging his empire by attacking Persia. His son and successor, Alexander, carried them out. He spent the ten years from 333 B.C. until his own death in 323 B.C. in an amazing series of campaigns across Asia, destroying the Persian Empire and reaching as far as India. The effects of the breakup of this new Macedonian empire after the death of Alexander were to be felt throughout the Hellenistic period that followed.

Philosophy in the Late Classical Period

The intellectual and cultural spirit of the new century was foreshadowed in its very first year in an event at Athens. In 399 B.C. the philosopher Socrates was charged with impiety and corruption of the young, found guilty, and executed. Yet the ideas that Socrates represented—concern with the fate of the individual and the questioning of traditional values—could not be killed so easily. They had already begun to spread at the end of the 5th century B.C. and came to dominate the culture of the 4th century B.C.

Socrates is one of the most important figures in

Greek history. He is also one of the most difficult to understand clearly. Much of the philosophy of the Greeks and of later ages and cultures has been inspired by his life and teachings. Yet Socrates himself wrote nothing; most of what we know of him comes from the works of his disciple, Plato. Socrates was born around 469 B.C., the son of a sculptor and a midwife; in later life he claimed to have followed his mother's profession in being a "midwife to ideas." He seems first to have been interested in natural science, but he soon turned to the problems of human behavior and morality. Unlike the sophists, the professional philosophers of the day, he never took money for teaching, nor did he ever found a school. Instead he went around Athens, to both public places like the markets and the gymnasia and private gatherings, talking and arguing, testing traditional ideas by subjecting them to a barrage of questions—as he put it, "following the argument wherever it led." Socrates gradually gained a circle of enthusiastic followers, drawn mainly from the young. At the same time he acquired many enemies, disturbed by both his challenge to established morality and the uncompromising persistence with which he interrogated those who upheld it. Socrates was no respecter of the pride or dignity of others, and his search for the truth inevitably exposed the ignorance of his opponents.

Among Socrates' supporters were a number who had taken part in an unpopular and tyrannical political coup at Athens immediately following the Peloponnesian War. The rule of the so-called Thirty Tyrants lasted only from 404 to 403 B.C.; it ended with the death or expulsion of its leading figures. The return of democracy gave Socrates' enemies a chance to take advantage of the hostility felt toward those who had "collaborated" with the tyrants; thus in 399 B.C. he was put on trial.

It seems probable that to some degree the proceedings were intended for show and that those who voted for the death sentence never seriously thought it would be carried out. Socrates was urged by his friends to escape from prison, and the authorities themselves offered him every opportunity. However, the strength of his own morality and his reverence for the laws of his city prohibited him from doing so. After a final discussion with his friends he was put to death by the administration of a draught of hemlock.

Many of Socrates' disciples tried to preserve his memory by writing accounts of his life and teachings. The works of only two have survived. One of these is the Greek historian Xenophon, whose *Apology, Symposium,* and *Memorabilia* are interesting, if superficial. The other is Plato, who, together with his pupil Aristotle, stands at the forefront of the whole intellectual tradition of Western civilization.

The dialogues of Plato claim to record the teachings of Socrates. Indeed, in almost all of them Socrates himself appears, arguing with his opponents and presenting his own ideas. How much of Plato's picture of Socrates is historical truth and how much is Plato's invention, however, is debatable. The Socratic problem has been almost as much discussed as the identity of Homer. In general, modern opinion supports the view that in the early dialogues Plato tried to preserve something of his master's views and methods, while in the later ones he used Socrates as the spokesman for his own ideas.

There can certainly be no doubt that Plato was deeply impressed by Socrates' life and death. Born in 428 B.C., he was drawn by other members of his aristocratic family into the Socratic circle. Plato was present at the trial of Socrates, whose speech in his own defense Plato records in the *Apology,* one of three works that describe Socrates' last days. In the *Crito,* set in prison, Socrates explains why he refuses to escape. The *Phaedo* gives an account of his last day spent discussing with his friends the immortality of the soul and his death.

After Socrates' death, Plato left Athens, horrified at the society that had sanctioned the execution, and spent a number of years traveling. He returned in 387 B.C. and founded the Academy, the first permanent institution in Western civilization devoted to education and research, and thus the forerunner of all our universities. Its curriculum concentrated on mathematics, law, and political theory. Its purpose was to produce experts for the service of the state. Some twenty years later, in 368 B.C., Plato was invited to Sicily to put his political theories into practice by turning Syracuse into a model kingdom and its young ruler, Dionysius II, into a philosopher king. Predictably, the attempt was a dismal failure, and by 366 B.C. he was back in Athens. Apart from a second visit to Syracuse in 362 B.C., equally unsuccessful, he seems to have spent the rest of his life in Athens, teaching and writing. He died there in 347 B.C.

Much of Plato's work deals with political theory and the construction of an ideal society. The belief in an ideal is, in fact, characteristic of most of his thinking. It is most clearly expressed in his Theory of Forms, according to which in a higher dimension of existence there are perfect Forms of which all the phenomena we perceive in the world around us represent pale reflections. There can be no doubt that Plato's vision of an ideal society is far too authoritarian for most tastes, involving among other restrictions the careful breeding of children, the censorship of music and poetry, and the abolition of private property. In fairness to Plato, however, it must be remembered that his works are intended not as a set of instructions to be followed literally but as a challenge to think seriously about how our lives should be organized. Furthermore, the disadvantages of democratic government had become all too clear during the last years of the 5th century B.C. If Plato's attempt to redress the balance seems to veer excessively in the other direction, it may in part have been inspired by the continuing chaos of 4th century Greek politics.

Plato's most gifted pupil, Aristotle (384–322 B.C.), continued to develop his master's doctrines, at first wholeheartedly and later critically, for at least twenty years. In 335 B.C., Aristotle founded a school in competition with Plato's Academy, the Lyceum, severing fundamental ties with Plato from then on. Aristotle in effect introduced a rival philosophy—one that has attracted thinking minds ever since. Indeed, in the 19th century the English poet Samuel Taylor Coleridge was to comment, with much truth, that one was born either a "Platonist" or an "Aristotelian."

The Lyceum seems to have been organized with typically Aristotelian efficiency. In the morning Aristotle himself lectured to the full-time students, many of whom came from other parts of Greece to attend his courses and work on the projects he was directing. In the afternoon the students pursued their research in the library, museum, and map collection attached to the Lyceum, while Aristotle gave more general lectures to the public. His custom of strolling along the Lyceum's circular walkways, immersed in profound contemplation or discourse, gained his school the name *Peripatetic,* or the "walking" school.

As a philosopher Aristotle was the greatest systematizer. He wrote on every topic of serious study of the time. Many of his classifications have remained valid to this day, although some of the disciplines, such as psychology and physics, have severed their ties with philosophy and have become important sciences in their own right.

The most complex of Aristotle's works is probably the *Metaphysics,* in which he deals with his chief dispute with Plato, which concerned the Theory of Forms. Plato had postulated a higher dimension of existence for the Ideal Forms and thereby created a split between the apparent reality that we perceive and the genuine reality that we can only know by philosophical contemplation. Moreover, knowledge of these forms depended on a theory of "remembering" them from previous existences. Aristotle, on the other hand, claimed that the forms were actually present in the objects we see around us, thereby eliminating the split between the two realities.

Elsewhere in the *Metaphysics* Aristotle discusses the nature of God, whom he describes as "thought thinking of itself" and "the Unmoved Mover." The nature of the physical world ruled over by this su-preme being is further explored in the *Physics,* which is concerned with the elements that compose the universe and the laws by which they operate.

Other important works by Aristotle include the *Rhetoric,* which prescribes the ideal model of oratory, and the *Poetics,* which does the same for poetry and includes the famous definition of tragedy mentioned earlier (see page 79). Briefly, Aristotle's formula for tragedy is as follows: the tragic hero, who must be noble, through some undetected "tragic flaw" in character meets with a bad end involving the reversal of fortune and sometimes death. The audience, through various emotional and intellectual relations with this tragic figure, undergoes a "cleansing" or "purgation" of the soul, called *catharsis.* Critics of this analysis sometimes complain that Aristotle was trying to read his own very subjective formulas into the Greek tragedies of the time. This is not entirely just, since Aristotle was probably writing for future tragedians, prescribing what ought to be rather than what was.

Aristotle's influence on later ages was vast, although not continuous. Philip of Macedon employed him to tutor young Alexander, but the effect on the young conqueror was probably minimal. Thereafter his works were lost and not recovered until the 1st century B.C., when they were used by the Roman statesman and thinker Cicero (106–43 B.C.). During the Middle Ages, they were translated into Latin and Arabic and became a philosophical basis for Christian theology. Saint Thomas Aquinas' synthesis of Aristotelian philosophy and Christian doctrine still remains the official philosophical position of the Roman Catholic Church.

In philosophy, theology, and scientific and intellectual thought as a whole, many of the distinctions first applied by Aristotle were rediscovered in the early Renaissance and are still valid today. Indeed, no survey such as this can begin to do justice to one described by Dante as "the master of those who know." In the more than two thousand years since his death only Leonardo da Vinci has come near to equaling his creative range.

Greek Music in the Classical Period

Both Plato and Aristotle found a place for music in their ideal states; their comments on it provide some information on the status of Greek music in the Classical period. Throughout the 5th century B.C. music played an important part in dramatic performances but was generally subordinated to the poetry. By the end of the Peloponnesian War, however, the musical aspect of tragedy had begun to predominate. It is interesting to note that Euripides was criticized by his contemporaries for the lack of form and symmetry and the overemotionalism of his music, not of his verse. With its release from the function of mere accompaniment, instrumental music became especially popular in the 4th century B.C.

The belief in the doctrine of *ethos* (page 58), whereby music had the power to influence human behavior, meant that the study of music played a vital part in the education and life style of Classical Greeks. In Plato's view, participation in musical activities molded the character for better or worse—thus the ban on certain kinds of music, those with the "wrong" ethos, in his ideal Republic. At the same time the musical scale, with its various ratios of pitches, reflected the proportions of the cosmos; music thereby provided a link between the real world and the abstract world of Forms.

For Aristotle music held a more practical, less mystical, value in the attainment of virtue. As a mathematician he believed that the numerical relationships which linked the various pitches could be used by a musician to compose works which imitated the highest state of reason, and thus virtue. Furthermore, just as individuals could create works with a virtuous, moral ethos, so too the State would be served by "ethical" music.

For all its importance in Greek life and thought, however, the actual sound of Greek music and the principles whereby it was composed are not easy to reconstruct or understand.

The numerical relationship of notes to one another established by Pythagoras (see page 61) was used to divide the basic unit of an octave (series of eight notes) into smaller intervals named after their positions in relation to the lowest note in the octave. The interval known as a *fourth,* for example, represents the space between the lowest note and the fourth note up the octave. The intervals were then combined to form a series of scales, or *modes.* Each was given a name and was associated with a particular emotional range. Thus the Dorian mode was serious and warlike, the Phrygian exciting and emotional, and the Mixolydian plaintive and pathetic.

The unit with which Greek music was constructed was the *tetrachord,* a group of four notes of which the two outer ones are a perfect fourth apart and the inner ones variably spaced. The combination of two tetrachords formed a mode. The Dorian mode, for example, consisted of the following two tetrachords:

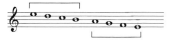

The Lydian mode was composed of two different tetrachords:

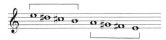

The origin of the modes and their relationship to one another is uncertain; it was disputed even in ancient times. The situation has not been made easier by the fact that medieval church music adopted the same system of mathematical construction and even some of the same names, but applied them to different modes.

The word *harmony* is Greek in origin; literally it means a "joining together," and in a musical context the Greeks used it to describe various kinds of scales. There is nevertheless no evidence that Greek music contained any element of harmony in a more modern sense—that is, of groups of notes (chords) sounded simultaneously. Throughout the fifth century B.C. musical rhythm was tied to that of the words or dance steps the music accompanied. Special instruments such as cymbals and tambourines were used to mark the rhythmical patterns, and Greek writers on music often discussed specific problems presented to composers by the nature of the Greek language and its accent system.

Although few traces have survived, a system of musical notation was used to write down compositions; the Greeks probably borrowed it, like their alphabet, from the Phoenicians. Originally used for lyre music, it used symbols to mark the position of fingers on the lyre strings, rather like modern guitar notation (tablature). The system was then adapted for vocal music and for nonstringed instruments such as the *aulos.* The oldest of the few examples to survive dates to around 250 B.C.

The Visual Arts in Classical Greece

Sculpture and Vase Painting in the 5th Century B.C.

Like the writers and thinkers of their time, artists of the mid-5th century B.C. were concerned with ideas of balance and order. Very early Classical works like the *Critian Boy* [2.15] revealed a new interest in realism, and the sculptors who came later began to explore the exciting possibilities of representing the human body in motion.

Among the most famous 5th-century sculptors working at Athens was Myron. Although none of his

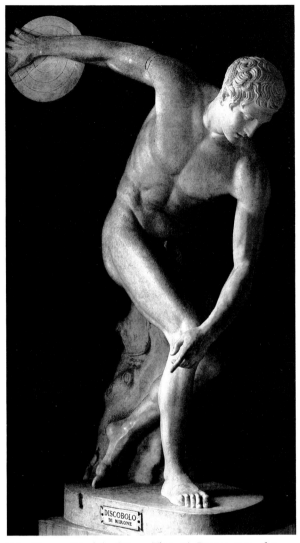

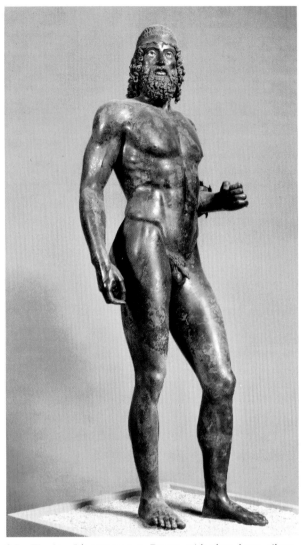

3.6 Myron. *Discobolos (Discus Thrower).* Roman copy after bronze original of c. 450 B.C. Marble, life-size. National Museum, Rome.

3.7 Warrior. 5th century B.C. Bronze with glass, bone, silver, and copper inlay, height 6′6″ (2 m). Museo Nazionale, Reggio Calabrio, Italy.

sculptures has survived, there are a number of later copies of one of his most famous pieces, the *Discus Thrower* [3.6]. The original, made around 450 B.C., is typical of its age in combining realistic treatment of an action with an idealized portrayal of the athlete himself.

While striving for naturalism, artists like Myron tried also to create a new standard of human beauty by controlling the human form according to principles of proportion, symmetry, and balance. Among the finest examples of mid-5th-century-B.C. sculpture are two bronze statues found off the coast of southeast Italy in the 1980s. Known as the Riace Bronzes, they were probably the work of a master sculptor on the Greek mainland. They represent war-

riors, although their precise subject, together with the reason for their presence in Italian water, remains a mystery. Around 440 B.C., one of the greatest of Classical sculptors, Polyclitus of Argos, devised a mathematical formula for representing the perfect male body, an ideal canon of proportion, and wrote a book about it. The idea behind *The Canon* was that ideal beauty consisted of a precise relationship between the various parts of the body. Polyclitus' book must have set forth the details of his system of proportion. To illustrate his theory, he also produced a bronze statue of a young man holding a spear, the *Doryphoros.* Both book and original statue are lost; only later copies of the *Doryphoros* survive [3.8].

We do not know, therefore, exactly what

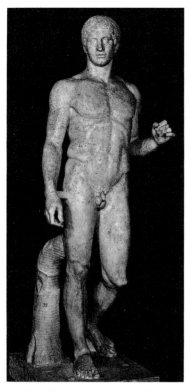

3.8 Polyclitus. *Doryphoros (Spear Bearer)*. Roman copy after bronze original of c. 450 B.C. Marble, life-size. Archaeological Museum, Naples.

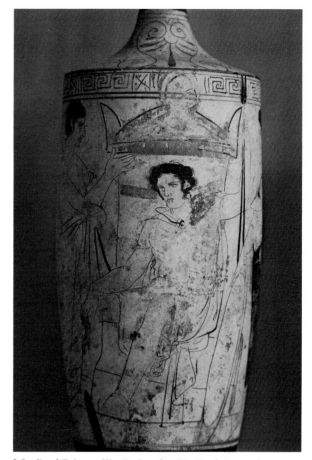

3.9 Reed Painter. *Warrior Seated at His Tomb*. Late 5th century B.C. White-ground lekythos, height 18⅞″ (48 cm). National Archaeological Museum, Athens. A youth is at one side. On the other side is a young woman who holds the warrior's shield and helmet.

Polyclitus' system was. Nevertheless, we have some indication in the writings of a later philosopher, Chrysippus (c. 280–207 B.C.), who wrote that "beauty consists of the proportion of the parts; of finger to finger; of all the fingers to the palm and the wrist; of those to the forearm; of the forearm to the upper arm; and of all these parts to one another, as set forth in *The Canon* of Polyclitus." Even if the exact relationships are lost, what was important about Polyclitus' ideal—and what made it so characteristic of the Classical vision as a whole—was that it depended on precisely ordered and balanced interrelationships of the various parts of the human body. Furthermore, the ideal beauty this created was not produced by nature, but by the power of the human intellect.

In the late 5th century B.C., as the Greeks became embroiled in the Peloponnesian War, sculpture and vase painting were characterized by a growing concern with the individual rather than a generalized ideal. Artists began to depict the emotional responses of ordinary people to life and death instead of approaching these responses indirectly through the use of myths. Thus, death and mourning became increasingly common subjects.

Among the most touching works to survive from the period are a number of oil flasks used for funerary offerings [3.9]. They are painted with mourning or graveside scenes on a white rather than red background. The figures are depicted with quiet and calm dignity but with considerable feeling. This personal rather than public response to death is found also on the gravemarkers of the very end of the 5th century B.C., which show a grief that is perhaps resigned but still intense [3.10].

Architecture in the 5th Century B.C.

In architecture, as in sculpture, designers were concerned with proportion and the interrelationship of the various parts that constitute a complete structure. Nowhere is this more apparent than in the Temple of Zeus at Olympia [3.11], the first great artistic achievement of the years following the Persian Wars,

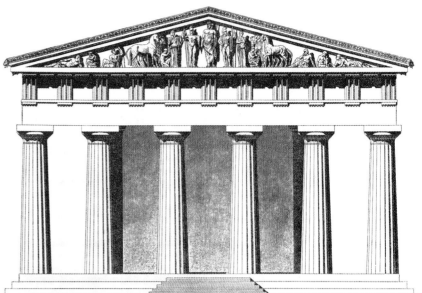

3.11 Reconstruction drawing of east façade, Temple of Zeus, Olympia. c. 470–456 B.C. The pediment shows Zeus between two contestants prior to a chariot race.

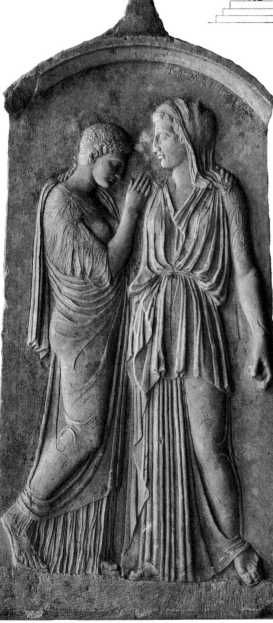

begun in 470 B.C. and finished by 456 B.C. By the time of its completion it was also the largest Doric temple in mainland Greece. The architect of this temple, Libon of Elis, clearly intended it to illustrate the new Classical preoccupation with proportion. The distance from the center of one column to the center of the next was the unit of measurement for the whole temple. Thus the height of each column is equal to two units, and the combined length of a triglyph and a metope equals half a unit.

The theme of order, implicit in the architecture of the temple, became explicit in the sculpture that decorated it. At the center of the west pediment, standing calmly amidst a fight raging between Lapiths and Centaurs, was the figure of Apollo, the god of reason, exerting his authority by a single confident gesture [3.12].

Like the works of Aeschylus, the sculptures from Olympia express a conviction that justice will triumph and that the gods will enforce it. The art of the second half of the 5th century B.C., however, is more concerned with human achievement than with divine will. Pericles' building program for the Acropolis, or citadel of Athens, represents the supreme expression in visual terms of Classical ideals [3.13].

This greatest of all Classical artistic achievements has a special grandeur and poignancy. The splendor of its conception and execution has survived the vicissitudes of time; the great temple to Athena, the Parthenon, remains to this day an incomparable sym-

3.10 Grave stele of Crito and Timarista. c. 420 B.C. Marble. Museum, Rhodes.

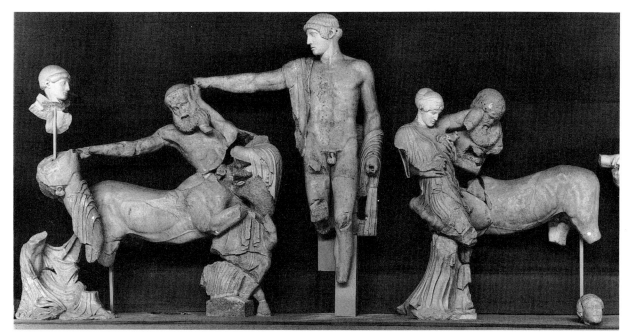

3.12 Apollo intervenes in the battle between the Lapiths and Centaurs, from the west pediment of the Temple of Zeus, Olympia. c. 470–456 B.C. Museum, Olympia.

bol of the Golden Age of Greece. Yet it was built during years of growing division and hostility in the Greek world—the last sculpture was barely in place before the outbreak of the Peloponnesian War in 431 B.C. Pericles died in 429 B.C., but fighting and building both dragged on. The Erechtheum, the final temple to be completed, was not finished until 406 B.C., two years before the end of the war and the fall of Athens. Pericles had intended the whole program to perpetuate the memory of Athens' glorious achievements, but instead it is a reminder of the gulf be-

tween Classical high ideals and the realities of political existence in 5th-century-B.C. Greece.

Even the funding of the Parthenon symbolizes this gap, since it was paid for at least in part from the treasury of the Delian League (see page 75). The transfer of the League's funds to Athens in 454 B.C. clearly indicated Pericles' imperialist intentions, as did the use to which he put them. In this way the supreme monument of Periclean Athens was built with money originally intended for a pan-Hellenic League. It is even more ironic that Athens' further

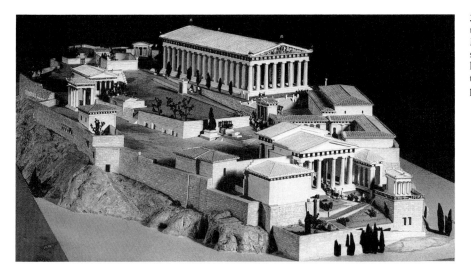

3.13 Model reconstruction of the Acropolis. Royal Ontario Museum, Toronto. Most of the smaller buildings no longer exist, leaving an unobstructed view of the Parthenon that was not possible in ancient times.

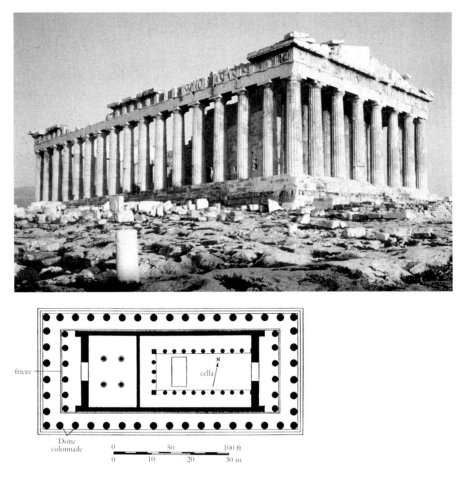

3.14 Ictinus and Callicrates. The Parthenon, Athens. 447–432 B.C. Height of columns 34′ (10.36 m). Below is a plan of the temple.

frieze

N

cella

Doric colonnade

| 0 | | 50 | | 100 ft |
| 0 | 10 | 20 | | 30 m |

highhanded behavior created a spirit of ill feeling and distrust throughout the Greek world that led inevitably to the outbreak of the Peloponnesian War—a war that effectively destroyed the Athenian glory the Parthenon had been intended to symbolize.

The great outcrop of rock that forms the Acropolis was an obvious choice by Pericles for the Parthenon and the other buildings planned with it. The site, which towers above the rest of the city, had served as a center for Athenian life from Mycenaean times, when a fortress was built on it. Throughout the Archaic period a series of temples had been constructed there, the last of them destroyed by the Persians in 480 B.C.

Work on the Acropolis was begun in 449 B.C. under the direction of Phidias, the greatest sculptor of his day and a personal friend of Pericles. The Parthenon [3.14] was the first building to be constructed; its architects were Ictinus and Callicrates (the name of the temple comes from the Greek *parthenos,* or virgin; that is, the goddess Athena). It was built between 447 and 438 B.C.; its sculptural decoration was complete by 432 B.C. Even larger than the Temple of Zeus at

Olympia, the building combines the Doric order of its columns (seventeen on the sides and eight on the ends) with some Ionic features, including a continuous running frieze inside the outer colonnade, at the top of the temple wall and inner colonnades. The design incorporates a number of refinements intended to prevent any sense of monotony or heaviness and gives to the building an air of richness and grace. Like earlier Doric columns, those of the Parthenon are thickest at the point one-third from the base and then taper to the top, a device called *entasis.* In addition, all the columns tilt slightly toward each other (it has been calculated that they would all meet if extended upward for 2 miles, or 3.2 kilometers). The columns at the corners are thicker and closer together than the others and the entablature leans outwards. The flat floor is not really flat at all but convex. All these refinements are, of course, extremely subtle and barely visible to the naked eye. The perfection of their execution, requiring incredible precision of mathematical calculation, is the highest possible tribute to the Classical search for order.

The sculptural decoration of the Parthenon occu-

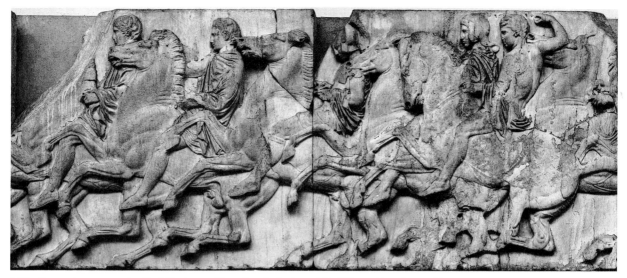

3.15 Equestrian group, detail of Parthenon frieze (north face). c. 442–432 B.C. Pentelic marble, height 41⅜″ (106 cm). British Museum, London (reproduced by courtesy of the Trustees). The composition is elaborate but clear. The riders, with their calm, typically Classical expressions, are shown in various positions: note especially the last figure on the right.

pied three parts of the building and made use of three different techniques of carving. The figures in the pediments are freestanding; the frieze is carved in low relief; the metopes are in high relief (see page 54). The Ionic frieze, 520 feet (158.6 meters) long, is carved in low relief; it depicts a procession that took place every four years on the occasion of the Great Panathenaic Festival. It shows Athenians walking and riding to the Acropolis in a ceremony during which an ancient wooden statue of Athena was presented with a new robe. The variety of movement, gesture, and rhythm achieved in the relatively limited technique of low relief makes the frieze among the greatest treasures of Greek art [3.15]. At the beginning of the 19th century, most of the frieze, together with other Parthenon sculptures, was removed from

the building by the British Ambassador to Constantinople, Lord Elgin; these are now in the British Museum. (All the sculptures from the Parthenon that are in the British Museum are generally known as the Elgin Marbles.)

Equally impressive are the surviving figures from the east and west pediments, which are freestanding. They show, respectively, the birth of Athena and her contest with Poseidon, god of the sea, to decide which of them should be patron deity of the city. They are badly damaged; even so, statues like the group of three goddesses [3.16], from the east pediment, show a combination of idealism and naturalism that has never been surpassed. The anatomy of the figures and the drapery, which in some cases covers them, are both treated realistically, even in places

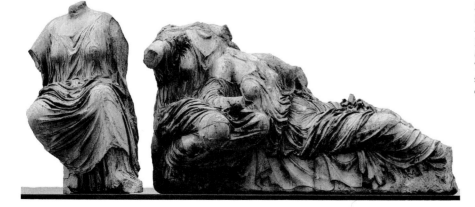

3.16 *Three Goddesses,* from Parthenon east pediment. c. 438–432 B.C. Marble, over life-size. British Museum, London (reproduced by courtesy of the Trustees). The robes show the sculptor's technical virtuosity in carving drapery.

where the details of the workmanship would have been barely visible to the spectator below. The realism is combined, however, with a characteristically Classical preoccupation with proportion and balance; the result is sculptures that achieve an almost perfect blend of the two elements of the Classical style: ideal beauty represented in realistic terms.

In contrast to the frieze, the technique employed on the metopes is high relief, so high, in fact, that some of the figures seem almost completely detached from their background. These metopes, which illustrate a number of mythological battles, represent a lower level of achievement, although some are more successful than others at reconciling scenes of violence and Classical idealism. The most impressive ones show episodes from the battle between Lapiths and Centaurs [3.17], the same story we saw on the west pediment at Olympia.

The monumental entrance to the Acropolis, the Propylaea [3.18], was begun in 437 B.C. and finished on the eve of the outbreak of war, although probably only by a modification of the architect Mnesicles' original plan. An unusual feature of its design is that both Doric and Ionic columns are used, the Doric ones visible from the front and the back and the Ionic ones lining the passageway through the outer porch.

The other major building on the Acropolis is the Erechtheum, an Ionic temple of complex design, which was begun in 421 B.C. but not completed until 406 B.C. The chief technical problem facing the archi-

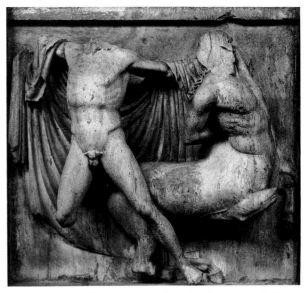

3.17 *Lapith and Centaur,* metope from Parthenon (south face). c. 448–442 B.C. Pentelic marble, height 4′4¼″ (1.34 m). British Museum, London (reproduced by courtesy of the Trustees). The assailed Lapith has dropped to one knee.

tect, whose identity is unknown, was the uneven ground level of the site. The problem was solved by creating a building with entrances on different levels. The nature of the building itself produced other design problems. The Erechtheum had to commemo-

3.18 Mnesicles. Propylaea, Athens (west front). 437–431 B.C. This is the view from the Temple of Athena Nike. Note the contrast between the simple Doric columns of the façade and the Ionic columns that line the center passageway.

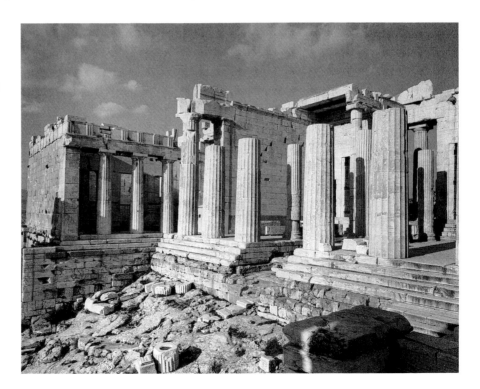

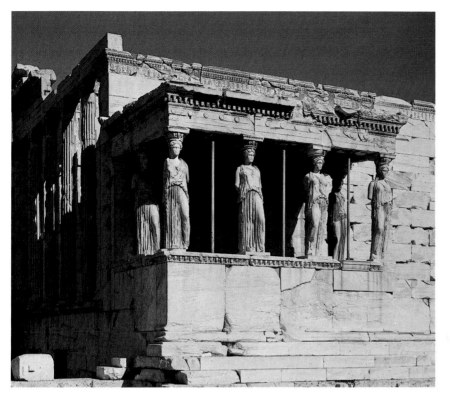

3.19 *Porch of the Maidens,* Erechtheum, Athens. 421–406 B.C. Height of caryatids 7′9″ (2.36 m).

rate a whole series of elaborate religious events and honor a number of different deities. One of its four chambers housed the ancient wooden statue of Athena that was at the center of the Great Panathenaic Festival shown on the Parthenon frieze. Elsewhere in the temple were altars to Poseidon and Erechtheus, an early Athenian king; to the legendary Athenian hero Butes; and to Hephaistos, the god of the forge. Furthermore, the design had to incorporate the marks in the ground made by Poseidon's trident during the competition with Athena, as shown on the west pediment of the Parthenon, and the site of the grave of another early and probably legendary Athenian king, Cecrops. The result of all this was a building whose complex plan is still not fully understood. In fact, the exact identification of the inner chambers remains in doubt.

The decoration of the temple is both elaborate and delicate, almost fragile. Its most well-known feature is the South Porch, where the roof rests not on columns but on the famous *caryatids,* statues of young women [3.19]. These graceful figures, who stand gravely upright with one knee slightly bent as if to sustain the weight of the roof, represent the most complete attempt until then to conceal the structural functions of a column behind its form.

In many respects innovations such as these make the Erechtheum as representative of the mood of the late 5th century B.C. as the confident Parthenon is of the mood of a generation earlier. The apparent lack of a coherent overall plan and the blurring of traditional distinctions between architecture and sculpture, structure and decoration, seem to question traditional architectural values in a way that parallels the doubts of Euripides and his contemporaries.

The Visual Arts in the 4th Century B.C.

As in the case of literature and philosophy, the confusion of Greek political life in the years following the defeat of Athens in 404 B.C. affected the development of the visual arts. In general, the idealism and heroic characters of High Classical art were replaced with a growing interest in realism and emotion. Our knowledge of the visual arts in the 4th century B.C. is, however, far from complete. Greek fresco painting of the period has been entirely lost, though recent discoveries in northern Greece at the Royal Cemetery of Vergina suggest that some of it may yet be found again [3.20]. In sculpture, fortunately, Roman copies of lost original statues enable us to form a fairly good estimate of the main developments. It is clear that Plato's interest in the fate of the individual soul finds its parallel in the sculptural treatment of the human form. Facial expressions become more emotional, often characterized by a mood of dreamy tenderness.

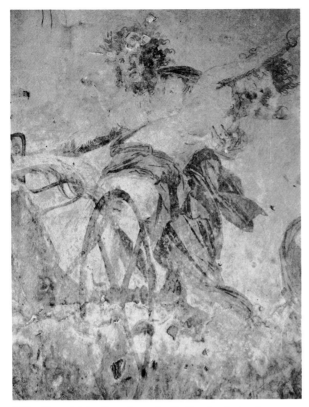

3.20 *Pluto Seizing Persephone,* detail of wall painting from Royal Tomb I, Vergina. Mid-4th century B.C. This unique example of Late Classical monumental painting was discovered by the Greek archaeologist Manolis Andronikos in 1977. It shows a remarkable fluency and freedom of technique.

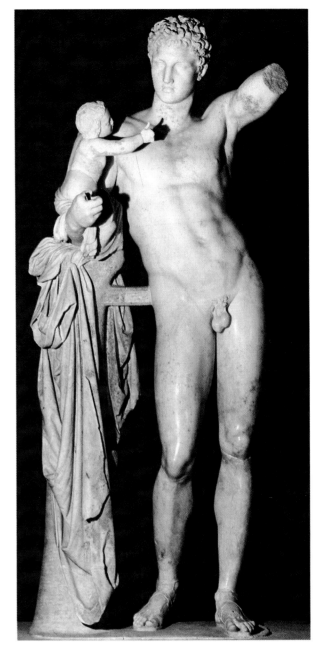

3.21 Praxiteles. *Hermes with the Infant Dionysus.* c. 340 B.C. Marble, height 7′1″ (2.16 m). Museum, Olympia. Hermes' missing right arm held a bunch of grapes just out of the baby's reach.

Technical skill in depicting drapery and the anatomy beneath are put to the service of a new virtuosity. The three sculptors who dominated the art of the 4th century B.C. are Praxiteles, Scopas, and Lysippus.

The influence of Praxiteles on his contemporaries was immense. His particular brand of gentle melancholy is well illustrated by the *Hermes* at Olympia [3.21] that is generally attributed to him. Equally important is his famous statue of Aphrodite nude [3.22], of which some fifty copies have survived. This represents the discovery of the female body as an object of beauty in itself; it was also one of the first attempts in Western art to introduce the element of sensuality into the portrayal of the female form.

The art of Scopas was more dramatic, with an emphasis on emotion and intensity. Roman copies of his statue of *Pothos,* or Desire [3.23], allow comparison of this yearning figure with Praxiteles' more relaxed *Hermes.*

The impact of Lysippus was as much on succeeding periods as on his own time. One of his chief claims to fame was as the official portraitist of Alex-

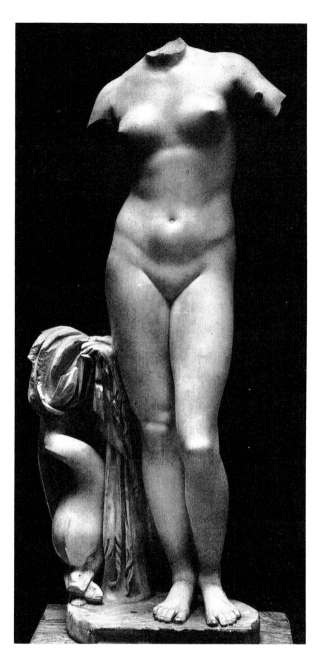

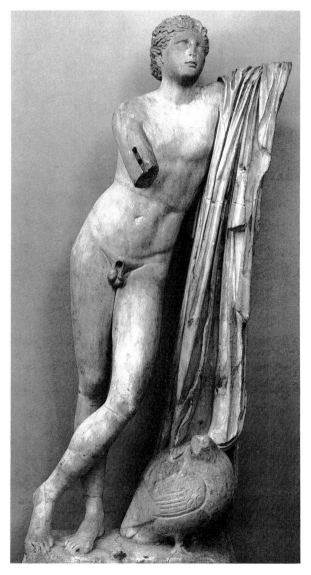

3.22 Praxiteles. *Aphrodite of Cyrene*. Roman copy of c. 100 B.C. Marble, height 5′ (1.52 m). National Museum, Rome. This copy was found by chance in the Roman baths at Cyrene, North Africa. The statue is also called *Venus Anadyomene,* the Roman name for Aphrodite and a Greek word meaning "rising up from the sea," often used in referring to Aphrodite because she was supposed to have arisen from the sea at her birth. The porpoise is a reminder of the goddess' marine associations.

3.23 Scopas. *Pothos*. Roman copy after original of c. 350 B.C. Marble. Palazzo dei Conservatori, Rome.

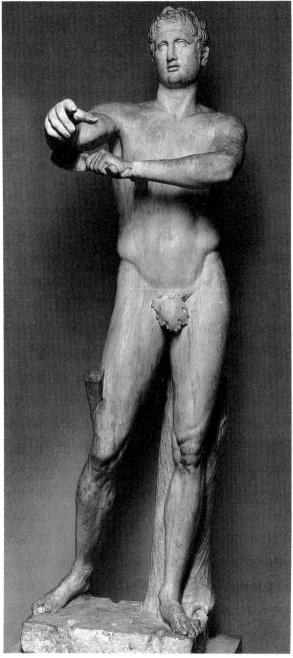

3.24 Lysippus. *Apoxyomenos (The Scraper).* Roman copy after bronze original of c. 330 B.C. Marble, height 6′9″ (2.06 m). Vatican Museums, Rome. The young athlete is cleaning off sweat and dirt with a tool called a strigil.

ander the Great. Lysippus' very individual characteristics—a new, more attenuated system of proportion, greater concern for realism, and the large scale of many of his works—had a profound effect later on Hellenistic art [3.24].

In architecture, as in the arts generally, the Late Classical period was one of innovation. The great sanctuaries at Olympia and Delphi were expanded and new cities were laid out at Rhodes, Cnidus, and Priene, using Classical principles of town planning.

The 4th century was also notable for the invention of building forms new to Greek architecture, including the *tholos,* or circular building [3.26]. The most grandiose work of the century was probably the Temple of Artemis at Ephesus, destroyed by fire in 356 B.C. and rebuilt on the same massive scale as before.

Although the Greeks of the 4th century B.C. lacked the certainty and self-confidence of their predecessors, their culture shows no lack of ideas or inspiration. Furthermore, even before Alexander's death the Macedonian empire had spread Greek culture throughout the Mediterranean world. If Athens itself had lost any real political or commercial importance, the ideas of its great innovators began to affect an ever-growing number of people.

When Alexander died in the summer of 323 B.C., the division of his empire into separate independent kingdoms spread Greek culture even more widely. The kingdoms of the Seleucids in Syria and the Ptolemies in Egypt are the true successors to Periclean Athens. Even as far away as India sculptors and town planners were influenced by ideas developed by Athenians of the 5th and 4th centuries B.C.

In due course, the cultural achievement of Classical Greece was absorbed and reborn in Rome, as Chapter 4 will show. Meanwhile, in the period known as the Hellenistic Age, which lasted from the death of Alexander to the Roman conquest of Greece in 146 B.C., that achievement took a new turn.

The Hellenistic Period

Alexander's generals' inability to agree on a single successor after his death made the division of the Macedonian empire inevitable. The four most important kingdoms that split off, Syria (the kingdom of the Seleucids), Egypt, Pergamum, and Macedonia itself (see map, page 96), were soon at loggerheads and remained so until they were finally conquered by Rome. Each of them, however, in its own way continued the spread of Greek culture, as the name of the period implies (it is derived from the verb "to Hellenize," or to spread Greek influence).

The greatest of all centers of Greek learning was in the Egyptian city of Alexandria, where King Ptolemy, Alexander's former personal staff officer and bodyguard, planned a large institute for scholarship known as the Temple of the Muses, or the Museum. The Library at the Museum contained everything of

THE ARTS AND INVENTION: *City Planning*

The oldest Greek cities grew up randomly around a shrine at some geographic feature such as the Athenian Acropolis. From the time of their early colonization in Southern Italy and Sicily, however, the Greeks began to experiment with ways of laying out their public buildings and residential quarters according to an orderly system. By the Classical period they had devised a plan that was used in new city projects throughout Greece and the Greek colonies in Asia Minor.

One of the finest examples can be seen at Miletus, where a new city was laid out in the mid-5th century B.C. [3.25]. The private houses are located in two distinct grids of blocks, divided by roads running approximately north–south and east–west. The principal public buildings are placed in the middle; they include a large market on the right and on the left a theater that held some 15,000 spectators.

Miletus was the birthplace of Hippodamus—who was, the Greeks believed, the inventor of this kind of formal city planning, although he probably only put into practice ideas that had been developing for a century or more. He almost certainly had a hand in the planning of his home city and was also credited with laying out the port city of Athens at Piraeus.

The grid plan of a Classical Greek city seems surprisingly modern, far more like Manhattan or many large American cities than like most of the medieval cities of Europe, with their winding streets and irregular public squares. The explanation is that the Greek system was adopted by the Romans. When Thomas Jefferson and the other founding fathers of the United States wanted artistic models for their new Republic they turned to the Roman Republic (as they perceived it) for examples. Thus, by Roman mediation, Greek notions of how cities should be organized continue to affect the lives of millions. Today's urban dwellers, caught in traffic jams at every intersection, are more likely to grumble than to be grateful—but neither the Greeks, the Romans, nor

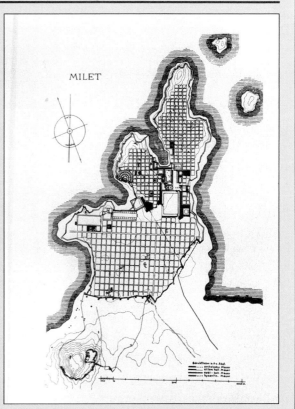

3.25 After *Milet, Ergebnisse d. Ausgrabungen*, II, 3 (1935). From J. B. Ward-Perkins, *Cities of Ancient Greece and Italy: Planning in Classical Antiquity*, 1974, fig. 7. Copyright © 1974 by J. B. Ward-Perkins. Reprinted by permission of George Braziller, Inc./NYPL.

the Americans of the 18th century could have imagined the consequences of the invention of the motorcar.

importance ever written in Greek, up to seven hundred thousand separate works, according to contemporary authorities. Its destruction by fire when Julius Caesar besieged the city in 47 B.C. must surely be one of the great intellectual disasters in the history of Western culture.

In Asia Minor and farther east in Syria the Hellenistic rulers of the new kingdoms fostered Greek art

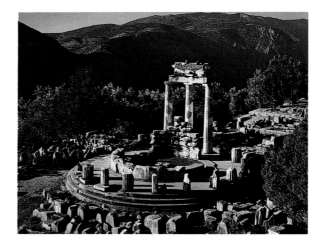

3.26 Theodoros of Phokaia. Tholos of the Sanctuary of Athena Pronaia, Delphi. c. 390 B.C. Marble and limestone; diameter of cella 28′2⅝″ (8.6 m), present height 27′2½″ (8.29 m). This is one of the first circular designs in Greek architecture. Originally, twenty Doric columns encircled the temple and ten Corinthian columns were set against the wall of the cella within.

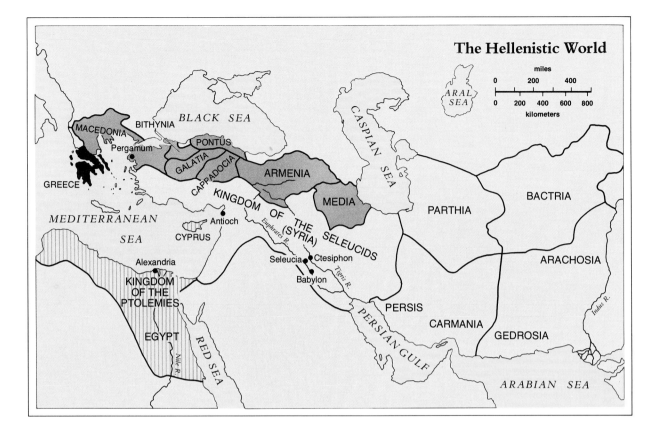

The Hellenistic World

and literature as one means of holding foreign influences at bay. Libraries were built at Pergamum and the Syrian capital of Antioch, and philosophers from Greece were encouraged to visit the new centers of learning and lecture there. In this way Greek ideas not only retained their hold but began to make an impression on more remote peoples even farther east. The first Buddhist monumental sculpture, called Gandharan after the Indian province of Gandhara where it developed, made use of Greek styles and techniques. There is even a classic Buddhist religious work called *The Questions of King Milinda* in which a

EAST MEETS WEST

The Greeks in India

The earliest known contact between Greeks and Indians occurred long before the time of Alexander, on Greek soil: according to Herodotus, a detachment of Indians fought in the Persian army during the Persian War of 480–479 B.C. Later, as Alexander drove his way across Asia in the decade preceding his death in 323 B.C., Indian troops continued to provide support to the Persians; their most valuable assets were the elephants they had trained for warfare.

By 326 B.C. Alexander's army had arrived in the Punjab in northwest India. There they fought, and barely defeated, the army of King Poros (probably a tribal name), which was equipped with no fewer than two hundred elephants. On hearing that the next kingdom, the Ganges, had a force of five thousand elephants, Alexander's men flatly refused to go on; even his charisma could not make them change their minds. Most returned westward, although some stayed on in the region known as Bactria in what is now Afghanistan and northwest India.

The Greek cities of Bactria served as a bridge between East and West in two ways: They lay astride the principal central Asian trade routes and thus controlled commercial exchange; some of the most splendid of Greek coins were minted by Bactrian Greeks. Secondly— and more significantly in the long run—they carried Western art and culture into India. In addition to the influence of Greek styles on Buddhist sculpture, Indian Sanskrit drama may well have been inspired by Classical Greek models. Western theories of science and medicine also passed east. Long after these scientific ideas had been forgotten in the West, almost a thousand years later they were reimported into medieval Europe by Muslim explorers.

local Greek ruler, probably called Menandros, is described exchanging ideas with a Buddhist sage, ending with the ruler's conversion to Buddhism—one example of the failure of Greek ideas to convince those exposed to them.

Yet, however much literature and philosophy could do to maintain the importance of Greek culture, it was primarily to the visual arts that Hellenistic rulers turned. In doing so they inaugurated the last great period of Greek art.

The most powerful influence on the period immediately following Alexander's death was the memory of his life. The daring and immensity of his conquests, his own heroic personality, the new world he had sought to create—all these produced a spirit of adventure and experiment. Artists of the Hellenistic period sought not so much to equal or surpass their Classical predecessors in the familiar forms as to discover new subjects and invent new techniques. The development of realistic portraiture dates to this period [3.27], as does the construction of buildings like the Lighthouse at Alexandria [3.28], in its day the tallest tower ever built and one of the Seven Wonders of the World.

The all-pervading spirit of the Classical Age had been order. Now artists began to discover the delights of freedom. Classical art was calm and restrained, but Hellenistic art was emotional and expressive. Classical artists sought clarity and balance

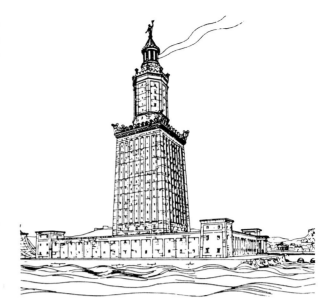

3.28 Reconstruction of the Lighthouse on Pharos, north of Alexandria harbor, 279 B.C. Original height 440′ (134.2 m). The beam of light from the lantern at top was intensified by a system of reflectors. The name of the island, Pharos, became, and still is, another word for lighthouse or beacon.

even in showing scenes of violence, but Hellenistic artists allowed themselves to depict riotous confusion involving strong contrasts of light and shade and the appearance of perpetual motion. It is not surprising that the term *baroque,* originally used to describe the extravagant European art of the 17th century A.D., is often applied to the art of the Hellenistic period.

The artists responsible for these innovations created their works for a new kind of patron. Most of the great works of the Classical period had been produced for the state, with the result that the principal themes and inspirations were religious and political. With the disintegration of the Macedonian Empire and the establishment of prosperous kingdoms at Pergamum, Antioch, and elsewhere, there developed a group of powerful rulers and wealthy businessmen who commissioned works either to provide lavish decoration for their cities or to adorn their private palaces and villas. Artists were no longer responsible to humanity and to the gods, but to whoever paid for the work. Their patrons encouraged them to develop new techniques and surpass the achievements of rivals.

At the same time, the change in the artist's social role produced a change in the function of the work. Whereas in the Classical period architects had devoted themselves to the construction of temples and religious sanctuaries, the Hellenistic age is notable for its marketplaces and theaters, as well as for scientific and technical buildings like the Tower of the Winds at Athens and the Lighthouse at Alexandria [3.28].

3.27 *Alexander the Great.* Pergamum, c. 160 B.C. Marble. Archaeological Museum, Istanbul. Note the emotional fire of the eyes and mouth, emphasized by the set of the head.

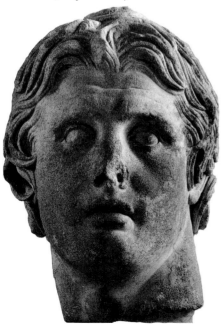

Among the rich cities of Hellenistic Asia, none was wealthier than Pergamum, ruled by a dynasty of kings known as the Attalids. Pergamum was founded in the early 3rd century B.C. and reached the high point of its greatness in the reign of Eumenes II (197–159 B.C.). The layout of the chief buildings in the city represents a rejection of the Classical concepts of order and balance. Unlike the Periclean buildings on the Athenian Acropolis, the buildings in Pergamum were placed independently of one another with a new and dramatic use of space. The theater itself, set on a steep slope, seemed to be falling headlong down the hillside [3.29].

The chief religious shrine of Pergamum was the immense altar to Zeus erected by Eumenes II around 180 B.C. to commemorate the victories of his father, Attalus I, over the Gauls. Its base is decorated with a colossal frieze depicting the battle of the gods and giants. The triumphant figure of Zeus presumably stands as a symbol for the victorious king of Pergamum. The drama and violence of the battle find perfect expression in the tangled, writhing bodies, which leap out of the frieze in high relief, and in the intensity of the gestures and facial expressions [3.30].

The immense emotional impact of the scenes may prevent us from appreciating the remarkable skill of the artists, some of whom were brought from Athens to work on the project. However, the movement of the figures is very far from random and the surface of the stone has been carefully worked to reproduce the texture of hair, skin, fabric, metal, and so on.

The Altar of Zeus represents the most complete illustration of the principles and practice of Hellenistic art. It is, of course, a work on a grand, even grandiose, scale, intended to impress a wide public. But many of its characteristics occur in freestanding pieces of sculpture like the *Laocoön* [3.31]. This famous work shows the Trojan priest Laocoön, punished by the gods for his attempt to warn his people against bringing into their city the wooden horse left by the Greeks. To silence the priest, Apollo sends two sea serpents to strangle him and his sons. The large piece is superbly composed, with the three figures bound together by the sinuous curves of the serpents; they pull away from one another under the agony of the creatures' coils.

By the end of the Hellenistic period both artists and public seemed a little weary of so much richness

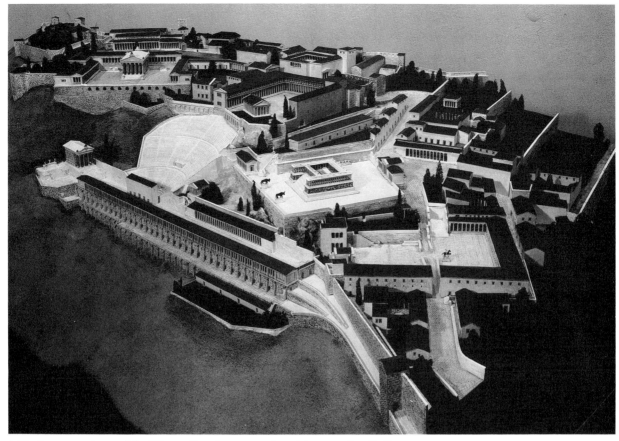

3.29 Reconstruction model of Upper City, Pergamum. State Museums, East Berlin. The steeply sloping theater is at left; the altar to Zeus is in the center foreground.

3.30 *Athena Slaying Giant,* detail of Altar to Zeus frieze, Pergamum. c. 180 B.C. Marble, height 7′6″ (2.29 m). State Museums, East Berlin. Athena is grasping the giant Alcyoneus by the hair to lift him off the ground, source of his strength. His mother Ge, the earth goddess, looks on despairingly from below.

3.31 Agesander, Athenodorus, and Polydorus of Rhodes. *Laocoön Group.* c. 150 B.C. Marble, height 8′ (2.44 m). Vatican Museums, Rome. This statue was uncovered in 1506 in the ruins of Nero's Golden House. Note the similarity between Laocoön's head and the head of the giant Alcyoneus on the Pergamum frieze.

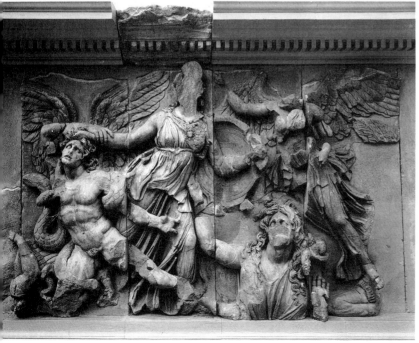

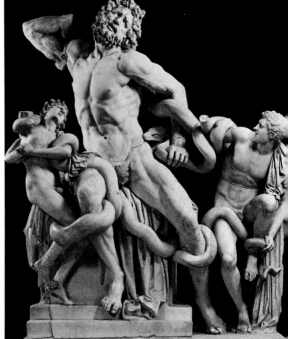

and elaboration and returned to some of the principles of Classical art. At the same time the gradual conquest of the Hellenistic kingdoms by Rome and their absorption into the Roman Empire produced a new synthesis in which the achievements of Classical and Hellenistic Greece fused with the native Italian culture and passed on to later ages.

Summary

The period covered in this chapter falls into three parts. The first, the years from 479 B.C. to 404 B.C., saw the growth of Athenian power and the consequent mistrust on the part of the rest of the Greek world of Athens' intentions. The same period was marked by major cultural developments at Athens. Sculptors such as Myron and Phidias created the High Classical blend of realism and idealism. Tragic drama, in which music played an important role, reached its highest achievement in the works of Aeschylus, Sophocles, and Euripides. In 449 B.C. work was begun on the buildings on the Athenian Acropolis planned by Pericles, Athens' ambitious leader. The Parthenon and the Propylea were completed in an atmosphere made increasingly tense by the deteriorating relations between Athens and the other leading Greek states, particularly Corinth and Sparta.

In 431 B.C. the Peloponnesian War broke out, with Athens and her few remaining allies on one side, and the rest of the Greek world on the other. In 429 B.C. Pericles was killed by a plague that ravaged the city. In the absence of firm leadership the war dragged on, and during a period of truce the Athenians launched a disastrous campaign against the Greek cities of Sicily. When hostilities resumed the Athenians were fatally weakened, and in 404 B.C. they surrendered to the Spartans and their allies.

The years of fighting profoundly affected cultural developments at Athens. Both the sculpture and the vase painting of the late 5th century show a new and somber interest in funerary subjects. In the theater the later plays of Euripides depicted the horrors of war, while the comedies of Aristophanes mocked the political leaders responsible for the turmoil. Thucidides wrote his *History of the Peloponnesian War* to try to analyze the motives and reactions of the participants. Socrates began to question his fellow Athenians about their moral and religious beliefs in a similar spirit of inquiry.

The second period, from 404 B.C. to 323 B.C., was marked by considerable upheaval. Athens was no longer the dominating force in the Greek world, but there was no successor among her rivals. First Sparta and then Thebes achieved an uneasy control of Greek political life. With the collapse of the optimism of the High Classical period the Late Classical age was marked by a new concern with the individual. The dreamy melancholy of Praxiteles' statues is in strong contrast to the idealism of a century earlier, while his figure of Aphrodite naked was one of the first examples in the Western tradition of sensuous female nudity. The most complete demonstration of the new interest in the fate of the individual can be found in the works of Plato, Socra-

tes' disciple, who spent much of his life studying the relationship between individuals and the state. Aristotle, Plato's younger contemporary, also wrote on political theory as well as on a host of other topics.

In 359 B.C. the northern kingdom of Macedon passed under the rule of Philip II and began to play an increasing part in Greek affairs. Despite Athenian resistance, led by the orator Demosthenes, Philip succeeded in uniting the cities of Greece in an alliance known as the League of Corinth; the only important city to remain independent was Sparta.

When Philip was assassinated in 336 B.C. he was succeeded by his son Alexander, who set out to expand the Macedonian empire. After defeating the Persians, he set out in an amazing series of campaigns across Asia that brought him to the borders of India. Only the revolt of his weary troops prevented him from going farther. In 323 B.C., in the course of the long journey home, Alexander died of fever.

The period from 323 B.C. to 146 B.C., marked by the spread of Greek culture throughout the parts of Asia conquered by Alexander, is known as the Hellenistic Age. In the confusion following his death, four kingdoms emerged: Syria, Egypt, Pergamum, and Macedon itself. Prosperous and aggressive and frequently at war with one another, they combined Greek intellectual ideas and artistic styles with native Eastern ones.

The chief characteristics of Hellenistic art were virtuosity and drama. Works such as the Altar of Zeus at Pergamum were commissioned by Hellenistic rulers to glorify their reigns. Artists were encouraged to develop elaborate new techniques and employ them in complex and dramatic ways. The principal buildings of the age were public works like markets and theaters or scientific constructions such as the lighthouse at Alexandria.

The inability of the Hellenistic kingdoms to present a united front caused them to fall victim one by one to a new force in the eastern Mediterranean: Rome. By the end of the 3rd century B.C. the Romans had secured their position in the western Mediterranean and begun an expansion into Asia that was to bring all the Hellenistic kingdoms under their control.

In 146 B.C. Roman troops captured the city of Corinth, center of the League of Corinth founded by Philip and symbol of Greek independence. Greece was made into a Roman province, and its subsequent history followed that of the Roman empire. If Greece was under Roman political control, however, Greek art and culture dominated much of Roman cultural life and were passed on by the Romans into the Western tradition.

Pronounciation Guide

Aegisthus: Ee-GISTH-us

Aeschylus: EESK-ill-us

Antigone: Ant-IG-owe-nee

Aristophanes: A-rist-OFF-an-ease

Caryatid: Ca-ree-AT-id

Catharsis: Cath-ARE-sis

Chaeronaea: Kai-ron-EE-a
Clytemnaestra: Klit-em-NESS-tra
Demosthenes: Dem-OSTH-en-ease
Doryphorus: Dor-IF-or-us
Elgin: EL-ghin
Entasis: ENT-ass-iss
Erechtheum: Er-EK-thee-um
Eumenides: You-MEN-id-ease
Euripides: You-RIP-id-ease
Ictinus: Ic-TINE-us
Laocoön: La-OK-owe-on
Mnesicles: MNEE-sik-lees
Oedipus: ED-ip-us
Panathenaic: Pan-ath-e-NAY-ic
Parthenon: PARTH-en-on
Pericles: PE-rik-lees
Phaedo: FEE-doe
Phidias: FID-i-ass
Polyclitus: Po-lic-LIE-tus
Propylea: Pro-pie-LEE-a
Ptolemy: PTOL-em-ee
Satyr: SAY-tr
Scopas: SKOWE-pass
Seleucids: Sell-YOU-sids
Thucydides: Thyou-SID-id-ease

Exercises

1. Explain the chief differences between the three principal Greek tragic dramatists. Illustrate with episodes in particular plays.
2. Discuss the contributions of Plato and Aristotle to the development of philosophy.
3. Describe Greek musical theory in the 5th and 4th centuries B.C.
4. How was sculpture used to decorate the buildings on the Athenian Acropolis? What is the significance of the myths it illustrates?
5. What are the features of a work of art that indicate it is Hellenistic? How does the Hellenistic style contrast with that of the Classical period?

Further Reading

Barnes, J. *Aristotle*. Oxford: Oxford University Press, 1982. In a mere eighty pages this remarkable book provides an excellent general introduction to Aristotle's vast range of works.

Casson, L. *Travel in the Ancient World*. New York: New York University Press, 1974. An absorbing description of the part played by travel and communication throughout antiquity.

Cawkwell, G. *Philip of Macedon*. Boston: Houghton Mifflin, 1978. A lively account, incorporating new discoveries, of the career of one of the most influential figures in Greek history.

Finley, M. I. (ed.) *The Legacy of Greece: A New Appraisal*. Oxford: Oxford University Press, 1981. A collection of essays by various authors that discuss Greek achievements in various fields—philosophy, art, literature, among others—and evaluate their relevance to the late 20th century.

Hammond, N. G. L. *Alexander the Great: King, Commander, and Statesman*. London: Methuen, 1981. Alexander is still a controversial figure. The author of this scholarly study, clearly an admirer, provides a vivid account of Alexander's life.

Lefkowitz, M. R. and M. B. Fant. *Women in Greece and Rome*. Toronto: University of Toronto Press, 1978. A collection of writings from classical antiquity by, about, sometimes even against women.

Lesky, A. *Greek Tragic Poetry,* 3rd ed.; trans. M. Dillon. New Haven: Yale University Press, 1983. The latest version of one of the standard works on Greek tragedy, analyzing it as literature rather than as theater.

Morford, M. P. O. and P. J. Lenardon. *Classical Mythology*. New York: Longman, 1977. A useful reference source for the many myths found in Greek art and literature, this book also discusses Greek religion and the Greeks' views of the afterlife.

Staveley, E. S. *Greek and Roman Voting and Elections*. London: Methuen, 1972. An absorbing introduction to the world of ancient politics and political practices.

Walbank, F. W. *The Hellenistic World*. Cambridge, Mass.: Harvard University Press, 1982. This book describes the various Hellenistic kingdoms and evaluates their cultural achievements. Includes a good section on Hellenistic science and technology.

Wycherley, R. E. *The Stones of Athens*. Princeton, N.J.: Princeton University Press, 1978. An authoritative description of the monuments of Classical Athens that includes an individual description as well as a bibliography for each important building.

Reading Selections

Sophocles
OEDIPUS THE KING

Sophocles' famous play recounts the tragic downfall of Oedipus, king of Thebes, fated even before birth to kill his father and marry his mother. In the course of the action he is transformed from the confident ruler of the first scene to the self-blinded helpless beggar of the play's conclusion. The inexorable drive of the action is accomplished in a series of dramatic encounters: Oedipus with the Thebans; Oedipus and Teiresias; Oedipus and Creon; Oedipus and his wife

Jocasta; the arrival of the first messenger with news that Jocasta understands only too well; the arrival of the second messenger, the old servant who finally opens Oedipus' eyes to the truth.

When at last all is clear, by a powerful stroke of Sophoclean irony Oedipus blinds himself. The whole play, in fact, is marked by the use of what is called dramatic irony. *The term is used to describe situations or speeches that have one meaning for the characters in the play but a very different one for the audience. Thus when in the opening scene Oedipus tells the chorus "None there is among you as sick as I," unknown to him his statement has a terrible truth. Similarly, in the central scene of the play Jocasta pours scorn on the warnings of oracles and prophets; we know, although she does not, that her own words contradict themselves and that everything she claims to be false is in fact true.*

The end of the play is a gradual unwinding of the tension. As the broken king prepares to go into exile, the chorus reminds us of the instability of success and happiness, leaving us to interpret for ourselves the moral of Oedipus' fate.

Characters

OEDIPUS, *king of Thebes*
A PRIEST
CREON, *brother-in-law of Oedipus*
CHORUS *of Theban elders*
TEIRESIAS, *a prophet*
JOCASTA, *sister of Creon, wife of Oedipus*
MESSENGER
SERVANT *of Laius, father of Oedipus*
SECOND MESSENGER
(*silent*) ANTIGONE *and* ISMENE, *daughters of Oedipus*

SCENE. *Before the palace of Oedipus at Thebes. In front of the large central doors, an altar; and an altar near each of the two side doors. On the altar steps are seated suppliants—old men, youths, and young boys—dressed in white tunics and cloaks, their hair bound with white fillets. They have laid on the altars olive branches wreathed with wool-fillets.*

The old PRIEST OF ZEUS *stands alone facing the central doors of the palace. The doors open, and* OEDIPUS, *followed by two attendants who stand at either door, enters and looks about.*

OEDIPUS O children, last born stock of ancient Cadmus,
What petitions are these you bring to me
With garlands on your suppliant olive branches?
The whole city teems with incense fumes,
Teems with prayers for healing and with groans.
Thinking it best, children, to hear all this
Not from some messenger, I came myself,
The world renowned and glorious Oedipus.

But tell me, aged priest, since you are fit
To speak before these men, how stand you here,   10
In fear or want? Tell me, as I desire
To do my all; hard hearted I would be
To feel no sympathy for such a prayer.
PRIEST O Oedipus, ruler of my land, you see
How old we are who stand in supplication
Before your altars here, some not yet strong
For lengthy flight, some heavy with age,
Priests, as I of Zeus, and choice young men.
The rest of the tribe sits with wreathed branches,
In market places, at Pallas' two temples,   20
And at prophetic embers by the river.
The city, as you see, now shakes too greatly
And cannot raise her head out of the depths
Above the gory swell. She wastes in blight,
Blight on earth's fruitful blooms and grazing flocks,
And on the barren birth pangs of the women.
The fever god has fallen on the city,
And drives it, a most hated pestilence
Through whom the home of Cadmus is made empty.
Black Hades is enriched with wails and groans.   30
Not that we think you equal to the gods
These boys and I sit suppliant at your hearth,
But judging you first of men in the trials of life,
And in the human intercourse with spirits:—
You are the one who came to Cadmus' city
And freed us from the tribute which we paid
To the harsh-singing Sphinx. And that you did
Knowing nothing else, unschooled by us.
But people say and think it was some god
That helped you to set our life upright.
Now Oedipus, most powerful of all,   40
We all are turned here toward you, we beseech you,
Find us some strength, whether from one of the gods
You hear an omen, or know one from a man.
For the experienced I see will best
Make good plans grow from evil circumstance.
Come, best of mortal men, raise up the state.
Come, prove your fame, since now this land of ours
Calls you savior for your previous zeal.
O never let our memory of your reign
Be that we first stood straight and later fell,   50
But to security raise up this state.
With favoring omen once you gave us luck;
Be now as good again; for if henceforth

You rule as now, you will be this country's
  king,
Better it is to rule men than a desert,
Since nothing is either ship or fortress tower
Bare of men who together dwell within.
OEDIPUS O piteous children, I am not ignorant
Of what you come desiring. Well I know
You are all sick, and in your sickness none   60
There is among you as sick as I,
For your pain comes to one man alone,
To him and to none other, but my soul
Groans for the state, for myself, and for you.
You do not wake a man who is sunk in sleep;
Know that already I have shed many tears,
And travelled many wandering roads of
  thought.
Well have I sought, and found one remedy;
And this I did: the son of Menoeceus,
Creon, my brother-in-law, I sent away   70
Unto Apollo's Pythian halls to find
What I might do or say to save the state.
The days are measured out that he is gone;
It troubles me how he fares. Longer than usual
He has been away, more than the fitting time.
But when he comes, then evil I shall be,
If all the god reveals I fail to do.
PRIEST You speak at the right time. These men
  just now
Signal to me that Creon is approaching.
OEDIPUS O Lord Apollo, grant that he may
  come   80
In saving fortune shining as in eye.
PRIEST Glad news he brings, it seems, or else his
  head
Would not be crowned with leafy, berried bay.
OEDIPUS We will soon know. He is close enough
  to hear.—
Prince, my kinsman, son of Menoeceus,
What oracle do you bring us from the god?
CREON A good one. For I say that even burdens
If they chance to turn out right, will all be well.
OEDIPUS Yet what is the oracle? Your present
  word
Makes me neither bold nor apprehensive.   90
CREON If you wish to hear in front of this crowd
I am ready to speak, or we can go within.
OEDIPUS Speak forth to all. The sorrow that I
  bear
Is greater for these men than for my life.
CREON May I tell you what I heard from the
  god?
Lord Phoebus clearly bids us to drive out,
And not to leave uncured within this country,
A pollution we have nourished in our land.
OEDIPUS With what purgation? What kind of
  misfortune?

CREON Banish the man, or quit slaughter with
  slaughter   100
In cleansing, since this blood rains on the state.
OEDIPUS Who is this man whose fate the god
  reveals?
CREON Laius, my lord, was formerly the guide
Of this our land before you steered this city.
OEDIPUS I know him by hearsay, but I never saw
  him.
CREON Since he was slain, the god now plainly
  bids us
To punish his murderers, whoever they may be.
OEDIPUS Where are they on the earth? How shall
  we find
This indiscernible track of ancient guilt?
CREON In this land, said Apollo. What is
  sought   110
Can be apprehended; the unobserved escapes.
OEDIPUS Did Laius fall at home on this bloody
  end?
Or in the fields, or in some foreign land?
CREON As a pilgrim, the god said, he left his
  tribe
And once away from home, returned no more.
OEDIPUS Was there no messenger, no fellow
  wayfarer
Who saw, from whom an inquirer might get
  aid?
CREON They are all dead, save one, who fled in
  fear
And he knows only one thing sure to tell.
OEDIPUS What is that? We may learn many facts
  from one   120
If we might take for hope a short beginning.
CREON Robbers, Apollo said, met there and killed
  him
Not by the strength of one, but many hands.
OEDIPUS How did the robber unless something
  from here
Was at work with silver, reach this point of
  daring?
CREON These facts are all conjecture. Laius dead,
There rose in evils no avenger for him.
OEDIPUS But when the king had fallen slain, what
  trouble
Prevented you from finding all this out?
CREON The subtle-singing Sphinx made us
  let go   130
What was unclear to search at our own feet.
OEDIPUS Well then, I will make this clear
  afresh
From the start. Phoebus was right, you were
  right
To take this present interest in the dead.
Justly it is you see me as your ally
Avenging alike this country and the god.

Not for the sake of some distant friends,
But for myself I will disperse this filth.
Whoever it was who killed that man
With the same hand may wish to do vengeance
    on me.   140
And so assisting Laius I aid myself.
But hurry quickly, children, stand up now
From the altar steps, raising these suppliant
    boughs.
Let someone gather Cadmus' people here
To learn that I will do all, whether at last
With Phoebus' help we are shown saved or
    fallen.

PRIEST   Come, children, let us stand. We came
    here
First for the sake of what this man proclaims.
Phoebus it was who sent these prophecies
And he will come to save us from the
    plague.   150

CHORUS
    Strophe A
    O sweet-tongued voice of Zeus, in what spirit
        do you come
    From Pytho rich in gold
    To glorious Thebes? I am torn on the rack,
        dread shakes my fearful mind,
    Apollo of Delos, hail!
    As I stand in awe of you, what need, either
        new
    Do you bring to the full for me, or old in the
        turning times of the year?
    Tell me, O child of golden Hope, undying
        Voice!

    Antistrophe A
    First on you do I call, daughter of Zeus,
        undying Athene
    And your sister who guards our land,   160
    Artemis, seated upon the throne renowned of
        our circled Place,
    And Phoebus who darts afar;
    Shine forth to me, thrice warder-off of death;
    If ever in time before when ruin rushed upon
        the state,
    The flame of sorrow you drove beyond our
        bounds, come also now.

    Strophe B
    O woe! Unnumbered that I bear
    The sorrows are! My whole host is sick, nor is
        there a sword of thought
    To ward off pain. The growing fruits   170
    Of glorious earth wax not, nor women
    Withstand in childbirth shrieking pangs.
    Life on life you may see, which, like the well-
        winged bird,

Faster than stubborn fire, speed
To the strand of the evening god.

    Antistrophe B
    Unnumbered of the city die.   180
    Unpitied babies bearing death lie unmoaned on
        the ground.
    Grey-haired mothers and young wives
    From all sides at the altar's edge
    Life up a wail beseeching, for their mournful
        woes.
    The prayer for healing shines blent with a
        grieving cry;
    Wherefore, O golden daughter of Zeus,
    Send us your succour with its beaming face.

    Strophe C
    Grant that fiery Ares, who now with no brazen
        shield   190
    Flames round me in shouting attack
    May turn his back in running flight from our
        land,
    May be borne with fair wind
    To Amphitrite's great chamber
    Or to the hostile port
    Of the Thracian surge.
    For even if night leaves any ill undone
    It is brought to pass and comes to be in the
        day.
    O Zeus who bear the fire   200
    And rule the lightning's might,
    Strike him beneath your thunderbolt with
        death!

    Antistrophe C
    O lord Apollo, would that you might come and
        scatter forth
    Untamed darts from your twirling golden bow;
    Bring succour from the plague; may the
        flashing
    Beams come of Artemis,
    With which she glances through the Lycian
        hills.
    Also on him I call whose hair is held in gold,
    Who gives a name to this land,   210
    Bacchus of winy face, whom maidens hail!
    Draw near with your flaming Maenad band
    And the aid of your gladsome torch
    Against the plague, dishonoured among the
        gods.

OEDIPUS   You pray; if for what you pray you
    would be willing
To hear and take my words, to nurse the
    plague,
You may get succour and relief from evils.
A stranger to this tale I now speak forth,
A stranger to the deed, for not alone   220

Could I have tracked it far without some clue,
But now that I am enrolled a citizen
Latest among the citizens of Thebes
To all you sons of Cadmus I proclaim
Whoever of you knows at what man's hand
Laius, the son of Labdacus, met his death,
I order him to tell me all, and even
If he fears, to clear the charge and he will suffer
No injury, but leave the land unharmed.
If someone knows the murderer to be an
    alien   230
From foreign soil, let him not be silent;
I will give him a reward, my thanks besides.
But if you stay in silence and from fear
For self or friend thrust aside my command,
Hear now from me what I shall do for this;
I charge that none who dwell within this land
Whereof I hold the power and the throne
Give this man shelter whoever he may be,
Or speak to him, or share with him in prayer
Or sacrifice, or serve him lustral rites,   240
But drive him, all, out of your homes, for he
Is this pollution on us, as Apollo
Revealed to me just now in oracle.
I am therefore the ally of the god
And of the murdered man. And now I pray
That the murderer, whether he hides alone
Or with his partners, may, evil coward,
Wear out in luckless ills his wretched life.
I further pray, that, if at my own hearth
He dwells known to me in my own home,   250
I may suffer myself the curse I just now
    uttered.
And you I charge to bring all this to pass
For me, and for the god, and for our land
Which now lies fruitless, godless, and corrupt.
Even if Phoebus had not urged this affair,
Not rightly did you let it go unpurged
When one both noble and a king was murdered!
You should have sought it out. Since now I
    reign
Holding the power which he had held before
    me,
Having the selfsame wife and marriage
    bed—   260
And if his seed had not met barren fortune
We should be linked by offspring from one
    mother;
But as it was, fate leapt upon his head.
Therefore in this, as if for my own father
I fight for him, and shall attempt all
Searching to seize the hand which shed that
    blood,
For Labdacus' son, before him Polydorus,
And ancient Cadmus, and Agenor of old.
And those who fail to do this, I pray the gods

May give them neither harvest from their
    earth   270
Nor children from their wives, but may they be
Destroyed by a fate like this one, or a worse.
You other Thebans, who cherish these
    commands,
May Justice, the ally of a righteous cause,
And all the gods be always on your side.
CHORUS   By the oath you laid on me, my king, I
    speak.
I killed not Laius, nor can show who killed
    him.
Phoebus it was who sent this question to us,
And he should answer who has done the deed.
OEDIPUS   Your words are just, but to compel the
    gods   280
In what they do not wish, no man can do.
CHORUS   I would tell what seems to me our
    second course.
OEDIPUS   If there is a third, fail not to tell it too.
CHORUS   Lord Teiresias I know, who sees this best
Like lord Apollo; in surveying this,
One might, my lord, find out from him most
    clearly.
OEDIPUS   Even this I did not neglect; I have done
    it already.
At Creon's word I twice sent messengers.
It is a wonder he has been gone so long.
CHORUS   And also there are rumors, faint
    and old.   290
OEDIPUS   What are they? I must search out every
    tale.
CHORUS   They say there were some travellers who
    killed him.
OEDIPUS   So I have heard, but no one sees a
    witness.
CHORUS   If his mind knows a particle of fear
He will not long withstand such curse as yours.
OEDIPUS   He fears no speech who fears not such a
    deed.
CHORUS   But here is the man who will convict the
    guilty.
Here are these men leading the divine prophet
In whom alone of men the truth is born.
OEDIPUS   O you who ponder all, Teiresias,   300
Both what is taught and what cannot be
    spoken,
What is of heaven and what trod on the earth,
Even if you are blind, you know what plague
Clings to the state, and, master, you alone
We find as her protector and her saviour.
Apollo, if the messengers have not told you,
Answered our question, that release would
    come
From this disease only if we make sure
Of Laius' slayers and slay them in return

Or drive them out as exiles from the land.
But you now, grudge us neither voice of
    birds   310
Nor any way you have of prophecy.
Save yourself and the state; save me as well.
Save everything polluted by the dead.
We are in your hands; it is the noblest task
To help a man with all your means and powers.
TEIRESIAS   Alas! Alas! How terrible to be wise,
  Where it does the seer no good. Too well I
    know
  And have forgot this, or would not have come
    here.
OEDIPUS   What is this? How fainthearted you have
    come!
TEIRESIAS   Let me go home; it is best for you to
    bear   320
  Your burden, and I mine, if you will heed me.
OEDIPUS   You speak what is lawless, and hateful to
    the state
  Which raised you, when you deprive her of
    your answer.
TEIRESIAS   And I see that your speech does not
    proceed
  In season; I shall not undergo the same.
OEDIPUS   Don't by the gods turn back when you
    are wise,
  When all we suppliants lie prostrate before you.
TEIRESIAS   And all unwise; I never shall reveal
  My evils, so that I may not tell yours.
OEDIPUS   What do you say? You know, but will
    not speak?   330
  Would you betray us and destroy the state?
TEIRESIAS   I will not hurt you or me. Why in vain
  Do you probe this? You will not find out from
    me.
OEDIPUS   Worst of evil men, you would enrage
  A stone itself. Will you never speak,
  But stay so untouched and so inconclusive?
TEIRESIAS   You blame my anger and do not see
    that
  With which you live in common, but upbraid
    me.
OEDIPUS   Who would not be enraged to hear these
    words
  By which you now dishonor this our city?   340
TEIRESIAS   Of itself this will come, though I hide it
    in silence.
OEDIPUS   Then you should tell me what it is will
    come.
TEIRESIAS   I shall speak no more. If further you
    desire,
  Rage on in wildest anger of your soul.
OEDIPUS   I shall omit nothing I understand
  I am so angry. Know that you seem to me
  Creator of the deed and worker too

In all short of the slaughter; if you were not
    blind,
I would say this crime was your work alone.
TEIRESIAS   Really? Abide yourself by the decree   350
  You just proclaimed, I tell you! From this day
  Henceforth address neither these men nor me.
  You are the godless defiler of this land.
OEDIPUS   You push so bold and taunting in your
    speech;
  And how do you think to get away with this?
TEIRESIAS   I have got away. I nurse my strength in
    truth.
OEDIPUS   Who taught you this? Not from your art
    you got it.
TEIRESIAS   From you. You had me speak against
    my will.
OEDIPUS   What word? Say again, so I may better
    learn.
TEIRESIAS   Didn't you get it before? Or do you
    bait me?   360
OEDIPUS   I don't remember it. Speak forth again.
TEIRESIAS   You are the slayer whom you seek, I
    say.
OEDIPUS   Not twice you speak such bitter words
unpunished.
TEIRESIAS   Shall I speak more to make you angrier
    still?
OEDIPUS   Do what you will, your words will be in
    vain.
TEIRESIAS   I say you have forgot that you are
    joined
  With those most dear to you in deepest shame
  And do not see where you are in sin.
OEDIPUS   Do you think you will always say such
    things in joy?
TEIRESIAS   Surely, if strength abides in what is
    true.
OEDIPUS   It does, for all but you, this not
    for you   370
  Because your ears and mind and eyes are blind.
TEIRESIAS   Wretched you are to make such taunts,
    for soon
  All men will cast the selfsame taunts on you.
OEDIPUS   You live in entire night, could do no
    harm
  To me or any man who sees the day.
TEIRESIAS   Not at my hands will it be your fate to
    fall.
  Apollo suffices, whose concern it is to do this.
OEDIPUS   Are these devices yours, or are they
    Creon's?
TEIRESIAS   Creon is not your trouble; you are
    yourself.
OEDIPUS   O riches, empire, skill surpassing
    skill   380
  In all the numerous rivalries of life,

How great a grudge there is stored up against
    you
If for this kingship, which the city gave,
Their gift, not my request, into my hands—
For this, the trusted Creon, my friend from the
    start
Desires to creep by stealth and cast me out
Taking a seer like this, a weaver of wiles,
A crooked swindler who has got his eyes
On gain alone, but in his art is blind.
Come, tell us, in what clearly are you a
    prophet?   390
How is it, when the weave-songed bitch was
    here
You uttered no salvation for these people?
Surely the riddle then could not be solved
By some chance comer; it needed prophecy.
You did not clarify that with birds
Or knowledge from a god; but when I came,
The ignorant Oedipus, I silenced her,
Not taught by birds, but winning by my wits,
Whom you are now attempting to depose,
Thinking to minister near Creon's throne.   400
I think that to your woe you and that plotter
Will purge the land, and if you were not old
Punishment would teach you what you plot.
CHORUS   It seems to us, O Oedipus our king,
    Both this man's words and yours were said in
        anger.
    Such is not our need, but to find out
    How best we shall discharge Apollo's orders.
TEIRESIAS   Even if you are king, the right to
        answer
    Should be free to all; of that I too am king.
    I live not as your slave, but as Apollo's.   410
    And not with Creon's wards shall I be counted.
    I say, since you have taunted even my
        blindness,
    You have eyes, but see not where in evil
        you are
    Nor where you dwell, nor whom you are
        living with.
    Do you know from whom you spring? And
        you forget
    You are an enemy to your own kin
    Both those beneath and those above the earth.
    Your mother's and father's curse, with double
        goad
    And dreaded foot shall drive you from this
        land.
    You who now see straight shall then be blind,
    And there shall be no harbour for your cry   420
    With which all Mount Cithaeron soon shall
        ring,
    When you have learned the wedding where you
        sailed

At home, into no port, by voyage fair.
A throng of other ills you do not know
Shall equal you to yourself and to your
    children.
Throw mud on this, on Creon, on my voice—
Yet there shall never be a mortal man
Eradicated more wretchedly than you.
OEDIPUS   Shall these unbearable words be heard
    from him?
    Go to perdition! Hurry! Off, away,   430
    Turn back again and from this house depart.
TEIRESIAS   If you had not called me, I should not
    have come.
OEDIPUS   I did not know that you would speak
    such folly
    Or I would not soon have brought you to my
    house.
TEIRESIAS   And such a fool I am, as it seems to
    you.
    But to the parents who bore you I seem wise.
OEDIPUS   What parents? Wait! What mortals gave
    me birth?
TEIRESIAS   This day shall be your birth and your
    destruction.
OEDIPUS   All things you say in riddles and unclear.
TEIRESIAS   Are you not he who best can search
    this out?   440
OEDIPUS   Mock, if you wish, the skill that made
    me great.
TEIRESIAS   This is the very fortune that destroyed
    you.
OEDIPUS   Well, if I saved the city, I do not care.
TEIRESIAS   I am going now. You, boy, be my
    guide.
OEDIPUS   Yes, let him guide you. Here you are in
    the way.
    When you are gone you will give no more
    trouble.
TEIRESIAS   I go when I have said what I came
    to say
    Without fear of your frown; you cannot
    destroy me.
    I say, the very man whom you long seek
    With threats and announcements about Laius'
        murder—   450
    This man is here. He seems an alien stranger,
    But soon he shall be revealed of Theban birth,
    Nor at this circumstance shall he be pleased.
    He shall be blind who sees, shall be a beggar
    Who now is rich, shall make his way abroad
    Feeling the ground before him with a staff.
    He shall be revealed at once as brother
    And father to his own children, husband
        and son
    To his mother, his father's kin and murderer.   460
    Go in and ponder that. If I am wrong,

Say then that I know nothing of prophecy.

CHORUS

Strophe A

Who is the man the Delphic rock said with
    oracular voice
Unspeakable crimes performed with his gory
    hands?
It is time for him now to speed
His foot in flight, more strong
Than horses swift as the storm.
For girt in arms upon him springs
With fire and lightning, Zeus' son   470
And behind him, terrible,
Come the unerring Fates.

Antistrophe A

From snowy Parnassus just now the word
    flashed clear
To track the obscure man by every way,
For he wanders under the wild
Forest, and into caves
And cliff rocks, like a bull,
Reft on his way, with care on care
Trying to shun the prophecy
Come from the earth's mid-navel;   480
But about him flutters the ever living doom.

Strophe B

Terrible, terrible things the wise bird-augur stirs.
I neither approve nor deny, at a loss for what to
    say,
I flutter in hopes and fears, see neither here nor
    ahead;
For what strife has lain
On Labdacus' sons or Polybus' that I have
    found ever before   490
Or now, whereby I may run for the sons of
    Labdacus
In sure proof against Oedipus' public fame
As avenger for dark death?

Antistrophe B

Zeus and Apollo surely understand and know
The affairs of mortal men, but that a mortal
    seer
Knows more than I, there is no proof. Though
    a man
May surpass a man in knowledge,
Never shall I agree, till I see the word true,
    when men blame Oedipus,
For there came upon him once clear the winged
    maiden   500
And wise he was seen, by sure test sweet for
    the state.
So never shall my mind judge him evil guilt.

CREON   Men of our city, I have heard dread
    words
That Oedipus our king accuses me.
I am here indignant. If in the present troubles

He thinks that he has suffered at my hands
One word or deed tending to injury
I do not crave the long-spanned age of life
To bear this rumor, for it is no simple wrong
The damage of this accusation brings me;   510
It brings the greatest, if I am called a traitor
To you and my friends, a traitor to the state.

CHORUS   Come now, for this reproach perhaps
    was forced
By anger, rather than considered thought.

CREON   And was the idea voiced that my advice
    Persuaded the prophet to give false accounts?

CHORUS   Such was said. I know not to what intent.

CREON   Was this accusation laid against me
    From straightforward eyes and straightforward
    mind?

CHORUS   I do not know. I see not what my
    masters do;   520
But here he is now, coming from the house.

OEDIPUS   How dare you come here? Do you own
    a face
So bold that you can come before my house
When you are clearly the murderer of this man
And manifestly pirate of my throne?
Come, say before the gods, did you see in me
A coward or a fool, that you plotted this?
Or did you think I would not see your wiles
Creeping upon me, or knowing, would not
    ward off?
Surely your machination is absurd   530
Without a crowd of friends to hunt a throne
Which is captured only by wealth and
    many men.

CREON   Do you know what you do? Hear answer
    to your charges
On the other side. Judge only what you know.

OEDIPUS   Your speech is clever, but I learn it ill
Since I have found you harsh and grievous
    toward me.

CREON   This very matter hear me first explain.

OEDIPUS   Tell me not this one thing: you are not
    false.

CREON   If you think stubbornness a good
    possession
Apart from judgment, you do not think
    right.   540

OEDIPUS   If you think you can do a kinsman evil
Without the penalty, you have no sense.

CREON   I agree with you. What you have said is
    just.
Tell me what you say you have suffered
    from me.

OEDIPUS   Did you, or did you not, advise my need
Was summoning that prophet person here?

CREON   And still is. I hold still the same opinion.

OEDIPUS   How long a time now has it been since
    Laius—

CREON   Performed what deed? I do not understand.

OEDIPUS   —Disappeared to his ruin at deadly hands.   550

CREON   Far in the past the count of years would run.

OEDIPUS   Was this same seer at that time practising?

CREON   As wise as now, and equally respected.

OEDIPUS   At that time did he ever mention me?

CREON   Never when I stood near enough to hear.

OEDIPUS   But did you not make inquiry of the murder?

CREON   We did, of course, and got no information.

OEDIPUS   How is it that this seer did not utter this then?

CREON   When I don't know, as now, I would keep still.

OEDIPUS   This much you know full well, and so should speak:—   560

CREON   What is that? If I know, I will not refuse.

OEDIPUS   This: If he had not first conferred with you
He never would have said that I killed Laius.

CREON   If he says this, you know yourself, I think;
I learn as much from you as you from me.

OEDIPUS   Learn then: I never shall be found a slayer.

CREON   What then, are you the husband of my sister?

OEDIPUS   What you have asked is plain beyond denial.

CREON   Do you rule this land with her in equal sway?

OEDIPUS   All she desires she obtains from me.   570

CREON   Am I with you two not an equal third?

OEDIPUS   In just that do you prove a treacherous friend.

CREON   No, if, like me, you reason with yourself.
Consider this fact first: would any man
Choose, do you think, to have his rule in fear
Rather than doze unharmed with the same power?
For my part I have never been desirous
Of being king instead of acting king.
Nor any other man has, wise and prudent.
For now I obtain all from you without fear.   580
If I were king, I would do much unwilling.
How then could kingship sweeter be for me
Than rule and power devoid of any pain?
I am not yet so much deceived to want
Goods besides those I profitably enjoy.
Now I am hailed and gladdened by all men.
Now those who want from you speak out to me,

Since all their chances' outcome dwells therein.
How then would I relinquish what I have
To get those gains? My mind runs not so bad.   590
I am prudent yet, no lover of such plots,
Nor would I ever endure others' treason.
And first as proof of this go on to Pytho;
See if I told you truly the oracle.
Next proof: see if I plotted with the seer;
If you find so at all, put me to death
With my vote for my guilt as well as yours.
Do not convict me just on unclear conjecture.
It is not right to think capriciously
The good are bad, nor that the bad are good.   600
It is the same to cast out a noble friend,
I say, as one's own life, which best he loves.
The facts, though, you will safely know in time,
Since time alone can show the just man just,
But you can know a criminal in one day.

CHORUS   A cautious man would say he has spoken well.
O king, the quick to think are never sure.

OEDIPUS   When the plotter, swift, approaches me in stealth
I too in counterplot must be as swift.
If I wait in repose, the plotter's ends   610
Are brought to pass and mine will then have erred.

CREON   What do you want then? To cast me from the land?

OEDIPUS   Least of all that. My wish is you should die,
Not flee to exemplify what envy is.

CREON   Do you say this? Will you neither trust nor yield?

OEDIPUS   [No, for I think that you deserve no trust.]

CREON   You seem not wise to me.

OEDIPUS   I am for me.

CREON   You should be for me too.

OEDIPUS   No, you are evil.   620

CREON   Yes, if you understand nothing.

OEDIPUS   Yet I must rule.

CREON   Not when you rule badly.

OEDIPUS   O city, city!

CREON   It is my city too, not yours alone.

CHORUS   Stop, princes. I see Jocasta coming
Out of the house at the right time for you.
With her you must settle the dispute at hand.

JOCASTA   O wretched men, what unconsidered feud
Of tongues have you aroused? Are you not   630
ashamed,
The state so sick, to stir up private ills?
Are you not going home? And you as well?
Will you turn a small pain into a great?

CREON My blood sister, Oedipus your husband
   Claims he will judge against me two
      dread ills:
   Thrust me from the fatherland or take and
      kill me.
OEDIPUS I will, my wife; I caught him in the act
   Doing evil to my person with evil skill.
CREON Now may I not rejoice but die accursed
   If ever I did any of what you accuse me.   640
JOCASTA O, by the gods, believe him, Oedipus.
   First, in reverence for his oath to the gods,
   Next, for my sake and theirs who stand before
      you.
CHORUS Hear my entreaty, lord. Consider and
   consent.
OEDIPUS What wish should I then grant?
CHORUS Respect the man, no fool before, who
   now in oath is strong.
OEDIPUS You know what you desire?
CHORUS I know.
OEDIPUS Say what you mean.
CHORUS Your friend who has sworn do not
   dishonour   650
   By casting guilt for dark report.
OEDIPUS Know well that when you ask this grant
   from me,
   You ask my death or exile from the land.
CHORUS No, by the god foremost among the
   gods,
   The Sun, may I perish by the utmost doom
   Godless and friendless, if I have this in mind.
   But ah, the withering earth wears down
   My wretched soul, if to these ills
   Of old are added ills from both of you.
OEDIPUS Then let him go, though surely I must
   die   660
   Or be thrust dishonoured from this land by
      force.
   Your grievous voice I pity, not that man's;
   Wherever he may be, he will be hated.
CREON Sullen you are to yield, as you are heavy
   When you exceed in wrath. Natures like these
   Are justly sorest for themselves to bear.
OEDIPUS Will you not go and leave me?
CREON I am on my way.
   You know me not, but these men see me just.
CHORUS O queen, why do you delay to bring this
   man indoors?   670
JOCASTA I want to learn what happened here.
CHORUS Unknown suspicion rose from talk, and
   the unjust devours.
JOCASTA In both of them?
CHORUS Just so.
JOCASTA What was the talk?
CHORUS Enough, enough! When the land is pained
   It seems to me at this point we should stop.
OEDIPUS Do you see where you have come?

   Though your intent
   Is good, you slacken off and blunt my heart.   680
CHORUS O lord, I have said not once alone,
   Know that I clearly would be mad
   And wandering in mind, to turn away
   You who steered along the right,
   When she was torn with trouble, our beloved
      state.
   O may you now become in health her guide.
JOCASTA By the gods, lord, tell me on what
   account
   You have set yourself in so great an anger.
OEDIPUS I shall tell you, wife; I respect you more
   than these men.
   Because of Creon, since he has plotted against
      me.   690
JOCASTA Say clearly, if you can; how started the
   quarrel?
OEDIPUS He says that I stand as the murderer of
   Laius.
JOCASTA He knows himself, or learned from
   someone else?
OEDIPUS No, but he sent a rascal prophet here.
   He keeps his own mouth clean in what concerns
   him.
JOCASTA Now free yourself of what you said, and
   listen.
   Learn from me, no mortal man exists
   Who knows prophetic art for your affairs,
   And I shall briefly show you proof of this:
   An oracle came once to Laius. I do not say   700
   From Phoebus himself, but from his ministers
   That his fate would be at his son's hand to
      die—
   A child, who would be born from him and me.
   And yet, as the rumor says, they were strangers,
   Robbers who killed him where three highways
      meet.
   But three days had not passed from the child's
      birth
   When Laius pierced and tied together his ankles,
   And cast him by others' hands on a pathless
      mountain.
   Therein Apollo did not bring to pass
   That the child murder his father, nor for
      Laius   710
   The dread he feared, to die at his son's hand.
   Such did prophetic oracles determine.
   Pay no attention to them. For the god
   Will easily make clear the need he seeks.
OEDIPUS What wandering of soul, what stirring of
   mind
   Holds me, my wife, in what I have just heard!
JOCASTA What care has turned you back that you
   say this?
OEDIPUS I thought I heard you mention this, that
   Laius

Was slaughtered at the place where three
   highways meet.
JOCASTA   That was the talk. The rumour has not
   ceased.   720
OEDIPUS   Where is this place where such a sorrow
   was?
JOCASTA   The country's name is Phocis. A split
   road
   Leads to one place from Delphi and Daulia.
OEDIPUS   And how much time has passed since
   these events?
JOCASTA   The news was heralded in the city
   scarcely
   A little while before you came to rule.
OEDIPUS   O Zeus, what have you planned to do
   to me?
JOCASTA   What passion is this in you, Oedipus?
OEDIPUS   Don't ask me that yet. Tell me about
   Laius.
   What did he look like? How old was he when
   murdered?   730
JOCASTA   A tall man, with his hair just brushed
   with white.
   His shape and form differed not far from yours.
OEDIPUS   Alas! Alas! I think unwittingly
   I have just laid dread curses on my head.
JOCASTA   What are you saying? I shrink to behold
   you, lord.
OEDIPUS   I am terribly afraid the seer can see.
   That will be clearer if you say one thing more.
JOCASTA   Though I shrink, if I know what you
   ask, I will answer.
OEDIPUS   Did he set forth with few attendants then,
   Or many soldiers, since he was a king?   740
JOCASTA   They were five altogether among them.
   One was a herald. One chariot bore Laius.
OEDIPUS   Alas! All this is clear now. Tell me, my
   wife,
   Who was the man who told these stories to
   you?
JOCASTA   One servant, who alone escaped,
   returned.
OEDIPUS   Is he by chance now present in our
   house?
JOCASTA   Not now. Right from the time when he
   returned
   To see you ruling and Laius dead,
   Touching my hand in suppliance, he implored
   me
   To send him to fields and to pastures of
   sheep   750
   That he might be farthest from the sight of this
   city.
   So I sent him away, since he was worthy
   For a slave, to bear a greater grant than this.
OEDIPUS   How then could he return to us with
   speed?

JOCASTA   It can be done. But why would you
   order this?
OEDIPUS   O lady, I fear I have said too much.
   On this account I now desire to see him.
JOCASTA   Then he shall come. But I myself
   deserve
   To learn what it is that troubles you, my
   lord.
OEDIPUS   And you shall not be prevented, since
   my fears   760
   Have come to such a point. For who is closer
   That I may speak to in this fate than you?
   Polybus of Corinth was my father,
   My mother, Dorian Merope. I was held there
   Chief citizen of all, till such a fate
   Befell me—as it is, worthy of wonder,
   But surely not deserving my excitement.
   A man at a banquet overdrunk with wine
   Said in drink I was a false son to my father.
   The weight I held that day I scarcely bore,   770
   But on the next day I went home and asked
   My father and mother of it. In bitter anger
   They took the reproach from him who had let
   it fly.
   I was pleased at their actions; nevertheless
   The rumour always rankled; and spread abroad.
   In secret from mother and father I set out
   Toward Delphi. Phoebus sent me away
   ungraced
   In what I came for, but other wretched things
   Terrible and grievous, he revealed in answer;
   That I must wed my mother and produce   780
   An unendurable race for men to see,
   That I should kill the father who begot me.
   When I heard this response, Corinth I fled
   Henceforth to measure her land by stars alone.
   I went where I should never see the disgrace
   Of my evil oracles be brought to pass,
   And on my journey to that place I came
   At which you say this king had met his death.
   My wife, I shall speak the truth to you. My
   way
   Led to a place close by the triple road.   790
   There a herald met me, and a man
   Seated on colt-drawn chariot, as you said.
   There both the guide and the old man himself
   Thrust me with driving force out of the path.
   And I in anger struck the one who pushed me,
   The driver. Then the old man, when he saw
   me,
   Watched when I passed, and from his chariot
   Struck me full on the head with double goad.
   I paid him back and more. From this very
   hand
   A swift blow of my staff rolled him right
   out   800
   Of the middle of his seat onto his back.

I killed them all. But if relationship
Existed between this stranger and Laius,
What man now is wretcheder than I?
What man is cursed by a more evil fate?
No stranger or citizen could now receive me
Within his home, or even speak to me,
But thrust me out; and no one but myself
Brought down these curses on my head.
The bed of the slain man I now defile   810
With hands that killed him. Am I evil by birth?
Am I not utterly vile if I must flee
And cannot see my family in my flight
Nor tread my homeland soil, or else be joined
In marriage to my mother, kill my father,
Polybus, who sired me and brought me up?
Would not a man judge right to say of me
That this was sent on me by some cruel spirit?
O never, holy reverence of the gods,
May I behold that day, but may I go   820
Away from mortal men, before I see
Such a stain of circumstance come to me.

CHORUS   My lord, for us these facts are full of
        dread.
    Until you hear the witness, stay in hope.

OEDIPUS   And just so much is all I have of hope,
    Only to wait until the shepherd comes.

JOCASTA   What, then, do you desire to hear him
        speak?

OEDIPUS   I will tell you, if his story is found to be
    The same as yours, I would escape the
        sorrow.

JOCASTA   What unusual word did you hear
        from me?   830

OEDIPUS   You said he said that they were highway
        robbers
    Who murdered him. Now, if he still says
    The selfsame number, I could not have killed
        him,
    Since one man does not equal many men.
    But if he speaks of a single lonely traveller,
    The scale of guilt now clearly falls to me.

JOCASTA   However, know the word was set forth
        thus
    And it is not in him now to take it back;
    This tale the city heard, not I alone.
    But if he diverges from his previous story,   840
    Even then, my lord, he could not show Laius'
        murder
    To have been fulfilled properly. Apollo
    Said he would die at the hands of my own son.
    Surely that wretched child could not have killed
        him,
    But he himself met death some time before.
    Therefore, in any prophecy henceforth
    I would not look to this side or to that.

OEDIPUS   Your thoughts ring true, but still let
        someone go

To summon the peasant. Do not neglect
    this.

JOCASTA   I shall send without delay. But let us
        enter.   850
    I would do nothing that did not please you.

CHORUS
    Strophe A
    May fate come on me as I bear
    Holy pureness in all word and deed,
    For which the lofty striding laws were set
        down,
    Born through the heavenly air
    Whereof the Olympian sky alone the father
        was;
    No mortal spawn of mankind gave them birth,
    Nor may oblivion ever lull them down;   860
    Mighty in them the god is, and he does not
        age.

    Antistrophe A
    Pride breeds the tyrant.
    Pride, once overfilled with many things in vain,
    Neither in season nor fit for man,
    Scaling the sheerest height
    Hurls to a dire fate
    Where no foothold is found.
    I pray the god may never stop the rivalry
    That works well for the state.   870
    The god as my protector I shall never cease to
        hold.

    Strophe B
    But if a man goes forth haughty in word or
        deed
    With no fear of the Right
    Nor pious to the spirits' shrines,
    May evil doom seize him
    For his ill-fated pride,
    If he does not fairly win his gain
    Or works unholy deeds,
    Or, in bold folly lays on the sacred profane
        hands.   880
    For when such acts occur, what man may boast
    Ever to ward off from his life darts of the gods?
    If practices like these are in respect,
    Why then must I dance the sacred dance?

    Antistrophe B
    Never again in worship shall I go
    To Delphi, holy navel of the earth,
    Nor to the temple at Abae,
    Nor to Olympia,
    If these prophecies do not become   890
    Examples for all men.
    O Zeus, our king, if so you are rightly called,
    Ruler of all things, may they not escape
    You and your forever deathless power.
    Men now hold light the fading oracles

Told about Laius long ago
And nowhere is Apollo clearly honored;
Things divine are going down to ruin.

JOCASTA   Lords of this land, the thought has come
    to me
    To visit the spirits' shrines, bearing in hand   900
    These suppliant boughs and offerings of
        incense.
    For Oedipus raises his soul too high
    With all distresses; nor, as a sane man should,
    Does he confirm the new by things of old,
    But stands at the speaker's will if he speaks
        terrors.
    And so, because my advice can do no more,
    To you, Lycian Apollo—for you are nearest—
    A suppliant, I have come here with these
        prayers,
    That you may find some pure deliverance for us:
    We all now shrink to see him struck in fear,   910
    That man who is the pilot of our ship.
MESSENGER   Strangers, could I learn from one of
    you
    Where is the house of Oedipus the king?
    Or best, if you know, say where he is himself.
CHORUS   This is his house, stranger; he dwells
    inside;
    This woman is the mother of his children.
MESSENGER   May she be always blessed among the
    blest,
    Since she is the fruitful wife of Oedipus.
JOCASTA   So may you, stranger, also be. You
    deserve
    As much for your graceful greeting. But tell
        me   920
    What you have come to search for or to show.
MESSENGER   Good news for your house and your
    husband, lady.
JOCASTA   What is it then? And from whom have
    you come?
MESSENGER   From Corinth. And the message I will
    tell
    Will surely gladden you—and vex you,
        perhaps.
JOCASTA   What is it? What is this double force it
    holds?
MESSENGER   The men who dwell in the Isthmian
    country
    Have spoken to establish him their king.
JOCASTA   What is that? Is not old Polybus still
    ruling?
MESSENGER   Not he. For death now holds him in
    the tomb.   930
JOCASTA   What do you say, old man? Is Polybus
    dead?
MESSENGER   If I speak not the truth, I am ready to
    die.

JOCASTA   O handmaid, go right away and tell
    your master
    The news. Where are you, prophecies of the
        gods?
    For this man Oedipus has trembled long,
    And shunned him lest he kill him. Now the
        man
    Is killed by fate and not by Oedipus.
OEDIPUS   O Jocasta, my most beloved wife,
    Why have you sent for me within the house?
JOCASTA   Listen to this man, and while you hear
    him, think   940
    To what have come Apollo's holy prophecies.
OEDIPUS   Who is this man? Why would he speak
    to me?
JOCASTA   From Corinth he has come, to announce
    that your father
    Polybus no longer lives, but is dead.
OEDIPUS   What do you say, stranger? Tell me this
    yourself.
MESSENGER   If I must first announce my message
    clearly,
    Know surely that the man is dead and gone.
OEDIPUS   Did he die by treachery or chance
    disease?
MESSENGER   A slight scale tilt can lull the old to
    rest.
OEDIPUS   The poor man, it seems, died by
    disease.   950
MESSENGER   And by the full measure of lengthy
    time.
OEDIPUS   Alas, alas! Why then do any seek
    Pytho's prophetic art, my wife, or hear
    The shrieking birds on high, by whose report
    I was to slay my father? Now he lies
    Dead beneath the earth, and here am I
    Who have not touched the blade. Unless in
        longing
    For me he died, and in this sense was killed by
        me.
    Polybus has packed away these oracles
    In his rest in Hades. They are now worth
        nothing.   960
JOCASTA   Did I not tell you that some time ago?
OEDIPUS   You did, but I was led astray by fear.
JOCASTA   Henceforth put nothing of this on your
    heart.
OEDIPUS   Why must I not still shrink from my
    mother's bed?
JOCASTA   What should man fear, whose life is
    ruled by fate,
    For whom there is clear foreknowledge of
        nothing?
    It is best to live by chance, however you can.
    Be not afraid of marriage with your
        mother;
    Already many mortals in their dreams

Have shared their mother's bed. But he who counts 970
This dream as nothing, easiest bears his life.

OEDIPUS   All that you say would be indeed propitious,
If my mother were not alive. But since she is,
I still must shrink, however well you speak.

JOCASTA   And yet your father's tomb is a great eye.

OEDIPUS   A great eye indeed. But I fear her who lives.

MESSENGER   Who is this woman that you are afraid of?

OEDIPUS   Merope, old man, with whom Polybus lived.

MESSENGER   What is it in her that moves you to fear?

OEDIPUS   A dread oracle, stranger, sent by the god. 980

MESSENGER   Can it be told, or must no other know?

OEDIPUS   It surely can. Apollo told me once
That I must join in intercourse with my mother
And shed with my own hands my father's blood.
Because of this, long since I have kept far
Away from Corinth—and happily—but yet
It would be most sweet to see my parents' faces.

MESSENGER   Was this your fear in shunning your own city?

OEDIPUS   I wished, too, old man, not to slay my father. 990

MESSENGER   Why then have I not freed you from this fear,
Since I have come with friendly mind, my lord?

OEDIPUS   Yes, and take thanks from me, which you deserve.

MESSENGER   And this is just the thing for which I came,
That when you got back home I might fare well.

OEDIPUS   Never shall I go where my parents are.

MESSENGER   My son, you clearly know not what you do.

OEDIPUS   How is that, old man? By the gods, let me know.

MESSENGER   If for these tales you shrink from going home. 1000

OEDIPUS   I tremble lest what Phoebus said comes true.

MESSENGER   Lest you incur pollution from your parents?

OEDIPUS   That is the thing, old man, that always haunts me.

MESSENGER   Well, do you know that surely you fear nothing?

OEDIPUS   How so? If I am the son of those who bore me.

MESSENGER   Since Polybus was no relation to you.

OEDIPUS   What do you say? Was Polybus not my father?

MESSENGER   No more than this man here but just so much.

OEDIPUS   How does he who begot me equal nothing?

MESSENGER   That man was not your father, any more than I am. 1010

OEDIPUS   Well then, why was it he called me his son?

MESSENGER   Long ago he got you as a gift from me.

OEDIPUS   Though from another's hand, yet so much he loved me!

MESSENGER   His previous childlessness led him to that.

OEDIPUS   Had you bought or found me when you gave me to him?

MESSENGER   I found you in Cithaeron's folds and glens.

OEDIPUS   Why were you travelling in those regions?

MESSENGER   I guarded there a flock of mountain sheep.

OEDIPUS   Were you a shepherd, wandering for pay?

MESSENGER   Yes, and your saviour too, child, at that time 1020

OEDIPUS   What pain gripped me, that you took me in your arms?

MESSENGER   The ankles of your feet will tell you that.

OEDIPUS   Alas, why do you mention that old trouble?

MESSENGER   I freed you when your ankles were pierced together.

OEDIPUS   A terrible shame from my swaddling clothes I got.

MESSENGER   Your very name you got from this misfortune.

OEDIPUS   By the gods, did my mother or father do it? Speak.

MESSENGER   I know not. He who gave you knows better than I.

OEDIPUS   You didn't find me, but took me from another?

MESSENGER   That's right. Another shepherd gave you to me. 1030

OEDIPUS   Who was he? Can you tell me who he was?

MESSENGER   Surely. He belonged to the household of Laius.

OEDIPUS   The man who ruled this land once long ago?

MESSENGER   Just so. He was a herd in that man's service.

OEDIPUS   Is this man still alive, so I could see him?

MESSENGER   You dwellers in this country should know best.

OEDIPUS   Is there any one of you who stand before me
Who knows the shepherd of whom this man speaks?
If you have seen him in the fields or here,
Speak forth; the time has come to find this out.   1040

CHORUS   I think the man you seek is no one else
Than the shepherd you were so eager to see before.
Jocasta here might best inform us that.

OEDIPUS   My wife, do you know the man we just ordered
To come here? Is it of him that this man speaks?

JOCASTA   Why ask of whom he spoke? Think nothing of it.
Brood not in vain on what has just been said.

OEDIPUS   It could not be that when I have got such clues,
I should not shed clear light upon my birth.

JOCASTA   Don't, by the gods, investigate this more   1050
If you care for your own life. I am sick enough.

OEDIPUS   Take courage. Even if I am found a slave
For three generations, your birth will not be base.

JOCASTA   Still, I beseech you, hear me. Don't do this.

OEDIPUS   I will hear of nothing but finding out the truth.

JOCASTA   I know full well and tell you what is best.

OEDIPUS   Well, then, this best, for some time now, has given me pain.

JOCASTA   O ill-fated man, may you never know who you are.

OEDIPUS   Will someone bring the shepherd to me here?
And let this lady rejoice in her opulent birth.   1060

JOCASTA   Alas, alas, hapless man. I have this alone
To tell you, and nothing else forevermore.

CHORUS   O Oedipus, where has the woman gone
In the rush of her wild grief? I am afraid
Evil will break forth out of this silence.

OEDIPUS   Let whatever will break forth. I plan to see
The seed of my descent, however small.
My wife, perhaps, because a noblewoman
Looks down with shame upon my lowly birth.

I would not be dishonoured to call myself   1070
The son of Fortune, giver of the good.
She is my mother. The years, her other children,
Have marked me sometimes small and sometimes great.
Such was I born! I shall prove no other man,
Nor shall I cease to search out my descent.

CHORUS
   Strophe
If I am a prophet and can know in mind,
Cithaeron, by tomorrow's full moon
You shall not fail, by mount Olympus,
To find that Oedipus, as a native of your land,
Shall honour you for nurse and mother.   1080
And to you we dance in choral song because you bring
Fair gifts to him our king.
Hail, Phoebus, may all this please you.

   Antistrophe
Who, child, who bore you in the lengthy span of years?
One close to Pan who roams the mountain woods,
One of Apollo's bedfellows?
For all wild pastures in mountain glens to him are dear.
Was Hermes your father, who Cyllene sways,
Or did Bacchus, dwelling on the mountain peaks,
Take you a foundling from some nymph   1090
Of those by springs of Helicon, with whom he sports the most?

OEDIPUS   If I may guess, although I never met him,
I think, elders, I see that shepherd coming
Whom we have long sought, as in the measure
Of lengthy age he accords with him we wait for.
Besides, the men who lead him I recognize
As servants of my house. You may perhaps
Know better than I if you have seen him before.

CHORUS   Be assured, I know him as a shepherd
As trusted as any other in Laius' service.   1100

OEDIPUS   Stranger from Corinth, I will ask you first,
Is this the man you said?

MESSENGER   You are looking at him.

OEDIPUS   You there, old man, look here and answer me
What I shall ask you. Were you ever with Laius?

SERVANT   I was a slave, not bought but reared at home.

OEDIPUS   What work concerned you? What was
      your way of life?
SERVANT   Most of my life I spent among the flocks.
OEDIPUS   In what place most of all was your usual
      pasture?   1110
SERVANT   Sometimes Cithaeron, or the ground
      nearby.
OEDIPUS   Do you know this man before you here
      at all?
SERVANT   Doing what? And of what man do you
      speak?
OEDIPUS   The one before you. Have you ever had
      congress with him?
SERVANT   Not to say so at once from memory.
MESSENGER   That is no wonder, master, but I shall
      remind him,
   Clearly, who knows me not; yet will I know
   That he knew once the region of Cithaeron.
   He with a double flock and I with one
   Dwelt there in company for three whole
      years   1120
   During the six months' time from spring to fall.
   When winter came, I drove into my fold
   My flock, and he drove his to Laius' pens.
   Do I speak right, or did it not happen so?
SERVANT   You speak the truth, though it was long
      ago.
MESSENGER   Come now, do you recall you gave
      me then
   A child for me to rear as my own son?
SERVANT   What is that? Why do you ask me this?
MESSENGER   This is the man, my friend, who then
      was young.
SERVANT   Go to destruction! Will you not be
      quiet?   1130
OEDIPUS   Come, scold him not, old man. These
      words of yours
   Deserve a scolding more than this man's do.
SERVANT   In what, most noble master, do I
      wrong?
OEDIPUS   Not to tell of the child he asks
      about.
SERVANT   He speaks in ignorance, he toils in vain.
OEDIPUS   If you will not speak freely, you will
      under torture.
SERVANT   Don't, by the gods, outrage an old man
      like me.
OEDIPUS   Will someone quickly twist back this
      fellow's arms?
SERVANT   Alas, what for? What do you want to
      know?   1140
OEDIPUS   Did you give this man the child of
      whom he asks?
SERVANT   I did. Would I had perished on that day!
OEDIPUS   You will come to that unless you tell the
      truth.
SERVANT   I come to far greater ruin if I speak.

OEDIPUS   This man, it seems, is trying
      to delay.
SERVANT   Not I. I said before I gave it to him.
OEDIPUS   Where did you get it? At home or from
      someone else?
SERVANT   It was not mine. I got him from a man.
OEDIPUS   Which of these citizens? Where did he
      live?
SERVANT   O master, by the gods, ask me no
      more.   1150
OEDIPUS   You are done for if I ask you this again.
SERVANT   Well then, he was born of the house of
      Laius.
OEDIPUS   One of his slaves, or born of his own
      race?
SERVANT   Alas, to speak I am on the brink of
      horror.
OEDIPUS   And I to hear. But still it must
      be heard.
SERVANT   Well, then, they say it was his child.
      Your wife
   Who dwells within could best say how this
      stands.
OEDIPUS   Was it she who gave him to you?
SERVANT   Yes, my lord.
OEDIPUS   For what intent?   1160
SERVANT   So I could put it away.
OEDIPUS   When she bore him, the wretch.
SERVANT   She feared bad oracles.
OEDIPUS   What were they?
SERVANT   They said he should kill his father.
OEDIPUS   Why did you give him up to this old
      man?
SERVANT   I pitied him, master, and thought he
      would take him away
   To another land, the one from which he came.
   But he saved him for greatest woe. If you are
      he
   Whom this man speaks of, you were born
      curst by fate.   1170
OEDIPUS   Alas, alas! All things are now come true.
   O light, for the last time now I look upon you;
   I am shown to be born from those I ought not
      to have been.
   I married the woman I should not have
      married,
   I killed the man whom I should not have killed.

CHORUS
   Strophe A
   Alas, generations of mortal men!
   How equal to nothing do I number you in life!
   Who, O who, is the man
   Who bears more of bliss
   Than just the seeming so,   1186
   And then, like a waning sun, to fall away?
   When I know your example,

Your guiding spirit, yours, wretched Oedipus,
I call no mortal blest.

Antistrophe A

He is the one, O Zeus,
Who peerless shot his bow and won well–fated
  bliss,
Who destroyed the hook–clawed maiden,
The oracle–singing Sphinx,
And stood a tower for our land from death;
For this you are called our king,   1190
Oedipus, are highest–honoured here,
And over great Thebes hold sway.

Strophe B

And now who is more wretched for men to
  hear,
Who so lives in wild plagues, who dwells in
  pains,
In utter change of life?
Alas for glorious Oedipus!
The selfsame port of rest
Was gained by bridegroom father and his
  son,
How, O how did your father's furrows ever
  bear you, suffering man?
How have they endured silence for so long?   1200

Antistrophe B

You are found out, unwilling, by all seeing
  Time.
It judges your unmarried marriage where for
  long
Begetter and begot have been the same.
Alas, child of Laius,
Would I had never seen you.
As one who pours from his mouth a dirge I
  wail,
To speak the truth, through you I breathed new
  life,
And now through you I lulled my eye to sleep.
SECOND MESSENGER   O men most honoured always
  of this land
What deeds you shall hear, what shall you
  behold!   1210
What grief shall stir you up, if by your kinship
You are still concerned for the house of
  Labdacus!
I think neither Danube nor any other river
Could wash this palace clean, so many ills
Lie hidden there which now will come to light.
They were done by will, not fate; and sorrows
  hurt
The most when we ourselves appear to choose
  them.
CHORUS   What we heard before causes no little
  sorrow.
What can you say which adds to that a burden?

SECOND MESSENGER   This is the fastest way to tell
  the tale;   1220
Hear it: Jocasta, your divine queen, is dead.
CHORUS   O sorrowful woman! From what cause
  did she die?
SECOND MESSENGER   By her own hand. The most
  painful of the action
Occurred away, not for your eyes to see.
But still, so far as I have memory
You shall learn the sufferings of that wretched
  woman:
How she passed on through the door enraged
And rushed straight forward to her nuptial bed,
Clutching her hair's ends with both her hands.
Once inside the doors she shut herself in   1230
And called on Laius, who has long been dead,
Having remembrance of their seed of old
By which he died himself and left her a mother
To bear an evil brood to his own son.
She moaned the bed on which by double curse
She bore husband to husband, children to child.
How thereafter she perished I do not know,
For Oedipus burst in on her with a shriek,
And because of him we could not see her woe.
We looked on him alone as he rushed
  around.   1240
Pacing about, he asked us to give him a sword,
Asked where he might find the wife no wife,
A mother whose plowfield bore him and his
  children.
Some spirit was guiding him in his frenzy,
For none of the men who are close at hand did
  so.
With a horrible shout, as if led on by someone,
He leapt on the double doors, from their
  sockets
Broke hollow bolts aside, and dashed within.
There we beheld his wife hung by her neck
From twisted cords, swinging to and fro.   1250
When he saw her, wretched man, he terribly
  groaned
And slackened the hanging noose. When the
  poor woman
Lay on the ground, what happened was dread
  to see.
He tore the golden brooch pins from her clothes,
And raised them up, and struck his own
  eyeballs,
Shouting such words as these "No more shall
  you
Behold the evils I have suffered and done.
Be dark from now on, since you saw before
What you should not, and knew not what you
  should."
Moaning such cries, not once but many
  times   1260
He raised and struck his eyes. The bloody pupils

Bedewed his beard. The gore oozed not in
  drops,
But poured in a black shower, a hail of blood.
From both of them these woes have broken out,
Not for just one, but man and wife together.
The bliss of old that formerly prevailed
Was bliss indeed, but now upon this day
Lamentation, madness, death, and shame—
No evil that can be named is not at hand.
CHORUS   Is the wretched man in any rest now
    from pain?   1270
SECOND MESSENGER   He shouts for someone to
    open up the doors
  And show to all Cadmeans his father's slayer,
  His mother's—I should not speak the unholy
    word.
  He says he will hurl himself from the land, no
    more
  To dwell cursed in the house by his own curse.
  Yet he needs strength and someone who will
    guide him.
  His sickness is too great to bear. He will show
    it to you
  For the fastenings of the doors are opening up,
  And such a spectacle you will soon behold
  As would make even one who abhors it take
    pity.   1280
CHORUS   O terrible suffering for men to see,
  Most terrible of all that I
  Have ever come upon. O wretched man,
  What madness overcame you, what springing
    daimon
  Greater than the greatest for men
  Has caused your evil-daimoned fate?
  Alas, alas, grievous one,
  But I cannot bear to behold you, though I
    desire
  To ask you much, much to find out,
  Much to see,   1290
  You make me shudder so!
OEDIPUS   Alas, alas, I am grieved!
  Where on earth, so wretched, shall I go?
  Where does my voice fly through the air,
  O Fate, where have you bounded?
CHORUS   To dreadful end, not to be heard or seen.

Strophe A
OEDIPUS   O cloud of dark
  That shrouds me off, has come to pass,
    unspeakable,
  Invincible, that blows no favoring blast.
  Woe,   1300
  O woe again, the goad that pierces me,
  Of the sting of evil now, and memory of
    before.
CHORUS   No wonder it is that among so many
    pains

You should both mourn and bear a double
  evil.
    Antistrophe A
OEDIPUS   Ah, friend,
  You are my steadfast servant still,
  You still remain to care for me, blind.
  Alas! Alas!
  You are not hid from me; I know you clearly,
  And though in darkness, still I hear your
    voice.   1310
CHORUS   O dreadful doer, how did you so endure
  To quench your eyes? What daimon drove you
    on?
    Strophe B
OEDIPUS   Apollo it was, Apollo, friends
  Who brought to pass these evil, evil woes of
    mine.
  The hand of no one struck my eyes but
    wretched me.
  For why should I see,
  When nothing sweet there is to see with sight?
CHORUS   This is just as you say.
OEDIPUS   What more is there for me to see,
  My friends, what to love,   1320
  What joy to hear a greeting?
  Lead me at once away from here,
  Lead me away, friends, wretched as I am,
  Accursed, and hated most
  Of mortals to the gods.
CHORUS   Wretched alike in mind and in your
    fortune,
  How I wish that I had never known you.
    Antistrophe B
OEDIPUS   May he perish, whoever freed me
  From fierce bonds on my feet,
  Snatched me from death and saved me, doing
    me no joy.   1330
  For if then I had died, I should not be
  So great a grief to friends and to myself.
CHORUS   This also is my wish.
OEDIPUS   I would not have come to murder my
    father,
  Nor have been called among men
  The bridegroom of her from whom I was born.
  But as it is I am godless, child of
    unholiness,
  Wretched sire in common with my father.
  And if there is any evil older than evil left,
  It is the lot of Oedipus.   1340
CHORUS   I know not how I could give you good
    advice,
  For you would be better dead than living blind.
OEDIPUS   That how things are was not done for
    the best—
  Teach me not this, or give me more
    advice.

If I had sight, I know not with what eyes
I could ever face my father among the dead,
Or my wretched mother. What I have done to
    them
Is too great for a noose to expiate.
Do you think the sight of my children would
    be a joy
For me to see, born as they were to me?   1350
No, never for these eyes of mine to see.
Nor the city, nor the tower, nor the sacred
Statues of gods; of these I deprive myself,
Noblest among the Thebans, born and bred,
Now suffering everything. I tell you all
To exile me as impious, shown by the gods
Untouchable and of the race of Laius.
When I uncovered such a stain on me,
Could I look with steady eyes upon the people?
No, No! And if there were a way to block   1360
The spring of hearing, I would not forbear
To lock up wholly this my wretched body.
I should be blind and deaf.—For it is sweet
When thought can dwell outside our evils.
Alas, Cithaeron, why did you shelter me?
Why did you not take and kill me at once, so I
Might never reveal to men whence I was born?
O Polybus, O Corinth, O my father's halls,
Ancient in fable, what an outer fairness,
A festering of evils, you raised in me.   1370
For now I am evil found, and born of evil.
O the three paths! Alas the hidden glen,
The grove of oak, the narrow triple roads
That drank from my own hands my father's
    blood.
Do you remember any of the deeds
I did before you then on my way here
And what I after did? O wedlock, wedlock!
You gave me birth, and then spawned in return
Issue from the selfsame seed; you revealed
Father, brother, children, in blood relation,   1380
The bride both wife and mother, and whatever
Actions are done most shameful among men.
But it is wrong to speak what is not good to
    do.
By the gods, hide me at once outside our
    land,
Or murder me, or hurl me in the sea
Where you shall never look on me again.
Come, venture to lay your hands on this
    wretched man.
Do it. Be not afraid. No mortal man
There is, except myself, to bear my evils.
CHORUS   Here is Creon, just in time for what you
    ask   1390
To work and to advise, for he alone
Is left in place of you to guard the land.
OEDIPUS   Alas, what word, then, shall I tell this
    man?

What righteous ground of trust is clear
    in me,
As in the past in all I have done him evil?
CREON   Oedipus, I have not come to laugh at
    you,
Nor to reproach you for your former wrongs.
        (*To the attendants*)
If you defer no longer to mortal offspring,
Respect at least the all-nourishing flame   1400
Of Apollo, lord of the sun. Fear to display
So great a pestilence, which neither earth
Nor holy rain nor light will well receive.
But you, conduct him to the house at once.
It is most pious for the kin alone
To hear and to behold the family sins.
OEDIPUS   By the gods, since you have plucked me
    from my fear,
Most noble, facing this most vile man,
Hear me one word—I will speak for you, not
    me.
CREON   What desire do you so persist to get?   1410
OEDIPUS   As soon as you can, hurl me from this
    land
To where no mortal man will ever greet me.
CREON   I would do all this, be sure. But I want
    first
To find out from the god what must be done.
OEDIPUS   His oracle, at least, is wholly clear;
Leave me to ruin, an impious parricide.
CREON   Thus spake the oracle. Still, as we stand
It is better to find out sure what we should do.
OEDIPUS   Will you inquire about so wretched a
    man?
CREON   Yes. You will surely put trust in the
    god.   1420
OEDIPUS   I order you and beg you, give the
    woman
Now in the house such burial as you yourself
Would want. Do last rites justly for your kin.
But may this city never be condemned—
My father's realm—because I live within.
Let me live in the mountains where Cithaeron
Yonder has fame of me, which father and
    mother
When they were alive established as my
    tomb.
There I may die by those who sought to kill
    me.
And yet this much I know, neither a
    sickness   1430
Nor anything else can kill me. I would not
Be saved from death, except for some dread
    evil.
Well, let my fate go wherever it may.
As for my sons, Creon, assume no trouble;
They are men and will have no difficulty
Of living wherever they may be.

O my poor grievous daughters, who never
  knew
Their dinner table set apart from me,
But always shared in everything I touched—
Take care of them for me, and first of all   1440
Allow me to touch them and bemoan our ills.
Grant it, lord,
Grant it, noble. If with my hand I touch
  them
I would think I had them just as when I could
  see.

  (Creon's attendants bring in ANTIGONE *and*
  ISMENE.*)*

What's that?
By the gods, can it be I hear my dear ones
  weeping?
And have you taken pity on me, Creon?
Have you had my darling children sent to me?
Do I speak right?
CREON   You do. For it was I who brought them
  here,   1450
  Knowing this present joy your joy of old.
OEDIPUS   May you fare well. For their coming
  may the spirit
  That watches over you be better than mine.
My children, where are you? Come to me,
  come
Into your brother's hands, that brought about
Your father's eyes, once bright, to see like
  this.
Your father, children, who, seeing and knowing
  nothing,
Became a father whence he was got himself.
I weep also for you—I cannot see you—
To think of the bitter life in days to come   1460
Which you will have to lead among mankind.
What citizens' gatherings will you approach?
What festivals attend, where you will
  not cry
When you go home, instead of gay rejoicing?
And when you arrive at marriageable age,
What man, my daughters, will there be to
  chance you,
Incurring such reproaches on his head,
Disgraceful to my children and to yours?
What evil will be absent, when your father
Killed his own father, sowed seed in her who
  bore him,   1470
From whom he was born himself, and
  equally
Has fathered you whence he himself was born.
Such will be the reproaches. Who then will wed
  you?
My children, there is no one for you. Clearly
You must decay in barrenness, unwed.
Son of Menoeceus—since you are alone

Left as a father to them, for we who produced
  them
Are both in ruin—see that you never let
These girls wander as beggars without
  husbands,
Let them not fall into such woes as mine.   1480
But pity them, seeing how young they are
To be bereft of all except your aid.
Grant this, my noble friend, with a touch of
  your hand.
My children, if your minds were now mature,
I would give you much advice. But, pray this
  for me,
To live as the time allows, to find a life
Better than that your siring father had.
CREON   You have wept enough here, come, and
  go inside the house.
OEDIPUS   I must obey, though nothing sweet.
CREON   All things are good in their time.   1490
OEDIPUS   Do you know in what way I go?
CREON   Tell me, I'll know when I hear.
OEDIPUS   Send me outside the land.
CREON   You ask what the god will do.
OEDIPUS   But to the gods I am hated.
CREON   Still, it will soon be done.
OEDIPUS   Then you agree?
CREON   What I think not I would not say in
  vain.
OEDIPUS   Now lead me away.
CREON   Come then, but let the children go.   1500
OEDIPUS   Do not take them from me.
CREON   Wish not to govern all,
  For what you ruled will not follow you
    through life.
CHORUS   Dwellers in native Thebes, behold this
  Oedipus
  Who solved the famous riddle, was your
    mightiest man.
  What citizen on his lot did not with envy gaze?
  See to how great a surge of dread fate he has
    come!
  So I would say a mortal man, while he is
    watching
  To see the final day, can have no happiness
  Till he pass the bound of life, nor be relieved of
    pain.   1510

Plato
from PHAEDO

The Phaedo *describes Socrates' last hours, spent discussing
with his friends the immortality of the soul, and ends with
his death. A number of ideas Plato developed further in
later works appear in this extract. Belief in the immortal
nature of the soul is reinforced by a conviction that during
life the soul is trapped in the body and thereby prevented
from attaining its full powers. This emphasis on the superi-*

ority of spiritual to material values had a great appeal for later Christian philosophers.

[Socrates is speaking.] "Now then, I want to give the proof at once, to you as my judges, why I think it likely that one who has spent his life in philosophy should be confident when he is going to die, and have good hopes that he will win the greatest blessings in the next world when he has ended: so Simmias and Cebes my judges, I will try to show how this could be true.

"The fact is, those who tackle philosophy aright are simply and solely practising dying, practising death, all the time, but nobody sees it. If this is true, then it would surely be unreasonable that they should earnestly do this and nothing else all their lives, yet when death comes they should object to what they had been so long earnestly practising."

Simmias laughed at this, and said, "I don't feel like laughing just now, Socrates, but you have made me laugh. I think the many if they heard that would say, 'That's a good one for the philosophers!' And other people in my city would heartily agree that philosophers are really suffering from a wish to die, and now they have found them out, that they richly deserve it!"

"That would be true, Simmias," said Socrates, "except the words 'found out.' For they have not found out in what sense the real philosophers wish to die and deserve to die, and what kind of death it is. Let us say good-bye to them," he went on, "and ask ourselves: Do we think there is such a thing as death?"

"Certainly," Simmias put in.

"Is it anything more than the separation of the soul from the body?" said Socrates. "Death is, that the body separates from the soul, and remains by itself apart from the soul, and the soul, separated from the body, exists by itself apart from the body. Is death anything but that?"

"No," he said, "that is what death is."

"Then consider, my good friend, if you agree with me here, for I think this is the best way to understand the question we are examining. Do you think it the part of a philosopher to be earnestly concerned with what are called pleasures, such as these—eating and drinking, for example?"

"Not at all," said Simmias.

"The pleasures of love, then?"

"Oh no."

"Well, do you suppose a man like that regards the other bodily indulgences as precious? Getting fine clothes and shoes and other bodily adornments—ought he to price them high or low, beyond whatever share of them it is absolutely necessary to have?"

"Low, I think," he said, "if he is a true philosopher."

"Then in general," he said, "do you think that such a man's concern is not for the body, but as far as he can he stands aloof from that and turns towards the soul?"

"I do."

"Then firstly, is it not clear that in such things the philosopher as much as possible sets free the soul from communion with the body, more than other men?"

"So it appears."

"And I suppose, Simmias, it must seem to most men that he who has no pleasure in such things and takes no share in them does not deserve to live, but he is getting pretty close to death if he does not care about pleasures which he has by means of the body."

"Quite true, indeed."

"Well then, what about the actual getting of wisdom? Is the body in the way or not, if a man takes it with him as companion in the search? I mean, for example, is there any truth for men in their sight and hearing? Or as poets are forever dinning into our ears, do we hear nothing and see nothing exactly? Yet if these of our bodily senses are not exact and clear, the others will hardly be, for they are all inferior to these, don't you think so?"

"Certainly," he said.

"Then," said he, "when does the soul get hold of the truth? For whenever the soul tries to examine anything in company with the body, it is plain that it is deceived by it."

"Quite true."

"Then is it not clear that in reasoning, if anywhere, something of the realities becomes visible to it?"

"Yes."

"And I suppose it reasons best when none of these senses disturbs it, hearing or sight, or pain, or pleasure indeed, but when it is completely by itself and says good-bye to the body, and so far as possible has no dealings with it, when it reaches out and grasps that which really is."

"That is true."

"And is it not then that the philosopher's soul chiefly holds the body cheap and escapes from it, while it seeks to be by itself?"

"So it seems."

"Let us pass on, Simmias. Do we say there is such a thing as justice by itself, or not?"

"We do say so, certainly!"

"Such a thing as the good and beautiful?"

"Of course!"

"And did you ever see one of them with your eyes?"

"Never," said he.

"By any other sense of those the body has did you ever grasp them? I mean all such things, greatness, health, strength, in short everything that really is the nature of things whatever they are: Is it through the body that the real truth is perceived? Or is this better— whoever of us prepares himself most completely and most exactly to comprehend each thing which he examines would come nearest to knowing each one?"

"Certainly."

"And would he do that most purely who should approach each with his intelligence alone, not adding sight to intelligence, or dragging in any other sense along with reasoning, but using the intelligence uncontaminated alone by itself, while he tries to hunt out each essence uncontaminated, keeping clear of eyes and ears and, one might say, of the whole body, because he thinks the body disturbs him and hinders the soul from getting possession of truth and wisdom when body and soul are companions—is not this the man, Simmias, if anyone, who will hit reality?"

"Nothing could be more true, Socrates," said Simmias.

"Then from all this," said Socrates, "genuine philosophers must come to some such opinion as follows, so as to make to one another statements such as these: 'A sort of direct path, so to speak, seems to take us to the conclusion that so long as we have the body with us in our enquiry, and our soul is mixed up with so great an evil, we shall never attain sufficiently what we desire, and that, we say, is the truth. For the body provides thousands of busy distractions because of its necessary food; besides, if diseases fall upon us, they hinder us from the pursuit of the real. With loves and desires and fears and all kinds of fancies and much rubbish, it infects us, and really and truly makes us, as they say, unable to think one little bit about anything at any time. Indeed, wars and factions and battles all come from the body and its desires, and from nothing else. For the desire of getting wealth causes all wars, and we are compelled to desire wealth by the body, being slaves to its culture; therefore we have no leisure for philosophy, from all these reasons. Chief of all is that if we do have some leisure, and turn away from the body to speculate on something, in our searches it is everywhere interfering, it causes confusion and disturbance, and dazzles us so that it will not let us see the truth; so in fact we see that if we are ever to know anything purely we must get rid of it, and examine the real things by the soul alone; and then, it seems, after we are dead, as the reasoning shows, not while we live, we shall possess that which we desire, lovers of which we say we are, namely wisdom. For if it is impossible in company with the body to know anything purely, one thing of two follows: either knowledge is possible nowhere, or only after death; for then alone the soul will be quite by itself apart from the body, but not before. And while we are alive, we shall be nearest to knowing, as it seems, if as far as possible we have no commerce or communion with the body which is not absolutely necessary, and if we are not infected with its nature, but keep ourselves pure from it, until God himself shall set us free. And so, pure and rid of the body's foolishness, we shall probably be in the company of those like ourselves, and shall know through our own selves complete incontamination, and that is perhaps the truth. But for the impure to grasp the pure is not, it seems, allowed.' So we must think, Simmias, and so we must say to one another, all who are rightly lovers of learning; don't you agree?"

"Assuredly, Socrates."

"Then," said Socrates, "if this is true, my comrade, there is great hope that when I arrive where I am travelling, there if anywhere I shall sufficiently possess that for which all our study has been pursued in this past life. So the journey which has been commanded for me is made with good hope, and the same for any other man who believes he has got his mind purified, as I may call it."

"Certainly," replied Simmias.

"And is not purification really that which has been mentioned so often in our discussion, to separate as far as possible the soul from the body, and to accustom it to collect itself together out of the body in every part, and to dwell alone by itself as far as it can, both at this present and in the future, being freed from the body as if from a prison?"

"By all means," said he.

"Then is not this called death—a freeing and separation of soul from body?"

"Not a doubt of that," said he.

"But to set it free, as we say, is the chief endeavour of those who rightly love wisdom, nay of those alone, and the very care and practice of the philosophers is nothing but the freeing and separation of soul from body, don't you think so?"

"It appears to be so."

"Then, as I said at first, it would be absurd for a man preparing himself in his life to be as near as possible to death, so to live, and then when death came, to object?"

"Of course."

"Then in fact, Simmias," he said, "those who rightly love wisdom are practising dying, and death to them is the least terrible thing in the world. Look at it in this way: If they are everywhere at enmity with the body, and desire the soul to be alone by itself, and if, when this very thing happens, they shall fear and object—would not that be wholly unreasonable? Should they not willingly go to a place where there is good hope of finding what they were in love with all through life (and they loved wisdom), and of ridding themselves of the companion which they hated? When human favourites and wives and sons have died, many have been willing to go down to the grave, drawn by the hope of seeing there those they used to desire, and of being with them; but one who is really in love with wisdom and holds firm to this same hope, that he will find it in the grave, and nowhere else worth speaking of—will he then fret at dying and not go thither rejoicing? We must surely think, my comrade, that he will go rejoicing, if he is really a philosopher; he will surely believe that he will find wisdom in its purity there and there alone. If this is true, would it not be most unreasonable, as I said just now, if such a one feared death?"

"Unreasonable, I do declare," said he.

The Phaedo ends with one of the most famous of all passages in Greek literature, the description of Socrates' death. His last words have been interpreted in many different ways. Asclepius was the god of healing, and Socrates may perhaps be reminding his friends that death, by releasing the soul, is the final cure for bodily ills.

. . . he got up and retired into another room for the bath, and Criton went after him, telling us to wait. So we waited discussing and talking together about what had been said, or sometimes speaking of the great misfortune which had befallen us, for we felt really as if we had lost a father and had to spend the rest of our lives as orphans. When he had bathed, and his children had been brought to see him—for he had two little sons, and one big—and when the women of his family had come, he talked to them before Criton and gave what instructions he wished. Then he asked the women and children to go, and came back to us. It was now near sunset, for he had spent a long time within. He came and sat down after his bath, and he had not talked long after this when the servant of the Eleven came in, and standing by him said, "O Socrates! I have not to complain of you as I do of others, that they are angry with me, and curse me, because I bring them word to drink their potion, which my officers make me do! But I have always found you in this time most generous and gentle, and the best man who ever came here. And now too, I know well you are not angry with me, for you know who are responsible, and you keep it for them. Now you know what I came to tell you, so farewell, and try to bear as well as you can what can't be helped."

Then he turned and was going out, with tears running down his cheeks. And Socrates looked up at him and said, "Farewell to you also, I will do so." Then, at the same time turning to us, "What a nice fellow!" he said. "All the time he has been coming and talking to me, a real good sort, and now how generously he sheds tears for me! Come along, Criton, let's obey him. Someone bring the potion, if the stuff has been ground; if not, let the fellow grind it."

Then Criton said, "But, Socrates, I think the sun is still over the hills, it has not set yet. Yes, and I know of others who, having been told to drink the poison, have done it very late; they had dinner first and a good one, and some enjoyed the company of any they wanted. Please don't be in a hurry, there is time to spare."

But Socrates said, "Those you speak of have very good reason for doing that, for they think they will gain by doing it; and I have good reasons why I won't do it. For I think I shall gain nothing by drinking a little later, only that I shall think myself a fool for clinging to life and sparing when the cask's empty. Come along," he said, "do what I tell you, if you please."

And Criton, hearing this, nodded to the boy who stood near. The boy went out, and after spending a long time, came in with the man who was to give the poison carrying it ground ready in a cup. Socrates caught sight of the man and said, "Here, my good man, you know about these things; what must I do?"

"Just drink it," he said, "and walk about till your legs get heavy, then lie down. In that way the drug will act of itself."

At the same time, he held out the cup to Socrates, and he took it quite cheerfully, Echecrates, not a tremble, not a change in colour or looks; but looking full at the man under his brows, as he used to do, he asked him, "What do you say about this drink? What of a libation to someone? Is that allowed, or not?"

He said, "We only grind so much as we think enough for a moderate potion."

"I understand," he said, "but at least, I suppose, it is allowed to offer a prayer to the gods and that must be done, for good luck in the migration from here to there. Then that is my prayer, and so may it be!"

With these words he put the cup to his lips and, quite easy and contented, drank it up. So far most of us had been able to hold back our tears pretty well; but when we saw him begin drinking and end drinking, we could no longer. I burst into a flood of tears for all I could do, so I wrapped up my face and cried myself out; not for him indeed, but for my own misfortune in losing such a man and such a comrade. Criton had got up and gone out even before I did, for he could not hold the tears in. Apollodoros had never ceased weeping all this time, and now he burst out into loud sobs, and by his weeping and lamentations completely broke down every man there except Socrates himself. He only said, "What a scene! You amaze me. That's just why I sent the women away, to keep them from making a scene like this. I've heard that one ought to make an end in decent silence. Quiet yourselves and endure."

When we heard him we felt ashamed and restrained our tears. He walked about, and when he said that his legs were feeling heavy, he lay down on his back, as the man told him to do; at the same time the one who gave him the potion felt him, and after a while examined his feet and legs; then pinching a foot hard, he asked if he felt anything; he said no. After this, again, he pressed the shins; and, moving up like this, he showed us that he was growing cold and stiff. Again he felt him, and told us that when it came to his heart, he would be gone. Already the cold had come nearly as far as the abdomen, when Socrates threw off the covering from his face—for he had covered it over—and said, the last words he uttered, "Criton," he said, "we owe a cock to Asclepios; pay it without fail."

"That indeed shall be done," said Criton. "Have you anything more to say?"

When Criton had asked this, Socrates gave no further answer, but after a little time, he stirred, and the man uncovered him, and his eyes were still. Criton, seeing this, closed the mouth and eyelids.

This was the end of our comrade, Echecrates, a man, as we would say, of all then living we had ever met, the noblest and the wisest and most just.

Plato
THE REPUBLIC, Book VII

The Allegory of the Cave

In The Republic *Plato describes his version of the ideal society. The role of education and the function of the philosopher within this society are defined in an elaborate metaphor, the Allegory of the Cave. We are to imagine a group of people who live, as it were, chained to the ground in an underground cave in such a way that they can see only shadows of reality projected onto the inner wall of the cave by firelight behind them. Since they have been accustomed to seeing nothing but shadows all their lives they have no way of comprehending the real world outside the cave. It is therefore the task of the philosopher, who is already free from the chains of misconception, to liberate the others and educate them in such a way as to set them free from the imprisonment of the senses.*

"Next, then," I said, "take the following parable of education and ignorance as a picture of the condition of our nature. Imagine mankind as dwelling in an underground cave with a long entrance open to the light across the whole width of the cave; in this they have been from childhood, with necks and legs fettered, so they have to stay where they are. They cannot move their heads round because of the fetters, and they can only look forward, but light comes to them from fire burning behind them higher up at a distance. Between the fire and the prisoners is a road above their level, and along it imagine a low wall has been built, as puppet showmen have screens in front of their people over which they work their puppets."

"I see," he said.

"See, then, bearers carrying along this wall all sorts of articles which they hold projecting above the wall, statues of men and other living things, made of stone or wood and all kinds of stuff, some of the bearers speaking and some silent, as you might expect."

"What a remarkable image," he said, "and what remarkable prisoners!"

"Just like ourselves," I said. "For, first of all, tell me this: What do you think such people would have seen of themselves and each other except their shadows, which the fire cast on the opposite wall of the cave?"

"I don't see how they could see anything else," said he, "if they were compelled to keep their heads unmoving all their lives!"

"Very well, what of the things being carried along? Would not this be the same?"

"Of course it would."

"Suppose the prisoners were able to talk together, don't you think that when they named the shadows which they saw passing they would believe they were naming things?"

"Necessarily."

"Then if their prison had an echo from the opposite wall, whenever one of the passing bearers uttered a sound, would they not suppose that the passing shadow must be making the sound? Don't you think so?"

"Indeed I do," he said.

"If so," said I, "such persons would certainly believe that there were no realities except those shadows of handmade things."

"So it must be," said he.

"Now consider," said I, "what their release would be like, and their cure from these fetters and their folly; let us imagine whether it might naturally be something like this. One might be released, and compelled suddenly to stand up and turn his neck round, and to walk and look towards the firelight; all this would hurt him, and he would be too much dazzled to see distinctly those things whose shadows he had seen before. What do you think he would say, if someone told him that what he saw before was foolery, but now he saw more rightly, being a bit nearer reality and turned towards what was a little more real? What if he were shown each of the passing things, and compelled by questions to answer what each one was? Don't you think he would be puzzled, and believe what he saw before was more true than what was shown to him now?"

"Far more," he said.

"Then suppose he were compelled to look towards the real light, it would hurt his eyes, and he would escape by turning them away to the things which he was able to look at, and these he would believe to be clearer than what was being shown to him."

"Just so," said he.

"Suppose, now," said I, "that someone should

drag him thence by force, up the rough ascent, the steep way up, and never stop until he could drag him out into the light of the sun, would he not be distressed and furious at being dragged; and when he came into the light, the brilliance would fill his eyes and he would not be able to see even one of the things now called real?"

"That he would not," said he, "all of a sudden."

"He would have to get used to it, surely, I think, if he is to see the things above. First he would most easily look at shadows, after that images of mankind and the rest in water, lastly the things themselves. After this he would find it easier to survey by night the heavens themselves and all that is in them, gazing at the light of the stars and moon, rather than by day the sun and the sun's light."

"Of course."

"Last of all, I suppose, the sun; he could look on the sun itself by itself in its own place, and see what it is like, not reflections of it in water or as it appears in some alien setting."

"Necessarily," said he.

"And only after all this he might reason about it, how this is he who provides seasons and years, and is set over all there is in the visible region, and he is in a manner the cause of all things which they saw."

"Yes, it is clear," said he, "that after all that, he would come to this last."

"Very good. Let him be reminded of his first habitation, and what was wisdom in that place, and of his fellow-prisoners there; don't you think he would bless himself for the change, and pity them?"

"Yes, indeed."

"And if there were honours and praises among them and prizes for the one who saw the passing things most sharply and remembered best which of them used to come before and which after and which together, and from these was best able to prophesy accordingly what was going to come—do you believe he would set his desire on that, and envy those who were honoured men or potentates among them? Would he not feel as Homer says, and heartily desire rather to be serf of some landless man on earth and to endure anything in the world, rather than to opine as they did and to live in that way?"

"Yes indeed," said he, "he would rather accept anything than live like that."

"Then again," I said, "just consider; if such a one should go down again and sit on his old seat, would he not get his eyes full of darkness coming in suddenly out of the sun?"

"Very much so," said he.

"And if he should have to compete with those who had been always prisoners, by laying down the law about those shadows while he was blinking before his eyes were settled down—and it would take a good long time to get used to things—wouldn't they all laugh at him and say he had spoiled his eyesight by going up there, and it was not worth-while so much as to try to go up? And would they not kill anyone who tried to release them and take them up, if they could somehow lay hands on him and kill him?"

"That they would!" said he.

"Then we must apply this image, my dear Glaucon," said I, "to all we have been saying. The world of our sight is like the habitation in prison, the firelight there to the sunlight here, the ascent and the view of the upper world is the rising of the soul into the world of mind; put it so and you will not be far from my own surmise, since that is what you want to hear; but God knows if it is really true. At least, what appears to me is, that in the world of the known, last of all, is the idea of the good, and with what toil to be seen! And seen, this must be inferred to be the cause of all right and beautiful things for all, which gives birth to light and the king of light in the world of sight, and, in the world of mind, herself the queen produces truth and reason; and she must be seen by one who is to act with reason publicly or privately."

"I believe as you do," he said, "in so far as I am able."

"Then believe also, as I do," said I, "and do not be surprised, that those who come thither are not willing to have part in the affairs of men, but their souls ever strive to remain above; for that surely may be expected if our parable fits the case."

"Quite so," he said.

"Well then," said I, "do you think it surprising if one leaving divine contemplations and passing to the evils of men is awkward and appears to be a great fool, while he is still blinking—not yet accustomed to the darkness around him, but compelled to struggle in law courts or elsewhere about shadows of justice, or the images which make the shadows, and to quarrel about notions of justice in those who have never seen justice itself?"

"Not surprising at all," said he.

"But any man of sense," I said, "would remember that the eyes are doubly confused from two different causes, both in passing from light to darkness and from darkness to light; and believing that the same things happen with regard to the soul also, whenever he sees a soul confused and unable to discern anything he would not just laugh carelessly; he would examine whether it had come out of a more brilliant life, and if it were darkened by the strangeness; or whether it had come out of greater ignorance into a more brilliant light, and if it were dazzled with the brighter illumination. Then only would he congratulate the one soul upon its happy experience and way of life, and pity the other; but if he must laugh, his laugh would be a less downright laugh than his laughter at the soul which came out of the light above."

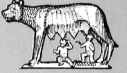

ROMAN REPUBLIC

753 B.C.

753 B.C. Founding of Rome (traditional date)

c. 700 Development of Etruscan culture

509

Conquest of Italy and Mediterranean

509 Expulsion of Etruscan kings and foundation of Roman Republic

c. 390 Sack of Rome by Gauls

264–241 First Punic War: Roman conquest of Sicily, Sardinia, Corsica

218–201 Second Punic War: Roman conquest of Spain

146 Destruction of Carthage: Africa becomes Roman province. Sack of Corinth: Greece becomes Roman province

c. 200–160 B.C. Ennius, *Annales*, epic poem; Plautus, *Mostellaria*, Roman comedy; Terence, Roman comedies

2nd cent. Epicureanism and Stoicism imported to Rome

133

Political Crisis at Rome

90–88 Social War

82–81 Sulla dictator at Rome

60 First Triumvirate: Pompey, Caesar, Crassus

58–56 Caesar conquers Gaul

48 Battle of Pharsalus: war of Caesar and Pompey ends in death of Pompey. Caesar meets Cleopatra in Egypt

46–44 Caesar rules Rome as dictator until assassinated

43 Second Triumvirate: Antony, Lepidus, Octavian

c. 65–43 Lucretius, *On the Nature of Things*, Epicurean poem; Cicero, orations and philosophical essays; Catullus, lyric poems; Caesar, *Commentaries*, on Gallic wars

31

31 Battle of Actium won by Octavian

30 Death of Antony and Cleopatra

27–14 Octavian under name of Augustus rules as first Roman emperor

c. 27 B.C.–A.D. 14 Horace, *Odes* and *Ars Poetica*; Vergil, *Aeneid, Georgics, Eclogues*; Ovid, *Metamorphoses*, mythological tales; Livy, *Annals of the Roman People*

B.C.

c. 6 Birth of Jesus; crucified c. A.D. 30

A.D.

ROMAN EMPIRE

Stability

A.D. 14–68 Julio-Claudian emperors: Tiberius, Caligula, Claudius, Nero

69–96 Flavian emperors: Vespasian, Titus, Domitian

70 Capture of Jerusalem by Titus; destruction of Solomon's Temple

79 Destruction of Pompeii and Herculaneum

96–138 Adoptive emperors: Nerva, Trajan, Hadrian, et al.

138–192 Antonine emperors: Antoninus Pius, Marcus Aurelius, et al.

c. A.D. 100–150 Tacitus, *History*; Juvenal, *Satires*; Pliny the Younger, *Letters*; Suetonius, *Lives of the Caesars*; Epictetus, *Enchiridion*, on Stoicism

c. 166–179 Marcus Aurelius, *Meditations*, on Stoicism

180

Disinte-gration

193–235 Severan emperors: Septimius Severus, Caracalla, et al.

212 Edict of Caracalla

284

Reconstruction and Decline

284–305 Reign of Diocletian; return of civil order

301 Edict of Diocletian, fixing wages and prices

307–337 Reign of Constantine; sole emperor after 324

330 Founding of Constantinople

392 Paganism officially suppressed; Christianity made state religion

409–455 Vandals and Visigoths invade Italy, Spain, Gaul, Africa

476 Romulus Augustulus forced to abdicate as last Western Roman emperor

476 A.D.

4

The Roman Legacy

c. 650–500 B.C.
Influence of Greek and
Orientalizing styles
on Etruscan art

late 6th cent.
Etruscan
Apollo,
from Veii

c. 616–509 B.C.
Etruscans drain
marshes, build temples,
construct roads

Extension of Greek
trumpet into Roman
tuba, used in games,
processions, battles

c. 2nd cent B.C. Greek
music becomes popular
at Rome

1st cent. Discovery
of concrete

1st cent. Realistic
portraiture; *Portrait
of Cicero*

c. 82 Sulla commissions
Sanctuary of Fortuna
Primagenia,
Praeneste

c. 30 B.C.–A.D. 30
Villa of Mysteries
frescoes, Pompeii

c. 20 *View of a Garden,*
fresco from Augustus'
villa, Prima Porta

13–9 *Ara Pacis*

Use of arch,
vault, dome,
principles of stress/
counterstress

c. A.D. 14
*Augustus
of Prima
Porta*

1st cent. A.D. Pont du
Gard, Nîmes; atrium-
style houses at Pompeii

c. 126 Pantheon,
Rome

Decline of realism

300–305 Diocletian's
palace, Split

306–315 Basilica of
Constantine, Rome

324–330 Colossal head
from Basilica of
Constantine, Rome

The Importance of Rome

The contribution of Rome to the development of Western civilization is tremendous. In fields like language, law, politics, religion, and art Roman culture continues to affect our lives. The road network of modern Europe is based on one planned and built by the Romans some two thousand years ago; the alphabet we use is the Roman alphabet; and the division of the year into twelve months of unequal length is a modified form of the calendar introduced by Julius Caesar in 45 B.C. Even after the fall of the Roman Empire the city of Rome stood for centuries as the symbol of civilization itself; later empires deliberately shaped themselves on the Roman model.

The enormous impact of Rome on our culture is partly the result of the industrious and determined character of the Romans themselves, who very early in their history saw themselves as the divinely appointed rulers of the world. In the course of fulfilling their mission they spread Roman culture from the north of England to Africa, from Spain to India (see map). This Romanization of the entire known world permitted the spread of ideas the Romans had drawn from other peoples. It was through the Romans that Greek art and literature were handed down into the Western tradition, not from the Greeks themselves. The rapid spread of Christianity in the 4th century A.D. was a result of the decision of the Roman emperors to adopt it as the official religion of the Roman Empire. In these and in other respects, the legacy Rome was to pass on to Western civilization had been inherited from its predecessors.

The Romans themselves were surprisingly modest about their own cultural achievements, in fact, believing that their strengths lay in good government and military prowess rather than in artistic and intellectual attainments. It was their view that Rome should get on with the job of ruling the world and leave luxuries like sculpture and astronomy to others.

It is easy but unfair to accept the Romans' estimate of themselves as uncreative without questioning it. True, in some fields the Roman contribution was not very impressive. What little we know about Roman music, for example, suggests that its loss is hardly a serious one. It was intended mainly for performance at religious events like weddings and funerals, and as a background for social occasions. Musicians were often brought into aristocratic homes to provide after-dinner entertainment at a party, and individual performers, frequently women, would play before small groups in a domestic setting. Small bands of traveling musicians, playing on pipes and such percussion instruments as cymbals and tambourines, provided background music for the acrobats and jugglers who performed in public squares and during gladiatorial contests [4.1].

Nonetheless, for the Romans music certainly had none of the intellectual and philosophical significance it bore for the Greeks, and when Roman writers mention musical performances it is often to complain about the noise. The only serious development in Roman music was the extension of the Greek trumpet into a longer and louder bronze instrument known as the *tuba,* which was used on public occasions like games and processions and in battle, when an especially powerful type some 4 feet (1.2 meters) long gave the signals for attack and retreat. The sound was not pleasant.

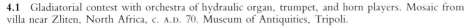

4.1 Gladiatorial contest with orchestra of hydraulic organ, trumpet, and horn players. Mosaic from villa near Zliten, North Africa, c. A.D. 70. Museum of Antiquities, Tripoli.

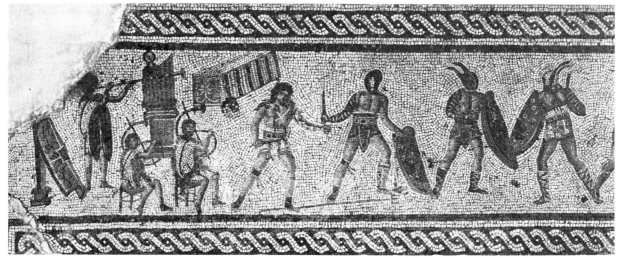

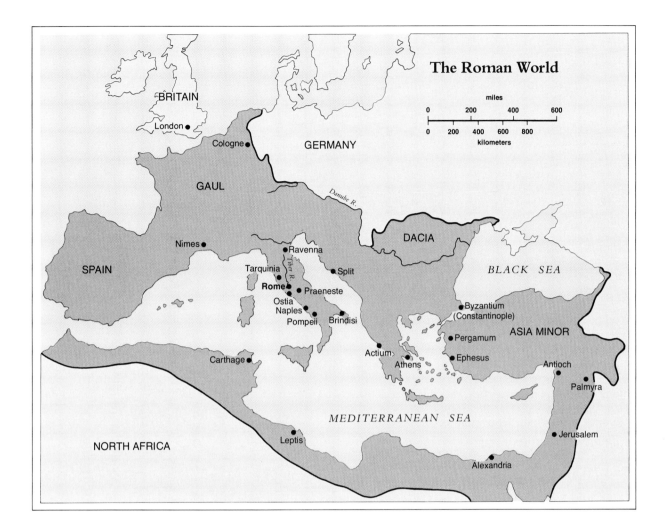

The Roman World

In general, Roman music-lovers contented themselves with Greek music played on Greek instruments. Although serious music began to grow in popularity with the spread of Greek culture, it always remained an aristocratic rather than popular taste. The emperor Nero's love of music, coupled with his insistence on giving public concerts on the lyre, may even have hastened his downfall.

In areas other than music, the Roman achievement is considerable. There is no doubt that Roman art and literature rarely show the originality of their Greek predecessors, but originality is not the only artistic virtue, nor is its absence always a defect. The Roman genius, in fact, lay precisely in absorbing and assimilating influences from outside and going on to create from them something typically Roman. The lyric poetry of 1st-century-B.C. writers like Catullus was inspired by the works of Sappho, Alcaeus, and other Greek poets of the 6th century B.C., but nothing could be more Roman in spirit than Catullus' poems.

In architecture, the Romans achieved a style that is one of the most impressive of all our legacies from the ancient world.

It is useful to emphasize the very real value of Roman art and literature because there has been a tendency since the 19th century to exalt the Greek cultural achievement at the expense of the Roman. All agree on the superior quality of Roman roads, sewers, and aqueducts; Roman sculpture or drama has in general been less highly rated, mainly because of comparisons with that of the Greeks. Any study of Roman culture inevitably involves examining the influences that went to make it up, and it is necessary always to remember the Roman ability to absorb and combine outside ideas and create something fresh from them.

Rome's history was a long one, beginning with the foundation of the city in the 8th century B.C. For the first two and a half centuries of its existence it was ruled by kings. The rest of the vast span of Roman

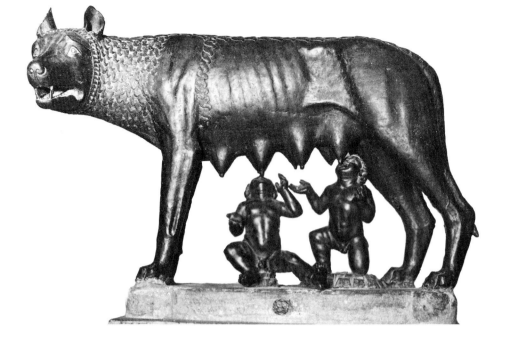

4.2 *Capitoline She-Wolf.* Etruscan, late 6th or early 5th century B.C. Bronze, length 4′4″ (1.32 m). Capitoline Museum, Rome. Although this statue or one very like it became the mascot of Rome, it was probably made by an Etruscan craftsman. The twins Romulus and Remus, legendary founders of the city, were added during the Renaissance.

history is divided into two long periods: Republican Rome (509–31 B.C.), during which time democratic government was first developed and then allowed to collapse; and Imperial Rome (31 B.C.–A.D. 476), during when the Roman world was ruled, at least in theory, by one man—the Emperor. The date A.D. 476 marks the deposition of the last Roman Emperor in the West; it forms a convenient, if artificial, terminus to the Imperial period (see page 152).

Shortly after the foundation of the Republic, the Romans began their conquest of neighboring peoples, first in Italy, then throughout Europe, Asia, and North Africa. As their territory grew, Roman civilization developed along with it, assimilating the cultures of the peoples who fell under Roman domination. But long before the Romans conquered Greece or anywhere else, they were themselves conquered by the Etruscans, and the story of Rome's rise to power truly begins with the impact on Roman life made by Etruscan rule there.

The Etruscans and Their Art

The late 8th century B.C. was a time of great activity in Italy. The Greeks had reached the south coast and Sicily. In the valley of the Tiber, farmers and herdsmen of a group of tribes known as the Latins (origin of the name of the language spoken by the Romans) were establishing small village settlements, one of

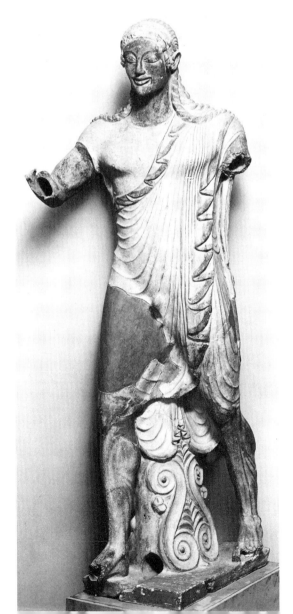

4.3 *Apollo of Veii.* Etruscan, late 6th or early 5th century B.C. Terra cotta, height 5′10″ (1.78 m). Museo Nazionale di Villa Giulia, Rome.

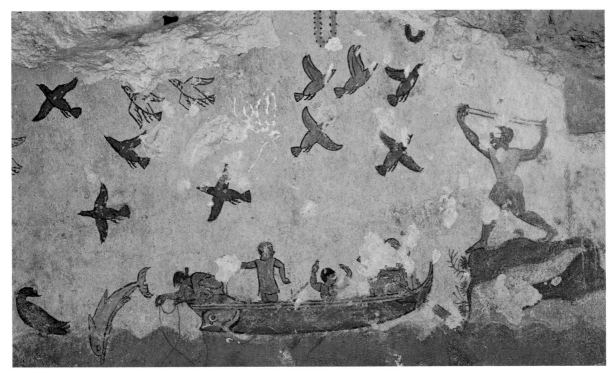

4.4 Wall painting from the Tomb of Hunting and Fishing, Tarquinia. c. 520 B.C. Fresco. Men, fish, and birds are all rendered naturalistically, with acute observation. Note the bird perched on the waves to the left of the diving fish and the hunter at right.

which was to become the future imperial city of Rome. The most flourishing area at the time, however, was to the north of Rome, where in central Italy a new culture—the Etruscan—was appearing.

The Etruscans are among the most intriguing of ancient peoples, and ever since early Roman times scholars have argued about who they were, where they came from, and what language they spoke. Even today, in spite of the discoveries of modern archaeologists, we still know little about the origins of the Etruscans and their language has still not been deciphered. By 700 B.C. they had established themselves in the part of Italy named for them, Tuscany; but it is not clear whether they arrived from abroad or whether their culture was a more developed form of an earlier Italian one. The ancient Greeks and Romans believed that the Etruscans had come to Italy from the East, perhaps from Lydia, an ancient kingdom in Asia Minor. Indeed, many aspects of their life and much of their art have pronounced Eastern characteristics. In other ways, however, the Etruscans have much in common with their predecessors in central Italy. Even so, no other culture related to the Etruscans' has ever been found. Whatever their origins, they were to have a major effect upon Italian life, and on the growth of Rome and its culture [4.2].

From the very beginning of their history the Etruscans showed an outstanding sophistication and technological ability. The sumptuous gold treasures buried in their tombs are evidence both of their material prosperity and of their superb craftsmanship. The commercial contacts of the Etruscans extended over most of the western Mediterranean, and in Italy itself Etruscan cities like Cerveteri and Tarquinia developed rich artistic traditions. Etruscan art has its own special character, a kind of elemental force almost primitive in spirit, although the craftsmanship and techniques are highly sophisticated. Unlike the Greeks, the Etruscans were less interested in intellectual problems of proportion or understanding how the human body works than in producing an immediate impact upon the viewer. The famous statue of Apollo found in 1916 at Veii [4.3] is unquestionably related to Greek models, but the tension of the god's pose and the sinister quality of his smile produce an effect of great power in a typically Etruscan way. Other Etruscan art is more relaxed, showing a love of nature rarely found in Greek art. The paintings in the Tomb of Hunting and Fishing at Tarquinia [4.4] convey a marvelous sense of light and air, the hazy blue background evoking the sensations of sea and spray.

This gifted people was bound to exert a strong influence on the development of civilization in Italy; Etruscan occupation of Rome from 616 to 510 B.C. marks a turning point in Roman history. According to later tradition, the city of Rome had been founded in 753 B.C. and was ruled in its earliest days by kings (in actual fact Rome was probably not much more than a small country town for most of this period). The later Romans' own grandiose picture of the early days of their city was intended to glamorize its origins, but only with the arrival of the Etruscans did anything like an urban center begin to develop. Etruscan engineers drained a large marshy area, previously uninhabitable, which became the community's center, the future Roman Forum. They built temples and shrines and constructed roads. Among other innovations the Etruscans introduced a number of things we are accustomed to think of as typically Roman, including public games like chariot racing and even the toga, the most characteristic form of Roman dress.

Most important, however, was the fact that under Etruscan domination the Romans found themselves for the first time in contact with the larger world. Instead of being simple villagers living in a small community governed by tribal chiefs they became part of a large cultural unit with links throughout Italy and abroad. Within a hundred years Rome had learned the lessons of Etruscan technology and culture, driven out the Etruscans, and begun her unrelenting climb to power.

The rise of Rome signaled the decline of the Etruscans throughout Italy. In centuries following their expulsion from Rome in 510 B.C., their cities were conquered and their territory taken over by the Romans. In the 1st century B.C. they automatically received the right of Roman citizenship and became absorbed into the Roman empire. The gradual collapse of their world is mirrored in later Etruscan art. The wall paintings in the tombs become increasingly gloomy, suggesting that for an Etruscan of the 3rd century B.C. the misfortunes of this life were followed by the tortures of the next. The old couple from Volterra whose anxious faces are so vividly depicted on the lid of their sarcophagus [4.5] give us some idea of the troubled spirit of the final days of Etruscan culture.

Republican Rome (509–31 B.C.)

With the expulsion of the Etruscans in 510 B.C., the Romans began their climb to power, free now to rule themselves. Instead of choosing a new king, Rome constituted itself a republic, governed by the people somewhat along the lines of the Greek city-states, although less democratically. Two chief magistrates or consuls were elected for a one-year term by all the male citizens, but the principal assembly, the Senate, drew most of its members from Roman aristocratic families. From the very beginning, therefore, power was concentrated in the hands of the upper class, the patricians, although the lower class (the plebeians) was permitted to form its own assembly. The leaders elected by the plebeian assembly, the tribunes, represented the plebeians' interests and protected them against state officials who treated them unjustly. The meeting place for both the Senate and the assemblies of the people was the *forum*, the large open space at the foot of the Palatine and Capitoline hills that had been drained and made habitable by the Etruscans [4.6].

From the founding of the Roman Republic to its

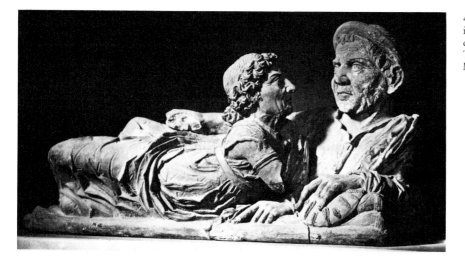

4.5 Lid of a funerary urn showing the dead couple whose ashes it contains. Etruscan, 1st century B.C. Terra cotta, length 18½″ (47 cm). Museo Guarnacci, Volterra.

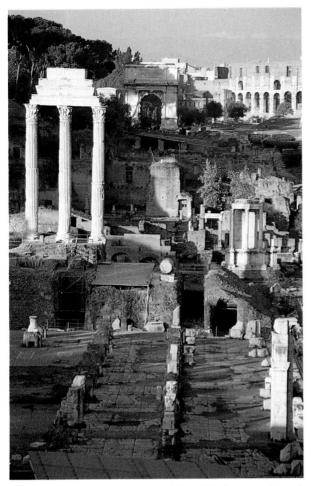

4.6 The Roman forum—center of the political, economic, and religious life of the Roman world—as it appears today.

the Middle East stretched a vast territory consisting of subject provinces, protectorates, and nominally free kingdoms, all of which depended on Roman good will and administrative efficiency.

Unfortunately, the Romans had been too busy in acquiring their empire to think very hard about how to rule it; the results were frequently chaotic. Provincial administration was incompetent and often corrupt. The long series of wars had hardened the Roman character, leading to insensitivity and, frequently, brutality in the treatment of conquered peoples. This situation was not helped by increasing political instability at home. The old balance of power struck between the patricians and plebeians was being increasingly disturbed by the rise of a middle class, many of whom were plebeians who had made their fortunes in the wars. Against this background were fought bitter struggles that eventually caused the collapse of the Republic.

By the 1st century B.C. it was apparent that the political system that had been devised for a thriving but small city five hundred years earlier was hopelessly inadequate for a vast empire. Discontent among Rome's Italian allies led to open revolt. Although the Romans were victorious in the Social War of 90–88 B.C. the cost in lives and economic stability was tremendous. The ineffectiveness of the Senate and the frustration of the Roman people led to a series of struggles among the leading statesmen for supreme power. The Roman general Sulla ruled as dictator for a brief and violent period beginning in 82 B.C., but suddenly resigned three years later, in 79 B.C. There followed a long-drawn-out series of political skirmishes between Pompey, the self-appointed defender of the Senate, and Julius Caesar, culminating in Caesar's withdrawal to Gaul and subsequent return to Rome in 49 B.C. After a short but bitter conflict Caesar defeated Pompey in 48 B.C. at the Battle of Pharsalus and returned to Rome as dictator, only to be assassinated himself in 44 B.C. The civil wars that followed brought the Republic to its unlamented end.

The years of almost uninterrupted violence had a profound effect upon the Roman character, and the relief felt when a new era dawned under the first emperor, Augustus, can only be fully appreciated in this light.

Literary Developments during the Republic

The Romans put most of their energy into political and military affairs, leaving little time for art or literature. By the 3rd century B.C., when most of the Mediterranean was under their control and they

bloody end in the civil wars following the murder of Julius Caesar in 44 B.C., its history was dominated by agitation for political equality. Yet the first major confrontation, the conflict between patricians and plebeians, never seriously endangered political stability in Rome or military campaigns abroad. Both sides showed a flexibility and spirit of compromise that produced a gradual growth in plebeian power while avoiding any split disastrous enough to interrupt Rome's growing domination of the Italian peninsula. The final plebeian victory came in 287 B.C. with the passage of the Hortensian Law, which made the decisions of the plebeian assembly binding on the entire Senate and Roman people. By then most of Italy had already fallen under Roman control.

Increasing power brought new problems. In the 3rd and 2nd centuries B.C. Rome began to build its empire abroad. By the 1st century B.C. the whole Hellenistic world had been conquered. From Spain to could afford to relax, they were overwhelmed intellectually and artistically by the Greeks. Conquest of the Hellenistic kingdoms of the East and of Greece itself brought the Romans into contact with Hellenistic Greek culture (see pages 94–100). Thus, from the 3rd century B.C. most Roman works of art followed Greek models in form and content. Roman plays were based on Greek originals, Roman temples imitated Greek buildings, and Roman sculpture and painting depicted episodes from Greek mythology.

Greek influence extends to the works of Ennius (239–169 B.C.), known to later Romans as the father of Roman poetry. Almost all of his works are lost, but from later accounts Ennius' tragedies appear to have been adapted from Greek models. His major work was the *Annals,* an epic chronicle of the history of Rome, in which for the first time a Greek metrical scheme was used to write Latin verse.

The two comic playwrights Plautus (c. 254–184 B.C.) and Terence (c. 195–159 B.C.) are the first Roman writers whose works have survived in quantity. Their plays are adaptations of Greek comedies; whereas the Greek originals are comic satires, the Roman versions turn human foibles into pure comedy. Plautus, the more boisterous of the two, is fond of comic songs and farcical intrigues. Terence's style is more refined and his characters show greater realism. It says something about the taste of the Roman public that Plautus was by far the more successful. In later times, however, Terence's sophisticated style was much admired. His plays were studied and imitated both during the Middle Ages and more recently. Both authors were fond of extremely elaborate plots involving mistaken identities, identical twins, and general confusion, with everything sorted out in the last scene.

In general, however, when educated Romans of the late Republic stopped to think about something other than politics it was likely to be love. Roman lyric poetry, often on a romantic theme, is one of the most rewarding genres of Latin literature. The first great Roman lyric poet, Catullus (c. 80–54 B.C.), is one of the best-loved of all Roman authors. Instead of philosophical or historical themes, he returned to a traditional subject from Sappho's time—personal experience—and charted the course of his own love affair with a girl whom he calls Lesbia. Among his works are 25 short poems describing the course of his relationship that range from the ecstasy of its early stages to the disillusionment and despair of the final breakup. The clarity of his style is the perfect counterpart to the direct expression of his emotions.

These poems, personal though they are, are not simply an outpouring of feelings. Catullus makes his own experiences universal. However trivial one man's unhappy love affair may seem in the context of the grim world of the late Republic, Lesbia's inconstancy has achieved a timelessness unequaled by many more serious events.

Two of the principal figures who dominated those events also made important contributions to Republican literature. Julius Caesar (100–44 B.C.) is perhaps the most famous Roman of them all. Brilliant politician, skilled general, expert administrator and organizer, he was also able to write the history of his own military campaigns in his *Commentaries,* in a simple but gripping style. In the four years during which he ruled Rome he did much to repair the damage of the previous decades. His assassination on March 15, 44 B.C., at the hands of a band of devoted republicans served only to prolong Rome's agony for another thirteen years—as well as providing Shakespeare with the plot for one of his best-known plays.

Among the most lasting achievements of Julius Caesar's dictatorship and of Roman culture in general was the creation of a single unified code of civil law, the *Ius Civile.* The science of law is one of the few original creations of Roman literature. The earliest legal code of the Republic was the so-called Law of the Twelve Tables of 451–450 B.C. By the time of Caesar, however, most of this law had become either irrelevant or out of date and had been replaced by a mass of later legislation, much of it contradictory and confusing. Caesar's *Ius Civile,* produced with the help of eminent legal experts of the day, served as the model for later times. The most complete collection of Roman law was, in fact, made during Byzantine times by the Byzantine emperor Justinian I (A.D. 527–565).

Perhaps the most endearing figure of the late Republic was Marcus Tullius Cicero (106–43 B.C.), who first made his reputation as a lawyer. He is certainly the figure of this period about whom we know the most, for he took part in a number of important legal cases and embarked on a political career. In 63 B.C. he served as consul. A few years later, the severity with which he had put down a plot against the government during his consulship earned him a short period in exile as the result of the scheming of a rival political faction. He returned in triumph, however, and in the struggle between Pompey and Caesar supported Pompey. Although Caesar seems to have forgiven him, Cicero never really trusted Caesar, in spite of his admiration for the dictator's abilities. His mixed feelings are well expressed in a letter to his friend Atticus after he had invited Caesar, by then the ruler of the Roman world, to dinner:

> Quite a guest, although I have no regrets and everything went very well indeed. . . . He was taking medicine for his digestion, so he ate and drank without worrying and seemed perfectly at ease. It was a lavish dinner, excellently served and in addition well prepared and seasoned

with good conversation, very agreeable, you know. What can I say? We were human beings together. But he's not the kind of guest to whom you'd say "it's been fun, come again on the way back." Once is enough! We talked about nothing serious, a lot about literature: he seemed to enjoy it and have a good time. So now you know about how I entertained him—or rather had him billeted on me. It was a nuisance, as I said, but not unpleasant.

From letters like these we can derive an incomparably vivid picture of Cicero and his world. Almost nine hundred were published, most of them after his death. If they often reveal Cicero's weaknesses—his vanity, his inability to make a decision, his stubbornness—they confirm his humanity and sensitivity. For his contemporaries and for later ages his chief fame was nevertheless as an orator. Although the cases and causes that prompted his speeches have ceased to have any but historical interest, the power of a Ciceronian oration can still thrill the responsive reader, especially when it is read aloud.

Roman Philosophy

The Romans produced little in the way of original philosophical writing. Their practical nature made them suspicious of professional philosophers and unable to appreciate the rather subtle delights involved in arguing both sides of a complex moral or ethical question. In consequence most of the great Roman philosophical writers devoted their energies to expounding Greek philosophy to a Roman audience. The two principal schools of philosophy to make an impact at Rome, *Epicureanism* and *Stoicism,* were both imported from Greece.

Epicureanism never really gained many followers, in spite of the efforts of the poet Lucretius (99–55 B.C.), who described its doctrines in his brilliant poem *On the Nature of Things* (*De Rerum natura*). A remarkable synthesis of poetry and philosophy, this work alone is probably responsible for whatever admiration the Romans could muster for a system of thought so different from their own traditional virtues of simplicity and seriousness. According to Epicurus (341–271 B.C.), the founder of the school, the correct goal and principle of human actions is pleasure. Although Epicureanism stresses moderation and prudence in the pursuit of pleasure, the Romans insisted on thinking of the philosophy as a typically Greek enthusiasm for self-indulgence and debauchery.

Lucretius tried to correct this impression by emphasizing the profoundly intellectual and rational aspects of Epicureanism. Its principal teaching was that the gods, if they exist, play no part in human affairs or in the phenomena of nature; as a result we can live our lives free from superstitious fear of the unknown and the threat of divine retribution. The Epicurean theory of matter explains the world in purely physical terms. It describes the universe as made up of two elements: small particles of matter, or atoms, and empty space. The atoms are completely solid, possessing the qualities of size, shape, and mass, and can be neither split nor destroyed. Their joining together to form complex structures is entirely caused by their random swerving in space, without interference from the gods. As a result, human life can be lived in complete freedom; we can face the challenges of existence and even natural disasters like earthquakes or plagues with complete serenity, since their occurrence is random and outside our control. According to Epicurus, at death the atoms that make up our body separate, and neither body, mind, nor soul survives. Since no part of us is in any way immortal, we should have no fear of death, which offers no threat of punishment in a future world but brings only the complete ending of any sensation.

Epicureanism's rejection of a divine force in the world and its campaign against superstition probably appealed to the Romans as little as its claim that the best life was one of pleasure and calm composure. The hardheaded practical moralizing of the Roman mentality found far more appeal in the other school of philosophy imported into Rome from Greece, Stoicism. The Stoics taught that the world was governed by Reason and that Divine Providence watched over the virtuous, never allowing them to suffer evil. The key to becoming virtuous lay in willing or desiring only that which was under one's own control. Thus riches, power, or even physical health—all subject to the whims of Fortune—were excluded as objects of desire. For the Stoic all that counted was that which was subject to the individual's will.

Although Stoicism had already won a following at Rome by the 1st century B.C. and was discussed by Cicero in his philosophical writings, its chief literary exponents came slightly later. Seneca (8 B.C.–A.D. 65) wrote a number of essays on Stoic morality. He had an opportunity, and the necessity, to practice the moral fortitude about which he wrote when his former pupil, the emperor Nero, ordered him to commit suicide, since the taking of one's own life was fully sanctioned by Stoic philosophers. Perhaps the most impressive of all Stoic writers is Epictetus (c. A.D. 50–134), a former slave who established a school of philosophy in Rome and then in Greece. In his *Encheiridion* (*Handbook*) he recommends an absolute trust in Divine Providence to be maintained through every misfortune. For Epictetus the philosopher represented the spokesman of Providence itself "taking the human race for his children."

TABLE 4.1 Principal Roman Deities and Their Greek Equivalents	
Roman	*Greek*
Jupiter	Zeus
Juno	Hera
Neptune	Poseidon
Vulcan	Hephaestus
Mars	Ares
Apollo	Apollo
Diana	Artemis
Ceres	Demeter
Venus	Aphrodite
Minerva	Athena
Mercury	Hermes
Bacchus	Dionysus

Epictetus' teachings exerted a profound influence on the last great Stoic, the emperor Marcus Aurelius (A.D. 121–180), who was constantly plagued with the difficulty of being a Stoic and an emperor at the same time. Delicate in health, sentimental, inclined to be disillusioned by the weaknesses of others, Marcus Aurelius struggled hard to maintain the balance between his public duty and his personal convictions. While on military duty he composed his *Meditations,* which are less a philosophical treatise than an account of his own attempt to live the life of a Stoic. As many of his observations make clear, this was no easy task: "Tell yourself every morning 'Today I shall meet the officious, the ungrateful, the bullying, the treacherous, the envious, the selfish. All of them behave like this because they do not know the difference between good and bad.'"

Yet, even though Stoicism continued to attract a number of Roman intellectuals, the great majority of Romans remained immune to the appeal of the philosophical life. Both in the 1st century B.C. and later, the very superstition both Stoicism and Epicureanism sought to combat remained deeply ingrained in the Roman character. Festivals in honor of traditional deities were celebrated until long after the advent of Christianity (Table 4.1). Rituals that tried to read the future by the traditional examination of animals' entrails and other time-honored methods continued to be popular. If the Romans had paused more often to meditate on the nature of existence, they would probably have had less time to civilize the world.

Republican Art and Architecture

In the visual arts as in literature, the late Republic shows the translation of Greek styles into new Roman forms. The political scene was dominated by individuals like Cicero and Caesar; their individualism was captured in portrait busts that were both realistic and psychologically revealing. To some extent these realistic sculptures are based on such Etruscan models as the heads of the old couple on the Volterra sarcophagus [see 4.5] rather than on Hellenistic portraits, which idealized their subjects. However, the subtlety and understanding shown in portraits like those of Cicero and Caesar represent a typically Roman combination and amplification of others' styles. In many respects, indeed, Roman portraiture represents Roman art at its most creative and sensitive. It certainly opened up new expressive possibilities, as artists discovered how to use physical appearance to convey something about character. Many of the best Roman portraits serve as revealing psychological documents, expressing, for example, Cicero's self-satisfaction as well as his humanity [4.7]. Realistic details like the lines at the corners of the eyes and mouth, the hollows in the cheeks, or the set of the lips are used to express both outer appearance and inner character. The new skill, as it developed, could of course be put to propaganda use, and statesmen

4.7 *Bust of Cicero.* Roman, 1st century B.C. Uffizi, Florence. This portrait of one of the leading figures of the late Republic suggests the ability of Roman sculptors of the period to capture both likeness and character. Cicero is portrayed as thoughtful and preoccupied.

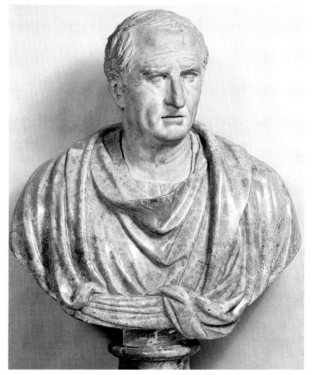

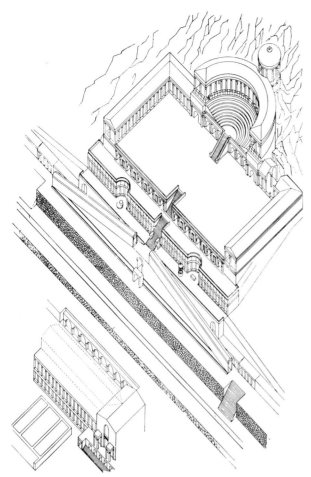

4.8 Plan of the Sanctuary of Fortuna Primigenia, Praeneste (Palestrina). This vast complex, constructed by Sulla after his destruction of the city in 82 B.C., is a series of six immense terraces crowned by a semicircular structure in front of which stood an altar.

has all the qualities of symmetry and grandeur we associate with later Roman imperial architecture, although it took its inspiration from massive Hellenistic building programs such as that at Pergamum. Caesar himself had a large area in the center of Rome cleared for the construction of a forum, or public meeting place, to be named after him. In time it was dwarfed by later monumental fora, but it had initiated the construction of public buildings for personal display and glory.

Imperial Rome (31 B.C.–A.D. 476)

With the assassination of Julius Caesar a brief respite from civil war was followed by further turmoil [4.9]. Caesar's lieutenant, Mark Antony, led the campaign to avenge his death and punish the conspirators. He was joined in this by Caesar's young great-nephew, Octavius, who had been named by Caesar as his heir and had recently arrived in Rome from the provinces. It soon became apparent that Antony and Octavius (or Octavian, to use the name he now took) were unlikely to coexist very happily. After the final defeat of the conspirators in 42 B.C. a temporary peace was obtained by putting Octavian in charge of the western provinces and sending Antony to the East. A final confrontation could not be long delayed, and Antony's fatal involvement with Cleopatra alienated much of his support at Rome. The end came in 31 B.C., at the Battle of Actium. The forces of Antony, reinforced by those of Cleopatra, were routed, and the couple committed suicide. Octavian was left as sole ruler of the Roman world, a world that was now in ruins. His victory marked the end of the Roman Republic.

When Octavian took supreme control after the Battle of Actium, Rome had been continuously involved both in civil and external wars for much of a century. The political and cultural institutions of Roman life were beyond repair, the economy was wrecked, and large areas of Italy were in complete turmoil. By the time of Octavian's death in A.D. 14,

and politicians soon learned that they could project their chosen self-image through their portraits.

The powerful political figures of the period also used the medium of architecture to express their authority. The huge sanctuary constructed by Sulla at Praeneste (modern Palestrina) around 82 B.C. [4.8]

4.9 Sacrificial scene from the frieze of Domitius Ahenobarbus, originally on the Temple of Neptune, Rome. 1st century B.C. Louvre, Paris. The sacrifice possibly commemorates a victory in the civil war that followed Julius Caesar's assassination. Mars, god of war, stands to the left of an altar toward which a huge bull is being led for sacrifice.

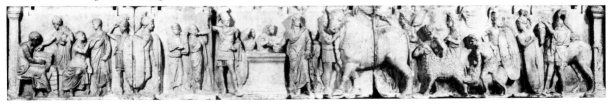

Rome had achieved a peace and prosperity unequaled in its history before or after. The art and literature created during his rule represents the peak of the Roman cultural achievement. To the Romans of his own time it seemed that a new Golden Age had dawned, and for centuries afterward his memory was revered. As the first Roman emperor, Octavian inaugurated the second great period in Roman history—the Empire, which lasted technically from 27 B.C., when he assumed the title Augustus, until A.D. 476, when the last Roman emperor was overthrown. In many ways, however, the period began with the Battle of Actium and continued in the subsequent Western and Byzantine empires (Table 4.2).

Augustus' cultural achievement was stupendous, but it could only have been accomplished in a world at peace. Perhaps Augustus' greatest achievement, then, was to restore calm and dignity to Roman life. Once again the Romans were inspired with a sense of destiny and purpose, and the results are visible in their art.

Augustan Literature: Vergil

Augustus himself played an active part in supporting and encouraging the writers and artists of his day; many of their works echo the chief themes of Augustan politics—the return of peace, the importance of the land and agriculture, the putting aside of ostentation and luxury in favor of a simple life, and above all the belief in Rome's destiny as world ruler. Some of the greatest works of Roman sculpture commemorate Augustus and his deeds; Horace and Vergil sing his praises in their poems. It is sometimes said that much of this art was propaganda, organized by the emperor to present the most favorable picture possible of his reign. Even the greatest works of the time do relate in some way or other to the Augustan world view, and it is difficult to imagine a poet whose philosophy differed radically from that of the emperor being able to give voice to it. But we have no reason to doubt the sincerity of the gratitude felt toward Augustus or the strength of what seems to have been an almost universal feeling that at last a new era had dawned. In any case, from the time of Augustus art at Rome became in large measure official. Most of Roman architecture and sculpture of the period was public, commissioned by the state, and served state purposes.

The greater the artist, the more subtle the response to the Augustan vision. The greatest of all Roman poets, Publius Vergilius Maro (70–19 B.C.), devoted the last ten years of his life to the composition of an epic poem intended to honor Rome, and, by implication, Augustus. The result was the *Aeneid,* one of the great poems of the world, not completely finished at

TABLE 4.2	The Principal Roman Emperors	
Augustus	27 B.C.–A.D. 14	Julio-Claudians
Tiberius	14–37	
Gaius (Caligula)	37–41	
Claudius	41–54	
Nero	54–68	
Year of the Four Emperors	69	
Vespasian	69–79	Flavians
Titus	79–81	
Domitian	81–96	
Nerva	96–98	Adoptive Emperors
Trajan	98–117	
Hadrian	117–138	
Antoninus Pius	138–161	Antonines
Marcus Aurelius	161–180	
Commodus	180–193	
Septimius Severus	193–211	
Alexander Severus	222–235	
Decius	249–251	
Diocletian	284–305	
Constantine	306–337	

the poet's death. For much of the Middle Ages, Vergil himself was held in the highest reverence. A succession of great poets has regarded him as their master—Dante, Tasso, Milton, among others. Probably no work of literature in the entire tradition of Western culture has been more loved and revered than the *Aeneid*—described by T. S. Eliot as *the classic* of Western society—yet its significance is complex and by no means universally agreed upon.

The *Aeneid* was not Vergil's first poem. The earliest authentic works that have survived are ten short pastoral poems known as the *Eclogues* or sometimes the *Bucolics,* which deal with the joys and sorrows of the country and the shepherds and herdsmen who live there. Vergil himself was the son of a farmer; his deep love of the land emerges also in his next work, the four books of the *Georgics* (29 B.C.). Their most obvious purpose is to serve as a practical guide to farming, and they offer helpful advice on such subjects as cattle breeding and beekeeping as well as a deep conviction that the strength of Italy lies in its agricultural richness. In a great passage in the second book of the *Georgics* Vergil hails the "ancient earth, great mother of crops and men." He does not disguise the hardships of the farmer's life, the poverty, hard work, and frequent disappointments, but still feels that only life in the country brings true peace and contentment [4.10].

The spirit of the *Georgics* clearly matched Augustus' plans for an agricultural revival. Indeed, it was probably the emperor himself who commissioned

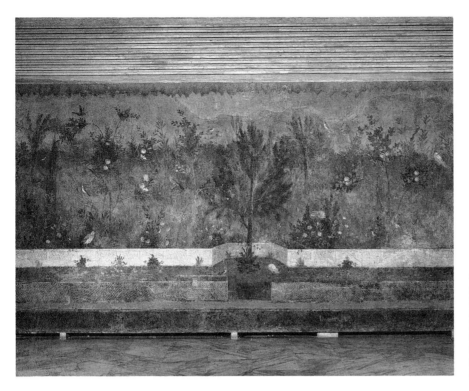

4.10 View of a garden, from the villa of Livia and Augustus at Prima Porta. c. 20 B.C. Fresco, detail, Museo delle Terme, Rome. The peaceful scene, with its abundance of fruit and flowers, reflects the interest in country life expressed in Vergil's *Eclogues* and *Georgics*.

Vergil to write an epic poem that would be to Roman literature what the *Iliad* and *Odyssey* were for Greek: a national epic. The task was immense. Vergil had to find a subject that would do appropriate honor to Rome and its past as well as commemorate the achievements of Augustus. The *Aeneid* is not a perfect poem (on his deathbed Vergil ordered his friends to destroy it), but in some ways it surpasses even the high expectations Augustus must have had for it. Vergil succeeded in providing Rome with its national epic and stands as a worthy successor to Homer. At the same time, he created a profoundly moving study of the nature of human destiny and personal responsibility.

The *Aeneid* is divided into twelve books. Its hero is a Trojan prince, Aeneas, who flees from the ruins of burning Troy and sails west to Italy to found a new city, the predecessor of Rome. Vergil's choice was significant: Aeneas' Trojan birth establishes connections with the world of Homer; his arrival in Italy involves the origins of Rome; and the theme of a fresh beginning born, as it were, out of the ashes of the past corresponds perfectly to the Augustan mood of revival. We first meet Aeneas and his followers in the middle of his journey from Troy to Italy, caught in a storm that casts them up on the coast of North Africa. They make their way to the city of Carthage, where they are given shelter by the Carthaginian ruler, Queen Dido. At a dinner in his honor Aeneas describes the fall of Troy (Book II) and his wanderings from Troy to Carthage (Book III), in the course of which his father Anchises had died.

In Book IV, perhaps the best known, the action resumes where it had broken off at the end of Book I. The tragic love that develops between Dido and Aeneas tempts Aeneas to stay in Carthage and thereby abandon his mission to found a new home in Italy. A divine messenger is sent to remind Aeneas of his responsibilities. He leaves after an agonizing encounter with Dido, and the distraught queen kills herself.

Book V brings the Trojans to Italy. In Book VI, Aeneas journeys to the underworld to hear from the spirit of his father the destiny of Rome. This tremendous episode provides the turning point of the poem. Before it we see Aeneas, and he sees himself, as a man prone to human weaknesses and subject to personal feelings. After Anchises' revelations, Aeneas' humanity is replaced by a sense of mission and the weary, suffering Trojan exile becomes transformed into a "man of destiny."

In Books VII and VIII, the Trojans arrive at the river Tiber and Aeneas visits the future site of Rome while the Italian peoples prepare to resist the Trojan invaders. The last four books describe in detail the war between the Trojans and the Latins, in the course of which there are losses on both sides. The *Aeneid* ends with the death of the great Italian warrior Turnus and the final victory of Aeneas.

It is tempting to see Aeneas as the archetype of Augustus; certainly Vergil must have intended for us to draw some parallels. Other historical analogies can also be found: Dido and Cleopatra, for example, have much in common. The *Aeneid* is, however, far more than an allegorical retelling of the events leading up to the foundation of the empire. Put briefly, Aeneas undertakes a responsibility for which initially he has no real enthusiasm and which costs him and others considerable suffering. It would have been much easier for him to have stayed in Carthage, or settled somewhere else along his way, rather than push forward under difficult circumstances into a foreign land where he and his followers were not welcome.

Once he has accepted his mission, however, he fulfills it conscientiously and in the process learns to sublimate his own personal desires to a common good. If this is indeed a portrait of Augustus, it represents a much more complex view of his character than we might expect. And Vergil goes further. If greatness can only be acquired by sacrificing human individuals, is it worth the price? Is the future glory of Rome a sufficient excuse for the cruel and unmanly treatment of Dido? Readers will provide their own answers. Vergil's might have been that the sacrifices were probably worth it, but barely. Much, of course, depends on individual views on the nature and purpose of existence, and for Vergil there is no doubt that life is essentially tragic. The prevailing mood of the poem is one of melancholy regret for the sadness of human lives and the inevitability of human suffering.

Augustan Sculpture

Many of the characteristics of Vergil's poetry can also be found in contemporary sculpture. In a relief from one of the most important works of the period, the *Ara Pacis* (Altar of Peace), Aeneas himself performs a sacrifice on his arrival in Italy before a small shrine that contains two sacred images brought from Troy [4.11]. More significantly, the *Ara Pacis* depicts the abundance of nature that could flourish again in the peace of the Augustan age. The altar, begun on Augustus' return to Rome in 13 B.C. after a visit to the provinces, was dedicated on January 30, 9 B.C., at a ceremony that is shown in the surrounding reliefs [4.12]. The procession making its way to the sacrifice is divided into two parts. On the south side Augustus leads the way, accompanied by priests and followed by the members of his family; the north side shows senators and other dignitaries. The lower part of the walls is decorated with a rich band of fruit and floral motifs, luxuriantly intertwined, amid which swans are placed. The actual entrance to the altar is flanked by two reliefs—on the right, the one showing Aeneas, and on the left, Romulus and Remus.

The *Ara Pacis* is perhaps the single most comprehensive statement of how Augustus wanted his con-

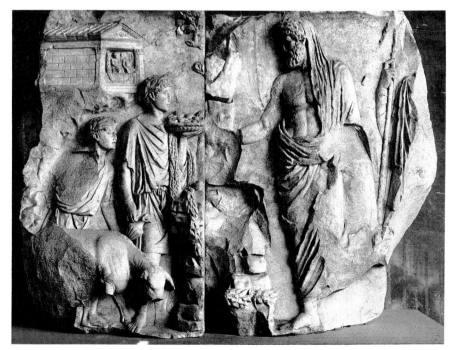

4.11 Aeneas sacrificing, from the *Ara Pacis,* Rome. 13–9 B.C. Marble. Aeneas is depicted in the manner of a Classical Greek god; the landscape and elaborate relief detail are typical of late Hellenistic art.

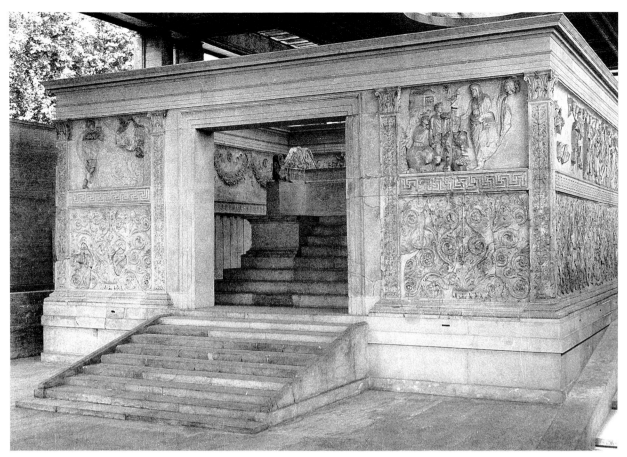

4.12 *Ara Pacis* of Augustus, Rome. 13–9 B.C. Marble, 36 × 33′ (11 × 10 m). The central doorway, through which the altar itself is just visible, is flanked by the reliefs showing Romulus and Remus and Aeneas. On the right-hand side is the procession led by Augustus. The altar originally stood on the ancient Via Flaminia. Fragments were discovered in the 16th century; the remaining pieces were located in 1937 and 1938 and the structure was reconstructed near the mausoleum of Augustus.

temporaries—and future generations—to see his reign. The altar is dedicated neither to Jupiter or Mars nor to Augustus himself but to the spirit of Peace. Augustus is shown as the first among equals rather than supreme ruler; although he leads the procession, he is marked by no special richness of dress. The presence of Augustus' family indicates that he intends his successor to be drawn from among them, and that they have a special role to play in public affairs. The reliefs of Aeneas and of Romulus and Remus relate the entire ceremony to Rome's glorious past. Further scenes at the back showing the Earth Mother and the goddess of war emphasize the abundance of the land and the need for vigilance. The rich vegetation of the lower band is a constant reminder of the rewards of agriculture, that can be enjoyed once more in the peace to which the whole altar is dedicated.

Amazingly enough, this detailed political and social message is expressed without pretentiousness and with superb workmanship. The style is deliberately and self-consciously "classical," based on works like the Parthenon frieze. To depict the New Golden Age of Augustus, his artists have chosen the artistic language of the Golden Age of Athens, although with a Roman accent. The figures in the procession, for instance, are portrayed far more realistically than those in the sculpture of 5th-century-B.C. Athens.

The elaborate message illustrated by the *Ara Pacis* can also be seen in the best-preserved statue of the emperor himself, the *Augustus of Prima Porta,* so called after the spot where an imperial villa containing the sculpture was excavated [4.13]. The statue probably dates from about the time of the emperor's death; the face is in the full vigor of life, calm and determined. The stance is one of quiet authority. The ornately carved breastplate recalls one of the chief events of Augustus' reign. In 20 B.C. he defeated the Parthians, an eastern tribe, and recaptured from them the Roman standards that had been lost in battle in

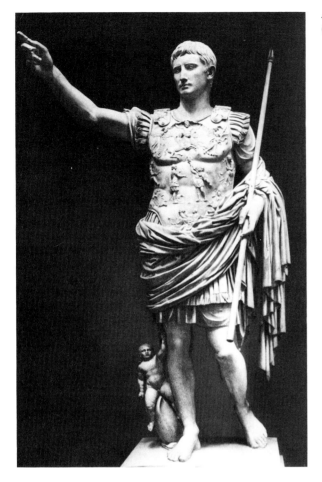

4.13 *Augustus of Prima Porta.* c. A.D. 14. Marble, height 6'8" (2.03 m). Vatican Museums, Rome.

53 B.C. On that former occasion Rome had suffered one of the greatest military defeats in its history, and Augustus' victory played an important part in restoring national pride. The breastplate shows a bearded Parthian handing back the eagle-crowned standard to a Roman soldier. The cupid on a dolphin at Augustus' feet serves two purposes. The symbol of the goddess Venus, it connects Augustus and his family with Aeneas (whose mother was Venus) and thereby with the origins of Rome. At the same time it looks to the future by representing Augustus' grandson Gaius, who was born the year of the victory over the Parthians and was at one time considered a possible successor to his grandfather.

The choice of his successor was the one problem that Augustus never managed to solve to his own satisfaction. The death of other candidates forced him to fall back reluctantly on his unpopular stepson Tiberius—a problem that was to recur throughout the long history of the empire, since no really effective mechanism was ever devised for guaranteeing a peaceful transfer of power. (As early as the reign of Claudius [A.D. 41–54], the right to choose a new emperor was seized by the army.) In every other respect the Augustan age was one of high attainment. In the visual arts, Augustan artists set the styles that dominated succeeding generations, while writers like the poets Vergil, Horace, Ovid, and Propertius, and

---

EAST MEETS WEST

Roman Traders in the Far East

Wealthy upper-class Romans provided a constant market for luxury goods imported from outside Italy. Some items could be found within the Empire: Spain supplied rare fruits such as dates or figs, and silk was imported from the Greek island of Cos. Yet the exotic always has a special appeal, and during the Augustan Age Roman merchants traveled as far as China to supply the demand for luxuries.

In the 1st century B.C. Roman navigators discovered for the first time that if they traveled during the monsoon season, when the winds blew favorably, they could sail from Egypt to India in about forty days. Commercial trading posts were set up on the Indian coast, where goods such as spices, ivory, incense, and pearls were paid for with Roman goods and money (hoards of Augustan coins have been found at Indian sites), and transported back to Rome. One of the hottest-selling items was pepper, for which the Romans developed an inordinate taste; great warehouses for its storage were built along the river Tiber.

The Indian connection provided access overland to an even more exotic and desirable market: that of China. The high quality of Chinese silk was already familiar to fashion-conscious Romans, but the overland Central Asian trade route passed through the hostile territory of the Parthians, whom Augustus had conquered but by no means subdued. Now it became possible to transport Chinese silks through Afghanistan and down the river Indus to the Indian Ocean; from there they and other luxury items were shipped back to Rome. On the outward voyage the Roman ships carried copper, lead, and Italian wine to trade with their new Chinese contacts. On the trip back to Rome many ships stopped off at the Horn of Africa (modern Ethiopia and Somalia) to pick up tortoiseshell and ivory.

The trade route to China remained in use until the collapse of the Roman Empire. Even in the most troubled times Roman high society demanded a constant supply of the latest in luxury Chinese silks.

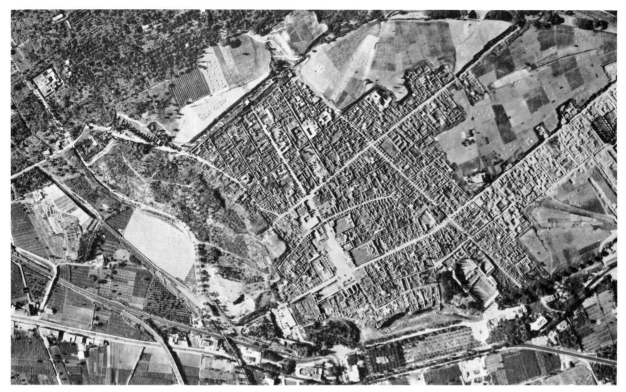

4.14 Aerial view of the excavated portion of Pompeii as it appears today. The long, open rectangular space in the lower center is the forum. The total area is 166 acres (67.23 hectares). Although excavations at Pompeii have been in progress for more than two hundred years, some two-fifths of the city is still buried.

the historian Livy established a Golden Age of Latin literature.

Curiously enough, perhaps the only person to have any real doubts about the Augustan achievement may have been Augustus himself. The Roman writer and gossip Suetonius (A.D. c. 69–c. 140) tells us that as the emperor lay dying he ordered a slave to bring a mirror so that he could comb his hair. He looked at himself, then turned to some friends standing by and asked, "Tell me, have I played my part in the comedy of life well enough?"

The Evidence of Pompeii

The 1st and 2nd centuries A.D. are probably the best-documented times in the whole of classical antiquity. From the many literary sources and the wealth of art and architecture that has survived, it is possible to reconstruct a detailed picture of life in imperial Rome. Even more complete is our knowledge of a prosperous but unimportant little town some 150 miles (240 kilometers) south of Rome that owes its worldwide fame to the circumstances of its destruction [4.14]. On August 24 in the year A.D. 79, the volcano Vesuvius above the Gulf of Naples erupted and a number of small towns were buried, the nearer ones under flowing lava and those some distance away under pumice and ash. By far the most famous is Pompeii, situated some 10 miles (16 kilometers) southeast of the erupting peak. Excavation first began there more than two hundred years ago. The finds preserved by the volcanic debris give us a rich and vivid impression of the way of life in a provincial town of the early empire—from the temples in which the Pompeians worshiped and the baths in which they cleaned themselves to their food on the fatal day [4.15, 4.16].

An eyewitness report about the eruption comes from two letters written by the Roman politician and literary figure Pliny the Younger (A.D. 62–before 114)—so called to distinguish him from his uncle, Pliny the Elder (A.D. 23–79). The two were in fact together at Misenum on the Bay of Naples on the day of the eruption. Pliny's uncle was much interested in natural phenomena (his chief work was a *Natural History* in 37 volumes); to investigate for himself the nature of the explosion he made his way toward Vesuvius, where he was suffocated to death by the fumes.

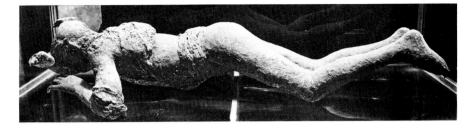

4.15 Cast of a woman trapped in volcanic pumice during the eruption of Mount Vesuvius at Pompeii, A.D. 79. Museo Nazionale, Naples.

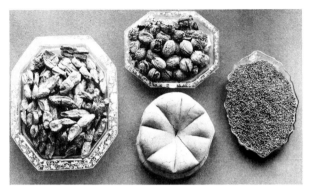

4.16 Carbonized dates, walnuts, sunflower seeds, and bread from Pompeii, August 24, A.D. 79. Museo Nazionale, Naples.

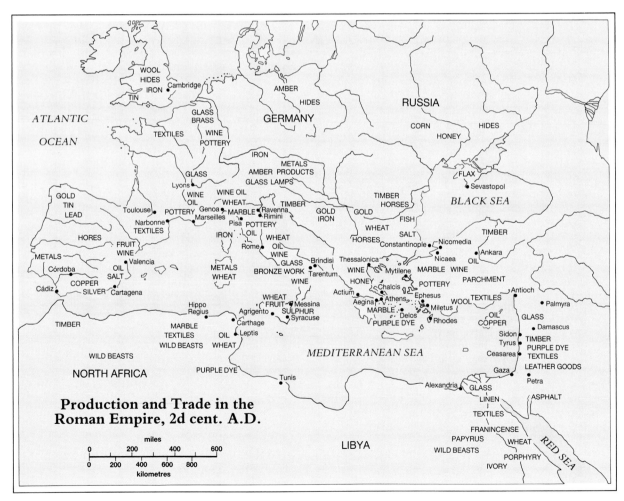

ATLANTIC

OCEAN

WOOL
HIDES
IRON
Cambridge
TIN

AMBER

HIDES

RUSSIA

GERMANY

GLASS
BRASS
TEXTILES
WINE
POTTERY

CORN
HONEY

HIDES

IRON
METALS
AMBER PRODUCTS
GLASS LAMPS

FLAX
Sevastopol

GLASS
Lyons

GOLD
TIN
LEAD

WINE
OIL

WINE OIL
WHEAT

TIMBER

TIMBER
HORSES

BLACK SEA

Toulouse
POTTERY
Genoa
Marseilles
MARBLE
Ravenna
Rimini

GOLD
IRON

GOLD

Narbonne
TEXTILES
Pisa
POTTERY

FISH

TIMBER

HORES

IRON
OIL

HORSES

SALT

Nicomedia
Ankara

FRUIT
WINE
Valencia

Rome
WHEAT
OIL
WINE

WHEAT

Constantinople
Nicaea

OIL

METALS
Córdoba
OIL
SALT

GLASS
BRONZE WORK

Thessalonica
WINE
Mytilene

MARBLE WINE

PARCHMENT

COPPER
SILVER
Cádiz
Cartagena

METALS
WHEAT

WINE
Tarentum

HONEY
Chalcis
Athens

POTTERY

Antioch

WHEAT
FRUIT
Agrigento
Hippo
Regius
SULPHUR
Syracuse
Messina

Actium
Aegina
MARBLE
Ephesus
Miletus
Delos

WOOL
TEXTILES

Palmyra

TIMBER

MARBLE
TEXTILES
WILD BEASTS
Carthage
OIL
Leptis
WHEAT

PURPLE DYE
Rhodes

OIL
COPPER
Sidon
Tyrus

GLASS
Damascus

TIMBER
PURPLE DYE
TEXTILES

WILD BEASTS

PURPLE DYE

MEDITERRANEAN SEA

Ceasarea
Gaza

LEATHER GOODS

NORTH AFRICA

Tunis

Alexandria
GLASS

Petra

**Production and Trade in the
Roman Empire, 2d cent. A.D.**

LIBYA

LINEN
TEXTILES

ASPHALT

FRANINCENSE
PAPYRUS
WILD BEASTS

WHEAT

RED SEA

PORPHYRY
IVORY

miles
0   200   400   600

0   200 400 600 800
kilometres

The younger Pliny stayed behind with his mother and in a letter to the historian Tacitus a little while later described the events of the next few hours:

Pliny the Younger
LETTER TO TACITUS ON THE ERUPTION OF VESUVIUS

You say that the letter I wrote at your request about the death of my uncle makes you want to hear about the terrors, and dangers as well, which I endured, having been left behind at Misenum—I had started on that topic but broken off. "Though my mind shudders to remember, I shall begin." After my uncle departed I spent the rest of the day on my studies; it was for that purpose I had stayed. Then I took a bath, ate dinner, and went to bed; but my sleep was restless and brief. For a number of days before this there had been a quivering of the ground, no so fearful because it was common in Campania. On that night, however, it became so violent that everything seemed not so much to move as to be overturned. My mother came rushing into my bedroom; I was just getting up, intending in my turn to arouse her if she were asleep. We sat down in the rather narrow courtyard of the house lying between the sea and the buildings. I don't know whether I should call it iron nerves or folly—I was only seventeen: I called for a book of Titus Livy and as if at ease I read it and even copied some passages, as I had been doing. Then one of my uncle's friends, who had recently come from Spain to visit him, when he saw my mother and me sitting there, and me actually reading a book, rebuked her apathy and my unconcern. But I was as intent on my book as ever.

It was now the first hour of day, but the light was still faint and doubtful. The adjacent buildings now began to collapse, and there was great, indeed inevitable, danger of being involved in the ruins; for though the place was open, it was narrow. Then at last we decided to leave the town. The dismayed crowd came after us; it preferred following someone else's decision rather than its own; in panic that is practically the same as wisdom. So as we went off we were crowded and shoved along by a huge mob of followers. When we got out beyond the buildings we halted. We saw many strange and fearful sights there. For the carriages we had ordered brought for us, though on perfectly level ground, kept rolling back and forth; even when the wheels were chocked with stones they would not stand still. Moreover the sea appeared to be sucked back and to be repelled by the vibration of the earth; the shoreline was much farther out than usual, and many specimens of marine life were caught on the dry sands. On the other side a black and frightful cloud, rent by twisting and quivering paths of fire, gaped open in huge patterns of flames; it was like sheet lightning, but far worse. Then indeed that friend from Spain whom I have mentioned spoke to us more sharply and insistently: "If your brother and uncle still lives, he wants you to be saved; if he has died, his wish was that you should survive him; so why do you delay to make your escape?" We replied

that we would not allow ourselves to think of our own safety while still uncertain of his. Without waiting any longer he rushed off and left the danger behind at top speed.

Soon thereafter the cloud I have described began to descend to the earth and to cover the sea; it had encircled Capri and hidden it from view, and had blotted out the promontory of Misenum. Then my mother began to plead, urge, and order me to make my escape as best I could, for I could, being young; she, weighed down with years and weakness, would die happy if she had not been the cause of death to me. I replied that I would not find safety except in her company; then I took her hand and made her walk faster. She obeyed with difficulty and scolded herself for slowing me. Now ashes, though thin as yet, began to fall. I looked back; a dense fog was looming up behind us; it poured over the ground like a river as it followed. "Let us turn aside," said I, "lest, if we should fall on the road, we should be trampled in the darkness by the throng of those going our way." We barely had time to consider the thought, when night was upon us, not such a night as when there is no moon or there are clouds, but such as in a closed place with the lights put out. One could hear the wailing of women, the crying of children, the shouting of men; they called each other, some their parents, others their children, still others their mates, and sought to recognize each other by their voices. Some lamented their own fate, others the fate of their loved ones. There were even those who in fear of death prayed for death. Many raised their hands to the gods; more held that there were nowhere gods any more and that this was that eternal and final night of the universe. Nor were those lacking who exaggerated real dangers with feigned and lying terrors. Men appeared who reported that part of Misenum was buried in ruins, and part of it in flames; it was false, but found credulous listeners.

It lightened a little; this seemed to us not daylight but a sign of approaching fire. But the fire stopped some distance away; darkness came on again, again ashes, thick and heavy. We got up repeatedly to shake these off; otherwise we would have been buried and crushed by the weight. I might boast that not a groan, not a cowardly word, escaped from my lips in the midst of such dangers, were it not that I believed I was perishing along with everything else, and everything else along with me; a wretched and yet a real consolation for having to die. At last the fog dissipated into smoke or mist, and then vanished; soon there was real daylight; the sun even shone, though wanly, as when there is an eclipse. Our still trembling eyes found everything changed, buried in deep ashes as if in snow. We returned to Misenum and attended to our physical needs as best we could; then we spent a night in suspense between hope and fear. Fear was the stronger, for the trembling of the earth continued, and many, crazed by their sufferings, were mocking their own woes and others' by awful predictions. But as for us, though we had suffered dangers and anticipated others, we had not even then any thought of going away until we should have word of my uncle.

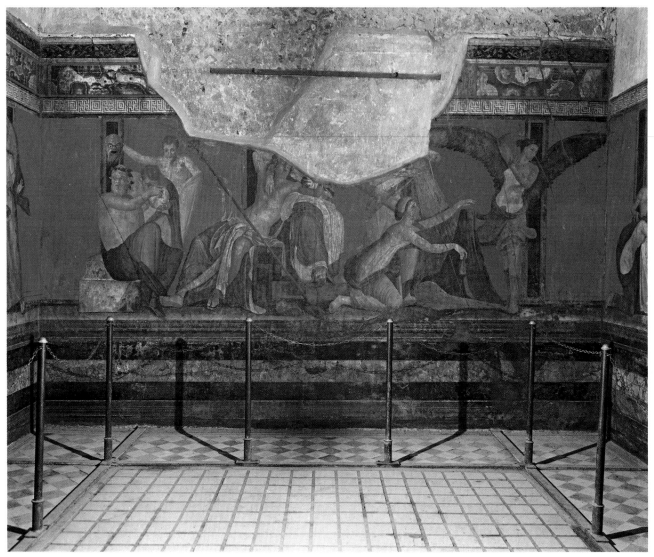

4.17 Wall paintings from the Villa of the Mysteries, Pompeii. c. 60 B.C. Frescoes. Probably no ancient work of art has been more argued about than these paintings. They seem to relate to the cult of the Greek god Dionysus and the importance of the cult for girls approaching marriage, but many of the details are difficult to interpret. There is no argument, however, about the high quality of the paintings.

You will read this account, far from worthy of history, without any intention of incorporating it; and you must blame yourself, since you insisted on having it, if it shall seem not even worthy of a letter.

With a few exceptions, like the frescoes in the Villa of the Mysteries [4.17], the works of art unearthed at Pompeii are not masterpieces. Their importance lies precisely in the fact that they show us how the ordinary Pompeian lived, worked, and played [4.18]. The general picture is very impressive. Cool, comfortable houses were decorated with charming frescoes and mosaics and included quiet gardens, remote from the noise of busy streets and watered by fountains. The household silver and other domestic ornaments found in the ruins of houses were often of very high quality. Although the popu-

lation of Pompeii was only twenty thousand, there were no fewer than three sets of public baths, a theater, a concert hall, an amphitheater large enough to seat the entire population, and a more-than-adequate number of brothels. The forum was closed to traffic, and the major public buildings ranged around it include a splendid basilica or large hall that served as both stock exchange and law courts. Life must have been extremely comfortable at Pompeii, even though it was by no means the most prosperous of the towns buried by Vesuvius. Although only a small part of Herculaneum has been excavated, some mansions found there far surpass the houses of Pompeii. In the last few years work has begun at Oplontis, where a superbly decorated villa has already come to light.

Apart from its historic importance, the excavation of Pompeii in the 18th and 19th centuries had a profound effect on contemporary writers and artists. Johann Wolfgang von Goethe visited the site in 1787 and wrote of the buried city that "of all the disasters there have been in this world, few have provided so much delight to posterity." Johann Winckelmann (1717–1768), sometimes called the father of archaeology and art history, used material from the excavations in his *History of Ancient Art*. Artists like Ingres, David, and Canova were influenced by Pompeian paintings and sculptures; on a more popular level a style of Wedgwood china was based on Pompeian motifs. Countless poets and novelists of the 19th century either set episodes in the excavations at Pompeii or tried to imagine what life there was like in Roman times.

Roman Imperial Architecture

All the charm and comfort of Pompeii pale before the grandeur of imperial Rome itself, where both public buildings and private houses were constructed in numbers and on a scale that still remains impressive [4.19]. The Roman achievement in both architecture and engineering had a lasting effect on the development of later architectural styles. In particular their use of the arch, probably borrowed from the Etruscans, was widely imitated, and pseudo-Roman triumphal arches have sprung up in such unlikely places as the Champs Élysées in Paris and Washington Square in New York. The original triumphal arches commemorated military victories [4.20]; each was a permanent version of the temporary wooden arch erected to celebrate the return to the capital of a victorious general.

Equally important was the use of internal arches and vaults [4.21] to provide roofs for structures of increasing size and complexity. Greek and Republican Roman temples had been relatively small, partly because of the difficulties involved in roofing a large space without supports. With the invention of concrete in the 1st century B.C. and growing understanding of the principles of stress and counterstress, Roman architects were able to experiment with elaborate new forms, many of which—like the barrel

4.18 Peristyle of the House of the Silver Wedding, Pompeii. 1st century A.D. The open plan of substantial houses such as this helped keep the interior cool in summer; the adjoining rooms were closed off by folding doors in winter.

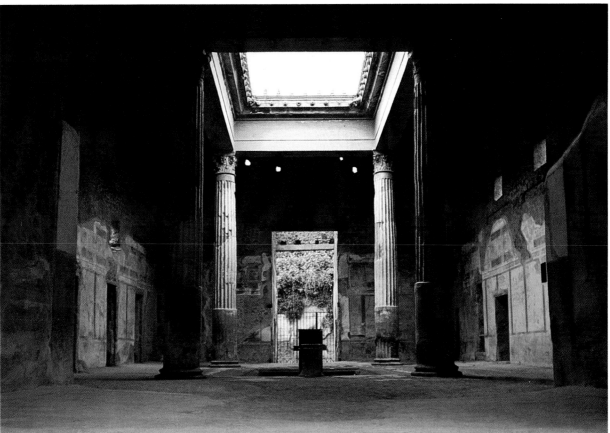

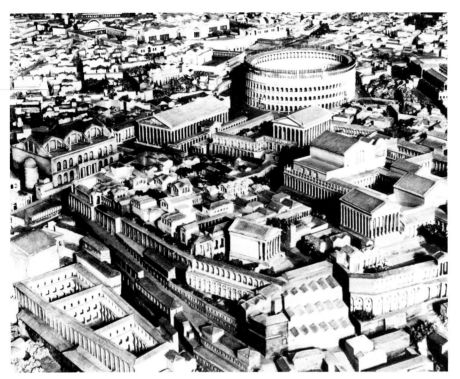

4.19 Model of ancient Rome as it was in about A.D. 320. Museo della Civiltà Romana, Rome. In the right center is the emperor's palace on the Palatine Hill, with the Colosseum above and the mammoth Basilica of Constantine at the upper left.

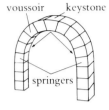

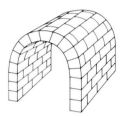

4.21 *Top:* Simple arch composed of wedge-shaped blocks (or *voussoirs*) and *keystone;* the curve of the arch rises from the *springers* on either side. *Center:* Tunnel or barrel vault composed of a series of arches. *Bottom:* Dome composed of a series of arches intersecting each other around a central axis.

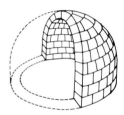

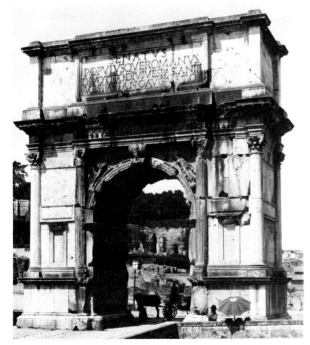

4.20 Arch of Titus, Rome. A.D. 81. Height 47′4″ (14.43 m). This structure commemorates the Roman capture of Jerusalem in A.D. 70.

vault and the dome—were to pass into the Western architectural tradition.

The Greeks had rarely built arches, but the Etruscans used them as early as the 5th century B.C., and the Romans may well have borrowed the arch form from them. From the 2nd century B.C. on, stone arches were regularly used for bridges and aqueducts. Vaults of small size were often used for domestic buildings, and by the time of Augustus architects had begun to construct larger-scale barrel vaults, semicylindrical in shape, two or more of which could intersect to roof a large area. The dome, which is really a hemispherical vault, became increasingly popular with the building of the vast public baths of imperial Rome. Using both bricks and concrete, architects could combine vaults, barrel vaults, and domes to construct very elaborate buildings capable of holding thousands of people at a time. The inside and outside surfaces of the buildings were then covered with a marble facing to conceal the elaborate internal support structures.

THE ARTS AND INVENTION: *Roman Concrete*

The domes, arches, and vaults typical of Roman architecture were only made possible by the Romans' invention of concrete. The Egyptians and Mesopotamians had used sun-dried bricks to build vaults. The Greeks, whose principal building material was stone, did not even attempt to solve the problem of cutting and balancing stone blocks to form domes or arches until the Hellenistic period. Etruscan arches were also made of stone; the blocks were so large and unwieldy that it must have been arduous and time-consuming to raise them into place.

Toward the end of the 2nd century B.C. Roman builders discovered that by mixing stone chips with quicklime and water, they could obtain a compound that could be laid wet and that would dry into a material of incomparable hardness. The quicklime was obtained by heating limestone; its effect is first to dissolve the stone fragments and then to solidify them.

In constructing concrete walls, Roman builders first built up the outer faces of the walls and then poured concrete between them; in this way the concrete became sandwiched between the outer faces and held the whole wall firm. In the case of vaults, or domes such as the Pantheon's, a wooden framework was probably erected on which the concrete was built up in layers. Quite apart from the vast range of architectural possibilities these techniques made possible, building in concrete had the great advantage of being inexpensive. The stone chips were the discarded waste material from masons' or sculptors' workshops, while the finest-quality quicklime was produced from the volcanic rock in which Italy is so rich. The only disadvantage of concrete is that it is damaged by moisture. The outsides of buildings were therefore lined with bricks or stones (or a combination) and the inside walls were covered either with stucco (a kind of plaster) or with a thin layer of marble or other stone.

The discovery of concrete revolutionized the history of architecture. Even though they have not always used concrete, architects of major buildings ever since Roman times have turned to the dome as a shape of especial grandeur and majesty.

Much of the work of these architects was destroyed during the barbarian invasions of the 5th and 6th centuries A.D. and more was wrecked in the Renaissance by builders looking for bricks or marble. By great good fortune one of the most superb of all imperial structures has been preserved almost intact.

The Pantheon [4.22] was built around 126, during the reign of Hadrian (117–138) to a design by the emperor himself. An austere and majestic exterior portico is supported on granite columns with Corinthian capitals [4.23]. It leads into the central rotunda, an astonishing construction approximately 142 feet

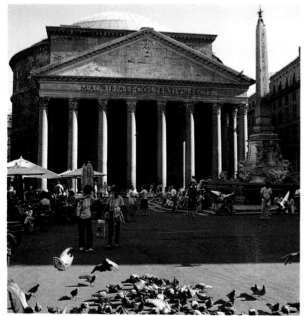

4.22   Pantheon, Rome. c. A.D. 126. Height of portico 59′ (17.98 m).

4.23   Corinthian capital. This elaborate bell-shape design, decorated with acanthus leaves, first became commonly used in Hellenistic times. It was especially popular with Roman architects, who in general preferred it to both the Doric and Ionic styles.

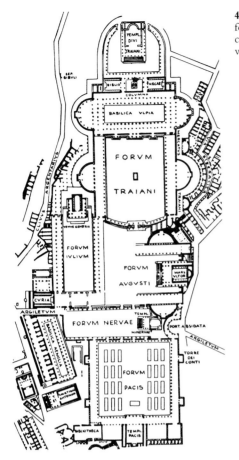

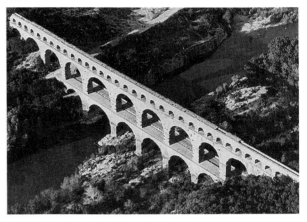

4.24 Plan of the imperial fora, Rome. Unlike the Republican forum, which served as a public meeting place, these huge complexes were constructed as monuments to the emperors who commissioned them.

4.25 Pont du Gard, near Nîmes in southern France. Late 1st century B.C. Length 902′ (274.93 m), height 161′ (49.07 m). Note the careful positioning of the three rows of arches along the top of which ran the water channel. The whole aqueduct was 25 miles (40 kilometers) long. This section carried the water over the river Gard.

(43.3 meters) high and wide in which a huge concrete dome rests on a wall interrupted by a series of niches. The building's only light source is a huge *oculus* (eye) at the top of the dome, an opening 30 feet (9.2 meters) across. The proportions of the building are very carefully calculated and contribute to its air of balance. The height of the dome from the ground, for example, is exactly equal to its width.

The Pantheon was dwarfed by the huge complex of buildings that made up the imperial fora. Completed by the beginning of the 2nd century A.D., they formed a vast architectural design unsurpassed in antiquity and barely equaled since [4.24]. Elsewhere in the city baths, theaters, temples, race tracks, and libraries catered to the needs and fancies of a huge urban population. In many of these structures, builders continued to experiment with new techniques of construction, and architectural principles developed in Rome were applied throughout the Roman Empire. From Spain to the Middle East theaters, amphitheaters, and other public buildings were erected according to the same basic designs, leaving a

permanent record of construction methods for later generations.

Urban life on such a scale required a constant supply of one of the basic human necessities, water. Their system of aqueducts is one of the most impressive of the Romans' engineering achievements. A vast network of pipes brought millions of gallons of water a day into Rome, distributing it to public fountains and baths and to the private villas of the wealthy. At the same time a system of covered street drains was built, eliminating the open sewers that had been usual before Roman times. These open drains were to return during the medieval period, when many of the Roman engineering skills were gone.

With the passage of time, most of the aqueducts that supplied ancient Rome have been demolished or have collapsed. Elsewhere in the Roman Empire, however, examples have survived that give some idea of Roman engineering skill. The famous Pont du Gard [4.25], which can still be seen in southern France, was probably first constructed during the

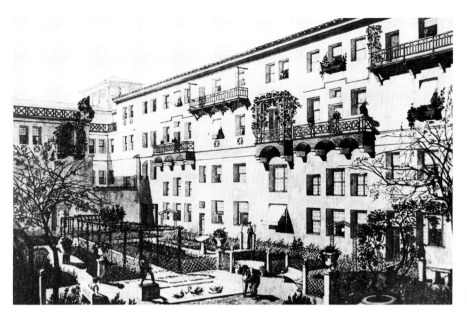

4.26 Reconstruction drawing of the garden facade of the Insula dei Dipinti, an apartment block in Ostia, the seaport of ancient Rome.

reign of Augustus. It carried the aqueduct that supplied the Roman city of Nîmes with water—a hundred gallons (387.5 liters) a day for each inhabitant—and was made of uncemented stone. The largest blocks weigh 2 tons (1.8 metric tons).

Even with the provision of such facilities, imperial Rome suffered from overcrowding. The average Roman lived in an apartment block, of which there were some 45,000. Most of these have long since disappeared, although their appearance can be reconstructed from examples excavated at Ostia, Rome's port [4.26]. The height of the apartment blocks was controlled by law to prevent the construction of unsafe buildings, but it was not unheard of for a building to collapse and fire was a constant danger. No doubt the grandeur of the public buildings in Rome was intended at least in part to distract the poorer Romans from thoughts of their humble private residences.

CONTEMPORARY VOICES

A Dinner Party in Imperial Rome

At the end of this course Trimalchio left the table to relieve himself, and so finding ourselves free from the constraint of his overbearing presence, we began to indulge in a little friendly conversation. Accordingly Dama began first, after calling for a cup of wine. "A day! what is a day?" he exclaimed, "before you can turn round, it's night again! So really you can't do better than go straight from bed to board. Fine cold weather we've been having; why! even my bath has hardly warmed me. But truly hot liquor is a good clothier. I've been drinking bumpers, and I'm downright fuddled. The wine has got into my head."

Seleucus then struck into the talk: "I don't bathe every day," he said; "your systematic bather's a mere fuller. Water's got teeth, and melts the heart away, a little every day; but there! when I've fortified my belly with a cup of mulled wine, I say 'Go hang!' to the cold. Indeed I couldn't bathe to-day, for I've been to a fu-

neral. A fine fellow he was too, good old Chrysanthus, but he's given up the ghost now. He was calling me just this moment, only just this moment; I could fancy myself talking to him now. Alas! alas! what are we but blown bladders on two legs? We're nor worth as much as flies; they are some use, but we're no better than bubbles." "He wasn't careful enough in his diet?" "I tell you, for five whole days not one drop of water, or one crumb of bread, passed his lips. Nevertheless he has joined the majority. The doctors killed him,—or rather his day was come; the very best of doctors is only a satisfaction to the mind. Anyhow he was handsomely buried, on his own best bed, with good blankets. The wailing was first class,—he did a trifle manumission before he died; though no doubt his wife's tears were a bit forced. A pity he always treated her so well. But woman! woman's of the kite kind. No man ought ever to do 'em a good turn; just as well pitch it in the well at once. Old love's an eating sore!"

From Petronius, *The Satyricon,* trans. attributed to Oscar Wilde (privately printed, 1928), p. 81.

Rome as the Object of Satire

Life in this huge metropolis had many of the problems of big-city living today: noise, traffic jams, dirty streets, and overcrowding were all constant sources of complaint. A particularly bitter protest comes from the Roman satirist Juvenal (A.D. c. 60–c. 130). Born in the provinces, he came to Rome, where he served as a magistrate and irritated the current emperor, Domitian—not a difficult task. After a period of exile, probably in Egypt, he returned to Rome and lived in considerable poverty. Toward the end of his life, however, his circumstances improved. His sixteen *Satires* make it perfectly clear that Juvenal liked neither Rome nor Romans. He tells us that he writes out of fierce outrage at the corruption and decadence of his day, the depraved aristocracy, the general greed and meanness. "At such a time who could *not* write satire?" His fiercest loathing is reserved for foreigners, although in the sixth *Satire* he launches a particularly virulent attack against women in one of the archetypal documents of misogyny.

Juvenal himself does not emerge as a very pleasant character and his obsessive hatred frequently verges on the psychopathic. As a satirical poet, though, he is among the greatest in Western literature, and strongly influenced many of his successors, including Jonathan Swift. Few other writers can make better or more powerful use of biting sarcasm, irony, and outright invective.

The End of the Roman Empire

Few historical subjects have been as much discussed as the fall of the Roman Empire. It is not even possible to agree on when it fell, let alone why. The traditional date, A.D. 476, marks the deposition of the last Roman emperor, Romulus Augustulus. By that time, however, the political unity of the empire had already disintegrated. Perhaps the beginning of the end was A.D. 330, when the emperor Constantine moved the capital from Rome to a new city on the Bosporus, Constantinople, although in another sense the transfer represented a new development as much as a conclusion. It might even be possible to argue that Constantine's successors in the East, the Byzantine emperors, were the successors of Augustus and that there is a continuous tradition from the beginning of the empire in 31 B.C. to the fall of Constantinople in A.D. 1453.

Fascinating though the question may be, in a sense it is theoretical rather than practical. The Roman Empire did not fall overnight. Many of the causes for its long decline are obvious though not always easy

to order in importance. One crucial factor was the growing power and changing character of the army. The larger it became, the more necessary it was to recruit troops from the more distant provinces—Germans, Illyrians, and others, the very people the army was supposed to be holding in check. Most of these soldiers had never been anywhere near Rome. They felt no loyalty to the empire, no reason to defend Roman interests. A succession of emperors had to buy their support by raising their pay and promising gifts of lands. At the same time, the army came to play an increasingly prominent part in the choice of a new emperor, and, since the army itself was largely non-Roman, so were many of the emperors chosen. Rulers of the 3rd and 4th centuries included Africans, Thracians, a Syrian, and an Arab, men unlikely to feel any strong reason to place the interests of Rome over those of themselves and their own men.

Throughout this late period the empire was increasingly threatened from outside. To the west, barbarian tribes like the Huns, the Goths, and the Alemanni began to penetrate farther and farther into its defenses and even to sack Rome itself. Meanwhile, in the East, Roman armies were continually involved in resisting the growing power of the Persians. In many parts of the empire it became clear that Rome could provide no help against invaders, and some of the provinces set themselves up as independent states with their own armies.

Problems like these inevitably had a devastating effect on the economy. Taxes increased and the value of money declined. The constant threat of invasion or civil war made trade impossible. What funds there were went for the support of the army, and the general standard of living suffered a steady decline. The eastern provinces, the old Hellenistic kingdoms, suffered rather less than the rest of the empire, since they were protected in part by the wealth accumulated over the centuries and by their long tradition of civilization. As a result, Italy sank to the level of a province rather than remaining the center of the imperial administration.

Total collapse was prevented by the efforts of two emperors: Diocletian, who ruled from A.D. 284 to 305, and Constantine, who ruled from 306 to 337. Both men were masterly organizers who realized that the only way to save the empire was to impose the most stringent controls on every aspect of life—social, administrative, and economic. In 301 the Edict of Diocletian was passed, establishing fixed maximums for the sale of goods and for wages. A vast bureaucracy was set up to collect taxes and administer the provinces. The emperor himself became once again the focal point of the empire, but to protect himself from the dangers of coups and assassina-

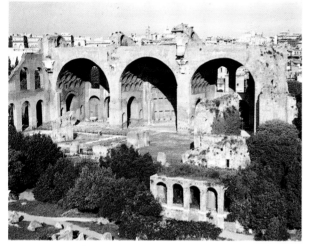

4.27 Basilica of Constantine, the last great imperial building in Rome. Begun in A.D. 306 by Maxentius, it was finished by Constantine after 315. Only the northern side is still standing; the central nave and south aisle collapsed during antiquity.

tions, he never appeared in public. As a result, an elaborate court with complex rituals developed, and the emperor's claim to semidivine status invested him with a new religious authority.

Late Roman Art and Architecture

Even if the emperor did not show himself to his subjects, he could impress them in other ways, and the reigns of Diocletian and Constantine marked the last great age of Roman architecture. The immense Basilica of Constantine [4.27], with its central nave rising to a height of 100 feet (30.5 meters), is now in ruins, but in its day this assembly hall must have been a powerful reminder of the emperor's authority. It also contained a 30-foot (9.2-meter) statue of the emperor himself [4.28]. The palace Diocletian had built for him at Split, on the Adriatic coast, is constructed on the plan of a military camp, with enormous central avenues dividing it into four quarters [4.29]. The decoration makes use of Eastern motifs, and the whole design is far from the classical style of earlier times.

4.28 Head of the colossal statue of Constantine that stood in the Basilica of Constantine, Rome. A.D. 324–330. Marble, height 8′6″ (2.59 m). Palazzo dei Conservatori, Rome. The massive and majestic simplicity of this portrait is very different from the detailed observation of earlier, much smaller Roman portraits like that of Cicero (figure 4.7), illustrating the new belief in the emperor as God's regent on earth.

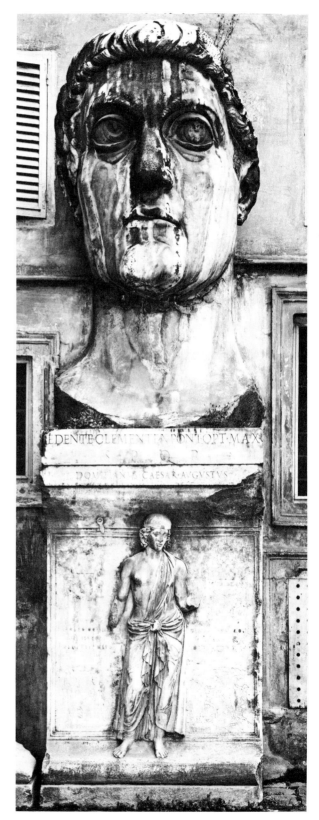

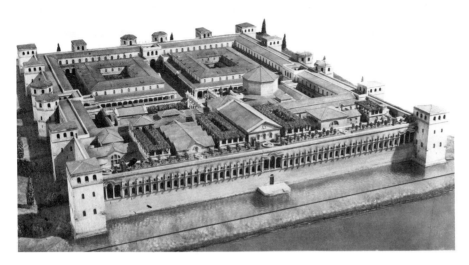

4.29 Reconstruction model of the Palace of Diocletian at Split, Yugoslavia. A.D. 300–305. Museo della Civiltà Romana, Rome. Note the octagonal dome of the emperor's mausoleum.

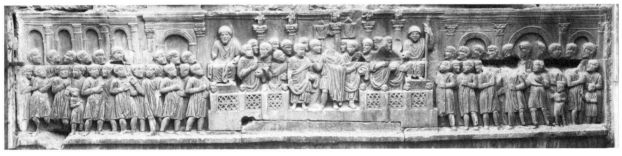

4.30 *Constantine Receiving Homage from the Senate,* frieze on the Arch of Constantine, Rome. A.D. 315. Marble, 3′4″ × 17′6″ (1.02 × 5.33 m). On both sides of the emperor (seated in the center) his officials distribute money to the crowds below. The simplified style, in which most of the puppetlike figures are shown frontally, foreshadows Byzantine and medieval art and is certainly very different from the style of earlier reliefs (figures 4.11, 4.12).

In sculpture, too, classical forms and styles were increasingly abandoned. Realistic portraiture and naturalistic drapery were neglected, and sculptors no longer tried to express depth or reality in their relief carving. The lack of perspective and precision in their work foreshadows the art of the early Middle Ages [4.30]. The general abandonment of classical ideas these artistic changes indicate went along with a waning of interest in Stoicism and Epicureanism and a new enthusiasm for Eastern religious cults. Traditional Roman religion had always been organized by the state, and from the time of the late Republic some Romans had sought a more personal religious satisfaction in the worship of Eastern deities. During the last stages of the empire strong cults developed around the Phygian goddess Cybele, the Egyptian Isis, and the sun god Mithras.

The appearance and eventual triumph of Christianity is outside the scope of this account, but its emergence as the official religion of the empire played a final and decisive part in bringing to an end the classical era. Pagan art, pagan literature, and pagan culture as a whole represented forces and ideals Christianity strongly rejected, and the art of the early Christians is fundamentally different in its inspiration. Yet even the fathers of the early Church, implacable opponents of paganism, could not fail to be moved by the end of so great a cultural tradition.

The memory of Rome's greatness lived on through the succeeding ages of turmoil and achievement and the classical spirit survived, to be reborn triumphantly in the Renaissance.

Summary

The vast extent of ancient Roman history—more than twelve hundred years—can be conveniently divided into three chief periods: the Monarchy (753 B.C.–510 B.C.); the Republic (509 B.C.–31 B.C.); and the Empire (31 B.C.–A.D. 476).

The city was founded in the mid-8th century, around the time the Greeks were setting up colonies in southern Italy and Sicily. Rome's first inhabitants were Latins, an Italian people native to central Italy, after whom the Roman language is named. Traditional accounts of the city's origins claimed that its first rulers were a series of seven kings. The first four were Latin, but in 616 B.C. Rome fell under Etruscan control. The Etruscans had developed in the region of central Italy to the north of Rome, although their origins are uncertain; they may have migrated to Italy from western Asia.

Etruscan art was strongly influenced by Greek and Orientalizing styles. Among the most striking works to survive are the tomb paintings at Tarquinia, one of the principal Etruscan cities, and the sculpture from the temple of Apollo at Veii. Although many Etruscan inscriptions can be deciphered, no Etruscan literature has been discovered. For the century during which they ruled Rome, the Etruscans expanded its trade contacts and introduced important technological innovations. In 510 B.C. the Romans drove out the last Etruscan king.

In 509 B.C. the Roman Republic was declared. The political system of the new state evolved from the need to achieve a balance of political power between the two classes of citizens: the aristocratic patricians and the people, or plebeians. There gradually developed two political institutions, the Senate and the Assembly of the people, while plebeians eventually won the right to run for election to virtually all offices of state. The growth of internal political stability was accompanied by the spread of Roman power throughout Italy. Among those to fall under Roman domination were the Etruscans, their former rulers. Little in the way of art or literature has survived from this early period, and most of what was produced seems to have been inspired by Etruscan or, more generally, Greek models.

In 264 B.C. there began a series of wars between Rome and her chief rival in the western Mediterranean, Carthage. By 201 B.C. the Romans had proved victorious, and Roman colonies were established in Spain and North Africa. Throughout the following century Roman power spread eastward. In 146 B.C. Greece was absorbed into the Roman empire, and the Hellenistic kingdom of Pergamum was bequeathed to Rome by its last king, Attalus III, on his death in 133 B.C. The 2nd century B.C. also saw the beginnings of the development of an independent Roman culture, although Greek influence remained strong. The Roman poet Ennius composed his epic, the *Annales,* while Plautus and Terence wrote comedies based on Greek originals. Greek music became popular at Rome, and the two chief schools of Greek philosophy, Stoicism and Epicureanism, began to attract Roman adherents.

With such vast territorial expansion, strains began to appear in Roman political and social life. The growth of a middle class, the equites, disturbed the old equilibrium, and the last century of the Republic (133 B.C. to 31 B.C.) was beset by continual crisis. A succession of powerful figures—Marius, Sulla, Pompey, Caesar—struggled to assume control of the state. The last of these proved victorious in 48 B.C., only to be assassinated four years later. Amid bitter fighting between Mark Antony, Caesar's lieutenant, and Octavius, the late dictator's nephew and heir, the Republic collapsed.

The political confusion of the Republic's last century was accompanied by important cultural developments. Among the major literary figures of the age were the Epicurean poet Lucretius, the lyric poet Catullus, and the orator and politician Cicero. Caesar himself combined his political and military career with the writing of accounts of his campaigns. In the visual arts realistic portrait sculpture became common, while the invention of concrete was to have enormous consequences both for Roman building and for the history of all later architecture in the West. Sulla's great Sanctuary at Praeneste inaugurated the tradition of large-scale public building projects that was to become common during the empire.

In 31 B.C. Octavius defeated the combined forces of Antony and Cleopatra to emerge as sole ruler of the Roman world; in 27 B.C., under the name Augustus, he became its first emperor. The Augustan age marked the high point of Roman art and literature, and many of its finest achievements were produced to celebrate the Augustan revolution. Vergil was commissioned to write a Roman national epic: the result was the *Aeneid.* Livy composed an account of Rome's early history in his *Annals of the Roman People.* Horace's *Carmen Saeculare* was written for Augustus' great popular festival of 17 B.C. Augustus himself was portrayed in numerous statues and portraits, including the Augustus of Prima Porta, and in the reliefs on the Ara Pacis. Important public works included the Pont du Gard near Nîmes, France.

From the time of Augustus until A.D. 476, the empire was ruled by a series of emperors who were increasingly dependent on an elaborate state bureaucracy. Augustus and his first four successors were from a single family, but with time Emperors either seized power for themselves or were imposed by the army. The empire continued to expand until the reign of Hadrian (A.D. 117–138), who fixed its borders to achieve stability abroad.

Some idea of the character of provincial daily life in the empire can be gained from the escavations at Pompeii and the other cities around the Bay of Naples, which were destroyed by an eruption of the volcano Vesuvius in A.D. 79. Writers of the early Empire included the historian Tacitus and the satirist Juvenal. Among the most impressive works of architecture of the period is the Pantheon, designed by Hadrian himself, which makes bold use of concrete.

The 3rd century was marked by continual struggles for imperial power. A brief peace was imposed in the reign of Aurelian (A.D. 270–275), but it proved temporary. Only the Emperor Diocletian (A.D. 284–305) managed to restore order by massive administrative and economic reform. After Diocletian's retirement to his palace at Split, one of his successors, Constantine (A.D. 307–337), transferred the imperial capital from Rome to the new city of Constantinople in A.D. 330, and the western part of the empire began its final decline. During this last period Roman art became less realistic as classical forms and styles were abandoned in favor of simpler, more massive effects. Finally Rome itself was shaken by barbarian assaults, and the last western emperor was forced to abdicate in A.D. 476.

Pronounciation Guide

Aeneid: Ee-NEE-id
Anchises: Ank-ICE-ease
Ara Pacis: ARE-a PAH-kiss
Ceres: SEAR-ease
Cerveteri: Cher-VET-er-ee
Cicero: SISS-er-owe
Cybele: KIB-e-lee
Dido: DIE-doe
Diocletian: Die-owe-KLEE-shan
Epictetus: Ep-ic-TEE-tus
Epicureanism: Ep-ik-you-REE-an-ism
Etruscans: Et-RUSK-ans
Gaius: GUY-us
Ius Civile: YUS kiv-EE-lay
Lydia: LID-i-a
Pantheon: PAN-thi-on
Plautus: PLOR-tus
Plebeians: Pleb-EE-ans
Pliny: PLIN-ee
Praeneste: Pry-NEST-ee
Stoicism: STOW-i-sism
Tacitus: TASS-it-us
Tarquinia: Tar-QUIN-i-a
Veii: VAY-ee
Winckelmann: VIN-kel-man

Exercises

1. What are the chief features of Etruscan culture and religion? What light do they cast on the problem of the Etruscans' origins?
2. "Roman art and culture are late and debased forms of Hellenistic art." Discuss.
3. In what ways does the *Aeneid* fulfill its aim to provide the Romans with a national epic? Compare it in this respect with the Greek epics, the *Iliad* and *Odyssey*, discussed in Chapter 2.
4. Describe in detail Augustus' use of the visual arts as instruments of propaganda. Are there comparable examples of the arts used for political purposes in recent times?
5. What do the discoveries at Rome and Pompeii tell us about daily life in the Roman Empire? In what significant respects did it differ from life today?

Further Reading

Brendel, O. J. *Etruscan Art*. Baltimore: Penguin, 1978. The most up-to-date survey of Etruscan painting and sculpture, with numerous illustrations.

Commager, S., ed. *Virgil, a Collection of Critical Essays*. Englewood Cliffs, N.J.: Prentice-Hall, 1966. The literature on Vergil is immense and wide-ranging, but this volume of essays provides a useful survey of modern critical approaches and suggests some further directions for the interested reader to explore.

Crawford, M. *The Roman Republic*. Cambridge, Mass.: Harvard University Press, 1982. An excellent survey of Republican history and culture, particularly good on coinage.

Grant, M. *Cities of Vesuvius: Pompeii and Herculaneum*. New York: American Heritage Press, 1971. This well-illustrated account describes the rediscovery of the buried cities, and analyzes the evidence they provide about Roman daily life.

Graves, Robert. *I, Claudius* and *Claudius the God*. Baltimore: Penguin, 1977. These two historical novels, originally published in 1934, are recreations of the Roman world that are both scholarly and thoroughly absorbing. Highly recommended.

Hanfmann, G. M. A. *Roman Art*. New York: Norton, 1975. The best introduction to the subject, with a very full selection of illustrations, sensitive comments, and up-to-date bibliographical notes.

Hooper, F. *Roman Realities*. Detroit: Wayne State University Press, 1980. A useful introduction to recent scholarship in Roman studies.

McKay, A. *Houses, Villas, and Palaces in the Roman World*. New York: Thames and Hudson, 1975. A guide to Roman domestic architecture, covering all parts of the Roman world. Good illustrations and diagrams.

Pallottino, M. *The Etruscans*. Baltimore: Penguin, 1975. A revised version of the standard work by the most eminent Etruscologist of our time, covering all aspects of Etruscan culture. Especially good on the language.

Potter, T. *The Changing Landscape of Southern Etruria*. New York: St. Martin's Press, 1979. A study of the material remains of central Italy, from the Etruscans and earlier to the present. An engrossing look at new archaeological techniques in action.

Scullard, H. H. *From the Gracchi to Nero*. Third edition. London: Methuen, 1970. A useful survey of the history of the late Republic and the early empire, reflecting the state of modern scholarly opinion.

Vermeule, C. *Greek Sculpture and Roman Taste*. Ann Arbor: University of Michigan Press, 1977. This book casts considerable light on Roman attitudes toward Greek culture by describing how the Romans used Greek sculpture, both originals and copies, in their own public buildings and private estates.

Ward-Perkins, J. B. *Cities of Ancient Greece and Italy*. New York: Braziller, 1974. A magisterial account of city planning in the ancient world, distilled in a mere 128 pages.

Vickers, M. *The Roman World*. Oxford: Elsevier/Phaidon, 1977. A fully illustrated account of Roman art and archaeology, also valuable for its discussion of the rediscovery of classical antiquity in the Renaissance.

Reading Selections

Catullus
Selected Poems

Many of Catullus' short poems trace the course of his relationship with a girl given the pseudonym of Lesbia; her real name was Clodia, and she was the sister of Cicero's archenemy Publius Clodius Pulcher. The poems written in the early days of their affair express Catullus' joy, in language of almost musical beauty.

The contentment was not to last. Lesbia lost interest, even as Catullus continued to protest his love. Driven to desperation by the hopelessness of his cause, he described in later poems his vain attempts to cure himself of the "fever" of his passion, until finally he could take no more: the last of the Lesbia poems expresses bitterness and hatred.

This short sequence follows their affair from rapturous beginning to hostile break-up; the reader inclined to sympathize with Catullus' pain should, of course, remember that Lesbia's (that is Clodia's) side of the story remains untold.

V

My darling, let us live
  And love for ever.
They with no love to give,
  Who feel no fever,
Who have no tale to tell
  But one of warning—
The pack of them might sell
  For half a farthing.
The sunset's dying ray
  Has its returning,
But fires of our brief day
  Shall end their burning
In night where joy and pain
  Are past recalling—
So kiss me, kiss again—
  The night is falling.

Kiss me and kiss again,
  Nor spare thy kisses.
Let thousand kisses rain
  A thousand blisses.
Then, when ten thousand more

Their strength have wasted,
Let's wipe out all the score
  Of what we've tasted:
Lest we should count our bliss
  To our undoing,
Or others grudge the kiss
  On kiss accruing.

LXXXVII

None could ever say that she,
Lesbia! was so loved by me.
Never all the world around
Faith so true as mine was found:
If no longer it endures
(Would it did!) the fault is yours.
I can never think again
Well of you: I try in vain:
But—be false—do what you will—
Lesbia! I must love you still.

LXXV

The office of my heart is still to love
  When I would hate.
Time and again your faithlessness I prove
  Proven too late.
Your ways might mend, yet my contempt could never
  Be now undone.
Yet crimes repeated cannot stop this fever
  From burning on.

LVIII

She that I loved, that face,
  Those hands, that hair,
Dearer than all my race,
  As dear as fair—
See her where throngs parade
  Th' imperial route,
Plying her skill unpaid—
  Rome's prostitute.

Vergil
from the AENEID, Book IV

The bitter confrontation between Dido and Aeneas in Book IV of the Aeneid *forms the emotional heart of the epic's first half. The scene begins as Aeneas has received the divine message to leave Carthage and continue on his journey. He says nothing to Dido for the moment and makes his preparations for departure. The queen cannot be fooled so easily; in a frenzy of grief and rage, she accuses him of deserting her. Aeneas' response seems cold and indicates the sacrifice of personal feelings his mission requires. His ap-*

peal to common sense and the will of the gods only enrages Dido further; she dismisses him with words of furious contempt. Yet at the end of the scene Vergil leaves no doubt as to Aeneas' terrible dilemma. Faced with the choice between love and duty he has chosen duty, but only at the price of personal anguish.

But who can ever hoodwink a woman in
    love? The queen,
Apprehensive even when things went well, now
    sensed his deception,
Got wind of what was going to happen. That
    mischievous Rumour,
Whispering the fleet was preparing to sail, put
    her in a frenzy.
Distraught, she witlessly wandered about the
    city, raving
Like some Bacchante driven wild, when the
    emblems of sanctity
Stir, by the shouts of "Hail, Bacchus!" and
    drawn to Cithaeron
At night by the din of revellers, at the triennial
    orgies.
Finding Aeneas at last, she cried, before he
    could speak:—
    Unfaithful man, did you think you could do
      such a dreadful thing   10
And keep it dark? yes, skulk from my land
    without one word?
Our love, the vows you made me—do these
    not give you pause,
Nor even the thought of Dido meeting a painful
    death?
Now, in the dead of winter, to be getting your
    ships ready
And hurrying to set sail when northerly gales
    are blowing,
You heartless one! Suppose the fields were not
    foreign, the home was
Not strange that you are bound for, suppose
    Troy stood as of old,
Would you be sailing for Troy, now, in this
    stormy weather?
Am I your reason for going? By these tears, by
    the hand you gave me—
They are all I have left, to-day, in my
    misery—I implore you,   20
And by our union of hearts, by our marriage
    hardly begun,
If I have ever helped you at all, if anything
About me pleased you, be sad for our broken
    home, forgo
Your purpose, I beg you, unless it's too late for
    prayers of mine!
Because of you, the Libyan tribes and the
    Nomad chieftains

Hate me, the Tyrians are hostile: because of you
    I have lost
My old reputation for faithfulness—the one
    thing that could have made me
Immortal. Oh, I am dying! To what, my guest,
    are you leaving me?
"Guest"—that is all I may call you now, who
    have called you husband.
Why do I linger here? Shall I wait till my
    brother, Pygmalion,   30
Destroys this place, or Iarbas leads me away
    captive?
If even I might have conceived a child by you
    before
You went away, a little Aeneas to play in the
    palace
And, in spite of all this, to remind me of you
    by his looks, oh then
I should not feel so utterly finished and desolate.
    She had spoken. Aeneas, mindful of Jove's
    words, kept his eyes
Unyielding, and with a great effort repressed his
    feeling for her.
In the end he managed to answer:—
    Dido, I'll never pretend
You have not been good to me, deserving of
    everything   40
You can claim. I shall not regret my memories
    of Elissa
As long as I breathe, as long as I remember my
    own self.
For my conduct—this, briefly: I did not look to
    make off from here
In secret—do not suppose it; nor did I offer you
    marriage
At any time or consent to be bound by a
    marriage contract.
If fate allowed me to be my own master, and
    gave me
Free will to choose my way of life, to solve my
    problems,
Old Troy would be my first choice: I would
    restore it, and honour
My people's relics—the high halls of Priam
    perpetuated,
Troy given back to its conquered sons, a
    renaissant city,   50
Had been my task. But now Apollo and the
    Lycian
Oracle have told me that Italy is our bourne.
There lies my heart, my homeland. You, a
    Phoenician, are held by
These Carthaginian towers, by the charm of
    your Libyan city:
So can you grudge us Trojans our vision of
    settling down

In Italy? We too may seek a kingdom abroad.
Often as night envelops the earth in dewy
    darkness,
Often as star-rise, the troubled ghost of my
    father, Anchises,
Comes to me in my dreams, warns me and
    frightens me.
I am disturbed no less by the wrong I am doing
    Ascanius,   60
Defrauding him of his destined realm in
    Hesperia.
What's more, just now the courier of heaven,
    sent by Jupiter—
I swear it on your life and mine—conveyed to
    me, swiftly flying,
His orders: I saw the god, as clear as day, with
    my own eyes,
Entering the city, and these ears drank in the
    words he uttered.
No more reproaches, then—they only torture
    us both.
God's will, not mine, says "Italy".
    All the while he was speaking she gazed at
    him askance,
Her glances flickering over him, eyes exploring
    the whole man
In deadly silence. Now, furiously, she burst
    out:—   70
    Faithless and false! No goddess mothered
    you, no Dardanus
Your ancestor! I believe harsh Caucasus begat
    you
On a flint-hearted rock and Hyrcanian tigers
    suckled you.
Why should I hide my feelings? What worse can
    there be to keep them for?
Not one sigh from him when I wept! Not a
    softer glance!
Did he yield an inch, or a tear, in pity for her
    who loves him?
I don't know what to say first. It has come to
    this,—not Juno,
Not Jove himself can view my plight with the
    eye of justice.
Nowhere is it safe to be trustful. I took him, a
    castaway,
A pauper, and shared my kingdom with him—I
    must have been mad—   80
Rescued his lost fleet, rescued his friends from
    death.
Oh, I'm on fire and drifting! And now Apollo's
    prophecies,
Lycian oracles, couriers of heaven sent by
    Jupiter
With stern commands—all these order you to
    betray me.
Oh, of course this is just the sort of transaction
    that troubles the calm of
The gods. I'll not keep you, nor probe the
    dishonest of your words,
Chase your Italy, then! Go, sail to your realm
    overseas!
I only hope that, if the just spirits have any power,
Marooned on some mid-sea rock you may
    drink the full cup of agony
And often cry out for Dido. I'll dog you, from
    far, with the death-fires;   90
And when cold death has parted my soul from
    my body, my spectre
Will be wherever you are. You shall pay for the
    evil you've done me.
The tale of your punishment will come to me
    down in the shades.
    With these words Dido suddenly ended, and
    sick at heart
Turned from him, tore herself away from his
    eyes, ran indoors,
While he hung back in dread of a still worse
    scene, although
He had much to say. Her maids bore up the
    fainting queen
Into her marble chamber and laid her down on
    the bed.
    But the god-fearing Aeneas, much as he
    longed to soothe
Her anguish with consolation, with words that
    would end her troubles,   100
Heavily sighing, his heart melting from love of
    her,
Nevertheless obeyed the gods and went off to
    his fleet.

Vergil
from the AENEID, Book VI

In Book VI of the Aeneid *Aeneas travels to the underworld led by his guide, the Sibyl of Cumae, to learn of the
future destiny both of himself and of Rome. The opening
lines of this extract evoke the melancholy gloom of the
scene; as Aeneas comes to the river of the dead the poet
emphasizes the sadness of those trying to cross it by a string
of pathetic images. Aeneas' journey is necessary because he
has to confront his past and come to terms with it before he
can move on to his future heroic destiny. As the Sibyl leads
him through the ranks of the dead he meets Palinurus, an
old comrade who had fallen overboard on the way from
Troy and drowned. The most emotional encounter, however, is the one that concludes this episode—Aeneas' meeting with Dido. Now it is Aeneas who weeps and pleads,
while Dido neither looks at him nor speaks.*

You gods who rule the kingdom of souls!
      You soundless shades!
Chaos, and Phlegethon! O mute wide leagues of
      Nightland!—
Grant me to tell what I have heard! With your
      assent
May I reveal what lies deep in the gloom of the
      Underworld!
      Dimly through the shadows and dark
            solitudes they wended,
Through the void domiciles of Dis, the bodiless
      regions:
Just as, through fitful moonbeams, under the
      moon's thin light,
A path lies in a forest, when Jove has palled the
      sky
With gloom, and the night's blackness has bled
      the world of colour.   10
See! At the very porch and entrance way to
      Orcus
Grief and ever-haunting Anxiety make their
      bed:
Here dwell pallid Diseases, here morose Old
      Age,
With Fear, ill-prompting Hunger, and squalid
      Indigence,
Shapes horrible to look at, Death and Agony;
Sleep, too, which is the cousin of Death; and
      Guilty Joys,
And there, against the threshold, War, the
      bringer of Death:
Here are the iron cells of the Furies, and lunatic
      Strife
Whose viperine hair is caught up with a
      headband soaked in blood.
      In the open a huge dark elm tree spreads
            wide its immemorial   20
Branches like arms, whereon, according to old
      wives' tales,
Roost the unsolid Dreams, clinging everywhere
      under its foliage.
Besides, many varieties of monsters can be found
Stabled here at the doors—Centaurs and
      freakish Scyllas,
Briareus with his hundred hands, the Lernaean
      Hydra
That hisses terribly and the flame-throwing
      Chimaera,
Gorgons and Harpies, and the ghost of three-
      bodied Geryon.
Now did Aeneas shake with a spasm of fear,
      and drawing
His sword, offered its edge against the creatures'
      onset:
Had not his learned guide assured him they
      were but incorporeal   30

Existences floating there, forms with no
      substance behind them,
He'd have attacked them, and wildly winnowed
      with steel mere shadows.
      From here is the road that leads to the dismal
            waters of Acheron.
Here a whirlpool boils with mud and immense
      swirlings
Of water, spouting up all the slimy sand of
      Cocytus.
A dreadful ferryman looks after the river crossing,
Charon: Appallingly filthy he is, with a bush of
      unkempt
White beard upon his chin, with eyes like jets
      of fire;
And a dirty cloak draggles down, knotted about
      his shoulders.
He poles the boat, he looks after the sails, he is
      all the crew   40
Of the rust-coloured wherry which takes the
      dead across—
An ancient now, but a god's old age is green
      and sappy.
This way came fast and streaming up to the
      bank the whole throng:
Matrons and men were there, and there were
      great-heart heroes
Finished with earthly life, boys and unmarried
      maidens,
Young men laid on the pyre before their
      parents' eyes;
Multitudinous as the leaves that fall in a forest
At the first frost of autumn, or the birds that
      out of the deep sea
Fly to land in migrant flocks, when the cold of
      the year
Has sent them overseas in search of a warmer
      climate.   50
So they all stood, each begging to be ferried
      across first,
Their hands stretched out in longing for the
      shore beyond the river.
But the surly ferryman embarks now this, now
      that group,
While others he keeps away at a distance from
      the shingle.
Aeneas, being astonished and moved by the
      great stir, said:—
      Tell me, O Sibyl, what means this
            rendezvous at the river?
What purpose have these souls? By what
      distinction are some
Turned back, while other souls sweep over the
      wan water?
      To which the long-lived Sibyl uttered this
            brief reply:—

O son of Anchises' loins and true-born
    offspring of heaven, 60
What you see is the mere of Cocytus, the
    Stygian marsh
By whose mystery even the gods, having
    sworn, are afraid to be forsworn.
All this crowd you see are the helpless ones, the
    unburied:
That ferryman is Charon: the ones he conveys
    have had burial.
None may be taken across from bank to
    awesome bank of
That harsh-voiced river until his bones are laid to rest.
Otherwise, he must haunt this place for a
    hundred years
Before he's allowed to revisit the longed-for
    stream at last.
    The son of Anchises paused and stood stock
    still, in deep
Meditation, pierced to the heart by pity for their
    hard fortune. 70
He saw there, sorrowing because deprived of
    death's fulfilment,
Leucaspis and Orontes, the commodore of the
    Lycian
Squadron, who had gone down, their ship being
    lost with all hands
In a squall, sailing with him the stormy seas
    from Troy.
    And look! yonder was roaming the
    helmsman, Palinurus,
Who, on their recent voyage, while watching
    the stars, had fallen
From the afterdeck, thrown off the ship there in
    mid-passage.
A sombre form in the deep shadows, Aeneas
    barely
Recognised him; then accosted:—
    Which of the gods, Palinurus, 80
Snatched you away from us and made you
    drown in the midsea?
Oh, tell me! For Apollo, whom never before
    had I found
Untruthful, did delude my mind with this one
    answer,
Foretelling that you would make your passage
    to Italy
Unharmed by sea. Is it thus he fulfils a sacred
    promise?
    Palinurus replied:—
    The oracle of Phoebus has not tricked you,
My captain, son of Anchises; nor was I
    drowned by a god.
It was an accident: I slipped, and the violent shock
Of my fall broke off the tiller to which I was
    holding firmly 90

As helmsman, and steering the ship. By the
    wild seas I swear
That not on my own account was I frightened
    nearly so much as
Lest your ship, thus crippled, its helmsman
    overboard,
Lose steerage-way and founder amid the
    mountainous waves.
Three stormy nights did the South wind
    furiously drive me along
Over the limitless waters: on the fourth day I just
Caught sight of Italy, being lifted high on a
    wave crest.
Little by little I swam to the shore. I was all but safe,
When, as I clung to the rough-edged cliff top,
    my fingers crooked
And my soaking garments weighing me down,
    some barbarous natives 100
Attacked me with swords, in their ignorance
    thinking that I was a rich prize.
Now the waves have me, the winds keep
    tossing me up on the shore again.
So now, by the sweet light and breath of
    heaven above
I implore you, and by your father, by your
    hopes for growing Ascanius
Redeem me from this doom, unconquered one!
    Please sprinkle
Dust on my corpse—you can do it and quickly
    get back to port Velia:
Or else, if way there is, some way that your
    heavenly mother
Is showing you (not, for sure, without the
    assent of deity
Would you be going to cross the swampy
    Stygian stream),
Give poor Palinurus your hand, take me with
    you across the water 110
So that at least I may rest in the quiet place, in
    death.
    Thus did the phantom speak, and the Sibyl
    began to speak thus:—
    This longing of yours, Palinurus, has carried
    you quite away.
Shall you, unburied, view the Styx, the austere
    river
Of the Infernal gods, or come to its bank
    unbidden?
Give up this hope that the course of fate can be
    swerved by prayer.
But hear and remember my words, to console
    you in your hard fortune.
I say that the neighbouring peoples, compelled
    by portents from heaven
Occurring in every township, shall expiate your
    death, 120

Shall give you burial and offer the solemn dues
    to your grave,
And the place shall keep the name of Palinurus
    for ever.
    Her sayings eased for a while the anguish of
      his sad heart;
He forgot his cares in the joy of giving his
    name to a region.
    So they resumed their interrupted journey,
      and drew near
The river. Now when the ferryman, from out
    on the Styx, espied them
Threading the soundless wood and making fast
    for the bank,
He hailed them, aggressively shouting at them
    before they could speak:—
    Whoever you are that approaches my river,
      carrying a weapon,
Halt there! Keep your distance, and tell me why
    you are come!   130
This is the land of ghosts, of sleep and
    somnolent night:
The living are not permitted to use the Stygian
    ferry.
Not with impunity did I take Hercules,
When he came, upon this water, nor Theseus,
    nor Pirithous,
Though their stock was divine and their powers
    were irresistible.
Hercules wished to drag off on a leash the
    watch-dog of Hades,
Even from our monarch's throne, and dragged
    it away trembling:
The others essayed to kidnap our queen from
    her lord's bedchamber.
    The priestess of Apollo answered him
      shortly, thus:—
    There is no such duplicity here, so set your
      mind at rest;   140
These weapons offer no violence: the huge
    watch-dog in his kennel
May go on barking for ever and scaring the
    bloodless dead,
Prosperpine keep her uncle's house,
    unthreatened in chastity.
Trojan Aeneas, renowned for war and a duteous
    heart,
Comes down to meet his father in the shades of
    the Underworld.
If you are quite unmoved by the spectacle of
    such great faith,
This you must recognise—
    And here she disclosed the golden
Bough which was hid in her robe. His angry
    mood calms down.
No more is said. Charon is struck with awe to see

After so long that magic gift, the bough fate-
    given;   150
He turns his sombre boat and poles it towards
    the bank.
Then, displacing the souls who were seated
    along its benches
And clearing the gangways, to make room for
    the big frame of Aeneas,
He takes him on board. The ramshackle craft
    creaked under his weight
And let in through its seams great swashes of
    muddy water.
At last, getting the Sibyl and the hero safe
    across,
He landed them amidst wan reeds on a dreary
    mud flat.
    Huge Cerberus, monstrously couched in a
      cave confronting them,
Made the whole region echo with his three-
    throated barking.
The Sibyl, seeing the snakes bristling upon his
    neck now,   160
Threw him for bait a cake of honey and wheat
    infused with
Sedative drugs. The creature, crazy with hunger,
    opened
Its three mouths, gobbled the bait; then its huge
    body relaxed
And lay, sprawled out on the ground, the whole
    length of its cave kennel.
Aeneas, passing its entrance, the watch-dog
    neutralised,
Strode rapidly from the bank of that river of no
    return.
    At once were voices heard, a sound of
      mewling and wailing,
Ghosts of infants sobbing there at the threshold,
    infants
From whom a dark day stole their share of
    delicious life,
Snatched them away from the breast, gave them
    sour death to drink.   170
Next to them were those condemned to death
    on a false charge.
Yet every place is duly allotted and judgment is
    given.
Minos, as president, summons a jury of the
    dead: he hears
Every charge, examines the record of each; he
    shakes the urn.
Next again are located the sorrowful ones who
    killed
Themselves, throwing their lives away, not
    driven by guilt
But because they loathed living: how they
    would like to be

In the world above now, enduring poverty and
    hard trials!
God's law forbids: that unlovely fen with its
    glooming water
Corrals them there, the nine rings of Styx corral
    them in.   180
Not far from here can be seen, extending in all
    directions,
The vale of mourning—such is the name it
    bears: a region
Where those consumed by the wasting torments
    of merciless love
Haunt the sequestered alleys and myrtle groves
    that give them
Cover; death itself cannot cure them of love's
    disease.
Here Aeneas descried Phaedra and Procris,
    sad
Eriphyle displaying the wounds her heartless
    son once dealt her,
Evadne and Pasiphae; with them goes
    Laodamia;
Here too is Caeneus, once a young man, but
    next a woman
And now changed back by fate to his original
    sex.   190
Amongst them, with her death-wound still
    bleeding, through the deep wood
Was straying Phoenician Dido. Now when the
    Trojan leader
Found himself near her and knew that the form
    he glimpsed through the shadows
Was hers—as early in the month one sees, or
    imagines he sees,
Through a wrack of cloud the new moon rising
    and glimmering—
He shed some tears, and addressed her in
    tender, loving tones:—
    Poor, unhappy Dido, so the message was
    true that came to me
Saying you'd put an end to your life with the
    sword and were dead?
Oh god! was it death I brought you, then? I
    swear by the stars,
By the powers above, by whatever is sacred in
    the Underworld,   200
It was not of my own will, Dido, I left your
    land.
Heaven's commands, which now force me to
    traverse the shades,
This sour and derelict region, this pit of
    darkness, drove me
Imperiously from your side. I did not, could not
    imagine
My going would ever bring such terrible agony
    on you.

Don't move away! Oh, let me see you a little
    longer!
To fly from me, when this is the last word fate
    allows us!
    Thus did Aeneas speak, trying to soften the
    wild-eyed,
Passionate-hearted ghost, and brought the tears
    to his own eyes.
She would not turn to him; she kept her gaze
    on the ground,   210
And her countenance remained as stubborn to
    his appeal
As if it were carved from recalcitrant flint or a
    crag of marble.
At last she flung away, hating him still, and
    vanished
Into the shadowy wood where her first
    husband, Sychaeus,
Understands her unhappiness and gives her an
    equal love.
None the less did Aeneas, hard hit by her
    piteous fate,
Weep after her from afar, as she went, with
    tears of compassion.

Horace
Centennial Hymn

By 17 B.C. Augustus had restored peace to most of the
empire. To celebrate his achievement and to encourage the
spirit of public optimism, he organized a great ceremony
known as the Secular Games; the tradition of such rituals
went back to Republican times. Horace was commissioned
to compose a hymn that would be part of the official liturgy,
and the Carmen Saeculare *(Secular Song) is the result.*

  The principal theme of the games was the dawning of a
new age. After invoking the protection of the gods, Horace
describes the hopes for the future in a world ruled by the
Romans in peace and prosperity, tactfully omitting any ref-
erence to the civil wars and turmoil that had preceded the
rule of Augustus. Appropriately enough for an occasion
intended to celebrate youth and rebirth, the poem was re-
cited by a chorus of girls and boys. Horace uses the character
of his performers by emphasizing the mood of simplicity,
even naïveté. Rather than striking a note of official gran-
deur, the Carmen Saeculare *expresses a spirit of innocent*
pride and shy wonder.

Diana, queen of forests, and Apollo,
O honoured and for ever to be honoured
Twin glories of the firmament, accord us
    All we beseech today—

Day of devotion, when the Sybil's verses
Enjoin the chaste, the chosen youths and maidens
To chant their hymns of worship to the patron
    Gods of our seven hills.

Kind sun, bright charioteer, bringer and hider
Of light, newborn each morning yet each morning   10
Unaltered, may thou never view a city
    Greater on earth than Rome.

Moon, gentle midwife, punctual in thy office,
Lucina, Ilithyia, Genitalis—
Be called whichever title is most pleasing—
    Care for our mothers' health,

Goddess, make strong our youth and bless the Senate's
Decrees rewarding parenthood and marriage,
That from the new laws Rome may reap a lavish
    Harvest of boys and girls,   20

So that the destined cycle of eleven
Decades may bring again great throngs to witness
The games and singing: three bright days and three long
    Nights of the people's joy.

And you, O Fates, who have proved truthful prophets,
Your promise stands—and may Time's sacred landmarks
Guard it immovably: add to our glorious
    History fresh renown.

May Mother Earth, fruitful in crops and cattle,
Crown Ceres' forehead with a wreath of wheat-ears,   30
And dews and rains and breezes, God's good agents,
    Nourish whatever grows.

Sun-god, put by thy bow and deign to listen
Mildly and gently to the boys' entreaties.
Moon, crescent sovereign of the constellations,
    Answer the virgins' prayers.

Rome if your handiwork; in your safe-keeping
The Trojan band reached an Etruscan haven,
That remnant which, at your command, abandoned
    City and hearth to make   40

The auspicious voyage, those for whom pure-hearted
Aeneas, the last pillar of royal manhood
Left standing in burnt Troy, paved paths to greater
    Fame than they left behind.

By these sure tokens make our young quick pupils
Of virtue, give the aged peace and quiet,
Rain on the race of Romulus wealth, offspring,
    Honours of every kind;

And when, tonight, with blood of milk-white oxen
The glorious son of Venus and Anchises   50
Invokes you, grant his prayers. Long may Augustus
    Conquer but spare the foe.

Now Parthia fears the fist of Rome, the fasces
Potent on land and sea; now the once haughty
Ambassadors from the Caspian and the Indus
    Sue for a soft reply.

Now Faith and Peace and Honour and old-fashioned
Conscience and unremembered Virtue venture

To walk again, and with them blessed Plenty,
    Pouring her brimming horn.   60

Apollo, augur, bright-bowed archer, well-loved
Music-master of the nine Muses, healer
Whose skill in medicine can ease the body's
    Ills and infirmities,

By thy affection for the Palatine altars
Prolong, we pray, the Roman State and Latium's
Prosperity into future cycles, nobler
    Eras, for evermore.

Diana, keeper of the sacred hilltops
Of Aventine and Algidus, be gracious   70
To the prayers of the Fifteen Guardians, to the children
    Bend an attentive ear.

That Jove and all the gods approve these wishes
We, the trained chorus, singers of the praises
Of Phoebus and Diana, carry homewards
    Happy, unshaken hope.

Juvenal
from the THIRD SATIRE

Juvenal tells us at the beginning of his first Satire that he turned to writing out of fierce outrage at the corruption and decadence of his day. In the third Satire he takes on Rome itself and the inconveniences (to say the least) of urban life. An imaginary friend has decided that he no longer can stand life in the big city, and as he leaves for the country (symbolized in the first lines of this extract by small towns such as Praeneste and Gabii) he catalogues some of the reasons for his departure.

"Who, in Praeneste's cool, or the wooded
    Volsinian uplands,
Who, on Tivoli's heights, or a small town
    like Gabii, say,
Fears the collapse of his house? But Rome is
    supported on pipestems,
Matchsticks; it's cheaper, so, for the landlord
    to shore up his ruins,
Patch up the old cracked walls, and notify all
    the tenants
They can sleep secure, though the beams are
    in ruins above them.
No, the place to live is out there, where no
    cry of *Fire!*
Sounds the alarm of the night, with a
    neighbor yelling for water,
Moving his chattels and goods, and the
    whole third story is smoking.
This you'll never know: for if the ground
    floor is scared first,   10
You are the last to burn, up there where the
    eaves of the attic

Keep off the rain, and the doves are brooding
    over their nest eggs. . . .
"Here in town the sick die from insomnia
    mostly.
Undigested food, on a stomach burning with
    ulcers,
Brings on listlessness, but who can sleep in a
    flophouse?
Who but the rich can afford sleep and a
    garden apartment?
That's the source of infection. The wheels
    creak by on the narrow
Streets of the wards, the drivers squabble and
    brawl when they're stopped,
More than enough to frustrate the drowsiest
    son of a sea cow.
When his business calls, the crowd makes
    way, as the rich man,   20
Carried high in his car, rides over them,
    reading or writing,
Even taking a snooze, perhaps, for the
    motion's composing.
Still, he gets where he wants before we do;
    for all of our hurry
Traffic gets in our way, in front, around and
    behind us.
Somebody gives me a shove with an elbow,
    or two-by-four scantling.
One clunks my head with a beam, another
    cracks down with a beer keg.
Mud is thick on my shins, I am trampled by
    somebody's big feet.
Now what?—a soldier grinds his hobnails
    into my toes.
    "Don't you see the mob rushing along to
    the handout?
There are a hundred guests, each one with
    his kitchen servant.   30
Even Samson himself could hardly carry
    those burdens,
Pots and pans some poor little slave tries to
    keep on his head, while he hurries
Hoping to keep the fire alive by the wind of
    his running.
Tunics, new-darned, are ripped to shreds;
    there's the flash of a fir beam
Huge on some great dray, and another carries
    a pine tree,
Nodding above our heads and threatening
    death to the people.
What will be left of the mob, if that cart of
    Ligurian marble
Breaks its axle down and dumps its load on
    these swarms?
Who will identify limbs or bones? The poor
    man's cadaver,

Crushed, disappears like his breath. And
    meanwhile, at home, his household   40
Washes the dishes, and puffs up the fire, with
    all kinds of clatter
Over the smeared flesh-scrapers, the flasks of
    oil, and the towels.
So the boys rush around, while their late
    master is sitting,
Newly come to the bank of the Styx, afraid
    of the filthy
Ferryman there, since he has no fare, not
    even a copper
In his dead mouth to pay for the ride
    through that muddy whirlpool.
    "Look at other things, the various dangers
    of nighttime.
How high it is to the cornice that breaks, and
    a chunk beats my brains out,
Or some slob heaves a jar, broken or
    cracked, from a window.   50
Bang! It comes down with a crash and
    proves its weight on the sidewalk.
You are a thoughtless fool, unmindful of
    sudden disaster,
If you don't make your will before you go
    out to have dinner.
There are as many deaths in the night as
    there are open windows
Where you pass by; if you're wise, you will
    pray, in your wretched devotions,
People may be content with no more than
    emptying slop jars."

Marcus Aurelius
The Meditations: Book II (complete)

The Meditations *of Marcus Aurelius consist of a philosophical journal or diary, in which the Emperor recorded his reflections and observations. Some parts were carefully composed; elsewhere he jotted down a few words or a quotation. Ideas were recorded in no logical order, and in places Marcus Aurelius contradicted himself—or at least changed his mind. The chief theme of the* Meditations *is that of self-examination and the search for spiritual happiness, inspired by the teachings of Stoicism.*

The tone of the book is not a happy one, and in places the emperor seems to come close to despair. Yet it is inspiring to share the thoughts of a man of high responsibilities and even higher ideals. Furthermore, on page after page we find observations that transcend Marcus Aurelius' historical period and remind us of the universality of human experience by their relevance to our own lives.

1. Say to yourself in the morning: I shall meet people who are interfering, ungracious, insolent, full of guile, deceitful and antisocial; they have all become like that because they have no understanding of

good and evil. But I who have contemplated the essential beauty of good and the essential ugliness of evil, who know that the nature of the wrongdoer is of one kin with mine—not indeed of the same blood or seed but sharing the same mind, the same portion of the divine—I cannot be harmed by any one of them, and no one can involve me in shame. I cannot feel anger against him who is of my kin, nor hate him. We were born to labor together, like the feet, the hands, the eyes, and the rows of upper and lower teeth. To work against one another is therefore contrary to nature, and to be angry against a man or turn one's back on him is to work against him.

2. Whatever it is which I am, it is flesh, breath of life, and directing mind. The flesh you should despise: blood, bones and a network woven of nerves, veins and arteries. Consider too the nature of the life-breath: wind, never the same, but disgorged and then again gulped in, continually. The third part is the directing mind. Throw away your books, be no longer anxious: that was not your given role. Rather reflect thus as if death were now before you: "You are an old man, let this third part be enslaved no longer, nor be a mere puppet on the strings of selfish desire; no longer let it be vexed by your past or present lot, or peer suspiciously into the future."

3. The works of the gods are full of Providence. The works of Chance are not divorced from Nature or from the spinning and weaving together of those things which are governed by Providence. Thence everything flows. There is also Necessity and what is beneficial to the whole ordered universe of which you are a part. That which is brought by the nature of the Whole, and preserves it, is good for every part. As do changes in the elements, so changes in their compounds preserve the ordered universe. That should be enough for you, these should ever be your beliefs. Cast out the thirst for books that you may not die growling, but with true graciousness, and grateful to the gods from the heart.

4. Remember how long you have delayed, how often the gods have appointed the day of your redemption and you have let it pass. Now, if ever, you must realize of what kind of ordered universe you are a part, of what kind of governor of that universe you are an emanation, that a time limit has now been set for you and that if you do not use it to come out into the light, it will be lost, and you will be lost, and there will be no further opportunity.

5. Firmly, as a Roman and a man should, think at all times how you can perform the task at hand with precise and genuine dignity, sympathy, independence, and justice, making yourself free from all other preoccupations. This you will achieve if you perform every action as if it was the last of your life, if you rid yourself of all aimless thoughts, of all emotional opposition to the dictates of reason, of all pretense, selfishness and displeasure with your lot. You see how few are the things a man must overcome to enable him to live a smoothly flowing and godly life; for even the gods will require nothing further from the man who keeps to these beliefs.

6. You shame yourself, my soul, you shame yourself, and you will have no further opportunity to respect yourself; the life of every man is short and yours is almost finished while you do not respect yourself but allow your happiness to depend upon the souls of others.

7. Do external circumstances to some extent distract you? Give yourself leisure to acquire some further good knowledge and cease to wander aimlessly. Then one must guard against another kind of wandering, for those who are exhausted by life, and have no aim at which to direct every impulse and generally every impression, are foolish in their deeds as well as in their words.

8. A man is not easily found to be unhappy because he takes no thought for what happens in the soul of another; it is those who do not attend to the disturbances of their own soul who are inevitably in a state of unhappiness.

9. Always keep this thought in mind: what is the essential nature of the universe and what is my own essential nature? How is the one related to the other, being so small a part of so great a Whole? And remember that no one can prevent your deeds and your words being in accord with nature.

10. Theophrastus speaks as a philosopher when, in comparing sins as a man commonly might, he states that offenses due to desire are worse than those due to anger, for the angry man appears to be in the grip of pain and hidden pangs when he discards Reason, whereas he who sins through desire, being overcome by pleasure, seems more licentious and more effeminate in his wrongdoing. So Theophrastus is right, and speaks in a manner worthy of philosophy, when he says that one who sins through pleasure deserves more blame than one who sins through pain. The latter is more like a man who was wronged first and compelled by pain to anger; the former starts on the path to sin of his own accord, driven to action by desire.

11. It is possible to depart from life at this moment. Have this thought in mind whenever you act, speak, or think. There is nothing terrible in leaving the company of men, if the gods exist, for they would not involve you in evil. If, on the other hand, they do not exist or do not concern themselves with human affairs, then what is life to me in a universe devoid of gods or of Providence? But they do exist and do care for humanity, and have put it altogether within a man's power not to fall into real evils. And if

anything else were evil they would have seen to it that it be in every man's power not to fall into it. As for that which does not make a man worse, how could it make the life of man worse?

Neither through ignorance nor with knowledge could the nature of the Whole have neglected to guard against this or correct it; nor through lack of power or skill could it have committed so great a wrong, namely that good and evil should come to the good and the evil alike, and at random. True, death and life, good and ill repute, toil and pleasure, wealth and poverty, being neither good nor bad, come to the good and the bad equally. They are therefore neither blessings nor evils.

12. How swiftly all things vanish; in the universe the bodies themselves, and in time the memories of them. Of what kind are all the objects of sense, especially those which entice us by means of pleasure, frighten us by means of pain, or are shouted about in vainglory; how cheap they are, how contemptible, sordid, corruptible and dead—upon this our intellectual faculty should fix its attention. Who are these men whose voice and judgment make or break reputations? What is the nature of death? When a man examines it in itself, and with his share of intelligence dissolves the imaginings which cling to it, he conceives it to be no other than a function of nature, and to fear a natural function is to be only a child. Death is not only a function of nature but beneficial to it.

How does man reach god, with what part of himself, and in what condition must that part be?

13. Nothing is more wretched than the man who runs around in circles busying himself with all kinds of things—investigating things below the earth, as the saying goes—always looking for signs of what his neighbors are feeling and thinking. He does not realize that it is enough to be concerned with the spirit within oneself and genuinely to serve it. This service consists in keeping it free from passions, aimlessness, and discontent with its fate at the hands of gods and men. What comes from the gods must be revered because of their goodness; what comes from men must be welcomed because of our kinship, although sometimes these things are also pitiful in a sense, because of men's ignorance of good and evil, which is no less a disability than to be unable to distinguish between black and white.

14. Even if you were to live three thousand years or three times ten thousand, remember nevertheless that no one can shed another life than this which he is living, nor live another life than this which he is shedding, so that the longest and the shortest life come to the same thing. The present is equal for all, and that which is being lost is equal, and that which is being shed is thus shown to be but a moment. No one can shed that which is past, nor what is still to come; for how could he be deprived of what he does not possess?

Therefore remember these two things always: first, that all things as they come round again have been the same from eternity, and it makes no difference whether you see the same things for a hundred years, or for two hundred years, or for an infinite time; second, that the longest-lived or the shortest-lived sheds the same thing at death, for it is the present moment only of which he will be deprived, if indeed only the present moment is his, and no man can discard what he does not have.

15. "All is but thinking so." The retort to the saying of Monimus the Cynic is obvious, but the usefulness of the saying is also obvious, if one accepts the essential meaning of it insofar as it is true.

16. The human soul violates itself most of all when it becomes, as far as it can, a separate tumor or growth upon the universe; for to be discontented with anything that happens is to rebel against that Nature which embraces, in some part of itself, all other natures. The soul violates itself also whenever it turns away from a man and opposes him to do him harm, as do the souls of angry men; thirdly, whenever it is overcome by pleasure or pain; fourthly, whenever it acts a part and does or says anything falsely and hypocritically; fifthly, when it fails to direct any action or impulse to a goal, but acts at random, without purpose, whereas even the most trifling actions must be directed toward the end; and this end, for reasonable creatures, is to follow the reason and the law of the most honored commonwealth and constitution.

17. In human life time is but a point, reality a flux, perception indistinct, the composition of the body subject to easy corruption, the soul a spinning top, fortune hard to make out, fame confused. To put it briefly: physical things are but a flowing stream, things of the soul dreams and vanity; life is but a struggle and the visit to a strange land, posthumous fame but a forgetting.

What then can help us on our way? One thing only: philosophy. This consists in guarding our inner spirit inviolate and unharmed, stronger than pleasures and pains, never acting aimlessly, falsely or hypocritically, independent of the actions or inaction of others, accepting all that happens or is given as coming from whence one came oneself, and at all times awaiting death with contented mind as being only the release of the elements of which every creature is composed. If it is nothing fearful for the elements themselves that one should continually change into another, why should anyone look with suspicion upon the change and dissolution of all things? For this is in accord with nature, and nothing evil is in accord with nature.

INTERLUDE

Antony and Cleopatra

Cleopatra (69–30 B.C.), who combined her personal romantic activities with her position as queen of Egypt, shocked beyond measure the Romans who knew about her—particularly since her lovers included such distinguished Roman leaders as Julius Caesar and Mark Antony. Women played an important role in the life of the Roman family and certain patrician women wielded formidable political and economic power behind the scenes, but they took an active part in public only rarely. The wives of public figures were expected to set an example of domestic rectitude and respectability that would both inspire others and aid their husbands' careers. Julius Caesar expressed the contemporary view succinctly when he divorced his wife after a widely discussed scandal in which she may have been involved: "Caesar's wife must be above suspicion."

At the same time, there was in operation a double standard that by no means disappeared with the fall of the Roman Empire. Men about town frequently turned to women other than their wives—often quite publicly—for sophisticated attentions

Claude Rains as Julius Caesar and Vivien Leigh, portraying a Cleopatra who is still a child, meet for the first time between the paws of the Sphinx in the 1946 film version of Bernard Shaw's *Caesar and Cleopatra. Right:* Leigh is a more mature and more regal queen of Egypt to Laurence Olivier's Antony in the production of Shakespeare's *Antony and Cleopatra* at the Ziegfeld Theatre, New York, 1951.

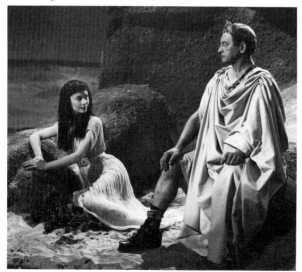

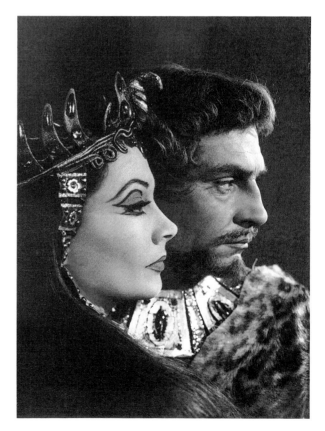

a Roman matron was hardly expected to cultivate. Among the most notorious of these courtesans was none other than Catullus' beloved Lesbia—almost certainly the infamous Clodia, a woman as beautiful and intelligent as she was ruthless.

Even so, in the Rome of the 1st century B.C. there was widespread respect for virtue and morality, and Cleopatra for the Romans was both a threat and a shocking figure. When her exotic career ended with a dramatic death, it was inevitable that she would become—for the Romans and for later ages—the symbol of the glamorous Eastern beauty, seductive but dangerous.

There is a considerable difference, however, between later legends and the facts of history. The real Cleopatra was chiefly interested in power, not in love. The last ruler of an independent Egypt, she was the culmination of two great traditions. By blood she was a Macedonian and thus the heir of Alexander the Great; her native tongue was Greek. At the same time she saw herself as the successor of the pharaohs and like them descended from the sun god Ra. Her self-appointed mission was to fulfill Alexander's dream of uniting East and West in a single great empire. The first stage in accomplishing this was to be the conquest of Rome, with subsequent victories intended to establish a worldwide kingdom with Cleopatra as supreme ruler. But Egypt, although rich, had little military power and could never have provided an army strong enough to challenge Roman might. Only by setting the Romans against themselves could she hope to overthrow the Roman Empire. To accomplish her vision of world domination she had to find herself a Roman with whom to join forces, and she threw all her considerable abilities into the attempt.

Her remarkable beauty was the most immediately visible of her advantages, and she was willing to exploit it, but she was in addition a woman of notable intellectual gifts, widely read in literature and philosophy, a brilliant administrator, and determined, even ruthless, in character. At the time of her alliance with Antony, contemporary Romans followed the lead of Octavian in describing her as an Oriental tyrant, sunk in depravity and prone to every vice. The intensity of their hatred for her reveals their genuine fear that, of all Rome's enemies, she could come the closest to overthrowing Roman rule.

Her first victim had been Julius Caesar. After his defeat of Pompey in 47 B.C. Caesar made his way to Egypt to arbitrate a dispute between the pharoah, Ptolemy XII, and his sister Cleopatra; in accordance with Egyptian custom, they were married to each other. Caesar also hoped to collect some money owed him by the couple's deceased father, Ptolemy XI. Both his financial demands and his support of Cleopatra naturally won him the enmity of the young Ptolemy. After a series of skirmishes, in the course of which Caesar himself narrowly escaped death several times, Ptolemy's troops were defeated and the king himself killed. By this time Rome was anxiously awaiting Caesar's return, but he delayed his departure and spent several weeks traveling in Egypt with Cleopatra. By the time he left, the queen was pregnant. When her son was born she named him Caesarion and took him to Rome to join his father. Although Caesar showered her with presents and honors, he was careful to go no further, and any hopes she might have had of an eventual marriage were ended by his assassination.

As Cleopatra surveyed the new situation created by Caesar's death, it must soon have been apparent to her than an even more likely candidate for her attentions was Mark Antony. Antony had been Caesar's faithful lieutenant and after the defeat of Caesar's assassins in 42 B.C. had been placed in command of the East. A man of great personality and abilities, he was characterized by moderation and good sense in his political and military achievements. His Roman virtues of leadership and courage were counterbalanced by a streak of sensuality and self-indulgence, and it was on these that Cleopatra counted. In 40 B.C., she traveled to Cydnus in Asia Minor, and there the two met for the first time.

At the banquet that followed Cleopatra made every effort to impress Antony with both her beauty and her wealth. According to one story, probably apocryphal, during the meal she removed a priceless pearl earring and dropped it into her glass of wine, in which it dissolved. She then casually drank the wine, showing her indifference to the value of the pearl.

Within a year Cleopatra had borne Antony twins, but her initial success was frustrated by the plans of Octavian, who in 39 B.C. persuaded Antony to try to patch up their growing differences by marrying his sister Octavia. By all accounts this remarkably diplomatic woman performed miracles in restraining Antony's wilder impulses and in keeping the peace between her new husband and her brother; from 39 to 37 B.C. Octavia and Antony lived peacefully at Athens, administering the Eastern provinces and strengthening the frontiers.

Cleopatra was shocked by the news of the marriage, but comforted by the realization that Antony would, in the end, probably choose a military alliance with herself rather than with Octavia. Her optimism was justified. After three years with Octavia Antony became restless. He had long had in mind an expedition that would accomplish Julius Caesar's dream of conquering the Parthians and at the same time increase his own prestige. In 36 B.C. he mustered an army of almost a hundred thousand men and set off, leaving Octavia behind and summoning Cleopatra to join him in Syria. The expedition was a complete failure, and the loss of a third of his forces seriously undermined Antony's reputation as a military leader. Back at Rome, the prestige of Octavian, by now embittered by Antony's treatment of his sister, was growing and Antony decided to strengthen his weakening position by cementing his alliance with Cleopatra. At an elaborate ceremony in Alexandria in 34 B.C. he formalized their political union by the so-called Donations of Alexandria. Cleopatra's eldest child, Caesarion, was publicly acknowledged Julius Caesar's son and was made joint ruler with his mother of Egypt and Cyprus. Antony's own children by Cleopatra were given other kingdoms.

The effect of this news at Rome was predictably disastrous for Antony's cause. Roman indignation at Antony's submission to the hated queen's plans for a universal kingdom under her rule was adroitly fanned by Octavian, who showed the same skillful control of propaganda he was later to demonstrate during his reign as Augustus. Octavian managed to obtain and publish his rival's will (in which Antony instructed that he be buried in Alexandria with Cleopatra at his side), which served to inflame still further Roman resentment against the noble Roman who had allowed himself to be so completely seduced. Although neither Octavian nor Antony had any legal political status by now, Octavian's agents organized the taking of an oath of allegiance to their master throughout Italy. Armed with this vote of confidence, Octavian formally declared war on Egypt and launched an expedition against

The fact that no authentic portrait of either Antony or Cleopatra has survived can probably be credited to the wishes of the emperor Augustus. The coins the couple had minted nevertheless give some idea of their appearance. *Right:* Coin with the profile of Mark Antony. 41 B.C. Silver, diameter ¾″ (1.9 cm). British Museum, London (reproduced by courtesy of the Trustees). *Left:* Coin with the profile of Cleopatra. Diameter 1″ (2.5 cm). Cabinet des Medailles, Paris.

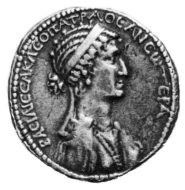 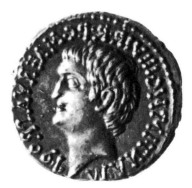

the joint forces of Antony and Cleopatra. The decisive engagement took place in September 31 B.C. at Actium in western Greece. Shortly after the beginning of the battle, which took place at sea, Antony's forces deserted. Antony and Cleopatra fled back to Egypt in total defeat.

Within a few months Octavian had followed Antony to Egypt and defeated the new forces remaining to him, leaving Antony little choice but suicide. A meeting was arranged between Octavian and Cleopatra, but if the queen made a last desperate attempt to win over her conqueror, it was unsuccessful. When it became clear that Octavian was only keeping her alive so he could exhibit her in his triumphal procession at Rome, she committed suicide. Her eldest son, Caesarion, was killed—Octavian was taking no chances—but her two children by Antony were taken to Rome, where they walked before Octavian's chariot in his triumphal procession.

Further Reading

Bradford, E. *Cleopatra*. New York: Harcourt Brace Jovanovich, 1972. Lavishly illustrated, readable if sometimes superficial description of Cleopatra's life and times.

Grant, M. *Cleopatra*. London: Weidenfeld and Nicolson, 1972. A more scholarly account of Cleopatra's career, well documented and with useful notes. The genealogical tables at the end are helpful.

Ludwig, Emil. *Cleopatra: The Story of a Queen*. New York: Bantam Books, 1959. The English translation of a book first published in German in 1937. More historical novel than accurate account, it provides a highly imaginative, and frequently imagined, picture of its subject.

Marsh, F. B. *A History of the Roman World 146–30 B.C.* 3rd ed. London: Methuen, 1963. This standard account of the fall of the Roman Republic discusses Cleopatra's life and character at some length.

Syme, R. *The Roman Revolution*. Oxford: Oxford University Press, 1939. A magnificent work of scholarship that traces the decline of freedom at Rome and the rise of Augustus and in the process throws much valuable light on Antony and Cleopatra.

		GENERAL EVENTS	**LITERATURE & PHILOSOPHY**	**ART**

BRONZE AGE

Before 1260 B.C.

1800–1600 Age of the Hebrew Patriarchs: Abraham, Isaac, Jacob

1600 Israelite tribes in Egypt

1280 Exodus of Israelites from Egypt under leadership of Moses

1260

Period of the Judges

1260 Israelites begin to penetrate land of Canaan

1040

1040–1000 Reign of Saul, first king of Israel

1000

Age of the Monarchy

1000–961 Reign of King David

961–922 Reign of Solomon; use of iron-tipped plow and iron war chariots; height of ancient Israel's cultural power: achievements form basis of Judaic, Christian, and Islamic religions

c. 1000 Formation of the Scriptures in written form

c. 950 Book of Psalms

10th–9th cent. Book of Kings

c. 961–c. 922 Hiram of Tyre constructs bronze "sea" in courtyard of Solomon's Temple

922

Age of the Two Kingdoms

922 Civil war after death of Solomon; split of Northern Kingdom (Israel) and Southern Kingdom (Judah); classical prophetic period begins

721 Northern Kingdom destroyed by Assyria

8th–6th cent. Old Testament books of Isaiah, Jeremiah, and Ezekiel

Depiction of divinity in art prohibited in Jewish religion

734 Oxen from bronze "sea" given to King of Assyria by King Achaz

587

IRON AGE (1000–)

Age of Exile, Return, and Occupations

587 Southern Kingdom defeated; Jews driven into captivity in Babylonia

539 Cyrus the Persian permits Jews to return to Jerusalem

516 Dedication of Second Temple in Jerusalem

332 Conquest of Jerusalem by Alexander the Great

2d. cent. Cult of Mithra in Rome

after 5th cent. Book of Job

end of 2d cent. Apocryphal Book of Judith

63

Roman Period

63 Conquest of Jerusalem by Romans under Pompey

37 B.C.–A.D. 4 Reign of Herod the Great under Roman tutelage

B.C.

c. 6 B.C. Birth of Jesus

A.D.

c. A.D. 30 Death of Jesus; beginnings of Christianity in Palestine

45–49 First missionary journeys of Saint Paul

66–70 Jewish rebellions against Romans

c. 70 Titus destroys Jerusalem and razes the Temple; Jews sent into exile

c. A.D. 70 "Sermon on the Mount" in Gospel of Saint Matthew, New Testament

c. A.D. 81 Reliefs from Arch of Titus, Rome, commemorate Roman victory in Jerusalem

324 A.D.

Dates before the 10th cent. B.C. are approximate and remain controversial

5

Jerusalem and Early Christianity

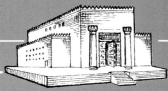

c. 961–c. 922 Building of Temple of Solomon; city of Megiddo rebuilt by Solomon

Music often accompanied the Psalms; musical instruments in use: drums, reed instruments, lyre, harp, horns

587 Solomon's Temple destroyed by Babylonians

c. 536–515 Second Temple of Solomon constructed

19 Herod the Great begins rebuilding Third Temple of Solomon

A.D. 70 Herod's Temple destroyed by the armies of Titus under Emperor Vespasian

c. 81 Arch of Titus, Rome, commemorates victory of Roman army in Jerusalem

Judaism and Early Christianity

One of the interesting ironies of history is the fact that, more than three thousand years ago in the Middle East, a small tribe turned nation became one of the central sources for the development of Western civilization. The fact is incontestable: the marriage of the biblical tradition and Graeco-Roman culture has produced, for better or worse, the West as we know it today.

The irony is all the more telling because this biblical people did not give to the world great art, significant music, philosophy, or science. Their language did not have a word for science. Their religion discouraged the plastic arts. We have the texts of their hymns, canticles, and psalms but we can only speculate how they were sung and how they were accompanied by instruments. What these people did give us was a book; more precisely, a collection of many different books we now call the Bible.

These people called themselves the Children of Israel or Israelites; at a later time they became known as the Jews (from the area around Jerusalem known as Judaea). In the Bible they are called Hebrews (most often by their neighbors), the name now most commonly used to describe the biblical people.

The history of the Hebrew people is long and complex, but the stages of their growth can be outlined as follows:

• **The Period of the Patriarchs.** According to the Bible, the Hebrew people had their origin in Abraham, the father (patriarch) of a tribe who took his people from ancient Mesopotamia to the land of Canaan on the east coast of the Mediterranean about 2000 B.C. After settling in this land, divided into twelve tribal areas, they eventually went to Egypt at the behest of Joseph, who had risen to high office in Egypt after his enslavement there.

• **The Period of the Exodus.** The Egyptians eventually enslaved the Hebrews (perhaps around 1750 B.C.), but they were led out of Egypt under the leadership of Moses. This "going out" (exodus) is one of the central themes of the Bible; this great event also gives its name to one of the books of the Old Testament.

• **The Period of the Conquest.** The biblical books of Joshua and Judges relate the struggles of the Hebrews to conquer the land of Canaan as they fought against the native peoples of that area and the competing "Sea People" (the Philistines) who came down from the north.

• **The United Monarchy.** The high point of the Hebrew political power came with the consolidation of Canaan and the rise of a monarchy. There were three kings: Saul, David, and Solomon. An ambitious flurry of building during the reign of Solomon (c. 961–922 B.C.) culminated in the construction of the great temple in Jerusalem [5.1].

• **Divided Kingdom and Exile.** After the death of Solomon a rift over the succession resulted in the separation of the Northern Kingdom and the Southern, the center of which was Jerusalem. Both were vulnerable to pressure from the surrounding great powers. The Northern Kingdom was destroyed by the Assyrians in the 8th century B.C. and its inhabitants (the so-called Lost Tribes of Israel) were swept away by death or exile. In 587 B.C. the Babylonians conquered the Southern Kingdom, destroyed Solomon's temple in Jerusalem, and carried the Hebrew people into an exile known to history as the Babylonian Captivity.

• **The Return.** The Hebrews returned from exile about 520 B.C. to rebuild their shattered temple and to resume their religious life. Their subsequent history was marked by a series of foreign (Greek, Egyptian, and Syrian) rulers, one brief period of political independence (c. 165 B.C.), and, finally, rule by Rome after the conquest of 63 B.C. In A.D. 70, after a Jewish revolt, the Romans destroyed Jerusalem and razed the rebuilt temple [5.2]. One small band of Jewish rebels that held off the Romans for two years at a mountain fortress called Masada was defeated in A.D. 73. Except for pockets of Jews who lived there over the centuries, not until 1948, when the state of Israel was established, would Jews hold political power in their ancestral home.

The Hebrew Bible and Its Message

The English word *bible* comes from the Greek name for the ancient city of Byblos, from which the papyrus reed used to make books was exported. As already noted, the Bible is a collection of books that took its present shape over a long period of time.

The ancient Hebrews divided the books of their Bible into three large groupings: the Law, the Prophets, and the Writings. The Law referred specifically to the first five books of the Bible, called the Torah (from the Hebrew for "law"). The Prophets consists of writings attributed to the great moral teachers of the Hebrews who were called prophets because they spoke with the authority of God (*prophet* is derived from a Greek word for "one who speaks for another"). The Writings contain the wisdom literature of the Bible, prose or poetry (like the book of Psalms) or a mixture of the two, as in the book of Job.

The list of books contained in the modern Bible was not established until A.D. 90, when an assembly of rabbis drew up such a list or *canon* even though its

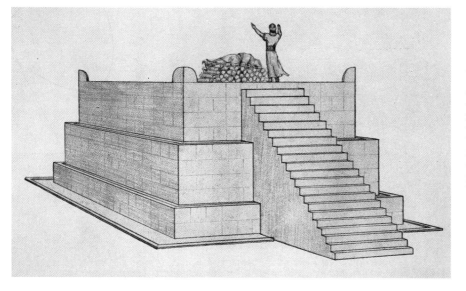

5.1 Reconstruction drawing of Solomon's Temple. The description in the Bible of this destroyed temple was an inspiration for sacred architecture well into the Middle Ages. The two bronze columns in front may have represented the columns of fire and smoke that guided the Israelites while they were in the desert.

main outline had been known for centuries. The Christians in turn accepted this canon and added the twenty-seven books that make up what we know as the Christian scriptures of the New Testament. (Roman Catholics and Orthodox Christians also accept as canonical some books of the Old Testament that are not in the Hebrew canon but are found in an ancient Greek version of the Hebrew scriptures known as the *Septuagint,* a version of the Bible widely used in the ancient world.)

One fundamental issue about the Bible must be emphasized: Both ancient Israel, subsequent Jewish history, and the Christian world have made the Bible *the* central document not only for worship and the rule of faith but also as moral guide and anchor for ethical and religious stability. The Bible, directly and indirectly, has shaped our law, literature, language, ethics, and social outlook. It permeates our culture. To cite one single example: at Solomon's temple the people sang hymns of praise (psalms) to God just as they are sung in Jewish synagogues today. Those same psalms were sung by Jesus and his followers in their time just as they are sung and recited in Christian churches in every part of the world. That ancient

5.2 *The Spoils of Jerusalem,* from the Arch of Titus, Rome. C. A.D. 81. Passageway relief. The seven-branched candelabrum (a *menorah*) is carried as part of the booty after the Romans sacked the city of Jerusalem.

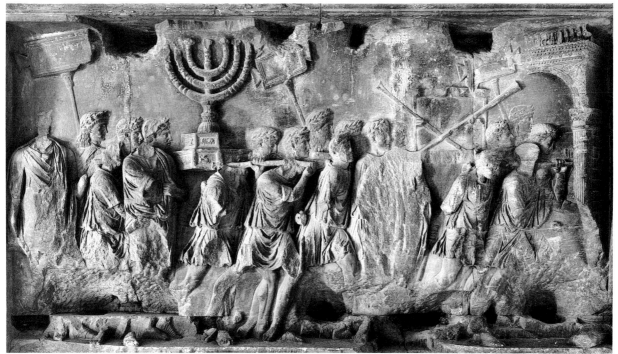

formulation is, in a deep sense, part of our common religious culture.

The Bible is not a philosophical treatise; it is a sacred book. It is, nonetheless, a book that contains ideas; those ideas have had an enormous impact on the way we think and the way we look at the world. Some of the basic motifs of the Bible have been so influential in our culture that they should be considered in some detail. We will examine three such motifs that run like strands throughout the Hebrew scriptures.

1. *Biblical monotheism.* A central conviction of biblical religion in that there is one God, that this God is good, and (most crucially) that this God is involved in the arena of human history. This God is conceived of as a person and not as some impersonal force in the world of nature. *Monotheism* (the belief in one god) can thus be distinguished both from *henotheism* (the belief that there may be other gods, although only one is singled out for worship) and *polytheism* (the belief that there are many gods).

The opening pages of the Bible set out a creation story (see Genesis 1:1–2:4a) that, properly understood, provides us with a rather complete vision of what the Bible believes about God. The creation story of Genesis makes three basic assertions about God. First, God exists before the world and called it into existence by the simple act of utterance. God, unlike the gods and goddesses of the Hebrews' ancient neighbors, is not born out of the chaos that existed before the world. God is not to be confused with the world, nor did God have to struggle with the forces of chaos to create. Second, God pronounces each part of creation and creation as a whole as "good." Thus the book of Genesis does not present the material universe as evil or, as certain Eastern religions teach, as an illusory world that conceals the true nature of reality. Finally, God creates human beings as the apex and crown of creation. The material world is a gift from God and they are obliged to care for it and be grateful for it. A basic motif of biblical prayer is gratitude to God for the gift of creation.

Biblical monotheism must not be thought of as a theory that simply sees God as the starting point or originator of all things after the fashion of a craftsperson who makes a chair and then forgets about it. The precise character of biblical monotheism is its conviction that God creates and sustains the world in general and chose a particular people to be both vehicle and sign of divine presence in the world. The precise character of that relationship can be found in the biblical notion of covenant.

Covenant is the crucial concept for setting out the relationship of God and the Hebrew people. The covenant can be summed up in the simple biblical phrases "I will be your God; you will be my people." In Hebrew history, the Bible insists, God has always been faithful to that covenant which was made with the people of Israel while the people must learn and relearn how to be faithful to it.

This strong portrait of single, deeply involved God who is beyond image or portrayal has had a profound impact on the shape of the Judeo-Christian world view. The notion of covenant religion not only gave form to Hebrew religion; the idea of a renewed covenant became the central claim of Christianity. (Remember that another word for covenant is *testament;* hence the popular Old/New-Testament split Christianity insists upon.) The idea has even spilled over from synagogues and churches into our national civil religion, where we affirm a belief in "One nation under God" and "In God we trust"—both sentiments rooted in the idea of covenant.

2. *Ethics.* The Bible is not primarily an ethical treatise; it is a theological one even though it does set out a moral code of behavior both for individuals and society. The Bible has a large number of rules for worship and ritual but its fundamental ethical world view lies in the idea that humans are created in "the image and likeness of God" (see Genesis 1:26). The more detailed formulation of that link between God and individual and social relationships is contained in the Ten Commandments, which the Bible depicts as being given by God to Moses after the latter brings the people out of the bondage of Egypt and before they reach the Promised Land (see Exodus 20). These commandments, consisting of both prohibitions (against murder, theft, idolatry, etc.) and positive commands (for worship, honoring of parents, etc.), are part of the larger ethical commands of all civilizations. The peculiarly monotheistic parts of the code appear in the first cluster, with the positive command to worship God alone and the prohibition of graven images and their worship.

Ancient Israel's ethics take on a more specific character in the writings of the prophets. The prophet (Hebrew *nabi*) speaks with God's authority. In Hebrew religion the prophet was not primarily concerned with the future (prophet and seer are thus not the same thing) even though the prophets do speak of a coming of peace and justice. The main prophetic task was to call people back to the observance of the covenant and to warn them about the ways in which they failed that covenant. The great 8th-century prophets who flourished in both the North and the South after the period of the monarchy left a great literature. They insisted that worship of God, for example, in the worship of the temple, was insufficient if that worship did not come from the heart and include a love and compassion for others. The prophets were radical critics of social injustice and defenders of the poor. They linked worship with a deep concern for ethics. They envisioned God as a God of all people and insisted on the connection between worship of God and just living.

Prophets were not a hereditary caste in ancient Israel, as the priest were. Prophets were called to preach. In many instances they even resisted that call and expressed reluctance to undertake the prophetic task. The fact that they had an unpopular message explains both why many of them suffered a violent end and why some were reluctant to undertake the task of preaching.

The prophetic element in religion was one of Israel's most enduring contributions to the religious sensibility of the world. The idea that certain people are called directly by God to preach peace and justice in the context of religious faith would continue beyond the biblical period in Judaism and Christianity. It is not accidental, to cite one modern example, that the civil rights leader Martin Luther King, Jr. (1929–1968) often cited the biblical prophets as the exemplars for his own struggle in behalf of black Americans. That King died a violent death in 1968 is an all-too-ready example of how disquieting the prophetic message can be.

3. *Models and types.* Until modern times relatively few Jews or Christians actually read the Bible on an individual basis. Literacy was rare, books expensive, and leisure at a premium. Bibles were read to people most frequently in public gatherings of worship in synagogues or churches. The one time that the New Testament reports Jesus as reading is from a copy of the prophet Isaiah kept in a synagogue (Luke 4:16ff.). The biblical stories were read over the centuries in a familial setting (as at the Jewish Passover) or in formal worship on the Sabbath. The basic point, however, is that for more than three thousand years the stories and (equally important) the persons in these stories have been etched in the Western imagination. The faith of Abraham, the guidance of Moses, the wisdom of Solomon, the sufferings of Job, the fidelity of Ruth have become proverbial in our culture.

These events and stories from the Bible are models of instruction and illumination; they have taken on a meaning far beyond their original significance. The events described in the book of Exodus, for example, are often invoked to justify a desire for freedom from oppression and slavery. It is not accidental that Benjamin Franklin suggested depicting the crossing of the reed sea (not the Red Sea as is often said) by the Children of Israel as the centerpiece of the Great Seal of the United States. Long before Franklin's day, the Pilgrims saw themselves as the new Children of Israel who had fled the oppression of Europe (read: Egypt) to find freedom in the land "flowing with milk and honey" that was America. At a later period in history the enslaved blacks of this country saw themselves as the oppressed Israelites in bondage. The desire of black Americans for freedom was couched in the language of the Bible as they sang "Go down, Moses. Tell old Pharaoh: Let my people go!"

No humanities student can ignore the impact of the biblical tradition on our common culture. Our literature echoes it; our art is saturated in it; our social institutions are shaped by it. Writers in the Middle Ages said that all knowledge came from God in the form of two great books: the book of nature and the book called the Bible. We have enlarged that understanding today but, nonetheless, we have absorbed much of the Hebrew scriptures into the very texture of our culture.

The Beginnings of Christianity

The fundamental fact with which to study the life of Jesus is to remember that he was a Jew, born during the reign of the Roman emperor Augustus in the Roman-occupied land of Judea. What we know about him, apart from a few glancing references in pagan and Jewish literature, comes from the four gospels (*gospel* derives from the Anglo-Saxon word meaning "good news") attributed to Matthew, Mark, Luke, and John. These gospels began to appear about a generation after the death of Jesus, which probably occurred in A.D. 30. The gospels are religious documents, not biographies, but they contain historical data about Jesus as well as theological reflections about the meaning of his life and the significance of his deeds.

Jesus must also be understood in the light of the Jewish prophetical tradition discussed above. He preached the coming of God's kingdom, which would be a reign of justice and mercy. Israel's enemies would be overcome. Until that kingdom arrived Jesus insisted on a life of repentance, an abandonment of earthly concerns, love of God and neighbor, compassion for the poor, downcast, and emarginated, and set forth his own life as an example. His identification with the poor and powerless antagonized his enemies—who included the leaders of his own religion and the governing authorities of the ruling Romans. Perhaps the most characteristic expression of the teachings of Jesus is to be found in his parables and in the moral code he expressed in what is variously called The Beatitudes or The Sermon on the Mount.

All of the teachings of Jesus reflect a profound grasp of the piety and wisdom of the Jewish traditions, but the Gospels make a further claim for Jesus, depicting him as the *Christ* (a Greek translation of the

EAST MEETS WEST

Mithraism

About a hundred years before the time of Christ a new religious deity began to be worshiped in the Roman Empire. Brought from Persia (modern Iran), the divinity was Mithra, a god who had been worshiped in Persia for centuries although the cult of Mithra probably came into Persia itself from India.

Mithra was identified with the sun (like the Greek god Apollo) and his birthday was celebrated on December 25th—just after the winter solstice, when the sun was "reborn" for another year. The Christian decision to celebrate the birth of Christ on that date was probably a strategy to combat Mithra worship.

The cult of Mithra had a strong appeal for the Roman military, who saw in the warrior figure killing a bull a model for their own life of masculine achievement. Archaeologists have found sites of Mithra worship (a *Mithraeum*) all over the Roman empire from the eastern Mediterranean to Italy and as far north as England and in what is present-day Hungary (ancient Pannonia).

Because the worship of Mithra was open only to those who had been initiated into its rites (a so-called mystery religion, it revealed mysteries concerning the gods) we do not have firm evidence concerning its ceremonies and their meaning. The rites did include the sacrifice of bulls, symbolic bathing, and communal meals. Because the rites of Mithra were connected with the signs of the Zodiac it is believed that the ceremonies were meant to act out a symbolic ascent into the heavens, where the devotees were freed from the bonds of fate and the influence of the stars.

Mithraism was a competitor of Christianity for the allegiance of the Romans. The cult died out in the 4th century under the pressure of an increasingly Christianized empire. While this Oriental religion had a wide appeal in the Roman period, it was hampered by its unremittingly masculine aspect. It did not permit women to be initiated into its mysteries. Nonetheless, its superficial resemblance to Christianity (a dying and reborn god; a kind of baptism; a ceremonial meal, and so on) made it a prime target for Christian polemicists who saw it as a demonic parody of their own religion. In many places churches were built over the remains of the sites of a Mithraeum as a symbol of the Christian victory over this pagan religion.

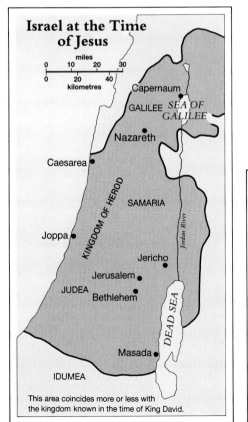

Israel at the Time of Jesus

This area coincides more or less with the kingdom known in the time of King David.

Hebrew *messiah,* "anointed one")—the savior promised by the ancient biblical prophets who would bring about God's kingdom. His tragic death by crucifixion (a punishment so degrading that it could not be inflicted on Roman citizens) would seem to have ended the public career of Jesus. The early Christian church, however, insisted that Jesus overcame death by rising from the tomb three days after his death. This belief in the resurrection became a centerpiece of Christian faith and preaching and the basis on which early Christianity proclaimed Jesus as Christ.

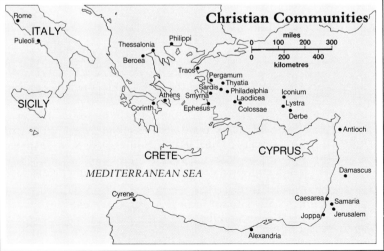

Christian Communities

message of the Christian movement (see Acts 17: 16–34).

TABLE 5.1 Books of the Old and New Testaments	
Genesis	*The Gospels:*
Exodus	Matthew
Leviticus	Mark
Numbers	Luke
Deuteronomy	John
Joshua	*The Acts of the Apostles*
Judges	*The Letters of Paul:*
Ruth	Romans
I and II Samuel	I Corinthians
I and II Kings	II Corinthians
I and II Chronicles	Galatians
Ezra	Ephesians
Nehemiah	Philippians
Esther	Colossians
Job	I Thessalonians
Psalms	II Thessalonians
Proverbs	I Timothy
Ecclesiastes	II Timothy
Song of Solomon	Titus
Isaiah	Philemon
Jeremiah	Hebrews
Lamentations	*The Letters of:*
Ezekiel	James
Daniel	I Peter
Hosea	II Peter
Joel	I John
Amos	II John
Obadiah	III John
Jonah	Jude
Micah	*The Book of Revelation*
Nahum	(also called *The Apocalypse*)
Habakkuk	
Zephaniah	
Haggai	
Zechariah	
Malachi	

Christianity Spreads

The slow growth of the Christian movement was given an early boost by the conversion of a Jewish zealot, Saul of Tarsus, around the year A.D. 35 near Damascus, Syria. Paul (his postconversion name) won a crucial battle in the early Christian church, insisting that non-Jewish converts to the movement would not have to adhere to Jewish religious customs, especially male circumcision. Paul's victory was to change Christianity from a religious movement within Judaism to a religious tradition that could embrace the non-Jewish world of the Roman empire. One dramatic example of Paul's approach to this pagan world was a public sermon he gave in the city of Athens in which he used the language of Greek culture to speak to the Athenians with the

Paul was a tireless missionary. He made at least three long journeys through the cities on the northern shore of the Mediterranean (and may once have gotten as far as Spain). On his final journey he reached Rome itself, where he met his death at the hands of a Roman executioner in A.D. 67 or 68. In many of the cities he visited he left small communities of believers. Some of his letters (Romans, Galatians, Corinthians, and so on) are addressed to believers in these places and provide details of his theological and pastoral concerns.

By the end of the 1st century communities of Christian believers existed in most of the cities of the vast Roman empire. Their numbers were sufficient enough that by A.D. 64 the emperor Nero could make Christians scapegoats for a fire that destroyed the city of Rome (probably set by the emperor's own agents). The Roman writer Tacitus provides a vivid description of the terrible tortures meted out against the Christians:

> . . . Nero charged, and viciously punished, people called Christians who were despised on account of their wicked practices. The founder of the sect, Christus, was executed by the procurator Pontius Pilate during the reign of Tiberius. The evil superstition was suppressed for a time but soon broke out afresh not only in Judea where it started but also in Rome where every filthy outrage arrives and prospers. First, those who confessed were seized and then, on their witness, a huge number was convicted, less for arson than for their hatred of the human race.
>
> In their death they were mocked. Some were sewn in animal skins and worried to death by dogs; others were crucified or burned so that, when daylight was over, they could serve as torches in the evening. Nero provided his own gardens for this show and made it into a circus. He mingled with the crowd dressed as a charioteer or posed in his chariot. As a result, the sufferers guilty and worthy of punishment although they were, did arouse the pity of the mob who saw their suffering resulted from the viciousness of one man and not because of some need for the common good. [*Annales* xv]

Two questions arise at this point: Why were the Christians successful in spreading their religion? Why did they become the object of persecution at the hands of the Romans?

A number of social factors aided the growth of Christianity: There was peace in the Roman empire; a good system of safe roads made travel easy; there was a common language in the empire (a form of common Greek called *koine:* the language of the New Testament) and Christianity was first preached in a network of Jewish centers. Scholars have also offered some religious reasons: the growing interest of pagans in monotheism; the strong Christian emphasis on salvation and freedom from sin; the Christian custom of offering mutual aid and charity for its members; and its relative freedom from class distinctions. Paul wrote that in this faith there was "neither Jew nor Gentile; male nor female; slave or free person."

This new religion met a good deal of resistance. The first martyrs died before the movement spread outside Jerusalem because of the resistance of the Jewish establishment. Very quickly, too, the Christians gained the enmity of the Romans. Even before Nero's persecution in 64, the Christians had been expelled from the city of Rome by the emperor Claudius. From those early days until the 3d century there were sporadic outbreaks of persecutions. In 250 under the emperor Decius there was an empire wide persecution, with two others coming in 257 (under Valerian) and under Diocletian in 303. Finally, in 312 the emperor Constantine issued a decree in Milan allowing Christianity toleration as a religion.

What was the basis for this long history of persecution?

The reasons are complex. Ordinarily, Rome had no interest in the religious beliefs of its subjects as long as these beliefs did not threaten public order. The Christian communities seemed secretive; they had their own network of communication in the empire; they kept away from active life in the political realm; most telling of all, they refused to pay homage to the state gods and goddesses. A common charge made against them was that they were atheists: they denied the existence of the Roman gods. Romans conceived of their society as bound together in a seamless web of *pietas,* a virtue that meant a combination of love and reverential fear. The Romans felt that one should express *pietas* to the parents of a family; the family should express that *pietas* toward the state, and the state in turn owed *pietas* to the gods.

That brought everything into harmony, and the state would flourish. The Christian refusal to express *pietas* to the gods seemed to the Romans to strike at the heart of civic order. The Christians, in short, were traitors to the state.

Christian writers of the 2nd century tried to answer these charges by insisting that the Christians wished to be good citizens and, in fact, could be. These writers (called *apologists*) wrote about the moral code of Christianity, about their beliefs and the reasons they could not worship the Roman deities. Their radical monotheism, inherited from Judaism, forbade such worship. Furthermore, they protested their roles as ready scapegoats for every ill, real and imagined, in society. The acid-tongued North African Christian writer Tertullian provided a sharp statement concerning the Christian grievance about such treatment: "If the Tiber floods its banks or the Nile doesn't flood; if the heavens stand still or the earth shakes, if there is hunger or drought, quickly the cry goes up, 'Christians to the lions!'"

Early Christian Art

Little significant Christian art or architecture dates from before the 4th century because of the illegal status of the Christian church and the clandestine life it was forced to lead. We do have art from the cemeteries of Rome and some other cities that were maintained by the Christian communities. These cemeteries (known as catacombs from the name of one of them, the *coemeterium ad catacumbas*) were the burial places of thousands of Christians. Contrary to romantic notion, these underground galleries, cut from the soft rock known as *tufa,* were never hiding places for Christians during the times of persecution, nor were they secret places for worship. Such ideas de-

---

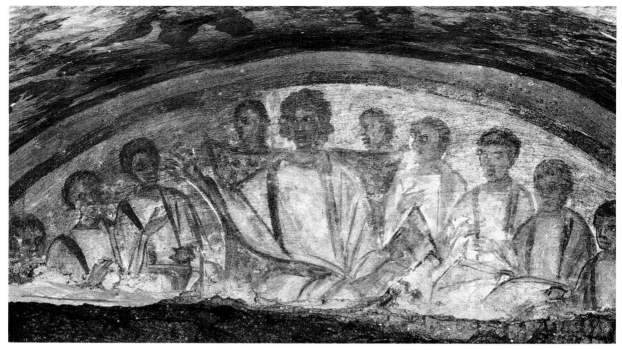

5.3 *Christ Teaching the Apostles.* c. A.D. 300. Wall painting. 1′3″ × 4′3″ (.38 × 1.3 m). Cemetery of Domitilla, Rome. The beardless Christ and the use of the Roman toga are characteristic. Partially destroyed; the original setting was meant to depict a eucharistic banquet.

rive not from fact but from 19th-century novels. Similarly, only a minuscule number of the tombs contained the bodies of martyrs; none do today, since the martyrs were reburied inside the walls of the city of Rome in the early Middle Ages.

These underground cemeteries are important, however, because they provide us some visual evidence about early Christian beliefs and customs. This artistic material falls into categories:

Frescoes (wall paintings done on fresh plaster) are found frequently in the catacombs. Most of these depict biblical subjects that reflect the Christian hope of salvation and eternal life. Thus, for example, common themes like the story of Jonah or the raising of Lazarus from the dead allude to the Christian belief that everyone would be raised at the end of time. Another common motif is the communion meal of Jesus at the Last Supper as an anticipation of the heavenly banquet that awaited all believers in the next life [5.3].

THE ARTS AND INVENTION: *Iconography*

Almost all art, and especially religious art, has both an obvious and an implied meaning. The latter may become intelligible only if we can enter into the symbol system assumed by artists and expressed in their work. *Iconography* is the study of the symbols and their meanings in a given piece of art.

The general principles of iconography apply to all artworks but are particularly useful for the study of Christian art because Christianity assumes the value of the Hebrew scriptures and then provides more significance, in light of its own beliefs, to those scriptures.

Following the path worked out by the art historian Irwin Panofsky we can interpret symbols in art in a threefold ascent: (1) The evident meaning of an object as it is depicted; (2) its conventional meaning in art (such as the Star of David as a symbol of Judaism), which is iconography in the narrow sense; and (3) the symbolic significance as a reflection of a state of mind or statement of significance.

A concrete example. The figure of Jonah is common in early Christian art. When we see that figure, if we have enough background, we might interpret it as follows:

Here is a depiction of a man being disgorged from the mouth of a sea monster. That evidently refers to the story of the prophet Jonah in the Hebrew Bible. We know that Jesus used that same story as a symbol of his stay in the tomb and of his resurrection; just as Jonah was in the belly of the sea monster so Jesus would be in the belly of the earth. Since Christians believed that they would share in this resurrection it would be natural for such a depiction to be found in a funeral setting. Thus the disgorged figure has behind it dense levels of symbolism that echo the Hebrew scriptures, the Christian scriptures, and the faith of the Roman Christian community where it was found. What we see depicted is one scene, but one who can "read" the symbol sees, at one time, various levels of meaning.

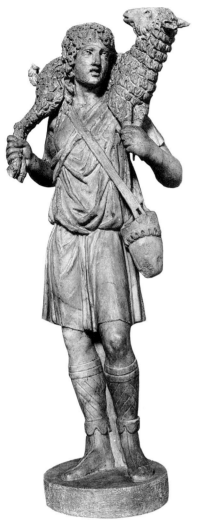

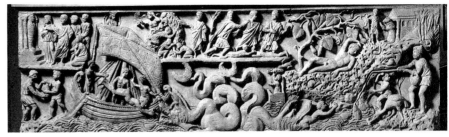

5.5 *Jonah Sarcophagus.* 4th century. Limestone. Museo Pio Cristiano, The Vatican. Besides the Jonah cycle there are other biblical scenes: at the top left, the raising of Lazarus; to the right of the sail at top, Moses striking the rock; at the far top right, a shepherd with a sheep.

such as an anchor (for hope) or a dove with an olive branch (peace) for decoration. One of the most common symbols was a fish. The Greek letters that spell out the word *fish* were considered an anagram for the phrase "Jesus Christ, Son of God and Savior" so that the fish symbol became a shorthand way of making that brief confession of faith [5.6].

Dura-Europos

Despite the persecutions of the Christians and the hostility of the Romans to the Jews, both religions

5.6 *Fish and Chalice.* 3rd century. Floor mosaic. Ostia Antica (Rome). This mosaic, and other evidence, led scholars to believe that a house excavated in the Roman port city of Ostia was a house church with a baptistery. The fish was a common symbol of Christ. This is one of the earliest uses of the symbol.

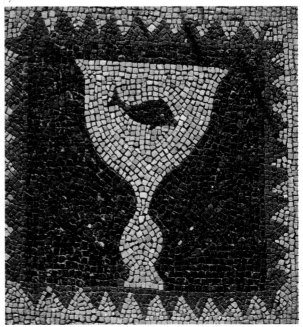

5.4 *Good Shepherd.* c. A.D. 300. Marble, height 39″ (99 cm.). Vatican Museums, Rome. This depiction of Christ is very common in early Christian art, although sculptural examples are rather rare.

Glass and sculpture. Although sculpture is quite rare before the 4th century, a statue of Christ as Good Shepherd [5.4], unbearded and with clearly classical borrowings, may be dated from this period. The figure repeats a common theme in the fresco art of the period. More common are the glass disks with gold paper cutouts pressed in them that are found in both Jewish and Christian catacombs as a decorative motif on individual tomb slots. After the period of Constantine carved sarcophagi also became both common and elaborate [5.5].

Inscriptions. Each tomb was covered by a slab of marble that was cemented in place. On those slabs would be carved the name and death date of the buried person. Quite frequently, there was also a symbol

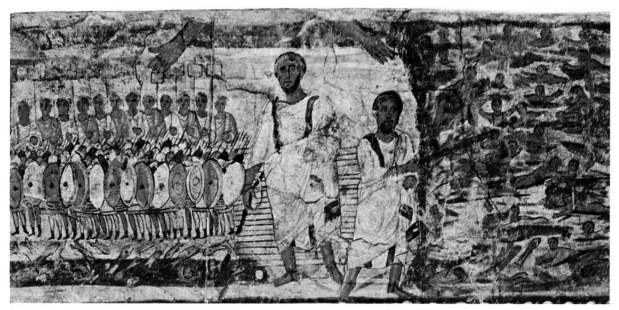

5.7 *The Crossing of the Red Sea.* Fresco. c. A.D. 245. Dura-Europos. National Archaeological Museum, Damascus, Syria. This extraordinary scene shows Moses and Aaron with Egyptian soldiers on their right and the drowning armies on their left. This is part of a huge wall mural depicting scenes from the Hebrew scriptures.

managed to exist and, to a certain extent, to thrive in the Roman Empire. One small indication of this fact can be seen in the spectacular archaeological finds made in the 1930s at a small town in present-day Syria called Dura-Europos. This small Roman garrison town, destroyed by Persian armies in A.D. 256, was covered by desert sands for nearly seventeen hundred years. The scholars who excavated it found a street that ran roughly north and south along the city wall (they called it Wall Street) and contained a Christian house church with some intact frescoes, a temple to a Semitic god called Aphlad, a temple to the god Zeus (Roman Jupiter), a meeting place for the worshipers of the cult of Mithra, and a Jewish synagogue with more than twenty well-preserved fresco paintings of scenes from the Hebrew scriptures [5.7].

The Dura-Europos discoveries both revealed the mingling of many religious cultures and demonstrated that the usual Jewish resistance to the visual arts was not total. Furthermore, the evidence of a building for Christian worship (part of a papyrus of the four gospels harmonized into one whole was found at the site) in place sixty years before Constantine's edict of toleration and in use during a time when there were empirewide persecutions of Christians is a significant discovery.

Scholars see in the art of Dura-Europos the mingling of both Eastern and Roman styles that might be the source for the art that would emerge more fully in the Byzantine world. Most significantly, the finds at Dura demonstrate how complex the religious situation of the time really was and how the neat generalizations of historians do not always correspond to the complicated realities of actual life.

Constantine and Early Christian Architecture

Two of the most famous churches in Christendom are associated with the reign of the Emperor Constantine. The present Saint Peter's Basilica in the Vatican rests on the remains of a basilica dedicated in 326. We do not have a fully articulated plan of that church, but its main outlines are clear. The faithful would enter into a courtyard called an *atrium* around which was a colonnaded arcade and from there through a vestibule into the church proper. The basilica, modeled after secular counterparts in Rome, featured a long central *nave* with two parallel side aisles. The nave was intersected at one end by a *transept,* the roof of which was pitched with wooden trusses and supported by the outer walls and the columned interiors. High up on the walls above the arches and below the roof was the so-called *clerestory,* windows that provided most of the interior illumina-

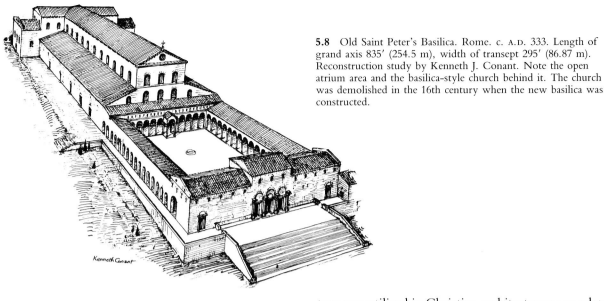

5.8 Old Saint Peter's Basilica. Rome. c. A.D. 333. Length of grand axis 835′ (254.5 m), width of transept 295′ (86.87 m). Reconstruction study by Kenneth J. Conant. Note the open atrium area and the basilica-style church behind it. The church was demolished in the 16th century when the new basilica was constructed.

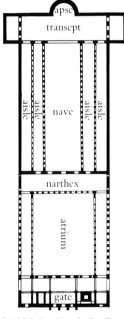

5.9 Floor plan of Old Saint Peter's Basilica.

tion. This basilica-type church [5.8, 5.9] became a model from which many of the features of later church architecture evolved.

The other famous church built in the Constantinian period is the church of the Holy Sepulchre in Jerusalem [5.10]. This church was also built in the basilica style, its atrium in front of the basilica hall, but with a significant addition. Behind the basilica was a domed structure that covered—it was believed—the rocky place where the body of Christ had been buried for three days. The domelike struc-

ture was utilized in Christian architecture as an adaptation of existing domed structures in pagan Rome, most notably the Pantheon and some of the vast baths.

Early Christian Music

If the visual arts of early Christianity turned to Graeco-Roman models for inspiration, the music of the early church drew on Jewish sources. The tradition of singing (or, rather, chanting) sacred texts at religious services was an ancient Jewish custom that appears to go back to Mesopotamian sources. What little we know of Jewish music, in fact, suggests that it was strongly influenced by the various peoples with whom the Jews came into contact. The lyre used by Jewish musicians was a common Mesopotamian instrument, while the harp for which King David was famous came to the Jews from Assyria by way of Egypt [5.11].

By early Christian times Jewish religious services consisted of a standardized series of prayers and scriptural readings organized in such a fashion as to create a cycle that fit the Jewish calendar. Many of these readings were taken over by early Christian congregations, particularly those where the number of converted Jews was high. In chanting the psalms the style of execution often depended on how well they were known by the congregation. Where the Jewish component of the congregation was strong the congregation would join in the chant. Increasingly, however, the singing was left to trained choruses with the other congregants joining in only for the standard response of *Amen* or *Alleluia*. As the music fell more into the hands of professionals it became increasingly complex.

This professionalization proved unpopular, however, with church authorities, who feared that the

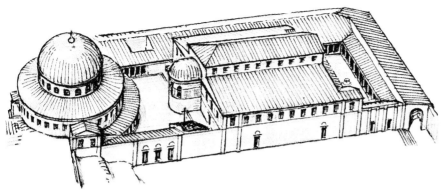

5.10 Church of the Holy Sepulchre, Jerusalem, as it appeared c. A.D. 345. Reconstruction by Kenneth J. Conant. In this drawing, both the domed area which covered the burial place of Christ and the detached basilica in front of it can be seen. In the present church there is no separation between the domed area and the basilica.

choirs were concerned more with performance than with worship. In 361 a provincial council of the Christian church in Laodicea ordered that there should be only one paid performer (a *cantor*) for each congregation. In Rome, the authorities discouraged poetic elaboration on the liturgical texts, a practice common among the Jews and the Christians of the East.

Part of the early Christian suspicion of music, in the West at least, was a reaction against the Greek doctrine of *ethos* in music, which claimed that music could have a profound effect on human behavior. That music might induce moods of passion or violence or might even be an agreeable sensation in itself was not likely to appeal to a church that required the *ethos* of its music to express religious truth alone. For this reason instrumental music was rejected as unsuitable for the Christian liturgy. Such instrumentation was, in the minds of many Christians, too reminiscent of pagan customs.

By the 4th century, then, the standard form of music in Christian churches was either *responsorial* singing, with a cantor intoning lines from the psalms and the congregation responding with a simple repeated refrain, or *antiphonal* singing, with parts of the congregation (or the cantor and the congregation) alternating verses of a psalm in a simple chant tone. By the beginning of the 5th century there is evidence of nonscriptural hymns being composed. Apart from some rare fragments, we have no illustration of music texts with notation before the 9th century.

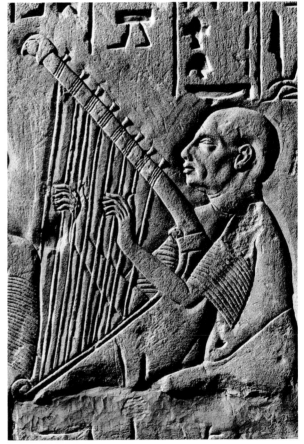

5.11 *The Blind Harper of Leiden,* detail from the tomb of Patenembveb, Saqqara. c. 1340–1330 B.C. Limestone bas-relief, Height 11 ½″ (29 cm). Rijksmuseum van Oudheden, Leiden, Netherlands. It is quite possible that the lyre depicted here is similar to those mentioned in the book of Psalms.

Summary

This chapter traces a very long history from the beginnings of the biblical tradition to the emergence of Christianity as a state religion in the Roman Empire, a history so complex that one hesitates to generalize about its shape and significance. Nonetheless, certain points deserve to be highlighted both because they are instructive in their own right and because of their continuing impact on the shape of Western culture.

First, the biblical tradition reflects the emergence of monotheism (a belief in one God) as a leading idea in Western culture. Judaism held the ideal of the uniqueness of God against the polytheistic cultures of Babylonia, Assyria, and Egypt. That idea carried over into Christianity and became a point of conflict with Roman culture. The Roman charge that Christians were atheists meant not that they denied the existence of God but that they rejected the Roman gods.

Second, the entire biblical tradition had a very strong ethical emphasis. The prophets never ceased to argue that the external practice of religion was worthless unless there was a "pure heart." Jesus preached essentially the same thing in his famous criticisms of those who would pray publicly but secretly, in his words, "devour the substance of widows."

This ethics was rooted in the biblical notion of *prophetism*—the belief that people could be called by God to denounce injustice in the face of hostility either from their own religious establishment or from equally hostile civil governments. Such prophetic protest, inspired by the biblical message, was always a factor in subsequent Judaism and Christianity.

Both Judaism and Christianity insisted on a personal God who was actively involved with the world of humanity to the degree that there was a *covenant* between God and people and that the world was created and sustained by God as a gift for humans. This was a powerful doctrine that flew in the face of the ancient belief in impersonal fate controlling the destiny of people or a pessimism about the goodness or reliability of the world as we have it and live in it.

The biblical belief in the providence of God would have an enormous impact on later Western culture in everything from shaping its philosophy of history (that history moves in a linear fashion and has a direction to it) to an optimism about the human capacity to understand the world and makes its secrets known for the benefit of people. Western culture never accepted, at least as a majority opinion, that the physical world itself was sacred or an illusion. It was, rather, a gift to be explored and at times exploited.

Finally, the Jewish and Christian tradition produced a work of literature: the *Bible*. The significance of that production can best be understood in the subsequent chapters of this book. It will soon become clear that a good deal of what the humanistic tradition of art, literature, and music produced until well into the modern period is unintelligible if not seen as an ongoing attempt to interpret that text in various artistic media according to the needs of the age.

Pronunciation Guide

Constantine: CON-stan-tine
catacombs: CAT-ah-combs
covenant: KUV-e-nent
Decius: DAY-see-us
Diocletian: Die-oh-KLE-shun
Dura-Europos: Dew-rah You-ROPE-us
Exodus: X-oh-dus

Laodicea: Lay-oh-de-SEE-ah
Messiah: Mess-EYE-ah
Mithraism: MYTH-rah-is-im
pietas: PEA-ah-tas
Torah: TOE-rah
tufa: TOO-fa

Exercises

1. Hebrew religion begins in a patriarchal culture (a tribe headed by a "father") and much of its language derives from that fact. What are the common titles for God that reflect that masculine dominance? Do some feminists have a case in their criticism of the overly patriarchal nature of biblical religion?
2. Biblical religion insists that God has no name and cannot be depicted in art. What do you think were the reasons behind that attitude (almost unique in the ancient world) and what were its cultural consequences?
3. The biblical covenant is summed up in "I will be your God; you will be my people." Can you suggest a short phrase to sum up a marriage covenant? a covenant between citizens and the state? What are the essential characteristics of a covenant?
4. Reread the Ten Commandments. Which of them make sense only to religious believers? Which have general applications? Could you suggest other commandments for inclusion in a modern version?
5. How would you characterize Jesus as a cultural type: teacher? philosopher? prophet? hero? martyr? other?
6. It is said that The Beatitudes are at the heart of the teaching of Jesus. Paraphrase those beatitudes in contemporary language. Which of them sound strangest to our ears?
7. Do you see any lessons about religious tolerance today from the history of the persecution of the Christians in the Roman Empire?
8. Constantine extended the aid of the state to Christians. What are the benefits of state support for religion? What are the problems?
9. In his famous praise of the virtue of love, Paul the Apostle says that love outlives both faith and hope. What kind of love is he talking about? How does love outlive both hope and faith?

Further Reading

Alter, Robert. *The Art of Biblical Narrative.* New York: Basic Books, 1981. An excellent work by a literary critic.

Alter, Robert and Frank Kermode. *The Literary Guide to the Bible.* Cambridge: Harvard University Press, 1987. Uneven but useful literary essays on all of the books of the Bible.

Anderson, Bernhard. *Understanding the Old Testament.* Englewood Cliffs, N.J.: Prentice-Hall, 1975. The standard college-level introduction to the Hebrew scriptures.

Buttrick, George, *et al. The Interpreter's Dictionary of the*

Bible, 4 vols. New York: Abingdon, 1962. Comprehensive and scholarly; reliable dictionary of the entire Bible.

Frend, W. H. C. *The Rise of Christianity.* Philadelphia: Fortress, 1983. An exhaustive treatment by an outstanding scholar.

Frye, Northrop. *The Great Code: The Bible and Literature.* New York: Harcourt Brace Jovanovich, 1981. A dense but rewarding study of biblical genre and Western literature.

Lane-Fox, Robert. *Pagans and Christians.* New York: Knopf, 1987. A brilliant study of the relationship of Roman culture and the emerging Christian movement in the first four centuries of the common era.

May, Herbert. *Oxford Bible Atlas.* New York: Oxford University Press, 1974. Invaluable for biblical geography.

Pelikan, Jaroslav. *Jesus Through the Centuries: His Place in the History of Culture.* New Haven, Conn.: Yale University Press, 1985. An account of the cultural interpretations of Jesus in Western culture by an eminent scholar.

Pritchard, J. B. *Ancient Near Eastern Texts Relating to the Old Testament.* Princeton, N.J.: Princeton University Press, 1969. An indispensable collection of texts for biblical study taken from the cultures of those who were in contact with the biblical peoples. A standard reference work.

Weitzmann, Kurt. *Age of Spirituality: Late Antique and Early Christian Art.* New York: Metropolitan Museum of Art, 1979. An exhaustive catalogue based on the definitive exhibit of the roots of Christian art.

Wilken, Robert. *The Christians as the Romans Saw Them.* New Haven, Conn.: Yale University Press, 1984. A well-written account of the rise of Christianity from the Roman point of view.

Reading Selections

Genesis 1–2

In this section we have two quite different accounts of God as the creator and sustainer of all things. The selections from the book of Genesis are the classic Hebrew accounts of creation; the first runs from 1.1 to 2.4a and the second to the end of the second chapter.

1 In the beginning God created the heavens and the earth. 2 The earth was without form and void, and darkness was upon the face of the deep; and the Spirit of God was moving over the face of the waters.

3 And God said, "Let there be light"; and there was light. 4 And God saw that the light was good; and God separated the light from the darkness. 5 God called the light Day, and the darkness he called Night. And there was evening and there was morning, one day.

6 And God said, "Let there be a firmament in the midst of the waters, and let it separate the waters from the waters." 7 And God made the firmament and separated the waters which were under the firmament from the waters which were above the firmament. And it was so. 8 And God called the firmament Heaven. And there was evening and there was morning, a second day.

9 And God said, "Let the waters under the heavens be gathered together into one place, and let the dry land appear." And it was so. 10 God called the dry land Earth, and the waters that were gathered together he called Seas. And God saw that it was good. 11 And God said, "Let the earth put forth vegetation, plants yielding seed, and fruit trees bearing fruit in which is their seed, each according to its kind, upon the earth." And it was so. 12 The earth brought forth vegetation, plants yielding seed according to their own kinds, and trees bearing fruit in which is their seed, each according to its kind. And God saw that it was good. 13 And there was evening and there was morning, a third day.

14 And God said, "Let there be lights in the firmament of the heavens to separate the day from the night; and let them be for signs and for seasons and for days and years, 15 and let them be lights in the firmament of the heavens to give light upon the earth." And it was so. 16 And God made the two great lights, the greater light to rule the day, and the lesser light to rule the night; he made the stars also. 17 And God set them in the firmament of the heavens to give light upon the earth, 18 to rule over the day and over the night, and to separate the light from the darkness. And God saw that it was good. 19 And there was evening and there was morning, a fourth day.

20 And God said, "Let the waters bring forth swarms of living creatures, and let birds fly above the earth across the firmament of the heavens," 21 So God created the great sea monsters and every living creature that moves, with which the waters swarm, according to their kinds, and every winged bird according to its kind. And God saw that it was good. 22 And God blessed them, saying, "Be fruitful and multiply and fill the waters in the seas, and let birds multiply on the earth." 23 And there was evening and there was morning, a fifth day.

24 And God said, "Let the earth bring forth living creatures according to their kinds: cattle and creeping things and beasts of the earth according to their kinds." And it was so. 25 And God made the beasts of the earth according to their kinds and the cattle according to their kinds, and everything that creeps upon the ground according to its kind. And God saw that it was good.

26 Then God said, "Let us make man in our image, after our likeness; and let them have domin-

ion over the fish of the sea, and over the birds of the air, and over the cattle, and over all the earth, and over every creeping thing that creeps upon the earth." [27] So God created man in his own image, in the image of God he created him; male and female he created them. [28] And God blessed them, and God said to them, "Be fruitful and multiply, and fill the earth and subdue it; and have dominion over the fish of the sea and over the birds of the air and over every living thing that moves upon the earth." [29] And God said, "Behold, I have given you every plant yielding seed which is upon the face of all the earth, and every tree with seed in its fruit; you shall have them for food. [30] And to every beast of the earth, and to every bird of the air, and to everything that creeps on the earth, everything that has the breath of life, I have given every green plant for food." And it was so. [31] And God saw everything that he had made, and behold, it was very good. And there was evening and there was morning, a sixth day.

2 Thus the heavens and the earth were finished, and all the host of them [2] And on the seventh day God finished his work which he had done, and he rested on the seventh day from all his work which he had done. [3] So God blessed the seventh day and hallowed it, because on it God rested from all his work which he had done in creation.

[4] These are the generations of the heavens and the earth when they were created.

In the day that the Lord God made the earth and the heavens, [5] when no plant of the field was yet in the earth and no herb of the field had yet sprung up— for the Lord God had not caused it to rain upon the earth, and there was no man to till the ground; [6] but a mist went up from the earth and watered the whole face of the ground—[7] then the Lord God formed man of dust from the ground, and breathed into his nostrils the breath of life; and man became a living being. [8] And the Lord God planted a garden in Eden, in the east; and there he put the man whom he had formed. [9] And out of the ground the Lord God made to grow every tree that is pleasant to the sight and good for food, the tree of life also in the midst of the garden, and the tree of the knowledge of good and evil.

[10] A river flowed out of Eden to water the garden, and there it divided and became four rivers. [11] The name of the first is Pishon; it is the one which flows around the whole land of Hav′i-lah, where there is gold; [12] and the gold of that land is good; bdellium and onyx stone are there. [13] The name of the second river is Gihon; it is the one which flows around the whole land of Cush. [14] And the name of the third river is Hid′de-kel, which flows east of Assyria. And the fourth river is the Eu-phra′tes.

[15] The Lord God took the man and put him in the garden of Eden to till it and keep it. [16] And the Lord God commanded the man, saying, "You may freely eat of every tree of the garden; [17] but of the tree of the knowledge of good and evil you shall not eat, for in the day that you eat of it you shall die."

[18] Then the Lord God said, "It is not good that the man should be alone; I will make him a helper fit for him." [19] So out of the ground the Lord God formed every beast of the field and every bird of the air, and brought them to the man to see what he would call them; and whatever the man called every living creature, that was its name. [20] The man gave names to all cattle, and to the birds of the air, and to every beast of the field; but for the man there was not found a helper fit for him. [21] So the Lord God caused a deep sleep to fall upon the man, and while he slept took one of his ribs and closed up its place with flesh; [22] and the rib which the Lord God had taken from the man he made into a woman and brought her to the man. [23] Then the man said,

"This at last is bone of my bones and flesh of my
    flesh;
she shall be called Woman, because she was taken
    out of Man."

[24] Therefore a man leaves his father and his mother and cleaves to his wife, and they become one flesh. [25] And the man and his wife were both naked, and were not ashamed.

Job 37–40

The selections from the book of Job constitute one of the finest poetic sections in the whole of the Bible. In answer to Job's questions about human sufferings God, speaking from a "whirlwind," catalogues the mystery of life itself. In essence, God says that the mystery of human suffering (the theme of Job) is paltry in the face of the wonders of creation. By a curious twist, God "answers" Job's questions not with an answer but by pointing to the deeper mysteries of existence itself.

37 "At this also my heart trembles,
    and leaps out of its place.
[2] Hearken to the thunder of his voice
    and the rumbling that comes from his mouth.
[3] Under the whole heaven he lets it go,
    and his lightning to the corners of the earth.
[4] After it his voice roars;
    he thunders with his majestic voice
    and he does not restrain the lightnings when
        his voice is heard.
[5] God thunders wondrously with his voice;
    he does great things which we cannot
        comprehend.
[6] For to the snow he says, 'Fall on the earth';
    and to the shower and the rain, 'Be strong.'
[7] He seals up the hand of every man,
    that all men may know his work.
[8] Then the beasts go into their lairs,

and remain in their dens.
⁹ From its chamber comes the whirlwind,
and cold from the scattering winds.
¹⁰ By the breath of God ice is given,
and the broad waters are frozen fast.
¹¹ He loads the thick cloud with moisture;
the clouds scatter his lightning.
¹² They turn round and round by his guidance,
to accomplish all that he commands them
on the face of the habitable world.
¹³ Whether for correction, or for his land,
or for love, he causes it to happen.

¹⁴ "Hear this, O Job;
stop and consider the wondrous works of
God.
¹⁵ Do you know how God lays his command
upon them,
and causes the lightning of his cloud to shine?
¹⁶ Do you know the balancings of the clouds,
the wondrous works of him who is perfect in
knowledge,
¹⁷ you whose garments are hot
when the earth is still because of the south
wind?
¹⁸ Can you, like him, spread out the skies,
hard as a molten mirror?
¹⁹ Teach us what we shall say to him;
we cannot draw up our case because of
darkness.
²⁰ Shall it be told him that I would speak?
Did a man ever wish that he would be
swallowed up?

²¹ "And now men cannot look on the light
when it is bright in the skies,
when the wind has passed and cleared them.
²² Out of the north comes golden splendor;
God is clothed with terrible majesty.
²³ The Almighty—we cannot find him;
he is great in power and justice,
and abundant righteousness he will not violate.
²⁴ Therefore men fear him;
he does not regard any who are wise in their
own conceit."

38
Then the LORD answered Job out of the
whirlwind:
² "Who is this that darkens counsel by words
without knowledge?
³ Gird up your loins like a man.
I will question you, and you shall declare to
me.

⁴ "Where were you when I laid the foundation of
the earth?
Tell me, if you have understanding.

⁵ Who determined its measurements—surely you
know!
Or who stretched the line upon it?
⁶ On what were its bases sunk,
or who laid its cornerstone,
⁷ when the morning stars sang together,
and all the sons of God shouted for joy?

⁸ "Or who shut in the sea with doors,
when it burst forth from the womb;
⁹ when I made clouds its garment,
and thick darkness its swaddling band,
¹⁰ and prescribed bounds for it,
and set bars and doors,
¹¹ and said, 'Thus far shall you come, and no
farther,
and here shall your proud waves be stayed'?

¹² "Have you commanded the morning since your
days began,
and caused the dawn to know its place,
¹³ that it might take hold of the skirts of the earth,
and the wicked be shaken out of it?
¹⁴ It is changed like clay under the seal,
and it is dyed like a garment.
¹⁵ From the wicked their light is withheld,
and their uplifted arm is broken.

¹⁶ "Have you entered into the springs of the sea,
or walked in the recesses of the deep?
¹⁷ Have the gates of death been revealed to you,
or have you seen the gates of deep darkness?
¹⁸ Have you comprehended the expanse of the
earth?
Declare, if you know all this.

¹⁹ "Where is the way to the dwelling of light,
and where is the place of darkness,
²⁰ that you may take it to its territory
and that you may discern the paths to its
home?
²¹ You know, for you were born then,
and the number of your days is great!

²² "Have you entered the storehouses of the snow,
or have you seen the storehouses of the hail,
²³ which I have reserved for the time of trouble,
for the day of battle and war?
²⁴ What is the way to the place where the light is
distributed,
or where the east wind is scattered upon the
earth?

²⁵ "Who has cleft a channel for the torrents of
rain,
and a way for the thunderbolt,
²⁶ to bring rain on a land where no man is,
on the desert in which there is no man;

²⁷ to satisfy the waste and desolate land,
and to make the ground put forth grass?

²⁸ "Has the rain a father,
or who has begotten the drops of dew?
²⁹ From whose womb did the ice come forth,
and who has given birth to the hoarfrost of
heaven?
³⁰ The waters become hard like stone,
and the face of the deep is frozen.

³¹ "Can you bind the chains of the Plei′ades,
or loose the cords of Orion?
³² Can you lead forth the Maz′zaroth in their
season,
or can you guide the Bear with its children?
³³ Do you know the ordinances of the heavens?
Can you establish their rule on the earth?

³⁴ "Can you lift up your voice to the clouds,
that a flood of waters may cover you?
³⁵ Can you send forth lightnings, that they may go
and say to you, 'Here we are'?
³⁶ Who has put wisdom in the clouds,
or given understanding to the mists?
³⁷ Who can number the clouds by wisdom?
Or who can tilt the waterskins of the heavens,
³⁸ when the dust runs into a mass
and the clods cleave fast together?

³⁹ "Can you hunt the prey for the lion,
or satisfy the appetite of the young lions,
⁴⁰ when they crouch in their dens,
or lie in wait in their covert?
⁴¹ Who provides for the raven its prey,
when its young ones cry to God,
and wander about for lack of food?

39 "Do you know when the mountain goats
bring forth?
Do you observe the calving of the hinds?
² Can you number the months that they fulfil,
and do you know the time when they bring
forth,
³ when they crouch, bring forth their offspring,
and are delivered of their young?
⁴ Their young ones become strong, they grow up
in the open;
they go forth, and do not return to them.

⁵ "Who has let the wild ass go free?
Who has loosed the bonds of the swift ass,
⁶ to whom I have given the steppe for his home,
and the salt land for his dwelling place?
⁷ He scorns the tumult of the city;
he hears not the shouts of the driver.
⁸ He ranges the mountains as his pasture,

and he searches after every green thing.
⁹ "Is the wild ox willing to serve you?
Will he spend the night at your crib?
¹⁰ Can you bind him in the furrow with ropes,
or will he harrow the valleys after you?
¹¹ Will you depend on him because his strength is
great,
and will you leave to him your labor?
¹² Do you have faith in him that he will return,
and bring your grain to your threshing floor?
¹³ "The wings of the ostrich wave proudly;
but are they the pinions and plumage of love?
¹⁴ For she leaves her eggs to the earth,
and lets them be warmed on the ground,
¹⁵ forgetting that a foot may crush them.
and that the wild beast may trample them.
¹⁶ She deals cruelly with her young, as if they
were not hers;
though her labor be in vain, yet she has no
fear;
¹⁷ because God has made her forget wisdom,
and given her no share in understanding.
¹⁸ When she rouses herself to flee,
she laughs at the horse and his rider.

¹⁹ "Do you give the horse his might?
Do you clothe his neck with strength?
²⁰ Do you make him leap like the locust?
His majestic snorting is terrible.
²¹ He paws in the valley, and exults in his
strength;
he goes out to meet the weapons.
²² He laughs at fear, and is not dismayed;
he does not turn back from the sword.
²³ Upon him rattle the quiver,
the flashing spear and the javelin.
²⁴ With fierceness and rage he swallows the
ground;
he cannot stand still at the sound of the
trumpet.
²⁵ When the trumpet sounds, he says 'Aha!'
He smells the battle from afar,
the thunder of the captains, and the shouting.

²⁶ "Is it by your wisdom that the hawk soars,
and spreads his wings toward the south?
²⁷ Is it at your command that the eagle mounts up
and makes his nest on high?
²⁸ On the rock he dwells and makes his home
in the fastness of the rocky crag.
²⁹ Thence he spies out the prey;
his eyes behold it afar off.
³⁰ His young ones suck up blood;
and where the slain are, there is he."

40 And the LORD said to Job:
² "Shall a faultfinder contend with the

Almighty?
He who argues with God, let him answer it."

3 Then Job answered the LORD:
4 "Behold, I am of small account; what shall I
  answer thee?
I lay my hand on my mouth.
5 I have spoken once, and I will not answer;
  twice, but I will proceed no further."

6 Then God answered Job out of the whirlwind:
7 "Gird up your loins like a man;
I will question you, and you declare to me.
8 Will you even put me in the wrong?
Will you condemn me that you may be
  justified?
9 Have you an arm like God,
and can you thunder with a voice like his?

10 "Deck yourself with majesty and dignity;
clothe yourself with glory and splendor.
11 Pour forth the overflowings of your anger,
and look on every one that is proud, and abase
  him.
12 Look on every one that is proud, and bring him
  low;
and tread down the wicked where they stand.
13 Hide them all in the dust together;
bind their faces in the world below.
14 Then will I also acknowledge to you,
that your own right hand can give you
  victory.

15 "Behold, Be'hemoth,
which I made as I made you;
he eats grass like an ox.
16 Behold, his strength in his loins,
and his power in the muscles of his belly.
17 He makes his tail stiff like a cedar;
the sinews of his thighs are knit together.
18 His bones are tubes of bronze,
his limbs like bars of iron.

19 "He is the first of the works of God;
let him who made him bring near his sword!
20 For the mountains yield food for him
where all the wild beasts play.
21 Under the lotus plants he lies,
in the covert of the reeds and in the marsh.
22 For his shade the lotus trees cover him;
the willows of the brook surround him.
23 Behold, if the river is turbulent he is not
  frightened;
he is confident though Jordan rushes against
  his mouth.
24 Can one take him with hooks,
or pierce his nose with a snare?

Exodus 19–20

This selection from the book of Exodus recounts the appearance of God (a theophany, a "showing forth" of God) and the giving of the Ten Commandments, which become the central core of the moral code of the Bible. When reading this passage note all the ways in which the author emphasizes the power and otherness of God in order to emphasize the awful solemnity of the events being described.

19 On the third new moon after the people of Israel had gone forth out of the land of Egypt, on that day they came into the wilderness of Sinai. 2 And when they set out from Reph'idim and came into the wilderness of Sinai, they encamped in the wilderness; and there Israel encamped before the mountain. 3 And Moses went up to God, and the LORD called him out of the mountain, saying, "Thus you shall say to the house of Jacob, and tell the people of Israel: 4 You have seen what I did to the Egyptians, and how I bore you on eagles' wings and brought you to myself. 5 Now therefore, if you will obey my voice and keep my covenant, you shall be my own possession among all peoples; for all the earth is mine, 6 and you shall be to me a kingdom of priests and a holy nation. These are the words which you shall speak to the children of Israel."

7 So Moses came and called the elders of the people, and set before them all these words which the LORD had commanded him. 8 And all the people answered together and said, "All that the LORD has spoken we will do." And Moses reported the words of the people to the LORD. 9 And the LORD said to Moses, "Lo, I am coming to you in a thick cloud, that the people may hear when I speak with you, and may also believe you for ever."

Then Moses told the words of the people to the LORD. 10 And the LORD said to Moses, "Go to the people and consecrate them today and tomorrow, and let them wash their garments, 11 and be ready by the third day; for on the third day the LORD will come down upon Mount Sinai in the sight of all the people. 12 And you shall set bounds for the people round about, saying, 'Take heed that you do not go up into the mountain or touch the border of it; whoever touches the mountain shall be put to death; 13 no hand shall touch him, but he shall be stoned or shot; whether beast or man, he shall not live.' When the trumpet sounds a long blast, they shall come up to the mountain." 14 So Moses went down from the mountain to the people, and consecrated the people; and they washed their garments. 15 And he said to the people, "Be ready by the third day; do not go near a woman."

16 On the morning of the third day there were thunders and lightnings, and a thick cloud upon the mountain, and a very loud trumpet blast, so that all

the people who were in the camp trembled. [17] Then Moses brought the people out of the camp to meet God; and they took their stand at the foot of the mountain. [18] And Mount Sinai was wrapped in smoke, because the LORD descended upon it in fire; and the smoke of it went up like the smoke of a kiln, and the whole mountain quaked greatly. [19] And as the sound of the trumpet grew louder and louder, Moses spoke, and God answered him in thunder. [20] And the LORD came down upon Mount Sinai, to the top of the mountain; and the LORD called Moses to the top of the mountain, and Moses went up. [21] And the LORD said to Moses, "Go down and warn the people, lest they break through to the LORD to gaze and many of them perish. [22] And also let the priests who come near to the LORD consecrate themselves, lest the LORD break out upon them," [23] And Moses said to the LORD, "The people cannot come up to Mount Sinai; for thou thyself didst charge us, saying, 'Set bounds about the mountain, and consecrate it.'" [24] And the LORD said to him, "Go down, and come up bringing Aaron with you; but do not let the priests and the people break through to come up to the LORD, lest he break out against them." [25] So Moses went down to the people and told them.

20 And God spoke all these words, saying, [2] "I am the LORD your God, who brought you out of the land of Egypt, out of the house of bondage.

[3] "You shall have no other gods before me.

[4] "You shall not make yourself a graven image, or any likeness of anything that is in heaven above, or that is in the earth beneath, or that is in the water under the earth; [5] you shall not bow down to them or serve them; for I the LORD your God am a jealous God, visiting the iniquity of the fathers upon the children to the third and the fourth generation of those who hate me, [6] but showing steadfast love to thousands of those who love me and keep my commandments.

[7] "You shall not take the name of the LORD your God in vain; for the LORD will not hold him guiltless who takes his name in vain.

[8] "Remember the sabbath day, to keep it holy. [9] Six days you shall labor, and do all your work; [10] but the seventh day is a sabbath to the LORD your God; in it you shall not do any work, you, or your son, or your daughter, or your manservant, or your maidservant, or your cattle, or the sojourner who is within your gates; [11] for in six days the LORD made heaven and earth, the sea, and all that is in them, and rested the seventh day; therefore the LORD blessed the sabbath day and hallowed it.

[12] "Honor your father and your mother, that your days may be long in the land which the LORD your God gives you.

[13] "You shall not kill.

[14] "You shall not commit adultery.

[15] "You shall not steal.

[16] "You shall not bear false witness against your neighbor.

[17] "You shall not covet your neighbor's house; you shall not covet your neighbor's wife, or his manservant, or his maidservant, or his ox, or his ass, or anything that is your neighbor's."

18 Now when all the people perceived the thunderings and the lightnings and the sound of the trumpet and the mountain smoking, the people were afraid and trembled; and they stood afar off, [19] and said to Moses, "You speak to us, and we will hear; but let not God speak to us, lest we die." [20] And Moses said to the people, "Do not fear; for God has come to prove you, and that the fear of him may be before your eyes, that you may not sin."

21 And the people stood afar off, while Moses drew near to the thick cloud where God was. [22] And the LORD said to Moses, "Thus you shall say to the people of Israel: 'You have seen for yourselves that I have talked with you from heaven. [23] You shall not make gods of silver to be with me, nor shall you make for yourselves gods of gold. [24] An altar of earth you shall make for me and sacrifice on it your burnt offerings and your peace offerings, your sheep and your oxen; in every place where I cause my name to be remembered I will come to you and bless you. [25] And if you make me an altar of stone, you shall not build it of hewn stones; for if you wield your tool upon it you profane it. [26] And you shall not go up by steps to my altar, that your nakedness be not exposed on it.'

Amos 3–6

Amos, an 8th-century prophet, reflects many of the characteristics of classical biblical prophetism: the prophet who speaks in the name of God: the warnings against social unjustice; the demand for a pure worship of God and fidelity to the biblical covenant; the judgment against neighboring people.

3 Hear this word that the LORD has spoken against you, O people of Israel, against the whole family which I brought up out of the land of Egypt:
[2] "You only have I known
    of all the families of the earth;
therefore I will punish you
    for all your iniquities.

[3] "Do two walk together,
    unless they have made an appointment?
[4] Does a lion roar in the forest,
    when he has no prey?

Does a young lion cry out from his den,
   if he has taken nothing?
5 Does a bird fall in a snare on the earth,
   when there is no trap for it?
Does a snare spring up from the ground,
   when it has taken nothing?
6 Is a trumpet blown in a city,
   and the people are not afraid?
Does evil befall a city,
   unless the LORD has done it?
7 Surely the LORD GOD does nothing,
   without revealing his secret
to his servants the prophets.
8 The lion has roared;
   who will not fear?
The LORD GOD has spoken;
   who can but prophesy?"

9 Proclaim to the strongholds in Assyria
   and to the strongholds in the land of Egypt,
   and say, "Assemble yourselves upon the
      mountains of Samar′ia,
   and see the great tumults within her,
   and the oppressions in her midst."
10 "They do not know how to do right," says the
   LORD,
   "those who store up violence and robbery in
      their strongholds."
11 Therefore thus says the Lord GOD:
   "An adversary shall surround the land,
      and bring down your defences from you,
      and your strongholds shall be plundered."

12 Thus says the LORD: "As the shepherd rescues
from the mouth of the lion two legs, or a piece of an
ear, so shall the people of Israel who dwell in
Samar′ia be rescued, with the corner of a couch and
part of a bed.

13 "Hear, and testify against the house of Jacob,"
   says the Lord GOD, the God of hosts,
14 "that on the day I punish Israel for his
   transgressions,
   I will punish the altars of Bethel,
   and the horns of the altar shall be cut off
      and fall to the ground.
15 I will smite the winter house with the summer
      house;
   and the houses of ivory shall perish,
   and the great houses shall come to an end,"
                              says the LORD.

4 "Hear this word, you cows of Bashan,
   who are in the mountain of Samar′ia,
who oppress the poor, who crush the needy,
   who say to their husbands, 'Bring, that we
      may drink!'
2 The Lord GOD has sworn by his holiness

that, behold, the days are coming upon you,
   when they shall take you away with hooks,
   even the last of you with fishhooks.
3 And you shall go out through the breaches,
   every one straight before her;
   and you shall be cast forth into Harmon,"
                              says the LORD.

4 "Come to Bethel, and transgress;
   to Gilgal, and multiply transgression;
   bring your sacrifices every morning,
      your tithes every three days;
5 offer a sacrifice of thanksgiving of that which is
      leavened,
   and proclaim freewill offerings, publish them;
   for so you love to do, O people of Israel!"
                              says the LORD GOD.

6 "I gave you cleanness of teeth in all your cities,
   and lack of bread in all your places,
   yet you did not return to me,"
                              says the LORD.

7 "And I also withheld the rain from you
   when there were yet three months to the
      harvest;
   I would send rain upon one city,
   and send no rain upon another city;
   one field would be rained upon,
   and the field on which it did not rain
      withered;
8 so two or three cities wandered to one city
   to drink water, and were not satisfied;
   yet you did not return to me,"
                              says the LORD.

9 "I smote you with blight and mildew;
   I laid waste your gardens and your vineyards;
   your fig trees and your olive trees the locust
      devoured;
   yet you did not return to me,"
                              says the LORD.

10 "I sent among you a pestilence after the manner
      of Egypt;
   I slew your young men with the sword;
   I carried away your horses;
   and I made the stench of your camp go up
      into your nostrils;
   yet you did not return to me,"
                              says the LORD.

11 "I overthrew some of you,
   as when God overthrew Sodom and
      Gomor′rah,
   and you were as a brand plucked out of the
      burning;

yet you did not return to me,"

says the LORD.

12 "Therefore thus I will do to you, O Israel;
    because I will do this to you,
    prepare to meet your God, O Israel!"

13 For lo, he who forms the mountains, and
        creates the wind,
    and declares to man what is his thought;
    who makes the morning darkness,
    and treads on the heights of the earth—
    the LORD, the God of hosts, is his name!

5 Hear this word which I take up over you in lamentation, O house of Israel:

2 "Fallen, no more to rise,
    is the virgin Israel;
    forsaken on her land,
    with none to raise her up."

3 For thus says the LORD GOD:
    "The city that went forth a thousand
    shall have a hundred left,
    and that which went forth a hundred
    shall have ten left
    to the house of Israel."

4 For thus says the LORD to the house of Israel:
    "Seek me and live;
5   but do not seek Bethel,
    and do not enter into Gilgal
    or cross over to Beer-sheba;
    for Gilgal shall surely go into exile,
    and Bethel shall come to nought."

6 Seek the LORD and live,
    lest he break out like fire in the house of
        Joseph,
    and it devour, with none to quench it for
        Bethel,
7 O you who turn justice to wormwood,
    and cast down righteousness to the earth!

8 He who made the Pleiades and Orion,
    and turns deep darkness into the morning,
    and darkens the day into night,
    who calls for the waters of the sea,
    and pours them out upon the surface of the
        earth,
    the LORD is his name,
9 who makes destruction flash forth against the
        strong,
    so that destruction comes upon the fortress.

10 They hate him who reproves in the gate,
    and they abhor him who speaks the truth.

11 Therefore because you trample upon the poor
    and take from him exactions of wheat,
    you have built houses of hewn stone,
    but you shall not dwell in them;
    you have planted pleasant vineyards,
    but you shall not drink their wine.
12 For I know how many are your transgressions,
    and how great are your sins—
    you who afflict the righteous, who take a bribe,
    and turn aside the needy in the gate.
13 Therefore he who is prudent will keep silent in
        such a time;
    for it is an evil time.

14 Seek good, and not evil,
    that you may live;
    and so the LORD, the God of hosts, will be with
        you,
    as you have said.
15 Hate evil, and love good,
    and establish justice in the gate;
    it may be that the LORD, the God of hosts,
    will be gracious to the remnant of Joseph.

16 Therefore thus says the LORD, the God of hosts,
        the Lord:
    "In all the squares there shall be wailing;
    and in all the streets they shall say, 'Alas! alas!'
    They shall call the farmers to mourning
    and to wailing those who are skilled in
        lamentation,
17 and in all vineyards there shall be wailing,
    for I will pass through the midst of you,"

says the LORD.

18 Woe to you who desire the day of the LORD!
    Why would you have the day of the LORD?
    It is darkness, and not light;
19   as if a man fled from a lion,
    and a bear met him;
    or went into the house and leaned
    with his hand against the wall,
    and a serpent bit him.
20 Is not the day of the LORD. darkness,
    and not light,
    and gloom with no brightness in it?

21 "I hate, I despise your feasts,
    and I take no delight in your solemn
        assemblies.
22 Even though you offer me your burnt offerings
        and cereal offerings,
    I will not accept them,
    and the peace offerings of your fatted beasts
    I will not look upon.
23 Take away from me the noise of your songs;
    to the melody of your harps I will not listen.

24 But let justice roll down like waters,
  and righteousness like an everflowing stream.

25 "Did you bring to me sacrifices and offerings the forty years in the wilderness, O house of Israel? 26 You shall take up Sakkuth your king, and Kaiwan your star-god, your images, which you made for yourselves; 27 therefore I will take you into exile beyond Damascus," says the LORD, whose name is the God of hosts.

6 "Woe to those who are at ease in Zion,
  and to those who feel secure on the mountain
    of Samar′ia.
  the notable men of the first of the nations,
    to whom the house of Israel come!
2 Pass over to Calneh, and see;
  and thence go to Hamath the great;
  then go down to Gath of the Philistines.
  Are they better than these kingdoms?
  Or is their territory greater than your
    territory,
3 O you put far away the evil day,
  and bring near the seat of violence?

4 Woe to those who lie upon beds of ivory,
  and stretch themselves upon their couches,
  and eat lambs from the flock,
  and calves from the midst of the stall;
5 who sing idle songs to the sound of the harp,
  and like David invent for themselves
    instruments of music;
6 who drink wine in bowls,
  and anoint themselves with the finest oils,
  but are not grieved over the ruin of Joseph!
7 Therefore they shall now be the first of those to
    go into exile,
  and the revelry of those who stretch
    themselves shall pass away."

8 The Lord GOD has sworn by himself
  (says the LORD, the God of hosts):
  "I abhor the pride of Jacob,
  and hate his strongholds;
  and I will deliver up the city and all that is in
    it."

9 And if ten men remain in one house, they shall die. 10 And when a man's kinsman, he who burns him, shall take him up to bring the bones out of the house, and shall say to him who is in the innermost parts of the house, "Is there still any one with you?" he shall say, "No"; and he shall say, "Hush! We must not mention the name of the LORD."

11 For behold, the LORD commands
  and the great house shall be smitten into

fragments,
  and the little house into bits.

Matthew 5–7

These sayings of Jesus, taken from the gospel of Matthew, reflect the core of the teachings of Jesus. In these sayings one finds not only The Beatitudes but also a prayer that is said to reflect perfectly the essential relationship of Jesus to Abba (the familiar Aramaic word for "Father," which Jesus used to describe God). Note too the demand Jesus makes to go beyond the mere observance of law. In asking for an interior conversion beyond law, Jesus stands in the tradition of the great Jewish prophets.

5 Seeing the crowds, he went up on the mountain, and when he sat down his disciples came to him. 2 And he opened his mouth and taught them, saying:
3 "Blessed are the poor in spirit, for theirs is the kingdom of heaven.
4 "Blessed are those who mourn, for they shall be comforted.
5 "Blessed are the meek, for they shall inherit the earth.
6 "Blessed are those who hunger and thirst for righteousness, for they shall be satisfied.
7 "Blessed are the merciful, for they shall obtain mercy.
8 "Blessed are the pure in heart, for they shall see God.
9 "Blessed are the peacemakers, for they shall be called sons of God.
10 "Blessed are those who are persecuted for righteousness' sake, for theirs is the kingdom of heaven.
11 "Blessed are you when men revile you and persecute you and utter all kinds of evil against you falsely on my account. 12 Rejoice and be glad, for your reward is great in heaven, for so men persecuted the prophets who were before you.
13 "You are the salt of the earth; but if salt has lost its taste, how shall its saltness be restored? It is no longer good for anything except to be thrown out and trodden under foot by men.
14 "You are the light of the world. A city set on a hill cannot be hid. 15 Nor do men light a lamp and put it under a bushel, but on a stand, and it gives light to all in the house. 16 Let your light so shine before men, that they may see your good works and give glory in your Father who is in heaven.
17 "Think not that I have come to abolish the law and the prophets; I have come not to abolish them but to fulfil them. 18 For truly, I say to you, till heaven and earth pass away, not an iota, not a dot, will pass from the law until all is accomplished. 19 Whoever then relaxes one of the least of these

commandments and teaches men so, shall be called least in the kingdom of heaven; but he who does them and teaches them shall be called great in the kingdom of heaven. 20 For I tell you, unless your righteousness exceeds that of the scribes and Pharisees, you will never enter the kingdom of heaven.

21 "You have heard that it was said to the men of old, 'You shall not kill; and whoever kills shall be liable to judgment.' 22 But I say to you that every one who is angry with his brother shall be liable to judgment; whoever insults his brother shall be liable to the council, and whoever says, 'You fool!' shall be liable to the hell of fire. 23 So if you are offering your gift at the altar, and there remember that your brother has something against you, 24 leave your gift there before the altar and go; first be reconciled to your brother, and then come and offer your gift. 25 Make friends quickly with your accuser, while you are going with him to court, lest your accuser hand you over to the judge, and the judge to the guard, and you be put in prison; 26 truly, I say to you, you will never get out till you have paid the last penny.

27 "You have heard that it was said, 'You shall not commit adultery.' 28 But I say to you that every one who looks at a woman lustfully has already committed adultery with her in his heart. 29 If your right eye causes you to sin, pluck it out and throw it away; it is better that you lose one of your members than that your whole body be thrown into hell. 30 And if your right hand causes you to sin, cut it off and throw it away; it is better that you lose one of your members than that your whole body go into hell.

31 "It was also said, 'Whoever divorces his wife, let him give her a certificate of divorce.' 32 But I say to you that every one who divorces his wife, except on the ground of unchastity, makes her an adulteress; and whoever marries a divorced woman commits adultery.

33 "Again you have heard that it was said to the men of old, 'You shall not swear falsely, but shall perform to the Lord what you have sworn.' 34 But I say to you, Do not swear at all, either by heaven, for it is the throne of God, 35 or by the earth, for it is his footstool, or by Jerusalem, for it is the city of the great King. 36 And do not swear by your head, for you cannot make one hair white or black. 37 Let what you say be simply 'Yes' or 'No'; anything more than this comes from evil.

38 "You have heard that it was said, 'An eye for an eye and a tooth for a tooth.' 39 But I say to you, Do not resist one who is evil. But if any one strikes you on the right cheek, turn to him the other also; 40 and if any one would sue you and take your coat, let him have your cloak as well; 41 and if any one forces you to go one mile, go with him two miles. 42 Give to him who begs from you, and do not refuse him who would borrow from you.

43 "You have heard that it was said, 'You shall love your neighbor and hate your enemy.' 44 But I say to you, Love your enemies and pray for those who persecute you, 45 so that you may be sons of your Father who is in heaven; for he makes his sun rise on the evil and on the good, and sends rain on the just and on the unjust. 46 For if you love those who love you, what reward have you? Do not even the tax collectors do the same? 47 And if you salute only your brethren, what more are you doing than others? Do not even the Gentiles do the same? 48 You, therefore, must be perfect, as your heavenly Father is perfect.

6 "Beware of practicing your piety before men in order to be seen by them; for then you will have no reward from your Father who is in heaven.

2 "Thus, when you give alms, sound no trumpet before you, as the hypocrites do in the synagogues and in the streets, that they may be praised by men. Truly, I say to you, they have their reward. 3 But when you give alms, do not let your left hand know what your right hand is doing, 4 so that your alms may be in secret; and your Father who sees in secret will reward you.

5 "And when you pray, you must not be like the hypocrites; for they love to stand and pray in the synagogues and at the street corners, that they may be seen by men. Truly, I say to you, they have their reward. 6 But when you pray, go into your room and shut the door and pray to your Father who is in secret; and your Father who sees in secret will reward you.

7 "And in praying do not heap up empty phrases as the Gentiles do; for they think that they will be heard for their many words. 8 Do not be like them, for your Father knows what you need before you ask him. 9 Pray then like this:

Our Father who art in heaven,
Hallowed be thy name.
10 Thy kingdom come,
Thy will be done,
On earth as it is in heaven.
11 Give us this day our daily bread;
12 And forgive us our debts,
As we also have forgiven our debtors;
13 And lead us not into temptation.
But deliver us from evil.

14 For if you forgive men their trespasses, your heavenly Father also will forgive you; 15 but if you do not forgive men their trespasses, neither will your Father forgive your trespasses.

16 "And when you fast, do not look dismal, like the hypocrites, for they disfigure their faces that their fasting may be seen by men. Truly, I say to you, they have their reward. 17 But when you fast, anoint your head and wash your face, 18 that your fasting may not be seen by men but by your Father who is in

secret; and your Father who sees in secret will reward you.

19 "Do not lay up for yourselves treasures on earth, where moth and rust consume and where thieves break in and steal, 20 but lay up for yourselves treasures in heaven, where neither moth nor rust consumes and where thieves do not break in and steal. 21 For where your treasure is, there will your heart be also.

22 "The eye is the lamp of the body. So, if your eye is sound, your whole body will be full of light; 28 but if your eye is not sound, your whole body will be full of darkness. If then the light in you is darkness, how great is the darkness!

24 "No one can serve two masters; for either he will hate the one and love the other, or he will be devoted to the one and despise the other. You cannot serve God and mammon.

25 "Therefore I tell you, do not be anxious about your life, what you shall eat or what you shall drink, nor about your body, what you shall put on. Is not life more than food, and the body more than clothing? 26 Look at the birds of the air: they neither sow nor reap nor gather into barns, and yet your heavenly Father feeds them. Are you not of more value than they? 27 And which of you by being anxious can add one cubit to his span of life? 28 And why are you anxious about clothing? Consider the lilies of the field, how they grow; they neither toil nor spin; 29 yet I tell you, even Solomon in all his glory was not arrayed like one of these. 30 But if God so clothes the grass of the field, which today is alive and tomorrow is thrown into the oven, will he not much more clothe you, O men of little faith? 31 Therefore do not be anxious, saying, 'What shall we eat?' or 'What shall we drink?' or 'What shall we wear?' 32 For the Gentiles seek all these things; and your heavenly Father knows that you need them all. 33 But seek first his kingdom and his righteousness, and all these things shall be yours as well.

34 "Therefore do not be anxious about tomorrow, for tomorrow will be anxious for itself. Let the day's own trouble be sufficient for the day.

7 "Judge not, that you be not judged. 2 For with the judgment you pronounce you will be judged, and the measure you give will be the measure you get. 3 Why do you see the speck that is in your brother's eye, but do not notice the log that is in your own eye? 4 Or how can you say to your brother, 'Let me take the speck out of your eye,' when there is the log in your own eye? 5 You hypocrite, first take the log out of your own eye, and then you will see clearly to take the speck out of your brother's eye.

6 "Do not give dogs what is holy; and do not throw your pearls before swine, lest they trample them underfoot and turn to attack you.

7 "Ask, and it will be given you; seek and you will find; knock, and it will be opened to you. 8 For every one who asks receives, and he who seeks finds, and to him who knocks it will be opened. 9 Or what man of you, if his son asks him for a loaf, will give him a stone? 10 Or if he asks for a fish, will give him a serpent? 11 If you then, who are evil, know how to give good gifts to your children, how much more will your Father who is in heaven give good things to those who ask him? 12 So whatever you wish that men would do to you, do so to them; for this is the law and the prophets.

13 "Enter by the narrow gate; for the gate is wide and the way is easy, that leads to destruction, and those who enter by it are many. 14 For the gate is narrow and the way is hard, that leads to life, and those who find it are few.

15 "Beware of false prophets, who come to you in sheep's clothing but inwardly are ravenous wolves. 16 You will know them by their fruits. Are grapes gathered from thorns, or figs from thistles? 17 So, every sound tree bears good fruit, but the bad tree bears evil fruit. 18 A sound tree cannot bear evil fruit, nor can a bad tree bear good fruit. 19 Every tree that does not bear good fruit is cut down and thrown into the fire. 20 Thus you will know them by their fruits.

21 "Not every one who says to me, 'Lord, Lord,' shall enter the kingdom of heaven, but he who does the will of my Father who is in heaven. 22 On that day many will say to me, 'Lord, Lord, did we not prophesy in your name, and cast out demons in your name, and do many mighty works in your name?' 23 And then will I declare to them, 'I never knew you; depart from me, you evildoers.'

24 "Every one then who hears these words of mine and does them will be like a wise man who built his house upon the rock; 25 and the rain fell, and the floods came, and the winds blew and beat upon that house, but it did not fall, because it had been founded on the rock. 26 And every one who hears these words of mine and does not do them will be like a foolish man who built his house upon the sand; 27 and the rain fell, and the floods came, and the winds blew and beat against that house, and it fell; and great was the fall of it."

28 And when Jesus finished these sayings, the crowds were astonished at his teaching, 29 for he taught them as one who had authority, and not as their scribes.

Acts 17:14–34

Paul's speech in Athens is a good example of Christianity's attempt to speak to the pagan world it encountered in its attempt to spread its message. The two additional passages from Paul's letters (Corinthians I and II) give us first an example of the powerful message he could articulate and a glimpse of Paul's own life as an early missionary of the infant Christian church.

14 Then the brethren immediately sent Paul off on his way to the sea, but Silas and Timothy remained there. 15 Those who conducted Paul brought him as far as Athens; and receiving a command for Silas and Timothy to come to him as soon as possible, they departed.

16 Now while Paul was waiting for them at Athens, his spirit was provoked within him as he saw that the city was full of idols. 17 So he argued in the synagogue with the Jews and the devout persons, and in the market place every day with those who chanced to be there. 18 Some also of the Epicurean and Stoic philosophers met him. And some said, "What would this babbler say?" Others said, "He seems to be a preacher of foreign divinities"— because he preached Jesus and the resurrection. 19 And they took hold of him, and brought him to the Are-op'agus, saying, "May we know what this new teaching is which you present? 20 For you bring some strange things to our ears; we wish to know therefore what these things mean." 21 Now all the Athenians and the foreigners who lived there spent their time in nothing except telling or hearing something new.

22 So Paul, standing in the middle of the Are-op' agus, said: "Men of Athens, I perceive that in every way you are very religious. 23 For as I passed along, and observed the objects of your worship, I found also an altar with this inscription, 'To an unknown god.' What therefore you worship as unknown, this I proclaim to you. 24 The God who made the world and everything in it, being Lord of heaven and earth, does not live in shrines made by man, 25 nor is he served by human hands, as though he needed anything, since he himself gives to all men life and breath and everything. 26 And he made from one every nation of men to live on all the face of the earth, having determined allotted periods and the boundaries of their habitation, 27 that they should seek God, in the hope that they might feel after him and find him. Yet he is not far from each one of us, 28 for

'In him we live and move and have our being';
as even some of your poets have said,

'For we are indeed his offspring.'

29 Being then God's offspring, we ought not to think that the Deity is like gold, or silver, or stone, a representation by the art and imagination of man. 30 The times of ignorance God overlooked, but now he commands all men everywhere to repent, 31 because he has fixed a day on which he will judge the world in righteousness by a man whom he has appointed, and of this he has given assurance to all men by raising him from the dead."

32 Now when they heard of the resurrection of the dead, some mocked; but others said, "We will hear you again about this." 33 So Paul went out from among them. 34 But some men joined him and believed, among them Dionys'ius the Are-op'agite and a woman named Dam'aris and others with them.

I Corinthians 13

And I will show you a still more excellent way.

13 If I speak in the tongues of men and of angels, but have not love, I am a noisy gong or a clanging cymbal. 2 And if I have prophetic powers, and understand all mysteries and all knowledge, and if I have all faith, so as to remove mountains, but have not love, I am nothing. 3 If I give away all I have, and if I deliver my body to be burned, but have not love, I gain nothing.

4 Love is patient and kind; love is not jealous or boastful; 5 it is not arrogant or rude. Love does not insist on its own way; it is not irritable or resentful; 6 it does not rejoice at wrong, but rejoices in the right. 7 Love bears all things, believes all things, hopes all things, endures all things.

8 Love never ends; as for prophecy, it will pass away; as for tongues, they will cease; as for knowledge, it will pass away. 9 For our knowledge is imperfect and our prophecy is imperfect; 10 but when the perfect comes, the imperfect will pass away. 11 When I was a child, I spoke like a child, I thought like a child, I reasoned like a child; when I became a man, I gave up childish ways. 12 For now we see in a mirror dimly, but then face to face. Now I know in part; then I shall understand fully, even as I have been fully understood. 13 So faith, hope, love abide, these three; but the greatest of these is love.

II Corinthians 11–12

11 I wish you would bear with me in a little foolishness. Do bear with me! 2 I feel a divine jealousy for you, for I betrothed you to Christ to present you as a pure bride to her one husband. 3 But I am afraid that as the serpent deceived Eve by his cunning, your thoughts will be led astray from a sincere and pure devotion to Christ. 4 For if some one comes and preaches another Jesus than the one we preached, or if you receive a different spirit from the one you received, or if you accept a different gospel from the one you accepted, you submit to it readily enough. 5 I think that I am not in the least inferior to these superlative apostles. 6 Even if I am unskilled in speaking, I am not in knowledge; in every way we have made this plain to you in all things.

7 Did I commit a sin in abasing myself so that you might be exalted, because I preached God's gospel without cost to you? 8 I robbed other churches by accepting support from them in order to serve you. 9 And when I was with you and was in want, I did not burden any one, for my needs were supplied by the brethren who came from Macedo'nia. So I refrained and will refrain from burdening you in any way. 10 As the truth of Christ is in me, this boast of

mine shall not be silenced in the regions of Acha'ia. [11] And why? Because I do not love you? God knows I do!

12 And what I do I will continue to do, in order to undermine the claim of those who would like to claim that in their boasted mission they work on the same terms as we do. [13] For such men are false apostles, deceitful workmen, disguising themselves as apostles of Christ. [14] And no wonder, for even Satan disguises himself as an angel of light. [15] So it is not strange if his servants also disguise themselves as servants of righteousness. Their end will correspond to their deeds.

16 I repeat, let no one think me foolish; but even if you do, accept me as a fool, so that I too may boast a little. [17] (What I am saying I say not with the Lord's authority but as a fool, in this boastful confidence; [18] since many boast of worldly things, I too will boast.) [19] For you gladly bear with fools, being wise yourselves! [20] For you bear it if a man makes slaves of you, or preys upon you, or takes advantage of you, or puts on airs, or strikes you in the face. [21] To my shame, I must say, we were too weak for that!

But whatever any one dares to boast of—I am speaking as a fool—I also dare to boast of that. [22] Are they Hebrews? So am I. Are they Israelites? So am I. Are they descendants of Abraham? So am I. [23] Are they servants of Christ? I am a better one—I am talking like a madman—with far greater labors, far more imprisonments, with countless beatings, and often near death. [24] Five times I have received at the hands of the Jews the forty lashes less one. [25] Three times I have been beaten with rods; once I was stoned. Three times I have been shipwrecked; a night and a day I have been adrift at sea; [26] on frequent journeys, in danger from rivers, danger from robbers, danger from my own people, danger from Gentiles, danger in the city, danger in the wilderness, danger at sea, danger from false brethren; [27] in toil and hardship, through many a sleepless night, in hunger and thirst, often without food, in cold and exposure. [28] And, apart from things, there is the daily pressure upon me of my anxiety for all the churches. [29] Who is weak, and I am not weak? Who is made to fall, and I am not indignant?

30 If I must boast, I will boast of the things that show my weakness. [31] The God and Father of the Lord Jesus, he who is blessed for ever, knows that I do not lie. [32] At Damascus, the governor under King Ar'etas guarded the city of Damascus in order to seize me, [33]but I was let down in a basket through a window in the wall, and escaped his hands.

12 I must boast; there is nothing to be gained by it, but I will go on to visions and revelations of the Lord. [2] I know a man in Christ who fourteen years ago was caught up to the third heaven—whether in the body or out of the body I do not know, God knows. [3] And I know that this man was caught up into Paradise—whether in the body or out of the body I do not know, God knows—[4] and he heard things that cannot be told, which man may not utter. [5] On behalf of this man I will boast, but on my own behalf I will not boast, except of my weaknesses. [6] Though if I wish to boast, I shall not be a fool, for I shall be speaking the truth. But I refrain from it, so that no one may think more of me than he sees in me or hears from me. [7] And to keep me from being too elated by the abundance of revelations, a thorn was given me in the flesh, a messenger of Satan, to harass me, to keep me from being too elated. [8] Three times I besought the Lord about this, that it should leave me; [9] but he said to me, "My grace is sufficient for you, for my power is made perfect in weakness." I will all the more gladly boast of my weaknesses, that the power of Christ may rest upon me. [10] For the sake of Christ, then, I am content with weaknesses, insults, hardships, persecutions, and calamities; for when I am weak, then I am strong.

11 I have been a fool! You forced me to it, for I ought to have been commended by you. For I am not at all inferior to these superlative apostles, even though I am nothing. [12] The signs of a true apostle were performed among you in all patience, with signs and wonders and mighty works. [13] For in what were you less favored than the rest of the churches, except that I myself did not burden you? Forgive me this wrong!

14 Here for the third time I am ready to come to you. And I will not be a burden, for I seek not what is yours but you; for children ought not to lay up for their parents, but parents for their children. [15] I will most gladly spend and be spent for your souls. If I love you the more, am I to be loved less? [16] But granting that I myself did not burden you, I was crafty, you say, and got the better of you by guile. [17] Did I take advantage of you through any of those whom I sent to you? [18] I urged Titus to go, and sent the brother with him. Did Titus take advantage of you? Did we not act in the same spirit? Did we not take the same steps?

19 Have you been thinking all along that we have been defending ourselves before you? It is in the sight of God that we have been speaking in Christ, and all for your upbuilding, beloved. [20] For I fear that perhaps I may come and find you not what I wish, and that you may find me not what you wish; that perhaps there may be quarreling, jealousy, anger, selfishness, slander, gossip, conceit, and disorder. [21] I fear that when I come again my God may humble me before you, and I may have to mourn over many of those who sinned before and have not repented of the impurity, immorality, and licentiousness which they have practiced.

		GENERAL EVENTS	LITERATURE & PHILOSOPHY	ART

64 A.D.

EARLY CHRISTIAN ERA

313

395

Period of Persecution

250 Persecution of Christians under Decius

286 Diocletion divides Roman Empire into East and West parts ruled by himself and Maximian

305 Abdication of Diocletian and Maximian; Constantius and Galerius rule as joint emperors

307–327 Reign of Constantine

c. 67 Apostle Paul, bearer of Christian message throughout Mediterranean, martyred at Rome

Period of Recognition

313 Edict of Milan, giving Christians freedom of religion

324 Constantine convenes Council of Nicaea

330 Constantine dedicates new capital of Roman Empire on site of Byzantium, naming it Constantinople

337 Constantine is baptized a Christian on his deathbed

383 Ostrogoths accept Christianity

c. 350 *Codex Sinaiticus*, earliest extant Greek codex of New Testament

c. 374–404 Saint John Chrysostom active as writer and preacher

c. 386 Saint Jerome translates Bible into Latin

c. 390 Obelisk of Theodosius erected in Hippodrome at Constantinople

BYZANTINE ERA

565

900

1100

1453

Growth of Empire

395 Division of Roman Empire begun by Diocletian becomes total separation

4th–5th cent. Decline of Western Roman Empire

410 Visigoths sack Rome

455 Vandals sack Rome

476 Romulus Augustulus forced to abdicate as last Western Roman emperor; Ostrogoths rule Italy

493–526 Theodoric the Ostrogoth reigns in Italy

527–565 Reign of Justinian as Eastern Roman emperor in Constantinople

532 Nika revolt; civil disorders in Constantinople

c. 533 Justinian codifies Roman Law

540 Belisarius conquers Ostrogoths in Italy for Justinian; Ravenna comes under Byzantine rule

397 Augustine of Hippo, *The Confessions*

413–426 Augustine of Hippo, *The City of God*

c. 522–524 Boethius, *The Consolation of Philosophy*, allegorical treatise; translation of Aristotle's writings

524 Execution of Boethius by Theodoric the Ostrogoth

c. 562 Procopius, *History of the Wars, The Buildings, Secret History*

c. 415 Theodosius II moves gilded horses and chariot from Rome to Hippodrome

c. 425 Mosaics at Mausoleum of Galla Placidia, Ravenna

c. 450 Dome mosaic in Orthodox Baptistery, Ravenna

6th cent. Art tied to theological doctrine and liturgical practice of Orthodox Church

c. 547 Ivory throne of Archbishop Maximian, given by Justinian for San Vitale

c. 550 Mosaics at Sant' Apollinare Nuovo and San Vitale, Ravenna; *Metamorphosis of Christ*, apse mosaic from Katholikon, Monastery of Saint Catherine, Mount Sinai

Territorial Decline

730–843 Iconoclastic Controversy: ban on religious imagery

800 Pope Leo III crowns first Western Roman emperor (Charlemagne) at Rome since 5th cent.

730–843 Ban on religious imagery; most earlier pictographic art destroyed

Second Growth

988–989 Russians accept Christianity

1054 Eastern and Western Church formally split

Renewal of icon tradition

Final Decline

1204 Crusaders sack Constantinople on way to Holy Land

1453 Constantinople falls to Ottoman Turks, ending Byzantine Empire; Church of Hagia Sophia becomes a mosque

12th cent. Mosaics at Palermo, Sicily

c. 1410 Rublev active as painter of icons in Moscow

6

The World of Byzantium

c. 324 Constantine has stadium in Constantinople enlarged to form Hippodrome

c. 326 Holy Sepulchre, Jerusalem

c. 333 Old Saint Peter's Basilica, Vatican

Use of basilica plan and central plan with dome

after 350 Beginnings of Byzantine music, based probably on Syriac and Hebrew music

386 Saint Ambrose of Milan begins use of vernacular hymns in church

c. 450 Mausoleum of Galla Placidia, Neonian and Arian Baptisteries, Ravenna

c. 493–526 Sant' Apollinare Nuovo, Ravenna

c. 526–547 San Vitale, Ravenna

526 Theodoric's Tomb, Ravenna

527 Hagia Eirene, Constantinople, begun

532–537 Anthemius of Tralles and Isidore of Miletus rebuild Hagia Sophia, Constantinople, combining basilica plan and central plan with dome

549 Sant' Apollinare in Classe

c. 550 Stephanos, Monastery of Saint Catherine, Mount Sinai

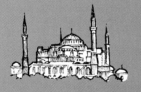

590–602 Gregorian Chant established at Rome during papacy of Gregory the Great

7th cent. Golden Age of Byzantine hymnody

1063 Saint Mark's, Venice, begun

11th cent. Codification of Greek liturgy; musical modifications decline

c. 1166 Church of the Intercession of the Virgin, near Vladimir, Russia; "onion dome" adapted from central dome

THE WORLD OF BYZANTIUM

The Decline of Rome

By the early 4th century the Roman Empire already had severe economic, political, and social problems. In 330 the emperor Constantine dedicated a Greek trading town on the Bosporus his eastern capital, changing its name from Byzantium to Constantinople. It was to be a New Rome. Constantinople had some obvious advantages for a major city: it straddled the most prominent land route between Asia and Europe. It had a deep-water port with natural shelter. It guarded the passage between the Mediterranean and the Black Sea. The surrounding countryside was rich in forests and water. The neighboring areas of both Europe (Thrace) and Asia (Bithynia) were rich agricultural areas that could supply the city's food needs.

Because of the tumultuous conditions in Rome the emperors spent less time there. By the beginning of the 5th century the emperor Honorius (in A.D. 402), moved the capital of the Western empire to the northern Italian city of Ravenna on the Adriatic coast. Seventy-four years later, in A.D. 476, the last Roman emperor in the West would die there. Goths would occupy the city; they in turn would be defeated by the imperial forces from Constantinople.

In the waning decades of the 4th and 5th centuries Christianity would continue to grow and expand in influence. During that period, in far different places, would live two writers who saw the decline of the West: Augustine in Roman North Africa and Boethius in the city of Ravenna. Their writings would have an enormous impact on the culture of Europe. Each deserves consideration.

Literature and Philosophy

Augustine of Hippo

The greatest writer of the Christian Latin West, Augustine of Hippo, was a witness to the decline of Roman power. Born in 354 in North Africa (then part of the Roman provinces), Augustine received a thorough classical education in Africa and in Rome. He was converted to Christianity in Milan and soon afterward returned to his native country, where he was named bishop of Hippo in 390. When the Visigoths sacked Rome in 410, the pagan world was aghast and many blamed the rise of Christianity for this event. Partially as a response to this charge, Augustine wrote *The City of God* as an attempt to show that history had a direction willed by God and that

"in the end" all would be made right as the city of man gave way to the city of God. This work, packed with reflections on scripture, philosophy, and pagan wisdom, is often cited as one of the most influential philosophies of history written in the Western world.

Indeed, it is difficult to overestimate the intellectual impact of Augustine of Hippo on the subsequent cultural history of the West. His influence within Christianity is without parallel. Until Thomas Aquinas in the 13th century, all Christian theologians started from explicitly Augustinian premises. Even Thomas did not shake off his debt to Augustine, although he replaced Augustine's strong Platonic orientation with a more empirical Aristotelian one. Augustine emphasized the absolute majesty of God, the immutability of God's will, and the flawed state of the human condition (notions derived from Saint Paul). These tenets received a powerful reformulation in the Protestant Reformation by Martin Luther (who as a Catholic friar had lived under the rule of Saint Augustine) and by John Calvin, a profound student of Augustine's theological writings.

Augustine also made a notable impact beyond theology. *The City of God,* begun about 412, was an attempt to formulate a coherent and all-embracing philosophy of history, the first such attempt in the West. For Augustine, history moves on a straight line in a direction from its origin in God until it ends, again in God, at the consummation of history in the Last Judgment. Augustine rejected the older notion that history repeats itself endlessly in cycles. His reading of the Bible convinced him that humanity had an origin, played out its story, and would terminate. The city of man would be judged and the city of God would be saved. Subsequent philosophers of history have secularized this view but, with very few exceptions (Vico, a 17th-century Italian philosopher, was one), have maintained the outlines of Augustine's framework to some extent. "A bright future," "an atomic wasteland of the future," and "classless society" are all statements about the end of history, all statements that echo, however dimly, the world view of Augustine.

Augustine also invented the genre of self-reflective writing in the West. "I would know myself that I might know Thee," Augustine writes of God in *The Confessions.* Before Augustine's time, memoirs related a life in terms of social, political, or military affairs (as Caesar's *Gallic Wars* did), but Augustine's intimate self-scrutiny of the significance of life was new in Western culture. There would not be another work like *The Confessions* until Petrarch, an indefatigable student of Augustine, wrote his *Letter to Posterity* in the mid-14th century. The Renaissance writers, an extremely self-conscious generation, were devoted students of Augustine's stately Latin prose;

even the great later autobiographies of our inherited culture—those of Gibbon, Mill, Newman—are literary and spiritual descendants of Augustine's.

Augustine's *The Confessions* is a compelling analysis of his spiritual and intellectual development from his youth until the time of his conversion to Christianity and readiness to return to his native Africa. The title must be understood in a triple sense—a confession of sin, an act of faith in God, and a confession of praise—so it is appropriate that Augustine wrote his book as a prayer to God.

Although strongly autobiographical, *The Confessions* is actually a long meditation by Augustine on the hidden grace of God as his life is shaped toward its appointed end. Augustine "confesses" to God (and the reader) how his early drive for fame as a teacher of rhetoric, his flirtation with the Manichean sect with its belief in two gods of evil and good, his liaison with a woman that resulted in the birth of a son, and his restless movement from North Africa to Rome and Milan were all part of a seamless web of circumstance that made up an individual life. Interspersed in the narrative line of his early life are Augustine's reflections on the most basic philosophical and theological questions of the day, always linked to his own experience.

If *The Confessions* can be said to be the beginning of autobiography, beyond that historic importance it is classic and singular in its balance of immense learning, searching speculation, and intense self-scrutiny. It is a work concerned first of all with meaning at the deepest philosophical level, and its full power is evident only to the reader who will take the time to enter Augustine's line of argument.

Boethius

In the twilight period in Ravenna between the death of the last Roman emperor and the arrival of Justinian's troops an important figure who bridged the gap between classical paganism and Christianity lived and died. Anicius Manlius Severinus Boethius was a highly educated Roman who entered the service of the Goth king Theodoric in 522. Imprisoned for reasons that are not clear, Boethius wrote a treatise called *The Consolation of Philosophy* while awaiting execution. Cast as a dialogue between Lady Philosophy and the author on the philosophical and religious basis for human freedom, the work blends the spirit of the Book of Job with Roman stoicism. Attempting to console him for his sad state of disgrace and imprisonment, Lady Philosophy demands that the author avoid self-pity, that he face his troubles with serenity and hope. Insisting that a provident God overcomes all evil, Philosophy insists that blind fate has no control over humanity. She explains that human freedom exists along with an all-knowing God and that good will triumph. Although Christian themes permeate the work, there is no explicit mention of Christian doctrine. What one does sense is the recasting of Roman thought into Christian patterns. In a way, *The Consolation of Philosophy* is one of the last works of the late Roman period. It reflects the elegance of Roman expression, the burgeoning hope of Christianity, and the terrible sadness that must have afflicted any sensitive Roman in this period.

The Consolation of Philosophy was one of the most widely read and influential works of the Middle Ages (Chaucer made an English translation of it from an already-existing French version). Its message of hope and faith was liberally quoted by every major medieval thinker from Thomas Aquinas to Dante Alighieri.

Boethius sets out a basic problem and provides an answer that would become normative Christian thought for subsequent centuries. In *The Consolation* Boethius asks how one can reconcile human freedom with the notion of an all-knowing God. To put it another way: If God knows what we do before we do it, how can we be said to be free agents who must accept responsibility for personal acts? The answer, Boethius insists through Lady Philosophy, is to look at the problem from the point of view of God, not from the human vantage point. God lives in eternity. Eternity does not mean a "long time" with a past and a future. Eternity means "no time": God lives in an eternal moment that for Him is a "now." In that sense God does not "foresee" the future. There is no future for God. God sees everything in one simple moment that is only past, present, and future from the human point of view. Boethius says that God does not exercise *praevidentia* (seeing things before they happen) but *providence* (seeing all things in the simultaneity of their happening). Thus God, in a single eternal, ineffable moment, grasps all activity, which for us is a long sequence of events. More specifically, in that moment, God sees our choices, the events that follow from them, and the ultimate consequences of those choices.

The consolation of Boethius, as Lady Philosophy explains it, rests in the fact that people do act with freedom, that they are not in the hands of an indifferent fate, and that the ultimate meaning of life rests with the all-seeing presence of a Person, not a blind force. Lady Philosophy sums up her discussion with Boethius by offering him this "consolation." It is her assurance that his life, even while awaiting execution in a prison cell, was not the product of a blind fate or an uncaring force in the universe.

The language of Boethius, with its discussion of time, eternity, free will, and the nature of God, echoes the great philosophical tradition of Plato and Ar-

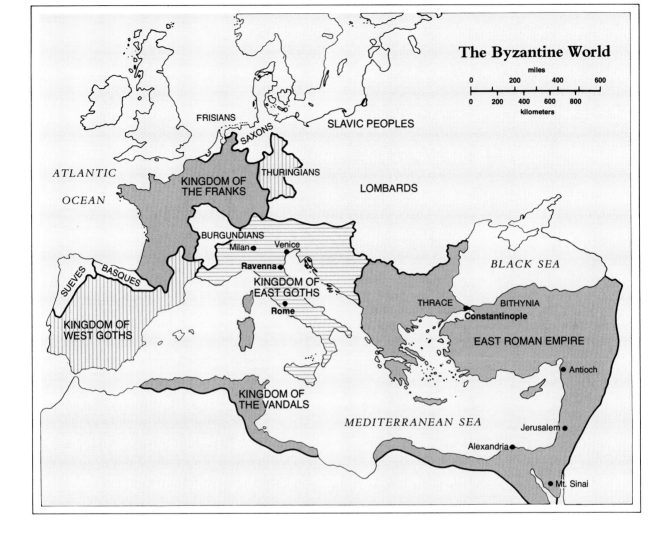

The Byzantine World

istotle (Boethius had translated the latter's works) as well as the stoicism of Cicero and the theological reflections of Augustine. It is a fitting end to the intellectual tradition of the late Roman Empire in the West.

The Ascendancy of Byzantium

The city of Constantinople became the center of imperial life in the early 5th century and reached its highest expression of power in the early 6th century with the ascension of Justinian to the throne in 527. His stated intention was to restore the empire to a state of grandeur. In this project he was aided by his wife Theodora. A former dancer and prostitute, Theodora was a tough-minded and capable woman who added strength and resolve to the grandiose plans of the emperor. She was Justinian's equal, perhaps more.

The reign of Justinian and Theodora was impressive, if profligate, by any standard. The emperor encouraged Persian monks residing in China to bring back silkworms for the introduction of the silk indus-

try into the West. Because the silk industry of China was a fiercely guarded monopoly, the monks accomplished this rather dangerous mission by smuggling silkworm eggs out of the country in hollow tubes, and within a decade the silk industry in the Western world rivaled that of China.

Justinian also revised and codified Roman Law, a gigantic undertaking of scholarship and research. Roman law had evolved over a thousand-year period, and by Justinian's time was a vast jumble of disorganized and often contradictory decisions, decrees, statutes, opinions, and legal codes. Under the aegis of the emperor, a legal scholar named Tribonian produced order out of this chaos. First a *Code* that summarized all imperial decrees from the time of Hadrian (in the 2nd century) to the time of Justinian was published. The *Code* was followed by the *Pandects* (digest), which synthesized a vast quantity of legal opinion and scholarship from the past. Finally came the *Institutes,* a legal collection broken down into four categories by which the laws concerning persons, things, actions, and personal wrongs (in other words, criminal law) were set forth. The body of this legal revision became the basis for the law courts of the empire and, in later centuries, the basis for the use of Roman law in the West.

Justinian and Theodora were fiercely partisan Christians who took a keen interest in theology and ecclesiastical governance. Justinian's fanatical devotion prompted him to shut down the last surviving Platonic academy in the world on the grounds that its paganism was inimical to the true religion. His own personal life—despite evidences of cruelty and capriciousness—was austere and abstemious, influenced by the presence of so many monks in the city of Constantinople. His generosity to the church was great, with his largess shown most clearly in openhanded patronage of church-building. Hagia Sophia, his most famous project, has become legendary for the beauty and opulence of its decoration.

Hagia Sophia: Monument and Symbol

Hagia Sophia (Greek for "Holy Wisdom") was the principal church of Constantinople. It had been destroyed twice, once by fire and—during Justinian's reign—during the terrible civil disorders of the Nika revolt in 532 that devastated most of the European side of the city. Soon afterward Justinian decided to rebuild the church using the plans of two architects, Anthemius of Tralles and Isidore of Miletus. Work began in 532 and the new edifice was solemnly dedicated five years later in the presence of Justinian and Theodora.

The church of Hagia Sophia was a stunning architectural achievement that combined the longitudinal shape of the Roman basilica with a domed central

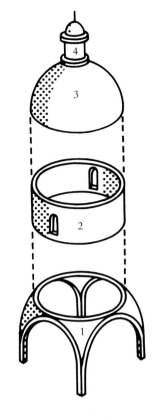

6.1 Dome construction:
1. pendentive; 2. drum;
3. cupola; 4. lantern.

plan. Two centuries earlier Constantine had used both the dome and basilica shapes in the church of the Holy Sepulchre in Jerusalem, as we have seen, but he had not joined them into a unity. In still earlier domed buildings in the Roman world such as the Pantheon and Santa Costanza, the dome rested on a circular drum. This gave the dome solidity but limited its height and expansiveness. Anthemius and Isidore solved this problem by the use of *pendentives* [6.1], triangular masonry devices that carried the

THE ARTS AND INVENTION: *The Dome*

The dome of Hagia Sophia is such a conspicuous achievement that it would be well to focus on its importance in architecture.

The dome was known in antiquity. Primitive people made domes by bending poles that were then covered with hides as dwelling places. The "beehive" domes of ancient Mycenae were concentric rings of corbeled stones. The Greeks knew the dome but did not make wide use of it.

The Romans quite rightly get the credit for the development of the dome, which grew out of their skill at making arches. The dome is simply a more sophisticated variation of the barrel vault. The greatest Roman dome was, of course, the Pantheon, but the architects of Hagia Sophia developed the pendentive in order to place a dome over a large square or rectangular space. The pendentive gave way to the *squinch* (a support carrying

across the corners of a room angle) which the Moslems, borrowing from Byzantine architecture, used to great advantage in such buildings as the Dome of the Rock in Jerusalem.

The dome developed a new grandeur in the Renaissance with Michelangelo's design for Saint Peter's in the 16th century, borrowing from Brunelleschi's ingenious dome for the cathedral in Florence done in the preceding century. That Michelangelo's achievement was influential can be judged by the impact it had on the architects who designed the Capitol building in Washington, D.C.

The versatility of the dome as an architectural tool can be seen in contemporary society by the use to which it has been put in many sports arenas of major cities; think of the Astrodome in Houston.

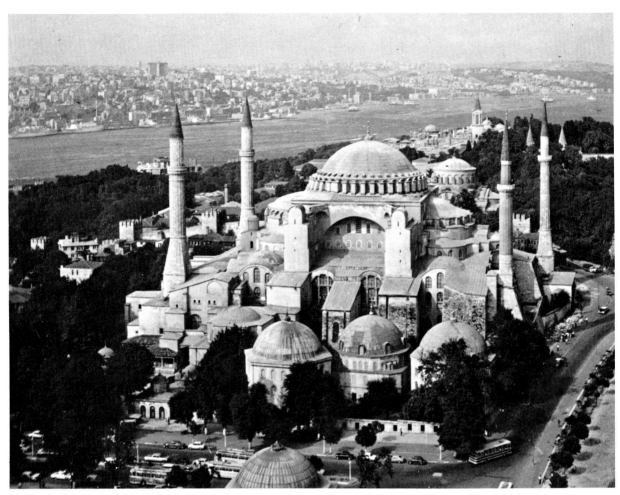

6.2 Anthemius of Tralles and Isidore of Miletus. Hagia Sophia, Constantinople (Istanbul).
532–537, 553–563. Exterior view from the southeast. The towers, of Turkish origin, are a later
addition as a comparison with figure 6.3 makes clear.

weight of the dome on massive piers rather than straight down to the drum. In the church of Hagia Sophia the central dome was abutted by two half-domes so that a person looking down at the building from above might see a nave in the form of an oval instead of a quadrangle [6.2].

The church—184 feet (55.2 meters) high, 41 feet (12.3 meters) higher than the Pantheon—retained a hint of the old basilica style as a result of the columned side aisles and the gallery for female worshipers in the triforium space above the arches of the aisles, but the overwhelming visual impression came from the massive dome. Since the pendentives reduced the weight of the dome, the area between drum and dome could be pierced by forty windows that made the dome seem to hang in space. Light streamed into the church from the windows and refracted off the rich mosaics and colored marbles that covered the interior [6.3].

Light, in fact, was a key theoretical element be-

hind the entire conception of Hagia Sophia. Light is the symbol of divine wisdom in the philosophy of Plato and in the New Testament. A common metaphor in pagan and biblical wisdom had the sun and its rays represent the eternity of God and his illumination of mortals. The suffusion of light was an element in the Hagia Sophia that went far beyond the functional need to illuminate the interior of the church. Light refracting in the church created a spiritual ambiance analogous to that of heaven, where the faithful would be bathed in the actual light of God.

The sequence of the various parts of the worship service at Constantinople—the *liturgy*—was developed from the efforts of Saint John Chrysostom (345–407), patriarch of the city in the century before Justinian. The official liturgy of Byzantine Christianity is still the Divine Liturgy of Saint John Chrysostom, modified and added to over the centuries. In that liturgy, the worshiping community visualized itself as standing in the forecourt of heaven when it

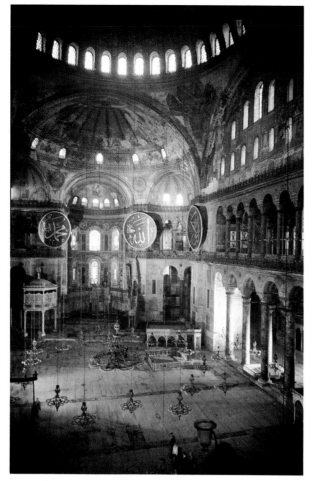

6.3 (plate) Anthemius of Tralles and Isidore of Miletus. Hagia Sophia, Constantinople (Istanbul). 532–537, 553–563. An interior view, looking toward the apse, shows how the windows between drum and dome give an impression of floating lightness that continues down to the floor.

worshiped in the church. Amid the swirling incense, the glittering light, and the stately chants of the clergy and people comes a sense of participation with the household of heaven standing before God. A fragment from the liturgy—added during the reign of Justinian's successor Justin II (565–578)—underscores the point dramatically. Note the characteristic cry of *Wisdom!* and the description of the congregation as mystically present in heaven:

> PRIEST Wisdom! That ever being guarded by Thy power, we may give glory to thee, Father, Son, and Holy Spirit, now and forevermore.

> CONGREGATION Amen. Let us here who represent the mystic Cherubim in singing the thrice holy hymn to the life-giving Trinity now lay aside every earthly care so that we may welcome the King of the universe who comes escorted by invisible armies of angels. Alleluia. Alleluia. Alleluia.

Hagia Sophia was enriched by subsequent emperors, and after repairs were made to the dome in 989 new mosaics were added to the church. After the fall of Constantinople in 1453 the Turks turned the church into a mosque; the mosaics were whitewashed or plastered over since the Koran prohibits the use of images. When the mosque was converted to a museum by the modern Turkish state, some of the mosaics were uncovered, and we can get some sense of the splendor of the original interior.

Other monuments bear the mark of Justinian's creative efforts. His church of the Holy Apostles, built on the site of an earlier church of the same name destroyed by an earthquake, did not survive the fall of the city in 1453 but did serve as a model for the

---

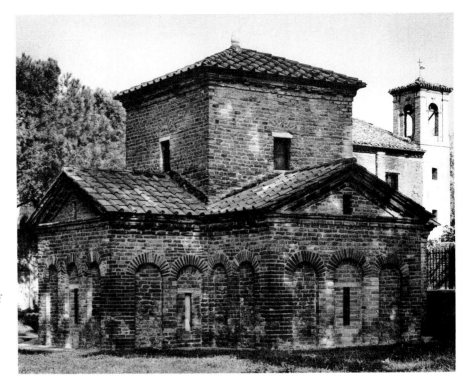

6.4 The so-called Mausoleum of Galla Placidia, Ravenna. Early 5th century. This building has sunk more than a meter (about 4') into the marshy soil, thus making it seem rather squat in appearance.

church of Saint Mark in Venice. Near the church of the Hagia Sophia is the church of Hagia Eirene (Holy Peace), now a mosque, whose architecture also shows the combination of basilica and dome. The church, dedicated to the martyr saints Sergius and Bacchus and begun in 527, was a preliminary study for the later Hagia Sophia. In all, Justinian built more than 25 churches and convents in Constantinople. His program of secular architecture included an impressive water-conduit system that still exists.

6.5 *The Good Shepherd* from the mausoleum of Galla Placidia, Ravenna. 5th century. Mosaic. The "Persian rug" motif can be seen in the vault. Note the beardless Christ dressed in a Roman toga.

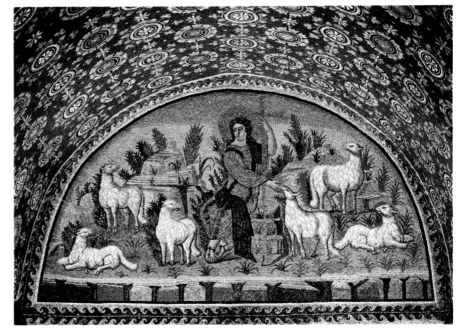

Ravenna

Art and Architecture

Ravenna is a repository of monuments that reflect its late-Roman, barbarian Gothic, and Byzantine history. The mausoleum (burial chapel) of Galla Placidia (who reigned as regent from 430 to 450) was built at the end of the Roman period of Ravenna's history [6.4]. Once thought to be the tomb of the empress (hence its name), it is more likely a votive chapel to Saint Lawrence originally attached to the nearby church of the Holy Cross. The huge sarcophagi in the building are probably medieval. This small chapel in the shape of a cross, very plain on the outside, shows the architectural tendency to combine the basilica-style nave with the structure of a dome (it even uses a modified pendentive form) used later in monumental structures like Hagia Sophia.

The importance of Galla Placidia rests in the complete and breathtakingly beautiful mosaics that decorate the walls and ceiling. The north niche, just above the entrance, has a *lunette* (a small arched space) mosaic depicting Christ as the Good Shepherd [6.5]. Clothed in royal purple and with a gold staff in his hand, the figure of Christ has a courtly, almost languid elegance that refines the more rustic depictions of the Good Shepherd theme in earlier Roman Christian art. The vaulting of both the *apse* (the altar end of the church) and the dome is covered with a deep blue mosaic interspersed with stylized sunbursts and stars in gold. This "Persian-rug" motif symbolized the heavens, the dwelling place of God. Since the *tesserae,* the small cubes that make up the mosaic, are not set fully flush in the wall, the surfaces of the mosaic are irregular. These surfaces thus refract and break up the light in the chapel, especially from flickering lamps and candles. (The translucent alabaster windows now in the chapel were installed in the 20th century.)

Opposite the lunette of the Good Shepherd is another lunette that depicts the deacon martyr of the Roman Church, Saint Lawrence, who stands next to the gridiron that was the instrument of his death. Beyond the gridiron is an open cabinet containing codices of the four gospels [6.6]. The spaces above these mosaics are filled with figures of the apostles. Between these are symbols of the search for religious understanding—deer, doves, fountains. In the arches, more spectacular and often overlooked are the abstract interlocking designs with their brightness and *trompe l'œil* (trick-the-eye) quality.

The two baptisteries of Ravenna represent a major religious division of the time between the Orthodox Christians, who accepted the divinity of Christ, and the Arian Christians, who did not. The Neonian

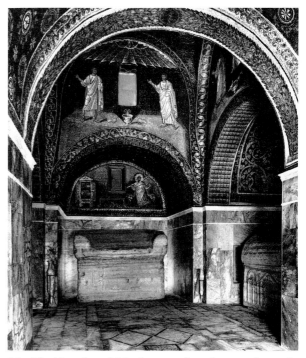

6.6 *The Martyrdom of Saint Lawrence,* from the mausoleum of Galla Placidia, Ravenna. 5th century. Mosaic. The window, a modern one, is made of alabaster. Saint Lawrence, with the gridiron on which legend said he was roasted, is at the lower right. The great stone sarcophagi in the niches are medieval.

Baptistery, built by Orthodox Christians in the early 5th century next to the ancient cathedral of the city, is octagonal—as were most baptisteries, because of their derivation from Roman bath houses. The ceiling mosaic, directly over the baptismal pool, is particularly striking. The lower register of the mosaic, above the windows, shows floral designs based on common Roman decorative motifs. Just above are a circle of empty thrones interspersed with altars with biblical codices open on them [6.7]. In the band above are the apostles, who seem to be walking in a stately procession around the circle of the dome. In the central disc is a mosaic of the baptism of Christ by John the Baptist in the Jordan River. The spirit of the river is depicted as Neptune.

The mosaic ensemble in the ceiling was designed to reflect the beliefs of the participants in the ceremonies below. The circling apostles reminded the candidates for baptism that the church was founded on the apostles; the convert's baptism was a promise that one day they would dwell with the apostles in heaven. Finally, the codices on the altars taught of the sources of their belief, while the empty thrones promised the new Christians a place in the heavenly Jerusalem. The art, then, was not merely decorative

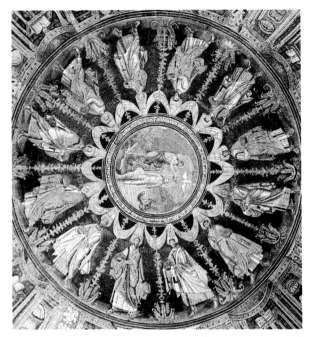

6.7 Ceiling mosaic of the Orthodox Baptistery, Ravenna. Mid-5th century.

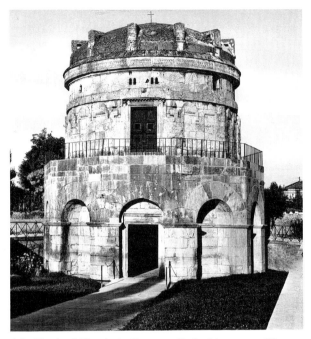

6.8 Tomb of Theodoric, Ravenna. Early 6th century. The cap of the mausoleum is a huge stone that measures 36′ × 10′ (11 × 3 m). The great porphyry tomb inside the mausoleum was pillaged in the early Middle Ages.

but, in the words of a modern Orthodox thinker, "theology in color."

The Arian Baptistery, built by the Goths toward the end of the 5th century, is much more severely decorated. Again the traditional scene of Christ's baptism is in the central disc of the ceiling mosaic.

Here the figure of the River Jordan has lobsterlike claws sprouting from his head—a curiously pagan marine touch. The twelve apostles in the lower register are divided into two groups, one led by Peter and the other by Paul. These two groups converge at a throne bearing a jeweled cross (the crucifix with the

6.9 South-wall mosaic, Sant' Apollinare Nuovo, Ravenna. Early 6th century. The procession of male saints is in the lower register. The prophets and apostles are placed between the windows. Scenes from the gospels are in the upper register. Detail appears in figure 6.11.

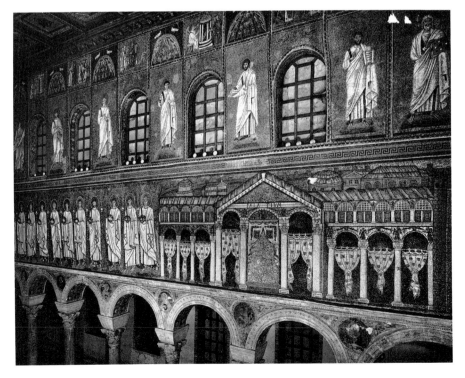

210

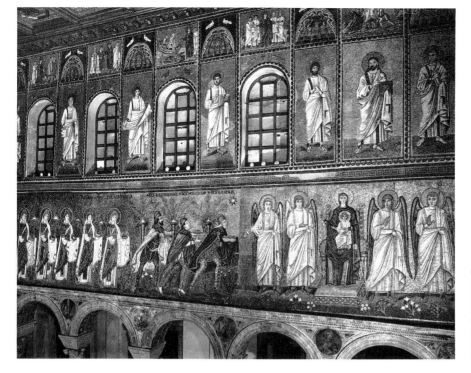

6.10 North-wall mosaic, Sant' Apollinare Nuovo, Ravenna. Early 6th century. Note the procession of female saints oriented behind the Three Magi, who all approach the enthroned Madonna. Details appear in figures 6.12 and 6.13.

body of Christ on the cross is very uncommon in this period) that represents in a single symbol the passion and the resurrection of Christ.

Theodoric, the emperor of the Goths who had executed Boethius and reigned from 493 to 526, was buried in a massive mausoleum that may still be seen on the outskirts of Ravenna [6.8]. The most famous extant monument of Theodoric's reign aside from his mausoleum is the church of Sant' Apollinare Nuovo, originally called the Church of the Redeemer, the palace church of Theodoric. This church is constructed in the severe basilica style: a wide nave with two side aisles partitioned off from the nave by double columns of marble. The apse decorations have been destroyed, but the walls of the basilica, richly ornamented with mosaics, can be seen. The mosaics,

however, are of two different dates and reflect in one building both the Roman and Byzantine styles of art. On each side of the aisles, in the spaces just above the aisle arches, are processions of male and female saints, each procession facing toward the apse and main altar [6.9] They move to an enthroned Christ on one side and toward a Madonna and Child on the other. These mosaics were added to the church when the building passed from the Goths into Byzantine hands in the reign of Justinian. The depiction of Theodoric's palace [6.10], in fact, still shows evidence of Orthodox censorship. In the arched spaces one can still see traces of halos of now-excised Arian saints (or perhaps members of Theodoric's court). On several columns of the mosaic can be seen the hands of figures that have now been replaced by dec-

6.11 Theodoric's palace; detail of south-wall mosaic, Sant' Apollinare Nuovo, Ravenna. The curtains replace earlier figures; fragments of their hands can still be seen on the columns.

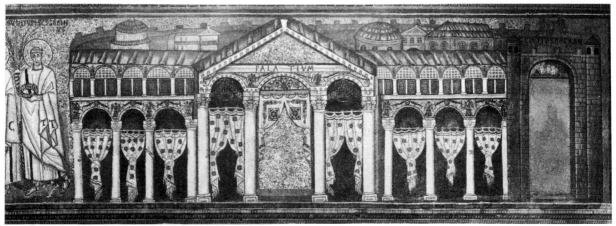

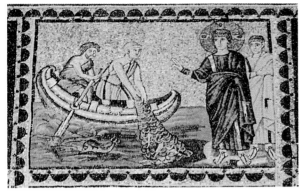

6.12 Jesus calls the apostles Peter and Andrew. North-wall upper-register mosaic, Sant' Apollinare Nuovo, Ravenna. Note the Christ figure in the royal-purple toga and his beardless appearance.

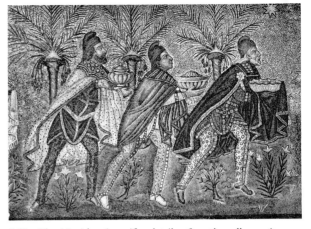

6.13 The Magi bearing gifts; details of north-wall mosaic, Sant' Apollinare Nuovo, Ravenna. Christian legend had already named these figures Balthasar, Melchior, and Caspar, which can be seen inscribed on the mosaic. Bishop Apollinaris was a 2nd-century apologist for Christianity who defended his faith in a treatise addressed to the emperor, Marcus Aurelius.

orative twisted draperies. The next register above has a line of prophetic figures. At the level of the clerestory windows are scenes from the New Testament—the miracles of Christ on one side [6.11–6.13] and scenes from his passion on the other. These mosaics are very different in style from the procession of sainted martyrs on the lower level. The gospel sequence is more Roman in inspiration, more severe and simple. Certain themes of earlier Roman Christian iconography are evident. The procession of saints, most likely erected by artists from a Constantinople studio, is much more lush, reverent, and static in tone. The Orientalizing element is especially noteworthy in the depiction of the Three Magi (with their Phrygian caps) who offer gifts to the Christ Child.

The church of San Vitale most clearly testifies to the presence of Justinian in Ravenna [6.14]. Dedicated by Bishop Maximian in 547, it had been begun by Bishop Ecclesius in 526, the year Justinian came to the throne, while the Goths still ruled Ravenna. The church is octagonal, with only the barest hint of basilica length. How different it is may be seen by comparing it with Sant' Apollinare in Classe (the ancient seaport of Ravenna), built at roughly the same time [6.15]. The octagon has another octagon within it. This interior octagon, supported by columned arches and containing a second-story women's gallery, is the structural basis for the dome. The dome is supported on the octagonal walls by small vaults called *squinches* that cut across the angles of each part of the octagon.

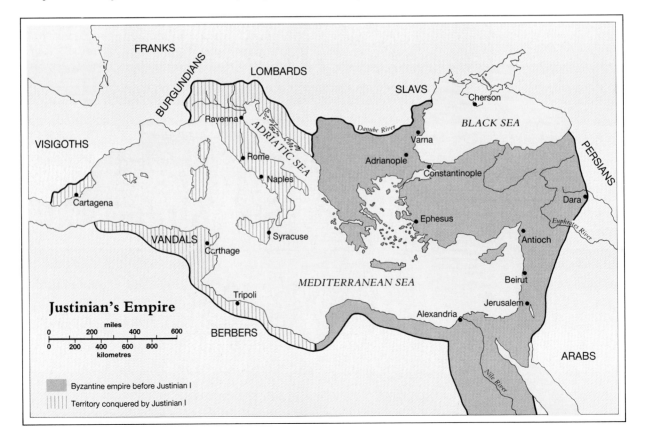

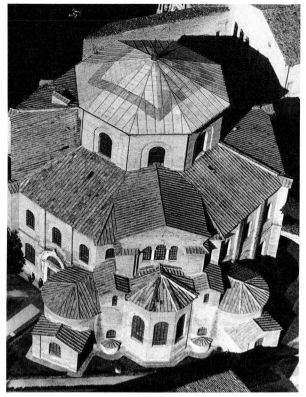

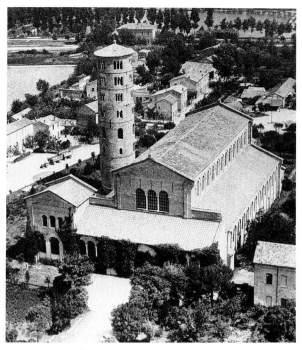

6.14 San Vitale, Ravenna. c. 530–548. Aerial view. This complex building, the inspiration for Charlemagne's church at Aachen, gives little exterior evidence that it is done in the basilica style.

6.15 Sant' Apollinare in Classe, Ravenna. c. 549. Aerial view. The tower is a medieval addition. The clear outlines of the basilica style, with its side aisles, can be clearly seen in this photograph.

6.16 Christ enthroned, with Saint Vitalis and Bishop Ecclesius, ceiling mosaic, San Vitale, Ravenna. c. 530. The bishop holds a model of the church at the extreme right while Christ hands the crown of martyrdom to the saint on the left.

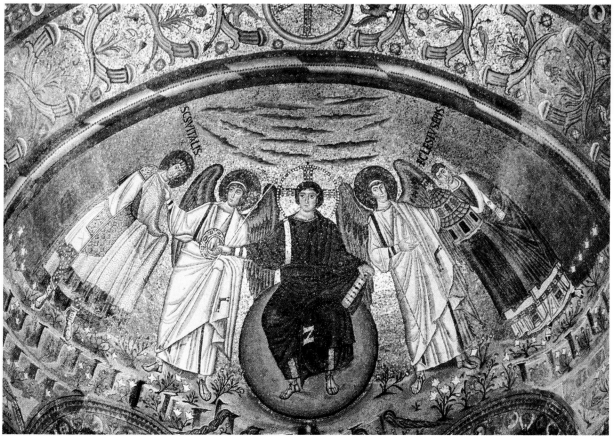

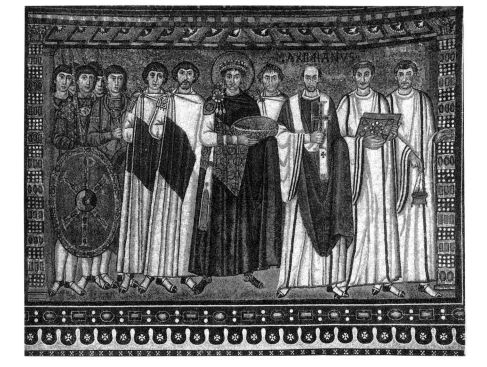

6.17 Emperor Justinian and courtiers, wall mosaic, San Vitale, Ravenna. c. 547. The church authorities stand at the emperor's left; the civil authorities at the right.

The most arresting characteristic of San Vitale, apart from its intricate and not fully understood architectural design, is its stunning program of mosaics. In the apse is a great mosaic of Christ the Pantocrator, the one who sustains all things in his hands [6.16]. Christ is portrayed as a beardless young man, clothed in royal purple. He holds in his left hand a book with seven seals (a reference to the book of Revelation) and offers the crown of martyrdom to Saint Vitalis with his right. Flanked by the two archangels, Christ is offered a model of the church by the bishop, Ecclesius, who laid its foundations. Above the figures are symbolic representations of the four rivers of paradise.

Mosaics to the left and right of the apse mosaic represent the royal couple as regents of Christ on earth. On the left wall of the sanctuary is a mosaic depicting Justinian and his attendants [6.17]. It is not

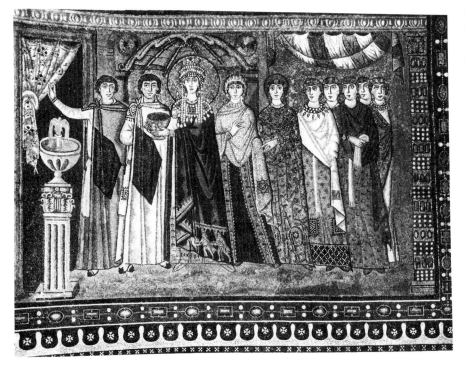

6.18 Empress Theodora and retinue, wall mosaic, San Vitale, Ravenna. c. 547. Note the Three Magi on the hem of the empress' gown.

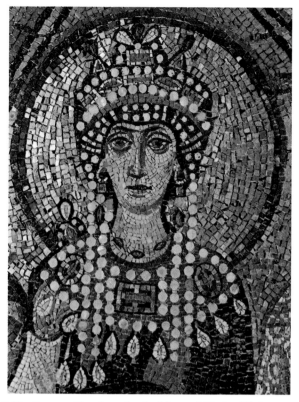

6.19 Empress Theodora; detail of figure 6.18, San Vitale, Ravenna, c. 547. Note the irregular placement of the tesserae in this mosaic.

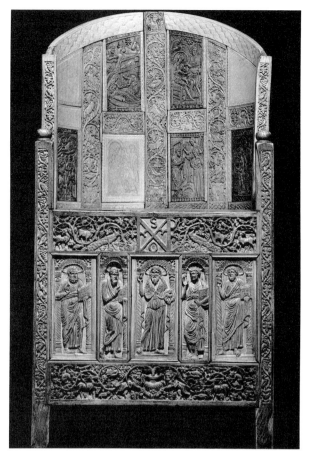

6.20 Bishop's *cathedra* (throne) of Maximian. c. 546–556. Ivory panels on wood frame. Height 4′11″ (1.5 m.), width 1′11⅝″ (.6 m.) Archepiscopal Museum, Ravenna. Maximian is portrayed with his name in the Justinian mosaic (see 6.17).

merely accidental nor an exercise of simple piety that the soldiers carry a shield with *chi* and *rho* (the first Greek letters in the name of Christ) or that there are twelve attendants or that the figure of the emperor divides clergy and laity. The emperor considered himself the regent of Christ, an attitude summed up in the *iconographic,* or symbolic, program: Justinian represents Christ on earth and his power balances both church and state. The only figure identified in the mosaic is Bishop (later Archbishop) Maximian flanked by his clergy, who include a deacon with a jeweled gospel and a subdeacon with a chained incense pot.

Opposite the emperor's retinue, the Empress Theodora and her attendants look across at the imperial group [6.18–6.19]. Theodora holds a chalice to complement the bread basket (paten) held by the emperor. At the hem of Theodora's gown is a small scene of the Magi bringing gifts to the Christ Child. Scholars disagree whether the two mosaics represent the royal couple bringing the eucharistic gifts for the celebration of the liturgy or the donation of the sacred vessels for the church. It was a custom for the rulers to give such gifts to the more important churches of their realm. The fact that the empress seems to be leaving her palace (two male functionar-

ies of the court are ushering her out) makes the latter interpretation the more probable one. The women at Theodora's left are striking; those to the extreme left are stereotyped, but the two closest to the empress appear more individualized, leading some art historians to suggest that they are idealized portraits of two of Theodora's closest friends: the wife and daughter of the conqueror of Ravenna, Belisarius.

The royal generosity extended not only to the building and decoration of the church of San Vitale. An ivory throne, now preserved in the episcopal museum of Ravenna, was a gift of the emperor to Bishop Maximian, the ecclesiastical ruler of Ravenna when San Vitale was dedicated [6.20]. A close stylistic analysis of the carving on the throne has led scholars to see the work of at least four different artists on the panels, all probably from Constantinople. The front of the throne bears portraits of John the Baptist and the four Evangelists, while the back has scenes from the New Testament with sides showing episodes from the Old Testament of the life of Joseph.

The purely decorative elements of trailing vines and animals show the style of a different hand, probably Syrian. The bishop's throne (*cathedra* in Latin; a cathedral is a church where a bishop presides) bears a small monogram: *Maximian, Bishop*.

The entire ensemble of San Vitale, with its pierced capitals typical of the Byzantine style, its elaborate mosaic portraits of saints and prophets, its lunette mosaics of Old Testament prefigurements of the Eucharist, and monumental mosaic scenes, is a living testimony to the rich fusion of imperial, Christian, and Middle Eastern cultural impulses. San Vitale is a microcosm of the sociopolitical vision of Byzantium fused with the religious world view of early Christianity.

Saint Catherine's Monastery at Mount Sinai

Justinian is remembered not only in Constantinople and Ravenna but also in the Near East, where he founded a monastery that is still in use some fifteen hundred years later—a living link back to the Byzantine world.

In her *Peregrinatio,* that wonderfully tireless traveler of the 4th century, Etheria, describes a visit to the forbidding desert of the Sinai to pray at the site where God appeared to Moses in a burning bush (that, Etheria assures us, "is still alive to this day and throws out shoots") and to climb the mountain where the Law was given to Moses. She says that there was a church at the spot of the burning bush with some hermits living nearby to tend it and see to the needs of pilgrim visitors. More than a century later, the Emperor Justinian built a monastery fortress at the foot of Mount Sinai and some pilgrimage chapels on the slopes of the mountain [6.21]. An Arabic inscription over one of the gates tells the story:

> The pious king Justinian, of the Greek Church, in the expectation of divine assistance and in the hope of divine promises, built the monastery of Mount Sinai and the Church of the Colloquy [a church over the spot where Moses spoke to God in the burning bush] to his eternal memory and that of his wife, Theodora, so that all the earth and all its inhabitants should become the heritage of God; for the Lord is the best of masters. The building was finished in the thirtieth year of his reign and he gave the monastery a superior named Dukhas. This took place in the 6021st year after Adam, the 527th year [by the calendar] of the era of Christ the Savior.

Because of the number of factors—most important its extreme isolation and the very dry weather—the monastery is an immense repository of ancient Byzantine art and culture. It preserves, as well as the oldest icons in Christianity, some of Justinian's architecture. The monastery is also famous as the site of the rediscovery of the earliest Greek codex of the New Testament hitherto found. Called the *Codex Sinaiticus,* it was discovered in the monastery by the German scholar Konstantin von Tischendorf in the 19th century. The codex—from the middle of the 4th century—was given by the monks to the Tsar of Russia. In 1933 the Soviet Government sold it for £100,000 to the British Museum, where it remains today, a precious document.

The monastery is surrounded by heavy, fortified walls, the main part of which date from before Justinian's time. Within those walls are some modern buildings, including a fireproof structure that houses the monastery's library and icon collections. The monastic church, the Katholikon, dates from the time of Justinian, as recently discovered inscriptions carved into the wooden trusses in the ceiling of the church prove. Even the name of the architect—Stephanos—was uncovered. This church thus is unique: signed 6th-century ecclesiastical architecture.

One of the more spectacular holdings of the monastery is its vast collections of religious icons. Be-

6.21 The fortress monastery of Saint Catherine in the Sinai Desert. 6th century. The church (called the *Katholikon*) from Justinian's time can be seen in the lower center of the walled enclosure, flanked by a belltower.

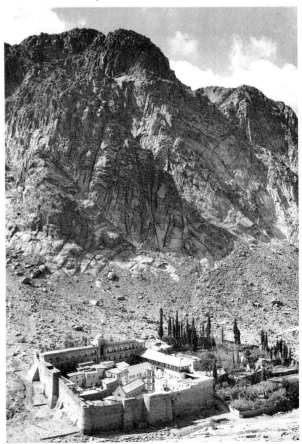

cause of the iconoclastic controversies of the 8th and 9th centuries in the Byzantine Empire almost no pictorial art remains from the period before the 8th century. Sinai survived the purges of the "image-breakers" (iconoclasts) that engulfed the rest of the Byzantine world because of its extreme isolation. At Sinai, a range of icons that date from Justinian's time to the modern period can be seen. In a real sense, the icons of the monastery of Saint Catherine show the entire evolution of icon painting.

The Greek word *icon* means image. In the Byzantine Christian tradition, *icon* refers to a painting of a religious figure or a religious scene that is used in the public worship (the liturgy) of the church. Icons are not primarily decorative and they are didactic only in a secondary sense: for the Orthodox Christian faithful the icon is a window into the world of the sacred. Just as Jesus Christ was in the flesh but imaged God in eternity, so the icon is a "thing," but it permits a glimpse into the timeless world of religious mystery. One stands before the icon and speaks through its image to the reality beyond it. This explains why the figures in an icon are usually portrayed full-front with no shadow or sense of three-dimensionality. The figures "speak" directly and frontally to the viewer against a hieratic background of gold.

This iconic style becomes clear by an examination of an icon of Christ that may well have been sent to his new monastery by Justinian himself [6.22]. The icon is done by the *encaustic* method of painting (a technique common in the Roman world for funerary portraits): painting with molten wax that has been colored by pigments. Christ, looking directly at the viewer, is robed in royal purple; in his left hand he holds a jeweled codex and with his right hand he blesses the viewer.

This icon is an example from a large number found at Sinai that can be dated from before the 10th century. The later icons of the same monastery have not yet been published, but the entire corpus represents a continuous tradition of Byzantine art and piety. Mount Sinai is unique in its great tradition of historical continuity. Despite the rise of Islam, the harshness of the atmosphere, the vicissitudes of history, and the changing culture of the modern world, the monastery fortress at Sinai is living testimony to a style of life and a religiosity with an unbroken history to the time of Justinian's building program.

The Persistence of Byzantine Culture

It is simplistic to describe Byzantine art as unchanging—it underwent regional, intellectual, social, and

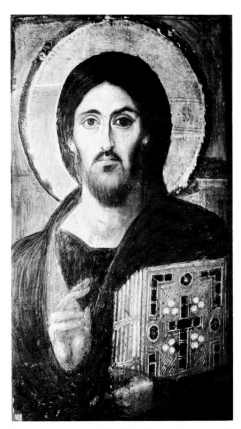

6.22 *Christ Pantocrater.* c. 500–530. Encaustic on wood panel. 32¼″ × 17¾″ (84 × 46 cm.). Monastery of Saint Catherine, Mount Sinai. The book is a complex symbol that symbolizes the Bible, Christ as the Word of God, and the record of human secrets that will be opened on the Last Day.

iconographic changes—but a person who visits a modern Greek or Russian Orthodox church is struck more by the similarities than by the dissimilarities with the art of early medieval Constantinople. Furthermore, the immediately recognizable Byzantine style can be found in the history of art in areas as geographically diverse as Sicily in southern Italy and the far-eastern reaches of Russia. What explains this basic persistence of style and outlook?

First of all, until it fell to the Turks in 1453, Constantinople exerted an extraordinary cultural influence over the rest of the Eastern Christian world. Russian emissaries sent to Constantinople in the late 10th century to inquire about religion brought back to Russia both favorable reports about Byzantine Christianity and a taste for the Byzantine style of religious art. It was the impact of services in Hagia Sophia that most impressed the delegates of Prince Vladimir, the first Christian ruler in Russia. Although art in Christian Russia was to develop its own regional variations, it was still closely tied to the art of Constantinople; Russian "onion-dome" churches, for example, are native adaptations of the central-dome churches of Byzantium.

Russia, in fact, accepted Christianity about 150 years after the ban on icons was lifted in Constantinople in 843. By this time the second "golden age" of Byzantine art was well under way. By the 11th century Byzantine artists were not only working in Russia but had also established schools of icon painting in such centers as Kiev. By the end of century these schools had passed into the hands of Russian monks, but their stylistic roots remained the artistic ideas of Byzantium. Even after the Mongol invasions of Russia in 1240, Russian religious art continued to have close ties to the Greek world, although less with Constantinople than with the monastic centers of Mount Athos and Salonica in Greece.

Byzantine influence was also very strong in Italy. We have already seen the influence of Justinian's court on Ravenna. Although northern Italy fell to Lombard rule in the 8th century, Byzantine influence continued in the south of Italy for the next five hundred years. During the iconoclastic controversy in the East many Greek artisans went into exile in Italy, where their work is still to be seen. Even while the Kingdom of Sicily was under Norman rule in the 12th century, Byzantine artisans were still active—as the great mosaics of Monreale, Cefalù, and Palermo testify. In northern Italy, especially in Venice, the trade routes to the East and the effects of the Crusades permitted a strong presence of Byzantine art, as the mosaics of the church of Saint Mark's (as well as Byzantine art looted when the Crusaders entered Constantinople in 1204) and the cathedral on the nearby island of Torcello attest. We shall see in later chapters the impact of this artistic presence on panel painting in Italy. Until the revolutionary changes by Cimabue and Giotto at the end of the 13th century, the pervasive influence of this style was so great that Italian painting up to that time is often characterized as Italo-Byzantine.

There is another reason that Byzantine aesthetics seem so changeless over the centuries. From the time of Justinian (and even more so after controversies of the 8th and 9th centuries) Byzantine art was intimately tied to the theology and liturgical practices of the Orthodox church. The use of icons, for example, is not merely a pious practice but a deep-rooted part of the faith. Each year the Orthodox church celebrated a feast commemorating the triumph of the Icon party called the Feast of the Triumph of Orthodoxy.

Art, then, is tied to theological doctrine and liturgical practice. Because of the innate conservatism of the theological tradition, innovation either in theology or in art was discouraged. The ideal of the artist was not to try something new but to infuse his work with a spirit of deep spirituality and unwavering reverence. This art, while extremely conservative, was never stagnant. The artists strove for fidelity to the past as their aesthetic criterion. As art historian André Grabar has noted: "Their role can be compared to that of musical performers in our day, who do not feel that their importance is diminished by the fact that they limit their talent to the interpretation of other people's work, since each interpretation contains original nuances."

This attitude of theological conservatism and aesthetic stability helps explain why, for example, the art of icon painting is considered a holy occupation in the Eastern Orthodox church. Today, when a new Orthodox church is built the congregation may commission from a monk or icon painter the necessary icons for the interior of the church. The expeditions of scholars who went to Saint Catherine's monastery to study the treasures there recall the sadness they felt at the funeral of a monk, Father Demetrios, in 1958. The last icon painter in the monastery, he marked the end of a tradition that stretched back nearly fifteen hundred years.

Travelers to Mount Athos in Greece can visit (with some difficulty) the small monastic communities (sketes) on the south of the peninsula, where monastic icon painters still work at their art. In our century there has been a renaissance of the appreciation of this style of painting. In Greece there has been a modern attempt to purge icon painting of Western influences (especially those of the Renaissance and the Baroque periods) in order to recover a more authentic link with the great Byzantine tradition of the past. Even in the Soviet Union, which for decades was indifferent to its religious heritage, there has been a surge of interest in the treasures of past religious art. This has resulted in careful conservation of the icons in Russia, exhibits of the art in the museums of Russia and abroad, and an intense scholarly study of this heritage.

Byzantine culture was not confined to artistic concerns. We have already seen that Justinian made an important contribution to legal studies. Constantinople also had a literary, philosophical, and theological culture. Although Justinian closed the pagan academies, later Byzantine emperors encouraged humanistic and theological studies. While the links between Constantinople and the West were strained over the centuries, those links did remain. At first a good deal of Greek learning came into the West (after having been lost in the early Middle Ages) through the agency of Arabic sources. The philosophical writings of Aristotle became available to Westerners in the late 12th and early 13th centuries in the form of Latin translations or Arabic translations of the Greek: Aristotle came to the University of Paris from the Mos-

EAST MEETS WEST

The Rise of Islam

Mohammed was born in the Arabian city of Mecca in 570. At about age forty he claimed to have received a series of "recitations" (Arabic *qur'au,* hence their holy book is called the Koran) from the angel Gabriel. These recitations claimed to contain the final revelation of God, who had spoken earlier through both the Jewish prophets and Jesus of Nazareth. Mohammed's preaching was not well accepted in Mecca. In 622 he fled to the city of Medina. That flight (Arabic *hegira*) marks the beginning of the Islamic religion for Muslims; it is from that date that they begin their calendars. Mohammed died in 632, but not before seeing his religious ideas firmly entrenched in Arabia and spreading throughout the Mediterranean.

The word *islam* means "surrender." That gives us a fine clue as to the central message of this faith—that there is one God (Allah) to whom all people owe absolute adoration (surrender); hence the typical image of the follower of Islam at prayer: kneeling with the head bowed to the ground as a sign of surrender.

Islamic faith rests on five pillars:

• The basic profession of faith that "There is no God but God (Allah) and Mohammed is his prophet (better, messenger).
• The obligation of prayer five times a day.
• The observation of the month of fasting called *Ramadan,* with no food or drink taken from sunrise to sunset during that month.
• The giving of alms to the poor and needy.
• The obligation of making a pilgrimage (the *Haj*) to the holy city of Mecca at least once during one's lifetime.

The Koran taught the morality of spreading Islam through holy war. This militant attitude, combined with the attractive simplicity of Islamic beliefs, resulted in the rapid spread of the new religion. Within a few generations after the death of Mohammed Islam was not only the predominant faith of the Middle East but had established itself over most of North Africa and had penetrated into Europe through southern Spain.

---

lem centers of learning in Spain and northern Africa. Not until the 15th century did Greek become a widely known language in the West; Petrarch and Boccaccio in the 14th century had a difficult time finding anyone to teach them the language. By the 15th century this had changed. One factor contributing to the Renaissance love for the classics was the presence of Greek-speaking scholars from Constantinople in Italy.

The importance of this reinfusion of Greek culture can be seen easily enough by looking at the great libraries of 15th-century Italy. Of the nearly four thousand books in the Vatican library listed in a catalogue of 1484, a thousand were in Greek, most of them from Constantinople. The core of the great library of Saint Mark's in Venice was Cardinal Bessarion's collection of Greek books, brought from the East when he went to the Council of Ferrara-Florence to discuss the union of the Greek and Latin churches in 1438. Bessarion brought with him, in addition to his books, a noted Platonic scholar, Genistos Plethon, who lectured on Platonic philosophy for the delighted Florentines. This event prompted Cosimo de' Medici to subsidize the collection, translation, and study of Plato's philosophy under the direction of Marsilio Ficino. Ficino's Platonic Academy, supported by Medici money, became a rallying point for the study of philosophical ideas.

The fall of Constantinople to the Turks in 1453 brought a flood of émigré Greek scholars to the West, in particular to Italy. The presence of these scholars enhanced the already considerable interest in Greek studies. Green refugee scholars soon held chairs at the various *studia* (schools) of the leading Italian cities. These scholars taught language, edited texts, wrote commentaries, and fostered an interest not only in Greek pagan learning but also in the literature of the Greek Fathers of the Church. By the end of the 15th century the famous Aldine press in Venice was publishing a whole series of Greek classics to meet the great demand for such works. This new source of learning and scholarship spread rapidly throughout Western Europe so that by the early 16th century the study of Greek was an ordinary but central part of both humanistic and theological education.

The cultural world view of Justinian's Constantinople is preserved directly in the conservative traditionalism of Orthodox religious art [148] and indirectly by Constantinople's gift of Greek learning to Europe during the Renaissance. The great social and political power of the Byzantine Empire ended in the 15th century although it had been in decline since the end of the 12th century. Only the great monuments remain to remind us of a splendid and opulent culture now gone but once active and vigorous for nearly a thousand years.

Summary

This chapter traces briefly the slow waning of Roman power in the West by a focus on two late Roman writers who are both Christians: Boethius, who wrote in provincial Ravenna, and Augustine, who lived in Roman North Africa.

As the wheel of fortune turned Rome down, Byzantium began its ascent as the center of culture. Our focus was on the great builder and patron of Byzantine culture, the emperor Justinian and his consort, Theodora. The central feature of their reign is its blending of their political power with the Christian church so that church and state became a seamless whole. Christianity, which had been a despised and persecuted sect, now became the official religion of the state.

Byzantine Christianity had a readily recognizable look to it, a look most apparent in its art and architecture. It was an art that was otherworldly and formal and profoundly sacred. A contemporary Orthodox theologian has said that the proper attitude of a Byzantine worshipper is *gazing*. The mosaics and icons of this tradition were meant to be seen as windows through which the devout might see the eternal mysteries of religion. No conscious attempt was made to be innovative in this art. The emphasis was always on deepening the experience of sacred mystery.

The influence of this art was far-reaching. Italo-Byzantine styles of art persisted in the West up to the beginnings of the Italian Renaissance. The same styles entered Russia in the end of the 10th century and still persist. Contemporary students can visit Greek or Russian churches today and see these art forms alive as part of traditional Christian orthodox worship and practice.

Because Byzantium (centered in the city of Constantinople) was Greek-speaking, the culture of ancient Greece was kept alive in that center until the middle of the 15th century, when the city fell to the Ottoman Turks. The removal of much of that culture to the West was a strong influence on the development of the Renaissance, as we shall see in subsequent chapters.

One other factor to be noted in this chapter is the rise of Islam. Islam grew in the 7th century to be a shaping force on Western culture both because it supplanted traditional Roman/Christian areas of influence in North Africa and in the Middle East (especially the Holy Land) and because the growth of this alternative culture would exert pressure on Europe as it penetrated into the Iberian peninsula of present-day Spain and Portugal. That penetration would have both political consequences and a vast cultural influence on the West.

Pronunciation Guide

Anthemius: An-THEE-me-us
Boethius: Bow-A-thee-us
Galla Placidia: Gala Plah-SID-e-ah
Hagia Sophia: Ha-GE-ah So-FEE-ah
Honorius: Ho-NOR-e-us
John Chrysostom: Jon CHRIS-o-stam

Justinian: Jus-TIN-e-an
Maximian: Max-IM-e-an
Pantocrater: Pan-TAW-craw-ter [also: Pan-TOE-crater]
Ravenna: Raw-VEN-ah
San Apollinare: Sawn Ah-pole-in-ARE-a
San Vitale: Sawn Vee-TALL-a
Theodora: Thee-ah-DOOR-ah
Theodoric: Thee-AH-door-ick
Tribonian: Tree-BONE-e-an

Exercises

1. Augustine understood the word *confessions* to mean both an admission of sin and a statement of belief. Why is that term so useful and correct for an autobiography? Do most modern autobiographies constitute a confession in Augustine's sense of the term?
2. In the *City of God* Augustine defines peace as "the tranquillity of order." What does he mean? Is that definition a good one?
3. The outstanding art of the Byzantine period is the mosaic. What made mosaic such a desirable art form for the period? What do you see as its limitations?
4. Take a long look at the Ravenna mosaics of Justinian and Theodora and their court. What political and social values show through in the composition of the scenes, taken as a whole?
5. Look carefully at the various depictions of Christ found in Byzantine mosaics and icons. What religious values are underscored in those depictions? What values are neglected?
6. Define the term *icon* and be sure you understand its function in Orthodox Christianity. Is there anything comparable in contemporary art in terms of function?
7. Byzantine art prided itself on not changing its style but in preserving and perfecting it. Is there something to be said for continuity rather than change in artistic styles? What are the more apparent objections to such a philosophy?
8. The Byzantine empire saw and, ultimately, succumbed to the rise of Islam. What are the most obvious points of tension between Islam and the Orthodox church of Byzantium?

Further Reading

Beckwith, John, *The Art of Constantinople.* New York: Phaidon, 1961. A brief survey of Byzantine art from A.D. 330 to 1453 with good illustrations.

Brown, Peter. *Augustine of Hippo: A Biography.* Berkeley, Calif: University of California Press, 1967. Brilliant, definitive, and readable.

Gibbon, Edward. *The Decline and Fall of the Roman Empire.* Many editions; the standard version is in 9 vols., edited by J. Bury in 1914. This monumental work, first published in 1776, is still the single best work on the period of Rome's decline. For a panoramic view of the period in this chapter and an example of how English should be written, it is unparalleled.

Gibson, Margaret (ed.). *Boethius: His Life, Thought, and Influence*. Oxford: Basil Blackwell, 1981. An impressive collection of essays issued on the fifteen-hundredth anniversary of the birth of Boethius.

Grabar, André. *Byzantium: Byzantine Art in the Middle Ages*. London: Methuen, 1966. A sensitive and original study of Byzantine art and culture by an acknowledged expert in the field.

———. *The Golden Age of Justinian*. New York: Odyssey, 1967. A splendid work by one of the best scholars in the field.

MacDonald, William. *Early Christian and Byzantine Architecture*. New York: Braziller, 1967. A handy survey with good photographs and schematics of important buildings.

Sherrard, P. *Constantinople*. Oxford: Oxford University Press, 1965. A study important for its historical learning.

Simson, Otto von. *The Sacred Fortress*. Chicago: University of Chicago Press, 1948. The best book on the artistic heritage of Ravenna.

Talbot Rice, David, and Tamara Talbot Rice. *Icons and Their History*. London: Thames and Hudson, 1974. Fine scholarship with good bibliographies and beautiful plates.

Vidal, Gore. *Julian*. New York: Vintage, 1977. This novel, originally published in 1964, is a brilliant evocation of Christianity and Classicism in conflict toward the end of the Roman Empire.

Ware, Timothy. *The Orthodox Church*. Baltimore: Penguin, 1969. A reliable, nontechnical survey.

Reading Selections

Saint Augustine, *Confessions*

This selection from the Confessions *recounts the conversion experience of Augustine with the famous "garden scene" and then the subsequent conversation that Augustine had with his mother Monica as they await a ship at the Roman port of Ostia to take them back to their native North Africa. Monica dies before their departure which adds a sad note to this great religious conversation that the two had as they looked out over the port itself.*

from Book VIII

11

This was the nature of my sickness. I was in torment, reproaching myself more bitterly than ever as I twisted and turned in my chain. I hoped that my chain might be broken once and for all, because it was only a small thing that held me now. All the same it held me. And you, O Lord, never ceased to watch over my secret heart. In your stern mercy you lashed me with the twin scourge of fear and shame in case I should give way once more and the worn and slender remnant of my chain should not be broken but gain new strength and bind me all the faster. In my heart I kept saying "Let it be now, let it be now!," and merely by saying this I was on the point of making the resolution. I was on the point of making it, but I did not succeed. Yet I did not fall back into my old state. I stood on the brink of resolution, waiting to take fresh breath. I tried again and came a little nearer to my goal, and then a little nearer still, so that I could almost reach out and grasp it. But I did not reach it. I could not reach out to it or grasp it, because I held back from the step by which I should die to death and become alive to life. My lower instincts, which had taken firm hold of me, were stronger than the higher, which were untried. And the closer I came to the moment which was to mark the great change in me, the more I shrank from it in horror. But it did not drive me back or turn me from my purpose: it merely left me hanging in suspense.

I was held back by mere trifles, the most paltry inanities, all my old attachments. They plucked at my garment of flesh and whispered, "Are you going to dismiss us? From this moment we shall never be with you again, for ever and ever. From this moment you will never again be allowed to do this thing or that, for evermore." What was it, my God, that they meant when they whispered "this thing or that?" Things so sordid and so shameful that I beg you in your mercy to keep the soul of your servant free from them! These voices, as I heard them, seemed less than half as loud as they had been before. They no longer barred my way, blatantly contradictory, but their mutterings seemed to reach me from behind, as though they were stealthily plucking at my back, trying to make me turn my head when I wanted to go forward. Yet, in my state of indecision, they kept me from tearing myself away, from shaking myself free of them and leaping across the barrier to the other side, where you were calling me. Habit was too strong for me when it asked, "Do you think you can live without these things?"

But by now the voice of habit was very faint. I had turned my eyes elsewhere, and while I stood trembling at the barrier, on the other side I could see the chaste beauty of Continence in all her serene, unsullied joy, as she modestly beckoned me to cross over and to hesitate no more. She stretched out loving hands to welcome and embrace me, holding up a host of good examples to my sight. With her were countless boys and girls, great numbers of the young and people of all ages, staid widows and women still virgins in old age. And in their midst was Continence herself, not barren but a fruitful mother of children, of joys born of you, O Lord, her Spouse. She smiled at me to give me courage, as though she were saying, "Can you not do what these men and these women do? Do you think they find the strength to do it in themselves and not in the Lord their God? It was the Lord their God who gave me to them. Why do you try to stand in your own strength and fail? Cast yourself upon God and have no fear. He will not shrink away and let you fall. Cast yourself upon him without fear, for he will welcome you and cure you of your ills." I was overcome with shame, because I was still listening to the futile mutterings of my lower self and I was still hanging in suspense. And again Continence seemed to say, "Close your ears to the unclean whispers of your body, so that it may be mortified. It tells you of things that delight you, but not such things as the law of the Lord your God has to tell."

In this way I wrangled with myself, in my own heart, about my own self. And all the while Alypius stayed at my side, silently awaiting the outcome of this agitation that was new in me.

12

I probed the hidden depths of my soul and wrung its pitiful secrets from it, and when I mustered them all before the eyes of my heart, a great storm broke within me, bringing with it a great deluge of tears. I stood up and left Alypius so that I might weep and cry to my heart's content, for it occurred to me that tears were best shed in solitude. I moved away far enough to avoid being embarrassed even by his presence. He must have realized what my feelings were, for I suppose I had said something and he had known from the sound of my voice that I was ready to burst into tears. So I stood up and left him where we had been sitting, utterly bewildered. Somehow I flung myself down beneath a fig tree and gave way to the tears which now streamed from my eyes, the sacrifice that is acceptable to you. I had much to say to you, my God, not in these very words but in this strain: *Lord, will you never be content? Must we always taste your vengeance? Forget the long record of our sins.* For I felt that I was still the captive of my sins, and in my misery I kept crying "How long shall I go on saying 'tomorrow, tomorrow'? Why not now? Why not make an end of my ugly sins at this moment?"

I was asking myself these questions, weeping all the while with the most bitter sorrow in my heart, when all at once I heard the sing-song voice of a child in a nearby house. Whether it was the voice of a boy or a girl I cannot say, but again and again it repeated the refrain "Take it and read, take it and read." At this I looked up, thinking hard whether there was any kind of game in which children used to chant words like these, but I could not remember ever hearing them before. I stemmed my flood of tears and stood up, telling myself that this could only be a divine command to open my book of Scripture and read the first passage on which my eyes should fall. For I had heard the story of Antony, and I remembered how he had happened to go into a church while the Gospel was being read and had taken it as a counsel addressed to himself when he heard the words *Go home and sell all that belongs to you. Give it to the poor, and so the treasure you have shall be in heaven; then come back and follow me.* By this divine pronouncement he had at once been converted to you.

So I hurried back to the place where Alypius was sitting, for when I stood up to move away I had put down the book containing Paul's Epistles. I seized it and opened it, and in silence I read the first passage on which my eyes fell: *Not in revelling and drunkenness, not in lust and wantonness, not in quarrels and rivalries. Rather, arm yourselves with the Lord Jesus Christ; spend no more thought on nature and nature's appetites.* I had no wish to read more and no need to do so. For in an instant, as I came to the end of the sentence, it was as though the light of confidence flooded into my heart and all the darkness of doubt was dispelled.

I marked the place with my finger or by some other sign and closed the book. My looks now were quite calm as I told Alypius what had happened to me. He too told me what he had been feeling, which of course I did not know. He asked to see what I had read. I showed it to him and he read on beyond the text which I had read. I did not know what followed, but it was this: *Find room among you for a man of overdelicate conscience.* Alypius applied this to himself and told me so. This admonition was enough to give him strength, and without suffering the distress of hesitation he made his resolution and took this good purpose to himself. And it very well suited his moral character, which had long been far, far better than my own.

Then we went in and told my mother, who was overjoyed. And when we went on to describe how it had all happened, she was jubilant with triumph and glorified you, *who are powerful enough, and more than powerful enough, to carry out your purpose beyond all our hopes and dreams.* For she saw that you had granted her far more than she used to ask in her tearful prayers and plaintive lamentations. You converted me to yourself, so that I no longer desired a wife or placed any hope in this world but stood firmly upon the rule of faith, where you had shown me to her in a dream so many years before. And you *turned her sadness into rejoicing,* into joy far fuller than her dearest wish, far sweeter and more chaste than any she had hoped to find in children begotten of my flesh.

from **Book IX**

10

Not long before the day on which she was to leave this life—you knew which day it was to be, O Lord, though we did not—my mother and I were alone, leaning from a window which overlooked the garden in the courtyard of the house where we were staying at Ostia. We were waiting there after our long and tiring journey, away from the crowd, to refresh ourselves before our sea-voyage. I believe that what I am going to tell happened through the secret working of your providence. For we were talking alone together and our conversation was serene and joyful. *We had forgotten what we had left behind and were intent on what lay before us.* In the presence of Truth, which is yourself, we were wondering what the eternal life of the saints would be like, that life which *no eye has seen, no ear has heard, no human heart conceived.* But we laid the lips of our hearts to the heavenly stream that flows from your fountain, *the source of all life* which is *in you,* so that as far as it was in our power to do so we might be sprinkled with its waters and in some sense reach an understanding of this great mystery.

Our conversation led us to the conclusion that no bodily pleasure, however great it might be and whatever earthly light might shed lustre upon it, was worthy of comparison, or even of mention, beside the happiness of the life of the saints. As the flame of love burned stronger in us and raised us higher towards the eternal God, our thoughts ranged over the whole compass of material things in their various degrees, up to the heavens themselves, from which the sun and the moon and the stars shine down upon the earth. Higher still we climbed, thinking and speaking all the while in wonder at all that you have made. At length we came to our own souls and passed beyond them to that place of everlasting plenty, where you feed Israel for ever with the food of truth. There life is that Wisdom by which all these things that we know are made, all things that ever have been and all that are yet to be. But that Wisdom is not made: it is as it has always been and as it will be for ever—or, rather, I should not say that it *has been* or *will be,* for it simply *is,* because eternity is not in the past or in the future. And while we spoke of the eternal Wisdom, longing for it and straining for it with all the strength of our hearts, for one fleeting instant we reached out and touched it. Then with a sigh, leaving *our spiritual harvest* bound to it, we returned to the sound of our own speech, in which each word has a beginning and an ending—far, far different from your Word, our

Lord, who abides in himself for ever, yet never grows old and gives new life to all things.

And so our discussion went on. Suppose, we said, that the tumult of a man's flesh were to cease and all that his thoughts can conceive, of earth, of water, and of air, should no longer speak to him; suppose that the heavens and even his own soul were silent, no longer thinking of itself but passing beyond; suppose that his dreams and the visions of his imagination spoke no more and that every tongue and every sign and all that is transient grew silent—for all these things have the same message to tell, if only we can hear it, and their message is this: We did not make ourselves, but he who abides for ever made us. Suppose, we said, that after giving us this message and bidding us listen to him who made them, they fell silent and he alone should speak to us, not through them but in his own voice, so that we should hear him speaking, not by any tongue of the flesh or by an angel's voice, not in the sound of thunder or in some veiled parable, but in his own voice, the voice of the one whom we love in all these created things; suppose that we heard him himself, with none of these things between ourselves and him, just as in that brief moment my mother and I had reached out in thought and touched the eternal Wisdom which abides over all things; suppose that this state were to continue and all other visions of things inferior were to be removed, so that this single vision entranced and absorbed the one who beheld it and enveloped him in inward joys in such a way that for him life was eternally the same as that instant of understanding for which we had longed so much—would not this be what we are to understand by the words *Come and share the joy of your Lord?* But when is it to be? Is it to be when *we all rise again, but not all of us will undergo the change?*

This was the purport of our talk, though we did not speak in these precise words or exactly as I have reported them. Yet you know, O Lord, that as we talked that day, the world, for all its pleasures, seemed a paltry place compared with the life that we spoke of. And then my mother said, "My son, for my part I find no further pleasure in this life. What I am still to do or why I am here in the world, I do not know, for I have no more to hope for on this earth. There was one reason, and one alone, why I wished to remain a little longer in this life, and that was to see you a Catholic Christian before I died. God has granted my wish and more besides, for I now see you as his servant, spurning such happiness as the world can give. What is left for me to do in this world?"

11

I scarcely remember what answer I gave her. It was about five days after this, or not much more, that she took to her bed with a fever. One day during her illness she had a fainting fit and lost consciousness for a short time. We hurried to her bedside, but she soon regained consciousness and looked up at my brother and me as we stood beside her. With a puzzled look she asked, "Where was I?" Then watching us closely as we stood there speechless with grief, she said, "You will bury your mother here." I said nothing, trying hard to hold back my tears, but my brother said something to the effect that he wished for her sake that she would die in her own country, not abroad. When she heard this, she looked at him anxiously and her eyes reproached him for his worldly thoughts. She turned to me and said, "See how he talks!" and then, speaking to both of us, she went on, "It does not matter where you bury my body. Do not let that worry you! All I ask of you is that, wherever you may be, you should remember me at the altar of the Lord."

Although she hardly had the strength to speak, she managed to make us understand her wishes and then fell silent, for her illness was becoming worse and she was in great pain. But I was thinking of your gifts, O God. Unseen by us you plant them like seeds in the hearts of your faithful and they grow to bear wonderful fruits. This thought filled me with joy and I thanked you for your gifts, for I had always known, and well remembered now, my mother's great anxiety to be buried beside her husband's body in the grave which she had provided and prepared for herself. Because they had lived in the greatest harmony, she had always wanted this extra happiness. She had wanted it to be said of them that, after her journeyings across the sea, it had been granted to her that the earthly remains of husband and wife should be joined as one and covered by the same earth. How little the human mind can understand God's purpose! I did not know when it was that your good gifts had borne their full fruit and her heart had begun to renounce this vain desire, but I was both surprised and pleased to find that it was so. And yet, when we talked at the window and she asked, "What is left for me to do in this world?," it was clear that she had no desire to die in her own country. Afterwards I also heard that one day during our stay at Ostia, when I was absent, she had talked in a motherly way to some of my friends and had spoken to them of the contempt of this life and the blessings of death. They were astonished to find such courage in a woman—it was your gift to her, O Lord—and asked whether she was not frightened at the thought of leaving her body so far from her own country. "Nothing is far from God," she replied, "and I need have no fear that he will not know where to find me when he comes to raise me to life at the end of the world."

And so on the ninth day of her illness, when she was fifty-six and I was thirty-three, her pious and devoted soul was set free from the body.

Augustine, The City of God

This selection is from Augustine's massive meditation on history called The City of God. *Here Augustine meditates on a perennial subject for all people: the character of peace in both its personal and social context. This great reflection on peace is all the more compelling because it was written by Augustine against the background of the barbarian invasions of Europe and Roman North Africa as well as his own shock at the sack of the city of Rome, the occasion for his writing of this book in the first place.*

7. Human society divided by differences of language. The misery of war, even when just

After the city or town comes the world, which the philosophers reckon as the third level of human society. They begin with the household, proceed to the city, and then arrive at the world. Now the world, being like a confluence of waters, is obviously more full of danger than the other communities by reason of its greater size. To begin with, on this level the diversity of languages separates man from man. For if two men meet, and are forced by some compelling reason not to pass on but to stay in company, then if neither knows the other's language, it is easier for dumb animals, even of different kinds, to associate together than these men, although both are human beings. For when men cannot communicate their thoughts to each other, simply because of difference of language, all the similarity of their common human nature is of no avail to unite them in fellowship. So true is this that a man would be more cheerful with his dog for company than with a foreigner. I shall be told that the Imperial City has been at pains to impose on conquered peoples not only her yoke but her language also, as a bond of peace and fellowship, so that there should be no lack of interpreters but even a profusion of them. True; but think of the cost of this achievement! Consider the scale of those wars, with all that slaughter of human beings, all the human blood that was shed!

Those wars are now past history; and yet the misery of these evils is not yet ended. For although there has been, and still is, no lack of enemies among foreign nations, against whom wars have always been waged, and are still being waged, yet the very extent of the Empire has given rise to wars of a worse kind, namely, social and civil wars, by which mankind is more lamentably disquieted either when fighting is going on in the hope of bringing hostilities eventually to a peaceful end, or when there are fears that hostilities will break out again. If I were to try to describe, with an eloquence worthy of the subject, the many and multifarious disasters, the dour and dire necessities, I could not possibly be adequate to the theme, and there would be no end to this protracted discussion. But the wise man, they say, will wage just wars. Surely, if he remembers that he is a human being, he will rather lament the fact that he is faced with the necessity of waging just wars; for if they were not just, he would not have to engage in them, and consequently there would be no wars for a wise man. For it is the injustice of the opposing side that lays on the wise man the duty of waging wars; and this injustice is assuredly to be deplored by a human being, since it is the injustice of human beings, even though no necessity for war should arise from it. And so everyone who reflects with sorrow on such grievous evils, in all their horror and cruelty, must acknowledge the misery of them. And yet a man who experiences such evils, or even thinks about them, without heartfelt grief, is assuredly in a far more pitiable condition, if he thinks himself happy simply because he has lost all human feeling.

8. The friendship of good men can never be carefree, because of this life's dangers

If we are spared that kind of ignorance, akin to madness, which is a common affliction in the wretched condition of this life, an ignorance which leads men to believe an enemy to be a friend, or a friend an enemy, what consolation have we in this human society, so replete with mistaken notions and distressing anxieties, except the unfeigned faith and mutual affections of genuine, loyal friends? Yet the more friends we have and the more dispersed they are in different places, the further and more widely extend our fears that some evil may befall them from among all the mass of evils of this present world. For not only are we troubled and anxious because they may be afflicted by famine, war, disease, or captivity, fearing that in slavery they may suffer evils beyond our powers of imagination; there is the much more bitter fear, that their friendship be changed into treachery, malice and baseness. And when such things do happen (and the more numerous our friends, the more often they happen) and the news is brought to our ears, who, except one who has this experience, can be aware of the burning sorrow that ravages our hearts? Certainly we would rather hear that our friends were dead, although this also we could not hear without grief.

For if their life brought us the consoling delights of friendship, how could it be that their death should bring us no sadness? Anyone who forbids such sadness must forbid, if he can, all friendly conversation, must lay a ban on all friendly feeling or put a stop to it, must with a ruthless insensibility break the ties of all human relationships, or else decree that they must only be engaged upon so long as they inspire no delight in a man's soul. But if this is beyond all possibility, how can it be that a man's death should not be bitter if his life is sweet to us? For this is why the grief of a heart that has not lost human feeling is a thing like some wound or ulcer, and our friendly words of consolation are the healing application. And it does not follow that there is nothing to be healed simply because the nobler a man's spirit the quicker and easier the cure.

It is true, then, that the life of mortals is afflicted, sometimes more gently, sometimes more harshly, by the death of those most dear to us, and especially the death of those whose functions are necessary for human society; and yet we should prefer to hear, or even to witness, the death of those we love, than to become aware that they have fallen from faith or from moral conflict—that is, that they have died in their very soul. The earth is full of this vast mass of evils; that is why we find this in Scripture: 'Is man's life on earth anything but temptation?' And why the Lord himself says, 'Alas for the world, because of these obstacles'; and again, 'Because iniquity will increase beyond measure, the love of many will grow cold.' The result of this situation is that when good men die who are our friends we rejoice for them; and though their death brings us sadness, we find our surer consolation in this, that they have been spared those evils by which in this life even good men are crushed or corrupted, or at least are in danger of both these disasters.

9. The friendship of the holy angels, obscured by the deceit of demons

Our relationship with the society of the holy angels is quite another matter. Those philosophers, we observe, who insisted that the gods are our friends placed this angelic fellowship on the fourth level, as they proceeded in their scheme from the earth to the universe, intending by this method to include, in some fashion, even heaven itself. Now, with regard to the angels, we have, it is true, no manner of fear that such friends may bring us sorrow, either by their death or by their degradation. But they do not mix with us on the same familiar footing as do men—and this in itself is one of the disappointments involved in this life—and Satan, as Scripture tells us, transforms himself at times to masquerade as an angel of light, to tempt those men who are in need of this kind of training, or men who deserve to be thus deluded. Hence God's great mercy is needed to prevent anyone from supposing that he is enjoying the friendship of good angels when in fact it is evil demons that he has as his false friends, and when he thus suffers from the enmity of those whose harmfulness is in proportion to their cunning and deceit. In fact, where is God's great mercy needed if not by men in their most pitiable state, where they are so weighed down by ignorance that they are readily deluded by the pretences of those spirits? Now those philosophers in the ungodly city alleged that the gods were their friends; but it is quite certain that they had fallen in with these malignant demons, the powers to whom that city itself is wholly subjected, and in whose company it will suffer everlasting punishment. This is made quite clear by those beings who are worshipped in that city. It is revealed unmistakably by the sacred, or rather sacrilegious, rites by which the pagans think it right to worship them, and by the filthy shows by which they think those demons must be propitiated; and it is the demons themselves who suggest, and indeed demand, the performance of such vile obscenities.

10. The reward of victory over temptation

However, not even the saints and the faithful worshippers of the one true and supreme God enjoy exemption from the deceptions of the demons and from their multifarious temptations. In fact, in this situation of weakness and in these times of evil such anxiety is even not without its use in leading them to seek, with more fervent longing, that state of serenity where peace is utterly complete and assured. For there the gifts of nature, that is, the gifts bestowed on our nature by the Creator of all natures, will be not only good but also everlasting; and this applies not only to the spirit, which is healed by wisdom, but also to the body, which will be renewed by resurrection. There the virtues will not be engaged in conflict with any kind of vice or evil; they will be possessed of the reward of victory, the everlasting peace which no adversary can disturb. This is indeed the ultimate bliss, the end of ultimate fulfilment that knows no destructive end. Here in this world we are called blessed, it is true, when we enjoy peace, however little may be the peace—the peace of a good life—which can be enjoyed here. And yet such blessedness as this life affords proves to be utter misery when compared with that final bliss. And so, when we enjoy here, if we live rightly, such peace as can be the portion of mortal men under the conditions of mortality, virtue rightly uses the blessings of peace, and even when we do not possess that peace, virtue turns to a good use even the ills that man endures. But virtue is truly virtue when it refers all the good things of which it makes good use, all its achievements in making good use of good things and evil things, and when it refers itself also, to that end where our peace shall be so perfect and so great as to admit of neither improvement nor increase.

11. The bliss of everlasting peace, which is the fulfilment of the saints

It follows that we could say of peace, as we have said of eternal life, that it is the final fulfilment of all our goods; especially in view of what is said in a holy psalm about the City of God, the subject of this laborious discussion. These are the words: 'Praise the Lord, O Jerusalem; praise your God, O Sion: for he has strengthened the bolts of your gates; he has blessed your sons within your walls; he has made your frontiers peace.' Now when the bolts of her gates have been strengthened, that means that no one will any more enter or leave that City. And this implies that we must take her 'frontiers' (or 'ends') to stand here for the peace whose finality I am trying to establish. In fact, the name of the City itself has a mystic significance, for 'Jerusalem', as I have said already, means 'vision of peace'.

But the word 'peace' is freely used in application to the events of this mortal state, where there is certainly no eternal life; and so I have preferred to use the term 'eternal life' instead of 'peace' in describing the end of this City, where its Ultimate Good will be found. About this end the Apostle says, 'But now you have been set free from sin and have become the servants of God; and so you have your profit, a profit leading to sanctification, and the end is everlasting life.' On the other hand, the life of the wicked may also be taken to be eternal life by those who have no familiarity with the holy Scriptures. They may follow some of the philosophers in thinking in terms of the immortality of the soul, or they may be influenced by our Christian belief in the endless punishment of the ungodly, who obviously cannot be tortured for ever without also living for ever. Consequently, in order to make it easier for everyone to understand our meaning, we have to say that the end of this City, whereby it will possess its Supreme Good, may be called either 'peace in life everlasting' or 'life everlasting in peace'. For peace is so great a good that even in relation to the affairs of earth and of our mortal state no word ever falls more gratefully upon the ear, nothing is desired with greater longing, in fact, nothing better can be found. So if I decide to discourse about it at somewhat greater length, I shall not, I think, impose a burden on my readers, not only because I shall be speaking of the end of the City which is the subject of this work, but also because of the delightfulness of peace, which is dear to the heart of all mankind.

12. Peace is the instinctive aim of all creatures, and is even the ultimate purpose of war

Anyone who joins me in an examination, however slight, of human affairs, and the human nature we all share, recognizes that just as there is no man who does not wish for joy, so there is no man who does not wish for peace. Indeed, even when men choose war, their only wish is for victory; which shows that their desire in fighting is for peace with glory. For what is victory but the conquest of the opposing side? And when this is achieved, there will be peace. Even wars, then, are waged with peace as their object, even when they are waged by those who are concerned to exercise their warlike prowess, either in command or in the actual fighting. Hence it is an established fact that peace is the desired end of war. For every man is in quest of peace, even in waging war, whereas no one is in quest of war when making peace. In fact, even when men wish a present state of peace to be disturbed they do so not because they hate peace, but because they desire the present peace to be exchanged for one that suits their wishes. Thus their desire is not that there should not be peace but that it should be the kind of peace they wish for. Even in the extreme case when they have separated themselves from others by sedition, they cannot achieve their aim unless they maintain some sort of semblance of peace with their confederates in conspiracy. Moreover, even robbers, to ensure greater efficiency and security in their assaults on the peace of the rest of mankind, desire to preserve peace with their associates.

Indeed, one robber may be so unequalled in strength and so wary of having anyone to share his plans that he does not trust any associate, but plots his crimes and achieves his successes by himself, carrying off his booty after overcoming and dispatching such as he can; yet even so he maintains some kind of shadow of peace, at least with those whom he cannot kill, and from whom he wishes to conceal his activities. At the same time, he is anxious, of course, to be at peace in his own home, with his wife and children and any other members of his household; without doubt he is delighted to have them obedient to his beck and call. For if this does not happen, he is indignant; he scolds and punishes; and, if need be, he employs savage measures to impose on his household a peace which, he feels, cannot exist unless all the other elements in the same domestic society are subject to one head; and this head, in his own home, is himself. Thus, if he were offered the servitude of a larger number, of a city, maybe, or a whole nation, on the condition that they should all show the same subservience he had demanded from his household, then he would no longer lurk like a brigand in his hide-out;

he would raise himself on high as a king for all to see—although the same greed and malignity would persist in him.

We see, then, that all men desire to be at peace with their own people, while wishing to impose their will upon those people's lives. For even when they wage war on others, their wish is to make those opponents their own people, if they can—to subject them, and to impose on them their own conditions of peace.

Let us, however, suppose such a man as is described in the verse of epic legends, a creature so unsociable and savage that they perhaps preferred to call him a semi-human rather than a human being. Now although his kingdom was the solitude of a dreadful cavern, and although he was so unequalled in wickedness that a name was found for him derived from that quality (he was called Cacus, and *kakos* is the Greek word for 'wicked'); although he had no wife with whom to exchange endearments, no children to play with when little or to give orders to when they were a little bigger, no friends with whom to enjoy a chat, not even his father, Vulcan (he was happier than his father only in this important respect—that he did not beget another such monster as himself); although he never gave anything to anyone, but took what he wanted from anyone he could and removed, when he could, anyone he wished to remove; despite all this, in the very solitude of his cave, the floor of which, in the poet's description

reeked ever with the blood of recent slaughter

his only desire was for a peace in which no one should disturb him, and no man's violence, or the dread of it, should trouble his repose. Above all, he desired to be at peace with his own body; and in so far as he achieved this, all was well with him. He gave the orders and his limbs obeyed. But his mortal nature rebelled against him because of its insatiable desires, and stirred up the civil strife of hunger, intending to dissociate the soul from the body and to exclude it; and then he sought with all possible haste to pacify that mortal nature, and to that end he ravished, murdered, and devoured. And thus, for all his monstrous savagery, his aim was still to ensure peace, for the preservation of his life, by these monstrous and savage methods. Accordingly, if he had been willing to maintain, in relation to others also, the peace he was so busily concerned to preserve in his own case and in himself, he would not have been called wicked, or a monster, or semi-human. Or if it was his outward appearance and his belching of murky flames that frightened away human companions, it may be that it was not lust for inflicting injury but the necessity of preserving his life that made him so savage. Perhaps, after all, he never existed or, more probably, he was not like the description given by poetic fantasy; for if Cacus had not been excessively blamed, Hercules would have received inadequate praise. And therefore the existence of such a man, or rather semi-human, is discredited, as are many similar poetical fictions.

We observe, then, that even the most savage beasts, from whom Cacus derived the wild-beast side of his nature (he was in fact also called a semi-beast), safeguard their own species by a kind of peace, by coition, by begetting and bearing young, by cherishing them and rearing them; even though most of them are not gregarious but solitary—not, that is, like sheep, deer, doves, starlings, and bees, but like lions, wolves, foxes, eagles and owls. What tigress does not gently purr over her cubs, and subdue her fierceness to caress them? What kite, however solitary as he hovers over his prey, does not find a mate, build a nest, help to hatch the eggs, rear the young birds, and, as we may say, preserve with the mother of his family a domestic society as peaceful as he can make it? How much more strongly is a human being drawn by the laws of his nature, so to speak, to enter upon a fellowship with all his fellow-men and to keep peace with them, as far as lies in him. For even the wicked when they go to war do so to defend the peace of their own people, and desire to make all men their own people, if they can, so that all men and all things might together be subservient to one master. And how could that happen, unless they should consent to a peace of his dictation either through love or through fear? Thus pride is a perverted imitation of God. For pride hates a fellowship of equality under God, and seeks to impose its own dominion on fellow men, in place of God's rule. This means that it hates the just peace of God, and loves its own peace of injustice. And yet it cannot help loving peace of some kind or other. For no creature's perversion is so contrary to nature as to destroy the very last vestiges of its nature.

It comes to this, then; a man who has learnt to prefer right to wrong and the rightly ordered to the perverted, sees that the peace of the unjust, compared with the peace of the just, is not worthy even of the name of peace. Yet even what is perverted must of necessity be in, or derived from, or associated with— that is, in a sense, at peace with—some part of the order of things among which it has its being or of which it consists. Otherwise it would not exist at all. For instance if anyone were to hang upside-down, this position of the body and arrangement of the limbs is undoubtedly perverted, because what should be on top, according to the dictates of nature, is underneath, and what nature intends to be underneath is

on top. This perverted attitude disturbs the peace of the flesh, and causes distress for that reason. For all that, the breath is at peace with its body and is busily engaged for its preservation; that is why there is something to endure the pain. And even if the breath is finally driven from the body by its distresses, still, as long as the framework of the limbs holds together, what remains retains a kind of peace among the bodily parts; hence there is still something to hang there. And in that the earthly body pulls towards the earth, and pulls against the binding rope that holds it suspended, it tends towards the position of its own peace, and by what might be called the appeal of its weight, it demands a place where it may rest. And so even when it is by now lifeless and devoid of all sensation it does not depart from the peace of its natural position, either while possessed of it or while tending towards it. Again, if treatment with embalming fluids is applied to prevent the dissolution and disintegration of the corpse in its present shape, a kind of peace still connects the parts with one another and keeps the whole mass fixed in its earthly condition, an appropriate, and therefore a peaceable state.

On the other hand, if no preservative treatment is given, and the body is left for nature to take its course, there is for a time a kind of tumult in the corpse of exhalations disagreeable and offensive to our senses (for that is what we smell in putrefaction), which lasts until the body unites with the elements of the world as, little by little, and particle by particle, it vanishes into their peace. Nevertheless, nothing is in any way removed, in this process, from the control of the laws of the supreme Creator and Ruler who directs the peace of the whole scheme of things. For although minute animals are produced in the corpse of a larger animal, those little bodies, each and all of them, by the same law of their Creator, are subservient to their little souls in the peace that preserves their lives. And even if the flesh of dead animals is devoured by other animals, in whatever direction it is taken, with whatever substances it is united, into whatever substances it is converted and transformed, it still finds itself subject to the same laws which are diffused throughout the whole of matter for the preservation of every mortal species, establishing peace by a harmony of congruous elements.

13. The peace of the universe maintained through all disturbances by a law of nature: the individual attains, by God's ordinance, to the state he has deserved by his free choice

The peace of the body, we conclude, is a tempering of the component parts in duly ordered proportion; the peace of the irrational soul is a duly ordered repose of the appetites; the peace of the rational soul is the duly ordered agreement of cognition and action. The peace of body and soul is the duly ordered life and health of a living creature; peace between mortal man and God is an ordered obedience, in faith, in subjection to an everlasting law; peace between men is an ordered agreement of mind with mind; the peace of a home is the ordered agreement among those who live together about giving and obeying orders; the peace of the Heavenly City is a perfectly ordered and perfectly harmonious fellowship in the enjoyment of God, and a mutual fellowship in God; the peace of the whole universe is the tranquility of order—and order is the arrangement of things equal and unequal in a pattern which assigns to each its proper position.

It follows that the wretched, since, in so far as they are wretched, they are obviously not in a state of peace, lack the tranquillity of order, a state in which there is no disturbance of mind. In spite of that, because their wretchedness is deserved and just, they cannot be outside the scope of order. They are not, indeed, united with the blessed; yet it is by the law of order that they are sundered from them. And when they are free from disturbance of mind, they are adjusted to their situation, with however small a degree of harmony. Thus they have amongst them some tranquillity of order, and therefore some peace. But they are still wretched just because, although they enjoy some degree of serenity and freedom from suffering, they are not in a condition where they have the right to be serene and free from pain. They are yet more wretched, however, if they are not at peace with the law by which the natural order is governed. Now when they suffer, their peace is disturbed in the part where they suffer; and yet peace still continues in the part which feels no burning pain, and where the natural frame is not broken up. Just as there is life, then, without pain, whereas there can be no pain when there is no life, so there is peace without any war, but no war without some degree of peace. This is not a consequence of war as such, but of the fact that war is waged by or within persons who are in some sense natural beings—for they could have no kind of existence without some kind of peace as the condition of their being.

There exists, then, a nature in which there is no evil, in which, indeed, no evil can exist; but there cannot exist a nature in which there is no good. Hence not even the nature of the Devil himself is evil, in so far as it is a nature; it is perversion that makes it evil. And so the Devil did not stand firm in the truth, and yet he did not escape the judgement of the truth. He did not continue in the tranquillity of order; but that did not mean that he escaped from the power of the imposer of order. The good that God imparts, which the Devil has in his nature, does not withdraw him from God's justice by which his punishment is ordained. But God, in punishing, does not chastise the good which he created, but the evil which the Devil has committed. And God does not take away all that he gave to that nature; he takes something, and yet he leaves something, so that there may be some being left to feel pain at the deprivation.

Now this pain is in itself evidence of the good that was taken away and the good that was left. In fact, if no good has been left there could have been no grief for lost good. For a sinner is in a worse state if he rejoices in the loss of righteousness; but a sinner who feels anguish, though he may gain no good from his anguish, is at least grieving at the loss of salvation. And since righteousness and salvation are both good, and the loss of any good calls for grief rather than for joy (assuming that there is no compensation for the loss in the shape of a higher good—for example, righteousness of character is a higher good than health of body), the unrighteous man's grief in his punishment is more appropriate than his rejoicing in sin. Hence, just as delight in the abandonment of good, when a man sins, is evidence of a bad will, so grief at the loss of good, when a man is punished, is evidence of a good nature. For when a man grieves at the loss of the peace of his nature, his grief arises from some remnants of that peace, which ensure that his nature is still on friendly terms with itself. Moreover, it is entirely right that in the last punishment the wicked and ungodly should bewail in their agonies the loss of their 'natural' goods, and realize that he who divested them of these goods with perfect justice is God, whom they despised when with supreme generosity he bestowed them.

God then, created all things in supreme wisdom and ordered them in perfect justice; and in establishing the mortal race of mankind as the greatest ornament of earthly things, he has given to mankind certain good things suitable to this life. These are: temporal peace, in proportion to the short span of a mortal life—the peace that consists in bodily health and soundness, and in fellowship with one's kind; and everything necessary to safeguard or recover this peace—those things, for example, which are appropriate and accessible to our senses: light, speech, air to breathe, water to drink, and whatever is suitable for the feeding and clothing of the body, for the care of the body and the adornment of the person. And all this is granted under the most equitable condition: that every mortal who uses aright such goods, goods designed to serve the peace of mortal men, shall receive goods greater in degree and superior in kind, namely, the peace of immortality, and the glory and honour appropriate to it in a life which is eternal for the enjoyment of God and of one's neighbour in God, whereas he who wrongly uses those mortal goods shall lose them, and shall not receive the blessings of eternal life.

14. The order and law, earthly or heavenly, by which government serves the interests of human society

We see, then, that all man's use of temporal things is related to the enjoyment of earthly peace in the earthly city; whereas in the Heavenly City it is related to the enjoyment of eternal peace. Thus, if we were irrational animals, our only aim would be the adjustment of the parts of the body in due proportion, and the quieting of the appetites—only, that is, the repose of the flesh, and an adequate supply of pleasures, so that bodily peace might promote the peace of the soul. For if bodily peace is lacking, the peace of the irrational soul is also hindered, because it cannot achieve the quieting of its appetites. But the two together promote that peace which is a mutual concord between soul and body, the peace of an ordered life and of health. For living creatures show their love of bodily peace by their avoidance of pain, and by their pursuit of pleasure to satisfy the demands of their appetites they demonstrate their love of peace of soul. In just the same way, by shunning death they indicate quite clearly how great is their love of the peace in which soul and body are harmoniously united.

But because there is in man a rational soul, he subordinates to the peace of the rational soul all that part of his nature which he shares with the beasts, so that he may engage in deliberate thought and act in accordance with this thought, so that he may thus exhibit that ordered agreement of cognition and action which we called the peace of the rational soul. For with this end in view he ought to wish to be spared the distress of pain and grief, the disturbances of desire, the dissolution of death, so that he may come to some profitable knowledge and may order his life and his moral standards in accordance with this knowledge. But he needs divine direction, which he may obey with resolution, and divine assistance that he may obey it freely, to prevent him from falling, in his enthusiasm for knowledge, a victim to some fatal error, through the weakness of the human mind. And so long as he is in this mortal body, he is a pilgrim in a foreign land, away from God; therefore he walks by faith, not by sight. That is why he views all peace, of body or of soul, or of both, in relation to that peace which exists between mortal man and immortal God, so that he may exhibit an ordered obedience in faith in subjection to the everlasting Law.

Now God, our master, teaches two chief precepts, love of God and love of neighbour; and in them man finds three objects for his love: God, himself, and his neighbour; and a man who loves God is not wrong in loving himself. It follows, therefore, that he will be concerned also that his neighbour should love God, since he is told to love his neighbour as himself; and the same is true of his concern for his wife, his children, for the members of his household, and for all other men, so far as is possible. And, for the same end, he will wish his neighbour to be concerned for him, if he happens to need that concern. For this reason he will be at peace, as far as lies in him, with all men, in that peace among men, that ordered harmony; and the basis of this order is the observance of two rules: first, to do no harm to anyone, and, secondly, to help everyone whenever possible. To begin with, therefore, a man has a responsibility for his own household—obviously, both in the order of nature and in the framework of human society, he has easier and more immediate contact with them; he can exercise his concern for them. That is why the Apostle says, 'Anyone who does not take care of his own people, especially those in his own household, is worse than an unbeliever—he is a renegade.' This is where domestic peace starts, the ordered harmony about giving and obeying orders among those who live in the same house. For the orders are given by those who are concerned for the interests of others; thus the husband gives orders to the wife, parents to children, masters to servants. While those who are the objects of this concern obey orders; for example, wives obey husbands, the children obey their parents, the servants their masters. But in the household of the just man who 'lives on the basis of faith' and who is still on pilgrimage, far from that Heavenly City, even those who give orders are the servants of those whom they appear to command. For they do not give orders because of a lust for domination but from a dutiful concern for the interests of others, not with pride in taking precedence over others, but with compassion in taking care of others.

15. Man's natural freedom; and the slavery caused by sin

This relationship is prescribed by the order of nature, and it is in this situation that God created man. For he says, 'Let him have lordship over the fish of the sea, the birds of the sky . . . and all the reptiles that crawl on the earth.' He did not wish the rational being, made in his own image, to have dominion over any but irrational creatures, not man over man, but man over the beasts. Hence the first just men were set up as shepherds of flocks, rather than as kings of men, so that in this way also God might convey the message of what was required by the order of nature, and what was demanded by the deserts of sinners—for it is understood, of course, that the condition of slavery is justly imposed on the sinner. That is why we do not hear of a slave anywhere in the Scriptures until Noah, the just man, punished his son's sin with this word; and so that son deserved this name because of his misdeed, not because of his nature. The origin of the Latin word for slave, *servus,* is believed to be derived from the fact that those who by the laws of war could rightly be put to death by the conquerors, became *servi,* slaves, when they were preserved, receiving this name from their preservation. But even this enslavement could not have happened, if it were not for the deserts of sin. For even when a just war is fought it is in defence of his sin that the other side is contending; and victory, even when the victory falls to the wicked, is a humiliation visited on the conquered by divine judgement, either to correct or to punish their sins. We have a witness to this in Daniel, a man of God, who in captivity confesses to God his own sins and the sins of his people, and in devout grief testifies that they are the cause of that captivity. The first cause of slavery, then, is sin, whereby man was subjected to man in the condition of bondage; and this can only happen by the judgement of God, with whom there is no injustice, and who knows how to allot different punishments according to the deserts of the offenders.

Now, as our Lord above says, 'Everyone who commits sin is sin's slave', and that is why, though many devout men are slaves to unrighteous masters, yet the masters they serve are not themselves free men; 'for when a man is conquered by another he is also bound as a slave to his conqueror.' And obviously it is a happier lot to be slave to a human being than to a lust; and, in fact, the most pitiless domination that devastates the hearts of men, is that exercised by this very lust for domination, to mention no others. However, in that order of peace in which men are subordinate to other men, humility is as salutary for the servants as pride is harmful to the masters. And yet by nature, in the condition in which God created man, no man is the slave either of man or of sin. But it remains true that slavery as a punishment is also ordained by that law which enjoins the preservation of the order of nature, and forbids its disturbance; in fact, if nothing had been done to contravene that law, there would have been nothing to require the discipline of slavery as a punishment. That explains also the Apostle's admonition to slaves, that they should be subject to their masters, and serve them loyally and willingly. What he means is that if they cannot be set free by their masters, they themselves may thus make their slavery, in a sense, free, by serving not with the slyness of fear, but with the fidelity of affection, until all injustice disappears and all human lordship and power is annihilated, and God is all in all.

16. Equity in the relation of master and slave

This being so, even though our righteous fathers had slaves, they so managed the peace of their households as to make a distinction between the situation of children and the condition of slaves in respect of the temporal goods of this life; and yet in the matter of the worship of God—in whom we must place our hope of everlasting goods—they were concerned, with equal affection, for all the members of their household. This is what the order of nature prescribes, so that this is the source of the name *paterfamilias,* a name that has become so generally used that even those who exercise unjust rule rejoice to be called by this title. On the other hand, those who are genuine 'fathers of their household' are concerned for the welfare of all in their households in respect of the worship and service of God, as if they were all their children, longing and praying that they may come to the heavenly home, where it will not be a necessary duty to give orders to men, because it will no longer be a necessary duty to be concerned for the welfare of those who are already in the felicity of that immortal state. But until that home is reached, the fathers have an obligation to exercise the authority of masters greater than the duty of slaves to put up with their condition as servants.

However, if anyone in the household is, through his disobedience, an enemy to the domestic peace, he is reproved by a word, or by a blow, or any other kind of punishment that is just and legitimate, to the extent allowed by human society; but this is for the benefit of the offender, intended to readjust him to the domestic peace from which he had broken away. For just as it is not an act of kindness to help a man, when the effect of the help is to make him lose a greater good, so it is not a blameless act to spare a man, when by so doing you let him fall into a greater sin. Hence the duty of anyone who would be blameless includes not only doing no harm to anyone but also restraining a man from sin or punishing his sin, so that either the man who is chastised may be corrected by his experience, or others may be deterred by his example. Now a man's house ought to be the beginning, or rather a small component part of the city, and every beginning is directed to some end of its own kind, and every component part contributes to the completeness of the whole of which it forms a part. The implication is quite apparent, that domestic peace contributes to the peace of the city—that is, the ordered harmony of those who live together in a house in the matter of giving and obeying orders, contributes to the ordered harmony concerning authority and obedience obtaining among the citizens. Consequently it is fitting that the father of a household should take his rules from the law of the city, and govern his household in such a way that it fits in with the peace of the city.

17. The origin of peace between the heavenly society and the earthly city, and of discord between them

But a household of human beings whose life is not based on faith is in pursuit of an earthly peace based on the things belonging to this temporal life, and on its advantages, whereas a household of human beings whose life is based on faith looks forward to the blessings which are promised as eternal in the future, making use of earthly and temporal things like a pilgrim in a foreign land, who does not let himself be taken in by them or distracted from his course towards God, but rather treats them as supports which help him more easily to bear the burdens of 'the corruptible body which weighs heavy on the soul'; they must on no account be allowed to increase the load. Thus both kinds of men and both kinds of households alike make use of the things essential for this mortal life: but each has its own very different end in making use of them. So also the earthly city, whose life is not based on faith, aims at an earthly peace, and it limits the harmonious agreement of citizens concerning the giving and obeying of orders to the establishment of a kind of compromise between human wills about the things relevant to mortal life. In contrast, the Heavenly City—or rather that part of it which is on pilgrimage in this condition of mortality, and which lives on the basis of faith—must needs make use of this peace also, until this mortal state, for which this kind of peace is essential, passes away. And therefore, it leads what we may call a life of captivity in this earthly city as in a foreign land, although it has already received the promise of redemption, and the gift of the Spirit as a kind of pledge of it; and yet it does not hesitate to obey the laws of the earthly city by which those things which are designed for the support of this mortal life are regulated; and the purpose of this obedience is that, since this mortal condition is shared by both cities, a harmony may be preserved between them in things that are relevant to this condition.

But this earthly city has had some philosophers belonging to it whose theories are rejected by the teaching inspired by God. Either led astray by their own speculation or deluded by demons, these thinkers reached the belief that there are many gods who must be won over to serve human ends, and also that they have, as it were, different departments with different responsibilities attached. Thus the body is the department of one god, the mind that of another; and within the body itself, one god is in charge of the head, another of the neck and so on with each of the separate members. Similarly, within the mind, one is responsible for natural ability, another for learning, another for anger, another for lust; and in the accessories of life there are separate gods over the departments of flocks, grain, wine, oil, forests, coinage, navigation, war and victory, marriage, birth, fertility, and so on. The Heavenly City, in contrast, knows only one God as the object of worship, and decrees, with faithful devotion, that he only is to be served with that service which the Greeks call *latreia*, which is due to God alone. And the result of this difference has been that the Heavenly City could not have laws of religion common with the earthly city, and in defence of her religious laws she was bound to dissent from those who thought differently and to prove a burdensome nuisance to them. Thus she had to endure their anger and hatred, and the assaults of persecution; until at length that City shattered the morale of her adversaries by the terror inspired by her numbers, and by the help she continually received from God.

While this Heavenly City, therefore, is on pilgrimage in this world, she calls out citizens from all nations and so collects a society of aliens, speaking all languages. She takes no account of any difference in customs, laws, and institutions, by which earthly peace is achieved and preserved—not that she annuls or abolishes any of those, rather, she maintains them and follows them (for whatever divergences there are among the diverse nations, those institutions have one single aim—earthly peace), provided that no hindrance is presented thereby to the religion which teaches that the one supreme and true God is to be worshipped. Thus even the Heavenly City in her pilgrimage here on earth makes use of the earthly peace and defends and seeks the compromise between human wills in respect of the provisions relevant to the mortal nature of man, so far as may be permitted without detriment to true religion and piety. In fact, that City relates the earthly peace to the heavenly peace, which is so truly peaceful that it should be regarded as the only peace deserving the name, at least in respect of the rational creation; for this peace is the perfectly ordered and completely harmonious fellowship in the enjoyment of God, and of each other in God. When we arrive at that state of peace, there will be no longer a life that ends in death, but a life that is life in sure and sober truth; there will be no animal body to 'weigh down the soul' in its process of corruption; there will be a spiritual body with no cravings, a body subdued in every part to the will. This peace the Heavenly City possesses in faith while on its pilgrimage, and it lives a life of righteousness, based on this faith, having the attainment of that peace in view in every good action it performs in relation to God, and in relation to a neighbour, since the life of a city is inevitably a social life.

	GENERAL EVENTS	LITERATURE & PHILOSOPHY	ART

EARLY MIDDLE AGES

Rise of the Franks

711 Muslims invade Spain

714–741 Charles Martel, grandfather of Charlemagne, reigns as first ruler of Frankish kingdom

732 Charles Martel defeats Moslems at Battle of Poitiers

741–768 Reign of Pepin the Short, father of Charlemagne

735 Death of Venerable Bede, author of *Ecclesiastical History of the English People* and other religious writings

8th–9th cent. Irish *Book of Kells*

768

Carolingian Period

768 Charlemagne ascends Frankish throne

772–778 Charlemagne's military campaigns against Moslem Emirates

778 Battle of Roncesvalles

c. 790 Charlemagne settles his court at Aachen (Aix-la-Chapelle)

800 Charlemagne crowned Holy Roman emperor at Rome by Pope Leo III

814 Death of Charlemagne

910 Founding of monastery at Cluny

987–996 Reign of Hugh Capet in France ends Carolingian line of succession

after 780 Carolingian minuscule form of lettering developed

781 Charlemagne opens palace school, importing such scholars as Theodulf of Orléans and Alcuin of York

785 Alcuin, *Sacramentary*

after 814 Carolingian monasteries adopt *Rule* of Saint Benedict of Nursia (480–547?)

821 Einhard, *Vita Caroli (Life of Charlemagne)*

Illuminated manuscripts and carved ivories prevalent

c. 775 *Centula Evangeliary* and *Dagulf Psalter*

800–810 *Gospel Book of Charlemagne*

early 9th cent. *Crucifixion Ivory,* done at palace school of Charlemagne

c. 820–830 *Utrecht Psalter*

1000

Romanesque Period

11th cent. Pilgrimages become very popular

1066 Norman invasion of England by William the Conqueror

1096–1099 First Crusade; capture of Jerusalem by Christians

c. 1098 *Song of Roland,* *chanson de geste* inspired by Battle of Roncesvalles, written down after 300 yrs. of oral tradition

12th cent. Development of liturgical drama

c. 1125 Saint Bernard of Clairvaux denounces extravagances of Romanesque decoration

1100–1125 Sculptures at Abbey Church of Saint-Pierre, Moissac

1120–1132 Sculptures at Abbey Church of La Madeleine, Vézelay

c. 1140 Portal sculptures at Priory Church, Saint-Gilles-du-Gard

1140

GOTHIC PERIOD

1165 Charlemagne canonized at Cathedral of Aachen

1187 Sultan Saladin conquers Jerusalem

1202–1204 Fourth Crusade; sack of Constantinople by crusaders

1270 Eighth Crusade

1291 Fall of Acre, last Christian stronghold in Holy Land

14th–15th cent. Play cycles performed outside the church; *Everyman* (15th cent.), morality play

c. 1165 Reliquary of Charlemagne and candelabra commissioned for Aachen cathedral by Frederick Barbarossa for canonization of Charlemagne

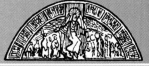

1400

7

The Age of Charlemagne

Monastic complexes become important centers in rural life

c. 795 Palace and chapel of Charlemagne at Aachen

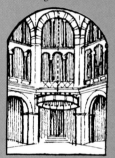

c. 820 Plan for Abbey of Saint Gall, the "ideal" monastery

c. 800 Monasteries become centers for encouragement of sacred music; theoretical study of music at Charlemagne's palace school

9th cent. Use of semi-dramatic trope in liturgical music; *Quem Quaeritis* trope introduced into Easter Mass

c. 810 Gregorian plain chant *(cantus planus)* obligatory in Charlemagne's churches

822 Earliest documented church organ

Use of massive walls and piers, rounded arches, and minimal windows

c. 1071–1112 Pilgrimage church at Santiago de Compostela, Spain

c. 1080–1130 Church of Saint Sernin, Toulouse, pilgrimage center

1088–1130 Great Third Church at Cluny

1096–1120 Abbey Church of La Madeleine, Vézelay

11th–12th cent. Gregorian chant codified

Charlemagne as Ruler and Diplomat

Charles the Great (742?–814)—known to subsequent history as Charlemagne—was crowned emperor of the Roman Empire in Saint Peter's Basilica in Rome on Christmas Day A.D. 800 by Pope Leo III, in the first imperial coronation in the West since the late 6th century. The papal coronation was rebellion in the eyes of the Byzantine court, and the emperor in Constantinople considered Charlemagne a usurper, but this act marked the revival of the Roman Empire in the West.

Charlemagne was an able administrator of lands brought under his subjugation. He modified and adapted the classic Roman administrative machinery to fit the needs of his own kingdom. Charlemagne's rule was essentially feudal—structured in a hierarchical fashion, with lesser rulers bound by acts of fealty to higher ones. Lesser rulers were generally large landowners who derived their right to own and rule their land from their tie to the emperor. Charlemagne also maintained a number of vassal dependents at his court who acted as counselors at home and as legates to execute and oversee the imperial will abroad. From his palace the emperor regularly issued legal decrees modeled on the old imperial Roman decrees [7.1]. These decrees were detailed sets of instructions that touched on a wide variety of secular and religious issues. Those that have survived give us some sense of what life was like in the very early medieval period. The legates of the emperor carried the decrees to the various regions of the empire and reported back on their acceptance and implementation. This burgeoning bureaucratic system required a class of civil servants with a reasonable level of literacy, an important factor in the cultivation of letters that was so much a part of the so-called Carolingian Renaissance.

The popular view of the early Middle Ages—often referred to as the Dark Ages—is of a period of isolated and ignorant peoples with little contact outside the confines of their own immediate surroundings, and at times that was indeed the general condition of life. Nonetheless, it is important to note that in the late 8th and early 9th centuries Charlemagne not only ruled over an immense kingdom (all of modern-day France, Germany, the Low Countries, and Italy as far south as Calabria) but also had extensive diplomatic contact outside that kingdom. Charlemagne maintained regular, if somewhat testy, diplomatic relations with the emperor in Constantinople (at one point he tried to negotiate a marriage between himself and the Byzantine empress Irene in order to consolidate the two empires). Envoys from Constantinople were regularly received in his palace at Aachen, and Charlemagne learned Greek well enough to understand the envoys speaking their own tongue.

Charlemagne's relationship with the rulers of Islamic kingdoms is interesting. Islam had spread all along the southern Mediterranean coast in the preceding century. Arabs were in complete command of all the Middle East, North Africa, and most of the Iberian peninsula. Charlemagne's grandfather Charles Martel (Charles the Hammer) had defeated the Muslims decisively at the battle of Poitiers in 732, thus halting an Islamic challenge from Spain to the rest of Europe. Charlemagne himself had fought the Muslims of the Córdoba caliphate on the Franco–Spanish borders; the battle of Roncesvalles (778) was the historical basis for the later epic poem the *Song of Roland*.

Despite his warlike relationship with Muslims in the West, Charlemagne had close diplomatic ties with the great Harun al-Rashid, the caliph of Baghdad. In 787 Charlemagne sent an embassy to the caliph to beg protection for the holy places of the Christians in Muslim-held Palestine. The caliph (of *Thousand and One Nights* fame) received the Frankish legates and their gifts (mainly bolts of the much-prized Frisian cloth) with welcome and sent an elephant back to the emperor as a gesture of friendship. This gift actually arrived at Aachen and lived there for a few years before succumbing to the harsh winter climate. Charlemagne's negotiations were successful. From a pair of Palestinian monks he received the keys to the church of the Holy Sepulchre and

7.1 Charlemagne's seal. 9th century. Archives Nationales, Paris. This Roman gem with the head of a philosopher or an emperor was used by Charlemagne to impress on wax on official documents. The inscription reads *Christ protect Charles King of the Franks.*

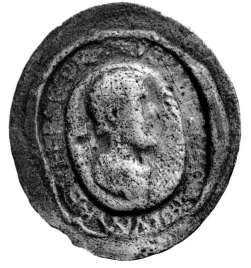

EAST MEETS WEST

Muslim Spain

In 711 Islamic troops from North Africa crossed the straits of Gibralter and conquered what is now a large portion of Spain. They called these lands *Al Andalus,* from which we get the name *Andalusia* for that part of modern Spain. These followers of Mohammed attempted to reach into what is present-day southern France until they were defeated by the grandfather of Charlemagne, Charles Martel, at the battle of Poiters in 732. The Muslims ruled Spain until overcome by Christian forces in the 13th century in a series of battles that have the generic name *Reconquista.*

What is most significant about the Muslim occupation of Spain is not the fact that they were there but that they were there when Islam as a whole was undergoing a dramatic cultural renaissance. Spanish cities like Cordoba, Seville, and Toledo still reflect the architectural influence of this period, while Islamic buildings like the Alcazar in Seville and the Alhambra in Granada demonstrate how successfully the Muslims used Arab and Byzantine architectural styles to create a stunningly beauti-

ful architecture. Despite the strong antipathy between the Christian West and Islamic Spain (reflected so vividly in the *Song of Roland*) a vigorous trade existed between the two cultures. Toledo steel for the making of swords and Cordova leather are only two of the products highly prized in the West.

Most significantly of all for medieval culture, Islamic Spain became a conduit to the West for Greek learning. In the city of Toledo translators turned Greek writers like Euclid, Ptolemy, Galen, Hippocrates, and Aristotle into Latin for scholars. One indelible remain of this work is the number of words that entered European languages as a direct result of this intellectual labor in the scientific learning of the time; our English words *zero, cipher, algebra, algorithm,* and *alcohol* (among many) are directly traceable back to Arabic. As we shall see in the next chapter, the university revolution of the 12th and 13th centuries would not have been possible without the flow of Aristotle's works which came to the West from translations done in Spain. Thomas Aquinas, for example, read Aristotle in a Latin translation done from Arabic manuscripts that had been, in turn, translated by Islamic scholars from the Greek originals.

---

other major Christian shrines, an important symbolic act that made the emperor the official guardian of the holiest shrines in Christendom.

Charlemagne's reign was also conspicuous for its economic developments. He stabilized the currency system of his kingdom. The silver *denier* struck at the royal mint in Frankfurt after 804 became the standard coin of the time; its presence in archaeological finds from Russia to England testifies to its widespread use and the faith traders had in it.

Trade and commerce were vigorous. Charlemagne welcomed Jewish immigration into his kingdom to provide a merchant class for commerce. There were annual trade fairs at Saint Denis near Paris, at which English merchants could buy foodstuffs, honey, and wine from the Carolingian estates. A similar fair was held each year at Pavia, an important town of the old Lombard kingdom of northern Italy. Port cities such as Marseilles provided mercantile contracts with the Muslims of Spain and North

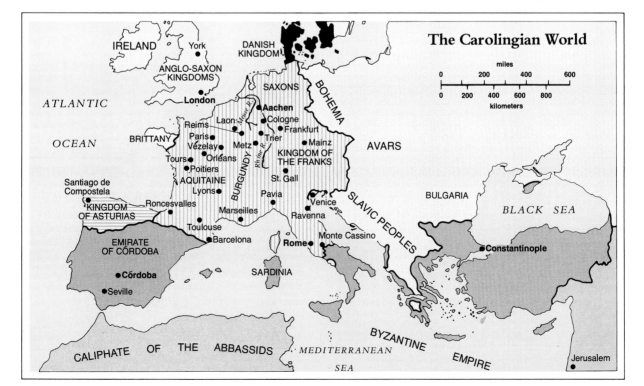

Africa. Jewish merchants operated as middlemen in France for markets throughout the Near East. The chief of Charlemagne's mission to Harun al-Rashid's court was a Jew named Isaac who had the linguistic ability and geographic background to make the trip to Baghdad and back—with an elephant—at a time when travel was a risky enterprise. Rivers such as the Rhine and the Moselle were utilized as important trade routes. One of the most sought-after articles from the Frankish kingdom was the iron broadsword produced from forges in and around the city of Cologne and sold to Arabs in the Middle East through Jewish merchants at the port cities. Vivid testimony to their value can be read in the repeated embargoes (imposed under penalty of death) decreed by Charlemagne against their export to the land of the Vikings, who put them too often to effective use against their Frankish manufacturers in coastal raids on North Sea towns and trading posts.

Learning in the Time of Charlemagne

At Aachen Charlemagne opened his famous "palace school," an institution that was a prime factor in initiating what has been called the Carolingian Renaissance. Literacy in Western Europe before the time of Charlemagne was rather spotty; it existed, but hardly thrived, in certain monastic centers that kept alive the old tradition of humanistic learning taken from ancient Rome. Original scholarship was rare, although monastic copyists did keep alive the tradition of literary conservation. Charlemagne himself could not write.

The scholars and teachers Charlemagne brought to Aachen provide some clues as to the various locales in which early medieval learning had survived. Peter of Pisa and Paul the Deacon (from Lombardy) came to teach grammar and rhetoric at his school since they had had contact with the surviving liberal arts curriculum in Italy. Theodulf of Orleans was a theologian and poet. He had studied in the surviving Christian kingdom of Spain and was an heir to the encyclopedic tradition of Isadore of Seville and his followers. Finally and most importantly, Charlemagne brought an Anglo-Saxon, Alcuin of York, to Aachen after meeting him in Italy in 781. Alcuin had been trained in the English intellectual tradition of the Venerable Bede (died 735), the most prominent intellectual of his day, a monk who had welded together the study of humane letters and biblical scholarship. These scholar-teachers were hired by Charlemagne for several purposes.

First, Charlemagne wished to establish a system of education for the young of his kingdom. The primary purpose of these schools was to develop literacy; Alcuin of York developed a curriculum for them. He insisted that humane learning should consist of those studies which developed logic and science. It was from this distinction that later medieval pedagogues developed the two courses of studies for all schooling prior to the university: the *trivium* (grammar, rhetoric, and dialectic) and the *quadrivium* (arithmetic, geometry, music, and astronomy). These subjects remained at the heart of the school curriculum from the medieval period until modern times. (The now much-neglected "classical education" has its roots in this basic plan of learning.)

Few books were available and writing was done on slates or waxed tablets since parchment was expensive. In grammar, some of the texts of the Latin Grammarian Priscian might be studied and then applied to passages from Latin prose writers. In rhetoric, the work of Cicero was studied, or Quintilian's *Institutio Oratoria* if available. For dialectics, some of the work of Aristotle might be read in the Latin translation of Boethius. In arithmetic, multiplication and division was learned and perhaps there was some practice on the *abacus* since the Latin numerals were clumsy to compute with pen and paper. Arithmetic also included some practice in chronology as students were taught to compute the variable dates of Easter. They would finish with a study of the allegorical meaning of numbers. Geometry was based on the study of Euclid. Astronomy was derived from the Roman writer Pliny, with some attention to Bede's work. Music was the theoretical study of scale, proportion, the harmony of the universe, and the "music of the spheres." Music at this period was distinguished from *cantus,* which was the practical knowledge of chants and hymns for church use. In general, all study was based largely on the rote mastery of texts.

Beyond the foundation of schools, Charlemagne needed scholars to reform existing texts and to halt their terrible corruption, especially those used in church worship. Literary revival was closely connected with liturgical revival. Part of Charlemagne's educational reform envisioned people who would read aloud and sing in church from decent, reliable texts. Literacy was conceived of as a necessary prelude for intelligible worship.

It was mainly Alcuin of York who worked at the task of revising the liturgical books. Alcuin published a book of extracts of Old and New Testament passages in Latin for public reading during Mass. He sent for books from Rome in order to publish a sacramentary, the book of prayers and rites for the administration of the sacraments of the church. Alcuin's *Sacramentary* was made obligatory for the churches of

An Abbot, an Irish Scholar, and Charlemagne's Biographer

Even as the sailor, fatigued with his labors, rejoices when he sights the familiar shore toward which he has long aspired, so does the scribe rejoice who sees the long-desired end of the book which has so overcome him with weariness. The man who does not know how to write makes light of the scribes' pains, but those who have done it know how hard is this work.

[A 9th-century monk-copyist describing labor in the scriptorium]

I love, better than all glory, to sit in diligent study over my little book. Pangur Ben has no envy of me, for he finds a mouse in his snares while only a difficult argument falls into mine. He bumps against the wall and I against the rigors of science. . . . He rejoices when he has a mouse in his paw as I rejoice when I have understood a difficult question. . . . Each of us loves our art.

[An Irish scholar and his cat]

He paid the greatest attention to the liberal arts. He had great respect for men who taught them, bestowing high honors on them. When he was learning the rules of grammar he received tuition from Peter the Deacon of Pisa who, by then, was an old man. For all other subjects he was taught by Alcuin, surnamed Albinus, a man of the Saxon race who came from Britain and was the most learned man anywhere to be found. Under him, the emperor spent much time and effort in studying rhetoric, dialectic, and especially astrology. He applied himself to mathematics and traced the course of the stars with great attention and care. He also tried to learn to write. With this end in view he used to keep writing tablets and notebooks under the pillows of his bed, so that he could try his hand at forming letters during his leisure moments; but, although he tried very hard, he had begun late in life and he made very little progress.

[Einhard in his biography of Charlemagne]

---

the Frankish kingdom in 785. Charlemagne made the Roman chant (called *Gregorian* after Pope Gregory the Great, who was said to have initiated such chants in the end of the 6th century) obligatory in all the churches of his realm. Alcuin also attempted to correct scribal errors in the Vulgate Bible (the Latin version of Saint Jerome) by a comparative reading of manuscripts, a gigantic task he never completed.

Beyond the practical need for literacy there was a further aim of education in this period. It was generally believed that all learning would lead to a better grasp of revealed truth—the Bible. The study of profane letters (by and large the literature of Rome) was a necessary first step toward the full study of the Bible. The study of grammar would set out the rules of writing, while dialectics would help distinguish true from false propositions. Models for such study were sought in the works of Cicero, Statius, Ovid, Lucan, and Vergil. These principles of correct writing and argumentation could then be applied to the study of the Bible in order to get closer to its truth. The pursuit of analysis, definition, and verbal clarity are the roots from which the scholastic form of philosophy would spring in the High Middle Ages. Scholasticism, which dominated European intellectual life until the eve of the Renaissance, had its first beginnings in the educational methodology established by Alcuin and his companions.

These educational enterprises were not centered exclusively at the palace school at Aachen. Under Charlemagne's direction Alcuin developed a system of schools throughout the Frankish Empire, schools centered in both monasteries and towns. Attempts were also made to attach them to parish churches in the rural areas. The monastic school at Metz became a center for singing and liturgical study; schools at Lyons, Orleans, Mainz, Tours, and Laon had centers for teaching children rudimentary literary skills and offered some opportunity for further study in the liberal arts and the study of scripture. The establishment of these schools was accomplished by a steady stream of decress and capitularies emanating from the Aachen palace. A circular letter, written most likely by Alcuin, called *On the Cultivation of Learning,* encouraged monks to study the Bible and to teach the young to do the same. A decree of 798 insisted that prelates and country clergy alike start schools for children.

This program of renewal in educational matters was an ideal set forth at a time when education was at a low ebb in Europe. Charlemagne tried to reverse the trend and in so doing encouraged real hope for an educated class in his time. His efforts were not entirely successful; many of his reforms came to naught in the generations after him when Europe slipped back into violence and ignorance.

Benedictine Monasticism

Monasticism—from the Greek *monos* (alone)—was an integral part of Christianity from the 3rd century on. Monasticism came into the West from the great Eastern tradition of asceticism (self-denial) and eremitism (the solitary life). Its development in the

West was very complex, and we cannot speak of any one form of monasticism as predominant before the time of Charlemagne.

Celtic monasticism in Ireland was characterized both by austere living and by a rather lively intellectual tradition. Monasticism in Italy was far more simple and rude. Some of the monasteries on the continent were lax, and Europe was full of wandering monks. No rule of life predominated in the 6th and 7th centuries. Monastic life styles varied not only from country to country but also from monastery to monastery.

The Rule of Saint Benedict

One strain of European monasticism derived from a rule of life written in Italy by Benedict of Nursia (480–547?) in the early 6th century. Although it borrows from early monastic rules and was applied only to a small proportion of monasteries for a century after its publication, the Rule of Saint Benedict eventually became the Magna Carta of monasticism in the West. Charlemagne had Alcuin of York bring the Rule to his kingdom and impose it on the monasteries of the Frankish kingdom to reform them and impose on them some sense of regular observance. In fact, the earliest copy of the Rule of Saint Benedict we possess today (a 9th-century manuscript preserved in the monastery of Saint Gall) is a copy of a copy Charlemagne had made in 814 from Saint Benedict's autograph copy preserved at the abbey of Monte Cassino in Italy (now lost).

The Rule of Saint Benedict consists of a prologue and 73 chapters (some only a few sentences long), which set out the ideal of monastic life. Monks (the brethren) are to live a family life in community under the direction of a freely elected father (the abbot) for the purpose of being schooled in religious perfection. They are to possess nothing of their own (poverty); they are to live in one monastery and not wander (stability); their life is to be one of obedience to the abbot; and they are to remain unmarried (chastity). Their daily life is to be a balance of common prayer, work, and study. Their prayer life centered around duly appointed hours of liturgical praise of God that were to mark the intervals of the day. This prayer, called the "Divine Office," consisted of the public recitation of psalms, hymns, and prayers with readings from the Holy Scriptures. The offices were interspersed throughout the day and were central to the monks' life. The periods of public liturgical prayer themselves set off the times for reading, study, and the manual labor that was done for the good of the community and its sustenance. The life style of Benedictine monasticism can be summed up in its motto: "pray and work."

The daily life of the monk was determined by sunrise and sunset (as it was for most people in those days). Here is a typical day—called the *horarium*—in an early medieval monastery. The italicized words designate the names for the liturgical hours of the day:

Horarium Monasticum

2:00 A.M.	Rise
2:10–3:30	*Nocturns* (later called *Matins;* the longest office of the day)
3:30–5:00	Private reading and study
5:00–5:45	*Lauds* (the second office; also called "morning prayer")
5:45–8:15	Private reading and *Prime* (the first of the short offices of the day); at times, there was communal Mass at this time and, in some places, a light breakfast, depending on the season
8:15–2:30	Work punctuated by short offices of *Tierce, Sext,* and *None* (literally the third, sixth, and ninth hours)
2:30–3:15	Dinner
3:15–4:15	Reading and private religious exercises
4:15–4:45	*Vespers*—break—*Compline* (night prayers)
5:15–6:00	To bed for the night

This daily regimen changed on feast days (less work and more prayer) and during the summer (earlier rising, work later in the day when the sun was down a bit, more food, and so on). While the schedule now seems harsh, it would not have surprised a person of the time. Benedict would have found it absurd for people to sleep while the sun is shining and then stay up under the glare of artificial light. When we look at the horarium closely we see a day in which prayer and reading get four hours each, while there are about six hours of work. The rest of the day was devoted to personal chores, eating, and the like.

The triumph of the Benedictine monastic style of life (the early Middle Ages has been called the Benedictine centuries by some historians) is to be found in its sensible balance between the extreme asceticism of Eastern monastic practices and the unstructured life of Western monasticism before the Benedictine reforms. There was an even balance of prayer, manual labor, and intellectual life.

Monasticism and Gregorian Chant

The main occupation of the monk was the *Opus Dei* (work of God)—the liturgical common prayer of the monasteric horarium; life centered around the monastic church where the monks gathered seven times a day for prayer. The centrality of the liturgy also explains why copying, correcting, and illuminating manuscripts was such an important part of monastic life. Texts were needed for religious services as well as for spiritual reading. The monks were encouraged to study the scriptures as a lifelong occupation. For the monk this study was *lectio divina* (divine reading) and was central to his development as a monk. This monastic imperative encouraged the study of the Bible and such ancillary disciplines (grammar, criticism, and the like) as necessary for the study of Scripture. From the 7th century on, monastic scriptoria were busily engaged in copying a wealth of material, both sacred and profane.

The monasteries were also centers for the development of sacred music. We have already seen that Charlemagne was interested in church music. His biographer Einhard tells us that the emperor "made careful reforms in the way in which the psalms were chanted and the lessons read. He was himself an expert at both of these exercises but he never read the lesson in public and he would sing only with the rest of the congregation and then in a low voice." Charlemagne's keen interest in music explains why certain monasteries of his reign—notably those at Metz and Trier—became centers for church music.

Charlemagne brought monks from Rome to stabilize and reform church music in his kingdom as part of his overall plan of liturgical renovation. In the earlier period of Christianity's growth quite diverse traditions of ecclesiastical music developed in various parts of the West. Roman music represented one tradition—later called *Gregorian* chant after Pope Gregory the Great (540–604), who was believed to have codified the music in the late 6th century. Milan had its own musical tradition, known as *Ambrosian* music—in honor of Saint Ambrose, who had been a noted hymn writer, as Saint Augustine attests in the *Confessions.* There was a peculiar regional style of music in Spain known as *Mozarabic* chant, while the Franks also had their own peculiar style of chant. All of these styles derive from earlier models of music which have their roots in Hebrew, Greco-Roman, and Byzantine styles. Lack of documentation permits only an educated reconstruction of this early music and its original development.

Gregorian chant as we know it today was not codified until the 11th and 12th centuries, so it is rather difficult to reconstruct precisely the music of Charlemagne's court. It was probably a mixture of Roman and Frankish styles of singing. It was *monophonic*—that is, one or many voices sang a single melodic line—and more often than not lacked musical accompaniment in the monastic churches. Most scholars believe that the majority of the music consisted of

simple chants for the recitation of the psalms at the Divine Office; more elaborate forms were used for the hymns of the Office and the Mass chants. The music was simply called *cantus planus,* plainsong or plainchant.

In its more elementary form the chant consisted of a single note for each syllable of a word. The basic symbols used to notate Gregorian chant were called *neums.* Using the Gregorian notational system with its four-line staff and the opening line of Psalm 109, *Dixit Dominus Domino Meo, sede a dextris meis* (The Lord said to my Lord: sit on my right hand), a line of syllabic chant would look like this:

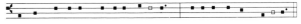

1. Di-xit Dóminus Dómino mé- o : * Séde a déxtris mé- is.

Even in the earliest form of chants, a cadence was created by emphasizing the final word of a phrase with the addition of one or two extra notes, as above. Later, more notes were added to the final words or syllables for elaboration and variation. For example:

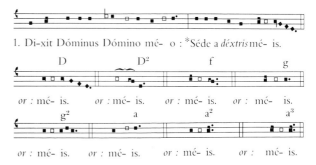

1. Di-xit Dóminus Dómino mé- o : *Séde a *déxtris* mé- is.

The simplicity of syllabic chant should not be regarded as useful only for the monotonous chanting of psalm verses. Very simple yet hauntingly melodic Gregorian compositions still exist that do not use elaborate cadences while relying on simple syllabic notes. A fine example is the Gregorian melody for the Lord's Prayer, reproduced here in modern notation. No rests are indicated in the musical text; the singer should simply breathe on a skipped note (it is presumed that not all would skip the same note) so that the music flows without pause. Ordinarily, these chants would be sung *a capella* (without musical accompaniment).

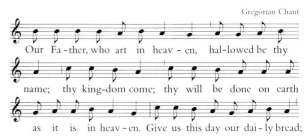

Gregorian Chant

Our Fa-ther, who art in heav-en, hal-lowed be thy name; thy king-dom come; thy will be done on earth as it is in heav-en. Give us this day our dai-ly bread;

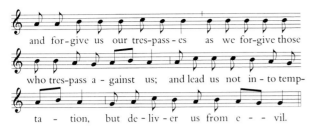

and for-give us our tres-pass-es as we for-give those

who tres-pass a - gainst us; and lead us not in - to temp-

ta - tion, but de - liv - er us from e - - vil.

Certain phrases, especially words of acclamation (like *Alleluia*) or the word at the end of a line, were elaborated beyond the few notes provided in syllabic chant. This extensive elaboration of a final syllable (or any syllable) by a chain of intricate notes was called a *melisma*. An example of melismatic chant may be noted in the elaboration of the final *ia* of the Easter *Alleluia* sung at the Easter Mass:

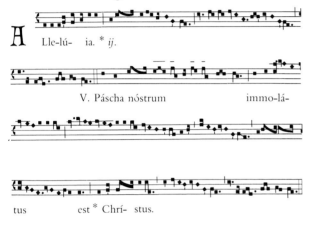

Lle-lú- ia. * ij.

V. Páscha nóstrum immo-lá-

tus est * Chrí- stus.

Liturgical Music and the Rise of Drama

The Liturgical Trope

One development connected with melismatic chant which evolved in the Carolingian period was the *trope*. Since books were scarce, monks memorized a great deal of liturgical chant. As an aid to memorization and, also, to provide some variety in the chant, words would be added to the long melismas. These words, tropes, would be verbal elaborations of the content of the text. Thus, for example, if there was a melismatic *Kyrie Eleison* (the Greek "Lord, have mercy on us" retained in the Latin Mass) with an elaboration of notes for the syllable *rie* of *Kyrie*, it became customary to add words such as *sanctus* (holy), *dominus* (lord), and the like, which were sung to the tune of the melisma. The use of tropes grew rapidly and became standard in liturgical music until they were removed from the liturgy at the time of the Counter-Reformation in the 16th century.

Scholars have pointed to the interpolation of tropes into liturgical music as the origin of drama in the Western world. There had been drama in the classical and Byzantine worlds, of course, but drama in Europe developed from the liturgy of the medieval church after it largely had been lost (or suppressed) in the very early Middle Ages.

A 9th-century manuscript (preserved at the monastery of Saint Gall) preserves an early trope that was added to the music of the Easter entrance hymn (the *Introit*) for Mass. It is in the form of a short dialogue and seems to have been sung by either two different singers or two choirs. It is called the *Quem Quæritis* trope from its opening lines:

THE *QUEM QUÆRITIS* TROPE

De Resurrectione Dom-ini	Of the Lord's Resurrection
Int[errogatio]: *Quem quæritis in sepulchro, {o} Christicolæ?*	Question [of the angels]: *Whom seek ye in the sepulchre, O followers of Christ?*
R[esponsio]: *Jesum Nazarenum crucifixum, o cœlicolæ.*	Answer [of the Marys]: *Jesus of Nazareth, which was crucified, O celestial ones.*
[Angeli:] *Non est hic; surrexit, sicut prædixerat.*	[The angels:] *He is not here; he is risen, just as he foretold.*
Ite, nuntiate quia surrexit de sepulchro.	*Go, announce that he is risen from the sepulchre.*

Very shortly after the introduction of this trope into the Easter Mass the short interrogation began to be acted, not at Mass but at the end of the night services preceding Easter dawn. The dialogue of the *Quem Quæritis* was not greatly enlarged but the directions for its singing were elaborated into the form of a short play. By the 11th and 12th centuries the dialogue was elaborated beyond the words of the Bible and more persons were added. By the 12th century the stories took on greater complexity.

It was a logical step to remove these plays from the church and peform them in the public square. By the 14th century sizable cycles of plays were performed in conjunction with various feast days and underwritten by the craft or merchants guilds. Some of these cycles acted out the major stories of the Bible, from Adam to the Last Judgment. The repertory also began to include plays about the lives of the saints and allegorical plays about the combats of virtue and vice, such as the 15th-century work *Every-*

man. These plays were a staple of public life well into the 16th century. William Shakespeare, for example, may well have seen such plays in his youth.

The Morality Play: *Everyman*

Everyman is a 15th-century play that may well be a translation from an earlier Dutch play. The subject is no longer a redoing of a biblical theme but rather the personification of abstractions representing a theme dear to the medieval heart: the struggle for the soul. The unprepared reader of *Everyman* will note the heavy-handed allegorizing and moralizing (complete with a "Doctor" who makes a final appearance to point up the moral of the play) with some sense of estrangement, but with a closer reading, students will also note the stark dignity of the play, the earnestness with which it is constructed, and the economy of its structure. Written in rather spare rhyming couplets, *Everyman* is a good example of the transitional play that forms a link between the earlier liturgical drama and the more secular drama that was to come at the end of the English medieval period.

The plot of *Everyman* is simplicity itself; it is quickly summarized by the messenger who opens the play. Everyman must face God in final judgment after death. None of the aids and friends of this life will support Everyman, as the speeches of the allegorical figures of Fellowship and others make clear. The strengths for Everyman come from the aiding virtues of Confession, Good Deeds, and Knowledge. The story, however, is not the central core of this play; the themes that run through the entire play are what should engage our attention. First is the common medieval notion of life itself as a pilgrimage, a notion that comes up again and again. It is embedded not only in the medieval penchant for pilgrimage but the use of that term (as one sees, for example, in Chaucer) as a metaphor. Second, the notion of the inevitability of death as the defining action of human life is omnipresent in medieval culture. *Everyman* has an extremely intense *memento mori* ("Keep death before your eyes!") motif. Finally, medieval theology puts great emphasis on the will of the human being in the attainment of salvation. It is not faith (this virtue is presumed) that will save Everyman; his or her willingness to learn (Knowledge), act (Good Deeds), and convert (Confession) will make the difference between salvation and damnation.

The Messenger says that *Everyman* is "By figure a moral play." It is meant not merely to instruct on the content of religion (as does a mystery play) but to instruct for the purposes of moral conversion. The

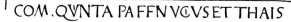

COM.QVNTA PAFFNVCVS ET THAIS

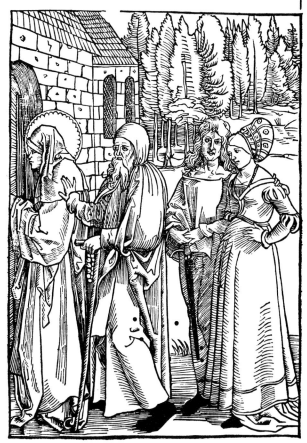

7.2 Woodcut of *Pafnutius and Thaïs* from the 16th-century edition of her plays by Conrad Celtis. Celtis, an early German humanist (died 1508), made an edition of Hrosvita's plays as a part of his program to exalt German contributions to literature.

earlier mystery plays usually point out a moral at the end of the performance. The morality uses its resources to moralize throughout the play.

The one lingering element from the liturgy in a play like *Everyman* is its pageant quality: the dramatic force of the presentation is enhanced by the solemn wearing of gowns, the stately pace of the speeches, and the seriousness of the message. The play depends less on props and place. Morality plays did not evolve directly out of liturgical drama (they may owe something to the study of earlier plays based on the classics studied in schools) but the liturgical overtones are not totally absent.

Nonliturgical Drama

At the end of the early Middle Ages we also have evidence of plays that were not dependent on liturgical worship. Thus a German nun-poet named Hrotsvitha (or Roswitha; the name is spelled variously) who lived at the aristocratic court of Gandersheim and died around the year 1000 has left us both a collection of legends written in Latin and six plays modeled on the work of the Roman dramatist Terence. What is interesting about this well-educated woman is the broad range of her learning and her mastery of classical Latin in an age that did not put a high premium on education of females. Scholars also point out that her prose legend called *Theophilus* is the first known instance in German literature of the Faust theme—the selling of one's soul to the devil for material gain and public glory.

Hrosvitha's plays were probably meant to be read aloud by a small circle of literate people, but there is some internal evidence that they may also have been acted out in some rudimentary fashion. They are heavily moralistic (typically involving a religious conversion or steadfastness in faith during a time of persecution) and very didactic. In the play *The Conversion of the Harlot Thaïs,* for example, the holy man Pafnutius begins with a long conversation with his disciples on a liberal education and the rules of musical proportion and harmony. Such a discussion would seem a wild digression to us today, but for her audience it would be a way of not only learning about the liberal arts but a reminder that their study leads, inevitably, to a consideration of God [see 7.2]. That her plays do not have finished dramatic quality underscores the fact that she was the *first* dramatist writing in Germany (as well as Germany's first female poet). Her model was the ancient drama of Rome as far as style was concerned, but her intention was to use that style to educate and convert. She was a direct heir of the humane learning that developed in the Carolingian and Ottonian periods.

The Legend of Charlemagne: *Song of Roland*

Charlemagne's kingdom did not long survive intact after the death of the emperor. By the 10th century, the Frankish kingdom was fractured and Europe reduced to a state worthy of the name "Dark Ages." Anarchy, famine, ignorance, war, and factionalism were constants in 10th-century Europe; Charlemagne's era was looked back to as a long-vanished Golden Age. By the 12th century Charlemagne's reputation was such that he was canonized (in Aachen on December 29, 1165) by the Emperor Frederick Barbarossa. Charlemagne's cult was immensely popular throughout France—especially at the royal abbey of Saint Denis in Paris, which made many claims of earlier links with the legendary emperor.

A 15th-century oil painting in Aachen depicts an idealized Charlemagne as saint, wearing the crown of

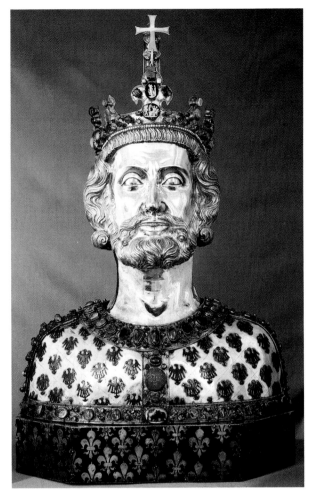

7.3 Reliquary of Charlemagne. Bust of Charlemagne after 1349; crown before 1349. Cathedral Treasury, Aachen. Reliquaries of this type are containers for some relic of the person depicted by the statue.

the Holy Roman Emperor and carrying a model of the church he had built at Aachen. Frederick Barbarossa commemorated the canonization by commissioning a great wrought-bronze candelabrum to hang in the Aachen cathedral. He also ordered a gold reliquary (now in the Louvre in Paris) to house the bones of one of his saintly predecessor's arms [see 7.3]; another reliquary in the form of a portrait bust that contains fragments of Charlemagne's skull is in the cathedral treasury at Aachen.

The memory of Charlemagne and his epoch was kept more vividly alive, however, in cycles of epic poems and in tales and memoirs developed, embroidered, and disseminated by poets and singers throughout Europe from shortly after Charlemagne's time until the late Middle Ages. These are the famous *chansons de geste* (songs of deeds) or, as some were called, *chanson d'histoire* (songs of history). Of these songs, the oldest extant—as well as the best and most famous—is the *Song of Roland.*

The *Song of Roland* was written sometime late in the 11th century, but behind it lay some three hundred years of oral tradition and earlier poems celebrating a battle between Charlemagne's army and a Muslim force at the Spanish border. Charlemagne did indeed campaign against the emirate of Spain in 777 and 778, without conclusive result. In August 778 Charlemagne's rear guard was ambushed by the Basques while making its way through the Pyrenees after the invasion of Spain. The real extent of that battle (later placed, on not too much evidence, at the town of Roncesvalles) is unclear. Some experts maintain that it was a minor skirmish, remembered in the area in local legends later told and retold (and considerably embroidered in the process) by monks of the monasteries and sanctuaries on the pilgrimage routes to the great shrine of Saint James at Santiago de Compostela in Spain. Other historians insist that the battle was a horrendous bloodbath for the army of Charlemagne and that the tale was carried back to the Frankish cities; the legend was transformed as it was repeated by the descendants of the few survivors.

In any event, by the 11th century the tale was widely known in Europe. Excerpts from the *Song of Roland* were sung to inspire the Norman army before the Battle of Hastings in 1066, and in 1096 Pope Urban II cited it in an appeal to French patriotism when he attempted to raise armies for a crusade to free the Hold Land. Medieval translations of the poem into German, Norse, and Italo-French attest to its widespread popularity outside the French-speaking area.

The *Song of Roland* is an epic poem; its unknown writer or writers had little interest in historical accuracy or geographic niceties. Its subject matter is the glory of the military campaign, the chivalric nature of the true knight, the constant possibility of human deviousness, the clash of good and evil. The poem, although set in the 8th century, reflects the military values and chivalric code of the 11th century.

The story is simple: Muslims attack the retreating rear portion of Charlemagne's army (through an act of betrayal) while it is under the command of Roland, a favorite nephew of the emperor. Roland's army is defeated, but not before he sounds his ivory horn to alert the emperor to the peril. The emperor in turn raises a huge army from throughout Christendom while the Muslims also raise a great force. An epic battle follows; Charlemagne, with divine aid, is victorious.

The *Song of Roland* is some four thousand lines long; it is divided into stanzas, and each line contains ten syllables. It is impossible to reproduce the rhyme in English, since each stanza ends with an assonance, so the poem is best read in blank-verse translation—although that loses the recitative quality of the original.

This poem was meant to be heard, not read. It was recited by wandering minstrels—*jongleurs*—to largely illiterate audiences. This fact explains the verse style, the immediacy of the adjectives describing the characters and the situations, and the somewhat repetitive language. The still-unexplained AOI at the end of many stanzas may have something to do with the expected reaction of the *jongleur* as he uttered that particular sound to give emphasis to a stanza. (Some sense of the immediacy of the original may be gained by a reader today who declaims some of these stanzas with gesture and appropriate pauses.)

Certain details of the poem merit particular attention. A portion of the poem recounts Charlemagne's arrival on the scene and his victory over the Saracens who are beleaguering the forces commanded by Roland. Most striking is the mixture of military and religious ideals, not an uncommon motif in the medieval period. This mixture is reflected not only in the imagery and in the plot (Charlemagne's prayer keeps the sun from setting in order to allow time for victory, an echo of the biblical siege of Jericho by Joshua) but also in the bellicose Archbishop Turpin. Christian valor is contrasted with Saracen wickedness and treachery; the anti-Muslim bias of the poem is clear. The Muslim Saracens are pagans and idolaters—an odd way to describe the rigidly monotheistic followers of Islam. The *Song of Roland,* like much of the epic tradition from which it springs, is nevertheless devoted to the martial virtues of courage and strength, the comradeship of the battlefield, and the power of great men as well as the venality of evil ones.

The *Song of Roland* was immensely popular in its own time. It spawned a number of other compositions like the *Pseudo Turpin* and the *Song of Aspremont* in order to continue the story or elaborate portions of it. At a much later time in Italy the story was redone in the telling of the exploits of Orlando (Roland). To this day, children in Sicily visit the traditional puppet shows in which the exploits of brave Roland and his mates are acted out with great clatter and verve. Spectators at those shows witness stories that go back to the beginnings of the medieval period.

The Visual Arts

The Illuminated Book

Given Charlemagne's preoccupation with literary culture, it should not be surprising that a great deal of artistic effort should have been expended on the production and illumination of manuscripts. Carolingian manuscripts were made of parchment (treated animal skins, mainly from cows and sheep) since papyrus was unavailable and the technical process of making

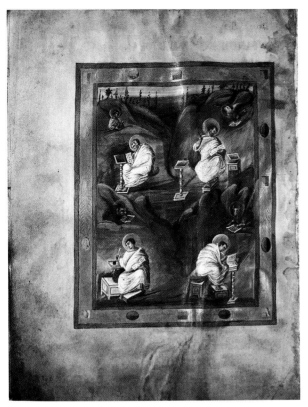

7.4 The four evangelists and their symbols, from the *Gospel Book of Charlemagne*. Palace School of Charlemagne, Aachen. Early 9th century. Manuscript illustration. Cathedral Treasury, Aachen.

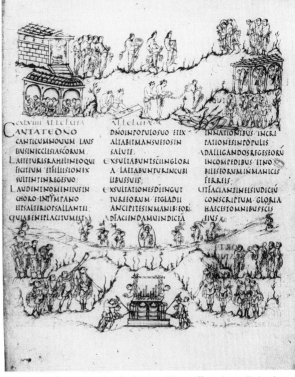

7.5 Page from the *Utrecht Psalter*. Hautvillers (near Reims). c. 820–840. Pen and ink on vellum. 12⅞ × 10″ (33 × 26 cm). University Library, Utrecht. This page is typical of the quick nervous style of the unknown illustrator, who did similar symbolic drawings for the entire psalter of 150 psalms.

paper was not known at this period. For very fine books the parchment was dyed purple and the letters were painted on with silver and gold pigments.

While a good deal of decoration of Carolingian manuscripts shows the influence of Irish models, the illustrations often show other influences. This is strikingly apparent in the illustrations of the *Gospel Book of Charlemagne* (800–810), where it is clear that the artists were conscious of the Roman style [7.4]. The page showing the four evangelists with their symbolic emblems is strikingly classical: the four evangelists are toga-clad like ancient Roman consuls. There is some evidence that the artists attempted some experiment in three-dimensionality. The wooded background in the receding part of the upper two illustrations tends to bring the evangelists forward and thus diminish the flatness we associate both with Byzantine and Celtic illustrations.

The *Utrecht Psalter* (so called because its present home is the University of Utrecht in Holland) has been called the masterpiece of the Carolingian Renaissance. Executed at Reims sometime around 820 to 840, it contains the whole psalter with wonderfully free and playful pen drawings around the text of the

psalms. The figures are free from any hieratic stiffness; they are mobile and show a nervous energy. The illustration for Psalm 148, for example, has a scene at the bottom of the page showing various figures "praising God with horn and cymbals" [7.5]. There are two other interesting aspects of the same illustration. One is that the figures are in the act of praising Christ, who stands at the apex of the illustration with the symbols of his resurrection (the stafflike cross in his hand). Although the psalms speak of the praise of God, for the medieval Christian the "hidden" or true meaning of the scriptures was that they speak in a prefigurative way of Christ. Thus the psalmist who praises God is a "shadow" of the church that praises Christ. A second thing to note in this illustration is the bottom-center scene of an organ with two men working the bellows to supply the air.

The style of the *Utrecht Psalter* has much in common with early Christian illustration. The lavish purple-and-silver manuscripts show a conscious imitation of Byzantine taste. We have also noted the influence of Celtic illustration. Carolingian manuscript art thus had a certain international flavor, and the

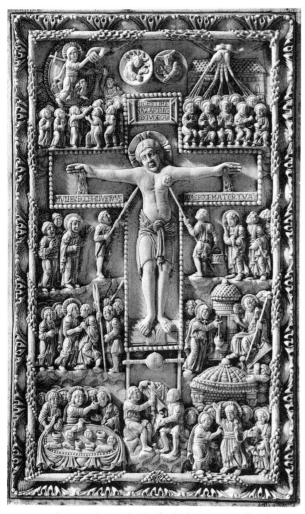

7.6 *Crucifixion*. Palace School of Charlemagne. Early 9th century. Ivory, 9⅞ × ½″ (25 × 16 cm). Cathedral Treasury of Saint Just, Narbonne. Such ivories were often used as covers for Gospel books and other liturgical works. They were often produced as gifts for special occasions.

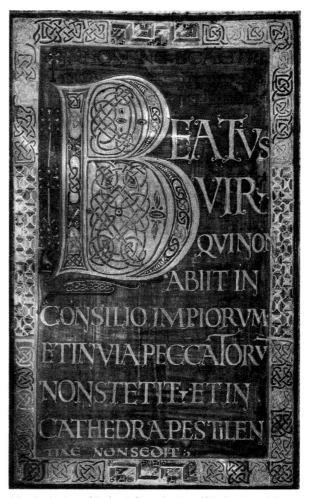

7.7 Beginning of Psalm 1 from the *Dagulf Psalter*. Late 8th century. Manuscript illustration, 7½ × 4⅝″ (19 × 12 cm). Austrian National Library. This psalter may well have been produced by a woman's hand at a convent.

various styles and borrowings give ample testimony to the cosmopolitan character of Charlemagne's culture. This universality diminished in the next century; not until the period of the so-called International Style in the 14th century would such a broad eclecticism again be seen in Europe.

One other art form that developed from the Carolingian love for the book is ivory carving. This technique was not unique to Charlemagne's time; it was known in the ancient world and highly valued in Byzantium. The ivories that have survived from Charlemagne's time were used for book covers. One beautiful example of the ivory carver's art is a crucifixion panel made at the palace workshop at Aachen sometime in the early 9th century [7.6]. Note the crowded scenes that surround the crucifixion event. Reading clockwise from the bottom left, one sees the Last Supper, the betrayal in the garden, and, at the

top, a soldier piercing Jesus' side. As a balance at the top right another soldier offers Jesus a wine-soaked sponge on a lance. Below that scene is one of the women at the tomb and, at the bottom, of the incredulity of Thomas. Framing these scenes above are the ascension of Christ on the left and the Pentecost on the right, the two scenes separated by a stylized sun and moon. The entire ivory is framed with geometric and abstract floral designs. The composition indicates that the carver had seen some examples of early Christian carving, while the beardless Christ and the flow of the drapery indicate familiarity with Byzantine art.

One surviving Carolingian manuscript that allows us to see both illumination and ivory work is the *Dagulf Psalter,* made as a gift for Pope Hadrian I, who reigned from 772 to 795. The psalms are not illustrated like the ones in the *Utrecht Psalter;* instead, the

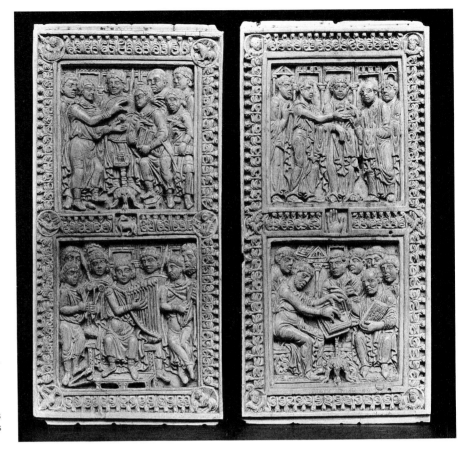

7.8 Cover panels for the *Dagulf Psalter*. Late 8th century. Ivory, 6⅛ × 3⅛″ (17 × 8 cm). Louvre, Paris. Jerome correcting the psalter (lower right panel) reflects common work in the monasteries of the Carolingian period.

illustrator begins a tradition that will be fairly normal for psalters in the future: he enlarges and illuminates the initial letter of the first, 51st, and 101st psalms. The *B* of the first word of Psalm 1, *Beatus vir qui* (Blessed is the man who), is enlarged and decorated in the swelling style of Celtic illumination; the same patterns are echoed on the page margin [7.7].

The ivory covers of the psalter have been preserved and are now in the Louvre [7.8]. Rather than the usual crowded scenes of most of these covers, the ivories from the *Dagulf Psalter* are composed of two scenes on each of the panels; the scenes make references to both the psalter and the papal connection. The panel on the left shows David and his court; below, David is shown singing one of his psalms to the accompaniment of his lyre. The right panel depicts Saint Jerome receiving a letter from Pope Damasus instructing him to correct the psalter; the

THE ARTS AND INVENTION: *Manuscript Illumination*

Manuscript illumination was one of the most common arts of the Middle Ages. Manuscripts were copied almost exclusively on what is called *parchment,* a fine animal skin especially treated for writing. The hide of an animal was soaked in lime to remove hair and flesh, not tanned as for making leather. Treated with powdered chalk, it was stretched on a frame to dry. The stretched hide was then smoothed with a pumice stone or some other abrasive. Both sides could be used to write on, so the book or *codex* soon replaced the scroll.

The term *vellum* is often used interchangeably with *parchment* but, technically speaking, vellum was made from the embryonic hides of calves, kids, or lambs whereas parchment was made from full-grown sheep or goats. Vellum produced a finer and thinner writing surface. The use of vellum and parchment came into existence some two centuries before the time of Christ, most likely in Pergamon in the Hellenistic world.

The writing of the text on a sheet of parchment was done with a notched pen (Latin *calamus*) in black ink made from soot and a fixative or brown ink developed from nuts. Initial letters were often highlighted in red, a process known as *rubrication*. Some manuscripts were then elaborately illuminated with painted scenes in an initial letter or decorative motif around the edges of the page. These illuminations were almost always done in *tempera* paint, a color ground from pigments mixed in water and then "fixed" by a substance such as egg white.

Needless to say, a parchment codex was an expensive object but, given the durability of parchment, many manuscripts have come down to us. Scrolls and sheets written on the flattened papyrus reed, on the other hand, have survived only in climates with very low humidity, like that of Egypt.

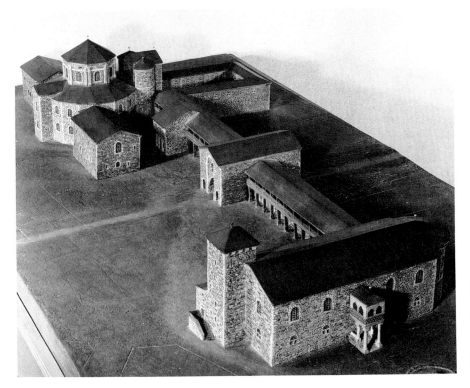

7.9 Model reconstruction of Charlemagne's palace at Aachen. Römisch-Germanisches Zentral Museum, Mainz. The royal hall with its long gallery is in the foreground. The octagonal royal chapel in the background should be compared with San Vitale in Ravenna.

scene below depicts Jerome in the act of working on the psalter while a grateful clergy looks on.

One other advance in manuscript production during the Carolingian period was in the area of fine handwriting or, as it is more technically known, calligraphy. Handwriting before the Carolingian period was cluttered, unformed, and cramped. It was very hard to read because of its erratic flourishes and its lack of symmetry. After 780 scribes in Carolingian scriptoria began to develop a precise and rounded form of lettering that became known as the Carolingian *minuscule,* as opposed to the *majuscule* or capital letter. This form of lettering was so crisp and legible that it soon became a standard form of manuscript writing. Even in the 15th century, the Florentine humanists preferred the minuscule calligraphy for their manuscripts. When printing became popular in the early 16th century, printers soon designed type fonts to conform to Carolingian minuscule. It overcame Gothic type in popularity and is the ancestor of modern standard lettering systems.

Charlemagne's Palace at Aachen

Beyond his immediate commercial, military, and political goals, Charlemagne had an overwhelming desire to model his kingdom on that of ancient Rome. His coronation in Rome symbolized the fu-

sion of the ancient imperial ideal with the notion of Christian destiny. It was not accidental that Charlemagne's favorite book—he had it read to him frequently at meals—was Augustine's *The City of God.* One highly visible way of making this ideal concrete was to build a capital.

At Aachen (in French it is called Aix-la-Chapelle) Charlemagne built his palace and royal chapel [7.9]. Except for the chapel (incorporated into the present cathedral), all the buildings of Charlemagne's palace have been destroyed and the Aachen city hall (itself built in the 14th century) covers the palace site. The palace itself was a long one-story building; its main room was the large royal hall, which measured roughly 140 by 60 feet (42.7 by 18.3 meters). So richly decorated that even the fastidious and sophisticated Byzantine legates were favorably impressed, the room had as its focal point at the western end the emperor's throne. In front of the palace was an open courtyard around which were outbuildings and apartments for the imperial retinue. Around the year 800 the courtyard held a great bronze statue of Theodoric, once king of the Ravenna Ostrogoths, that Charlemagne had brought back from Ravenna to adorn his palace.

The royal hall was joined to Charlemagne's chapel by a long wooden gallery. This royal chapel was probably built around 795. With sixteen exterior walls, the chapel was a central-plan church based on an octagon [7.10], its model undoubtedly the church of San Vitale in Ravenna, which Charlemagne had visited and admired. The octagon formed the main nave of the church, which was surrounded by *cloisters;* the building itself was two-storied. At the eastern end of the chapel was an altar dedicated to the Savior, with a chapel dedicated to the Virgin directly below it. The central space was crowned with an octagonal cupola, the lower part of which was pierced by windows, the main source of light in the church. The outside of the church was plain and severe; the inside was richly ornamented with marbles brought to Aachen from Ravenna and Rome. The interior of the cupola was decorated with a rich mosaic depicting Christ and the twenty-four elders of the Apocalypse (now destroyed; the present mosaics in the chapel are modern copies) while the other planes of the interior were covered with frescoes (now also destroyed). The railing of the upper gallery was made from bronze screens that are still in place, wrought in geometrical forms.

The chapel included two objects that emphasized its royal status: the most important relic of the kingdom, Saint Martin of Tours' cape, and a throne. Charlemagne's throne was on the second floor, opposite the chapel of the Savior. From this vantage point the emperor could observe the liturgical services being conducted in the Savior chapel and at the same time view the Virgin chapel with its rich collection of relics.

Charlemagne's throne, with its curved back and armrests, was mounted by six stone steps. This arrangement was obviously taken from King Solomon's throne as described in the Bible (I Kings 10:18–19). Charlemagne was to be thought of as the "new Solomon" who, like his ancient prototype, was an ambitious builder, a sagacious lawgiver, and the symbol of national unity. That this analogy was not an idle fancy is proved by a letter from Alcuin, Charlemagne's friend and tutor, to the emperor in anticipation of his return to Aachen: "May I soon be allowed to come with palms, accompanied with

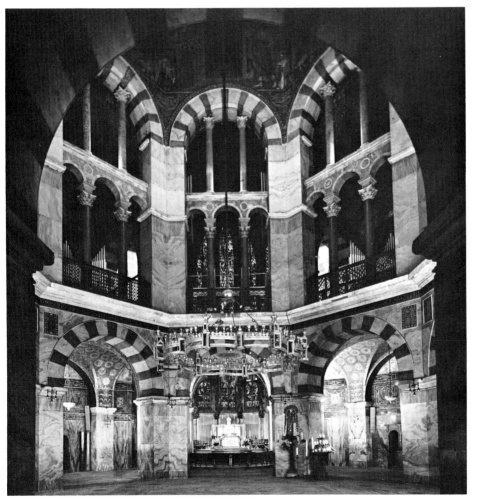

7.10 Interior of chapel of Charlemagne, Aachen. This view, toward the east, shows the emperor's tribune in the second story. The ceiling mosaics on the ceiling and the lower-level inscriptions are modern.

children singing psalms, to meet your triumphant glory, and to see once more your beloved face in the Jerusalem of our most dear fatherland, wherein is the temple set up to God by this most wise Solomon.''

The Carolingian Monastery

In the period between Saint Benedict and Charlemagne the Benedictine monastery underwent a complex evolution. Originally the monasteries were made up of small communities with fewer than fifteen members who led a life of prayer and work in a rather simple setting. With the decline of city life and the disorders brought on by the repeated invasions of the barbarians after the 5th century, the monastery became increasingly a center of life for rural populations. Monasteries not only kept learning alive and worship intact but were also called on to become a shelter for the traveler, a rudimentary hospital for the sick, a place of refuge in time of invasion, a granary for the farmer, a center of law for both religious and civil courts, and a place that could provide agricultural services such as milling and brewing.

This expansion of services, making the monastery into what has been called a "miniature civic center," inevitably changed the physical character of the monastery compound itself. By Charlemagne's time the monastery was an intricate complex of buildings suitable for the many tasks it was called on to perform (Table 7.1). One vivid example of the complexity of the Carolingian monastery can be gained by a study of a plan for an ideal monastery developed about 820 at the Benedictine abbey of Saint Gall in present-day Switzerland [7.11].

In the Saint Gall plan the monastic church dominated the area. Set off with its two round towers, it

7.11 Plan for an ideal monastery. c. 820. Reconstruction by Walter Horn and Ernest Born from the manuscript in the library of the monastery of Saint Gall in Switzerland. The original plan, 3'8″ (1.12 m) across, was drawn to scale on vellum. The monastery site would have been 480′ × 640′ (146 × 195 m) which would have housed 120 monks and 170 serfs. It was a plan for future monasteries and exerted, over the centuries, considerable influence on monastic construction.

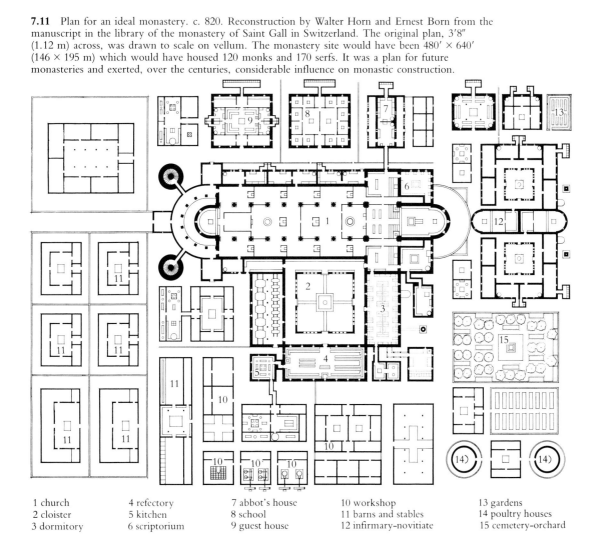

1 church	4 refectory	7 abbot's house	10 workshop	13 gardens
2 cloister	5 kitchen	8 school	11 barns and stables	14 poultry houses
3 dormitory	6 scriptorium	9 guest house	12 infirmary-novitiate	15 cemetery-orchard

TABLE 7.1 The Major Parts of the Monastery	
The Monastic Church	Site of the major religious services.
The Chapter House	Ordinary meeting room of the monastic community; the name comes from the custom of reading a chapter of the rule of St. Benedict aloud each day to the community.
The Cloister	Technically, the enclosed part of the monastery; more commonly, the enclosed garden and walkway in the interior of the monastery.
The Scriptorium	Library and copying area of the monastery.
The Refectory	Monks' dining hall.
The Novitiate	Quarters for aspirant monks not yet vowed in the community.
The Dormitory	Sleeping area for the monks.
The Infirmary	For sick, retired, and elderly monks.
The Guest House	For visitors, retreatants, and travelers.
The Outbuildings	Buildings for the farms and crafts of the monastery. Small buildings far from the main monastery that housed farmer monks were called *granges*.

warfare, Europe began to stir with new life. Pilgrimages became very popular as travel became safe. Pilgrimage routes—in particular to sites in Spain, England, and Italy—crisscrossed Europe. Crusades were mounted to free the holy places of the Middle East from the Muslims so that pilgrims could journey in peace to the most desired goal of the pilgrim: Jerusalem. In this period monks built and maintained pilgrimage churches and hostels on the major routes of the pilgrims.

The building style of this period (roughly from 1000 to 1200) is called Romanesque because the architecture was larger and more "Roman"-looking than the work done in the earlier medieval centuries. The two most striking characteristics of this architecture were the use of heavy stone arches and generous exterior decoration, mainly sculpture. The Romanesque style had two obvious advantages. One was

was a basilica-style church with numerous entrances for the use of the monks. To the south of the church was a rectangular garden space surrounded by a covered walkway (the *cloister*) from which radiated the monk's dormitory, dining hall (*refectory*), and kitchens. To the north of the church were a copying room (*scriptorium*), a separate house for the abbot, a school for youths and young novices, and a guest house. To the extreme south of the church were ranged workshops, barns, and other utilitarian outbuildings. To the east beyond the church were an infirmary and a separate house for aspirant monks (the *novitiate*), gardens, poultry houses, and the community cemetery.

The Romanesque Style

The plan of Saint Gall was never realized in stone, but the Benedictines did participate in ambitious architectural works after the Carolingian period. In the 11th century, after a long period of desolation and

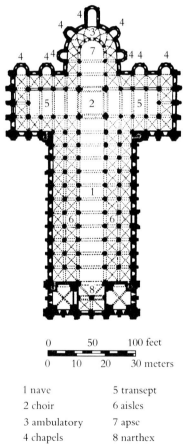

0	50	100 feet
0	10 20	30 meters

1 nave	5 transept
2 choir	6 aisles
3 ambulatory	7 apse
4 chapels	8 narthex

7.12 Floor plan of the church of Saint Sernin, Toulouse. Notice the ample aisles for easy passage of pilgrim groups around the entire church. The radiating chapels around the ambulatory permitted many priests to celebrate mass simultaneously.

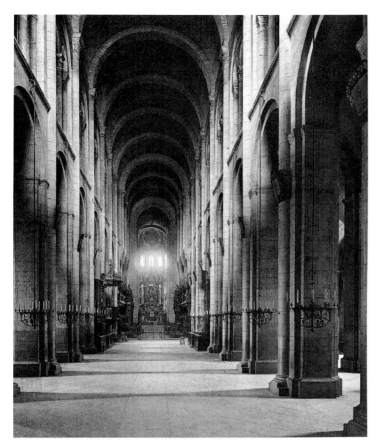

7.13 Interior of the church of Saint Sernin, Toulouse. c. 1080–1120. The massive ceiling vaults are called barrel or tunnel vaults. This heavy stonework required heavy walls to support the weight of the vaults. The galleries, with their own vaults, also helped with the support of the cut-stone ceiling vaults.

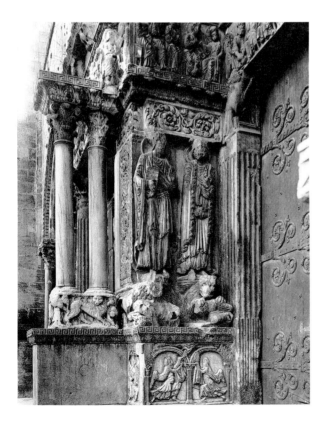

that the use of heavy stone and masonry walls permitted larger and more spacious interiors. Secondly, the heavy walls could support stone arches (mainly the Roman barrel arch), at least in France and Spain, which in turn permitted fireproof stone and masonry roofs. Long experience had shown that basilica-style churches, with their wooden trusses and wooden roofs, were notoriously susceptible to destruction by fire.

Romanesque architecture sprouted all over Europe, and while it showed great regional variation its main lines are clear enough. The Benedictine pilgrimage church of Saint Sernin in Toulouse was designed to accommodate the large number of pilgrims as they made their way to the famous shrine of Santiago de Compostela in Spain. A glimpse at the floor plan [7.12] and the interior [7.13] shows clearly that the generous interior space was articulated in such a manner that large numbers of persons besides the monastic community could move freely through the

7.14 Jamb on the central portal, Saint Gilles du Gard, France. c. 1140. Notice the echoes of classical column capitals and low-relief carving on the jambs.

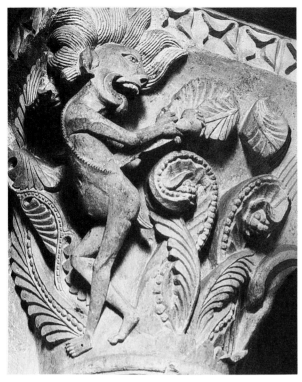

7.15 *Demon of Luxury,* nave capital sculpture, abbey church of La Madeleine, Vézelay. c. 1130. This kind of extravagant figure would be criticized by monastic reformers of the 12th century.

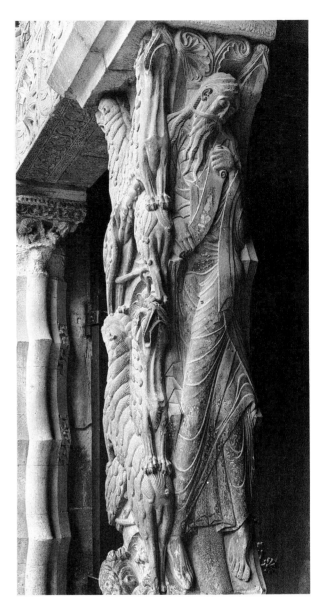

7.16 *Jeremiah the prophet,* trumeau of south portal, Saint Pierre, Moissac, France. Early 12th century. The serpentine figure of the prophet leans toward the church as he holds the scroll of his biblical book. The lions probably reflect the influence of Islamic art from Spain.

building. For example, the floor plan allows for an aisle parallel to the nave to go completely around the church. In that fashion the monastic choir, which extended out into the nave, was circumvented by the faithful—who could make a complete circle of the church without disturbing the monks.

Exterior church decoration was almost unknown in the Carolingian period, but during the Romanesque period there was a veritable explosion of exterior sculpture. The lack of interior light (precluded by the thick solid walls needed for the roof vaulting) drove the artist outside, in a sense. A favorite area of decoration was the *portal* or doorway, since the crowds would pass through the doors to enter the church and receive edifying instruction in the proc-

ess. The artist might decorate a door jamb [7.14], a capital [7.15], or the central supporting post of a portal, the *trumeau* [7.16].

The fullest iconographic program of the Romanesque sculptor can usually be found in the half moon-shaped space called the *tympanum* over the portal; Romanesque churches in France offer many splendid examples of this elaborated art. The sculptural program over the inner west door of the Benedictine abbey church of Sainte Madeleine at Vézelay is representative of the elaborated art in stone [7.17].

The Vézelay tympanum depicts Christ, ascending into heaven, giving his church the mission to preach the gospel to the entire world. Christ, in the center almond-shape called the *mandorla,* sends the power of

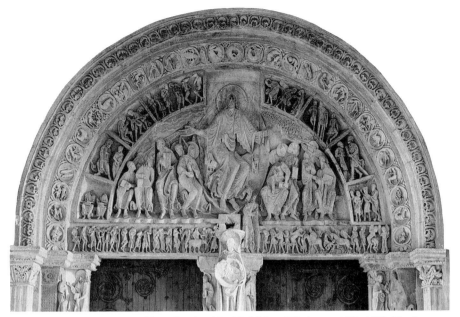

7.17 *Pentecost,* tympanum, abbey church of La Madeleine, Vézelay. c. 1120–1132. The lower band of figures reflects all of the peoples of the earth called to salvation by the central figure of Christ.

the Holy Spirit into the apostles who cluster on either side and just below with copies of the gospel in their hands. Below the apostles the lintel stone depicts the peoples of the world, including fanciful races known to the sculptor only through the legendary travel books and encyclopedias that circulated in Europe. The theme of the exotic peoples to be healed by the gospel is repeated in the eight arching compartments above the central scene, which depict strange peoples, lepers, cripples, and others who need to hear the gospel. The outer arches, or *archivolts,* depict the signs of the Zodiac and the symbolic seasons of the year, a reminder that the gospel depicted in the central scene is to be preached "in season and out"; these symbolic medallions are interspersed with mythical and fantastic beasts. The outer archivolts are purely decorative, derived perhaps from Islamic sources known to the artists through the Muslim architecture of Spain.

Romanesque style was a European phenomenon—its variant forms in Italy, Germany, and England give ample testimony—and a summing-up of much of European culture between the end of the Carolingian period and the rise of city life and the Gothic style in the late 12th century. The roots of the Romanesque were in the Benedictine tradition of service, scholarship, and solidity. Churches like Vézelay also manifest the period's concern with travel, expansion, and the attendant knowledge that comes from such mobility. When reaction came against the more extravagant forms of Romanesque decoration it came from Bernard of Clairvaux (1090–1153), who was primarily a monastic reformer. Bernard was horrified by the fantastic nature of Romanesque sculpture since he felt so many "and so marvelous are the varieties of diverse shapes that we are more tempted to read in the marbles than in the Book and to spend our whole day wondering at these things rather than meditating on the Law of God." Even Bernard's strictures testify to the close relationship between the Benedictines and the Romanesque (especially the French Romanesque), which is another reason the period after Charlemagne and before the primacy of the city can be called simply the Benedictine Age.

Summary

Our attention in this chapter shifted from Byzantium to the West and, more specifically, to the rise of the kingdom of the Franks under Charlemagne. The so-called Carolingian Renaissance rekindled the life of culture after the dark period following the fall of the last Roman emperor in the West in the late 5th century and the rise of the so-called barbarian tribes.

Charlemagne's reign saw the standardization of monasticism, worship, music, and education in the church. Those reforms would give general shape to Western Catholicism that, in some ways, endured into the modern period. Equally important was Charlemagne's assumption of the title of Holy Roman Emperor. That act would establish a political office that would exist in Europe until the end of World War I in the 20th century. It also became a cause for friction between Rome and Constantinople because the Byzantine emperors saw Charlemagne's act as an intrusion on their legitimate claim to be the successsors of the old Roman empire.

The Carolingian world was essentially rural and feudal. Society was based on a rather rigid hierarchy with the emperor at the top, the nobles and higher clergy below him, and the vast sea of peasants bound to the land at the bottom of the pyramid. There was little in the way of city life on any scale. The outpost of rural Europe was the miniature town known as the monastery or the stronghold of the nobles. The rise of the city and increased social mobility would eventually destroy the largely agricultural and feudal society as the High Middle Ages emerged in the 11th century.

Finally there was Charlemagne as a mythic figure who eventually became drawn larger than life in *The Song of Roland*. The growth of such myths always have some deep desires behind them. In the case of Charlemagne, the desire was to describe the ideal warrior who could perform two very fundamental tasks for Europe: vanquish the Islamic powers which threatened Christian Europe and provide a model for a unified empire (the Holy Roman Empire) that would be both a perfect feudal society and one strong enough to accomplish the first task of destroying Islam. Not without reason was the *Song of Roland* a central poem for the first Crusaders who turned their faces to the East.

Pronunciation Guide

Aachen: Aw-ken
Aix-la-Chapelle: Eye-lah-shap-el
Alcuin: Al-cue-in
Dagulf: Dah-gulf
Harun al-Rashid: Haw-RUNE all-raw-sheed
horarium: hoar-ARE-e-um
Hroswitha: Haw-ros-WITH-ah
psalter: SALT-er
Quem Quæritis: kwem-QUAY-re-tus
Roland: ROLL-on
Roncesvalles: Ron-sa-vals
trope: TROP
Utrecht: YOU-trek(t)
Vézelay: Vez-e-LAY

Exercises

1. The "seven liberal arts" are divided into the trivium and the quadrivium. How much of the trivium lingers in primary education today? What has been added to those "trivial" subjects?
2. Two subjects studied in the quadrivium were music and astronomy. Those subjects were quite different from what we understand by them today. How were they understood and how do we understand them?
3. One feature of the Carolingian period was the central place of monasticism. Why was monasticism exceptionally suited to a time when there was little urban life?
4. Many scholars have argued that monasticism is the living out of a utopian ideal. How is monasticism as an "utopian" society and to what degree is it also a form of countercultural living?
5. Why is plainchant (Gregorian chant) ideally suited for congregational singing, especially for the unaccompanied voice?
6. Contrast the place of books in early medieval culture and in our own beyond the obvious issue of our better production technologies.
7. Drama evolved out of worship in the early medieval period just as Greek tragedy evolved out of worship in its time. Speculate on why there should be this connection between worship and drama.
8. Byzantine churches tended to lavish their decorative efforts on the inside of churches while romanesque churches tended to decorate the outsides, more especially the façades. Suggest reasons for this widely observable fact.

Further Reading

Boussard, Jacques. *The Civilization of Charlemagne*. Translated by Frances Partridge. New York: McGraw-Hill, 1968. A well-illustrated survey with a detailed bibliography of more specialized sources.

Brault, Gerard. *The Song of Roland*. 2nd vol. University Park: University of Pennsylvania Press, 1978. A critical edition of the work with exhaustive notes. Essential.

Brondsted, Johannes. *The Vikings*. Translated by Kalle Skov. New York: Penguin Books, 1960. A basic survey of the Northmen; with some illustrations in black and white.

Bullough, Donald. *The Age of Charlemagne*. New York: Putnam, 1966. Well-written and lavishly illustrated.

Dunbabin, Jean. *France in the Making*. New York: Oxford University Press, 1985. An account of how the Frankish kingdom evolved into what we know as France.

Folz, Robert. *The Coronation of Charlemagne: 25th December 800*. Translated by J. E. Anderson. London: Routledge & Kegan Paul, 1974. A detailed but readable study of Charlemagne's imperial ideals.

Henderson, George. *Early Medieval*. New York: Penguin Books, 1972. Part of the "style and civilization" series; an extremely readable and thorough study of artistic styles in the early medieval period with 150 illustrations and a thorough bibliography.

Knowles, David. *Christian Monasticism*. New York: McGraw-Hill, 1969. A readable survey of the history of Christian monasticism by a distinguished monastic historian.

Price, Lorna. *The Plan of St. Gall in Brief*. Berkeley: University of California, 1982. An inexpensive condensed edition of the definitive study of Walter Horn and Ernest Born. Excellent drawings and floor plans. Very valuable.

Riche, Pierre. *Daily Life in the World of Charlemagne*. Translated by JoAnn MacNamara. Philadelphia: University of Pennsylvania Press, 1978. A fascinating and indispensable study of all facets of Carolingian life.

Thorpe, Lewis (trans.). *Einhard and Notker the Stammerer: Two Lives of Charlemagne*. New York: Penguin Books, 1969. Basic sources from the period with a good introduction.

Wallace-Hadrill, J. M. *The Frankish Church*. Oxford: The Clarendon Press, 1983. The definitive study of ecclesiastical life in the age of Charlemagne.

Reading Selections

Everyman

HERE BEGINNETH A TREATISE HOW THE HIGH FATHER OF HEAVEN SENDETH DEATH TO SUMMON EVERY CREATURE TO COME AND GIVE ACCOUNT OF THEIR LIVES IN THIS WORLD, AND IS IN MANNER OF A MORAL PLAY.

MESSENGER   I pray you all give your audience,
And hear this matter with reverence,
By figure° a moral play: *in form*
The *Summoning of Everyman* called it is,
That of our lives and ending shows   5
How transitory we be all day.°   *always*
This matter is wondrous precious,
But the intent of it is more gracious,
And sweet to bear away.
The story saith: Man, in the beginning   10
Look well, and take good heed to the ending,
Be you never so gay!
Ye think sin in the beginning full sweet,
Which in the end causeth the soul to weep,
When the body lieth in clay.   20
Here shall you see how Fellowship and Jollity,
Both Strength, Pleasure, and Beauty,
Will fade from thee as flower in May;
For ye shall hear how our Heaven King
Calleth Everyman to a general reckoning: 20
Give audience, and hear what he doth say.   [*Exit*]

[GOD *speaketh*]

GOD   I perceive, here in my majesty,
How that all creatures be to me unkind,°   *ungrateful*
Living without dread in worldly prosperity:
Of ghostly sight the people be so blind,   25
Drowned in sin, they know me not for their God;
In worldly riches is all their mind,
They fear not my righteousness, the sharp rod.
My law that I showed, when I for them died,
They forget clean, and shedding of my blood red;   30
I hanged between two, it cannot be denied;
To get them life I suffered to be dead;
I healed their feet, with thorns hurt was my head.
I could do no more than I did, truly;
And now I see the people do clean forsake me: 35
They use the seven deadly sins damnable,
As pride, covetise, wrath, and lechery°   *covetousness*
Now in the world be made commendable;
And thus they leave of angels the heavenly company.
Every man liveth so after his own pleasure,   40
And yet of their life they be nothing sure:
I see the more that I them forbear
The worse they be from year to year.
All that liveth appaireth° fast;   *degenerates*
Therefore I will, in all the haste,   45
Have a reckoning of every man's person;
For, and° I leave the people thus alone   *if*
In their life and wicked tempests,°   *tumults*
Verily they will become much worse than beasts;
For now one would by envy another up eat;   50
Charity they do all clean forget.
I hoped well that every man
In my glory should make his mansion,
And thereto I had them all elect;
But now I see, like traitors deject,°   *abject*
They thank me not for the pleasure that I to° them meant   *for*
Nor yet for their being that I them have lent.
I proffered the people great multitude of mercy,
And few there be that asketh it heartily.°   *earnestly*
They be so cumbered with wordly riches   60
That needs on them I must do justice,
On every man living without fear.
Where art thou, Death, thou mighty messenger?

[*Enter* DEATH]

DEATH   Almighty God, I am here at your
        will,
        Your commandment to fulfil.   65
GOD   Go thou to Everyman,
        And show him, in my name,
        A pilgrimage he must on him take,
        Which he in no wise may escape;
        And that he bring with him
        a sure reckoning   70
        Without delay or any tarrying. [GOD *withdraws*]
DEATH   Lord, I will in the world
        go run overall,°   *everywhere*
        And cruelly outsearch both great and
        small;
        Every man will I beset that liveth beastly
        Out of God's laws, and dreadeth not folly.   75
        He that loveth riches I will strike with my
        dart,
        His sight to blind, and from heaven
        to depart°—   *separate*
        Except that alms be his good friend—
        In hell for to dwell, world without end.
        Lo, yonder I see Everyman walking.   80
        Full little he thinketh on my coming;
        His mind is on fleshly lusts and his
        treasure,
        And great pain it shall cause him to
        endure
        Before the Lord, Heaven King.

[*Enter* EVERYMAN]

        Everyman, stand still!
        Whither art thou going   85
        Thus gaily? Hast thou thy Maker forget?
EVERYMAN   Why askest thou?
        Wouldest thou wit?°   *know*
DEATH   Yea, sir; I will show you:
        In great haste I am sent to thee   90
        From God out of his majesty.
EVERYMAN   What, sent to me?
DEATH   Yea, certainly.
        Though thou have forget him here,
        He thinketh on thee
        in the heavenly sphere,   95
        As, ere we depart, thou shalt know.
EVERYMAN   What desireth God of me?
DEATH   That shall I show thee:
        A reckoning he will needs have
        Without any longer respite.   100
EVERYMAN   To give a reckoning longer
        leisure I crave;
        This blind° matter troubleth my wit.   *obscure*
DEATH   On thee thou must take a long
        journey;

Therefore thy book of count°
        with thee thou bring,   *account*
For turn again° thou cannot by   *return*
        no way.
And look thou be sure of thy reckoning,
For before God thou shalt answer, and
        show
Thy many bad deeds, and good but a few;
How thou hast spent thy life, and in what
        wise,
Before the chief Lord of paradise.   110
Have ado that we were in that way,
For, wit thou well, thou shalt make none
        attorney.
EVERYMAN   Full unready I am such reckoning
        to give.
        I know thee not. What messenger art
        thou?
DEATH   I am Death,
        that no man dreadeth,   115
        For every man I rest,°   *arrest*
        and no man spareth;
        For it is God's commandment
        That all to me should be obedient.
EVERYMAN   O Death, thou comest when I
        had thee least in mind!
        In thy power it lieth me to save;   120
        Yet of my good° will I give thee,   *goods*
        if thou will be kind:
        Yea, a thousand pound shalt thou have,
        And defer this matter till another day.
DEATH   Everyman, it may not be, by no
        way.
        I set not by° gold, silver, nor   *care not for*
        riches,
        Ne by pope, emperor, king, duke, ne
        princes;
        For, and° I would receive gifts great,   *if*
        All the world I might get;
        But my custom is clean contrary.
        I give thee no respite.
        Come hence, and not tarry.   130
EVERYMAN   Alas, shall I have no longer
        respite?
        I may say Death giveth no warning!
        To think on thee, it maketh my heart sick,
        For all unready is my book of reckoning.
        But twelve year and I might have abiding,   135
        My counting-book I would make so clear
        That my reckoning I should not need to fear.
        Wherefore, Death, I pray thee, for God's
        mercy,
        Spare me till I be provided of remedy.
DEATH   Thee availeth not to
        cry, weep, and pray;   140
        But haste thee lightly that thou were gone

that journey,
And prove thy friends if thou can;
For, wit thou well,
    the tide° abideth no man,   *time*
And in the world each living creature
For Adam's sin must die of nature.   145

EVERYMAN   Death, if I should this pilgrimage
    take,
And my reckoning surely make,
Show me, for saint charity,
Should I not come again shortly?

DEATH   No, Everyman;
    and thou be once there,   150
Thou mayst never more come here,
Trust me verily.

EVERYMAN   O gracious God in the high seat
    celestial,
Have mercy on me in this most need!
Shall I have no company
    from this vale terrestrial   155
Of mine acquaintance, that way me to
    lead?

DEATH   Yea, if any be so hardy
That would go with thee and bear thee
    company.
Hie thee that thou were gone to God's
    magnificence,
Thy reckoning to give before his
    presence.   160
What, weenest° thou thy life   *suppose*
    is given thee,
And thy worldly goods also?

EVERYMAN   I had wend° so, verily.   *supposed*

DEATH   Nay, nay; it was but lent thee;
For as soon as thou art go,°   *gone*
Another a while shall have it,
    and then go therefro,°   *from it*
Even as thou hast done.
Everyman, thou art mad! Thou hast thy
    wits five,
And here on earth will not amend thy life;
For suddenly I do come.   170

EVERYMAN   O wretched caitiff, whither shall
    I flee,
That I might scape this endless sorrow?
Now, gentle Death, spare me till to-
    morrow,
That I may amend me
With good advisement.°   *reflection*

DEATH   Nay, thereto I will not consent,
Nor no man will I respite;
But to the heart suddenly I shall smite
Without any advisement.
And now out of thy sight I will me hie;   180
See thou make thee ready shortly,
For thou mayst say this is the day

That no man living may scape
    away. *Exit* DEATH]

EVERYMAN   Alas, I may well weep with sighs
    deep!
Now have I no manner of company   185
To help me in my journey,
    and me to keep;°   *guard*
And also my writing is full unready.
How shall I do now for to excuse me?
I would to God I had never
    be get!°   *been born*
To my soul a full great profit it had be;   190
For now I fear pains huge and great.
The time passeth. Lord, help, that all
    wrought!
For though I mourn it availeth nought.
The day passeth, and is almost ago;°   *gone*
I wot not well what for to do.   195
To whom were I best my complaint to
    make?
What and° I to Fellowship thereof spake,   *if*
And showed him of this sudden chance?
For in him is all mine affiance;°   *trust*
We have in the world so many a day   200
Be good friends in sport and play.
I see him yonder, certainly.
I trust that he will bear me company;
Therefore to him will I speak to ease my
    sorrow.
Well met, good Fellowship,
    and good morrow!   205

[FELLOWSHIP *speaketh*]

FELLOWSHIP   Everyman, good morrow, by
    this day!
Sir, why lookest thou so piteously?
If any thing be amiss, I pray thee me say,
That I may help to remedy.

EVERYMAN   Yea, good Fellowship, yea;   210
I am in great jeopardy.

FELLOWSHIP   My true friend, show to me
    your mind;
I will not forsake thee to my life's end,
In the way of good company.

EVERYMAN   That was well spoken,
    and lovingly.   215

FELLOWSHIP   Sir, I must needs know
    your heaviness;°   *sorrow*
I have pity to see you in any distress.
If any have you wronged, ye shall
    revenged be,
Though I on the ground be slain for
    thee—
Though that I know
    before that I should die.   220

EVERYMAN   Verily, Fellowship, gramercy.

FELLOWSHIP   Tush! by thy thanks I set not a straw.
Show me your grief, and say no more.

EVERYMAN   If I my heart should to you break,°   *open*
And then you to turn your mind from me,   225
And would not me comfort when ye hear me speak,
Then should I ten times sorrier be.

FELLOWSHIP   Sir, I say as I will do indeed.

EVERYMAN   Then be you a good friend at need:
I have found you true herebefore.   230

FELLOWSHIP   And so ye shall evermore;
For, in faith, and thou go to hell,
I will not forsake thee by the way.

EVERYMAN   Ye speak like a good friend; I believe you well.
I shall deserve° it, and I may.   *repay*

FELLOWSHIP   I speak of no deserving, by this day!
For he that will say, and nothing do,
Is not worthy with good company to go;
Therefore show me the grief of your mind,
As to your friend most loving and kind.   240

EVERYMAN   I shall show you how it is:
Commanded I am to go a journey,
A long way, hard and dangerous,
And give a strait count,°   *strict account*
without delay,
Before the high Judge, Adonai.   245
Wherefore, I pray you, bear me company,
As ye have promised, in this journey.

FELLOWSHIP   That is matter indeed. Promise is duty;
But, and I should take such a voyage on me,
I know it well, it should be to my pain;   250
Also it maketh me afeard, certain.
But let us take counsel here as well as we can,
For your words would fear°   *frighten*
a strong man.

EVERYMAN   Why, ye said if I had need
Ye would me never forsake, quick ne dead,   255
Though it were to hell, truly.

FELLOWSHIP   So I said, certainly,
But such pleasures be set aside, the sooth to say;
And also, if we took such a journey,
When should we come again?   260

EVERYMAN   Nay, never again, till the day of doom.

FELLOWSHIP   In faith, then will not I come there!
Who hath you these tidings brought?

EVERYMAN   Indeed, Death was with me here.

FELLOWSHIP   Now, by God   265
that all hath bought,°   *redeemed*
If Death were the messenger,
For no man that is living to-day
I will not go that loath° journey—   *loathsome*
Not for the father that begat me!

EVERYMAN   Ye promised otherwise, pardie.°   *by God*

FELLOWSHIP   I wot well I said so, truly;
And yet if thou wilt eat, and drink, and make good cheer,
Or haunt to women the lusty company,
I would not forsake you while the day is clear,
Trust me verily.   275

EVERYMAN   Yea, thereto ye would be ready!
To go to mirth, solace, and play,
Your mind will sooner apply,°   *attend*
Than to bear me company in my long journey.

FELLOWSHIP   Now, in good faith, I will not that way.   280
But and thou will murder, or any man kill,
In that I will help thee with a good will.

EVERYMAN   O, that is a simple advice indeed.
Gentle fellow, help me in my necessity!
We have loved long, and now I need;   285
And now, gentle Fellowship, remember me.

FELLOWSHIP   Whether ye have loved me or no,
By Saint John, I will not with thee go.

EVERYMAN   Yet, I pray thee, take the labour, and do so much for me
To bring me forward,° for   *escort me*
saint charity,
And comfort me till I come without the town.

FELLOWSHIP   Nay, and thou would give me a new gown,
I will not a foot with thee go;
But, and thou had tarried, I would not have left thee so.
And as now God speed thee in thy journey,   295
For from thee I will depart as fast as I may.

EVERYMAN   Whither away, Fellowship? Will thou forsake me?

FELLOWSHIP   Yea, by my fay°! To God I   *faith*
betake° thee.   *commend*

EVERYMAN   Farewell, good Fellowship; for thee my heart is sore.

Adieu for ever! I shall see thee no more.   300

FELLOWSHIP   In faith, Everyman, farewell
    now at the ending;
For you I will remember that parting is
    mourning.

[*Exit* FELLOWSHIP]

EVERYMAN   Alack! shall we thus depart°   *part*
    indeed—
Ah, Lady, help!—without any more
    comfort?
Lo, Fellowship forsaketh me in my most
    need.   305
For help in this world whither shall I
    resort?
Fellowship herebefore with me would
    merry make,
And now little sorrow for me doth he
    take.
It is said, "In prosperity men friends may
    find,
Which in adversity be full unkind."   310
Now whither for succour shall I flee,
Sith° that Fellowship hath forsaken me?   *since*
To my kinsmen I will, truly,
Praying them to help me in my necessity;
I believe that they will do so,   315
For kind will creep where it may not go.
I will go say,°   *essay, try*
    for yonder I see them.
Where be ye now, my friends and
    kinsmen?

[*Enter* KINDRED *and* COUSIN]

KINDRED   Here be we now at your
    commandment.
Cousin, I pray you show us your intent   320
In any wise, and do not spare.

COUSIN   Yea, Everyman, and to us declare
If ye be disposed to go anywhither;°   *anywhere*
For, wit you well, we will live and die
    together.

KINDRED   In wealth and woe   325
    we will with you hold,°   *side*
For over his kin a man may be bold.

EVERYMAN   Gramercy, my friends and
    kinsmen kind.
Now shall I show you the grief of my
    mind:
I was commanded by a messenger,
That is a high king's chief officer;   330
He bade me go a pilgrimage, to my pain,
And I know well I shall never come again;
Also I must give a reckoning strait,
For I have a great enemy that hath me in
    wait,

Which intendeth me for to hinder.   335

KINDRED   What account is that which ye
    must render?
That would I know.

EVERYMAN   Of all my works I must show
How I have lived and my days spent;
Also of ill deeds that I have used°   *practiced*
In my time, sith life was me lent;
And of all virtues that I have refused.
Therefore, I pray you, go thither with me
To help to make mine account, for saint
    charity.

COUSIN   What, to go thither?
    Is that the matter?   345
Nay, Everyman, I had liefer fast bread and
    water
All this five year and more.

EVERYMAN   Alas, that ever I was bore!°   *born*
For now shall I never be merry,
If that you forsake me.   350

KINDRED   Ah, sir, what ye be a merry man!
Take good heart to you, and make no
    moan.
But one thing I warn you, by Saint
    Anne—
As for me, ye shall go alone.

EVERYMAN   My Cousin,
    will you not with me go?   355

COUSIN   No, by our Lady! I have the cramp
    in my toe.
Trust not to me, for, so God me speed,
I will deceive you in your most need.

KINDRED   It availeth not us to tice.
Ye shall have my maid with all my heart;   360
She loveth to go to feasts, there to
    be nice,°   *wanton*
And to dance, and abroad to start:
I will give her leave to help you in that
    journey,
If that you and she may agree.

EVERYMAN   Now show me the very   365
    effect° of your mind: *tenor*
Will you go with me, or abide behind?

KINDRED   Abide behind? Yea, that will I, and
    I may!
Therefore farewell till another
    day. [*Exit* KINDRED]

EVERYMAN   How should I be merry or glad?
For fair promises men to me make,   370
But when I have most need they me
    forsake.
I am deceived; that maketh me sad.

COUSIN   Cousin Everyman, farewell now,
For verily I will not go with you.
Also of mine own an unready reckoning   375
I have to account; therefore I make

tarrying.
Now God keep thee, for now I
  go. [*Exit* COUSIN]

EVERYMAN Ah, Jesus, is all come hereto?
Lo, fair words maketh fools fain;
They promise, and nothing will do,
  certain.   380
My kinsmen promised me faithfully
For to abide with me steadfastly,
And now fast away do they flee:
Even so Fellowship promised me.
What friend were best me of to provide? 385
I lose my time here longer to abide.
Yet in my mind a thing there is:
All my life I have loved riches;
If that my Good° now help me might,   *Goods*
He would make my heart full light. 390
I will speak to him in this distress—
Where art thou, my Goods and riches?

[GOODS *speaks from a corner*]

GOODS Who calleth me? Everyman? What!
  hast thou haste?
I lie here in corners, trussed and piled so
  high,
And in chests I am locked so fast,   395
Also sacked in bags. Thou mayst see
  with thine eye
I cannot stir; in packs low I lie.
What would you have? Lightly° me   *quickly*
  say.
EVERYMAN Come hither, Good, in all the
  haste thou may,
For of counsel I must desire thee.   400
GOODS Sir, and ye in the world have sorrow
  or adversity,
That can I help you to remedy shortly.
EVERYMAN It is another disease°   *trouble*
  that grieveth me;
In this world it is not, I tell thee so.
I am sent for, another way to go,   405
To give a strait count general
Before the highest Jupiter of all;
And all my life I have had joy and
  pleasure in thee,
Therefore, I pray thee, go with me;
For, peradventure, thou mayst
  before God Almighty   410
My reckoning help to clean and purify;
For it is said ever among
That money maketh all right that is wrong.
GOODS Nay, Everyman, I sing another song.
I follow no man in such voyages;   415
For, and I went with thee,
Thou shouldst fare much the worse for
  me;

For because on me thou did set thy mind,
Thy reckoning I have made blotted°   *obscure*
  and blind,
That thine account thou cannot make
  truly;   420
And that hast thou for the love of me.
EVERYMAN That would grieve me full sore,
When I should come to that fearful
  answer.
Up, let us go thither together.
GOODS Nay, not so! I am too brittle,
  I may not endure;   425
I will follow no man one foot, be ye sure.
EVERYMAN Alas, I have thee loved, and had
  great pleasure
All my life-days on good and treasure.
GOODS That is to thy damnation, without
  leasing,
For my love is contrary to the love
  everlasting;   430
But if thou had me loved moderately
  during,
As to the poor to give part of me,
Then shouldst thou not in this
  dolour° be,   *distress*
Nor in this great sorrow and care.
EVERYMAN Lo, now was I deceived   435
  ere I was ware,°   *aware*
And all I may write misspending of time.
GOODS What, weenest thou that I am thine?
EVERYMAN I had wend° so.   *supposed*
GOODS Nay, Everyman, I say no.
As for a while I was lent thee;   440
A season thou hast had me in prosperity.
My condition° is man's soul to kill;   *nature*
If I save one, a thousand I do spill.°   *ruin*
Weenest thou that I will follow thee?
Nay, not from this world, verily.   445
EVERYMAN I had wend otherwise.
GOODS Therefore to thy soul Good is a
  thief;
For when thou art dead, this is
  my guise°—   *practice*
Another to deceive in this same wise
As I have done thee,   450
  and all to his soul's reprief.°—   *shame*
EVERYMAN O false Good, cursed may
  thou be,
Thou traitor to God, that hast deceived me
And caught me in thy snare!
GOODS Marry, thou brought thyself in care,
  Whereof I am glad;   455
I must needs laugh, I cannot be sad.
EVERYMAN Ah, Good, thou hast had
  long my heartly° love;   *heartfelt*
I gave thee that which should be the

Lord's above.
But wilt thou not go with me indeed?
I pray thee truth to say.   460
GOODS No, so God me speed!
Therefore farewell, and have good day.

[*Exit* GOODS]

EVERYMAN O, to whom shall I make my
        moan
    For to go with me in that heavy journey?
    First Fellowship said he would   465
        with me gone;°   *go*
    His words were very pleasant and gay,
    But afterward he left me alone.
    Then spake I to my kinsmen, all in
        despair,
    And also they gave me words fair;
    They lacked no fair speaking,   470
    But all forsook me in the ending.
    Then went I to my Goods, that I loved
        best,
    In hope to have comfort, but there had I
        least;
    For my Goods sharply did me tell
    That he bringeth many into hell.   475
    Then of myself I was ashamed,
    And so I am worthy to be blamed;
    Thus may I well myself hate.
    Of whom shall I now counsel take?
    I think that I shall never speed   480
    Till that I go to my Good Deed.
    But, alas, she is so weak
    That she can neither go° nor speak;   *walk*
    Yet will I venture° on her now.   *gamble*
    My Good Deeds, where be you?   485

[GOOD DEEDS *speaks from the ground*]

GOOD DEEDS Here I lie, cold in the ground;
    Thy sins hath me sore bound,
    That I cannot stir.
EVERYMAN O Good Deeds, I stand in fear!
    I must you pray of counsel,   490
    For help now should come right well.
GOOD DEEDS Everyman, I have
        understanding
    That ye be summoned account to make
    Before Messias, of Jerusalem King;
    And you do by me, that journey   495
        with you will I take.
EVERYMAN Therefore I come to you, my
        moan to make;
    I pray you that ye will go with me.
GOOD DEEDS I would full fain, but I cannot
        stand, verily.
EVERYMAN Why, is there anything on
        you fall°?   *befallen*

GOOD DEEDS Yea, sir, I may thank you
        of° all;   *for*
    If ye had perfectly cheered me,
    Your book of count full ready had be.
    Look, the books of your works and deeds
        eke°!   *also*
    Behold how they lie under the feet,
    To your soul's heaviness.   505
EVERYMAN Our Lord Jesus help me!
    For one letter here I cannot see.
GOOD DEEDS There is a blind reckoning in
        time of distress.
EVERYMAN Good Deeds, I pray you help me
        in this need,
    Or else I am for ever damned indeed;   510
    Therefore help me to make reckoning
    Before the Redeemer of all thing,
    That King is, and was, and ever shall.
GOOD DEEDS Everyman, I am sorry of your
        fall,
    And fain would I help you, and I were
        able.   515
EVERYMAN Good Deeds, your counsel I pray
        you give me.
GOOD DEEDS That shall I do verily;
    Though that on my feet I may not go,
    I have a sister that shall with you also,
    Called Knowledge, which shall with you
        abide,   520
    To help you to make that dreadful
        reckoning.

[*Enter* KNOWLEDGE]

KNOWLEDGE Everyman, I will go with thee,
        and be thy guide,
    In thy most need to go by thy side.
EVERYMAN In good condition I am now in
        every thing,
    And am wholly content with this good
        thing,
    Thanked be God my creator.
GOOD DEEDS And when she hath brought
        you there
    Where thou shalt heal thee of thy
        smart,°   *pain*
    Then go you with your reckoning and
        your Good Deeds together,
    For to make you joyful at heart   530
    Before the blessed Trinity.
EVERYMAN My Good Deeds, gramercy!
    I am well content, certainly,
    With your words sweet.
KNOWLEDGE Now go we together lovingly   535
    To Confession, that cleansing river.
EVERYMAN For joy I weep; I would we were
        there!

But, I pray you, give me cognition°   *knowledge*
Where dwelleth that holy man,
  Confession.
KNOWLEDGE   In the house of salvation: 540
We shall find him in that place,
That shall us comfort, by God's grace.

[KNOWLEDGE *takes* EVERYMAN *to* CONFESSION]

Lo, this is Confession. Kneel down and
  ask mercy,
For he is in good conceit° with   *esteem*
  God Almighty.
EVERYMAN   O glorious fountain,
  that all uncleanness doth clarify,   545
Wash from me the spots of vice unclean,
That on me no sin may be seen.
I come with Knowledge for my
  redemption,
Redempt with heart and full contrition;
For I am commanded a pilgrimage to take,   550
And great accounts before God to make.
Now I pray you, Shrift,° mother   *confession*
  of salvation,
Help my Good Deeds for my piteous
  exclamation.
CONFESSION   I know your sorrow well,
  Everyman.
Because with Knowledge ye come to me,   555
I will you comfort as well as I can,
And a precious jewel I will give thee,
Called penance, voider° of adversity;   *expeller*
Therewith shall your body chastised be,
With abstinence and perseverance   560
  in God's service.
Here shall you receive that scourge of me,
Which is penance strong that ye must
  endure,
To remember thy Saviour was scourged
  for thee
With sharp scourges, and suffered it
  patiently;
So must thou, ere thou scape that   565
  painful pilgrimage.
Knowledge, keep him in this voyage,
And by that time Good Deeds will be
  with thee.
But in any wise be siker° of mercy,   *sure*
For your time draweth fast;
  and° ye will saved be,   *if*
Ask God mercy, and he will grant truly.   570
When with the scourge of penance
  man doth him° bind,   *himself*
The oil of forgiveness then shall he find.
EVERYMAN   Thanked be God for his gracious
  work!
For now I will my penance begin;

This hath rejoiced and lighted° my   *lightened*
  heart,
Though the knots be painful and hard
  within.
KNOWLEDGE   Everyman, look your penance
  that ye fulfil,
What pain that ever it to you be;
And Knowledge shall give you counsel at
  will
How your account ye shall make clearly.   580
EVERYMAN   O eternal God, O heavenly
  figure,
O way of righteousness, O goodly vision,
Which descended down in a virgin pure
Because he would every man redeem,
Which Adam forfeited by his disobedience: 585
O blessed Godhead,
  elect and high divine,   *divinity*
Forgive my grievous offence;
Here I cry thee mercy in this presence.
O ghostly treasure, O ransomer and
  redeemer,
Of all the world hope and conductor,   590
Mirror of joy, and founder of mercy,
Which enlumineth heaven
  and earth thereby,°   *besides*
Hear my clamorous complaint, though it
  late be;
Receive my prayers, of thy benignity;
Though I be a sinner most abominable,   595
Yet let my name be written in Moses'
  table.
O Mary, pray to the Maker of all thing,
Me for to help at my ending;
And save me from the power of my
  enemy,
For Death assaileth me strongly.   600
And, Lady, that I may by mean of thy
  prayer
Of your Son's glory to be partner,
By the means of his passion, I it crave;
I beseech you help my soul to save.
Knowledge, give me the scourge of
  penance;   605
My flesh therewith shall give acquittance:
I will now begin, if God give me grace.
KNOWLEDGE   Everyman, God give you
  time and space!°   *opportunity*
Thus I bequeath you in the hands of our
  Saviour;
Now may you make your reckoning sure.   610
EVERYMAN   In the name of the Holy Trinity,
My body sore punished shall be:
Take this, body, for the sin of the flesh!

[*Scourges himself*]

Also° thou delightest to go gay and fresh,   *as*
And in the way of damnation thou did me
    bring,   615
Therefore suffer now strokes and
    punishing.
Now of penance I will wade the water
    clear,
To save me from purgatory, that sharp
    fire.

        [GOOD DEEDS *rises from the ground*]

GOOD DEEDS   I thank God, now I can walk
    and go,
And am delivered of my sickness and woe.   620
Therefore with Everyman I will go, and
    not spare;
His good works I will help him to declare.
KNOWLEDGE   Now, Everyman, be merry and
    glad!
Your Good Deeds whole and sound,   625
Going upright upon the ground.
EVERYMAN   My heart is light, and shall be
    evermore;
Now will I smite faster than I did before.
GOOD DEEDS   Everyman, pilgrim, my special
    friend,
Blessed be thou without end;   630
For thee is preparate° the eternal glory.   *prepared*
Ye have me made whole and sound,
Therefore I will bide by thee
    in every stound.°   *trial*
EVERYMAN   Welcome, my Good Deeds; now I
    hear thy voice,
I weep for very sweetness of love.   635
KNOWLEDGE   Be no more sad, but ever
    rejoice;
God seeth thy living in his throne above.
Put on this garment to thy behoof,°   *advantage*
Which is wet with your tears,
Or else before God you may it miss,   640
When ye to your journey's end come shall.
EVERYMAN   Gentle Knowledge, what do ye it
    call?
KNOWLEDGE   It is a garment of sorrow:
From pain it will you borrow;°   *release*
Contrition it is,   645
That geteth forgiveness;
It pleaseth God passing° well.   *exceedingly*
GOOD DEEDS   Everyman, will you wear it
for your heal?°   *salvation*
EVERYMAN   Now blessed be Jesu, Mary's
    Son,
For now have I on true contrition.   650
And let us go now without tarrying;
Good Deeds, have we clear our reckoning?
GOOD DEEDS   Yea, indeed, I have it here.

EVERYMAN   Then I trust we need not fear;
Now, friends, let us not part in twain.   655
KNOWLEDGE   Nay, Everyman, that will we
    not, certain.
GOOD DEEDS   Yet must thou lead with thee
Three persons of great might.
EVERYMAN   Who should they be?
GOOD DEEDS   Discretion and Strength   660
    they hight,°   *are called*
And thy Beauty may not abide behind.
KNOWLEDGE   Also ye must call to mind
Your Five Wits° as for your   *senses*
    counsellors.
GOOD DEEDS   You must have them ready at
all hours.
EVERYMAN   How shall I get them hither?   665
KNOWLEDGE   You must call them all together,
And they will hear you
    incontinent.°   *immediately*
EVERYMAN   My friends, come hither and be
    present,
Discretion, Strength, my Five Wits, and
    Beauty.

[*Enter* BEAUTY, STRENGTH, DISCRETION, *and* FIVE
              WITS]

BEAUTY   Here at your will we be all ready.   670
What will ye that we should do?
GOOD DEEDS   That ye would with Everyman
    go,
And help him in his pilgrimage.
Advise° you, will ye with him or   *consider*
    not in that voyage?
STRENGTH   We will bring him all thither,   675
To his help and comfort, ye may believe me.
DISCRETION   So will we go with him all
    together.
EVERYMAN   Almighty God, lofed° may   *praised*
    thou be!
I give thee laud that I have hither brought
Strength, Discretion, Beauty, and Five
    Wits.   680
    Lack I nought.
And my Good Deeds, with Knowledge clear,
All be in my company at my will here;
I desire no more to° my business.   *for*
STRENGTH   And I, Strength, will by you
    stand in distress,
Though thou would in battle fight   685
    on the ground.
FIVE WITS   And though it were through the
    world round,
We will not depart for sweet ne sour.
BEAUTY   No more will I unto° death's   *until*
    hour,
Whatsoever thereof befall.

DISCRETION   Everyman, advise you first of all;   690
  Go with a good advisement°   *reflection*
    and deliberation.
  We all give you virtuous monition°   *forewarning*
  That all shall be well.
EVERYMAN   My friends, harken what I will tell:
  I pray God reward you in his   695
    heavenly sphere.
  Now harken, all that be here,
  For I will make my testament
  Here before you all present:
  In alms half my good I will give with my
    hands twain
  In the way of charity, with good intent,   700
  And the other half still shall remain
  In queth,° to be returned   *bequest*
    there° it ought to be.   *where*
  This I do in despite of the fiend of hell,
  To go quit out of his peril
  Ever after and this day.   705
KNOWLEDGE   Everyman, harken what I say:
  Go to priesthood, I you advise,
  And receive of him in any wise°   *without fail*
  The holy sacrament and ointment
    together.
  Then shortly see ye turn again hither;   710
  We will all abide you here.
FIVE WITS   Yea, Everyman, hie you that ye
    ready were.
  There is no emperor, king, duke, ne
    baron,
  That of God hath commission°   *authority*
  As hath the least priest in the world   715
    being;°   *living*
  For of the blessed sacraments pure and
    benign
  He beareth the keys,
    and thereof hath the cure°   *charge*
  For man's redemption—it is ever sure—
  Which God for our soul's medicine
  Gave us out of his heart with great   720
    pine.°   *suffering*
  Here in this transitory life, for thee and me,
  The blessed sacraments seven there be:
  Baptism, confirmation, with priesthood
    good,
  Which God their Saviour do buy or sell,
  Or they for any money do take or
    tell.°   *count out*
  Sinful priests giveth the sinners example
    bad;
  Their children sitteth by other men's fires,   760
    I have heard;
  And some haunteth women's company

With unclean life, as lusts of lechery:
These be with sin made blind.
FIVE WITS   I trust to God no such may we
    find;
  Therefore let us priesthood honour,   765
  And follow their doctrine for our souls'
    succour.
  We be their sheep, and they shepherds be
  By whom we all be kept in surety.
  Peace, for yonder I see Everyman come,
  Which hath made true satisfaction.   770
GOOD DEEDS   Methinks it is he indeed.

                [Re-enter EVERYMAN]

EVERYMAN   Now Jesu be your alder speed!
  I have received the sacrament for my
    redemption,
  And then mine extreme unction:
  Blessed be all they that counselled   775
    me to take it!
  And now, friends, let us go without
    longer respite;
  I thank God that ye have tarried so long.
  Now set each of you on this rood° your   *cross*
    hand,
  And shortly follow me:
  I go before there I would be;   780
    God be our guide!
STRENGTH   Everyman, we will not from you
    go
  Till ye have done this voyage long.
DISCRETION   I, Discretion, will bide by you
    also.
KNOWLEDGE   And though this pilgrimage
    be never so strong,°   *grievous*
  I will never part you fro.°   *from you*
STRENGTH   Everyman, I will be as sure by
    thee
  As ever I did by Judas Maccabee.

            [EVERYMAN *comes to his grave*]

EVERYMAN   Alas, I am so faint I may not
    stand;
  And the sacrament of God's precious flesh
    and blood,
  Marriage, the holy extreme unction,   725
    and penance;
  These seven be good to have in
    remembrance,
  Gracious sacraments of high divinity.
EVERYMAN   Fain would I receive that holy
    body,
  and meekly to my ghostly° father   *spiritual*
    I will go.
FIVE WITS   Everyman, that is the best that ye   730
    can do.

God will you to salvation bring,
To us Holy Scripture they do teach,
And converteth man from sin heaven to
reach;
God hath to them more power given   735
Than to any angel that is in heaven.
With five words he may consecrate,
God's body in flesh and blood to make,
And handleth his Maker between his
hands.
The priest bindeth and unbindeth all bands,   740
Both in earth and in heaven.
Thou ministers° all the sacraments   *administer*
seven;
Though we kissed thy feet, thou were
worthy;
Thou art surgeon that cureth sin deadly:
No remedy we find under God   745
But all only priesthood.
Everyman, God gave priests that dignity,
And setteth them in his stead among us to
be;
Thus be they above angels in degree.

[EVERYMAN *goes to the priest to receive
the last sacraments*]

KNOWLEDGE   If priests be good, it is so,
surely.   750
But when Jesus hanged on the cross with
great smart,
There he gave out of his blessed heart
The same sacrament in great torment:
He sold them not to us, that Lord
omnipotent.
Therefore Saint Peter the apostle doth say   755
That Jesu's curse hath all they
My limbs under me doth fold.
Friends, let us not turn again to this land,   790
Not for all the world's gold;
For into this cave must I creep
And turn to earth, and there to sleep.
BEAUTY   What, into this grave? Alas!
EVERYMAN   Yea, there shall ye consume,   795
more and less.
BEAUTY   And what, should I smother here?
EVERYMAN   Yea, by my faith, and never
more appear.
In this world live no more we shall,
But in heaven before the highest Lord of
all.
BEAUTY   I cross out all this; adieu,   800
by Saint John!
I take my cap in my lap, and am gone.
EVERYMAN   What, Beauty, whither will ye?
BEAUTY   Peace, I am deaf; I look not behind
me,

Not and thou wouldest give me all the
gold in thy chest.

[*Exit* BEAUTY]

EVERYMAN   Alas, whereto may I trust?   805
Beauty goeth fast away from me;
She promised with me to live and die.
STRENGTH   Everyman, I will thee also forsake
and deny;
Thy game liketh° me not at all.   *pleases*
EVERYMAN   Why, then, ye will forsake me   810
all?
Sweet Strength, tarry a little space.°   *while*
STRENGTH   Nay, sir, by the rood of grace!
I will hie me from thee fast,
Though thou weep till thy heart
to-brast.°   *break*
EVERYMAN   Ye would ever bide by me, ye   815
said.
STRENGTH   Yea, I have you far enough
conveyed.
Ye be old enough, I understand,
Your pilgrimage to take on hand;
I repent me that I hither came.
EVERYMAN   Strength, you to displease   820
I am to blame;
Yet promise is debt, this ye well wot.
STRENGTH   In faith, I care not.
Thou art but a fool to complain;
You spend your speech and waste your
brain.
Go thrust thee into the ground!   825

[*Exit* STRENGTH]

EVERYMAN   I had wend surer I should you
have found.
He that trusteth in his Strength
She him deceiveth at the length.
Both Strength and Beauty forsaketh me;
Yet they promised me fair and lovingly.   830
DISCRETION   Everyman, I will after Strength
be gone;
As for me, I will leave you alone.
EVERYMAN   Why, Discretion, will ye forsake me?
DISCRETION   Yea, in faith, I will go from
thee,
For when Strength goeth before   835
I follow after evermore.
EVERYMAN   Yet, I pray thee, for the love of
the Trinity,
Look in my grave once piteously.
DISCRETION   Nay, so nigh will I not come;
Farewell, every one!   840

[*Exit* DISCRETION]

EVERYMAN   O, all thing faileth, save God

alone—
Beauty, Strength, and Discretion;
For when Death bloweth his blast,
They all run from me full fast.

FIVE WITS   Everyman, my leave now   845
of thee I take;
I will follow the other, for here I thee
forsake.

EVERYMAN   Alas, then may I wail and weep,
For I took you for my best friend.

FIVE WITS   I will no longer thee keep;
Now farewell, and there an end.   850

[*Exit* FIVE WITS]

EVERYMAN   O Jesu, help! All hath forsaken me.

GOOD DEEDS   Nay, Everyman; I will bide
with thee.
I will not forsake thee indeed;
Thou shalt find me a good friend at need.

EVERYMAN   Gramercy, Good Deeds!   855
Now may I true friends see.
They have forsaken me, every one;
I loved them better than my Good Deeds
alone.
Knowledge, will ye forsake me also?

KNOWLEDGE   Yea, Everyman, when ye to   860
Death shall go;
But not yet, for no manner of danger.

EVERYMAN   Gramercy, Knowledge, with all
my heart.

KNOWLEDGE   Nay, yet I will not from hence
depart
Till I see where ye shall become.

EVERYMAN   Methink, alas, that I must be   865
gone
To make my reckoning and my debts pay,
For I see my time is nigh spent away.
Take example, all ye that this do hear or
see,
How they that I loved best do forsake me,
Except my Good Deeds that bideth truly.   870

GOOD DEEDS   All earthly things is but vanity:
Beauty, Strength, and Discretion do man
forsake,
Foolish friends, and kinsmen, that fair
spake—
All fleeth save Good Deeds, and that am I.

EVERYMAN   Have mercy on me, God most   875
mighty;
And stand by me, thou mother and maid,
holy Mary.

GOOD DEEDS   Fear not; I will speak for thee.

KNOWLEDGE   Here I cry God mercy.

GOOD DEEDS   Short our end, and minish our
pain;
Let us go and never come again.   880

EVERYMAN   Into thy hands, Lord,
my soul I commend;
Receive it, Lord, that it be not lost.
As thou me boughtest, so me defend,
And save me from the fiend's boast,
That I may appear with that blessed host   885
That shall be saved at the day of doom.
In manus tuas, of mights most
For ever, *commendo spiritum meum.*

[*He sinks into his grave.*]

KNOWLEDGE   Now hath he suffered that we
all shall endure;
The Good Deeds shall make all sure.   890
Now hath he made ending;
Methinketh that I hear angels sing,
And make great joy and melody
Where Everyman's soul received shall be.

ANGEL   Come, excellent elect spouse, to Jesu!   895
Hereabove thou shalt go
Because of thy singular virtue.
Now the soul is taken the body fro,
Thy reckoning is crystal-clear.
Now shalt thou into the heavenly sphere,   900
Unto the which all ye shall come
That liveth well before the day of doom.

[*Enter* DOCTOR]

DOCTOR   This moral men may have in mind
Ye hearers, take it of worth,° old and   *value it*
young,
And forsake Pride, for he deceiveth you in   905
the end;
And remember Beauty, Five Wits,
Strength, and Discretion,
They all at the last do every man forsake,
Save his Good Deeds there° doth he   *unless*
take.
But beware, for and they be small
Before God, he hath no help at all;   910
None excuse may be there for every man.
Alas, how shall he do then?
For after death amends may no man make,
For then mercy and pity doth him forsake
If his reckoning be not clear when he doth   915
come,
God will say: "*Ite, maledicti, in ignem
eternum.*"
And he that hath his account whole and
sound,
High in heaven he shall be crowned;
Unto which place God bring us all thither,
That we may live body and soul together.   920
Thereto help the Trinity!
Amen, say ye, for saint charity.

THUS ENDETH THIS MORAL PLAY OF EVERYMAN

Hrosvitha, *The Conversion of the Harlot Thaïs*

This rather "aristocratic" play was written in conscious imitation of the classical Roman playwright Terence. The opening part is strongly didactic; the nature of music (taken from the treatise De Musica *of Boethius) is discussed as part of a liberal arts education. Given the very rudimentary stage directions it is easy to imagine this play being read aloud by a circle of people (the nuns of Hrosvitha's convent?) for mutual edification and instruction. We reproduce the second half of the play here.*

The story of Thaïs is a very old one that Hrosvitha adapts from the legends of the saints. Like many of her plays, it deals with a woman who triumphs in the life of virtue. The same story was turned into an opera titled Thaïs *by Jules Massenet in 1894.*

Pafnutius:	A certain shameless woman dwells in this land./
Disciples:	For all citizens a grave peril at hand./
Pafnutius:	She shines forth in wondrous beauty, but threatens men with foul shame./
Disciples:	How misfortunate. What is her name?/
Pafnutius:	Thais.
Disciples:	Thais, the whore?/
Pafnutius:	That is her name./
Disciples:	No one is unaware of her sordid fame./
Pafnutius:	No wonder, because she is not satisfied with leading only a few men to damnation/but is ready to ensnare all men with the allurement of her beauty and drag them along with her to eternal perdition./
Disciples:	A doleful situation./
Pafnutius:	And not only frivolous youths dissipate their family's few possessions on her,/ but even respected men waste their costly treasures by lavishing gifts on her./ Thus they harm themselves.
Disciples:	We are horrified to hear./
Pafnutius:	Crowds of lovers flock to her, wishing to be near./
Disciples:	Damning themselves in the process.
Pafnutius:	These fools that come to her are blind in their hearts; they contend and quarrel and fight each other./
Disciples:	One vice gives birth to another./
Pafnutius:	Then, when the fight has started they fracture each other's faces and noses with their fists; they attack each other with their weapons and drench the threshold of the brothel with their blood gushing forth./
Disciples:	What detestible wrong!/
Pafnutius:	This is the injury to our Maker which I bewail./ This is the cause of my grief and ail./
Disciples:	Justifiably you grieve thereof, and doubtlessly the citizens of heaven grieve with you.
Pafnutius:	What if I visit her, disguised as a lover, to see if perchance she might be recovered from her worthless and frivolous life?
Disciples:	He who instilled the desire for this undertaking in you,/ may He make this worthy desire come true./
Pafnutius:	Stand by me with your constant prayers all the while/ so that I won't be overcome by the vicious serpent's guile./
Disciples:	He who overcame the prince of the dark, may He grant you triumph over the fiend.
Pafnutius:	Here I see some young men in the forum. First I will go to them and ask, where I may find her whom I seek./
Young men:	Hm, a stranger approaches, let's enquire what he wants.
Pafnutius:	Young men, who are you?/
Young men:	Citizens of this town.
Pafnutius:	Greetings to you./
Young men:	Greetings to you whether you are from these parts or stranger./
Pafnutius:	I just arrived. I am a stranger./
Young men:	Why did you come? What do you seek?/
Pafnutius:	Of that, I cannot speak./
Young men:	Why not?
Pafnutius:	Because that is my secret.
Young men:	It would be better if you told us,/ because as you are not one of us,/ you will find it very difficult to accomplish your business without the inhabitants' advice.
Pafnutius:	What if I told you and by telling an obstacle for myself procured?
Young men:	Not from us—rest assured!/
Pafnutius:	Then, trusting in your promise I will yield,/ and my secret no longer shield./
Young men:	We will not betray our promise; we

	will not lay an obstacle in your way./
Pafnutius:	Rumors reached my ear/ that a certain woman lives here/ which surpasses all in amiability,/ surpasses all in affability./
Young men:	Do you know her name?/
Pafnutius:	I do.
Young men:	What is her name?/
Pafnutius:	Thais.
Young men:	For her, we too are aflame./
Pafnutius:	They say she is the most beautiful woman on earth,/ greater than all in delight and mirth./
Young men:	Whoever told you that, did not tell a lie.
Pafnutius:	It was for her sake that I decided to make this arduous journey; I came to see her today./
Young men:	There are no obstacles in your way./
Pafnutius:	Where does she stay?/
Young men:	In that house, quite near./
Pafnutius:	The one you are pointing out to me here?/
Young men:	Yes.
Pafnutius:	I will go there.
Young men:	If you like, we'll go along./
Pafnutius:	No, I'd rather go alone./
Young men:	As you wish.
Pafnutius:	Are you inside, Thais, whom I'm seeking?/
Thais:	Who is the stranger speaking?/
Pafnutius:	One who loves you.
Thais:	Whoever seeks me in love/ finds me returning his love./
Pafnutius:	Oh Thais, Thais, what an arduous journey I took to come to this place/ in order to speak with you and to behold your face./
Thais:	I do not deny you the sight of my face nor my conversation/
Pafnutius:	The secret nature of our conversation/ necessitates the solitude of a secret location./
Thais:	Look, here is a room well furnished for a pleasant stay./
Pafnutius:	Isn't there another room, where we can converse more privately, one that is hidden away?/
Thais:	There is one so hidden, so secret, that no one besides me knows its inside except for God./
Pafnutius:	What God?/

Thais:	The true God./
Pafnutius:	Do you believe He knows what we do?/
Thais:	I know that nothing is hidden from His view./
Pafnutius:	Do you believe that He overlooks the deeds of the wicked or that He metes out justice as its due?/
Thais:	I believe that He weighs the merits of each person justly in His scale/ and that, each according to his deserts receives reward or travail./
Pafnutius:	Oh Christ, how wondrous is the patience, of Thy great mercy! Thou seest that some sin with full cognition,/ yet Thou delay their deserved perdition./
Thais:	Why do you tremble? Why the change of color? Why all these tears?
Pafnutius:	I shudder at your presumption,/ I bewail your sure perdition/ because you know all this so well,/ and yet you sent many a man's soul to Hell./
Thais:	Woe is me, wretched woman!
Pafnutius:	You deserve to be damned even more,/ as you offended the Divine Majesty haughtily, knowing of Him before./
Thais:	Alas, alas, what do you do? What calamity do you sketch?/ Why do you threaten me, unfortunate wretch?/
Pafnutius:	Punishment awaits you in Hell/ if you continue in sin to dwell./
Thais:	Your severe reproach's dart/ pierces the inmost recesses of my heart./
Pafnutius:	Oh, how I wish you were pierced through all your flesh with pain/ so that you wouldn't dare to give yourself to perilous lust again./
Thais:	How can there be place now for appalling lust in my heart when it is filled entirely with the bitter pangs of sorrow/ and the new awareness of guilt, fear, and woe?/
Pafnutius:	I hope that when the thorns of your vice are destroyed at the root,/ the winestock of penitence may then bring forth fruit./
Thais:	If only you believed/ and the hope conceived/ that I who am so stained,/ with thousands and thousands of sins enchained,/ could expiate my sins or could perform due penance to gain forgiveness!

Pafnutius:	Show contempt for the world, and flee the company of your lascivious lovers' crew./
Thais:	And then, what am I to do?/
Pafnutius:	Withdraw yourself to a secret place,/ where you may reflect upon yourself and your former ways/ and lament the enormity of your sins.
Thais:	If you have hopes that I will succeed,/ then I will begin with all due speed./
Pafnutius:	I have no doubt that you will reap benefits.
Thais:	Give me just a short time to gather what I long saved:/ my wealth, ill-gotten and depraved./
Pafnutius:	Have no concern for your treasure,/ there'll be those who will use them for pleasure./
Thais:	I was not planning on saving it for myself nor giving it to friends. I don't even wish to give it to the poor because I don't think that the prize of sin is fit for good.
Pafnutius:	You are right. But how do you plan to dispose of your treasure and cash?/
Thais:	To feed all to the fire, until it is turned to ash./
Pafnutius:	Why?
Thais:	So that nothing is left of what I acquired through sin,/ wronging the world's Maker therein./
Pafnutius:	Oh how you have changed from your prior condition/ when you burned with illicit passions/ and were inflamed with greed for possessions./
Thais:	Perhaps, God willing,/ I'll be changed into a better being./
Pafnutius:	It is not difficult for Him, Himself unchangeable, to change things according to His will./
Thais:	I will now leave and what I planned fulfill./
Pafnutius:	Go forth in peace and return quickly.
Thais:	Come, hurry along,/ my worthless lovers' throng!/
Lovers:	The voice of Thais calls us, let us hurry, let us go/ so that we don't offend her by being slow./
Thais:	Be quick, come here, and don't

	delay,/ there is something I wish to say./
Lovers:	Oh Thais, Thais, what do you intend to do with this pile, why did you gather all these riches around the pyre yonder?/
Thais:	Do you wonder?
Lovers:	We are much surprised./
Thais:	You'll be soon apprised./
Lovers:	That's what we hope for.
Thais:	Then watch me!
Lovers:	Stop it Thais; refrain!/ What are you doing? Are you insane?/
Thais:	I am not insane, but savoring good health again./
Lovers:	But why this destruction of four-hundred pounds of gold,/ and of these treasures manifold?/
Thais:	All that I extorted from you unjustly, I now wish to burn,/ so that no spark of hope is left that I will ever again return/ and give in to your lust.
Lovers:	Wait for a minute, wait,/ and the cause of your distress relate!
Thais:	I will not stay,/ for I have nothing more to say./
Lovers:	Why do you dismiss us in obvious disgust?/ Do you accuse any one of us of breaking trust?/ Have we not always satisfied your every desire,/ and yet you reward us with hate and with ire!/
Thais:	Go away, depart!/ Don't tear my robe apart./ It's enough that I sinned with you in the past;/ this is the end of my sinful life, it is time to part at last./
Lovers:	Whereto are you bound?/
Thais:	Where I never can be found./
Lovers:	What incredible plight/ . . . that Thais, our only delight,/ the same Thais who was always eager to accumulate wealth, who always had lascivious things on her mind,/ and who abandoned herself entirely to voluptuousness of every kind,/ has now destroyed her jewels and her gold and all of a sudden scorns us,/ and wants to leave us./
Thais:	Here I come, father Pafnutius, eager to follow you.
Pafnutius:	You took so long to arrive here,/

	that I was tortured by grave fear/ that you may have become involved once again in worldly things.
Thais:	Do not fear; I had different things planned namely to dispose of my possessions according to my wish and to renounce my lovers publicly.
Pafnutius:	Since you have abandoned those/ you may now make your avowals/ to the Heavenly Bridegroom.
Thais:	It is up to you to tell me what I ought to do. Chart my course as if drawing a circle.
Pafnutius:	Then, come along./
Thais:	I shall follow you, I'm coming along:/ Oh, how I wish to avoid all wrong,/ and imitate your deeds!

Pafnutius:	Here is the cloister where the noble company of holy virgins stays./ Here I want you to spend your days/ performing your penance.
Thais:	I will not contradict you.
Pafnutius:	I will enter and ask the abbess, the virgins' leader, to receive you./
Thais:	In the meantime, what shall I do?
Pafnutius:	Come with me./
Thais:	As you command, it shall be./
Pafnutius:	But look, the abbess approaches. I wonder who told her so promptly of our arrival./
Thais:	Some rumor, bound by no hindrance and in speed without a rival./

Pafnutius:	Noble abbess, Providence brings you,/ for I came to seek you./
Abbess:	Honored father Pafnutius, our most welcome guest,/ your arrival, beloved of God, is manifoldly blest./
Pafnutius:	May the felicity of eternal bliss/ grant you the Almighty's grace and benefice./
Abbess:	For what reason does your holiness deign to visit my humble abode?/
Pafnutius:	I ask for your aid; in a situation of need I took to the road./
Abbess:	Give me only a hint of what you wish me to do, and I will fulfill it forthright./ I will try to satisfy your wish with all my might.
Pafnutius:	I have brought you a half-dead little she-goat, recently snatched from the

	teeth of wolves. I hope that by your compassion its shelter will be ensured,/ and that by your care, it will be cured,/ until, having cast aside the rough pelt of a goat, she will be clothed with the soft wool of the lamb.
Abbess:	Please, explain it more./
Pafnutius:	She whom you see before you, led the life of a whore./
Abbess:	What a wretched life she bore!/
Pafnutius:	She gave herself entirely to vice./
Abbess:	At the cost of her salvation's sacrifice!/
Pafnutius:	But now urged by me and helped by Christ, she renounced her former frivolous way of life and seeks to embrace chastity./
Abbess:	Thanks be to the Lord for the change./
Pafnutius:	But because the sickness of both body and soul must be cured by the medicine of contraries, it follows that she must be sequestered from the tumult of the world,/ obscured in a small cell, so that she may contemplate her sins undisturbed./
Abbess:	That cure will work very well./
Pafnutius:	Then have them build such a cell./
Abbess:	It will be completed promptly./
Pafnutius:	Make sure it has no entry and no exit, only a tiny window through which she may receive some modest food on certain days at set hours and in small quantity./
Abbess:	I fear that the softness of her delicate disposition/ will find it difficult to suffer such harsh conditions./
Pafnutius:	Do not fear; such a grave offense certainly requires a strong remedy.
Abbess:	That is quite plain./
Pafnutius:	I am loath to delay any longer, because I fear she might be seduced by visitors again./
Abbess:	Why do you worry? Why don't you hurry/ and enclose her? Look, the cell you ordered is built./
Pafnutius:	Well done. Enter, Thais, your tiny cell, just right for deploring your sins and guilt./
Thais:	How narrow, how dark is the room!/ For a tender woman's dwelling, how full of gloom!/
Pafnutius:	Why do you complain about the place?/ Why do you shudder and your steps retrace?/ It is only proper

	that you who for so long were wandering unrestrained/ in a solitary place should be detained./
Thais:	A mind used to comfort and luxury,/ is rarely able to bear such austerity./
Pafnutius:	All the more reason to restrain it by the reins of discipline, until it desist from rebellion.
Thais:	Whatever your fatherly concern prescribes for my reform,/ my wretched self does not refuse to perform;/ but in this dwelling there is one unsuitable thing however/ which would be difficult for my weak nature to bear./
Pafnutius:	What is this cause of care?/
Thais:	I am embarrassed to speak./
Pafnutius:	Don't be embarrassed, but speak!/
Thais:	What could be more unsuitable/ what could be more uncomfortable,/ than that I would have to perform all necessary functions of the body in the very same room? I am sure that it will soon be uninhabitable because of the stench.[11]
Pafnutius:	Fear rather the eternal tortures of Hell,/ and not the transitory inconveniences of your cell./
Thais:	My frailty makes me afraid.
Pafnutius:	It is only right/ that you expiate the evil sweetness of alluring delight/ by enduring this terrible smell./
Thais:	And so I shall./ I, filthy myself, do not refuse to dwell/ in a filthy befouled cell/ —that is my just due./ But it pains me deeply that there is no spot left dignified and pure,/ where I could invoke the name of God's majesty.
Pafnutius:	And how can you have such great confidence that you would presume to utter the name of the unpolluted Divinity with your polluted lips?
Thais:	But how can I hope for grace, how can I be saved by His mercy if I am not allowed to invoke Him, against Whom alone I sinned, and to Whom alone I should offer my devotion and prayer?
Pafnutius:	Clearly you should pray not with words but with tears; not with your tinkling voice's melodious art/ but with the bursting of your penitent heart./
Thais:	But if I am prohibited from praying

	with words, how can I ever hope for forgiveness?/
Pafnutius:	The more perfectly you humiliate yourself, the faster you will earn forgiveness./ Say only: Thou Who created me,/ have mercy upon me!/
Thais:	I will need His mercy not to be overcome in this uncertain struggle.
Pafnutius:	Struggle manfully so that you may gloriously attain your triumph.
Thais:	You must pray for me so that I may deserve the palm of victory./
Pafnutius:	No need to admonish me./
Thais:	I hope so.
Pafnutius:	Now it is time that I return to my longed-for retreat and visit my dear disciples. Noble abbess,/ I commit my charge to your care and kindness,/ so that you may nourish her delicate body with a few necessities occasionally/ and nourish her soul with profitable admonitions frequently./
Abbess:	Don't worry about her, because I will look after her, and my maternal affections will never cease./
Pafnutius:	I will then leave.
Abbess:	Go forth in peace!/
Disciples:	Who knocks at the door?
Pafnutius:	Hello!/
Disciples:	Our father's, Pafnutius' voice!
Pafnutius:	Unlock the door!/
Disciples:	Oh father, greetings to you!/
Pafnutius:	Greetings to you, too./
Disciples:	We were worried about your long stay./
Pafnutius:	It was good that I went away./
Disciples:	What happened with Thais?
Pafnutius:	Just the event for which I was praying./
Disciples:	Where is she now staying?/
Pafnutius:	She is bewailing her sins in a tiny cell, quite nigh./
Disciples:	Praise be to the Trinity on High./
Pafnutius:	And blessed be His formidable name, now and forever.
Disciples:	Amen.
Pafnutius:	Behold, three years of Thais' penitence have passed and I don't know whether or not her penance was

	deemed acceptable. I will rise and go to my brother Antonius, so that through his intercession I may find out.

Antonius:	What unexpected pleasure, what surprising delight:/ it is my brother and co-hermit Pafnutius whom I sight!/ He is coming near./
Pafnutius:	I am here./
Antonius:	How good of you to come, brother, your arrival gives me great joy.
Pafnutius:	I am as delighted in seeing you as you are with my visit.
Antonius:	And what happy and for both of us welcome cause brings you here away from your solitary domain?/
Pafnutius:	I will explain./
Antonius:	I'd like to know./
Pafnutius:	Three years ago/ a certain whore/ by the name of Thais lived in this land/ who not only damned herself but dragged many a man to his miserable end./
Antonius:	What an abominable way one's life to spend!/
Pafnutius:	I visited her, disguised as a lover, secretly/ and won over her lascivious mind first with kind admonitions and flattery,/ then I frightened her with harsh threats.
Antonius:	A proper measure,/ necessary for this whore of pleasure./
Pafnutius:	Finally she yielded,/ scorning the reprehensible way of life she formerly wielded/ and she chose a life of chastity consenting to be enclosed in a narrow cell./
Antonius:	I am delighted to hear what you tell/ so much so that my veins are bursting, and my heart beats with joy.
Pafnutius:	That becomes your saintliness, and while I am overjoyed by her change of heart,/ I am still disturbed by a decision on my part:/ I fear that her frailty/ can bear the long penance only with great difficulty./
Antonius:	Where true affection reigns,/ kind compassion never wanes./
Pafnutius:	Therefore I'd like to implore you that you and your disciples pray together with me until Heaven reveals to our sight or ears/ whether

	or not Divine Mercy has been moved to forgiveness by the penitent's tears./
Antonius:	We are happy to comply with your request./
Pafnutius:	I have no doubt that God will graciously listen and grant your behest./

Antonius:	Look, the Gospel's promise is fulfilled in us.
Pafnutius:	What promise?
Antonius:	The one that promises that communal prayer can achieve all./
Pafnutius:	What did befall?/
Antonius:	A vision was granted to my disciple, Paul./
Pafnutius:	Call him!
Antonius:	Come hither, Paul, and tell Pafnutius what you saw.
Paul:	In my vision of Heaven, I saw a bed/ with white linen beautifully spread/ surrounded by four resplendent maidens who stood as if guarding the bed./ And when I beheld the beauty of this marvelous brightness I said to myself: This glory belongs to no one more than to my father and my lord Antonius.
Antonius:	I am not worthy so such beautitude to soar./
Paulus:	After I spoke, a Divine voice spoke: "This glory is not as you hope for Antonius, but is meant for Thais the whore."/
Pafnutius:	Praised be Thy sweet mercy, Oh Christ, only begotten Son of God, for Thou hast deigned to deliver me from my sadness' plight./
Antonius:	To praise Him is meet and right./
Pafnutius:	I shall go and visit my prisoner.
Antonius:	It is proper to give her hope for forgiveness without further remiss,/ and assure her of the comfort of Heavenly bliss./

Pafnutius:	Thais, my adoptive daughter, open your window so I may see you and rejoice./
Thais:	Who speaks? Whose is this voice?

Pafnutius:	It is Pafnutius, your father.
Thais:	To what do I owe the bliss of such great joy that you deign to visit me, poor sinful soul?/
Pafnutius:	Even though I was absent in body for three years, yet I was constantly concerned about how you would achieve your goal./
Thais:	I do not doubt that at all./
Pafnutius:	Tell me of these past three years' course,/ and how you practised your remorse./
Thais:	This is all I can tell:/ I have done nothing worthy of God, and that I know full well./
Pafnutius:	If God would consider our sins only/ no one would stand up to scrutiny./
Thais:	But if you wish to know how I spent my time, in my conscience I enumerated my manifold sins and wickedness and gathered them as in a bundle of crime./ Then I continuously went over them in my mind,/ so that just as the nauseating smell here never left my nostrils, so the fear of Hell never departed from my heart's eyes.
Pafnutius:	Because you punished yourself with such compunction/ you have earned forgiveness' unction./
Thais:	Oh, how I wish I did!
Pafnutius:	Give me your hand so I can lead you out.
Thais:	Venerable Father, do not take me, stained and foul wretch, from this filth; let me remain in this place/ appropriate for my sinful ways./
Pafnutius:	It is time for you to lessen your fear/ and to begin to have hopeful cheer./
Thais:	All angels sing His praise and His kindness, because He never scorns the humility of a contrite soul.
Pafnutius:	Remain steadfast in fearing God, and continue to love Him forever. After fifteen days you will leave your human body/ and, having completed your happy journey,/ by the favor of Heavenly grace you will reach the stars.
Thais:	Oh, how I desire to avoid Hell's tortures, or rather how I aspire/ to suffer by some less cruel fire!/ For my merits do not suffice/ to secure me the bliss of paradise./
Pafnutius:	Grace is God's gift and a free award,/ and not human merit's reward;/ because if it were simply a payment for merits, it wouldn't be called grace.
Thais:	Therefore praise Him all the company of heaven, and on earth the least little sprout or bush,/ not only all living creatures but even the waterfall's crush/ because He not only suffers men to live in sinful ways/ but rewards the penitent with the gift of grace./
Pafnutius:	This has been His custom from time immemorial, to have mercy on sinners rather than to slay them.
Thais:	Do not leave, venerable father, but stand by me with consolation in my hour of death.
Pafnutius:	I am not leaving,/ I am staying/ until your soul rejoices in Heaven's gains/ and I bury your earthly remains./
Thais:	Death is near./
Pafnutius:	Then we must begin our prayer./
Thais:	Thou Who made me, Have mercy upon me/ and grant that my soul which Thou breathed into me,/ may return happily to Thee.
Pafnutius:	Thou Who art created by no one, Thou only art truly without material form, one God in Unity of Substance,/ Thou Who created man, unlike Thee, to consist of diverse substances;/ grant that the dissolving, diverse parts of this human being/ may happily return to the source of their original being; that the soul, divinely imparted, live on in heavenly bliss,/ and that the body, may rest in peace/ in the soft lap of earth, from which it came,/ until ashes and dirt combine again/ and breath animates the revived members; that Thais be resurrected exactly as she was,/ a human being, and joining the white lambs may enter eternal joys./ Thou Who alone art what Thou art, one God in the Unity of the Trinity who reigns and is glorified, world without end.

The Song of Roland

The selection from The Song of Roland *reproduced here recounts the death of Roland, Oliver, Archbishop Turpin, and their loyal followers and the return of Charlemagne to take up the battle against the pagans. Pay particular attention to the epic qualities of the narrative: the stark distinction between the battling forces; the bravery of the combatants in the face of death; the sacred nature of weapons and horses (indicated by their being named); and, peculiar to postclassical epic poetry, the blending of martial and biblical language. To get the full force of the poem, read some of the stanzas aloud in a declamatory fashion; this is the way they were originally meant to be "read." The phrase AOI appended to the end of many of the stanzas is of uncertain meaning. It may have been a ritual shout, but scholars do not agree.*

128

Count Roland sees the slaughter of his men.
He calls aside Olivier, his comrade:
"Fair lord, dear comrade, in the name of God,
    what now?
You see what good men lie here on the ground.
We well may mourn sweet France the Beautiful,
to be deprived of barons such as these.
Oh king, my friend—if only you were here!
Olivier, my brother, what can we do?
By what means can we get this news to him?"
"I have no notion," says Olivier,   10
"but I'd rather die than have us vilified." AOI

129

Then Roland says: "I'll sound the oliphant,
and Charles, who's moving through the pass,
    will hear it.
I promise you the Franks will then return."
Olivier says: "That would bring great shame
and reprobation down on all your kin,
and this disgrace would last throughout their
    lives!
You wouldn't do a thing when I implored you,
so don't act now to win my gratitude.
No courage is involved in sounding it;   20
already you have bloodied both your arms."
The count replies: "I've struck some lovely
    blows!" AOI

130

Then Roland says: "Our fight is getting rough:
I'll sound my horn—King Charles is sure to
    hear it."
Olivier says: "That would not be knightly.
You didn't deign to, comrade, when I asked
    you,

and were the king here now, we'd be
    unharmed.
The men out yonder shouldn't take the blame."
Olivier says: "By this beard of mine,
if I should see my lovely sister Alde,
then *you* shall never lie in her embrace." AOI   30

131

Then Roland says: "You're angry with
    me—why?"
And he replies: "Companion, you're to blame,
for bravery in no sense is bravado,
and prudence is worth more than recklessness.
Those French are dead because of your caprice;
King Charles will have our services no more.
My lord would be here now, if you'd believed me,
and we'd have put an end to this affray;
Marsilla would be dead or taken captive.   40
But we were doomed to see your prowess,
    Roland;
now Charlemagne will get no help from us
(there'll be no man like him until God judges)
and you shall die, and France shall be disgraced.
Today our loyal comradeship will end:
before the evening falls we'll part in grief." AOI

132

The archbishop overhears them quarreling:
he rakes his horse with spurs of beaten gold,
comes over, and begins to reprimand them:
"Lord Roland, you too, Lord Olivier,   50
I beg of you, for God's sake do not quarrel!
A horn blast cannot save us any more,
but nonetheless it would be well to sound it;
the king will come, and then he can avenge
    us—
the men from Spain will not depart in joy.
Our Frenchmen will dismount here, and on foot
they'll come upon us, dead and hacked to
    pieces,
and lift us up in coffins onto pack-mules,
and weep for us in pity and in grief.
They'll bury us beneath the aisles of churches,   60
where wolves and pigs and dogs won't gnaw
    on us."
"You've spoken very well, sire," answers
    Roland. AOI

133

Count Roland brought the horn up to his
    mouth:
he sets it firmly, blows with all his might.
The peaks are high, the horn's voice carries far;
they hear it echo thirty leagues away.
Charles hears it, too, and all his company:

the king says then: "Our men are in a fight."
And Ganelon replies contentiously:
"Had someone else said that, he'd seem a liar."
AOI   70

134

Count Roland, racked with agony and pain
and great chagrin, now sounds his ivory horn:
bright blood leaps in a torrent from his mouth:
the temple has been ruptured in his brain.
The horn he holds emits a piercing blast:
Charles hears it as he crosses through the pass;
Duke Naimes has heard it, too; the Franks give
        ear.
The king announces: "I hear Roland's horn!
He'd never sound it if he weren't embattled."
Says Ganelon: "There isn't any battle!   80
You're getting old, your hair is streaked and
        white;
such speeches make you sound just like a child.
You're well aware of Roland's great conceit;
it's strange that God has suffered him so long.
Without your orders he once captured Naples:
the Saracens inside came riding out
and then engaged that worthy vassal Roland,
who later flushed the gory field with water—
he did all this to keep it out of sight.
He'll blow that horn all day for just one hare.   90
He's showing off today before his peers—
no army under heaven dares to fight him.
So keep on riding!—Why do you stop here?
For Tere Majur lies far ahead of us." AOI

135

Count Roland's mouth is filling up with blood;
the temple has been ruptured in his brain.
In grief and pain he sounds the oliphant;
Charles hears it, and his Frenchmen listen, too.
The king says then, "That horn is long of
        wind."
Duke Naimes replies, "The baron is attacking!   100
A fight is taking place, of that I'm sure.
This man who tries to stall you has betrayed
        them.
Take up your arms, sing out your battle cry,
and then go save your noble retinue:
you've listened long enough to Roland's plaint!"

136

The emperor has let his horns be sounded:
the French dismount, and then they arm
        themselves
with hauberks and with casques and gilded
        swords.
Their shields are trim, their lances long and
stout,
their battle pennants crimson, white, and blue.   110
The barons of the army mount their chargers
and spur them briskly, all down through the
        passes.
There is not one who fails to tell his neighbor:
"If we see Roland prior to his death,
we'll stand there with him, striking mighty
        blows."
But what's the use?—for they've delayed too
        long.

137

The afternoon and evening are clear:
the armor coruscates against the sun,
those casques and hauberks throw a dazzling
        glare,
as do those shields, ornate with painted flowers, 120
those spears, those battle flags of gold brocade.
Impelled by rage, the emperor rides on,
together with the French, chagrined and
        grieved.
No man there fails to weep with bitterness,
and they are much afraid for Roland's sake.
The king has had Count Ganelon arrested,
and turns him over to his household cooks.
He tells Besgun, the leader of them all:
"Keep watch on him, like any common thug,
for he's betrayed the members of my house."   130
He turned him over to a hundred comrades,
the best and worst together, from the kitchen.
These men plucked out his beard and his
        moustache,
and each one hit him four times with his fist;
they whipped him thoroughly with sticks and
        clubs,
and then they put a chain around his neck
and chained him up exactly like a bear;
in ridicule, they set him on a pack-horse.
They'll guard him this way until Charles
        returns.

138

The hills are high and shadowy and large,   140
the valleys deep, with swiftly running streams.
The trumpets ring out to the front and rear,
all racketing reply to the oliphant.
The emperor rides on, impelled by rage,
as do the Franks, chagrined and furious:
no man among them fails to weep and mourn
and pray to God that He may safeguard Roland
until they all arrive upon the field.
Together with him there, they'll really fight.
But what's the use? They cannot be of help;   150
they stayed too long; they can't get there in
        time. AOI

139

Impelled by rage, King Charles keeps riding on,
his full white beard spread out upon his byrnie.
The Frankish barons all have used their spurs;
not one of them but bitterly regrets
that he is not beside the captain Roland,
now fighting with the Saracens from Spain,
and injured so, I fear his soul won't stay.
But, God—the sixty in his company!
No king or captain his commanded better. AOI 160

140

Count Roland scans the mountains and the hills:
he sees so many dead French lying there,
and like a noble knight he weeps for them.
"My lords and barons, God be merciful,
deliver all your souls to Paradise
and let them lie among the blessed flowers!
I've never seen more worthy knights than
        you—
you all have served me long and faithfully,
and conquered such great lands for Charles's
        sake!
The emperor has raised you, all for naught. 170
My land of France, how very sweet you are—
today laid waste by terrible disaster!
French lords, because of me I see you dying—
I can't reprieve you now, nor save your lives.
May God, who never lied, come to your aid!
Olivier, I won't fail *you,* my brother;
if no one kills me, I shall die of grief.
My lord companion, let's attack once more."

141

Count Roland now goes back into the field,
with Durendal in hand, fights gallantly: 180
he then has cut Faldrun of Pui in two,
as well as twenty-four among their best;
no man will ever want revenge so badly.
Just as the stag will run before the hounds,
the pagans break and run away from Roland.
The archbishop says: "You're doing rather well!
Such gallantry a chevalier should have,
if he's to carry arms and ride a horse.
He must be fierce and powerful in combat—
if not, he isn't worth four deniers— 190
should be instead a monastery monk
and pray the livelong day for all our sins."
"Lay on, don't spare them!" Roland says in
        answer,
and at these words the Franks attack again.
The Christians suffered very heavy losses.

142

The man who knows no captives will be taken,

in such a fight puts up a stout defense:
because of this, the Franks are fierce as lions.
Now see Marsilla make a gallant show.
He sits astride the horse he calls Gaignon; 200
he spurs him briskly, then attacks Bevon
(this man was lord of Beaune and of Dijon).
He breaks his shield and smashes through his
        hauberk
and drops him dead without a *coup de grâce.*
And then he killed Ivon and Ivorie,
together with Gerard of Roussillon.
Count Roland isn't very far away;
he tells the pagan: "May the Lord God damn
        you!
So wrongfully you've slaughtered my
        companions;
before we separate, you'll take a stroke, 210
and from my sword today you'll learn its
        name."
He goes to strike him with a gallant show:
the count swings down and cuts his right hand
        off,
then takes the head of Jurfaleu the Blond
(this pagan was the son of King Marsilla).
The pagans raise the cry: "Help us,
        Mohammed!
And you, our gods, give us revenge on Charles.
He's sent such villains to us in this land—
they'd rather die than leave the battlefield."
One tells another: "Let's get out of here!" 220
And at that word a hundred thousand run.
No matter who may call, they won't come
        back. AOI

145

The pagans, when they see the French are few,
feel proud and reassured among themselves:
"The emperor is wrong," one tells another.
Astride a sorrel horse sits Marganice;
he rakes him briskly with his golden spurs
and strikes Olivier on the back,
lays bare the flesh beneath the shining hauberk
and shoves his lance entirely through his chest, 230
and then he says: "You took a mortal blow!
Great Charles should not have left you at the
        pass,
he's done us wrong, he has no right to boast;
through you alone, our side is well avenged."

146

Olivier feels wounded unto death,
but gripping Halteclere, whose blade was
        polished,
strikes Marganice's high-peaked golden casque;
he smashes downward through fleurons and

gems
and splits the skull wide open to the teeth.
He wrenches free and lets the dead man fall,   240
and afterward he tells him: "Damn you, pagan!
I do not say that Charles has had no loss,
but neither to your wife nor any woman
you've seen back where you came from shall
          you brag
you took a denier of loot from me,
or injured me or anybody else."
Then afterward he calls for help to Roland. AOI

147

Olivier feels injured unto death,
yet he will never have his fill of vengeance:
he battles in the thick crowd like a baron,   250
still shearing through those shafts of spears,
          those bucklers,
and feet and wrists and shoulder-bones and ribs.
Whoever saw him maiming Saracens
and piling dead men one upon the other
would be reminded of a worthy knight.
Not wanting Charles's battle cry forgotten,
he sings out in a loud, clear voice: "Monjoy!"
He calls to him his friend and peer, Count
          Roland:
"My lord companion, come fight here by me;
today in bitter anguish we shall part." AOI   260

148

Count Roland contemplates Olivier:
his face is gray and bloodless, wan and pale,
and from his trunk bright blood is surging out
and dripping down in pools upon the ground.
The count says: "God, I don't know what to
          do.
Your valor was for naught, my lord
          companion—
there'll never be another one like you.
Sweet France, today you're going to be robbed
of loyal men, defeated and destroyed:
all this will do the emperor great harm."   270
And at this word he faints, still on his horse.
          AOI

149

See Roland, who has fainted on his horse,
and, wounded unto death, Olivier,
his vision so impaired by loss of blood
that, whether near or far, he cannot see
enough to recognize a living man;
and so, when he encounters his companion,
he hits him on his jeweled golden casque
and splits it wide apart from crown to nasal,

but doesn't cut into his head at all.   280
On being struck so, Roland studied him,
then asked him in a soft and gentle voice:
"My lord companion, did you mean to do that?
It's Roland, who has been your friend so long:
you gave no sign that you had challenged me."
Olivier says: "Now I hear you speak.
Since I can't see you, God keep you in sight!
I hit you, and I beg you to forgive me."
And Roland says: "I've not been hurt at all,
and here before the Lord I pardon you."   290
And with these words, they bowed to one
          another:
in friendship such as this you see them part.

150

Olivier feels death-pangs coming on;
his eyes have both rolled back into his head,
and his sight and hearing are completely gone.
Dismounting, he lies down upon the ground,
and then confesses all his sins aloud,
with both hands clasped and lifted up toward
          heaven.
He prays that God may grant him Paradise
and give His blessing to sweet France and
          Charles   300
and, most of all, to his companion Roland.
His heart fails; his helmet tumbles down;
his body lies outstretched upon the ground.
The count is dead—he could endure no more.
The baron Roland weeps for him and mourns:
on earth you'll never hear a sadder man.

151

Now Roland, when he sees his friend is dead
and lying there face down upon the ground,
quite softly starts to say farewell to him:
"Your valor was for naught, my lord
          companion!   310
We've been together through the days and years,
and never have you wronged me, nor I you;
since you are dead, it saddens me to live."
And having said these words, the marquis faints
upon his horse, whose name is Veillantif;
but his stirrups of fine gold still hold him on:
whichever way he leans, he cannot fall.

153

Now, Roland, grown embittered in his pain,
goes slashing through the middle of the crowd;
he throws down lifeless twenty men from
          Spain,   320
while Gautier kills six, and Turpin five.
The pagans say: "These men are infamous;

don't let them get away alive, my lords:
whoever fails to rush them is a traitor,
who lets them save themselves, a renegade."
So once more they renew the hue and cry;
from every side they go to the attack. AOI

154

Count Roland is a noble man-at-arms.
Gautier of Hum a splendid chevalier,
the archbishop an experienced campaigner: 330
no one of them will ever leave the others.
Engulfed within the crowd, they cut down
          pagans.
A thousand Saracens get down on foot,
and forty thousand stay upon their horses:
they do not dare come closer, that I know,
but they hurl at them their javelins and spears
and darts and wigars, mizraks, and agers.
The first barrage has killed Count Gautier;
Turpin of Reims—his shield is pierced clear
          through,
his helmet broken, injuring his head,   340
his hauberk torn apart and stripped of mail;
his body has been wounded by four spears;
they kill his destrier from under him.
Great sorrow comes as the archbishop falls.
          AOI

155

Turpin of Reims, when he sees that he's been
          downed
by four spears driven deep into his body,
the brave man leaps back quickly to his feet
and looks toward Roland, then runs up to him
and says this word: "By no means am I beaten;
no loyal man gives up while still alive."   350
He draws Almace, his sword of polished steel;
in the crowd he strikes a thousand blows or
          more.
Charles later on will say he spared no one—
he found about four hundred, all around him,
some only wounded, some who'd been run
          through,
and others who had had their heads cut off.
Thus says the *geste* and he who was afield,
the noble Giles, for whom God brought forth
          wonders.
At the minster of Laon he wrote the charter;
whoever doesn't know that much knows little.   360

156

Count Roland keeps on fighting skillfully,
although his body's hot and drenched with
          sweat:

he feels great pain and torment in his head,
since, when he blew his horn, his temple burst.
Yet he has to know if Charles is coming back:
he draws the ivory horn and sounds it feebly.
The emperor pulled up so he might listen:
"My lords," he says, "it's very bad for us;
today my nephew Roland will be lost.
From his horn blast I can tell he's barely living;   370
whoever wants to get there must ride fast.
So sound your trumpets, all this army has!"
And sixty thousand of them blare so loud,
the mountains ring, the valleys echo back.
The pagans hear it, take it as no joke.
One tells another: "Now we'll have King
          Charles."

157

The pagans say: "The emperor's returning; AOI
just listen to the Frenchmen's trumpets blare!
If Charles comes, it will be the ruin of us—
if Roland lives, our war will start again,   380
and we'll have forfeited our land of Spain."
About four hundred, wearing casques,
          assemble—
and launch one brutal, grim assault on Roland.
This time the count has got his work cut out.
          AOI

158

Count Roland, when he sees them drawing
          near,
becomes so strong and bold and vigilant!
As long as he's alive, he'll never yield.
He sits astride the horse called Veillantif
and rakes him briskly with his fine gold spurs
and wades into the crowd to fight them all,   390
accompanied by Turpin, the archbishop.
One tells another: "Friend, get out of here!
We've heard the trumpets of the men from
          France;
now Charles, the mighty king, is coming back."

159

Count Roland never cared much for a coward
nor a swaggerer nor evil-minded man
nor a knight, if he were not a worthy vassal.
He called out then to Turpin, the archbishop:
"My lord, you are on foot and I am mounted;
for love of you I'll make my stand right here.   400
Together we shall take the good and bad;
no mortal man shall ever make me leave you.
Today, in this assault, the Saracens
shall learn the names Almace and Durendal."
The archbishop says: "Damn him who won't

fight hard!
When Charles comes back here, he'll avenge us
    well."

160

The pagans cry out: "We were doomed at birth;
a bitter day has dawned for us today!
We've been bereft of all our lords and peers,
the gallant Charles is coming with his host,   410
we hear the clear-voiced trumpets of the French
and the uproar of the battle cry 'Monjoy.'
So great is the ferocity of Roland,
no mortal man will ever vanquish him;
so let us lance at him, then let him be."
They hurl at him a multitude of darts,
befeathered mizraks, wigars, lances, spears—
they burst and penetrated Roland's shield
and ripped his hauberk, shearing off its mail,
but not a one went through into his body.   420
They wounded Veillantif in thirty places
and killed him out from underneath the count.
The pagans take flight then and let him be:
Count Roland is still there upon his feet. AOI

161

The pagans, galled and furious, take flight
and head for Spain, as fast as they can go.
Count Roland is unable to pursue them,
for he has lost his charger Veillantif
and now, despite himself, is left on foot.
He went to give Archbishop Turpin help,   430
unlaced his gilded helmet from his head,
then pulled away his gleaming, lightweight
    hauberk
and cut his under-tunic all to shreds
and stuffed the strips into his gaping wounds.
This done, he took him up against his chest
and on the green grass gently laid him down.
Most softly Roland made him this request:
"Oh noble lord, if you will give me leave—
all our companions, whom we held so dear,
are dead now; we should not abandon them.   440
I want to seek them out, identify them,
and lay them out before you, side by side."
The archbishop tells him: "Go and then return;
this field is yours, I thank God, yours and mine."

162

Now Roland leaves and walks the field alone:
he seaches valleys, searches mountain slopes.
He found there Gerier, his friend Gerin,
and then he found Aton and Berenger,
and there he found Sanson and Anseïs;

he found Gerard the Old of Roussillon.   450
The baron picked them up then, pair by pair,
and brought them every one to the archbishop
and placed them in a row before his knees.
The archbishop cannot help himself; he weeps,
then lifts his hand and makes his benediction,
and says thereafter: "Lords, you had no chance;
may God the Glorious bring all your souls
to Paradise among the blessed flowers!
My own death causes me great pain, for I
shall see the mighty emperor no more."   460

163

Now Roland leaves, goes searching through the
    field:
he came upon Olivier, his comrade,
and holding him up tight against his chest
returned as best he could to the archbishop.
He laid him on a shield beside the others;
the archbishop blessed him, gave him
    absolution.
Then all at once despair and pain well up,
and Roland says: "Olivier, fair comrade,
you were the son of wealthy Duke Renier,
who ruled the frontier valley of Runers.   470
To break a lance-shaft or to pierce a shield,
to overcome and terrify the proud,
to counsel and sustain the valorous,
to overcome and terrify the gluttons,
no country ever had a better knight."

164

Count Roland, looking on his lifeless peers
and Olivier, whom he had cared for so,
is seized with tenderness, begins to weep.
The color has all vanished from his face;
he cannot stand, the pain is so intense;   480
despite himself, he falls to earth unconscious.
The archbishop says: "Brave lord, you've come
    to grief."

165

The archbishop, upon seeing Roland faint,
feels sorrow such as he has never felt,
extends his hand and takes the ivory horn.
At Roncesvals there is a running stream;
he wants to fetch some water there for Roland;
with little, stumbling steps he turns away,
but can't go any farther—he's too weak
and has no strength, has lost far to much
    blood.   490
Before a man could walk across an acre,
his heart fails, and he falls upon his face.
With dreadful anguish death comes over him.

166

Count Roland, now regaining consciousness,
gets on his feet, in spite of dreadful pain,
and scans the valleys, scans the mountainsides,
across the green grass, out beyond his
    comrades.
He sees the noble baron lying there—
the archbishop, sent by God in His own name.
Confessing all his sins, with eyes upraised   500
and both hands clasped and lifted up toward
    Heaven,
he prays that God may grant him Paradise.
Now Turpin, Charles's warrior, is dead:
in mighty battles and in moving sermons
he always took the lead against the pagans.
May God bestow on him His holy blessing! AOI

167

Count Roland sees the archbishop on the ground:
he sees the entrails bulging from his body.
His brains are boiling out upon his forehead.
Upon his chest, between the collarbones,   510
he laid crosswise his beautiful white hands,
lamenting him, as was his country's custom:
"Oh noble vassal, well-born chevalier,
I now commend you to celestial Glory.
No man will ever serve Him with such zeal;
no prophet since the days of the Apostles
so kept the laws and drew the hearts of men.
Now may your soul endure no suffering;
may Heaven's gate be opened up for you!"

168

Count Roland realizes death is near: 520
his brains begin to ooze out through his ears.
He prays to God to summon all his peers,
and to the angel Gabriel, himself.
Eschewing blame, he takes the horn in hand
and in the other Durendal, his sword,
and farther than a crossbow fires a bolt,
heads out across a fallow field toward Spain
and climbs a rise. Beneath two lovely trees
stand four enormous marble monoliths.
Upon the green grass he has fallen backward   530
and fainted, for his death is near at hand.

169

The hills are high, and very high the trees;
four massive blocks are there, of gleaming
    marble;
upon green grass Count Roland lies
    unconscious.
And all the while a Saracen is watching:
he lies among the others, feigning death;
he smeared his body and his face with blood.
He rises to his feet and starts to run—

a strong, courageous, handsome man he was;
through pride he enters into mortal folly—   540
and pinning Roland's arms against his chest,
he cries out: "Charles's nephew has been
    vanquished;
I'll take this sword back to Arabia."
And as he pulls, the count revives somewhat.

170

Now Roland feels his sword is being taken
and, opening his eyes, he says to him:
"I know for certain you're not one of us!"
He takes the horn he didn't want to leave
and strikes him on his jeweled golden casque;
he smashes through the steel and skull and
    bones,   550
and bursting both his eyeballs from his head,
he tumbles him down lifeless at his feet
and says to him: "How dared you, heathen
    coward,
lay hands on me, by fair means or by foul?
Whoever hears of this will think you mad.
My ivory horn is split across the bell,
and the crystals and the gold are broken off."

171

Now Roland feels his vision leaving him,
gets to his feet, exerting all his strength;
the color has all vanished from his face.   560
In front of him there is a dull gray stone;
ten times he strikes it, bitter and dismayed:
the steel edge grates, but does not break or
    nick.
"Oh holy Mary, help me!' says the count,
"Oh Durendal, good sword, you've come to
    grief!
When I am dead, you won't be in my care.
I've won with you on many battlefields
and subjugated many spacious lands
now ruled by Charles, whose beard is shot with
    gray.
No man who flees another should possess you!   570
A loyal knight has held you many years;
your equal holy France will never see."

172

Roland strikes the great carnelian stone:
the steel edge grides, but does not break or chip.
And when he sees that he cannot destroy it,
he makes this lamentation to himself:
"Oh Durendal, how dazzling bright you are—
you blaze with light and shimmer in the sun!
King Charles was in the Vales of Moriane
when God in Heaven had His angel tell him   580
that he sould give you to a captain-count:

the great and noble king then girded me.
With this I won Anjou and Brittany,
and then I won him both Poitou and Maine.
with this I won him Normandy the Proud,
and then I won Provence and Aquitaine,
and Lombardy, as well as all Romagna.
With this I won Bavaria, all Flanders,
and Burgundy, the Poliani lands,
Constantinople, where they did him homage—   590
in Saxony they do what he commands.
With this I won him Scotland, Ireland too,
and England, which he held as his demesne.
With this I've won so many lands and countries
which now are held by Charles, whose beard is
      white.
I'm full of pain and sorrow for this sword;
I'd rather die than leave it to the pagans.
Oh God, my Father, don't let France be
      shamed!"

173

Roland hammers on a dull gray stone
and breaks off more of it than I can say: 600
the sword grates, but it neither snaps nor splits,
and only bounces back into the air.
The count, on seeing he will never break it,
laments it very softly to himself:
"Oh Durendal, so beautiful and sacred,
within your golden hilt are many relics—
Saint Peter's tooth, some of Saint Basil's blood,
some hair belonging to my lord, Saint Denis,
a remnant, too, of holy Mary's dress.
It isn't right that pagans should possess you;   610
you ought to be attended on by Christians.
You never should be held by one who cowers!
With you I've conquered many spacious lands
now held by Charles, whose beard is streaked
      with white;
through them the emperor is rich and strong."

174

Now Roland feels death coming over him,
descending from his head down to his heart.
He goes beneath a pine tree at a run
and on the green grass stretches out, face down.
He puts his sword and ivory horn beneath him   620
and turns his head to face the pagan host.
He did these things in order to be sure
that Charles, as well as all his men, would say:
"This noble count has died a conqueror."
Repeatedly he goes through his confession,
and for his sins he proffers God his glove. AOI

175

Now Roland is aware his time is up:

he lies upon a steep hill, facing Spain,
and with one hand he beats upon his chest:
"Oh God, against Thy power I have sinned,   630
because of my transgressions, great and small,
committed since the hour I was born
until this day when I have been struck down!"
He lifted up his right-hand glove to God:
from Heaven angels came to him down there.
      AOI

176

Count Roland lay down underneath a pine,
his face turned so that it would point toward
      Spain:
he was caught up in the memory of things—
of many lands he'd valiantly subdued,
of sweet France, of the members of his line,   640
of Charlemagne, his lord, who brought him up;
he cannot help but weep and sigh for these.
But he does not intend to slight himself;
confessing all his sins, he begs God's mercy:
"True Father, Who hath never told a lie,
Who resurrected Lazarus from the dead,
and Who protected Daniel from the lions,
protect the soul in me from every peril
brought on by wrongs I've done throughout
      my life!"
He offered up his right-hand glove to God: 650
Saint Gabriel removed it from his hand.
And with his head inclined upon his arm,
hands clasped together, he has met his end.
Then God sent down his angel Cherubin
and Saint Michael of the Sea and of the Peril;
together with Saint Gabriel they came
and took the count's soul into Paradise.

177

Roland is dead, his soul with God in Heaven.
The emperor arrives at Roncesvals.
There's not a single trace nor footpath there,   660
nor ell, nor even foot of vacant ground,
on which there's not a pagan or a Frank.
"Fair nephew," Charles cries loudly, "where are
      you?
Where's the archbishop, and Count Olivier?
Where is Gerin, and his comrade Gerier?
Where is Anton? and where's Count Berenger?
Ivon and Ivorie, I held so dear?
What's happened to the Gascon, Engelier?
and Duke Sanson? and gallant Anseïs?
and where is Old Gerard of Roussillon?   670
—the twelve peers I permitted to remain?"
But what's the use, when none of them reply?
The king says: "God! I've cause enough to grieve
that I was not here when the battle started!"

He tugs upon his beard like one enraged;
the eyes of all his noble knights shed tears,
and twenty thousand fall down in a faint.
Duke Naimes profoundly pities all of them.

178

There's not a chevalier or baron there
who fails to shed embittered tears of grief;   680
they mourn their sons, their brothers, and their
    nephews,
together with their liege-lords and their friends;
and many fall unconscious to the ground.
Duke Naimes displayed his courage through all
    this,
for he was first to tell the emperor:
"Look up ahead of us, two leagues away—
along the main road you can see the dust,
so many of the pagan host are there.
So ride! Take vengeance for this massacre!"
"Oh God! says Charles, "already they're so
    far!   690
Permit me what is mine by right and honor;
they've robbed me of the flower of sweet
    France."
The king gives orders to Geboin, Oton,
Thibaud of Reims, and to the count Milon:
"You guard the field—the valleys and the hills.
Leave all the dead exactly as they lie,
make sure no lion or other beast comes near,
and let no groom or serving-man come near.
Prohibit any man from coming near them
till God grants our return upon this field."   700
In fond, soft-spoken tones these men reply:
"Dear lord and rightful emperor, we'll do it!"
They keep with them a thousand chevaliers.
    AOI

179

The emperor has had his trumpets sounded;
then, with his mighty host, the brave lord rides.
The men from Spain have turned their backs to
    them;
they all ride out together in pursuit.
The king, on seeing dusk begin to fall,
dismounts upon the green grass in a field,
prostrates himself, and prays Almighty God   710
that He will make the sun stand still for him,
hold back the night, and let the day go on.
An angel he had spoken with before
came instantly and gave him this command:
"Ride on, Charles, for the light shall not desert
    you.
God knows that you have lost the flower of
    France;
you may take vengeance on the guilty race."

And at these words, the emperor remounts. AOI

180

For Charlemagne God worked a miracle,
because the sun is standing motionless.   720
The pagans flee, the Franks pursue them hard,
and overtake them at Val-Tenebrus.
They fight them on the run toward Saragossa;
with mighty blows they kill them as they go;
they cut them off from the main roads and the
    lanes.
The river Ebro lies in front of them,
a deep, swift-running, terrifying stream;
there's not a barge or boat or dromond there.
The pagans call on Termagant, their god,
and then leap in, but nothing will protect them.   730
The men in armor are the heaviest,
and numbers of them plummet to the bottom;
the other men go floating off downstream.
The best equipped thus get their fill to drink;
they all are drowned in dreadful agony.
The Frenchmen cry out: "You were luckless,
    Roland!" AOI

181

As soon as Charles sees all the pagans dead
(some killed, a greater number of them drowned)
and rich spoils taken off them by his knights,
the noble king then climbs down to his feet,   740
prostrates himself, and offers thanks to God.
When he gets up again, the sun has set.
"It's time to pitch camp," says the emperor.
"It's too late to go back to Roncesvals.
Our horses are fatigued and ridden down;
unsaddle them and then unbridle them
and turn them out to cool off in this field."
The Franks reply: "Sire, you have spoken well."
    AOI

182

The emperor has picked a place to camp.
The French dismount upon the open land   750
and pull the saddles off their destriers
and take the gold-trimmed bridles from their
    heads;
then turn them out to graze the thick green grass;
there's nothing else that they can do for them.
The tiredest go to sleep right on the ground:
that night they post no sentinels at all.

183

The emperor has lain down in a meadow.
The brave lord sets his great lance at his head—
tonight he does not wish to be unarmed—
keeps on his shiny, saffron-yellow hauberk,   760

and his jeweled golden helmet, still laced up,
and at his waist Joyeuse, which has no peer:
its brilliance alters thirty times a day.
We've heard a great deal spoken of the lance
with which Our Lord was wounded on the cross;
that lance's head is owned by Charles, thank God;
he had its tip inletted in the pommel.
Because of this distinction and this grace,
the name "Joyeuse" was given to the sword.
The Frankish lords will not forget this fact: 770
they take from it their battle cry, "Monjoy."
Because of this, no race can stand against them.

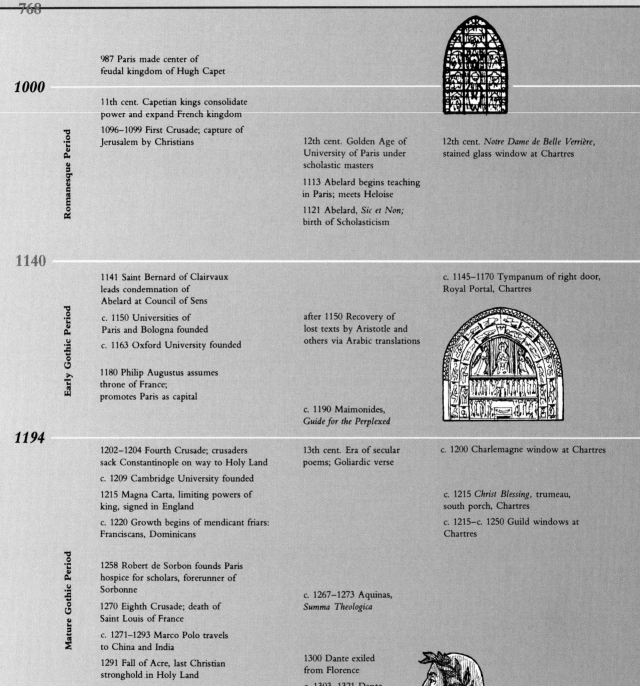

		GENERAL EVENTS	**LITERATURE & PHILOSOPHY**	**ART**

768

EARLY MIDDLE AGES

Romanesque Period

1000

987 Paris made center of feudal kingdom of Hugh Capet

11th cent. Capetian kings consolidate power and expand French kingdom

1096–1099 First Crusade; capture of Jerusalem by Christians

12th cent. Golden Age of University of Paris under scholastic masters

1113 Abelard begins teaching in Paris; meets Heloise

1121 Abelard, *Sic et Non;* birth of Scholasticism

12th cent. *Notre Dame de Belle Verrière,* stained glass window at Chartres

1140

Early Gothic Period

1141 Saint Bernard of Clairvaux leads condemnation of Abelard at Council of Sens

c. 1150 Universities of Paris and Bologna founded

c. 1163 Oxford University founded

1180 Philip Augustus assumes throne of France; promotes Paris as capital

after 1150 Recovery of lost texts by Aristotle and others via Arabic translations

c. 1190 Maimonides, *Guide for the Perplexed*

c. 1145–1170 Tympanum of right door, Royal Portal, Chartres

1194

HIGH MIDDLE AGES

Mature Gothic Period

1202–1204 Fourth Crusade; crusaders sack Constantinople on way to Holy Land

c. 1209 Cambridge University founded

1215 Magna Carta, limiting powers of king, signed in England

c. 1220 Growth begins of mendicant friars: Franciscans, Dominicans

1258 Robert de Sorbon founds Paris hospice for scholars, forerunner of Sorbonne

1270 Eighth Crusade; death of Saint Louis of France

c. 1271–1293 Marco Polo travels to China and India

1291 Fall of Acre, last Christian stronghold in Holy Land

1348–1367 Universities based on Paris model founded in Prague, Vienna, Cracow, Pecs

13th cent. Era of secular poems; Goliardic verse

c. 1267–1273 Aquinas, *Summa Theologica*

1300 Dante exiled from Florence

c. 1303–1321 Dante, *Divine Comedy*

c. 1385–1400 Chaucer, *The Canterbury Tales*

c. 1200 Charlemagne window at Chartres

c. 1215 *Christ Blessing,* trumeau, south porch, Chartres

c. 1215–c. 1250 Guild windows at Chartres

1400

8

The High Middle Ages: The Search for Synthesis

10th cent. Organum develops

11th cent. Guido of Arezzo invents musical notation used today

c. 1130 Halt of construction at Great Third Abbey Church of Cluny

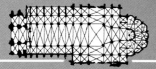

12th cent. Notre Dame School of Paris is center of music study and composition

1140 Abbot Suger begins rebuilding Abbey Church of Saint Denis; Gothic style evolves: use of pointed arch, flying buttress, window tracery

12th–13th cent. French troubadours and trouvères flourish

c. 1163–1250 Cathedral of Notre Dame, Paris

1160 Léonin of Paris, *Magnus Liber Organi*

c. 1180 Philip Augustus commissions Louvre as royal residence and treasury

1181 Pérotin "the Great," director of Notre Dame School of Paris

1194 Chartres cathedral destroyed by fire; rebuilding begins 1195 (ends 1260)

1220–1269 Cathedral of Amiens

13th cent. German minnesingers flourish

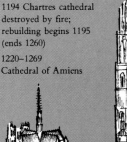

c. 1250 Polyphonic motets are principal form of composition

c. 1235 Honnecourt, notebook

1243–1248 Sainte Chapelle, Paris

1247–1568 Cathedral of Beauvais; cathedral of Strasbourg

1399–1439 Spire of Strasbourg cathedral erected

The Significance of Paris

From about 1150 to 1300 Paris could well claim to be the center of Western civilization. Beyond its position as a royal seat, it was a strong mercantile center. Its annual trade fair was famous. In addition, Paris gave birth to Gothic architecture, the philosophical and theological traditions known as scholasticism, and the educational community that in time became known as the university. These three creations have their own distinct history but they sprang from a common intellectual impulse: the desire to articulate all knowledge in a systematic manner.

The culture of the Middle Ages derives from the twin sources of all Western high culture: the humane learning inherited from the culture of Greece and Rome and the accepted faith of the West, which has its origin in the world view of the Judeo-Christian scriptures and religious world view.

The flowering of a distinct expression of culture in and around medieval Paris was made possible by a large number of factors. There was a renewed interest in learning, fueled largely by the discovery of hitherto lost texts from the classical world—especially the writings of Aristotle—which came to the West via the Moslem world. The often ill-fated crusades begun in the 11th century to recover the Holy Land and the increasing vogue for pilgrimages created a certain cosmopolitanism that, in turn, weakened the static feudal society. Religious reforms initiated by new religious orders like that of the Cistercians in the 12th century and the begging friars in the 13th breathed new life into the church.

Beyond these more generalized currents one can also point to individuals of genius who were crucial in the humanistic renaissance of the time. The University of Paris is inextricably linked with the name of Peter Abelard just as scholasticism is associated with the name of Thomas Aquinas. The Gothic style, unlike most art movements, can be pinpointed to a specific time at a particular place and with a single individual. Gothic architecture began near Paris at the Abbey of Saint Denis in the first half of the 12th century under the sponsorship of the head of the abbey, the Abbot Suger (1080–1151).

The Gothic Style

Suger's Building Program for Saint Denis

The Benedictine Abbey of Saint Denis over which Abbot Suger presided from 1122 until his death nearly 29 years later was the focal point for French patriotism. The abbey church—built in the Carolingian times—housed the relics of Saint Denis, a 5th-century martyr who had evangelized the area of Paris before his martyrdom. The crypts of the church served as burial places for Frankish kings and nobles from before the reign of Charlemagne, although it lacked the tomb of Charlemagne himself. One concrete link between the Abbey of Saint Denis and Charlemagne came through a series of literary works. The fictitious *Pèlerinage de Charlemagne* claimed that the relics of the Passion housed at the abbey had been brought there by Charlemagne himself when he returned from a pilgrimage-crusade to the Holy Land. Another work, the *Pseudo-Turpin,* has Charlemagne returning to the Abbey of Saint Denis after his Spanish campaign and proclaiming all France to be under the protection and tutelage of the saint. These two legends were widely believed in the Middle Ages; there is fair evidence that Suger himself accepted their authenticity. The main themes of the legends—pilgrimage, crusades, and the mythical presence of Charlemagne—created a story about the abbey that made it a major Christian shrine as well as one worthy of the royal city of Paris.

Pilgrims and visitors came to Paris to visit Saint Denis either because of the fame of the abbey's relics or because of the annual *Lendit,* the trade fair held near the precincts of the abbey. Accordingly, in 1124 Suger decided to build a new church to accommodate those who flocked to the popular pilgrimage center. This rebuilding program took the better part of fifteen years and never saw completion. Suger mentions as models two sacred buildings that by his time already had archetypal significance for Christianity. He wanted his church to be as lavish and brilliant as Hagia Sophia in Constantinople, which he knew only by reputation, and as loyal to the will of God as the Temple of Solomon as it was described in the Bible.

The first phase of Suger's project was basically a demolition and repair job; he had to tear down the more deteriorated parts of the old church and replace them. He reconstructed the western facade of the church and added two towers. In order better to handle the pilgrimage crowds and the increasingly elaborate processions called for in the medieval liturgy, the entrance was given three portals. The *narthex,* the part of the church one enters first, before the nave, was rebuilt and the old nave was to be extended by about 40 feet (12.2 meters). About 1140 Suger abruptly stopped work on the narthex to commence work at the opposite end, the *choir,* the area of the church where the monks sang the Office. By his own reckoning, he spent three years and three months at this new construction. The finished choir made a revolutionary change in architecture in the West.

Suger's choir was surrounded by a double *ambulatory,* an aisle around the apse and behind the high altar. The outer ambulatory had seven radiating chapels to accommodate the increasing number of monks who were priests and thus said Mass on a daily basis. Two tall windows pierced the walls of each chapel so that there was little external masonry wall in relation to the amount of space covered by windows. The chapels were shallow enough to permit the light from the windows to fall on the inner ambulatory [8.1].

Although Suger's nave was never completed there is some evidence that it would have had characteristics similar to that of the choir: crossed rib vaults with an abundance of stained-glass windows to permit the flooding of light into the church. We can get some idea of what that nave might have looked like by looking at churches directly inspired by Saint Denis: the cathedrals of Senlis and Noyons [8.2] (their bishops were both at the consecration of Saint Denis in 1144), begun respectively in 1153 and 1157, as well as the cathedral of Notre Dame in Paris, the first stone of which was laid in 1163. This quick emulation of the style of Saint Denis blossomed by the end of the century into a veritable explosion of cathedral-building in the cities and towns radiating out from Paris, the so-called Île-de-France. The Gothic impulse so touched other countries as well that by the

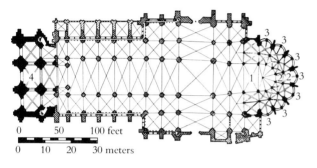

0   50   100 feet
0   10   20   30 meters

8.1 Plan of the abbey church of Saint Denis, built around 1140, and photograph of the ambulatory. Parts of the existing church shaded black in the plan are those rebuilt by Abbot Suger. The photograph shows how use of the ribbed vault and pointed arches gives scope for the passage of light through the lancet windows.

1. choir   3. radiating chapels
2. ambulatory   4. narthex

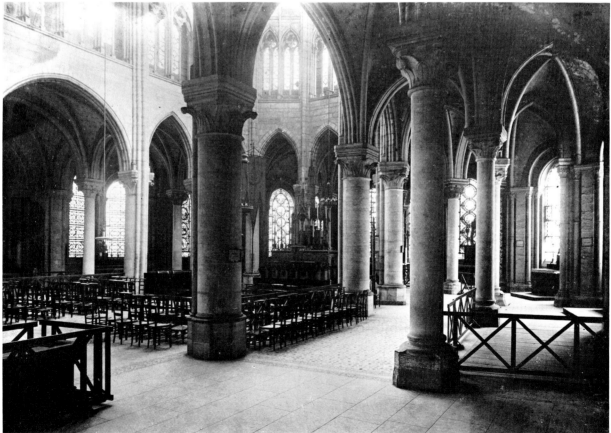

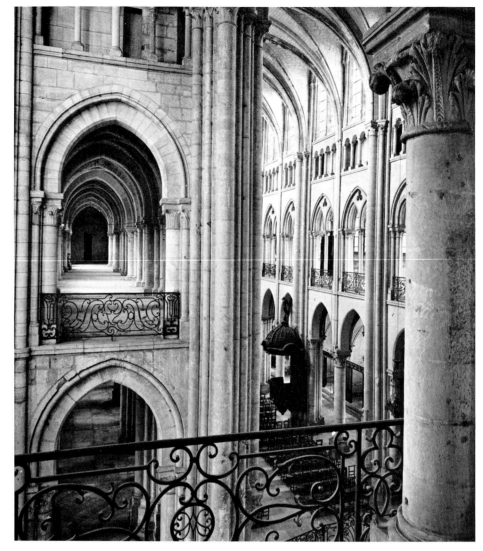

8.2 Interior of Noyons Cathedral. The nave was finished between 1285 and 1330. A fine example of the older style of Gothic architecture. The walls have four rather than the typical three levels: the nave arcade at floor level; the tribune gallery; a triforium; the clerestory with its windows. The rather thick walls of the triforium level would give way, in other Gothic churches, to thinner walls and more pointed arches.

end of the 13th century there were fine examples of Gothic architecture in England, Germany, and Italy.

The term *Gothic* merits a word of explanation. It was used first in the 17th century as a pejorative term meaning "barbarous" or "rude" to distinguish buildings that did not follow the classical models of Greece and Rome, a use still current in the mid-18th century. It was only as a result of the reappraisal of the medieval period in the last century that the word lost its negative meaning.

It is tempting to say that the common characteristic of these cathedrals was the desire for verticality. We tend to identify the Gothic style with the pointed arch, pinnacles and columns, and increasingly higher walls buttressed from the outside by flying arches to accommodate the weight of a pitched roof and the sheer size of the ascending walls [8.3]. It is a truism

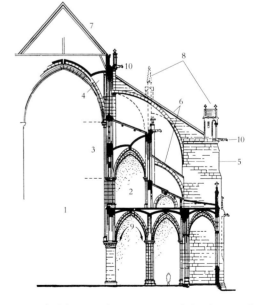

8.3 Transverse half-sectional drawing of the cathedral of Notre Dame in Paris. The height is about 140′ (42.7 m). The tiny figure at the lower right gives some sense of scale.

1 nave arcade	3 clerestory	5 buttress	7 pitched roof	9 pointed arch
2 triforium	4 vault	6 flying buttress	8 pinnacle	10 gargoyle

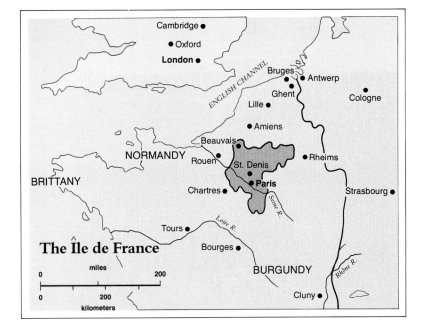

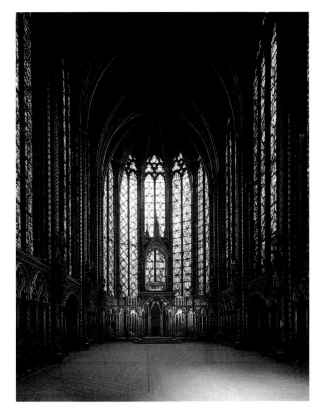

that the medieval builders seem to engage in contests to build higher and higher almost as a matter of civic pride: Chartres (begun in 1194) reached a height of 122 feet (37.2 meters); almost as a response the builders of Amiens (begun 1220) stretched that height to 140 feet (42.7 meters), while Beauvais (begun 1247) pushed verticality almost to the limit with a height of 157 feet (47.9 meters) from the cathedral pavement to the roof arch; indeed, Beauvais had a serious collapse of the roof when the building was barely completed.

That verticality typified Gothic architecture is indisputable, yet Romanesque architects only a generation before Suger had attempted the same verticality, as is evident in such churches as the proposed third abbey church of Cluny or the pilgrimage church at Santiago de Compostela in Spain. What prevented the Romanesque architect from attaining greater verticality was not lack of desire but insufficient technical means. The pointed arch was known in Romanesque architecture but not fully understood. It distributed weight more thoroughly in a downward direction and lessened the need for the massive interior piers of the typical Romanesque church. The size of the piers was further reduced by using buttresses outside the building to prop the interior piers and absorb some of the downward thrust. Furthermore, the downward thrust of the exterior buttresses themselves could be increased by the addition of heavy decorative devices such as spires.

The net result of these technical innovations was to lessen the thickness, weight, and mass of the walls of the Gothic cathedral. This reduction provided an opportunity for greater height with less bulk to absorb the weight of the vaulted roof. Such a reduction made the walls more available as framing devices for the windows that are so characteristic of the period. It has been said, perhaps with some exaggeration, that walls in Gothic cathedrals were replaced by masonry scaffolding for windows [8.4]. In any case, the basic characteristic of Gothic architecture is not verticality but luminosity. The Gothic may be described as transparent—diaphanous—architecture.

8.4 Interior of the upper chapel of La Sainte Chapelle, Paris. 1243–1248. Built to house relics of Christ's passion, this is an exquisite example of Gothic luminosity. Restored heavily, the overall effect is nonetheless maintained of skeletal architecture used as a frame for windows.

THE GOTHIC STYLE **291**

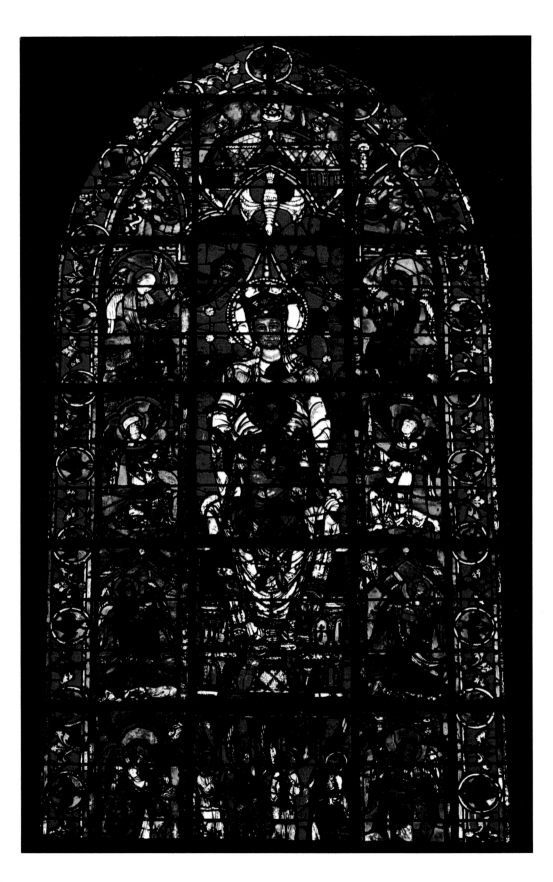

8.5 *Notre Dame de Belle Verrière,* Chartres Cathedral. Early 13th century. The heavy vertical and horizontal lines are iron reinforcing rods to hold the window in place. The thinner lines are the leading. Details such as the Virgin's eyes, nose, and mouth are painted in. The red is a distinctive characteristic of the Chartres stained-glass workshops.

The Mysticism of Light

Abbot Suger wrote two short booklets about his stewardship of the abbey and his ideas about the building and decorating program he initiated for the abbey church—extremely important sources for our understanding of the thought that stood behind the actual work of the builder and artist. Underlying Suger's description of the abbey's art treasures and architectural improvements was a theory or (perhaps better) a theology of beauty. Suger was heavily indebted to his reading of certain mystical treatises written by Dionysius the Areopagite (whom Suger and many of his contemporaries assumed was the Saint Denis for whom the abbey was named), a 5th-century Syrian monk whose works on mystical theology were strongly influenced by neo-Platonic philosophers as well as by Christian doctrine. In the doctrine of the Pseudo-Dionysius (as later generations have called him), every created thing partakes, however imperfectly, of the essence of God. There is an ascending hierarchy of existence that ranges from inert mineral matter to the purity of light, which is God. The Pseudo-Dionysius described all of creation under the category of light: every created thing is a small light that illumines the mind a bit. Ultimately, as light becomes more pure (as one ascends the hierarchy) one gets closer to pure light, which is God.

The high point of this light mysticism is expressed in the stained-glass window. Suger himself believed that when he finished his nave with its glass windows (never completed in fact) to complement his already finished choir he would have a total structure that would make a single statement: "Bright is that which is brightly coupled with the bright, and bright is the noble edifice which is pervaded by the new light [*lux nova*]." The *lux nova* is an allusion to the biblical description of God as the God of light. Suger did not invent stained glass but he fully exploited its possibilities both by encouraging an architecture that could put it to its most advantageous employment and at the same time providing a theory to justify and enhance its use.

No discussion of light and glass in this period can overlook the famous windows of the cathedral of Chartres, a small but important commercial town just south of Paris. When the cathedral was rebuilt after a disastrous fire in 1194 (which destroyed everything except the west facade of the church), the new building gave wide scope to the glazier's art.

When the walls were rebuilt more than 173 windows were installed covering an area of about 2000 square yards (1672 square meters) of surface. It is important to note that, except for some fine details like facial contours, the glass is not painted. The glaziers produced the colors (the blues and reds of Chartres are famous and the tones were never again reproduced exactly) by adding metallic salts to molten glass. Individual pieces were fitted together like a jigsaw puzzle and fixed by leading the pieces together. Individual pieces were rarely larger than 8 feet (2.4 meters) square, but 30-foot (9.2 meter) sections could be bonded together safely in the leading process. The sections were set into stone frames (mullions) and reinforced in place by the use of iron retaining rods. Windows as large as 60 feet (18.3 meters) high could be created in this fashion.

It would be useful at this point to compare the aesthetics of the stained-glass window to the mosaics discussed in Chapter 6. There was a strong element of light mysticism in the art of Byzantine mosaic decoration, derived from some of the same sources later utilized by Abbot Suger: neo-Platonism and the allegorical reading of the Bible. The actual perception of light in the two art forms, however, was radically different. The mosaic refracted light off an opaque surface. The "sacred" aura of the light in a Byzantine church comes from the oddly mysterious breaking up of light as it strikes the irregular surface of the mosaic tesserae. The stained-glass window was the medium through which the light was seen directly, even if it was subtly muted into diverse colors and combinations of colors.

You can only "read" the meaning of the window by looking at it from the inside with an exterior light source—the sun—illuminating it. It was a more perfectly Platonic analogy of God's relationship to the world and its creatures. The viewer sees an object (the illustrated window) but "through it" is conscious of a distant unseen source (the sun—God) that illumines it and gives it its intelligibility. (*Read* is not a rhetorical verb in this context. It was a commonplace of the period to refer to the stained-glass windows as the "Bible of the Poor" since the illiterate could "read" the biblical stories in their illustrated form in the cathedral.)

A close examination of one window at Chartres will illustrate the complexity of this idea. The *Notre Dame de Belle Verrière* (Our Lady of the Beautiful Window) [8.5], one of the most famous works in the cathedral, is a 12th-century work saved from the rubble of the fire of 1194 and reinstalled in the south choir. The window, with its characteristic pointed arch frame, depicts the Virgin enthroned with the Christ Child surrounded by worshiping angels bearing candles and censers. Directly above her is the

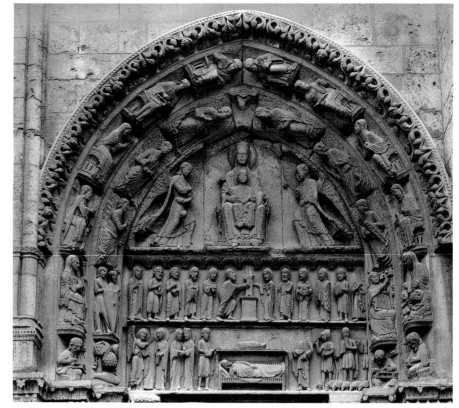

8.6 Scenes from the life of the Virgin Mary. Tympanum of the right door of the royal portal, west façade, Chartres Cathedral. Done between 1145 and 1170, the central panel shows the Virgin and Child as an almost mirror image of the Belle Verrière (figure 8.5). The arch has adoring angels while the outer arch (the archivolt) depicts the Seven Liberal Arts. At the lower left is Aristotle dipping his pen in ink with the female figure of Dialectic above him. Under the central figure of the Virgin are scenes from the life of Mary and the young Christ. At the lower left one can see the scene of the Annunciation.

dove that represents the Holy Spirit and at the very top a stylized church building representing the cathedral built in her honor.

To the simple viewer the window honored the Virgin, to whom one prayed in time of need and to whom the church was dedicated. The person of some theological sophistication would further recognize the particular scene of the Virgin enthroned as the symbol of Mary as the Seat of Wisdom, a very ancient motif in religious art. The window also has a conceptual link with the exterior sculptural program. In the tympanum of the portal is an enthroned Madonna and Christ Child with two censer-bearing angels. This scene is surrounded by sculptured arches, called *archivolts,* in which there is a symbolic representation of the Seven Liberal Arts [8.6], which together constitute a shorthand version of the window.

The Blessed Virgin depicted as the Seat of Wisdom would be an especially attractive motif for the town of Chartres. The cathedral school was a flourishing center of literary and philosophical studies, studies which emphasized that human learning became wisdom only when it led to the source of wisdom, God. The fact that Mary was depicted here in glass would also call to mind an oft-repeated *exemplum* (moral example) used in medieval preaching and theology: Christ was born of a virgin. He passed through her body as light passes through a window, completely intact without changing the

glass. The Christ/light—Mary/glass analogy is an apt and deepened metaphor to be seen in the *Belle Verrière* of Chartres.

That kind of interpretation can be applied profitably to many aspects of Gothic art and architecture. Builders and theologians worked closely while a cathedral was under construction. The church authorities felt it a primary duty not only to build a place suitable for divine worship but also to utilize every opportunity to teach and edify the participating worshiper. The famous Gothic gargoyles [8.7] are a good example of this blend of functionality and didacticism. These carved beasts served the practical purpose of funneling rainwater off the roofs while, in their extended and jutting positions on the roofs and buttresses, signifying that evil flees the sacred precincts of the church. At a far more ambitious level, the whole decorative scheme of a cathedral was an attempt to tell an integrated story about the history of salvation, a story alluded to in both profane and divine learning. The modern visitor may be overwhelmed by what appears a chaotic jumble of sculptures depicting biblical scenes, allegorical figures, symbols of the labors of the month, signs of the Zodiac, representatives of pagan learning, and panoramic views of Last Judgments; for the medieval viewer the variegated scenes represented a patterned whole. The decoration of the cathedral was, as it were, the common vocabulary of sermons, folk wisdom, and school learning fleshed out in stone.

The Many Meanings of the Gothic Cathedral

Some theological and philosophical background is crucial for an appreciation of the significance of the Gothic cathedral, but it is a serious oversimplification to view the cathedral only in the light of its intellectual milieu. The cathedral was, after all, the preeminent building in the episcopal towns of the Île-de-France, as a view of any of the towns shows. The cathedral overwhelms the town either by crowning a hilly site, as at Laon, or rising up above the town plain, as at Amiens. The cathedrals were *town* buildings (Saint Denis, a monastic church, is a conspicuous exception) and one might well inquire into their functional place in the life of the town. It is simplistic to think that their presence in the town reflected a credulous faith on the part of the populace or the egomania of the civil and religious builders. In fact, the cathedral served vital social and economic functions in medieval society.

A modern analogy illustrates the social function of architecture and building. Many small towns in America, especially those in rural areas of the South and the Northeast, center their civic and commercial life around a town square. The courthouse symbolically emanates social control (justice), social structures (births, weddings, and deaths are registered there), power (the sheriff, commissioners or aldermen, and the mayor are housed there), and—to a degree—culture, with its adjacent park and military or civic monuments to the founders and war dead. The better stores, the "uptown" churches, and the other appurtenances of respectability—banks, lawyers' and physicians' offices—cluster about the square. (The urbanization and suburbanization of America has steadily destroyed this basic symmetry, replacing it with a far more diffuse city or suburban pattern where the concept of "center" is less easy to identify.) The cathedral square of the typical European or Latin American town is the ancestor of the courthouse square. The difference is that the medieval cathedral exercised a degree of social control and integration more comprehensive than that of the courthouse.

The cathedral and its power were a serious force that shaped both individual and social life in the town. The individual was baptized in, made a communicant of, married in, and buried from, the cathedral. Schooling was obtained from the cathedral school and social services (hospitals, poor relief, orphanages, and so on) directed by the decisions of the cathedral staff (the *chapter*). The daily and yearly round of life was regulated by the horarium of the cathedral. People rose and ate and went to bed in rhythm with the tolling of the cathedral bell just as they worked or played in line with the feast days of the liturgical calendar of the church year. Citizens could sue and be sued in the church courts, and those same courts dispensed justice on a par with the civil courts; the scenes of the Last Judgment over the cen-

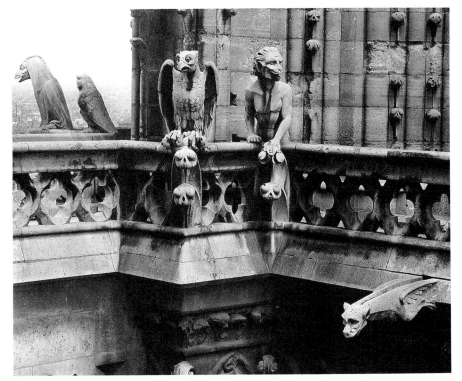

8.7 Grotesques and a gargoyle waterspout on a tower terrace of the cathedral of Notre Dame, Paris. Many of these figures are modern representations of originals that were badly damaged during the French Revolution.

295

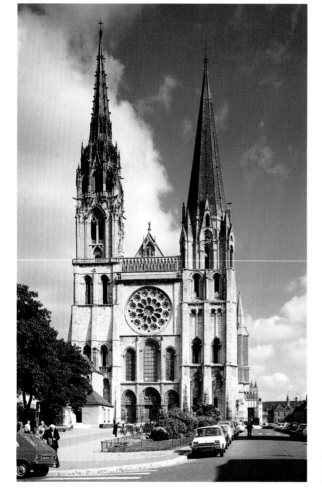

8.8 West Front and floor plan of Chartres Cathedral. 1194–1240. The towers were done at different times and reflect quite different styles of architecture.

0   50   100 feet

0 10 20   30 meters

1 nave   5 transept
2 choir   6 aisles
3 ambulatory   7 apse
4 chapels   8 narthex

tral portals of medieval cathedrals referred to more than divine justice.

Far more significant than the social interaction of town and cathedral was the economic impact of the cathedral on the town. The building of a cathedral was an extremely expensive enterprise. When the people of Chartres decided to rebuild their cathedral in 1194 the bishop pledged all of the diocesan revenues for three years (three to five million dollars!) simply to initiate the project [8.8]. It should be remembered that a town like Chartres was very small in the late 12th century, with no more than ten to fifteen thousand residents in the town itself. Some economic historians have attempted to show that the combination of civic pride and religious enthusiasm that motivated the town to build a cathedral was economically ruinous in the long run. The majority of scholars, however, insist that it was precisely economic gain that was the significant factor in construction. This was surely the case with Chartres.

From the late 9th century Chartres had been a major pilgrimage site. The cathedral possessed a relic of the Virgin (the tunic she wore when Jesus was born) given by Charles the Bald, the great-grandson of Charlemagne, in 876. Relics were very popular throughout the Middle Ages and this particular one was specially important to the pilgrims of the time. The relic had not been destroyed by the fire of 1194, a sure sign in the eyes of the populace that the Virgin wished the church rebuilt. Furthermore, the four great feasts of the Blessed Virgin in the liturgical year (the Purification of Mary on February 2, the Annunciation on March 25, the Assumption on August 15, and the Nativity of the Virgin on September 8) were celebrated in Chartres in conjunction with large trade fairs that drew merchants and customers from all over Europe.

These fairs were held in the shadow of the cathedral and their conduct was protected by legislation issued by the cathedral chapter. Regulations from the chapter, for example, stated that the prized textiles of the area were to be sold near the north portal while the purveyors of fuel, vegetables, fruit, and wine were to be located by the south portal. There were also sellers of images, medals, and other religious objects (forerunners of the modern souvenir) to the pilgrims who came both for the fair and for reasons of devotion. The church, then, was as much a magnet for outsiders as it was a symbol for the townspeople.

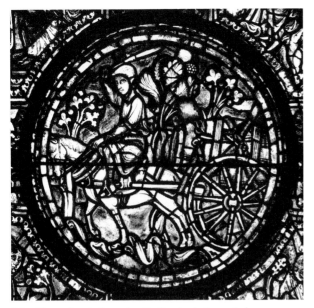

8.9 Vintner's window, detail of stained glass window, Chartres. c. 1215. This panel from a window donated by the winemakers of the area shows a carter taking wine casks to market.

The patrons who donated the windows of Chartres Cathedral also give some indication of the economics of the place. It was only natural that some of the large windows—like a rose window—would be the gift of a royal family or that a tall, pointed *lancet* window like those in the choir would be given by the nobility or the higher clergy. A large number of the windows, however, were donated by the members of the various craft and commercial guilds in the town; their "signature frames" can be found at the bottoms of the windows. The fact that the five large windows in honor of the Virgin in the *chevet,* the east end of the cathedral, were donated by merchants—principally the bakers, butchers, and vintners—indicates the significant power of the guilds [8.9].

The guild, a fraternal society of craftsmen or merchants, was a cross between a modern-day union and a fraternal organization like the Elks or the Knights of Columbus. Members of the guilds put themselves under the patronage of a saint, promised to perform certain charitable works, and acted as a mutual-aid society. Many of the economic guilds appear to have developed out of earlier, more purely religious confraternities. One had to belong to a guild to work at any level beyond day labor. The guild accepted and instructed apprentices; certified master craftsmen; regulated prices, wages, working conditions; and maintained funds for the care of older members and the burial of their dead. The guilds were a crucial part of town life and would remain so well into the mod-

ern period. And, as we shall see, the university developed from the guild idea in the 12th century.

The motivation for the building of a medieval cathedral, then, came from the theological vision, religious devotion, civic pride, and socioeconomic interest. The actual construction depended on a large number of people. The cathedral chapter decided to construct a building, raised the money, and hired the master-builder-architect. He in turn was responsible for hiring the various master craftsmen, designing the building, and creating the decorative scheme from ideas generated and approved by the theologians or church officials of the chapter. A great workshop was set up near the proposed site, with each master (mason, stonecutter, glazier) hiring his crew, obtaining his material, and setting up work quarters. Manual and occasional labor was recruited from the local population, but the construction crews were usually migratory groups who traveled from job to job.

The names of a number of master builders, including the builder of Chartres, have been lost, but others have survived in funerary inscriptions, commemorative plaques, and building records. Notes intended for students of buildings written by Villard de Honnecourt (about 1235), an architect from northern France, preserved in a unique copy at the Bibliothèque Nationale in Paris, provide us a rare glimpse into the skills of a medieval cathedral builder. Villard says in his book that he could teach a willing apprentice a wide range of skills ranging from carpentry and masonry to the more demanding skills of practical geometry [8.10] and plan drafting. The notebook also has random sketches and ideas jotted down for his own personal use; they include religious figures to serve as models for stonecarvers; animals and buildings that caught his eye; a perpetual-motion machine (which didn't work); the first example of clockworks in the West; and a self-operating saw for cutting huge timbers for buttressing and roofing, among others. He visited Rheims and made sketches of the cathedral. He tells of traveling as far as Hungary to get work. While not as complete and wide-ranging as the Renaissance notebooks of Leonardo da Vinci (with which they have often been compared), Villard's notebook reveals a highly skilled, persistently inquisitive, and very inventive man.

A look through Villard's notebook forcefully reminds us that because our tendency is to emphasize the religious and social significance of a cathedral (as that is what first strikes us about it), we easily overlook the basic fact that a cathedral is a stunning technological achievement. A prime example of the technological virtuosity of such buildings is the elegant spire of Strasbourg Cathedral. Finished in 1439, the spire is 466 feet (142.1 meters) high from pavement

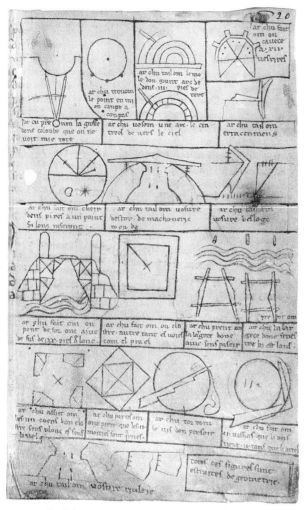

8.10 Villard de Honnecourt. Page on "practical geometry" from his *Album.* c. 1275. Pen and ink. Bibliothèque Nationale, Paris. *Top row:* Measuring the diameter of a partially visible column; finding the middle of a circle; cutting the mold of an arch; arching a vault with an outer covering; making an apse with twelve windows; cutting the spring stone of an arch. *Second row:* Bringing together two stones; cutting a voussoir for a round building; cutting an oblique voussoir. *Third row:* Bridging a stream with timers; laying out a cloister without plumb line or level; measuring the width of river without crossing it; measuring the width of a distant window. *Bottom row:* Cutting a regular voussoir.

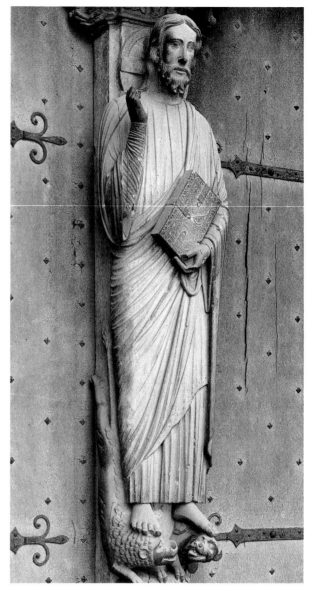

8.11 Christ in the act of blessing. Figure on trumeau of main portal, Chartres Cathedral. c. 1215. This statue symbolically blesses all pilgrims who pass through the door, the "Gates of Heaven."

to tip—as high as a forty-story building. This stone structure remained the tallest in Europe until the mid-1960s, when the London Post Office Tower was completed.

The Gothic cathedral is an almost perfect artifact for the study of the humanistic enterprise since it may be approached from so many angles and at so many levels. It was first an architectural and technological achievement. Its ensemble of walls, windows, sculpture, and decoration demonstrated a peculiar way of combining human knowledge and religious faith that provides a basic aesthetic experience to the viewer. It had a fundamental economic and social significance for the community in which it was located. Finally, it was, for those who entered it in faith, a transcendental religious experience of passing from the profane to the sacred world. Henry Adams, in his wonderfully eccentric book *Mont-Saint-Michel and Chartres,* says that only a person coming to Chartres as a pilgrim could understand the building. The pilgrim is a central metaphor for the period whether one speaks of the actual pilgrim on the road to Santiago de Compostela or Canterbury or life itself as a pilgrimage toward God. Pilgrims to Chartres or the other cathedrals were pilgrims in both senses: they traveled to visit a real monument and, at the same time, hoped to find rest and salvation through the act [8.11]. It is no wonder Abbot Suger should have called Saint Denis the "Gate of Heaven": that is exactly what it was meant to be.

Music: The School of Notre Dame

It should not be surprising that in an age of artistic and architectural development such as the Gothic the rather austere music of the early church should also undergo development and change. From the time Charlemagne introduced Gregorian chant into the church life of the Frankish kingdom there had been further developments of that musical form. In the 11th century, Guido of Arezzo had worked out a system of musical notation that provided the basis for the development of the musical notation used today. Church musicians from the 10th century on also experimented with a single melodic line of plainchant by adding parallel voices at different musical intervals above the line of chant. This first step toward *polyphony,* a musical term for "many voices," is called *orga-*

num. Outside the church, the knightly classes also composed and performed secular music. Some of the melodies of the *troubadours* and *trouvères* have survived, giving us an idea of secular music in the 12th and 13th centuries. The German *minnesingers* (*minne* means "love") of the 13th century utilized traditional church modes and melodies to create both secular and sacred songs.

The school of Notre Dame in Paris was the center of systematic musical study and composition in the 12th century. Léonin's *Magnus Liber Organi* (about 1160) is an important source for our knowledge of music in the period of the Gothic cathedral. Léonin's book was a collection of organum compositions for use during the liturgical services throughout the church year. Léonin's work was carried on by the other great composer of the century, Pérotin, who assumed the directorship of the music school of Notre Dame sometime around 1181.

In Pérotin's music, the Notre Dame organum utilized the basic melodic line of the traditional chant (the *cantus firmus*) while a second melodic line (the *duplum*), a third (*triplum*), and in some cases a fourth (*quadruplum*) voice was added above the melody. These added lines mirrored the rhythmic flow of the cantus firmus. It was soon learned, however, that pleasing and intricate compositions could be created by having the duplum and triplum move in opposition to the cantus firmus. This *counterpoint* (from *contrapunctum,* against the note) meant, at its most basic level, that a descending series of notes in the cantus

THE ARTS AND INVENTION: *Musical Notation*

With the development of music of greater complexity, musicians began to devise a system of notation to indicate the pitch and duration of each note. The earliest stages of musical notation can be seen in Gregorian chant manuscripts of the ninth century. Above the lines of the text are symbols, known as *neums* (Greek *neuma,* "sign"), which represent single notes or groups of notes. These could not indicate precise pitches but did give a general indication of the shape of the melody; thus the performers of the chant would have a reminder of its basic contours.

By the 13th century a new, more precise method had been devised; it still forms the basis of modern musical notation. Invention is generally attributed to Guido of Arezzo (c. 990–1050), but it was probably the result of experiments carried out by musicians throughout western Europe. The notes were placed on a four-line staff, with the distance from line to space (or space to line) representing the interval of a second. This system by itself would be able to convey only relative pitches. The

absolute pitch of the music notated is indicated by a mark known as a *clef,* which indicates the rate represented by a particular line; once one note was fixed, the others could be deduced automatically. The note indicated by the clef was virtually always C or F. Thus, in the Easter *Alleluia* quoted in Chapter 7, page 299, the first three notes are G, three steps below the C indicated on the second line down at the beginning of the staff.

There remained the problem of notating the length of the notes, indicating the rhythm of the music. The problem was discussed at length by writers on musical theory of the time. The solution chosen by the Notre Dame school of composers was to adapt symbols from Gregorian chant that had served a melodic purpose (like those at the end of the third staff of the *Alleluia,* for example) and use them to express a rhythmic, or metrical, relation between notes. The progress made by the end of the 13th century in developing an accurate system was summarized in the *Art of Measurable Song,* published around 1280 by Franco of Colgone.

firmus would have an ascending series of notes in the melodic lines above it.

One development in the Gothic period deriving from the polyphony of organum was the *motet*. The motet usually had three voices (in some cases, four). The tenor—from the Latin *tenere* (to hold), another term for cantus firmus—maintained the traditional line, usually derived from an older ecclesiastical chant. Since some of the manuscripts from the period show no words for this tenor position, it has been thought that for many motets the tenor line was the musical accompaniment (perhaps the organ, then an instrument of increasing popularity). Above the tenor were two voices who sang interweaving melodies. In the early 13th century, these melodies were invariably in Latin and were exclusively religious in content. In the late 13th century it was not uncommon to sing the duplum in Latin and the triplum in French. Indeed, the two upper voices could be singing quite distinct songs: a hymn in Latin with a love lyric in French with a tenor voice (or instrument) maintaining an elaborated melody based on the melismas of Gregorian chant.

This increasingly sophisticated music, built on a monastic basis but with a new freedom of its own, is indicative of many of the intellectual currents of the period. It is a technically complex music rooted in the distant past but open to new and somewhat daring innovation, a blend of the traditional and the vernacular—all held together in an intellectually complicated balance of competing elements. Gothic music was an aural expression of the dynamism inherent in the medieval Gothic cathedral.

Scholasticism

The Rise of the Universities

A number of our contemporary institutions have roots in the Middle Ages. Trial by jury is one, constitutional monarchy another. By far the best-known and most widely diffused cultural institution that dates from the Middle Ages, however, is the university. In fact, some of the most prestigious centers of European learning today stand where they were founded eight hundred years ago: Oxford and Cambridge in England; the University of Paris in France; the University of Bologna in Italy. There is also a remarkable continuity between the organization and purposes of the medieval university and our own, except that we have coeducation. The medieval student would be puzzled, to be sure, by the idea of football games, coeducation, degrees in business or agriculture, and well-manicured campuses, were he

to visit a modern American university. He would find himself at home with the idea of a liberal arts curriculum, the degrees from the baccalaureate through the master's to the doctorate, and the high cost of textbooks. At a less serious level, he would be well acquainted with drinking parties, fraternities, and friction between town and gown (the phrase itself has a medieval ring). The literature that has come down to us from the period is full of complaints about poor housing, high rents, terrible food, and lack of jobs after graduation. Letters from the Middle Ages between students and parents have an almost uncanny contemporaneity about them.

European universities developed in the late 12th and early 13th centuries along with the emergence of city life. In the earlier medieval period schools were most often associated with the monasteries, which were perforce situated in rural areas. As cities grew in importance, schools also developed at urban monasteries or, increasingly, under the aegis of bishops whose cathedrals were in the towns. The episcopal or cathedral school was a direct offshoot of the increasing importance of towns and the increasing power of bishops, the spiritual leaders of town life. In Italy, where town life had been relatively strong throughout the early Middle Ages and where feudalism never took hold, there was also a tradition of schools controlled by the laity. The center of medical studies in Salerno and the law faculty of Bologna had been in secular hands since the 10th century.

A number of factors help to explain the rapid rise of formal education institutions in the 12th century. First, the increasing complexity of urban life created a demand for an educated class who could join the ranks of administrators and bureaucrats. Urban schools were not simply interested in providing basic literacy. They were designed to produce an educated class who could give support to the socioeconomic structures of society. Those who completed the arts curriculum of a 12th-century cathedral school (like the one at Chartres) could find ready employment in either the civil or the ecclesiastical bureaucracy as lawyers, clerks, or administrators.

There were also intellectual and cultural reasons for the rise of the universities. In the period from 1150 to 1250 came a wholesale discovery and publication of texts from the ancient world. Principal among these were lost books by Aristotle that came to the West through Muslim sources in Spain. Aristotle's writings covered a vast range of subjects ranging from meteorology and physics to logic and philosophy. Furthermore, with a closer relationship between Christian and Arabic scholars, a large amount of scientific and mathematical material was coming into Europe [8.12]. There was also a renaissance of legal studies centered primarily at Bologna, the one intel-

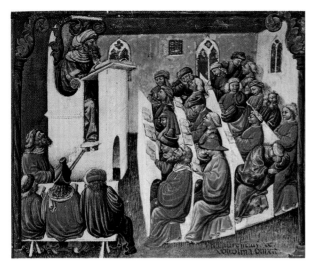

8.12 A university lecture; detail from the compendium of Aristotle's *Nichomachean Ethics*. German. 14th century. Manuscript illumination. State Museums, West Berlin. The professor expounds his text from the professorial chair (*cathedra*). Note the sleeping student at the lower right.

lectual center that could nearly rival Paris. Finally, there was a new tool being refined by such scholars as Peter Abelard and Peter Lombard: dialectics. Theologians and philosophers began to apply the principles of logic to the study of philosophy and theology. Abelard's book *Sic et Non* (1121) put together conflicting opinions concerning theological matters with contradictory passages from the Bible and the Church Fathers and then attempted to mediate and reconcile the apparent divergences. This method was later refined and stylized into the method which was to become *scholasticism,* so called because it was the philosophical method of the schools, the communities of scholars at the nascent universities.

The most famous and representative university to emerge in the Middle Ages was the University of Paris. The eminence of Paris rested mainly on the fame of the teachers who came there to teach. At this state of educational development, the teacher really was the school. Students in the 12th century flocked from all over Europe to frequent the lectures of teachers like William the Champeaux (1070–1121) and, later, his formal student and vehement critic, Peter Abelard (1079–1142). Besides these famous individual teachers Paris also had some established centers of learning that enjoyed a vast reputation. There was a cathedral school attached to the cathedral of Notre Dame, a theological center associated with the canons of the church of Saint Victor, and a school of arts maintained at the ancient monastery of Sainte Geneviève.

Although it is difficult to assign precise dates, it is safe to say that the university at Paris developed in the final quarter of the 12th and early part of the 13th centuries. Its development began with the masters (*magistri,* teachers) of the city forming a corporation after the manner of the guilds. At this time the word *universitas* simply meant a guild or corporation. The masters formed the *universitas* in Paris in order to exercise some "quality control" over the teaching profession and the students entrusted to their care. At Bologna the reverse was true. The students formed the *universitas* in order to hire the teachers with the best qualifications and according to the most advantageous financial terms.

The *universitas* soon acquired a certain status in law with a corporate right to borrow money, to sue (and be sued), and to issue official documents. As a legal body it could issue stipulations for the conduct of both masters and students. When a student finished the course of studies and passed his examinations the *universitas* would grant him a teaching certificate that enabled him to enter the ranks of the masters: he was a master of arts (our modern degree has its origin in that designation). After graduation a student could go on to specialized training in law, theology, or medicine. The completion of this specialized training entitled one to be called *doctor* (from the Latin *doctus* [learned]) in his particular field. The modern notion that a professional person (doctor, lawyer, and the like) should be university-trained is an idea derived directly from the usages of the medieval university.

Since the Carolingian period—indeed, earlier— the core of education was the arts curriculum. In the last 12th century in Paris the arts began to be looked on as a prelude to the study of theology. This inevitably caused a degree of tension between the arts faculty and the theology masters. This tension resulted in 1210 in a split, with the masters and students of arts moving their faculty to the Left Bank of the Seine, where they settled in the area intersected by the rue du Fouarre (Straw Street—so named because the students sat on straw during lectures). That part of the Left Bank has traditionally been a student haunt. The Latin Quarter name reminds us of the old language that was once the only tongue used at the university.

By the end of the 12th century Paris was the intellectual center of Europe. Students came from all over Europe to study there. We do not have reliable statistics about their number, but an estimate of five to eight thousand students would not be far from the mark for the early 13th century. The students were organized into *nationes* by their place of national origin. By 1294 there were four recognized *nationes* in Paris: the French, the Picard, the Norman, and the Anglo-German. Student support came from families, pious benefactors, church stipends, or civic grants to underwrite an education. Certain generous patrons

I have recently discovered that you live dissolutely and slothfully, preferring license to restraint and play to work and strumming a guitar while the others are at their studies, whence it happens that you have but one volume of law while more industrious companions have read several. I have decided to exhort you herewith to repent utterly of your dissolute and careless ways that you may no longer be called a waster and that your shame may be turned to good repute.

[parent to a son at the university in Orleans, 14th century]

We occupy a good and comely dwelling, next door but one from the schools and marketplace, so that we can go to school each day without wetting our feet. We have good companions in the house with us, well advanced in their studies, and of excellent habits—an advantage which we appreciate for, as the psalmist says, "with an upright man thou will show thyself upright." Wherefore, lest production should cease for lack of material, we beg your paternity to send us by the bearer money for the purchase of parchment, ink, a desk, and the other things which we need, in sufficient amount that we may suffer no want on your account (God forbid!) but finish our studies and return home with honor. The bearer will also take charge of the shoes and stockings which you will send us, and any news at all.

[scholar to his father, Orleans, 14th century]

provided funds for hospices for scholars, the most famous of which was that underwritten by Robert de Sorbon in 1258 for graduate students in theology; his hospice was the forerunner of the Sorbonne in Paris.

By our standards student life in the 13th century was harsh. Food and lodging were primitive, heating scarce, artificial lighting nonexistent, and income sporadic. The daily schedule was rigorous, made more so by the shortage of books and writing material. An "ideal" student's day, as sketched out in a late medieval pamphlet for student use, now seems rather grim:

A Student's Day at the University of Paris

4:00 A.M.	Rise
5:00–6:00	Arts lectures
6:00	Mass and breakfast
8:00–10:00	Lectures
11:00–12:00	Disputations before the noon meal
1:00–3:00	"Repetitions"—study of morning lectures with tutors
3:00–5:00	Cursory lectures (generalized lectures on special topics) or disputations
6:00	Supper
7:00–9:00	Study and repetitions; bed at 9:00 P.M.

The masters' lectures consisted of detailed commentaries on certain books the master intended to cover in a given term. Since books were expensive, emphasis was put on note-taking and copying so that the student might build up his own collection of books. Examinations were oral, before a panel of masters. Students were also expected to participate in formal debates (called disputations) as part of their training.

Geoffrey Chaucer provides us an unforgettable, albeit idealized, portrait of the medieval student (the clerk or cleric—many of the students were members of the minor clerical orders of the church) in his Prologue to the *Canterbury Tales*:

> A clerk from Oxford was with us also,
> Who'd turned to getting knowledge, long ago.
> As meagre was his horse as is a rake,
> Nor he himself too fat, I'll undertake,
> But he looked hollow and went soberly.
> Right threadbare was his overcoat; for he
> Had got him yet no churchly benefice,
> Nor was so worldly as to gain office.
> For he would rather have at his bed's head
> Some twenty books, all bound in black and red,
> Of Aristotle and his philosophy
> Than rich robes, fiddle, or gay psaltery.
> Yet, and for all he was philosopher,
> He had but little gold within his coffer;
> But all that he might borrow from a friend
> On books and learning he would swiftly spend,
> And then he'd pray right busily for the souls
> Of those who gave him wherewithal for
>   schools.
> Of study took he utmost care and heed.
> Not one word spoke he more than was his
>   need;
> And that was said in fullest reverence
> And short and quick and full of high good
>   sense.
> Pregnant of moral virtue was his speech;
> And gladly would he learn and gladly teach.

Chaucer's portrait of the lean, pious, poor, zealous student was highly idealized to create a type. We get probably a far more realistic picture of what students were actually doing and thinking about from the considerable amount of popular poetry that comes from the student culture of the medieval period. This poetry depicts a student life we are all familiar with: a poetry of wine, women, song, sharp satires at the expense of pompous professors or poor accommodations, and the occasional episodes of cruelty that most individuals are capable of only when they are banded into groups.

The student subculture had also invented a mythical Saint Golias, who was the patron saint of wandering scholars. Verses (called Goliardic verse) were written in honor of the "saint." The poems that have come down to use are a far cry from the sober commentaries on Aristotle's *Metaphysics* that we usually associate with the medieval scholar.

One of the more interesting collections of these medieval lyrics was discovered in a Bavarian monastery in the early 19th century. The songs in this collection were written in Latin, Old French, and German and seem to date from the late 12th and the 13th centuries. Their subject range was wide but, given the nature of such songs, predictable. There were drinking songs, laments over the loss of love or the trials of fate, hymns in honor of nature, salutes to the end of winter and the coming of the spring, and cheerfully obscene songs of exuberant sexuality. The lyrics reveal a shift of emotions ranging from the happiness of love to the despair of disappointment just as the allusions range from classical learning to medieval piety. One famous song, for example, praises the beautiful powerful virgin in language that echoes the piety of the church. The last line reveals, however, that the poem salutes not Mary but generous Venus.

In 1935 and 1936 the German composer Carl Orff set a number of these poems to music under the title *Carmina Burana*. His brilliantly lively blending of heavy percussion, snatches of ecclesiastical chant, strong choral voices, and vibrant rhythms have made this work a modern concert favorite. The listener gets a good sense of the vibrancy of these medieval lyrics by the use of the modern setting. Since the precise character of student music has not come down to us, Orff's new setting of these lyrics is a fine beginning for learning about the musicality of this popular poetry from the medieval university.

Thomas Aquinas

The Golden Age of the University of Paris was the 13th century, since in that period Paris could lay fair claim to being the intellectual center of the Western world. It is a mark of the international character of medieval university life that some of its most distinguished professors were from outside France: Albert the Great was German; Alexander of Hales was English; Bonaventure and Thomas Aquinas were Italian.

Thomas Aquinas (1225?–1274) was the most famous and influential of the Parisian masters of the 13th century [8.13]. His intellectual influence went

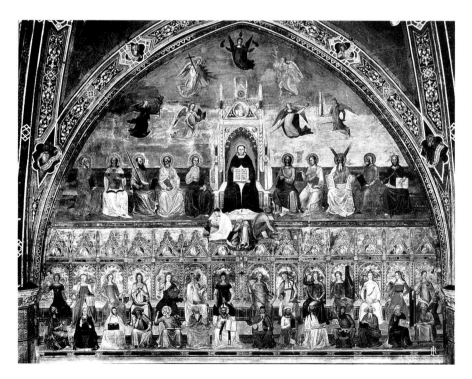

8.13 Andrea da Firenze. *The Triumph of Saint Thomas Aquinas.* c. 1365. Fresco. Santa Maria Novella, Florence. The saint is enthroned between figures of the Old and New Testaments with the personification of the Virtues, Sciences, and Liberal Arts below. This Florentine church had a school of studies attended by Dante Alighieri in his youth.

far beyond the lecture halls of Paris and is felt to the present. Born of noble parentage in southern Italy, Thomas joined the Preaching Friars of Saint Dominic (the Dominicans) in 1243. From 1245 to 1248 he studied with Albert the Great at both Paris and Cologne. He was made a *magister* of theology in 1258 after completing his doctoral studies. During this same period (from roughly 1256 to 1259) he lectured on theology in Paris. From 1259 to 1268 he was back in Italy, where he lectured and wrote at Orvieto (the papal court for a time), Rome, and Naples. From 1268 to 1272 he held a chair of theology again, when he returned to Naples to teach there. He died two years later on his way to a church council at Lyons in France.

Thomas Aquinas' life ended before he was fifty, but in that span he produced a vast corpus of writings (they fill forty folio volumes) on theology, philosophy, and biblical studies. It is a mark of his mobility that his masterpiece—the *Summa Theologica*—was composed at Rome, Viterbo, Paris, and Naples, although it was unfinished at his death. While his writings touched on a wide variety of subjects, at root Thomas Aquinas was interested in and made a lifetime study of a very basic problem: How does one harmonize those things that are part of human learning (reason) with those supernatural truths revealed by God in the Bible and through the teaching of the church (revelation)? Aquinas' approach was to steer a middle path through two diametrically opposed opinions, both of which had avid supporters in the Middle Ages: the position of *fideism,* which held that religious faith as an absolute is indifferent to the efforts of human reason (*credo quia absurdum est*—I believe because it is absurd) and *rationalism,* which insists that everything, revelation included, must meet the test of rational human scrutiny. Aquinas wanted to demonstrate what the Gothic cathedral illustrated: that the liberal arts, the things and seasons of the world, and the mysteries revealed by God could be brought into some kind of intellectual harmony based on a single criterion of truth.

For Aquinas, reason finds truth when it sees evidence of truth. The mind judges something true when it has observed a sufficient number of facts to compel it to make that judgment. The mind gives assent to truth on the basis of evidence. Aquinas was convinced that there was a sufficient amount of observable evidence in the world to conclude the existence of God. He proposed five arguments in support of such a position. Still he recognized that such argumentation only yields a very limited understanding of God. Aquinas did not believe that the naked use of reason could ever discover or prove the mysteries about God revealed in the Bible: that God became a man in Jesus Christ or that there was a Trinity of persons in God. God had to tell us that. Our assent to it is not based on evidence, but on the authority of God who reveals it to us. If we could prove the mysteries of faith, there would have been no need of a revelation and no need of faith.

Thus for Aquinas there is an organic relationship between reason and revelation. Philosophy perfects the human capacity to know and revelation perfects one beyond self by offering salvation and eternal life. Aquinas stated this relationship between reason and revelation at the very beginning of his great work of theology, the *Summa Theologica.*

When we read Aquinas today we get some sense of his stark and rigorous attempt to think things through. For one thing, he offers no stylistic adornment to relieve his philosophical and rational discourse. For another, he makes clear that philosophical reasoning is difficult; it is not a pastime for the incompetent or the intellectually lazy. Yet Aquinas was not a mere machine for logic. He had the temperament of a mystic. Some months before he died he simply put down his pen; when his secretary asked him why he had stopped writing, Aquinas simply said that in prayer and quiet he had had a vision and that what he had written "seemed as straw." Aquinas was a rare combination of intellectual and mystic.

The philosophical tradition Aquinas used in his writing was that of the Greek philosopher Aristotle. He first knew Aristotle's work in Latin translations based on Arabic texts done by Muslim scholars in the south of Spain and North Africa. Later Aquinas was able to use texts translated directly out of Greek by a Flemish friar and sometime companion, William of Moerbeke. Aquinas' use of Aristotle was certainly not a novelty in the Middle Ages. Such Arabic scholars as Avicenna (980–1036) and Averröes of Córdova (1126–1198) commented on Aristotle's philosophy and its relationship to the faith of Islam. Jewish thinkers like the famous Moses Maimonides (born in Córdova in 1135, died in Egypt in 1204) made similar attempts to bridge Greek thought and their religious faith. Maimonides wrote his famous *Guide for the Perplexed* to demonstrate the essential compatibility of the Hebrew scriptures with the thought of Aristotle. Maimonides was determined that essentials of the biblical message not be compromised, but he likewise felt that in nonessentials there was room for human reflection. In this task of distinguishing the place of intellect and faith Maimonides anticipated the work of Thomas Aquinas by two generations.

Two other characteristics of the thought of Aquinas should be noted. First, his world view was strongly hierarchical. Everything has its place in the universe, and that place is determined in relationship

Islamic Medicine and Science

In the early Middle Ages the Muslims not only translated and commented on Greek learning in the fields of philosophy, medicine, science, and mathematics but also produced new advances in those fields.

It is safe to say that until the High Middle Ages Muslim scholars kept the art of medicine alive. Doctors like Rhazes (d. 932) gave a clinical description of measles and smallpox, while others like Avicenna (d. 1037) and Averröes (d. 1198) wrote influential medical treatises whose translations formed the basis for medicine in the West. The great Jewish physician Moses Maimonides (d. 1204) was trained in the Islamic tradition. He insisted on the value of personal and social hygiene (not always appreciated in those days) and was an expert on poisons. He would be an influential figure for the development of medicine among the Jews. (The popes in Rome used Jewish physicians exclusively well into the Renaissance period because of their great reputation in medicine.) Maimonides left his native Spain to serve as the personal physician to the Sultan of Baghdad, Saladin, which says something about the cross-fertilization of cultures in this period.

Muslim scholars centered in Baghdad after the year 800 did extremely influential work. They adapted the numerical system we use today from the Hindus of India, who invented it. We still refer to Arabic numerals. The sheer utility of this system can be seen by taking a sheet of paper and multiplying 55 by 40, then trying to do the same exercise by using Roman numerals (which lack the zero): LV × XL! The most famous of the Muslim mathematicians was Al Khwarizmi (circa 825), whose treatise gave us the word *algebra* and from whose name we get the word *algorithm*.

Mention should also be made of certain technological advances that came to the West from the world of Islam. Two such developments were of incalculable importance: from the Chinese the Muslims learned the art of making paper and the chemical composition of gunpowder. Finally, the Egyptian scholar Al Hazen (d. 1038) did important work on optics and became expert in the theory of lenses.

to God. A rock is good because it *is* (to Aquinas existence was a gift), but an animal is more perfect because it has life and thus shares more of divine attributes. In turn, men and women are better still because they possess mind and will. Angels are closer yet to God because they, like God, are pure spirit.

This hierarchical world view explains other characteristics of Aquinas' thought in particular and medieval thought in general: it is wide-ranging, it is encyclopedic, and in interrelating everything it is synthetic. Everything fits and has its place, meaning, and truth. That a person would speak on psychology, physics, politics, theology, and philosophy with equal authority would strike us as presumptuous, just as any building decorated with symbols from the classics, astrology, the Bible, and scenes from everyday life would now be considered a hodgepodge. Such was not the case in the 13th century, since it was assumed that everything ultimately pointed to God.

Dante's *Divine Comedy*

In any discussion of the culture of the High Middle Ages two descriptive adjectives come immediately to mind: hierarchical and synthetic. It is a commonplace, for example, to compare the Gothic cathedral and the systematic treatises on philosophy and theology like the *Summa Theologica* of Saint Thomas Aquinas. On close inspection such comparisons may be facile, but they point to the following truths about this period that are relatively secure. Both the Gothic cathedral and the theology of Aquinas, for example, started from the tangible and sensual ("Nothing comes to the mind except through the senses" is a basic axiom for Aquinas) in order to mount in a hierarchical manner to the light that is God. Again, both writer and architect felt it possible to be universal in their desire to synthesize all human knowledge as prelude and pointer to the full revelation of God. Finally, they both constructed their edifices by the juxtaposition of tensions and syntheses.

If the Gothic cathedral and the *Summa* represent two masterpieces of the hierarchical and synthetic religious humanism of the Middle Ages, the *Divine Comedy* of Dante Alighieri (1265–1321) represents the same masterly achievement in literature. Dante [8.14] was a Florentine. He was nonetheless deeply influenced by the intellectual currents that emanated from the Paris of his time. As a comfortably fixed young man he devoted himself to a rigorous program of philosophical and theological study in order

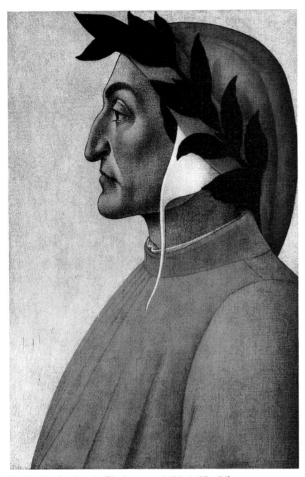

8.14 Sandro Botticelli. *Dante* c. 1480–1485. Oil on canvas, 24¼ × 18½″ (54 × 47 cm). Collection Dr. Martin Bodmer, Cologny/Geneva. Like most portraits of Dante, Botticelli's depicts him wearing the traditional laurel wreath of the poet.

TABLE 8.1   The Structure of Dante's Comedy

Hell

The Anteroom of the Neutrals

Circle 1:   *The Virtuous Pagans (Limbo)*
Circle 2:   *The Lascivious*
Circle 3:   *The Gluttonous*
Circle 4:   *The Greedy and the Wasteful*
Circle 5:   *The Wrathful*
Circle 7:   *The Violent against Others, Self, God/ Nature/ and Art*
Circle 8:   *The Fraudulent (subdivided into ten classes, each of which dwells in a separate ditch)*
Circle 9:   *The Lake of the Treacherous against kindred, country, guests, lords and benefactors. Satan is imprisoned at the center of this frozen lake.*

Purgatory

Ante-Purgatory: The Excommunicated/The Lazy/The Unabsolved/Negligent Rulers
The Terraces of the Mount of Purgatory

1. *The Proud*
2. *The Envious*
3. *The Wrathful*
4. *The Slothful*
5. *The Avaricious*
6. *The Gluttonous*
7. *The Lascivious*

The Earthly Paradise

Paradise

1. *The Moon: The Faithful who were inconstant*
2. *Mercury: Service marred by ambition*
3. *Venus: Love marred by lust*
4. *The Sun: Wisdom; the theologians*
5. *Mars: Courage; the just warriors*
6. *Jupiter: Justice; the great rulers*
7. *Saturn: Temperance; the contemplatives and mystics*
8. *The Fixed Stars: The Church Triumphant*
9. *The Primum Mobile: The Order of Angels*
10. *The Empyrean Heavens: Angels, Saints, The Virgin, and the Holy Trinity*

to enhance his already burgeoning literary talent. His published work gives evidence of a profound culture and a deep love for study. He wrote on the origin and development of language (*De Vulgari Eloquentia*), political theory (*De Monarchia*), and generalized knowledge (*Convivio*) as well as his own poetic aspirations (*Vita Nuova*). His masterpiece is the *Divine Comedy*.

Dante was exiled from Florence for political reasons in 1300. In his bitter wanderings in the north of Italy he worked on—and finally brought to conclusion—a long poem to which he gave a bitingly ironical title: *The Comedy of Dante Alighieri, A Florentine by Birth but Not in Behavior.* Dante called his poem a comedy since, as he noted, it had a happy ending and it was written in the popular language of the people.

The adjective *divine* was added later; some say by Boccaccio, who in the next generation lectured on the poem in Florence and wrote one of the first biographies of the great poet.

The *Divine Comedy* relates a symbolic journey that the poet begins on Good Friday, 1300, through the world of hell, purgatory, and heaven (Table 8.1). In the first two parts of his journey, Dante is guided by the ancient Roman poet Vergil, whose *Aeneid* was such an inspiration to him and from which he borrowed (especially from Book VI, which tells of Aeneas' own journey to the Underworld). From the border at the top of the Mount of Purgatory to the pinnacle of heaven where Dante glimpses the "still point of light" that is God, Dante's guide is Beatrice, a young woman Dante had loved passionately if platonically in his youth [8.15].

Every significant commentator on the *Comedy* has noted its careful organization. The poem is made up of one hundred cantos. The first canto of the *Inferno* serves as an introduction to the whole poem. There are then 33 cantos for each of the three major sections (*Inferno, Purgatorio,* and *Paradiso*). The entire poem is written in a rhyme scheme called *terza rima* (*aba, bcb, cdc,* and so on) that is almost impossible to duplicate in English because of the shortage of rhyming words in our language. The number three and its multiples, symbols of the Trinity, occur over and over. The *Inferno* is divided into nine regions plus a vestibule, and the same number is found in the *Purgatorio*. Dante's *Paradiso* is constituted by the nine heavens of the Ptolemaic system plus the Empyrean, the highest heaven. This scheme mirrors the whole poem of 99 cantos plus one. The sinners in the *Inferno* are arranged according to whether they sinned by incontinence, violence, or fraud (a division Dante derived from Aristotle's *Ethics*), while the yearning souls of

8.15 Domenico di Michelino. *Dante and His Poem*. 1465. Fresco. Florence Cathedral. Dante, with an open copy of the *Comedy*, points to Hell with his right hand. The mount of Purgatory with its seven terraces is behind him. Florence's cathedral (with its newly finished dome) represents Paradise on the poet's left.

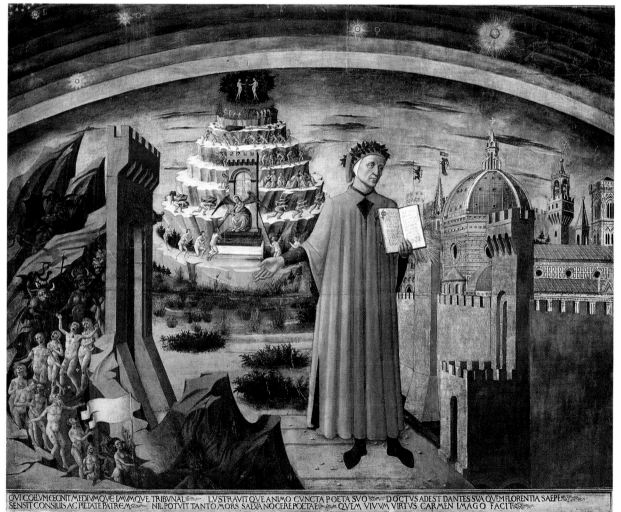

QVI COELVM CECINIT MEDIVMQVE IMVMQVE TRIBVNAL ⬥ LVSTRAVITQVE ANIMO CVNCTA POETA SVO ⬥ DOCTVS ADEST DANTES SVA QVEM FLORENTIA SAEPE ⬥ SENSIT CONSILIIS AC PIETATE PATREM ⬥ NIL POTVIT TANTO MORS SAEVA NOCERE POETAE ⬥ QVEM VIVVM VIRTVS CARMEN IMAGO FACIT ⬥

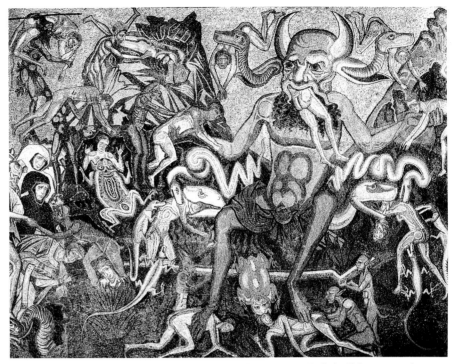

8.16 Hell, detail of mosaic in vault of baptistery of Florence Cathedral. 13th century. As a young man Dante would have seen this mosaic, which adorned the baptistery ("My beautiful San Giovanni," he calls it in his poem) of his native city.

purgatory are divided in three ways according to how they acted or failed to act in relation to love. The saved souls in the *Paradiso* are divided into the lay folk, the active, and the contemplative. Nearest the throne of God, but reflected in the circles of heaven, are the nine categories of angels.

Dante's interest in the symbolic goes beyond his elaborate manipulation of numbers. In the *Inferno* sinners suffer punishments that have symbolic value; their sufferings both punish and instruct. The gluttonous live on heaps of garbage under driving storms of cold rain, while the flatterers are immersed in pools of sewage and the sexually perverse walk burning stretches of sand in an environment as sterile as their attempts at love. Conversely, in the *Paradiso,* the blessed dwell in the circles most symbolic of their virtue. The theologians are in the circle of the sun since they provided such enlightenment to the world, and the holy warriors dwell in the sphere of Mars.

We can better appreciate the density and complexity of Dante's symbolism by looking at a single example. Our common image of Satan is that of a sly tempter (in popular art he is often in formal dress whispering blandishments in a willing ear with just a whiff of sulphur about him) after the manner of Milton's proud, perversely tragic, heroic Satan in *Paradise Lost*. For Dante, Satan is a huge, stupid beast, frozen in a lake of ice in the pit of hell. He beats six batlike wings (a demonic leftover from his angelic existence; see Isaiah 6:1–5) in an ineffectual attempt to escape the frozen pond that is watered by the four rivers of hell. He is grotesquely three-headed (a parody of the Trinity) and his slavering mouths remorselessly chew the bodies of three infamous traitors from sacred and secular history (Judas, Cassius, and Brutus).

Why does Dante portray Satan so grotesquely? It is clear that Dante borrowed some of the picture of Satan from Byzantine mosaics with which he would have been familiar in the Baptistery of Florence [8.16]. Beyond that, the whole complex of Satan is heavily weighted with symbolic significance. Satan lies in frozen darkness at a point in the universe farthest from the warmth and light of God. He is the fallen angel of light (Lucifer means "light-bearer"), now encased in a pit in the center of the earth excavated by the force of his own fall from heaven. Satan is immobile in contrast to God who is the mover of all things in the universe. He is totally inarticulate and stupid because he represents, par excellence, all of the souls of hell who have lost what Dante calls "the good of intellect." Satan, and all of the souls in hell, will remain totally unfulfilled as created rational beings because they are cut off from the final source of rational understanding and fulfillment: God. Intellectual estrangement from God is for Dante, as it was for Thomas Aquinas, the essence of damnation. This estrangement is most evident in the case of Satan, who symbolizes in his very being the loss of rationality and all that derives from that fact.

Dante, following a line of thought already developed by Suger and Aquinas, conceived the human journey as a slow ascent to the purity of God by means of the created things of this world. To settle for less than God was, in essence, to fail to return to the natural source of life, God. This explains why light is such a crucial motif in the *Divine Comedy* as it had been in the theories of Abbot Suger. Neither light nor the sources of light (the sun) is ever mentioned in the *Inferno*. The overwhelming visual impression of the *Inferno* is darkness—a darkness that begins when Dante is lost in the "dark wood" of Canto I and continues until he climbs from hell and sees above his head the stars (the word *stars* ends each of the three major parts of the poem) of the Southern Hemisphere. In the ascent of the mountain of purgatory, daylight and sunset are controlling motifs to symbolize the reception and rejection of divine light. In the *Paradiso* the blessed are bathed in the reflected light that comes from God. At the climax of the *Paradiso* the poet has a momentary glimpse of God as a point of light and rather obscurely understands that God, the source of all intelligibility, is the power that also moves the "sun and the other stars."

Within the broad reaches of Dante's philosophical and theological preoccupations the poet still has the concentrated power to sketch unforgettable portraits: the doomed lovers Paolo and Francesca—each of the tercets that tell their story starts with the word *amore* (love)—the haughty political leader Farinata degli Umberti, the pitiable suicide Pier delle Vigne, or the caricatures of gluttons like Ciacco the Hog. Damned, penitent, or saved, the characters are by turns both symbols and persons. Saint Peter represents the church in the *Paradiso* but also explodes with ferociously human anger at its abuses. Brunetto Latini in the *Inferno* with "his brown-baked features" is a condemned sodomite but still anxious that posterity at least remember his literary accomplishments.

It has been said that a mastery of the *Divine Comedy* would be a mastery of all that was significant about the intellectual culture of the Middle Ages. It is certainly true that the poem, encyclopedic and complex as it is, would provide a primer for any reader interested in the science, political theory, philosophy,

literary criticism, and theology of the 13th century as well as a detailed acquaintance with the burning questions of Dante's time. The very comprehensiveness of the poem has often been its major obstacle for the modern reader. Beyond that hurdle is the strangeness of the Dantean world, so at variance with our own: earth-centered, manageably small, sure of its ideas of right and wrong, orthodox in its theology, prescientific in its outlook, Aristotelean in its philosophy. For all that, Dante is not to be read only for his store of medieval lore; he is, as T. S. Eliot once wrote, the most universal of poets. He had a deeply sympathetic appreciation of human aspiration, love and hate, the destiny of humanity, and the meaning of nature and history.

Summary

The High Middle Ages saw the growth of a number of institutions that stood in sharp contrast to those of the Carolingian period. Foremost was the rise of the city. Urbanization brought with it a lessening of the importance of monastic life as a cultural center and the emergence of the influence of the bishop and the cathedral school. The increased need for a "knowledge class" triggered an expansion in education that would eventually lead to the university of scholars. Urbanization also warred against the old feudal values; it fostered trade and commerce; it made possible the growth of what today we would call a "middle class" who stood on the social ladder between the rural peasant/city worker and the landed royalty or hereditary aristocracy.

The 12th and 13th centuries were times of intense intellectual ferment and advance. New sources of knowledge came through Arabic sources either as original contributions (e.g., in medicine and science) or in the form of lost works of the classical past (e.g., the writings of Aristotle) to fuel the work of scholars. Advances in technology as "spinoffs" from the ambitious plans of both romanesque and Gothic architects had their impact. The increase of a money economy aided the growth of artistic and musical culture.

One conspicuous characteristic of medieval culture was its belief that everything knowable could be expressed in a manageable and rational whole. Whether it appeared in stone (Chartres) or technical prose (Thomas Aquinas) or in poetry (Dante), the medieval mind saw hierarchy, order, intelligibility, and, above all, God in all of observable creation. This hierarchy expressed itself in its emphasis on advancing steps of understanding. The sculptural program of Chartres, for example, is a revelation of the Old Testament figures who point us to their proper fulfillment in the New. In the theology of Aquinas we move from the plane of natural reason to a fuller truth taught by revelation. In Dante we progress from an awareness of our sinful nature to an intuition into the nature of God. In all of these cases the emphasis is on harmony and gradation and a final purpose of all knowledge, which is to become aware of God. In that sense, at least, much of medieval culture could be said to be oriented in an otherworldly manner.

Pronunciation Guide

Abelard: AB-eh-lard

Aligheri (Dante): Al-e-GARY

Aquinas: Ah-KWI-nas

Averroes: Av-ER-row-es

Avicenna: Av-e-CHENA

Carmina Burana: CAR-me-nah Bur-RAN-ah

Chartres: CHART-reh

Divina Commedia: Dee-VEE-nah Com-EH-dee-ah

Guido of Arezzo: GWE-dough of Ah-RET-so

Leonin: LEE-oh-nin

Maimonides: my-MON-id-eze

Perotin: PEAR-oh-tin

Pseudo-Dionysius: SUE-dough Die-oh-NY-sis

Suger: SUE-jay

Universitas: u-knee-VER-see-tas

Villard de Honnecourt: VEE-yard deh HO-knee-cor

Exercises

1. Is it possible to think of a building or complex of buildings serving as an organizing metaphor for a contemporary city in the way a cathedral served in the Middle Ages?
2. What positive and/or negative outcomes do you see deriving from the medieval cult of the Virgin?
3. Compare the use and role of light in the atmosphere of Hagia Sophia and the cathedral of Chartres.
4. Set out some of the technological problems medieval builders had to solve in an age with limited power sources, no tempered metals, no computers or slide rules for calculations, and so on.
5. The medieval university was organized around the body of scholars who made up the faculty. To what degree does that model hold up today? What is the organizing principle of the modern college or university?
6. A good deal of medieval education utilized *dialectics*. What does that term mean? Where do dialectics, broadly understood, find their usefulness today?
7. Thomas Aquinas had no doubt that all knowledge was both interrelated and capable of being synthesized into a whole. Everything from science and philosophy to theology would fit into that synthesis. Would that view find many supporters today? If not, why not?

8. If you were to organize a contemporary hell for the great villains of our day, would you use Dante's classification or would you construct another schema? On what basis would it be organized?
9. Dante looks back to Vergil as the model for his great work of poetry. If we were to write a work today to celebrate our culture and destiny, would we feel the need to invoke a past model to do so? Who might it be?

Further Reading

Adams, Henry. *Mont-Saint-Michel and Chartres.* Garden City, N.Y.: Doubleday, 1959. A brilliant albeit eccentric work on the culture of the Gothic world. While its scholarship has been superseded in this century, it is still an aesthetic classic.

Aubert, Marcel. *Gothic Cathedrals of France and Their Treasures.* London: Nicholas Kaye, 1959. A handy encyclopedia of Gothic architecture by a noted French scholar of the era.

Bony, Jean. *French Gothic Architecture of the 12th and 13th Centuries.* Berkeley: University of California Press, 1983. Authoritative and lavishly illustrated.

Daly, Lowrie. *The Medieval University: 1200–1400.* New York: Sheed & Ward, 1961. Less scholarly than Cobban's work but a handy and readable introduction.

Gilson, Etienne. *Reason and Revelation in the Middle Ages.* New York: Scribner, 1966. A brief but excellent survey of the intellectual milieu of the period by one of the foremost authorities of our century.

Gimpel, Jean. *The Medieval Machine: The Industrial Revolution of the Middle Ages.* New York: Penguin, 1977. A wonderful introduction to technology in medieval times.

Golding, William. *The Spire.* New York: Harcourt, 1964. A brilliant fictional evocation of medieval cathedral building.

Holmes, Urban T. *Daily Living in the Twelfth Century.* Madison: University of Wisconsin, 1966. An extremely readable account of ordinary life in medieval London and Paris drawn from documentary evidence.

Knowles, David. *The Evolution of Medieval Thought.* New York: Vintage, 1962. A classic study of medieval thought from Augustine to the eve of the Reformation.

Macauley, David. *Cathedral: The Story of Its Construction.* Boston: Houghton Mifflin, 1973. A book for young and old readers on the construction of a cathedral, with pen-and-ink drawings by the author. A fascinating and lovely work that is simple but richly informative.

Panofsky, Erwin. *Abbot Suger.* Princeton, N.J.: Princeton University Press, 1946. A translation of Suger's booklets on Saint Denis with an important introduction and full notes. Indispensable for the period.

Simson, Otto von. *The Gothic Cathedral*. New York: Harper, 1964. A classic work on the aesthetics of the Gothic era in the Île-de-France. The work is quite valuable for its study of Saint Denis and Chartres.

Singleton, Charles. *The Divine Comedy of Dante Alighieri*. 6 vols. Princeton, N.J.: Princeton University Press, 1972. The commentary in English by the foremost authority on Dante in America. There are separate volumes of the poem in English with companion volumes of commentary. Excellent and indispensable.

Weisheipl, James. *Friar Thomas D'Aquino: His Life, Thought, and Work*. Garden City, N.Y.: Doubleday, 1974. Reflects the current state of Thomistic studies; scholarly, with good notes and bibliography.

Reading Selections

Dante Alighieri
The Divine Comedy

These selections from the Divine Comedy *include cantos from all three parts of Dante's poem: The* Inferno, *the* Purgatorio, *and the* Paradiso. *They represent a fair sample of Dante's sources and his highly visual imagination. In these cantos there are mythical monsters, demons, angels, saints, heroes from the classical past, and figures from Dante's Italy. Those figures do not exist in solitude. The figure of Satan only makes sense in juxtaposition with the vision of God, the haughty pride of Farinata in contrast to the figure of Francis of Assisi.*

While reading these selections keep in mind Dante's powerful use of language: a single sentence can sketch a scene; one image can set a mood; an individual can stand for a class. While the poem as a whole is immensely long, the thing that most leaps out from these pages is Dante's economy, his ability to say so much in so few words. Coupled with his near-total control of classical and religious learning Dante makes this poem a veritable encyclopedia of medieval culture.

The translation and notes are by the late American poet John Ciardi.

Inferno

Canto I
The Dark Wood of Error
Midway in his allotted threescore years and ten, Dante comes to himself with a start and realizes that he has strayed from the True Way into the Dark Wood of Error (Worldliness). As soon as he has realized his loss, Dante lifts his eyes and sees the first light of the sunrise (the Sun is the Symbol of Divine Illumination) lighting the shoulders of a little hill (The Mount of Joy). It is the Easter Season, the time of resurrection, and the sun is in its equinoctial rebirth. This juxtaposition of joyous symbols fills Dante with hope and he sets out at once to climb directly up the Mount of Joy, but almost immediately his way is blocked by the Three Beasts of Worldliness: *The Leopard of Malice and Fraud, The Lion of Violence and Ambition,* and *The She-Wolf of Incontinence.* These beasts, and especially the She-Wolf, drive him back despairing into the darkness of error. But just as all seems lost, a figure appears to him. It is the shade of *Virgil,* Dante's symbol of *Human Reason.*

Virgil explains that he has been sent to lead Dante from error. There can, however, be no direct ascent past the beasts: the man who would escape them must go a longer and harder way. First he must descend through Hell (The Recognition of Sin), then he must ascend through Purgatory (The Renunciation of Sin), and only then may he reach the pinnacle of joy and come to the Light of God. Virgil offers to guide Dante, but only as far as Human Reason can go. Another guide (*Beatrice,* symbol of *Divine Love*) must take over for the final ascent, for Human Reason is self-limited. Dante submits himself joyously to Virgil's guidance and they move off.

Midway in our life's journey, I went astray
   from the straight road and woke to find myself
   alone in a dark wood. How shall I say   3

what wood that was! I never saw so drear,
   so rank, so arduous a wilderness!
   Its very memory gives a shape to fear.   6

Death could scarce be more bitter than that place!
   But since it came to good, I will recount
   all that I found revealed there by God's   9
   grace.

How I came to it I cannot rightly say,
   so drugged and loose with sleep had I become
   when I first wandered there from the   12
   True Way.

But at the far end of that valley of evil
   whose maze had sapped my very heart with fear
   I found myself before a little hill   15

and lifted up my eyes. Its shoulders glowed
   already with the sweet rays of that planet
   whose virtue leads men straight on every   18
   road,

and the shining strengthened me against the fright

whose agony had wracked the lake of my
    heart
    through all the terrors of that piteous night.   21

Just as a swimmer, who with his last breath
    flounders ashore from perilous seas, might
    turn
    to memorize the wide water of his death—   24

so did I turn, my soul still fugitive
    from death's surviving image, to stare down
    that pass that none had ever left alive.   27

And there I lay to rest from my heart's race
    till calm and breath returned to me. Then
    rose
    and pushed up that dead slope at such a pace   30

each footfall rose above the last. And lo!
    almost at the beginning of the rise
    I faced a spotted Leopard, all tremor and   33
    flow

and gaudy pelt. And it would not pass, but
    stood
    so blocking my every turn that time and
    again
    I was on the verge of turning back to the   36
    wood.

This fell at the first widening of the dawn
    as the sun was climbing Aries with those
    stars
    that rode with him to light the new creation.   39

Thus the holy hour and the sweet season
    of commemoration did much to arm my fear
    of that bright murderous beast with their   42
    good omen.

Yet not so much but what I shook with dread
    at sight of a great Lion that broke upon me
    raging with hunger, its enormous head   45

held high as if to strike a mortal terror
    into the very air. And down his track,
    a She-Wolf drove upon me, a starved horror   48

ravening and wasted beyond all belief.
    She seemed a rack for avarice, gaunt and
    craving.
    Oh many the souls she has brought to   51
    endless grief!

She brought such heaviness upon my spirit
    at sight of her savagery and desperation,
    I died from every hope of that high summit.   54

And like a miser—eager in acquisition
    but desperate in self-reproach when Fortune's
    wheel
    turns to the hour of his loss—all tears and   57
    attrition

I wavered back; and still the beast pursued,
    forcing herself against me bit by bit
    till I slid back into the sunless wood.   60

And as I fell to my soul's ruin, a presence
    gathered before me on the discolored air,
    the figure of one who seemed hoarse   63
    from long silence.

At sight of him in that friendless waste I cried:
    "Have pity on me, whatever thing you are,
    whether shade or living man." [265]   66
    And it replied:

"Not man, though man I once was, and my blood
    was Lombard, both my parents Mantuan.
    I was born, though late, *sub Julio,* and bred   69

in Rome under Augustus in the noon
    of the false and lying gods. I was a poet
    and sang of old Anchises' noble son   72

who came to Rome after the burning of Troy.
    But you—why do *you* return to these
    distresses
    instead of climbing that shining Mount   75
    of Joy

which is the seat and first cause of man's bliss?"
    "And are you then that Virgil and that
    fountain
    of purest speech?" My voice grew tremulous: 78

"Glory and light of poets! now may that zeal
    and love's apprenticeship that I poured out
    on your heroic verses serve me well!   81

For you are my true master and first author,
    the sole maker from whom I drew the breath
    of that sweet style whose measures have   84
    brought me honor.

See there, immortal sage, the beast I flee.
    For my soul's salvation, I beg you, guard me
    from her,
    for she has struck a mortal tremor   87
    through me."

And he replied, seeing my soul in tears:
    "He must go by another way who would
    escape
    this wilderness, for that mad beast that fleers   90

before you there, suffers no man to pass.
    She tracks down all, kills all, and knows no
    glut,
    but, feeding, she grows hungrier than   93
    she was.

She mates with any beast, and will mate with
    more
    before the Greyhound comes to hunt her
    down.

He will not feed on lands nor loot, but honor 96

and love and wisdom will make straight
    his way.
  He will rise between Feltro and Feltro,
    and in him
  shall be the resurrection and new day 99

of that sad Italy for which Nisus died,
  and Turnus, and Euryalus, and the maid
    Camilla.
  He shall hunt her through every nation of 102
    sick pride

till she is driven back forever to Hell
  whence Envy first released her on the world.
  Therefore, for your own good, I think it well 105

you follow me and I will be your guide
  and lead you forth through an eternal place.
  There you shall see the ancient spirits tried 108

in endless pain, and hear their lamentation
  as each bemoans the second death of souls.
  Next you shall see upon a burning mountain 111

souls in fire and yet content in fire,
  knowing that whensoever it may be
  they yet will mount into the blessed choir. 114

To which, if it is still your wish to climb,
  a worthier spirit shall be sent to guide you.
  With her shall I leave you, for the King of 117
    Time,

who reigns on high, forbids me to come there
  since, living, I rebelled against his law.
  He rules the waters and the land and air 120

and there holds court, his city and his throne.
  Oh blessed are they he chooses!" And I
    to him:
  "Poet, by that God to you unknown, 123

lead me this way. Beyond this present ill
  and worse to dread, lead me to Peter's gate
  and be my guide through the sad halls of 126
    Hell."

And he then: "Follow." And he moved ahead
  in silence, and I followed where he led.

NOTES

1. *midway in our life's journey:* The Biblical life span is three-score years and ten. The action opens in Dante's thirty-fifth year, i.e., 1300 A.D.

17. *that planet:* The sun. Ptolemaic astronomers considered it a planet. It is also symbolic of God as He who lights man's way.

31. *each footfall rose above the last:* The literal rendering would be: "So that the fixed foot was ever the lower." "Fixed" has often been translated "right" and an ingenious reasoning can support that reading, but a simpler explanation offers itself and seems more competent: Dante is saying that he climbed with such zeal and

haste that every footfall carried him above the last despite the steepness of the climb. At a slow pace, on the other hand, the rear foot might be brought up only as far as the forward foot. This device of selecting a minute but exactly-centered detail to convey the whole of a larger action is one of the central characteristics of Dante's style.

THE THREE BEASTS: These three beasts undoubtedly are taken from *Jeremiah* v. 6. Many additional and incidental interpretations have been advanced for them, but the central interpretation must remain as noted. They foreshadow the three divisions of Hell (incontinence, violence, and fraud) which Virgil explains at length in Canto XI, 16–111.

38–9. *Aries . . . that rode with him to light the new creation:* The medieval tradition had it that the sun was in Aries at the time of the Creation. The significance of the astronomical and religious conjunction is an important part of Dante's intended allegory. It is just before dawn of Good Friday 1300 A.D. when he awakens in the Dark Wood. Thus his new life begins under Aries, the sign of creation, at dawn (rebirth) and in the Easter season (resurrection). Moreover the moon is full and the sun is in the equinox, conditions that did not fall together on any Friday of 1300. Dante is obviously constructing poetically the perfect Easter as a symbol of his new awakening.

69. *sub Julio:* In the reign of Julius Caesar.

95. *The Greyhound . . . Feltro and Feltro:* Almost certainly refers to Can Grande della Scala (1290–1329), great Italian leader born in Verona, which lies between the towns of Feltre and Montefeltro.

100–101. *Nisus, Turnus, Euryalus, Camilla:* All were killed in the war between the Trojans and the Latins when, according to legend, Aeneas led the survivors of Troy into Italy. Nisus and Euryalus (*Aeneid* IX) were Trojan comrades-in-arms who died together. Camilla (*Aeneid* XI) was the daughter of the Latin king and one of the warrior women. She was killed in a horse charge against the Trojans after displaying great gallantry. Turnus (*Aeneid* XII) was killed by Aeneas in a duel.

110. *the second death:* Damnation. "This is the second death, even the lake of fire." (*Revelation* xx, 14)

118. *forbids me to come there since, living, etc.:* Salvation is only through Christ in Dante's theology. Virgil lived and died before the establishment of Christ's teachings in Rome, and cannot therefore enter Heaven.

125. *Peter's gate:* The gate of Purgatory. (See *Purgatorio* IX, 76 ff.) The gate is guarded by an angel with a gleaming sword. The angel is Peter's vicar (Peter, the first Pope, symbolized all Popes; i.e., Christ's vicar on earth) and is entrusted with the two great keys.

Some commentators argue that this is the gate of Paradise, but Dante mentions no gate beyond this one in his ascent to Heaven. It should be remembered, too, that those who pass the gate of Purgatory have effectively entered Heaven.

The three great gates that figure in the entire journey are: the gate of Hell (Canto III, 1–11), the gate of Dis (Canto VIII, 79–113, and Canto IX, 86–87), and the gate of Purgatory, as above.

Canto III
The Vestibule of Hell
The Opportunists

The Poets pass the Gate of Hell and are immediately assailed by cries of anguish. Dante sees the first of the souls in torment. They are *The Opportunists,* those souls who in life were neither for good nor evil but only for themselves. Mixed with them are those outcasts who took no sides in the Rebellion of the Angels. They are neither in Hell nor out of it. Eternally unclassified, they race round and round pursuing a wavering banner that runs forever before them through the dirty air; and as they run they are pursued by swarms of wasps and hornets, who sting them and produce a constant flow of blood and putrid matter which trickles down the bodies of the sinners and is feasted upon by loathsome worms and maggots who coat the ground.

The law of Dante's Hell is the law of symbolic retribution. As they sinned so are they punished. They took no sides, therefore they are given no place. As they pursued the ever-shifting illusion of their own advantage, changing their courses with every changing wind, so they pursue eternally an elusive, ever-shifting banner. As their sin was a darkness, so they move in darkness. As their own guilty conscience pursued them, so they are pursued by swarms of wasps and hornets. And as their actions were a moral filth, so they run eternally through the filth of worms and maggots which they themselves feed.

Dante recognizes several, among them *Pope Celestine* V, but without delaying to speak to any of these souls, the Poets move on to *Acheron,* the first of the rivers of Hell. Here the newly-arrived souls of the damned gather and wait for monstrous *Charon* to ferry them over to punishment. Charon recognizes Dante as a living man and angrily refuses him passage. Virgil forces Charon to serve them, but Dante swoons with terror, and does not reawaken until he is on the other side.

I AM THE WAY INTO THE CITY OF WOE.
I AM THE WAY TO A FORSAKEN PEOPLE.
I AM THE WAY INTO ETERNAL SORROW.   3

SACRED JUSTICE MOVED MY ARCHITECT.
I WAS RAISED HERE BY DIVINE OMNIPOTENCE,
PRIMORDIAL LOVE AND ULTIMATE INTELLECT.   6

ONLY THOSE ELEMENTS TIME CANNOT WEAR
WERE MADE BEFORE ME, AND BEYOND TIME I STAND.
ABANDON ALL HOPE YE WHO ENTER HERE.   9

These mysteries I read cut into stone
    above a gate. And turning I said: "Master,
    what is the meaning of this harsh   12
        inscription?"

And he then as initiate to novice:
    "Here must you put by all division of spirit
    and gather your soul against all cowardice.   15

This is the place I told you to expect.
    Here you shall pass among the fallen people,
    souls who have lost the good of intellect."   18

So saying, he put forth his hand to me,
    and with a gentle and encouraging smile
    he led me through the gate of mystery.   21

Here sighs and cries and wails coiled and
        recoiled
    on the starless air, spilling my soul to tears.
    A confusion of tongues and monstrous   24
        accents toiled

in pain and anger. Voices hoarse and shrill
    and sounds of blows, all intermingled, raised
    tumult and pandemonium that still   27

whirls on the air forever dirty with it
    as if a whirlwind sucked at sand. And I,
    holding my head in horror, cried: "Sweet   30
        Spirit,

what souls are these who run through this black
        haze?"
    And he to me: "These are the nearly soulless
    whose lives concluded neither blame nor   33
        praise.

They are mixed here with that despicable corps
    of angels who were neither for God nor
        Satan,
    but only for themselves. The High Creator   36

scourged them from Heaven for its perfect
        beauty,
    and Hell will not receive them since the
        wicked
    might feel some glory over them." And I: 39

"Master, what gnaws at them so hideously
    their lamentation stuns the very air?"
    "They have no hope of death," he   42
        answered me,

"and in their blind and unattaining state
    their miserable lives have sunk so low
    that they must envy every other fate.   45

No word of them survives their living season.
    Mercy and Justice deny them even a name.
    Let us not speak of them: look,   48
        and pass on."

I saw a banner there upon the mist.
    Circling and circling, it seemed to scorn all
        pause.
    So it ran on, and still behind it pressed   51

a never-ending rout of souls in pain.
    I had not thought death had undone so many
    as passed before me in that mournful train.   54

And some I knew among them; last of all
  I recognized the shadow of that soul
  who, in his cowardice, made the Great
    Denial.   57

At once I understood for certain: these
  were of that retrograde and faithless crew
  hateful to God and to His enemies.   60

These wretches never born and never dead
  ran naked in a swarm of wasps and hornets
  that goaded them the more the more they
    fled,   63

and made their faces stream with bloody gouts
  of pus and tears that dribbled to their feet
  to be swallowed there by loathsome   66
    worms and maggots.

Then looking onward I made out a throng
  assembled on the beach of a wide river,
  whereupon I turned to him: "Master, I long   69

to know what souls these are, and what strange
    usage
  makes them as eager to cross as they seem
    to be
  in this infected light." At which the Sage: 72

"All this shall be made known to you when we
    stand
  on the joyless beach of Acheron." And I
  cast down my eyes, sensing a reprimand   75

in what he said, and so walked at his side
  in silence and ashamed until we came
  through the dead cavern to that sunless tide.   78

There, steering toward us in an ancient ferry
  came an old man with a white bush of hair,
  bellowing: "Woe to you depraved souls!   81
    Bury

here and forever all hope of Paradise:
  I come to lead you to the other shore,
  into eternal dark, into fire and ice.   84

And you who are living yet, I say begone
  from these who are dead." But when he saw
    me stand
  against his violence he began again: 87

"By other windings and by other steerage
  shall you cross to that other shore. Not here!
    Not here!
  A lighter craft than mine must give you   90
    passage."

And my Guide to him: "Charon, bite back your
    spleen:
  this has been willed where what is willed
    must be,
  and is not yours to ask what it may mean."   93

The steersman of that marsh of ruined souls,
  who wore a wheel of flame around each eye,
  stifled the rage that shook his woolly jowls.   96

But those unmanned and naked spirits there
  turned pale with fear and their teeth began to
    chatter
  at sound of his crude bellow. In despair   99

they blasphemed God, their parents, their time
    on earth,
  the race of Adam, and the day and the hour
  and the place and the seed   102
    the womb that gave them birth.

But all together they drew to that grim shore
  where all must come who lose the fear
    of God.
  Weeping and cursing they come for   105
    evermore,

and demon Charon with eyes like burning coals
  herds them in, and with a whistling oar
  flails on the stragglers to his wake of souls. 108

As leaves in autumn loosen and stream down
  until the branch stands bare above its tatters
  spread on the rustling ground, so one by one 111

the evil seed of Adam in its Fall
  cast themselves, at his signal, from the shore
  and streamed away like birds who hear their   114
    call.

So they are gone over that shadowy water,
  and always before they reach the other shore
  a new noise stirs on this, and new throngs   117
    gather.

"My son," the courteous Master said to me,
  "all who die in the shadow of God's wrath
  converge to this from every clime and   120
    country.

And all pass over eagerly, for here
  Divine Justice transforms and spurs them so
  their dread turns wish: they yearn for what   123
    they fear.

No soul in Grace comes ever to this crossing;
  therefore if Charon rages at your presence
  you will understand the reason for his   126
    cursing."

When he had spoken, all the twilight country
  shook so violently, the terror of it
  bathes me with sweat even in memory: 129

the tear-soaked ground gave out a sigh of wind
  that spewed itself in flame on a red sky,
  and all my shattered senses left me. Blind,   132

like one whom sleep comes over in a swoon,
I stumbled into darkness and went down.

7–8. *Only those elements time cannot wear:* The Angels, the Empyrean, and the First Matter are the elements time cannot wear, for they will last to all time. Man, however, in his mortal state, is not eternal. The Gate of Hell, therefore, was created before man. The theological point is worth attention. The doctrine of Original Sin is, of course, one familiar to many creeds. Here, however, it would seem that the preparation for damnation predates Original Sin. True, in one interpretation, Hell was created for the punishment of the Rebellious Angels and not for man. Had man not sinned, he would never have known Hell. But on the other hand, Dante's God was one who knew all, and knew therefore that man would indeed sin. The theological problem is an extremely delicate one.

It is significant, however, that having sinned, man lives out his days on the rind of Hell, and that damnation is forever below his feet. This central concept of man's sinfulness, and, opposed to it, the doctrine of Christ's ever-abounding mercy, are central to all of Dante's theology. Only as man surrenders himself to Divine Love may he hope for salvation, and salvation is open to all who will surrender themselves.

8. *and beyond time I stand:* So odious is sin to God that there can be no end to its just punishment.

9. *Abandon all hope ye who enter here:* The admonition, of course, is to the damned and not to those who come on Heaven-sent errands. The Harrowing of Hell provided the only exemption from this decree, and that only through the direct intercession of Christ.

57. *who, in his cowardice, made the Great Denial:* This is almost certainly intended to be Celestine V, who became Pope in 1294. He was a man of saintly life, but allowed himself to be convinced by a priest named Benedetto that his soul was in danger since no man could live in the world without being damned. In fear for his soul he withdrew from all worldly affairs and renounced the papacy. Benedetto promptly assumed the mantle himself and became Boniface VIII, a Pope who became for Dante a symbol of all the worst corruptions of the church. Dante also blamed Boniface and his intrigues for many of the evils that befell Florence. We shall learn in Canto XIX that the fires of Hell are waiting for Boniface in the pit of the Simoniacs, and we shall be given further evidence of his corruption in Canto XXVII. Celestine's great guilt is that his cowardice (in selfish terror for his own welfare) served as the door through which so much evil entered the church.

80. *an old man:* Charon. He is the ferryman of dead souls across the Acheron in all classical mythology.

88–90. *By other windings:* Charon recognizes Dante not only as a living man but as a soul in grace, and knows, therefore, that the Infernal Ferry was not intended for him. He is probably referring to the fact that souls destined for Purgatory and Heaven assemble not at his ferry point, but on the banks of the Tiber, from which they are transported by an Angel.

110. *they blasphemed God:* The souls of the damned are not permitted to repent, for repentance is a divine grace.

123. *they yearn for what they fear:* Hell (allegorically Sin) is what the souls of the damned really wish for. Hell is their actual and deliberate choice, for divine grace is denied to none who wish for it in their hearts. The damned must, in fact, deliberately harden their hearts to God in order to become damned. Christ's grace is sufficient to save all who wish for it.

133–34. DANTE'S SWOON: This device (repeated at the end of Canto V) serves a double purpose. The first is technical: Dante uses it to cover a transition. We are never told how he crossed Acheron, for that would involve certain narrative matters he can better deal with when he crosses Styx in Canto VII. The second is to provide a point of departure for a theme that is carried through the entire descent: the theme of Dante's emotional reaction to Hell. These two swoons early in the descent show him most susceptible to the grief about him. As he descends, pity leaves him, and he even goes so far as to add to the torments of one sinner. The allegory is clear: we must harden ourselves against every sympathy for sin.

Canto V
Circle Two
The Carnal

The Poets leave Limbo [the dwelling place of the unbaptized] and enter the *Second Circle*. Here begin the torments of Hell proper, and here, blocking the way, sits *Minos,* the dread and semi-bestial judge of the damned who assigns to each soul its eternal torment. He orders the Poets back; but Virgil silences him as he earlier silenced Charon, and the Poets move on.

They find themselves on a dark ledge swept by a great whirlwind, which spins within it the souls of the *Carnal,* those who betrayed reason to their appetites. Their sin was to abandon themselves to the tempest of their passions: so they are swept forever in the tempest of Hell, forever denied the light of reason and of God. Virgil identifies many among them. *Semiramis* is there, and *Dido, Cleopatra, Helen, Achilles, Paris,* and *Tristan.* Dante sees *Paolo* and *Francesca* swept together, and in the name of love he calls to them to tell their sad story. They pause from their eternal flight to come to him, and Francesca tells their history while Paolo weeps at her side. Dante is so stricken by compassion at their tragic tale that he swoons once again.

So we went down to the second ledge alone;
    a smaller circle of so much greater pain
    the voice of the damned rose in a bestial   3
        moan.

There Minos sits, grinning, grotesque, and hale.
    He examines each lost soul as it arrives
    and delivers his verdict with his coiling tail.   6

That is to say, when the ill-fated soul
    appears before him it confesses all,
    and that grim sorter of the dark and foul   9

decides which place in Hell shall be its end,
    then wraps his twitching tail about himself
    one coil for each degree it must descend.   12

The soul descends and others take its place:
    each crowds in its turn to judgment, each
        confesses,
    each hears its doom and falls away through   15
        space.

"O you who come into this camp of woe,"
  cried Minos when he saw me turn away
  without awaiting his judgment, 18
    "watch where you go

once you have entered here, and to whom you
    turn!
  Do not be misled by that wide and easy
    passage!"
  And my Guide to him: "That is not your 21
    concern;

it is his fate to enter every door.
  This has been willed where what is willed
    must be,
  and is not yours to question. Say no more." 24

Now the choir of anguish, like a wound,
  strikes through the tortured air. Now I
    have come
  to Hell's full lamentation, sound beyond 27
    sound.

I came to a place stripped bare of every light
  and roaring on the naked dark like seas
  wracked by a war of winds. Their hellish 30
    flight

of storm and counterstorm through time
    foregone,
  sweeps the souls of the damned before its
    charge.
  Whirling and battering it drives them on, 33

and when they pass the ruined gap of Hell
  through which we had come, their shrieks
    begin anew.
  There they blaspheme the power of God 36
    eternal.

And this, I learned, was the never ending flight
  of those who sinned in the flesh, the carnal
    and lusty
  who betrayed reason to their appetite. 39

As the wings of wintering starlings bear
    them on
  in their great wheeling flights, just so the
    blast
  wherries these evil souls through time 42
    foregone.

Here, there, up, down, they whirl and whirling,
    strain
  with never a hope of hope to comfort them,
  not of release, but even of less pain. 45

As cranes go over sounding their harsh cry,
  leaving the long streak of their flight in air,
  so come these spirits, wailing as they fly. 48

And watching their shadows lashed by wind, I
  cried:

"Master, what souls are these the very air
  lashes with its black whips from side to 51
  side?"

"The first of these whose history you would
    know,"
  he answered me, "was Empress of many
    tongues.
  Mad sensuality corrupted her so 54

that to hide the guilt of her debauchery
  she licensed all depravity alike,
  and lust and law were one in her decree. 57

She is Semiramis of whom the tale is told
  how she married Ninus and succeeded him
  to the throne of that wide land the Sultans 60
  hold.

The other is Dido; faithless to the ashes
  of Sichaeus, she killed herself for love.
  The next whom the eternal tempest lashes 63

is sense-drugged Cleopatra. See Helen there,
  from whom such ill arose. And great
    Achilles,
  who fought at last with love in the house of 66
  prayer.

And Paris. And Tristan." As they whirled above
  he pointed out more than a thousand shades
  of those torn from the mortal life by love. 69

I stood there while my Teacher one by one
  named the great knights and ladies of dim
    time;
  and I was swept by pity and confusion. 72

At last I spoke: "Poet, I should be glad
  to speak a word with those two swept
    together
  so lightly on the wind and still so sad." 75

And he to me: "Watch them. When next they
    pass,
  call to them in the name of love that drives
  and damns them here. In that name they will 78
  pause."

Thus, as soon as the wind in its wild course
  brought them around, I called: "O wearied
    souls!
  if none forbid it, pause and speak to us." 81

As mating doves that love calls to their nest
  glide through the air with motionless raised
    wings,
  borne by the sweet desire that fills each 84
    breast—

Just so those spirits turned on the torn sky
  from the band where Dido whirls across
    the air;
  such was the power of pity in my cry. 87

"O living creature, gracious, kind, and good,
    going this pilgrimage through the sick night,
    visiting us who stained the earth with blood,   90

were the King of Time our friend, we would
        pray His peace
    on you who have pitied us. As long as the
        wind
    will let us pause, ask of us what you please.   93

The town where I was born lies by the shore
    where the Po descends into its ocean rest
    with its attendant streams in one long   96
        murmur.

Love, which in gentlest hearts will soonest
        bloom
    seized my lover with passion for that sweet
        body
    from which I was torn unshriven to my   99
        doom.

Love, which permits no loved one not to love,
    took me so strongly with delight in him
    that we are one in Hell, as we were above.   102

Love led us to one death. In the depths of Hell
    Caïna waits for him who took our lives."
    This was the piteous tale they stopped to tell.   105

And when I had heard those world-offended
        lovers
    I bowed my head. At last the Poet spoke:
    "What painful thoughts are these   108
        your lowered brow covers?"

When at length I answered, I began: "Alas!
    What sweetest thoughts, what green and
        young desire
    led these two lovers to this sorry pass."   111

Then turning to those spirits once again,
    I said: "Francesca, what you suffer here
    melts me to tears of pity and of pain.   114

But tell me: in the time of your sweet sighs
    by what appearances found love the way
    to lure you to his perilous paradise?"   117

And she: "The double grief of a lost bliss
    is to recall its happy hour in pain.
    Your Guide and Teacher knows the truth of   120
        this.

But if there is indeed a soul in Hell
    to ask of the beginning of our love
    out of his pity, I will weep and tell: 123

On a day for dalliance we read the rhyme
    of Lancelot, how love had mastered him.
    We were alone with innocence and dim   126
        time.

Pause after pause that high old story drew
    our eyes together while we blushed and
        paled;
    but it was one soft passage overthrew   129

our caution and our hearts. For when we read
    how her fond smile was kissed by such a lover,
    he who is one with me alive and dead   132

breathed on my lips the tremor of his kiss.
    That book, and he who wrote it, was a
        pander.
    That day we read no further." As she said   135
        this,

the other spirit, who stood by her, wept
    so piteously, I felt my senses reel
    and faint away with anguish. I was swept   138

by such a swoon as death is, and I fell,
as a corpse might fall, to the dead floor of Hell.

NOTES

2. *a smaller circle:* The pit of Hell tapers like a funnel. The circles of ledges accordingly grow smaller as they descend.

4. *Minos:* Like all the monsters Dante assigns to the various offices of Hell, Minos is drawn from classical mythology. He was the son of Europa and of Zeus, who descended to her in the form of a bull. Minos became a mythological king of Crete, so famous for his wisdom and justice that after death his soul was made judge of the dead. Virgil presents him fulfilling the same office at Aeneas' descent to the underworld. Dante, however, transforms him into an irate and hideous monster with a tail. The transformation may have been suggested by the form Zeus assumed for the rape of Europa—the monster is certainly bullish enough here—but the obvious purpose of the brutalization is to present a figure symbolic of the guilty conscience of the wretches who come before it to make their confessions. Dante freely reshapes his materials to his own purposes.

8. *It confesses all:* Just as the souls appeared eager to cross Acheron, so they are eager to confess even while they dread. Dante is once again making the point that sinners elect their Hell by an act of their own will.

27. *Hell's full lamentation:* It is with the second circle that the real tortures of Hell begin.

34. *the ruined gap of Hell:* See note to Canto II, 53. At the time of the Harrowing of Hell a great earthquake shook the underworld shattering rocks and cliffs. Ruins resulting from the same shock are noted in Canto XII, 34, and Canto XXI, 112 ff. At the beginning of Canto XXIV, the Poets leave the *bolgia* of the Hypocrites by climbing the ruined slabs of a bridge that was shattered by this earthquake.

THE SINNERS OF THE SECOND CIRCLE (THE CARNAL): Here begin the punishments for the various sins of Incontinence (The sins of the She-Wolf). In the second circle are punished those who sinned by excess of sexual passion. Since this is the most natural sin and the sin most nearly associated with love, its punishment is the lightest of all to be found in Hell proper. The Carnal are whirled and buffeted endlessly through the murky air (symbolic of the beclouding of their reason by passion) by a great gale (symbolic of their lust).

53. *Empress of many tongues:* Semiramis, a legendary queen of Assyria who assumed full power at the death of her husband, Ninus.

61. *Dido:* Queen and founder of Carthage. She had vowed to remain faithful to her husband, Sichaeus, but she fell in love with Aeneas. When Aeneas abandoned her she stabbed herself on a funeral pyre she had had prepared.

According to Dante's own system of punishments, she should be in the Seventh Circle (Canto XIII) with the suicides. The only clue Dante gives to the tempering of her punishment is his statement that "she killed herself for love." Dante always seems readiest to forgive in that name.

65. *Achilles:* He is placed among this company because of his passion for Polyxena, the daughter of Priam. For love of her, he agreed to desert the Greeks and to join the Trojans, but when he went to the temple for the wedding (according to the legend Dante has followed) he was killed by Paris.

74. *those two swept together:* Paolo and Francesca (PAH-oe-loe: Frahn-CHAY-ska).

Dante's treatment of these two lovers is certainly the tenderest and most sympathetic accorded any of the sinners in Hell, and legends immediately began to grow about this pair.

The facts are these. In 1275 Giovanni Malatesta (Djoe-VAH-nee Mahl-ah-TEH-stah) of Rimini, called Giovanni the Lame, a somewhat deformed but brave and powerful warrior, made a political marriage with Francesca, daughter of Guido da Polenta of Ravenna. Francesca came to Rimini and there an amour grew between her and Giovanni's younger brother Paolo. Despite the fact that Paolo had married in 1269 and had become the father of two daughters by 1275, his affair with Francesca continued for many years. It was sometime between 1283 and 1286 that Giovanni surprised them in Francesca's bedroom and killed both of them.

Around these facts the legend has grown that Paolo was sent by Giovanni as his proxy to the marriage, that Francesca thought he was her real bridegroom and accordingly gave him her heart irrevocably at first sight. The legend obviously increases the pathos, but nothing in Dante gives it support.

102. *that we are one in Hell, as we were above:* At many points of *The Inferno* Dante makes clear the principle that the souls of the damned are locked so blindly into their own guilt that none can feel sympathy for another, or find any pleasure in the presence of another. The temptation of many readers is to interpret this line romantically: *i.e.,* that the love of Paolo and Francesca survives Hell itself. The more Dantean interpretation, however, is that they add to one another's anguish (a) as mutual reminders of their sin, and (b) as insubstantial shades of the bodies for which they once felt such great passion.

104. *Caïna waits for him:* Giovanni Malatesta was still alive at the writing. His fate is already decided, however, and upon his death, his soul will fall to Caïna, the first ring of the last circle (Canto XXXII), where lie those who performed acts of treachery against their kin.

124–5. *the rhyme of Lancelot:* The story exists in many forms. The details Dante makes use of are from an Old French version.

126. *dim time:* The original simply reads "We were alone, suspecting nothing." "Dim time" is rhyme-forced, but not wholly outside the legitimate implications of the original, I hope. The old courtly romance may well be thought of as happening in the dim ancient days. The apology, of course, comes after the fact: one does the possible, then argues for justification, and there probably is none.

134. *that book, and he who wrote it, was a pander:* "Galeotto," the Italian word for "pander," is also the Italian rendering of the name of Gallehault, who in the French Romance Dante refers to here, urged Lancelot and Guinevere on to love.

Canto X
Circle Six
The Heretics

As the Poets pass on, one of the damned hears Dante speaking, recognizes him as a Tuscan, and calls to him from one of the fiery tombs. A moment later he appears. He is *Farinata degli Uberti,* a great war-chief of the Tuscan Ghibellines. The majesty and power of his bearing seem to diminish Hell itself. He asks Dante's lineage and recognizes him as an enemy. They begin to talk politics, but are interrupted by another shade, who rises from the same tomb.

This one is *Cavalcante dei Cavalcanti,* father of Guido Cavalcanti, a contemporary poet. If it is genius that leads Dante on his great journey, the shade asks, why is Guido not with him? Can Dante presume to a greater genius than Guido's? Dante replies that he comes this way only with the aid of powers Guido has not sought. His reply is a classic example of many-leveled symbolism as well as an overt criticism of a rival poet. The senior Cavalcanti mistakenly infers from Dante's reply that Guido is dead, and swoons back into the flames.

Farinata, who has not deigned to notice his fellow-sinner, continues from the exact point at which he had been interrupted. It is as if he refuses to recognize the flames in which he is shrouded. He proceeds to prophesy Dante's banishment from Florence, he defends his part in Florentine politics, and then, in answer to Dante's question, he explains how it is that the damned can foresee the future but have no knowledge of the present. He then names others who share his tomb, and Dante takes his leave with considerable respect for his great enemy, pausing only long enough to leave word for Cavalcanti that Guido is still alive.

We go by a secret path along the rim
    of the dark city, between the wall and the
      torments.
    My master leads me and I follow him.   **3**

"Supreme Virtue, who through this impious
    land
    wheel me at will down these dark gyres," I
      said,
    "speak to me, for I wish to understand.   **6**

Tell me, Master, is it permitted to see

the souls within these tombs? The lids are raised,
and no one stands on guard." And he to me:

"All shall be sealed forever on the day
these souls return here from Jehosaphat
with the bodies they have given once to clay.

In this dark corner of the morgue of wrath
lie Epicurus and his followers,
who make the soul share in the body's death.

And here you shall be granted presently
not only your spoken wish, but that other as well,
which you had thought perhaps to hide from me."

And I: "Except to speak my thoughts in few
and modest words, as I learned from your example,
dear Guide, I do not hide my heart from you."

"O Tuscan, who go living through this place
speaking so decorously, may it please you pause
a moment on your way, for by the grace

of that high speech in which I hear your birth,
I know you for a son of that noble city
which perhaps I vexed too much
in my time on earth."

These words broke without warning from inside
one of the burning arks. Caught by surprise,
I turned in fear and drew close to my Guide.

And he: "Turn around. What are you doing?
Look there:
it is Farinata rising from the flames.
From the waist up his shade will be made clear."

My eyes were fixed on him already. Erect,
he rose above the flame, great chest, great brow;
he seemed to hold all Hell in disrespect.

My Guide's prompt hands urged me among the dim
and smoking sepulchres to that great figure,
and he said to me: "Mind how you speak to him."

And when I stood alone at the foot of the tomb,
the great soul stared almost contemptuously,

before he asked: "Of what line do you come?"

Because I wished to obey, I did not hide
anything from him: whereupon as he listened,
he raised his brows a little, then replied:

"Bitter enemies were they to me,
to my fathers, and to my party, so that twice
I sent them scattering from high Italy."

"If they were scattered, still from every part
they formed again and returned both times,"
I answered,
"but yours have not yet wholly learned that art."

At this another shade rose gradually,
visible to the chin. It had raised itself,
I think, upon its knees, and it looked around me

as if it expected to find through that black air
that blew about me, another traveler.
And weeping when it found no other there,

turned back. "And if," it cried, "you travel through
this dungeon of the blind by power of genius,
where is my son? why is he not with you?"

And I to him: "Not by myself am I borne
this terrible way. I am led by him who waits there,
and whom perhaps your Guido held in scorn."

For by his words and the manner of his torment
I knew his name already, and could, therefore,
answer both what he asked and what he meant.

Instantly he rose to his full height:
"He *held*? What is it you say? Is he dead, then?
Do his eyes no longer fill with that sweet light?"

And when he saw that I delayed a bit
in answering his question, he fell backwards
into the flame, and rose no more from it.

But that majestic spirit at whose call
I had first paused there, did not change expression,
nor so much as turn his face to watch him fall.

"And if," going on from his last words, he said,
"men of my line have yet to learn that art,
that burns me deeper than this flaming bed. 78

But the face of her who reigns in Hell shall not
be fifty times rekindled in its course
before you learn what griefs attend that art. 81

And as you hope to find the world again,
tell me: why is that populace so savage
in the edicts they pronounce against my 84
strain?"

And I to him: "The havoc and the carnage
that dyed the Arbia red at Montaperti
have caused these angry cries in our 87
assemblage."

He sighed and shook his head. "I was not alone
in that affair," he said, "nor certainly
would I have joined the rest without good 90
reason.

But I *was* alone at that time when every other
consented to the death of Florence; I
alone with open face defended her." 93

"Ah, so may your soul sometime have rest,"
I begged him, "solve the riddle that pursues
me
through this dark place and leaves 96
my mind perplexed:

you seem to see in advance all time's intent,
if I have heard and understood correctly;
but you seem to lack all knowledge of the 99
present."

"We see asquint, like those whose twisted sight
can make out only the far-off," he said,
"for the King of All still grants us that much 102
light.

When things draw near, or happen, we perceive
nothing of them. Except what others
bring us
we have no news of those who are alive. 105

So may you understand that all we know
will be dead forever from that day and hour
when the portal of the Future is swung to." 108

Then, as if stricken by regret, I said:
"Now, therefore, will you tell that fallen one
who asked about his son, that he is not 111
dead,

and that, if I did not reply more quickly,
it was because my mind was occupied
with this confusion you have solved for 114
me."

And now my Guide was calling me. In haste,
therefore, I begged that mighty shade to
name
the others who lay with him in that chest. 117

And he: "More than a thousand cram this tomb.
The second Frederick is here, and the
Cardinal
of the Ubaldini. Of the rest let us be 120
dumb."

And he disappeared without more said, and I
turned back and made my way to the ancient
Poet,
pondering the words of the dark 123
prophecy.

He moved along, and then, when we had
started,
he turned and said to me, "What troubles
you?
Why do you look so vacant and 126
downhearted?"

And I told him. And he replied: "Well may you
bear
those words in mind." Then, pausing, raised
a finger:
"Now pay attention to what I tell you 129
here:

when finally you stand before the ray
of that Sweet Lady whose bright eye sees all,
from her you will learn the turnings of 132
your way."

So saying, he bore left, turning his back
on the flaming walls, and we passed deeper
yet
into the city of pain, along a track 135

that plunged down like a scar into a sink
which sickened us already with its stink.

NOTES

11. *Jehosaphat:* A valley outside Jerusalem. The popular belief that it would serve as the scene of the Last Judgment was based on *Joel* iii, 2, 12.

14. *Epicurus:* The Greek philosopher. The central aim of his philosophy was to achieve happiness, which he defined at the absence of pain. For Dante this doctrine meant the denial of the Eternal life, since the whole aim of the Epicurean was temporal happiness.

17. *not only your spoken wish, but that other as well:* "All knowing" Virgil is frequently presented as being able to read Dante's mind. The "other wish" is almost certainly Dante's desire to speak to someone from Florence with whom he could discuss politics. Many prominent Florentines were Epicureans.

22. *Tuscan:* Florence lies in the province of Tuscany. Italian, to an extent unknown in America, is a language of dialects, all of them readily identifiable even when they are not well understood by the hearer. Dante's native Tuscan has become the main source of modern official Italian. Two very common sayings still current

in Italy are: *"Lingua toscana, lingua di Dio"* (the Tuscan tongue is the language of God) and—to express the perfection of Italian speech—*"Lingua toscana in bocca romana"* (the Tuscan tongue in a Roman mouth).

32–51. Farinata: Farinata degli Uberti (DEH-lyee Oob-EHR-tee) was head of the ancient noble house of the Uberti. He became leader of the Ghibellines of Florence in 1239, and played a large part in expelling the Guelphs in 1248. The Guelphs returned in 1251, but Farinata remained. His arrogant desire to rule single-handed led to difficulties, however, and he was expelled in 1258. With the aid of the Manfredi of Siena, he gathered a large force and defeated the Guelphs at Montaperti on the River Arbia in 1260. Re-entering Florence in triumph, he again expelled the Guelphs, but at the Diet of Empoli, held by the victors after the battle of Montaperti, he alone rose in open counsel to resist the general sentiment that Florence should be razed. He died in Florence in 1264. In 1266 the Guelphs once more returned and crushed forever the power of the Uberti, destroying their palaces and issuing special decrees against persons of the Uberti line. In 1283 a decree of heresy was published against Farinata.

26. that noble city: Florence.

39. "Mind how you speak to him": The surface interpretation is clearly that Virgil means Dante to show proper respect to so majestic a soul. But the allegorical level is more interesting here. Virgil (as Human Reason) is urging Dante to go forward on his own. These final words then would be an admonition to Dante to guide his speech according to the highest principles.

52. another shade: Cavalcante dei Cavalcanti was a famous Epicurean ("like lies with like"). He was the father of Guido Cavalcanti, a poet and friend of Dante. Guido was also Farinata's son-in-law.

61. Not by myself: Cavalcanti assumes that the resources of human genius are all that are necessary for such a journey. (It is an assumption that well fits his character as an Epicurean.) Dante replies as a man of religion that other aid is necessary.

63. whom perhaps your Guido held in scorn: This reference has not been satisfactorily explained. Virgil is a symbol on many levels—of Classicism, of Religiosity, of Human Reason. Guido might have scorned him on any of these levels, or on all of them. One interpretation might be that Dante wished to present Guido as an example of how skepticism acts as a limitation upon a man of genius. Guido's skepticism does not permit him to see beyond the temporal. He does not see that Virgil (Human Reason expressed as Poetic Wisdom) exists only to lead one to Divine Love, and therefore he cannot undertake the final journey on which Dante has embarked.

70. and when he saw that I delayed: Dante's delay is explained in lines 112–114.

79. her who reigns in Hell: Hecate or Proserpine. She is also the moon goddess. The sense of this prophecy, therefore, is that Dante will be exiled within fifty full moons. Dante was banished from Florence in 1302, well within the fifty months of the prophecy.

83. that populace: The Florentines.

97–108. THE KNOWLEDGE OF THE DAMNED: Dante notes with surprise that Farinata can foresee the future, but that Cavalcanti does not know whether his son is presently dead or alive. Farinata explains by outlining a most ingenious detail of the Divine Plan: the damned can see far into the future, but nothing of what is present or *of what has happened.* Thus, after Judgment, when there is no longer any Future, the intellects of the damned will be void.

119. the second Frederick: The Emperor Frederick II. In Canto XIII Dante has Pier delle Vigne speak of him as one worthy of honor, but he was commonly reputed to be an Epicurean.

119–120. the Cardinal of the Ubaldini: In the original Dante refers to him simply as "il Cardinale." Ottaviano degli Ubaldini (born *circa* 1209, died 1273) became a Cardinal in 1245, but his energies seem to have been directed exclusively to money and political intrigue. When he was refused an important loan by the Ghibellines, he is reported by many historians as having remarked: "I may say that if I have a soul, I have lost it in the cause of the Ghibellines, and no one of them will help me now." The words "If I have a soul" would be enough to make him guilty in Dante's eyes of the charge of heresy.

131. that Sweet Lady: Beatrice.

Canto XIII
Circle Seven: Round Two
The Violent Against Themselves

Nessus [a centaur] carries the Poets across the river of boiling blood and leaves them in the Second Round of the Seventh Circle, *The Wood of the Suicides.* Here are punished those who destroyed their own lives and those who destroyed their substance.

The souls of the Suicides are encased in thorny trees whose leaves are eaten by the odious *Harpies,* the overseers of these damned. When the Harpies feed upon them, damaging their leaves and limbs, the wound bleeds. Only as long as the blood flows are the souls of the trees able to speak. Thus, they who destroyed their own bodies are denied a human form; and just as the supreme expression of their lives was self-destruction, so they are permitted to speak only through that which tears and destroys them. Only through their own blood do they find voice. And to add one more dimension to the symbolism, it is the Harpies—defilers of all they touch—who give them their eternally recurring wounds.

The Poets pause before one tree and speak with the soul of *Pier delle Vigne.* In the same wood they see *Jacomo da Sant' Andrea,* and *Lano da Siena,* two famous *Squanderers* and *Destroyers of Goods* pursued by a pack of savage hounds. The hounds overtake *Sant' Andrea,* tear him to pieces and go off carrying his limbs in their teeth, a self-evident symbolic retribution for the violence with which these sinners destroyed their substance in the world. After this scene of horror, Dante speaks to an *Unknown Florentine Suicide* whose soul is inside the bush which was torn by the hound pack when it leaped upon Sant' Andrea.

Nessus had not yet reached the other shore
    when we moved on into a pathless wood
        that twisted upward from Hell's broken   3
            floor.

Its foliage was not verdant, but nearly black.
  The unhealthy branches, gnarled and
      warped and tangled,
    bore poison thorns instead of fruit. The track 6

of those wild beasts that shun the open spaces
  men till between Cecina and Corneto
    runs through no rougher nor more tangled 9
      places.

Here nest the odious Harpies of whom my
      Master
    wrote how they drove Aeneas and his
      companions
    from the Strophades with prophecies of 12
      disaster.

Their wings are wide, their feet clawed, their
      huge bellies
    covered with feathers, their necks and faces
      human.
    They croak eternally in the unnatural trees. 15

"Before going on, I would have you
      understand,"
    my Guide began, "we are in the second
      round
    and shall be till we reach the burning sand. 18

Therefore look carefully and you will see
  things in this wood, which, if I told them to
      you
    would shake the confidence you have placed 21
      in me."

I heard cries of lamentation rise and spill
  on every hand, but saw no souls in pain
    in all that waste; and, puzzled, I stood still. 24

I think perhaps he thought that I was thinking
  those cries rose from among the twisted
      roots
    through which the spirits of the damned 27
      were slinking

to hide from us. Therefore my Master said:
  "If you break off a twig, what you will learn
    will drive what you are thinking from your 30
      head."

Puzzled, I raised my hand a bit and slowly
  broke off a branchlet from an enormous
      thorn:
    and the great trunk of it cried: "Why do 33
      you break me?"

And after blood had darkened all the bowl
  of the wound, it cried again: "Why do you
      tear me?
    Is there no pity left in any soul? 36

Men we were, and now we are changed to
      sticks;

well might your hand have been more
      merciful
    were we no more than souls of lice and 39
      ticks."

As a green branch with one end all aflame
  will hiss and sputter sap out of the other
    as the air escapes—so from that trunk there 42
      came

words and blood together, gout by gout.
  Startled, I dropped the branch that I was
      holding
    and stood transfixed by fear, half turned 45
      about

to my Master, who replied: "O wounded soul,
  could he have believed before what he has seen
    in my verses only, you would yet be whole, 48

for his hand would never have been raised
      against you.
    But knowing this truth could never be
      believed
    till it was seen, I urged him on to do 51

what grieves me now; and I beg to know your
      name,
    that to make you some amends in the sweet
      world
    when he returns, he may refresh your 54
      fame."

And the trunk: "So sweet those words to me
      that I
    cannot be still, and may it not annoy you
    if I seem somewhat lengthy in reply. 57

I am he who held both keys to Frederick's
      heart,
    locking, unlocking with so deft a touch
    that scarce another soul had any part 60

in his most secret thoughts. Through every
      strife
    I was so faithful to my glorious office
    that for it I gave up both sleep and life. 63

That harlot, Envy, who on Caesar's face
  keeps fixed forever her adulterous stare,
    the common plague and vice of court and 66
      palace,

inflamed all minds against me. These inflamed
  so inflamed him that all my happy honors
    were changed to mourning. Then, unjustly 69
      blamed,

my soul, in scorn, and thinking to be free
  of scorn in death, made me at last, though
      just,
    unjust to myself. By the new roots of this 72
      tree

I swear to you that never in word or spirit
    did I break faith to my lord and emperor
    who was so worthy of honor in his merit.   75

If either of you return to the world, speak for
        me,
    to vindicate in the memory of men
    one who lies prostrate from the blows of   78
        Envy."

The Poet stood. Then turned. "Since he is
        silent,"
    he said to me, "do not you waste this hour,
    if you wish to ask about his life or torment."   81

And I replied: "Question him for my part,
    on whatever you think I would do well to hear;
    I could not, such compassion chokes my   84
        heart."

The Poet began again: "That this man may
    with all his heart do for you what your
        words
    entreat him to, imprisoned spirit, I pray,   87

tell us how the soul is bound and bent
    into these knots, and whether any ever
    frees itself from such imprisonment."   90

At that the trunk blew powerfully, and then
    the wind became a voice that spoke these
        words:
    "Briefly is the answer given: when   93

out of the flesh from which it tore itself,
    the violent spirit comes to punishment,
    Minos assigns it to the seventh shelf.   96

It falls into the wood, and landing there,
    wherever fortune flings it, it strikes root,
    and there it sprouts, lusty as any tare,   99

shoots up a sapling, and becomes a tree.
    The Harpies, feeding on its leaves then, give it
    pain and pain's outlet simultaneously.   102

Like the rest, we shall go for our husks on
        Judgment Day,
    but not that we may wear them, for it is not
        just
    that a man be given what he throws away.   105

Here shall we drag them and in this mournful
        glade
    our bodies will dangle to the end of time,
    each on the thorns of its tormented shade."   108

We waited by the trunk, but it said no more;
    and waiting, we were startled by a noise
    that grew through all the wood. Just such a   111
        roar

and trembling as one feels when the boar and
        chase

approach his stand, the beasts and branches
        crashing
    and clashing in the heat of the fierce race.   114

And there on the left, running so violently
    they broke off every twig in the dark wood,
    two torn and naked wraiths went plunging
        by me.   117

The leader cried, "Come now, O Death! Come
        now!"
    And the other, seeing that he was outrun,
    cried out: "Your legs were not so ready,   120
        Lano,

in the jousts at the Toppo." And suddenly in
        his rush,
    perhaps because his breath was failing him,
    he hid himself inside a thorny bush   123

and cowered among its leaves. Then at his back,
    the wood leaped with black bitches, swift as
        greyhounds
    escaping from their leash, and all the pack   126

sprang on him; with their fangs they opened
        him
    and tore him savagely, and then withdrew,
    carrying his body with them, limb by limb.   129

Then, taking me by the hand across the wood,
    my Master led me toward the bush.
        Lamenting,
    all its fractures blew out words and blood: 132

"O Jacomo da Sant' Andrea!" it said,
    "what have you gained in making me your
        screen?
    What part had I in the foul life you led?"   135

And when my Master had drawn up to it
    he said: "Who were you, who through all
        your wounds
    blow out your blood with your lament, sad   138
        spirit?"

And he to us: "You who have come to see
    how the outrageous mangling of these
        hounds
    has torn my boughs and stripped my leaves   141
        from me,

O heap them round my ruin! I was born
    in the city that tore down Mars and raised
        the Baptist.
    On that account the God of War has sworn   144

her sorrow shall not end. And were it not
    that something of his image still survives
    on the bridge across the Arno, some have   147
        thought

those citizens who of their love and pain

afterwards rebuilt it from the ashes
left by Attila, would have worked in vain.　　**150**

I am one who has no tale to tell:
I made myself a gibbet of my own lintel."

NOTES

6–10. The reference here is to the Maremma district of Tuscany which lies between the mountains and the sea. The river Cecina is the northern boundary of this district; Corneto is on the river Marta, which forms the southern boundary. It is a wild district of marsh and forest.

10–15. THE HARPIES: These hideous birds with the faces of malign women were often associated with the Erinyes (Furies). Their original function in mythology was to snatch away the souls of men at the command of the Gods. Later, they were portrayed as defilers of food, and, by extension, of everything they touched. The islands of the Strophades were their legendary abode. Aeneas and his men landed there and fought with the Harpies, who drove them back and pronounced a prophecy of unbearable famine upon them.

18. *The burning sand:* The Third Round of this Circle.

25. *I think perhaps he thought that I was thinking:* The original is "Cred' io ch' ei *credette ch'io credesse.*" This sort of word play was considered quite elegant by medieval rhetoricians and by the ornate Sicilian School of poetry. Dante's style is based on a rejection of all such devices in favor of a sparse and direct diction. The best explanation of this unusual instance seems to be that Dante is anticipating his talk with Pier delle Vigne, a rhetorician who, as we shall see, delights in this sort of locution. (An analogous stylistic device is common in opera, where the musical phrase identified with a given character may be sounded by the orchestra when the character is about to appear.)

48. *In my verses only:* The *Aeneid,* Book III, describes a similar bleeding plant. There, Aeneas pulls at a myrtle growing on a Thracian hillside. It bleeds where he breaks it and a voice cries out of the ground. It is the voice of Polydorus, son of Priam and friend of Aeneas. He has been treacherously murdered by the Thracian king.

58. *I am he, etc.:* Pier delle Vigne (Pee-YAIR deh-leh VEE-nyeh) 1190–1249. A famous and once-powerful minister of Emperor Frederick II. He enjoyed Frederick's whole confidence until 1247 when he was accused of treachery and was imprisoned and blinded. He committed suicide to escape further torture. (For Frederick see Canto X.) Pier delle Vigne was famous for his eloquence and for his mastery of the ornate Provencal-inspired Sicilian School of Italian Poetry, and Dante styles his speech accordingly. The double balanced construction of line 59, the repetition of key words in lines 67–69 and 70–72, are characteristic of this rhetorical fashion. It is worth noting, however, that the style changes abruptly in the middle of line 72. There his courtly preamble finished, delle Vigne speaks from the heart, simply and passionately.

58. *who held both keys:* The phrasing unmistakably suggests the Papal keys; delle Vigne may be suggesting that he was to Frederick as the Pope is to God.

64. *Caesar:* Frederick II was of course Caesar of the Roman Empire, but in this generalized context "Caesar" seems to be used as a generic term for any great ruler, *i.e.,* "The harlot, Envy, never turns her attention from those in power."

72. *new roots:* Pier delle Vigne had only been in Hell fifty-one years, a short enough time on the scale of eternity.

98. *wherever fortune flings it:* Just as the soul of the suicide refused to accept divine regulation of its mortal life span, so eternal justice takes no special heed of where the soul falls.

102. *pain and pain's outlet simultaneously:* Suicide also gives pain and its outlet simultaneously.

117 ff. THE VIOLENT AGAINST THEIR SUBSTANCE: They are driven naked through the thorny wood pursued by ravening bitches who tear them to pieces and carry off the limbs. (Obviously the limbs must re-form at some point so that the process can be repeated. For a parallel see Canto XXVIII, the Schismatics. Boccaccio uses an identical device in the Decameron V, vi.) The bitches may be taken as symbolizing conscience, the last besieging creditors of the damned who must satisfy their claims by dividing their wretched bodies, since nothing else is left them. It is not simply prodigality that places them here but the *violence* of their wasting. This fad of violent wasting, scandalously prevalent in Dante's Florence, is hard to imagine today.

120. *Lano:* Lano da Siena, a famous squanderer. He died at the ford of the river Toppo near Arezzo in 1287 in a battle against the Aretines. Boccaccio writes that he deliberately courted death having squandered all his great wealth and being unwilling to live on in poverty. Thus his companion's jeer probably means: "You were not so ready to run then, Lano: why are you running now?"

133. *Jacomo da Sant' Andrea* (YAH-coe-moe): A Paduan with an infamous lust for laying waste his own goods and those of his neighbors. Arson was his favorite prank. On one occasion, to celebrate the arrival of certain noble guests, he set fire to all the workers' huts and outbuildings of his estate. He was murdered in 1239, probably by assassins hired by Ezzolino (for whom see Canto XII).

131–152. AN ANONYMOUS FLORENTINE SUICIDE: All that is known of him is what he says himself.

143. *the city that tore down Mars and raised the Baptist:* Florence. Mars was the first patron of the city and when the Florentines were converted to Christianity they pulled down his equestrian statue and built a church on the site of his temple. The statue of Mars was placed on a tower beside the Arno. When Totila (see note to line 150) destroyed Florence the tower fell into the Arno and the statue with it. Legend has it that Florence could never have been rebuilt had not the mutilated statue been rescued. It was placed on the Ponte Vecchio but was carried away in the flood of 1333.

150. *Attila:* Dante confuses Attila with Totila, King of the Ostrogoths (died 552). He destroyed Florence in 542. Attila (d. 453), King of the Huns, destroyed many cities of northern Italy, but not Florence.

Canto XXXIII
Circle Nine: Cocytus
Compound Fraud
Round Two: Antenora
The Treacherous to Country
Round Three: Ptolomea
The Treacherous to Guests and Hosts

The sinner who is gnawing his companion's head looks up, wipes his bloody mouth on his victim's hair, and tells his harrowing story. He is *Count Ugolino* and the wretch he gnaws is *Archbishop Ruggieri.* Both are in Antenora for treason. In life they had once plotted together. Then Ruggieri betrayed his fellow-plotter and caused his death, by starvation, along with his four "sons." In the most pathetic and dramatic passage of the *Inferno,* Ugolino details how their prison was sealed and how his "sons" dropped dead before him one by one, weeping for food. His terrible tale serves only to renew his grief and hatred, and he has hardly finished it before he begins to gnaw Ruggieri again with renewed fury. In the immutable Law of Hell, the killer-by-starvation becomes the food of his victim.

The Poets leave Ugolino and enter *Ptolomea,* so named for the Ptolomaeus of *Maccabees,* who murdered his father-in-law at a banquet. Here are punished those who were *Treacherous Against the Ties of Hospitality.* They lie with only half their faces above the ice and their tears freeze in their eye sockets, sealing them with little crystal visors. Thus even the comfort of tears is denied them. Here Dante finds *Friar Alberigo* and *Branca d'Oria,* and discovers the terrible power of Ptolomea: so great is its sin that the souls of the guilty fall to its torments even before they die, leaving their bodies still on earth, inhabited by Demons.

The sinner raised his mouth from his grim
 repast
  and wiped it on the hair of the bloody head
  whose nape he had all but eaten away. At
  last   3

he began to speak: "You ask me to renew
 a grief so desperate that the very thought
 of speaking of it tears my heart in two. 6

But if my words may be a seed that bears
 the fruit of infamy for him I gnaw,
 I shall weep, but tell my story through my 9
 tears.

Who you may be, and by what powers you
 reach
  into this underworld, I cannot guess,
  but you seem to me a Florentine by your 12
  speech.

I was Count Ugolino, I must explain;
 this reverend grace is the Archbishop
  Ruggieri:
  now I will tell you why I gnaw his brain. 15

That I, who trusted him, had to undergo
 imprisonment and death through his
  treachery,
  you will know already. What you cannot 18
  know—

that is, the lingering inhumanity
 of the death I suffered—you shall hear in full:
 then judge for yourself if he has injured me. 21

A narrow window in that coop of stone
 now called the Tower of Hunger for my sake
 (within which others yet must pace alone) 24

had shown me several waning moons already
 between its bars, when I slept the evil sleep
 in which the veil of the future parted for me. 27

This beast appeared as master of a hunt
 chasing the wolf and his whelps across the
  mountain
  that hides Lucca from Pisa. Out in front 30

of the starved and shrewd and avid pack he had
  placed
  Gualandi and Sismondi and Lanfranchi
  to point his prey. The father and sons had 33
  raced

a brief course only when they failed of breath
 and seemed to weaken; then I thought I saw
 their flanks ripped open by the hounds' fierce 36
 teeth.

Before the dawn, the dream still in my head,
 I woke and heard my sons, who were there
  with me,
  cry from their troubled sleep, asking for 39
  bread.

You are cruelty itself if you can keep
 your tears back at the thought of what
  foreboding
  stirred in my heart; and if you do not weep, 42

at what are you used to weeping?—The hour
 when food
  used to be brought, drew near. They were
  now awake,
  and each was anxious from his dream's dark 45
  mood.

And from the base of that horrible tower I
 heard
  the sound of hammers nailing up the gates:
  I stared at my sons' faces without a word. 48

I did not weep: I had turned stone inside.
 They wept. 'What ails you, Father, you look
  so strange,'
  my little Anselm, youngest of them, cried. 51

But I did not speak a word nor shed a tear:
 not all that day nor all that endless night,
 until I saw another sun appear. 54

When a tiny ray leaked into that dark prison
 and I saw staring back from their four faces
 the terror and the wasting of my own, 57

I bit my hands in helpless grief. And they,
 thinking I chewed myself for hunger, rose
 suddenly together. I heard them say: 60

'Father, it would give us much less pain
   if you ate us: it was you who put upon us
   this sorry flesh; now strip it off again.   63

I calmed myself to spare them. Ah! hard earth,
   why did you not yawn open? All that day
   and the next we sat in silence. On the fourth,   66

Gaddo, the eldest, fell before me and cried,
   stretched at my feet upon that prison floor:
   'Father, why don't you help me?' There he   69
   died.

And just as you see me, I saw them fall
   one by one on the fifth day and the sixth.
   Then, already blind, I began to crawl   72

from body to body shaking them frantically.
   Two days I called their names, and they were
   dead.
   Then fasting overcame my grief and me."   75

His eyes narrowed to slits when he was done,
   and he seized the skull again between his
   teeth
   grinding it as a mastiff grinds a bone.   78

Ah, Pisa! foulest blemish on the land
   where "si" sound sweet and clear,
      since those nearby you are slow to blast
      the ground on which you stand,   81

may Caprara and Gorgona drift from place
   and dam the flooding Arno at its mouth
   until it drowns the last of your foul race!   84

For if to Ugolino falls the censure
   for having betrayed your castles, you for
   your part
   should not have put his sons to such a   87
   torture:

you modern Thebes! those tender lives you
   spilt—
   Brigata, Uguccione, and the others
   I mentioned earlier—were too young for   90
   guilt!

We passed on further, where the frozen mine
   entombs another crew in greater pain;
   these wraiths are not bent over, but lie   93
   supine.

Their very weeping closes up their eyes;
   and the grief that finds no outlet for its tears
   turns inward to increase their agonies: 96

for the first tears that they shed knot instantly
   in their eye-sockets, and as they freeze they
   form
   a crystal visor above the cavity.   99

And despite the fact that standing in that place
   I had become as numb as any callus,
   and all sensation had faded from my face,   102

somehow I felt a wind begin to blow,
   whereat I said: "Master, what stirs this wind?
   Is not all heat extinguished here below?"   105

And the Master said to me: "Soon you will be
   where your own eyes will see the source and
   cause
   and give you their own answer to the   108
   mystery."

And one of those locked in that icy mall
   cried out to us as we passed: "O souls so
   cruel
   that you are sent to the last post of all,   111

relieve me for a little from the pain
   of this hard veil; let my heart weep a while
   before the weeping freeze my eyes again."   114

And I to him: "If you would have my service,
   tell me your name; then if I do not help you
   may I descend to the last rim of the ice."   117

"I am Friar Alberigo," he answered therefore,
   "the same who called for the
      fruits from the bad garden.
   Here I am given dates for figs full store."   120

"What! Are you dead already?" I said to him.
   And he then: "How my body stands in the
   world
   I do not know. So privileged is this rim   123

of Ptolomea, that often souls fall to it
   before dark Atropos has cut their thread.
   And that you may more willingly free my   126
   spirit

of this glaze of frozen tears that shrouds my
   face,
   I will tell you this: when a soul betrays as I
   did,
   it falls from flesh, and a demon takes its   129
   place,

ruling the body till its time is spent.
   The ruined soul rains down into this cistern.
   So, I believe, there is still evident   132

in the world above, all that is fair and mortal
   of this black shade who winters here behind
   me.
   If you have only recently crossed the portal   135

from that sweet world, you surely must have
   known
   his body: Branca D'Oria is its name,
   and many years have passed since he   138
   rained down."

"I think you are trying to take me in," I said,
   "Ser Branca D'Oria is a living man;
   he eats, he drinks, he fills his clothes and his   141
   bed."

"Michel Zanche had not yet reached the ditch
　　of the Black Talons," the frozen wraith replied,
　　"there where the sinners thicken in hot pitch, 144

when this one left his body to a devil,
　　as did his nephew and second in treachery,
　　and plumbed like lead through space 147
　　　　to this dead level.

But now reach out your hand, and let me cry."
　　And I did not keep the promise I had made,
　　for to be rude to him was courtesy. 150

Ah, men of Genoa! souls of little worth,
　　corrupted from all custom of righteousness,
　　why have you not been driven from the 153
　　　　earth?

For there beside the blackest soul of all
　　Romagna's evil plain, lies one of yours
　　bathing his filthy soul in the eternal 156

glacier of Cocytus for his foul crime,
　　while he seems yet alive in world and time!

NOTES

1–90. *Ugolino and Ruggieri:* (Oog-oh-LEE-noe: Roo-DJAIR-ee) Ugolino, Count of Donoratico and a member of the Guelph family della Gherardesca. He and his nephew, Nino de' Visconti, led the two Guelph factions of Pisa. In 1288 Ugolino intrigued with Archbishop Ruggieri degli Ubaldini, leader of the Ghibellines, to get rid of Visconti and to take over the command of all the Pisan Guelphs. The plan worked, but in the consequent weakening of the Guelphs, Ruggieri saw his chance and betrayed Ugolino, throwing him into prison with his sons and his grandsons. In the following year the prison was sealed up and they were left to starve to death. The law of retribution is clearly evident: in life Ruggieri sinned against Ugolino by denying him food; in Hell he himself becomes food for his victim.

18. *you will know already:* News of Ugolino's imprisonment and death would certainly have reached Florence, *what you cannot know:* No living man could know what happened after Ugolino and his sons were sealed in the prison and abandoned.

22. *coop:* Dante uses the word *muda,* in Italian signifying a stone tower in which falcons were kept in the dark to moult. From the time of Ugolino's death it became known as The Tower of Hunger.

25. *several waning moons:* Ugolino was jailed late in 1288. He was sealed in to starve early in 1289.

28. *This beast:* Ruggieri.

29–30. *the mountain that hides Lucca from Pisa:* These two cities would be in view of one another were it not for Monte San Giuliano.

32. *Gualandi and Sismondi and Lanfranchi:* (Gwah-LAHN-dee . . . Lahn-FRAHN-kee) Three Pisan nobles, Ghibellines and friends of the Archbishop.

51–71. UGOLINO'S "SONS": Actually two of the boys were grandsons and all were considerably older than one would gather from Dante's account. Anselm, the younger grandson, was fifteen. The others were really young men and were certainly old enough for guilt despite Dante's charge in line 90.

75. *Then fasting overcame my grief and me:* i.e., He died. Some interpret the line to mean that Ugolino's hunger drove him to cannibalism. Ugolino's present occupation in Hell would certainly support that interpretation but the fact is that cannibalism is the one major sin Dante does not assign a place to in Hell. So monstrous would it have seemed to him that he must certainly have established a special punishment for it. Certainly he could hardly have relegated it to an ambiguity. Moreover, it would be a sin of bestiality rather than of fraud, and as such it would be punished in the Seventh Circle.

79–80. *the land where "sì" sound sweet and clear:* Italy.

82. *Caprara and Gorgona:* These two islands near the mouth of the Arno were Pisan possessions in 1300.

86. *betrayed your castles:* In 1284, Ugolino gave up certain castles to Lucca and Florence. He was at war with Genoa at the time and it is quite likely that he ceded the castles to buy the neutrality of these two cities, for they were technically allied with Genoa. Dante, however, must certainly consider the action as treasonable, for otherwise Ugolino would be in Caïna for his treachery to Visconti.

88. *you modern Thebes:* Thebes, as a number of the foregoing notes will already have made clear, was the site of some of the most hideous crimes of antiquity.

91. *we passed on further:* Marks the passage into Ptolomea.

105. *is not all heat extinguished:* Dante believed (rather accurately, by chance) that all winds resulted from "exhalations of heat." Cocytus, however, is conceived as wholly devoid of heat, a metaphysical absolute zero. The source of the wind, as we discover in the next Canto, is Satan himself.

117. *may I descend to the last rim of the ice:* Dante is not taking any chances; he has to go on to the last rim in any case. The sinner, however, believes him to be another damned soul and would interpret the oath quite otherwise than as Dante meant it.

118. *Friar Alberigo:* (Ahl-beh-REE-ghoe) Of the Manfredi of Faenza. He was another Jovial Friar. In 1284 his brother Manfred struck him in the course of an argument. Alberigo pretended to let it pass, but in 1285 he invited Manfred and his son to a banquet and had them murdered. The signal to the assassins was the words: "Bring in the fruit." "Friar Alberigo's bad fruit," became a proverbial saying.

125. *Atropos:* The Fate who cuts the thread of life.

137. *Branca d'Oria:* (DAW-ree-yah) A Genoese Ghilbelline. His sin is identical in kind to that of Friar Alberigo. In 1275 he invited his father-in-law, Michel Zanche, to a banquet and had him and his companions cut to pieces. He was assisted in the butchery by his nephew.

Canto XXXIV
Circle Nine: Cocytus
Compound Fraud
Round Four: Judecca
The Treacherous to Their Masters
The Center
Satan

"On march the banners of the King," Virgil begins as the Poets face the last depth. He is quoting a medieval hymn, and to it he adds the distortion and perversion of all that lies about him. "On march the banners of the King—of Hell." And there before them, in an infernal parody of

Godhead, they see Satan in the distance, his great wings beating like a windmill. It is their beating that is the source of the icy wind of Cocytus, the exhalation of all evil.

All about him in the ice are strewn the sinners of the last round, *Judecca,* named for Judas Iscariot. These are the *Treacherous to Their Masters.* They lie completely sealed in the ice, twisted and distorted into every conceivable posture. It is impossible to speak to them, and the Poets move on to observe Satan.

He is fixed into the ice at the center to which flow all the rivers of guilt; and as he beats his great wings as if to escape, their icy wind only freezes him more surely into the polluted ice. In a grotesque parody of the Trinity, he has three faces, each a different color, and in each mouth he clamps a sinner whom he rips eternally with his teeth. *Judas Iscariot* in the central mouth: *Brutus* and *Cassius* in the mouths on either side.

Having seen all, the Poets now climb through the center, grappling hand over hand down the hairy flank of Satan himself—a last supremely symbolic action—and at last, when they have passed the center of all gravity, they emerge from Hell. A long climb from the earth's center to the Mount of Purgatory awaits them, and they push on without rest, ascending along the sides of the river Lethe, till they emerge once more to see the stars of Heaven, just before dawn on Easter Sunday.

"On march the banners of the King of Hell,"
   my Master said. "Toward us. Look straight
     ahead:
   can you make him out at the core   3
    of the frozen shell?"

Like a whirling windmill seen afar at twilight,
   or when a mist has risen from the ground—
   just such an engine rose upon my sight   6

stirring up such a wild and bitter wind
   I cowered for shelter at my Master's back,
   there being no other windbreak I could find.   9

I stood now where the souls of the last class
   (with fear my verses tell it) were covered
     wholly;
   they shone below the ice like straws in glass.   12

Some lie stretched out; others are fixed in place
   upright, some on their heads, some on their
     soles;
   another, like a bow, bends foot to face.   15

When we had gone so far across the ice
   that it pleased my Guide to show me the foul
     creature
   that once had worn the grace of Paradise,   18

he made me stop, and, stepping aside, he said:
   "Now see the face of Dis! This is the place
   where you must arm your soul against all   21
    dread."

Do not ask, Reader, how my blood ran cold
   and my voice choked up with fear. I cannot
     write it:
   this is a terror that cannot be told.   24

I did not die, and yet I lost life's breath:
   imagine for yourself what I became,
   deprived at once of both my life and death.   27

The Emperor of the Universe of Pain
   jutted his upper chest above the ice;
   and I am closer in size to the great mountain   30

the Titans make around the central pit,
   than they to his arms. Now, starting from
     this part,
   imagine the whole that corresponds to it!   33

If he was once as beautiful as now
   he is hideous, and still turned on his Maker,
   well may he be the source of every woe!   36

With what a sense of awe I saw his head
   towering above me! for it had three faces:
   one was in front, and it was fiery red;   39

the other two, as weirdly wonderful,
   merged with it from the middle of each
     shoulder
   to the point where all converged   42
    at the top of the skull;

the right was something between white and
     bile;
   the left was about the color one observes
   on those who live along the banks of the   45
    Nile.

Under each head two wings rose terribly,
   their span proportioned to so gross a bird:
   I never saw such sails upon the sea.   48

They were not feathers—their texture and their
     form
   were like a bat's wings—and he beat them so
   that three winds blew from him in one   51
    great storm:

it is these winds that freeze all Cocytus.
   He wept from his six eyes, and down three
     chins
   the tears ran mixed with bloody froth and   54
    pus.

In every mouth he worked a broken sinner
   between his rake-like teeth. Thus he kept
     three
   in eternal pain at his eternal dinner.   57

For the one in front the biting seemed to play
  no part at all compared to the ripping: at
    times
  the whole skin of his back was flayed away.   60

"That soul that suffers most," explained my
    Guide,
  "is Judas Iscariot, he who kicks his legs
  on the fiery chin and has his head inside.   63

Of the other two, who have their heads thrust
    forward,
  the one who dangles down from the black
    face
  is Brutus: note how he writhes without a   66
    word.

And there, with the huge and sinewy arms, is
    the soul
  of Cassius.—But the night is coming on
  and we must go, for we have seen the   69
    whole."

Then as he bade, I clasped his neck, and he,
  watching for a moment when the wings
  were opened wide, reached over dexterously   72

and seized the shaggy coat of the king demon;
  then grappling matted hair and frozen crusts
  from one tuft to another, clambered down.   75

When we had reached the joint where the great
    thigh
  merges into the swelling of the haunch,
  my Guide and Master, straining terribly,   78

turned his head to where his feet had been
  and began to grip the hair as if he were
    climbing;
  so that I thought we moved toward Hell   81
    again.

"Hold fast!" my Guide said, and his breath
    came shrill
  with labor and exhaustion. "There is no way
  but by such stairs to rise above such evil."   84

At last he climbed out through an opening
  in the central rock, and he seated me on the
    rim;
  then joined me with a nimble backward   87
    spring.

I looked up, thinking to see Lucifer
  as I had left him, and I saw instead
  his legs projecting high into the air.   90

Now let all those whose dull minds are still
    vexed
  by failure to understand what point it was
  I had passed through, judge if I was   93
    perplexed.

"Get up. Up on your feet," my Master said.
  "The sun already mounts to middle tierce,
  and a long road and hard climbing lie   96
    ahead."

It was no hall of state we had found there,
  but a natural animal pit hollowed from rock
  with a broken floor and a close and sunless   99
    air.

"Before I tear myself from the Abyss,"
  I said when I had risen, "O my Master,
  explain to me my error in all this: 102

where is the ice? and Lucifer—how has he
  been turned from top to bottom: and how
    can the sun
  have gone from night to day so suddenly?"   105

And he to me: "You imagine you are still
  on the other side of the center where I
    grasped
  the shaggy flank of the Great Worm of Evil   108

which bores through the world—you *were*
  while I climbed down,
  but when I turned myself about, you passed
  the point to which all gravities are drawn.   111

You are under the other hemisphere where you
    stand;
  the sky above us is the half opposed
  to that which canopies the great dry land.   114

Under the midpoint of that other sky
  the Man who was born sinless and who lived
  beyond all blemish, came to suffer and die.   117

You have your feet upon a little sphere
  which forms the other face of the Judecca.
  There it is evening when it is morning here.   120

And this gross Fiend and Image of all Evil
  who made a stairway for us with his hide
  is pinched and prisoned in the ice-pack still. 123

On this side he plunged down from heaven's
    height,
  and the land that spread here once hid in the
    sea
  and fled North to our hemisphere for fright;   126

and it may be that moved by that same fear,
  the one peak that still rises on this side
  fled upward leaving this great cavern here."   129

Down there, beginning at the further bound
  of Beelzebub's dim tomb, there is a space
  not known by sight, but only by the sound   132

of a little stream descending through the hollow
  it has eroded from the massive stone
  in its endlessly entwining lazy flow.   135

My Guide and I crossed over and began
    to mount that little known and lightless road
    to ascend into the shining world again.   **138**

He first, I second, without thought of rest
    we climbed the dark until we reached the
        point
    where a round opening brought in sight the   **141**
        blest

and beauteous shining of the Heavenly cars.
And we walked out once more beneath the
    Stars.

NOTES

1. *On march the banners of the King:* The hymn (*Vexilla regis prodeunt*) was written in the sixth century by Venantius Fortunatus, Bishop of Poitiers. The original celebrates the Holy Cross, and is part of the service for Good Friday to be sung at the moment of uncovering the cross.

17. *the foul creature:* Satan.

38. *three faces:* Numerous interpretations of these three faces exist. What is essential to all explanation is that they be seen as perversions of the qualities of the Trinity.

54. *bloody froth and pus:* The gore of the sinners he chews which is mixed with his slaver.

62. *Judas:* Note how closely his punishment is patterned on that of the Simoniacs.

67. *huge and sinewy arms:* The Cassius who betrayed Caesar was more generally described in terms of Shakespeare's "lean and hungry look." Another Cassius is described by Cicero (*Catiline* III) as huge and sinewy. Dante probably confused the two.

68. *the night is coming on:* It is now Saturday evening.

95. *middle tierce:* In the canonical day tierce is the period from about six to nine A.M. Middle tierce, therefore, is seven-thirty. In going through the center point, they have gone from night to day. They have moved ahead twelve hours.

128. *the one peak:* The Mount of Purgatory.

129. *this great cavern:* The natural animal pit of line 98. It is also "Beelzebub's dim tomb," line 131.

133. *a little stream:* Lethe. In classical mythology, the river of forgetfulness, from which souls drank before being born. In Dante's symbolism it flows down from the top of Purgatory, where it washes away the memory of sin from the souls that have achieved purity. That memory it delivers to Hell, which draws all sin to itself.

143. *Stars:* As part of his total symbolism Dante ends each of the three divisions of the *Commedia* with this word. Every conclusion of the upward soul is toward the stars, God's shining symbols of hope and virtue. It is just before dawn of Easter Sunday that the Poets emerge—a further symbolism.

Purgatory

Canto I

Ante-Purgatory: the Shore of the Island
Cato of Utica

The Poets emerge from Hell just before dawn of Easter Sunday (April 10, 1300), and Dante revels in the sight of the rediscovered heavens. As he looks eagerly about at the stars, he sees nearby an old man of impressive bearing. The ancient is *Cato of Utica,* guardian of the shores of Purgatory. Cato challenges the Poets as fugitives from Hell, but Virgil, after first instructing Dante to kneel in reverence, explains Dante's mission and Beatrice's command. Cato then gives them instructions for proceeding.

The Poets have emerged at a point a short way up the slope of Purgatory. It is essential, therefore, that they descend to the lowest point and begin from there, an allegory of Humility. Cato, accordingly, orders Virgil to lead Dante to the shore, to wet his hands in the dew of the new morning, and to wash the stains of Hell from Dante's face and the film of Hell's vapors from Dante's eyes. Virgil is then to bind about Dante's waist one of the pliant reeds (symbolizing Humility) that grow in the soft mud of the shore.

Having so commanded, Cato disappears. Dante arises in silence and stands waiting, eager to begin. His look is all the communication that is necessary. Virgil leads him to the shore and performs all that Cato has commanded. Dante's first purification is marked by a miracle: when Virgil breaks off a reed, the stalk immediately regenerates a new reed, restoring itself exactly as it had been.

For better waters now the little bark
    of my indwelling powers raises her sails,
    and leaves behind that sea so cruel and dark.   **3**

Now shall I sing that second kingdom given
    the soul of man wherein to purge its guilt
    and so grow worthy to ascend to Heaven.   **6**

Yours am I, sacred Muses! To you I pray.
    Here let dead poetry rise once more to life,
    and here let sweet Calliope rise and play   **9**

some far accompaniment in that high strain
    whose power the wretched Pierides once felt
    so terribly they dared not hope again.   **12**

Sweet azure of the sapphire of the east
    was gathering on the serene horizon
    its pure and perfect radiance—a feast   **15**

to my glad eyes, reborn to their delight,
    as soon as I had passed from the dead air
    which had oppressed my soul and   **18**
        dimmed my sight.

The planet whose sweet influence strengthens
        love
    was making all the east laugh with her rays,
    veiling the Fishes, which she swam above.   **21**

I turned then to my right and set my mind
    on the other pole, and there I saw four stars
    unseen by mortals since the first mankind.   **24**

The heavens seemed to revel in their light.
　　O widowed Northern Hemisphere, bereft
　　forever of the glory of that sight!　　27

As I broke off my gazing, my eyes veered
　　a little to the left, to the other pole
　　from which, by then, the Wain had　　30
　　　disappeared.

I saw, nearby, an ancient man, alone.
　　His bearing filled me with such reverence,
　　no father had had more from any son.　　33

His beard was long and touched with strands of
　　　white,
　　as was his hair, of which two tresses fell
　　over his breast. Rays of the holy light　　36

that fell from the four stars made his face glow
　　with such a radiance that he looked to me
　　as if he faced the sun. And standing so,　　39

he moved his venerable plumes and said:
　　"Who are you two who climb by the dark
　　　stream
　　to escape the eternal prison of the dead?　　42

Who led you? or what served you as a light
　　in your dark flight from the eternal valley,
　　which lies forever blind in darkest night?　　45

Are the laws of the pit so broken? Or is new
　　　counsel
　　published in Heaven that the damned may
　　　wander
　　onto my rocks from the abyss of Hell?"　　48

At that my Master laid his hands upon me,
　　instructing me by word and touch and
　　　gesture
　　to show my reverence in brow and knee,　　51

then answered him: "I do not come this way
　　of my own will or powers. A Heavenly Lady
　　sent me to this man's aid in his dark day.　　54

But since your will is to know more, my will
　　cannot deny you; I will tell you truly
　　why we have come and how. This man has　　57
　　　still

to see his final hour, though in the burning
　　of his own madness he had drawn so near it
　　his time was perilously short for turning.　　60

As I have told you, I was sent to show
　　the way his soul must take for its salvation;
　　and there is none but this by which I go.　　63

I have shown him the guilty people. Now I
　　　mean
　　to lead him through the spirits in your keep-
　　　ing,
　　to show him those whose suffering makes　　66
　　　them clean.

By what means I have led him to this strand
　　to see and hear you, takes too long to tell:
　　from Heaven is the power and the command.　　69

Now may his coming please you, for he goes
　　to win his freedom; and how dear that is
　　the man who gives his life for it best knows.　　72

You know it, who in that cause found death
　　　sweet
　　in Utica where you put off that flesh
　　which shall rise radiant at the Judgment Seat.　　75

We do not break the Laws: this man lives yet,
　　and I am of that Round not ruled by Minos,
　　with your own Marcia, whose chaste eyes　　78
　　　seem set

in endless prayers to you. O blessed breast
　　to hold her yet your own! for love of her
　　grant us permission to pursue our quest　　81

across your seven kingdoms. When I go
　　back to her side I shall bear thanks of you,
　　if you will let me speak your name below."　　84

"Marcia was so pleasing in my eyes
　　there on the other side," he answered then
　　"that all she asked, I did. Now that she lies　　87

beyond the evil river, no word or prayer
　　of hers may move me. Such was the Decree
　　pronounced upon us when I rose from there.　　90

But if, as you have said, a Heavenly Dame
　　orders your way, there is no need to flatter:
　　you need but ask it of me in her name.　　93

Go then, and lead this man, but first see to it
　　you bind a smooth green reed about his
　　　waist
　　and clean his face of all trace of the pit.　　96

For it would not be right that one with eyes
　　still filmed by mist should go before the
　　　angel
　　who guards the gate: he is from Paradise.　　99

All round the wave-wracked shore-line, there
　　　below,
　　reeds grow in the soft mud. Along that edge
　　no foliate nor woody plant could grow.　　102

for what lives in that buffeting must bend.
　　Do not come back this way: the rising sun
　　will light an easier way you may ascend."　　105

With that he disappeared; and silently
　　I rose and moved back till I faced my Guide,
　　my eyes upon him, waiting. He said to me:　　108

"Follow my steps and let us turn again:
　　along this side there is a gentle slope
　　that leads to the low boundaries of the　　111
　　　plain."

The dawn, in triumph, made the day-breeze flee
   before its coming, so that from afar
   I recognized the trembling of the sea.   **114**

We strode across that lonely plain like men
   who seek the road they strayed from and
      who count
   the time lost till they find it once again.   **117**

When we had reached a place along the way
   where the cool morning breeze shielded the
      dew
   against the first heat of the gathering day,   **120**

with gentle graces my Sweet Master bent
   and laid both outspread palms upon the
      grass.
   Then I, being well aware of his intent,   **123**

lifted my tear-stained cheeks to him, and there
   he made me clean, revealing my true color
   under the residues of Hell's black air.   **126**

We moved on then to the deserted strand
   which never yet has seen upon its waters
   a man who found his way back to dry land.   **129**

There, as it pleased another, he girded me.
   Wonder of wonders! when he plucked a reed
   another took its place there instantly,   **132**

arising from the humble stalk he tore
   so that it grew exactly as before.

NOTES

4. *that second kingdom:* Purgatory.

5. *to purge its guilt:* (See also line 66: *those whose suffering makes them clean.*) There is suffering in Purgatory but no torment. The torment of the damned is endless, produces no change in the soul that endures it, and is imposed from without. The suffering of the souls in Purgatory, on the other hand, is temporary, is a means of purification, and is eagerly embraced as an act of the soul's own will. Demons guard the damned to inflict punishment and to prevent escape. In Purgatory, the sinners are free to leave off their sufferings: nothing but their own desire to be made clean moves them to accept their pains, and nothing more is needed. In fact, it is left to the suffering soul itself (no doubt informed by Divine Illumination) to decide at what point it has achieved purification and is ready to move on.

8. *dead poetry:* The verses that sang of Hell. Dante may equally have meant that poetry as an art has long been surpassed by history as the medium for great subjects. Here poetry will return to its classic state.

7–12. THE INVOCATION. Dante invokes all the Muses, as he did in *Inferno,* II, 7, but there the exhortation was to his own powers, to High Genius, and to Memory. Here he addresses his specific exhortation to Calliope, who, as the Muse of Epic Poetry, is foremost of the Nine. In *Paradiso* (I, 13) he exhorts Apollo himself to come to the aid of the poem.

Dante exhorts Calliope to fill him with the strains of the music she played in the defeat of the Pierides, the nine daughters of Pierius, King of Thessaly. They presumed to challenge the Muses

to a contest of song. After their defeat they were changed into magpies for their presumption. Ovid (*Metamorphoses,* V, 294–340 and 662–678) retells the myth in detail.

Note that Dante not only calls upon Calliope to fill him with the strains of highest song, but that he calls for that very song that overthrew the arrogant pretensions of the Pierides, the strains that humbled false pride. The invocation is especially apt, therefore, as a first sounding of the theme of Humility.

17. *the dead air:* Of Hell.

19–21. *the planet whose sweet influence strengthens love:* Venus. Here, as morning star, Venus is described as rising in Pisces, the Fishes, the zodiacal sign immediately preceding Aries. In Canto I of the *Inferno* Dante has made it clear that the Sun is in Aries. Hence it is about to rise.

Allegorically, the fact that Venus represents love is, of course, indispensable to the mood of the *Purgatory.* At no time in April of 1300 was Venus the morning star. Rather, it rose after the sun. Dante's description of the first dawn in Canto I of the *Inferno* similarly violates the exact detail of things. But Dante is no bookkeeper of the literal. In the *Inferno* he violated fact in order to compile a perfect symbol of rebirth. Here, he similarly violates the literal in order to describe an ideal sunrise, and simultaneously to make the allegorical point that Love (Venus) leads the way and that Divine Illumination (the Sun) follows upon it.

23. *four stars:* Modern readers are always tempted to identify these four stars as the Southern Cross, but it is almost certain that Dante did not know about that formation. In VIII, 89, Dante mentions three other stars as emphatically as he does these four and no one has been tempted to identify them on the star-chart. Both constellations are best taken as allegorical. The four stars represent the Four Cardinal Virtues: Prudence, Justice, Fortitude, and Temperance. Dante will encounter them again in the form of nymphs when he achieves the Earthly Paradise.

24. *the first mankind:* Adam and Eve. In Dante's geography, the Garden of Eden (the Earthly Paradise) was at the top of the Mount of Purgatory, which was the only land in the Southern Hemisphere. All of what were called "the southern continents" were believed to lie north of the equator. When Adam and Eve were driven from the Garden, therefore, they were driven into the Northern Hemisphere, and no living soul since had been far enough south to see those stars.

Ulysses and his men had come within sight of the Mount of Purgatory, but Ulysses mentioned nothing of having seen these stars.

29. *the other pole:* The North Pole. The Wain (Ursa Major, *i.e.,* the Big Dipper) is below the horizon.

31 ff. CATO OF UTICA. Marcus Porcius Cato the Younger, 95–46 B.C. In the name of freedom, Cato opposed the policies of both Caesar and Pompey, but because he saw Caesar as the greater evil joined forces with Pompey. After the defeat of his cause at the Battle of Thapsus, Cato killed himself with his own sword rather than lose his freedom. Virgil lauds him in the *Aeneid* as a symbol of perfect devotion to liberty, and all writers of Roman antiquity have given Cato a similar high place. Dante spends the highest praises on him both in *De Monarchia* and *II Convivio.*

Why Cato should be so signally chosen by God as the special guardian of Purgatory has been much disputed. Despite his suicide (and certainly one could argue that he had less excuse for it than had Pier delle Vigne—see *Inferno,* XIII—for his) he was sent to Limbo as a Virtuous Pagan. From Limbo he was especially summoned to his present office. It is clear, moreover, that he will find a special triumph on Judgment Day, though he will probably not be received into Heaven.

The key to Dante's intent seems to lie in the four stars, the Four Cardinal Virtues, that shine so brightly on Cato's face when Dante first sees him. Once Cato is forgiven his suicide (and a partisan could argue that it was a positive act, a death for freedom), he may certainly be taken as a figure of Prudence, Justice, Fortitude, and Temperance. He does very well, moreover, as a symbol of the natural love of freedom; and Purgatory, it must be remembered, is the road to Ultimate Freedom. Cato may be taken, therefore, as representative of supreme virtue short of godliness. He has accomplished everything but the purifying total surrender of his will to God. As such he serves as an apt transitional symbol, being the highest rung on the ladder of natural virtue, but the lowest on the ladder of those godly virtues to which Purgatory is the ascent. Above all, the fact that he took Marcia (see line 78, note) back to his love, makes him an especially apt symbol of God's forgiveness in allowing the strayed soul to return to him through Purgatory.

53. *A Heavenly Lady:* Beatrice.

77. *Minos:* The Judge of the Damned. The round in Hell not ruled by Minos is Limbo, the final resting place of the Virtuous Pagans. Minos (see *Inferno, V*) is stationed at the entrance to the second circle of Hell. The souls in Limbo (the first circle) have never had to pass before him to be judged.

78. *Marcia.* The story of Marcia and of Cato is an extraordinary one. She was the daughter of the consul Philippus and became Cato's second wife, bearing his three children. In 56 B.C., in an unusual transaction approved by her father, Cato released her in order that she might marry his friend Hortensius (Hence line 87: "that all she asked I did.") After the death of Hortensius, Cato took her back.

In *II Convivio,* IV, 28, Dante presents the newly widowed Marcia praying to be taken back in order that she may die the wife of Cato, and that it may be said of her that she was not cast forth from his love. Dante treats that return as an allegory of the return of the strayed soul to God (that it may die "married" to God, and that God's love for it be made manifest to all time). Virgil describes Marcia as still praying to Cato.

89. *the Decree:* May be taken as that law that makes an absolute separation between the damned and the saved. Cato cannot be referring here to *Mark,* xii, 25 ("when they shall rise from the dead, they neither marry, nor are given in marriage") for that "decree" was not pronounced upon his ascent from Limbo.

98. *filmed by mist:* Of Hell.

100. ff. THE REED. The pliant reed clearly symbolizes humility, but other allegorical meanings suggest themselves at once. First, the Reed takes the place of the Cord that Dante took from about his waist in order to signal Geryon. The Cord had been intended to snare and defeat the Leopard with the Gaudy Pelt, a direct assault upon sin. It is now superseded by the Reed of submission to God's will. Second, the reeds are eternal and undiminishable. As such they must immediately suggest the redemption purchased by Christ's sufferings (ever-abounding grace), for the quantity of grace available to mankind through Christ's passion is, in Christian creed, also eternal and undiminishable. The importance of the fact that the reeds grow at the lowest point of the Island and that the Poets must descend to them before they can begin, has already been mentioned. Curiously, the reed is never again mentioned, though it must remain around Dante's waist. See also *Matthew,* xxvii, 29.

119. *breeze shielded the dew:* The dew is a natural symbol of God's grace. The morning breeze shields it in the sense that, being cool, it retards evaporation.

Even more naturally, being bathed in the dew may be taken to signify baptism. The structure of Purgatory certainly suggests a parable of the soul's stages of sacred development: the dew, baptism; the gate of Purgatory, above, first communion; Virgil's certification of Dante as lord of himself (XXVII, 143), confirmation; and Dante's swoon and awakening as extreme unction and the reception into the company of the blessed.

Canto IX
The Gate of Purgatory
The Angel Guardian

Dawn is approaching. Dante has a dream of A GOLDEN EAGLE that descends from the height of Heaven and carries him up to the Sphere of Fire. He wakes to find he has been transported in his sleep, that it was LUCIA [Divine Light] who bore him, laying him down beside an enormous wall, through an opening in which he and Virgil may approach THE GATE OF PURGATORY.

Having explained these matters, Virgil leads Dante to the Gate and its ANGEL GUARDIAN. The Angel is seated on the topmost of THREE STEPS that symbolize the three parts of a perfect ACT OF CONFESSION. Dante prostrates himself at the feet of the Angel, who cuts SEVEN P'S in Dante's forehead with the point of a blazing sword. He then allows the Poets to enter. As the Gates open with a sound of thunder, the mountain resounds with a great HYMN OF PRAISE.

Now pale upon the balcony of the East
    ancient Tithonus' concubine appeared,
    but lately from her lover's arms released.   3

Across her brow, their radiance like a veil,
    a scroll of gems was set, worked in the shape
    of the cold beast whose sting is in his tail.   6

And now already, where we were, the night
    had taken two steps upward, while the third
    thrust down its wings in the first stroke of   9
      flight;

when I, by Adam's weight of flesh defeated,
    was overcome by sleep, and sank to rest
    across the grass on which we five were   12
      seated.

At that new hour when the first dawn light
      grows
    and the little swallow starts her mournful cry,
    perhaps in memory of her former woes;   15

and when the mind, escaped from its
      submission
    to flesh and to the chains of waking thought,
    becomes almost prophetic in its vision;   18

in a dream I saw a soaring eagle hold
   the shining height of heaven, poised to strike,
   yet motionless on widespread wings of gold.   21

He seemed to hover where old history
   records that Ganymede rose from his friends,
   borne off to the supreme consistory.   24

I thought to myself: "Perhaps his habit is
   to strike at this one spot; perhaps he scorns
   to take his prey from any place but this."   27

Then from his easy wheel in Heaven's spire,
   terrible as a lightning bolt, he struck
   and snatched me up high as the Sphere of
      Fire. [266]   30

It seemed that we were swept in a great blaze,
   and the imaginary fire so scorched me
   my sleep broke and I wakened in a daze.   33

Achilles must have roused exactly thus—
   glancing about with unadjusted eyes,
   now here, now there, not knowing
      where he was—   36

when Thetis stole him sleeping, still a boy,
   and fled with him from Chiron's care to
      Scyros,
   whence the Greeks later lured him off to   39
      Troy.

I sat up with a start; and as sleep fled
   out of my face, I turned the deathly white
   of one whose blood is turned to ice by dread.   42

There at my side my comfort sat—alone.
   The sun stood two hours high, and more. I sat
   facing the sea. The flowering glen was gone.   45

"Don't be afraid," he said. "From here our
      course
   leads us to joy, you may be sure. Now,
      therefore,
   hold nothing back, but strive with all your   48
      force.

You are now at Purgatory. See the great
   encircling rampart there ahead. And see
   that opening—it contains the Golden Gate.   51

A while back, in the dawn before the day,
   while still your soul was locked in sleep
      inside you,
   across the flowers that made the valley gay,   54

a Lady came. 'I am Lucia,' she said.
   'Let me take up this sleeping man and bear him
   that he may wake to see his hope ahead.'   57

Sordello and the others stayed. She bent
   and took you up. And as the light grew full,
   she led, I followed, up the sweet ascent.   60

Here she put you down. Then with a sweep

of her sweet eyes she marked that open
   entrance.
   Then she was gone; and with her went your   63
   sleep."

As one who finds his doubt dispelled, sheds fear
   and feels it change into new confidence
   as bit by bit he sees the truth shine clear—   66

so did I change; and seeing my face brim
   with happiness, my Guide set off at once
   to climb the slope, and I moved after him.   69

Reader, you know to what exalted height
   I raised my theme. Small wonder if I now
   summon still greater art to what I write.   72

As we drew near the height, we reached a place
   from which—inside what I had first believed
   to be an open breach in the rock face—   75

I saw a great gate fixed in place above
   three steps, each its own color; and a guard
   who did not say a word and did not move.   78

Slow bit by bit, raising my lids with care,
   I made him out seated on the top step,
   his face more radiant than my eyes could   81
   bear.

He held a drawn sword, and the eye of day
   beat such a fire back from it, that each time
   I tried to look, I had to look away.   84

I heard him call: "What is your business here?
   Answer from where you stand. Where is
      your Guide?
   Take care you do not find your coming   87
   dear."

"A little while ago," my Teacher said,
   "A Heavenly Lady, well versed in these
      matters,
   told us 'Go there. That is the Gate ahead.'"   90

"And may she still assist you, once inside,
   to your soul's good! Come forward to our
      three steps,"
   the courteous keeper of the gate replied.   93

We came to the first step: white marble
      gleaming
   so polished and so smooth that in its mirror
   I saw my true reflection past all seeming.   96

The second was stained darker than blue-black
   and of a rough-grained and a fire-flaked
      stone,
   its length and breadth crisscrossed   99
   by many a crack.

The third and topmost was of porphyry,
   or so it seemed, but of a red as flaming
   as blood that spurts out of an artery.   102

The Angel of the Lord had both feet on
  this final step and sat upon the sill
  which seemed made of some adamantine   105
    stone.

With great good will my Master guided me
  up the three steps and whispered in my ear;
  "Now beg him humbly that he turn the   108
    key."

Devoutly prostrate at his holy feet,
  I begged in mercy's name to be let in,
  but first three times upon my breast I beat. 111

Seven *P*'s, the seven scars of sin,
  his sword point cut into my brow. He said:
  "Scrub off these wounds when you have   114
    passed within."

Color of ashes, of parched earth one sees
  deep in an excavation, were his vestments,
  and from beneath them he drew out two   117
    keys.

One was of gold, one silver. He applied
  the white one to the gate first, then the
    yellow,
  and did with them what left me satisfied.   120

"Whenever either of these keys is put
  improperly in the lock and fails to turn it,"
  the Angel said to us, "the door stays shut. 123

One is more precious. The other is so wrought
  as to require the greater skill and genius,
  for it is that one which unties the knot.   126

They are from Peter, and he bade me be
  more eager to let in than to keep out
  whoever cast himself prostrate before me."   129

Then opening the sacred portals wide:
  "Enter. But first be warned: do not look
    back
  or you will find yourself once more outside." 132

The Tarpeian rock-face, in that fatal hour
  that robbed it of Metellus, and then the
    treasure,
  did not give off so loud and harsh a roar   135

as did the pivots of the holy gate—
  which were of resonant and hard-forged
    metal—
  when they turned under their enormous   138
    weight.

At the first thunderous roll I turned half-round,
  for it seemed to me I heard a chorus singing
  Te deum laudamus mixed with that sweet   141
    sound.

I stood there and the strains that reached my
    ears

left on my soul exactly that impression
  a man receives who goes to church and hears 144

the choir and organ ringing out their chords
  and now does, now does not, make out the
    words.

NOTES

1–9. There is no wholly satisfactory explanation of this complex opening description. Dante seems to be saying that the third hour of darkness is beginning (hence, if sunset occurred at 6:00 it is now a bit after 8:00 P.M.) and that the aurora of the rising moon is appearing above the horizon.

He describes the moon as the concubine of Tithonus. Tithonus, however, married the daughter of the sun, Aurora (dawn), and it was she who begged Jove to give her husband immortality while forgetting to ask perpetual youth for him. Thus Tithonus lived but grew older and older beside his ageless bride. (In one legend he was later changed into a grasshopper.) Despite his advanced years, however, he seems here to be philandering with the moon as his concubine. Dante describes the moon as rising from Tithonus' bed and standing on the balcony of the East (the horizon) with the constellation Scorpio gemmed on her forehead, that "cold [blooded] beast whose sting is in his tail" being the scorpion.

Having given Tithonus a double life, Dante now adds a mixed metaphor in which the "steps" of the night have "wings." Two of the steps (hours) have flown, and the third has just completed the first downstroke of its wings (i.e., has just begun its flight).

15. *former woes:* Tereus, the husband of Procne, raped her sister Philomela, and cut out her tongue so that she could not accuse him. Philomela managed to communicate the truth to Procne by means of her weaving. The two sisters thereupon took revenge by killing Itys, son of Procne and Tereus, and serving up his flesh to his father. Tereus, learning the truth, was about to kill the sisters when all were turned into birds. Ovid (*Metamorphoses,* VI, 424 ff.) has Tereus changed into a hoopoe, and probably (though the text leaves some doubt) Procne into a swallow and Philomela into a nightingale. Dante clearly takes the swallow to be Philomela.

18. *prophetic in its vision:* It was an ancient belief that the dreams that came toward dawn were prophetic.

19–33. DANTE'S DREAM. Each of Dante's three nights on the Mount of Purgatory ends with a dream that comes just before dawn. The present dream is relatively simple in its symbolism, and as we learn shortly after Dante's awakening, it parallels his ascent of the mountain in the arms of Lucia. The dream is told, however, with such complexities of allusion that every reference must be carefully weighed.

To summarize the symbolism in the simplest terms, the Golden Eagle may best be rendered in its attributes. It comes from highest Heaven (from God), its feathers are pure gold (Love? God's splendor?), its wings are outspread (the open arms of Divine Love?), and it appears poised to descend in an instant (as is Divine Grace). The Eagle snatches Dante up to the Sphere of Fire (the presence of God? the beginning of Purgatorial purification? both?), and both are so consumed by the fire that Dante, in his unpurified state, cannot bear it.

On another level, of course, the Eagle is Lucia (Divine Light), who has descended from Heaven, and who bears the sleeping Dante from the Flowering Valley to the beginning of the true Purgatory. Note that Lucia is an anagram for *acuila,* "eagle."

On a third level, the dream simultaneously connects with the earlier reference to Ganymede, also snatched up by the eagle of God, but the two experiences are contrasted as much as they are compared. Ganymede was carried up by Jove's eagle, Dante by Lucia. Ganymede was out hunting in the company of his worldly associates; Dante was laboring for grace, had renounced worldliness, and was in the company of great souls who were themselves awaiting purification. Ganymede was carried to Olympus; Dante to the beginning of a purification which, though he was still too unworthy to endure it, would in time make him a perfect servant of the true God. Thus, his experience is in the same pattern as Ganymede's, but surpasses it as Faith surpasses Human Reason, and as Beatrice surpasses Virgil.

23. *Ganymede:* Son of Tros, the mythical founder of Troy, was reputedly the most beautiful of mortals, so beautiful that Jove sent an eagle (or perhaps went himself in the form of an eagle) to snatch up the boy and bring him to Heaven, where he became cupbearer to the gods. The fact that Dante himself is about to begin the ascent of Purgatory proper (and hence to Heaven) inevitably suggests an allegory of the soul in the history of Ganymede. God calls to Himself what is most beautiful in man.

The fact that Dante always thought of the Trojans as an especially chosen people is also relevant. Ganymede was the son of the founder of Troy; Troy, in Dante's Virgilian view, founded Rome. And through the Church of Rome men's souls were enabled to mount to Heaven.

24. *consistory:* Here, the council of the gods on Olympus. Dante uses the same term to describe Paradise.

30. *Sphere of Fire:* The four elemental substances are earth, water, fire, and air. In Dante's cosmography, the Sphere of Fire was located above the Sphere of Air and just under the Sphere of the Moon. Hence the eagle bore him to the top of the atmosphere. The Sphere of Fire, however, may also be taken as another symbol for God.

34–39. ACHILLES' WAKING. It had been prophesied that Achilles would be killed at Troy. Upon the outbreak of the Trojan War, his mother, Thetis, stole him while he was sleeping, from the care of the centaur Chiron who was his tutor and fled with him to Scyros, where she hid him disguised as a girl. He was found there and lured away by Ulysses and Diomede, who burn for that sin (among others) in Malebolge. Thus Achilles, like Dante, was borne off in his sleep and awoke to find himself in a strange place.

51. *that opening:* The Gate, as the Poets will find, is closed and guarded. Dante (here and in line 62, below) can only mean "the opening in which the gate was set" and not "an open entrance." At this distance, they do not see the Gate itself but only the gap in the otherwise solid wall.

55. *Lucia* (Loo-TCHEE-ya): Symbolizes Divine Light, Divine Grace.

77. *three steps:* (See also lines 94–102, below.) The entrance into Purgatory involves the ritual of the Roman Catholic confessional with the Angel serving as the confessor. The three steps are the three acts of the perfect confession: candid confession (mirroring the whole man), mournful contrition, and burning gratitude for God's mercy. The Angel Guardian, as the priestly confessor, does not move or speak as the Poets approach, because he can admit to purification only those who ask for admission.

86. *Where is your Guide?* It must follow from the Angel's question that souls ready to enter Purgatory are led up the mountain by another Angel. Dante and Virgil are arriving in an irregular way, as they did to the shore below, where they were asked essentially

the same question by Cato. Note, too, that Virgil answers for the Poets, as he did to Cato. The allegory may be that right thinking answers for a man, at least to start with, though the actual entrance into the state of Grace requires an act of Faith and of Submission.

90. *told us:* Lucia spoke only with her eyes, and what Virgil is quoting is her look. What he is quoting is, in essence, correct, but it does seem he could have been a bit more accurate in his first actual conversation with an Angel.

94–96. *the first step:* Contrition of the heart. White for purity, shining for hope, and flawless for perfection. It is not only the mirror of the soul, but it is that mirror in which the soul sees itself as it truly is and not in its outward seeming.

97–99. *the second:* Contrition of the mouth, i.e., confession. The color of a bruise for the shame that envelops the soul as it confesses, rough-grained and fire-flaked for the pain the confessant must endure, and cracked for the imperfection (sin) the soul confesses.

100–102. *the third:* Satisfaction by works. Red for the ardor that leads to good works. Porphyry is, of course, a purple stone, but Dante does not say the stone was porphyry; only that it resembled it, though red in color.

"Artery" here is, of course, an anachronism, the circulation of the blood having yet to be discovered in Dante's time. Dante uses the word *vena* (vein), but it seems to me the anachronism will be less confusing to a modern reader than would be the idea of bright red and spurting venous blood.

103–105. The Angel, as noted, represents the confessor, and, more exactly, the Church Confessant. Thus the Church is founded on adamant and rests its feet on Good Works.

112. *Seven P's:* P is for the Latin *peccatum*. Thus there is one P for each of the Seven Deadly Sins for which the sinners suffer on the seven ledges above: Pride, Envy, Wrath, Acedia (Sloth), Avarice (Hoarding and Prodigality), Gluttony, and Lust.

Dante has just completed the act of confession and the Angel confessor marks him to indicate that even in a shriven soul there remain traces of the seven sins which can be removed only by suffering.

115–117. *Color of ashes, of parched earth:* The colors of humility which befit the office of the confessor. *two keys:* (Cf. the Papal Seal, which is a crown above two crossed keys.) The keys symbolize the power of the confessor (the Church, and hence the Pope) to grant or to withhold absolution. In the present context they may further be interpreted as the two parts of the confessor's office of admission: the gold key may be taken to represent his ordained authority, the silver key as the !earning and reflection with which he must weigh the guilt before assigning penance and offering absolution.

126. *unties the knot:* Another mixed metaphor. The soul-searched judgment of the confessor (the silver key) decides who may and who may not receive absolution, and in resolving that problem the door is opened, provided that the gold key of ordained authority has already been turned.

133–138. *The Tarpeian rock-face:* The public treasury of Rome was kept in the great scarp of Tarpeia on the Campidoglio. The tribune Metellus was its custodian when Caesar, returned to Rome after crossing the Rubicon, moved to seize the treasury. Metellus opposed him but was driven away and the great gates were opened. Lucan (*Pharsalia*, III, 154–156 and 165–168) describes the scene and the roar that echoed from the rock face as the gates were forced open.

139–141. The thunder of the opening of the Gates notifies the souls within that a new soul has entered, and they burst into the hymn "We Praise Thee, O God." (Contrast these first sounds of Purgatory with the first sounds of Hell—*Inferno,* III, 22–24.) Despite the thunderous roar right next to him, Dante seems to hear with his "allegorical ear" what certainly could not have registered upon his physical ear.

This seeming incongruity has long troubled me. I owe Professor MacAllister a glad thanks for what is certainly the essential clarification. The whole *Purgatorio,* he points out, is built upon the structure of a Mass. The Mass moreover is happening not on the mountain but in church with Dante devoutly following its well-known steps. I have not yet had time to digest Professor MacAllister's suggestion, but it strikes me immediately as a true insight and promises another illuminating way of reading the *Purgatorio.*

Paradise

Canto XI
The Fourth Sphere: the Sun
Doctors of the Church
The First Garland of Souls: Aquinas • Praise of St. Francis • Degeneracy of Dominicans

Aquinas reads Dante's mind and speaks to make clear several points about which Dante was in doubt. He explains that Providence sent two equal princes to guide the Church, St. Dominic, the wise law-giver, being one, and St. Francis, the ardent soul, being the other. Aquinas was himself a Dominican. To demonstrate the harmony of Heaven's gift and the unity of the Dominicans and Franciscans, Aquinas proceeds to pronounce a *Praise of the Life of St. Francis.* His account finished, he returns to the theme of the unity of the Dominicans and Franciscans, and proceeds to illustrate it further by himself lamenting the *Degeneracy of the Dominican Order.*

O senseless strivings of the mortal round!
　　how worthless is that exercise of reason
　　that makes you beat your wings into the　　　3
　　　　ground!

One man was giving himself to law, and one
　　to aphorisms; one sought sinecures,
　　and one to rule by force or sly persuasion;　　6

one planned his business, one his robberies;
　　one, tangled in the pleasure of the flesh,
　　wore himself out, and one lounged at his　　9
　　　　ease;

while I, of all such vanities relieved
　　and high in Heaven with my Beatrice,
　　arose to glory, gloriously received.　　　　12

—When each had danced his circuit and come
　　　　back
　　to the same point of the circle, all stood still,
　　like votive candles glowing in a rack.　　　15

And I saw the splendor of the blazing ray

that had already spoken to me, smile,
　　and smiling, quicken; and I heard it say:　　18

"Just as I take my shining from on high,
　　so, as I look into the Primal Source,
　　I see which way your thoughts have turned,　21
　　and why.

You are uncertain, and would have me find
　　open and level words in which to speak
　　what I expressed too steeply for your mind　24

when I said 'leads to where all plenty is,'
　　and 'no mortal ever rose to equal this one.'
　　And it is well to be exact in this.　　　　27

The Providence that governs all mankind
　　with wisdom so profound that any creature
　　who seeks to plumb it might as well be　　30
　　blind,

in order that the Bride seek her glad good
　　in the Sweet Groom who, crying from on
　　　　high,
　　took her in marriage with His blessed blood,　33

sent her two Princes, one on either side
　　that she might be secure within herself,
　　and thereby be more faithfully His Bride.　36

One, in his love, shone like the seraphim.
　　The other, in his wisdom, walked the earth
　　bathed in the splendor of the cherubim.　39

I shall speak of only one, though to extol
　　one or the other is to speak of both
　　in that their works led to a single goal.　42

Between the Tupino and the little race
　　sprung from the hill blessed Ubaldo chose,
　　a fertile slope spreads up the mountain's face.　45

Perugia breathes its heat and cold from there
　　through Porta Sole, and Nocera and Gualdo
　　behind it mourn the heavy yoke they bear.　48

From it, at that point where the mountainside
　　grows least abrupt, a sun rose to the world
　　as this one does at times from Ganges' tide.　51

Therefore, let no man speaking of that place
　　call it *Ascesi*—'I have risen'—but rather,
　　Oriente—so to speak with proper grace.　54

Nor was he yet far distant from his birth
　　when the first comfort of his glorious powers
　　began to make its warmth felt on the earth:　57

a boy yet, for that lady who, like death
　　knocks on no door that opens to her gladly,
　　he had to battle his own father's wrath.　60

With all his soul he married her before
　　the diocesan court *et coram patre;*
　　and day by day he grew to love her more.　63

Bereft of her First Groom, she had had to stand
   more than eleven centuries, scorned, obscure;
   and, till he came, no man had asked her   66
    hand:

none, at the news that she had stood beside
   the bed of Amyclas and heard, unruffled,
   the voice by which the world was terrified;   69

and none, at word of her fierce constancy,
   so great, that even when Mary stayed below,
   she climbed the Cross to share Christ's   72
    agony.

But lest I seem obscure, speaking this way,
   take Francis and Poverty to be those lovers.
   That, in plain words, is what I meant to say.   75

Their harmony and tender exultation
   gave rise in love, and awe, and tender glances
   to holy thoughts in blissful meditation.   78

The venerable Bernard, seeing them so,
   kicked off his shoes, and toward so great a
    peace
   ran, and running, seemed to go too slow.   81

O wealth unknown! O plentitude untried!
   Egidius went unshod. Unshod, Sylvester
   followed the groom. For so it pleased the   84
    bride!

Thenceforth this father and this happy lord
   moved with his wife and with his family,
   already bound round by the humble cord.   87

He did not grieve because he had been born
   the son of Bernardone; he did not care
   that he went in rags, a figure of passing   90
    scorn.

He went with regal dignity to reveal
   his stern intentions to Pope Innocent,
   from whom his order first received the seal.   93

There as more souls began to follow him
   in poverty—whose wonder-working life
   were better sung among the seraphim—   96

Honorius, moved by the Eternal Breath,
   placed on the holy will of this chief shepherd
   a second crown and everflowering wreath.   99

Then, with a martyr's passion, he went forth
   and in the presence of the haughty Sultan
   he preached Christ and his brotherhood on   102
    earth;

but when he found none there would take
    Christ's pardon,
   rather than waste his labors, he turned back
   to pick the fruit of the Italian garden.   105

On the crag between Tiber and Arno then, in
    tears

of love and joy, he took Christ's final seal,
   the holy wounds of which he wore two   108
    years.

When God, whose loving will had sent him
    forward
   to work such good, was pleased to call him
    back
   to where the humble soul has its reward,   111

he, to his brothers, as to rightful heirs
   commended his dearest Lady and he bade
    them
   to love her faithfully for all their years.   114

Then from her bosom, that dear soul of grace
   willed its return to its own blessed kingdom;
   and wished its flesh no other resting place.   117

Think now what manner of man was fit to be
   his fellow helmsman, holding Peter's ship
   straight to its course across the dangerous   120
    sea.

Such was our patriarch. Hence, all who rise
   and follow his command will fill the hold,
   as you can see, with fruits of paradise.   123

But his flock has grown so greedy for the taste
   of new food that it cannot help but be
   far scattered as it wanders through the waste.   126

The more his vagabond and distant sheep
   wander from him, the less milk they bring
    back
   when they return to the fold. A few do keep   129

close to the shepherd, knowing what wolf
    howls
   in the dark around them, but they are so few
   it would take little cloth to make their cowls.   132

Now, if my words have not seemed choked and
    blind,
   if you have listened to me and taken heed,
   and if you will recall them to your mind,   135

your wish will have been satisfied in part,
   for you will see how the good plant is broken,
   and what rebuke my words meant to impart   138

when I referred, a while back in our talk,
to 'where all plenty is' and to 'bare rock.'"

NOTES

15. *rack:* Dante says "candellier," which may be taken to mean candlestick, but equally to mean the candle-racks that hold votive candles in churches. The image of the souls as twelve votive candles in a circular rack is certainly apter than that of twelve candles in separate candlesticks.

25–26. *lead to . . . all plenty:* X, 95. *no mortal ever:* X, 114.

28–42. INTRODUCTION TO THE LIFE OF ST. FRANCIS. Compare the words of Bonaventura in introducing the life of St. Dominic, XII, 31–45.

31. *the Bride:* The Church.

32. *crying from on high: Matthew,* XXVII. 46, 50; *Mark* XV, 34, 37; *Luke,* XXIII, 46; and *John,* XIX, 26–30; all record Christ's dying cries upon the cross.

34. *two Princes, one on either side:* St. Dominic and St. Francis. Dominic, on one side (line 39 equates his wisdom with the cherubic), by his wisdom and doctrinal clarity made the church secure within itself by helping to defend it against error and heresy. Francis, on the other hand (line 37 ascribes to him seraphic ardor of love), set the example that made her more faithfully the bride of Christ.

43–51. ASSISI AND THE BIRTH OF ST. FRANCIS. The passage, in Dante's characteristic topophiliac style, is full of local allusions, not all of them relevant to St. Francis, but all describing the situation of Assisi, his birthplace. Perugia stands to the east of the upper Tiber. The Tiber at this point runs approximately north to south. Mt. Subasio, a long and many spurred crest, runs roughly parallel to the Tiber on the west. Assisi is on the side of Subasio, and it was from Assisi that the sun of St. Francis rose to the world, as "this one" (the actual sun in which Dante and Aquinas are standing) rises from the Ganges. The upper Ganges crosses the Tropic of Cancer, the line of the summer solstice. When the sun rises from the Ganges, therefore, it is at its brightest.

the Tupino: Skirts Mt. Subasio on the south and flows roughly west into the Tiber. *the little race:* The Chiascio [KYAH-show] flows south along the length of Subasio and empties into the Tupino below Assisi. *blessèd Ubaldo:* St. Ubaldo (1084–1160), Bishop of Gubbio from 1129. He chose a hill near Gubbio as a hermitage in which to end his days, but died before he could retire there. *Porta Sole:* Perugia's west gate. It faces Mt. Subasio; in summer its slopes reflect the sun's ray through Porta Sole; in winter, covered with snow, they send the cold wind. *Nocera* [NAW-teheh-ra], *Gualdo* [GWAHL-doe]: Towns on the other side of (behind) Subasio. Their heavy yoke may be their subjugation by Perugia, or Dante may have meant by it the taxes imposed by Robert of Naples and his Spanish brigands.

51–54. It is such passages that certify the failures of all translation. *Ascesi,* which can mean "I have risen," was a common name for Assisi in Dante's day. *Oriente,* of course, is the point at which the sun rises. Let no man, therefore, call Assisi "I have risen" (i.e., a man has risen), but let him call it, rather, the dawning east of the world (a sun has risen).

55 ff. *yet far distant:* While he was still young. The phrasing continues the figure of the new-risen sun.

Francis, born Bernardone, was the son of a relatively prosperous merchant and, early in life, assisted his father. In a skirmish between Assisi and Perugia he was taken prisoner and later released. On his return to Assisi (he was then twenty-four) he abandoned all worldly affairs and gave himself entirely to religious works.

a boy yet: Here, as in line 55, Aquinas is overdoing it a bit: twenty-four is a bit old for being a boy yet. *that lady:* Poverty. *his own father's wrath:* In 1207 (Francis was then twenty-five) he sold one of his father's horses along with a load of bread and gave the money to a church. In a rage, his father forced the church to return the money, called Francis before the Bishop of Assisi, and there demanded that he renounce his right to inherit. Francis not only agreed gladly but removed his clothes and gave them back to his father saying, "Until this hour I called you my father on earth; from this hour I can say in full truth 'our Father which art in Heaven.'"

he married: In his "Hymn to Poverty" Francis himself celebrated his union to Poverty as a marriage. He had married her before the diocesan court of Assisi, *et coram patre* (before the court, i.e., in the legal presence of, his father). The marriage was solemnized by his renunciation of all possessions.

64–66. *her First Groom:* Christ. *he:* St. Francis.

68. *Amyclas:* Lucan reported (see also *Convivio,* IV, 13) how the fisherman Amyclas lay at his ease on a bed of seaweed before Caesar himself, being so poor that he had nothing to fear from any man. Not even this report of the serenity Mistress Poverty could bring to a man, and not even the fact that she outdid even Mary in constancy, climbing the very cross with Christ, had moved any man to seek her in marriage.

79. *Bernard:* Bernard di Quintavalle, a wealthy neighbor, became the first disciple of Francis, kicking off his shoes to go barefoot in imitation of the master.

82–84. *unknown:* To men. Holy Poverty is the wealth none recognize, the plentitude none try. *Egidius . . . Sylvester:* The third and fourth disciples of Francis. Peter, the second disciple, seems not to have been known to Dante. *the groom:* Francis. *the bride:* Poverty.

87. *the humble cord:* Now a symbol of the Franciscans but then in general use by the poor as a makeshift belt.

88. *grieve:* At his humble origins.

93. *his order first received the seal:* In 1210. But Innocent III thought the proposed rule of the order so harsh that he granted only provisional approval.

96. *among the seraphim:* In the Empyrean, rather than in this Fourth Heaven.

97–99. *Honorius . . . second crown:* In 1223, Pope Honorius III gave his fully solemnized approval of the Franciscan Order.

100–105. In 1219, St. Francis and eleven of his followers made missionary pilgrimage to Greece and Egypt. Dante, whose facts are not entirely accurate, may have meant that pilgrimage; or he may have meant Francis's projected journey to convert the Moors (1214–1215) when Francis fell ill in southern Spain and had to give up his plans.

106–108. In 1224, on a crag of Mt. Alverna (on the summit of which the Franciscans have reared a commemorative chapel), St. Francis received the stigmata in a rapturous vision of Christ. He wore the wound two years before his death in 1226, at the age of (probably) forty-four.

109–117. The central reference here is to Dame Poverty. *her bosom:* The bare ground of Poverty. *no other resting place:* Than in the bare ground.

119. *his fellow helmsman:* St. Dominic. *Peter's ship:* The Church.

121–132. THE DEGENERACY OF THE DOMINICANS IN DANTE'S TIME. Aquinas was a Dominican. As a master touch to symbolize the harmony of Heaven and the unity of Franciscans and Dominicans, Dante puts into the mouth of a Dominican the praise of the life of St. Francis. That praise ended, he chooses the Dominican to lament the degeneracy of the order. In XII, Dante will have the Franciscan, St. Bonaventure, praise the life of St. Dominic and lament the degeneracy of the Franciscans.

122. *his command:* The rule of the Dominicans. *will fill his hold:* With the treasures of Paradise. Dante is carrying forward the helmsman metaphor of lines 118–120, though the ship is now commanded by a patriarch. Typically, the figure changes at once to a shepherd-and-flock metaphor.

136. *in part:* In X, 95–96, in identifying himself as a Domini-

can, Aquinas said the Dominican rule "leads to where all plenty is" unless the lamb itself stray to "bare rock." In lines 25–26, above, he refers to these words and also to his earlier statements (X, 114) about Solomon's wisdom (that "no mortal ever rose to equal this one"). What he has now finished saying about the degeneracy of the Dominicans will satisfy part of Dante's wish (about "plenty" and "bare rock"). The other part of his wish (about "no mortal ever rose to equal this one") will be satisfied later.

137. *the good plant:* Of the Dominican rule strictly observed.

Canto XXXIII
The Empyrean
St. Bernard • Prayer to the Virgin • The Vision of God

St. Bernard offers a lofty *Prayer to the Virgin,* asking her to intercede in Dante's behalf, and in answer Dante feels his soul swell with new power and grow calm in rapture as his eyes are permitted the Direct Vision of God.

There can be no measure of how long the vision endures. It passes, and Dante is once more mortal and fallible. Raised by God's presence, he had looked into the Mystery and had begun to understand its power and majesty. Returned to himself, there is no power in him capable of speaking the truth of what he saw. Yet the impress of the truth is stamped upon his soul, which he now knows will return to be one with God's Love.

"Virgin Mother, daughter of thy son;
　humble beyond all creatures and more exalted;
　predestined turning point to God's intention; 　3

thy merit so ennobled human nature
　that its divine Creator did not scorn
　to make Himself the creature of His creature. 　6

The Love that was rekindled in Thy womb
　sends forth the warmth of the eternal peace
　within whose ray this flower has come to bloom. 　9

Here, to us, thou art the noon and scope
　of Love revealed; and among mortal men,
　the living fountain of eternal hope. 　12

Lady, thou art so near God's reckonings
　that who seeks grace and does not first seek thee
　would have his wish fly upward without wings. 　15

Not only does thy sweet benignity
　flow out to all who beg, but oftentimes
　thy charity arrives before the plea. 　18

In thee is pity, in thee munificence,
　in thee the tenderest heart, in thee unites
　all that creation knows of excellence! 　21

Now comes this man who from the final pit
　of the universe up to this height has seen,
　one by one, the three lives of the spirit. 　24

He prays to thee in fervent supplication
　for grace and strength, that he may raise his eyes
　to the all-healing final revelation. 　27

And I, who never more desired to see
　the vision myself than I do that he may see It,
　add my own prayer, and pray that it may be 　30

enough to move you to dispel the trace
　of every mortal shadow by thy prayers
　and let him see revealed the Sum of Grace. 　33

I pray thee further, all-persuading Queen,
　keep whole the natural bent of his affections
　and of his powers after his eyes have seen. 　36

Protect him from the stirrings of man's clay;
　see how Beatrice and the blessèd host
　clasp reverent hands to join me as I pray." 　39

The eyes that God reveres and loves the best
　glowed on the speaker, making clear the joy
　with which true prayer is heard by the most blest. 　42

Those eyes turned then to the Eternal Ray,
　through which, we must indeed believe, the eyes
　of others do not find such ready way. 　45

And I, who neared the goal of all my nature,
　felt my soul, at the climax of its yearning,
　suddenly, as it ought, grow calm with rapture. 　48

Bernard then, smiling sweetly, gestured to me
　to look up, but I had already become
　within myself all he would have me be. 　51

Little by little as my vision grew
　it penetrated further through the aura
　of the high lamp which in Itself is true 　54

What then I saw is more than tongue can say.
　Our human speech is dark before the vision.
　The ravished memory swoons and falls away. 　57

As one who sees in dreams and wakes to find
　the emotional impression of his vision
　still powerful while its parts fade from his mind— 　60

just such am I, having lost nearly all
　the vision itself, while in my heart I feel
　the sweetness of it yet distill and fall. 　63

So, in the sun, the footprints fade from snow.

On the wild wind that bore the tumbling
    leaves
    the Sybil's oracles were scattered so. 66

O Light Supreme who doth Thyself withdraw
    so far above man's mortal understanding,
    lend me again some glimpse of what I saw; 69

make Thou my tongue so eloquent it may
    of all Thy glory speak a single clue
    to those who follow me in the world's day; 72

for by returning to my memory
    somewhat, and somewhat sounding in these
      verses,
    Thou shalt show man more of Thy victory. 75

So dazzling was the splendor of that Ray,
    that I must certainly have lost my senses
    had I, but for an instant, turned away. 78

And so it was, as I recall, I could
    the better bear to look, until at last
    my vision made one with the Eternal Good. 81

Oh grace abounding that had made me fit
    to fix my eyes on the eternal light
    until my vision was consumed in it! 84

I saw within Its depth how It conceives
    all things in a single volume bound by Love,
    of which the universe is the scattered leaves; 87

substance, accident, and their relation
    so fused that all I say could do no more
    than yield a glimpse of that bright revelation. 90

I think I saw the universal form
    that binds these things, for as I speak these
      words
    I feel my joy swell and my spirits warm. 93

Twenty-five centuries since Neptune saw
    the Argo's keel have not moved all mankind,
    recalling that adventure, to such awe 96

as I felt in an instant. My tranced being
    stared fixed and motionless upon that vision,
    ever more fervent to see in the act of seeing. 99

Experiencing that Radiance, the spirit
    is so indrawn it is impossible
    even to think of ever turning from It. 102

For the good which is the will's ultimate object
    is all subsumed in It; and, being removed,
    all is defective which in It is perfect. 105

Now in my recollection of the rest
    I have less power to speak than any infant
    wetting its tongue yet at its mother's breast; 108

and not because that Living Radiance bore
    more than one semblance, for It is
      unchanging
    and is forever as it was before; 111

rather, as I grew worthier to see,
    the more I looked, the more unchanging
      semblance
    appeared to change with every change 114
      in me.

Within the depthless deep and clear existence
    of that abyss of light three circles shown—
    three in color, one in circumference: 117

the second from the first, rainbow from
      rainbow;
    the third, an exhalation of pure fire
    equally breathed forth by the other two. 120

But oh how much my words miss my
      conception,
    which is itself so far from what I saw
    that to call it feeble would be rank 123
      deception!

O Light Eternal fixed in Itself alone,
    by Itself alone understood, which from Itself
    loves and glows, self-knowing and self- 126
      known;

that second aureole which shone forth in Thee,
    conceived as a reflection of the first—
    or which appeared so to my scrutiny— 129

seemed in Itself of Its own coloration
    to be painted with man's image. I fixed my
      eyes
    on that alone in rapturous contemplation. 132

Like a geometer wholly dedicated
    to squaring the circle, but who cannot find,
    think as he may, the principle indicated— 135

so did I study the supernal face.
    I yearned to know just how our image
      merges
    into that circle, and how it there finds place; 138

but mine were not the wings for such a flight.
    Yet, as I wished, the truth I wished for came
    cleaving my mind in a great flash of light. 141

Here my powers rest from their high fantasy,
    but already I could feel my being turned—
    instinct and intellect balanced equally 144

as in a wheel whose motion nothing jars—
by the Love that moves the Sun and the other
      stars.

NOTES

1–39. ST. BERNARD'S PRAYER TO THE VIRGIN MARY. No reader who has come this far will need a lengthy gloss of Bernard's prayer. It can certainly be taken as a summarizing statement of the special place of Mary in Catholic faith. For the rest only a few turns of phrase need underlining. 3. *predestined turning point of God's intention:* All-forseeing God built his whole scheme for mankind with Mary as its pivot, for through her He would become man. 7. *The Love that was rekindled in thy womb:* God. In a sense he withdrew from man when Adam and Eve sinned. In Mary He returned and Himself became man. 35. *keep whole the natural bent of his affections:* Bernard is asking Mary to protect Dante lest the intensity of the vision overpower his faculties. 37. *Protect him from the stirrings of man's clay:* Protect him from the stirrings of base human impulse, especially from pride, for Dante is about to receive a grace never before granted to any man and the thought of such glory might well move a mere mortal to an hybris that would turn glory to sinfullness.

40. *the eyes:* Of Mary.

50. *but I had already become:* i.e., "But I had already fixed my entire attention upon the vision of God." But if so, how could Dante have seen Bernard's smile and gesture? Eager students like to believe they catch Dante in a contradiction here. Let them bear in mind that Dante is looking directly at God, as do the souls of Heaven, who thereby acquire—insofar as they are able to contain it—God's own knowledge. As a first stirring of that heavenly power, therefore, Dante is sharing God's knowledge of St. Bernard.

54. *which in Itself is true:* The light of God is the one light whose source is Itself. All others are a reflection of this.

65–66. *tumbling leaves . . . oracles:* The Cumean Sybil (Virgil describes her in *Aeneid,* III, 441 ff.) wrote her oracles on leaves, one letter to a leaf, then sent her message scattering on the wind. Presumably, the truth was all contained in that strew, could one only gather all the leaves and put the letters in the right order.

76–81. How can a light be so dazzling that the beholder would swoon if he looked away for an instant? Would it not be, rather, in looking at, not away from, the overpowering vision that the viewer's senses would be overcome? So it would be on earth. But now Dante, with the help of all heaven's prayers, is in the presence of God and strengthened by all he sees. It is by being so strengthened that he can see yet more. So the passage becomes a parable of grace. Stylistically it once more illustrates Dante's genius: even at this height of concept, the poet can still summon and invent new perceptions, subtlety exfoliating from subtlety.

The simultaneous metaphoric statement, of course, is that no man can lose his good in the vision of God, but only in looking away from it.

85–87. The idea here is Platonic: the essence of all things (form) exists in the mind of God. All other things exist as exempla.

88. *substance:* Matter, all that exists in itself. *accident:* All that exists as a phase of matter.

92. *these things:* Substance and accident.

109–114. In the presence of God the soul grows ever more capable of perceiving God. Thus, the worthy soul's experience of God is a constant expansion of awareness. God appears to change as He is better seen. Being perfect, He is changeless within himself, for any change would be away from perfection.

130–144. The central metaphor of the entire *Comedy* is the image of God and the final triumphant in Godding of the elected soul returning to its Maker. On the mystery of that image, the metaphoric symphony of the *Comedy* comes to rest.

In the second aspect of Trinal-unity, in the circle reflected from the first, Dante thinks he sees the image of mankind woven into the very substance and coloration of God. He turns the entire attention of his soul to that mystery, as a geometer might seek to shut out every other thought and dedicate himself to squaring the circle. In *Il Convivio,* II, 14, Dante asserted that the circle could not be squared, but that impossibility had not yet been firmly demonstrated in Dante's time and mathematicians still worked at the problem. Note, however, that Dante assumes the impossibility of squaring the circle as a weak mortal example of mortal impossibility. How much more impossible, he implies, to resolve the mystery of God, study as man will.

The mystery remains beyond Dante's mortal power. Yet, there in Heaven, in a moment of grace, God revealed the truth to him in a flash of light—revealed it, that is, to the God-enlarged power of Dante's emparadised soul. On Dante's return to the mortal life, the details of that revelation vanished from his mind but the force of the revelation survives in its power on Dante's feelings.

So ends the vision of the *Comedy,* and yet the vision endures, for ever since that revelation, Dante tells us, he feels his soul turning ever as one with the perfect motion of God's love.

INTERLUDE

Abelard and Heloise

Well before the first real stirrings of the Renaissance there lived and loved Peter Abelard and Heloise, about whom Etienne Gilson wrote: "This story of flesh and blood, carried along by a passion at once brutal and ardent to its celebrated conclusion, we know from within, as, indeed, we know few others. Its heroes observe themselves, analyze themselves as only Christian consciences fallen prey can do it. Nor do they merely analyze themselves, but they talk about themselves as well. What Renaissance autobiographies can be compared with the correspondence of Abelard and Heloise?"

Beyond the forceful portraits of their personalities reflected in their letters to each other, the story of Heloise and Abelard is significant for the times in which they lived, the myth their story generated, and the people with whom they had contact during their stormy careers. Peter Abelard (1079–1142) can be described as the single most important personality in establishing 12th-century Paris as the university center of Europe. Among his many books, his *Sic et Non* (*Yes and No*) marks the beginning of the application of dialects to theology, permitting the rise of the whole scholastic movement in philosophy and theology. Both Heloise and Abelard crossed paths (and, on occasion, intellectual swords) with some of the most notable figures of the time. Abelard had a noteworthy antagonist in Bernard of Clairvaux, the most influential churchman and theologian of the century. For a time Abelard was a monk at the famous abbey of Saint Denis in Paris when its fortunes were being guided by the celebrated Abbot Suger, the founder of Gothic architecture. Both Heloise and Abelard had been friendly with Peter the Venerable; Abelard, in fact, was sheltered at Peter's abbey of Cluny at the end of his life. When Abelard died it was Peter who sent the body to Heloise for burial. Subsequent centuries would look back on their story and create from it a whole fabric legend that would inevitably color our understanding and change our perception of what the 12th century was all about. Today scholars are beginning better to understand Abelard and his place in medieval intellectual life, but for two hundred years people of many diverse backgrounds have been far more interested in the complexities of the couple's "star-crossed" love for each other.

In 1113 Abelard, then nearly 35 years old, began teaching in Paris. His early, stormy career had been marked by clashes with his own teachers and masters, a succession of schools he founded in various towns outside Paris, and a physical breakdown triggered by his own overwrought activity. Shortly after Abelard began his Paris career he was the most sought-after and lionized teacher in the city. This brilliant and handsome figure, with his masterful style of lecturing and his easy command of critical analysis, heard of a young girl named Heloise who lived with her uncle, the Canon Fulbert, in the same city. Heloise was distinguished not only for her beauty but also for her learning. For a young girl to have a reputation for scholarly attainment was quite rare, given the limited opportunities for female education in the period. Although certain noblewomen and a few cloistered nuns could make claim to an education, it was virtually unheard of for a girl still in her teens to have an arts education. In a letter to Heloise many years later Peter the Venerable (himself a student in Paris during Abelard's period there) would remember this about her: "When wisdom has difficulty in finding a haven—I will not say among the female sex, from where it is utterly banished, but even in the minds of men— your burning zeal has raised you above all women, and there are few men whom you have not surpassed."

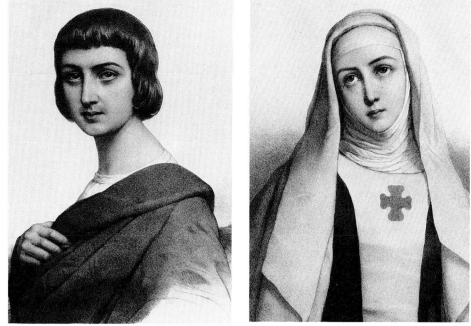

"Portraits" of Abelard and Heloise. 19th-century engravings by Grevedon. Bibliothèque Nationale, Paris. An excellent illustration of the sentimental regard the Romantics had for the medieval couple. Abelard—35 when he met Heloise—is depicted as a youth and Heloise is presented as a demure nun living as a "prisoner of love."

Abelard's interest in Heloise could hardly be called strictly academic, although it was her reputation as an intellectual that had first piqued his rather egocentric curiosity. With some calculation, Abelard took rooms at Canon Fulbert's house. It was an easy thing to do; the canon was greedy for more income and hopeful that a noted scholar would consent to tutor his precocious niece. With the handsome professor and the beautiful young girl under the same roof, the outcome was predictable. Abelard, never reticent in these matters, describes it.

> We were first together in one house and then one in mind. Under the pretext of work we made ourselves entirely free for love and the pursuit of her studies provided the secret privacy which love desired. We opened our books but more words of love than of the lessons asserted themselves. There was more kissing than teaching; my hands found themselves at her breasts more often than on the book. Love brought us to gaze into each other's eyes more than reading kept them on the text. . . . No sign of love was omitted by us in our ardor and whatever unusual love could devise, that was added too. And the more such delights were new to us, the more ardently we indulged in them, and the less did we experience satiety.

Heloise became pregnant and Abelard sent her to his family home, where she bore him a son whom they named Peter Astralabe. Heloise's uncle, wild with grief and shame over the affair, demanded satisfaction. Abelard brought Heloise back to Paris and proposed marriage in order to placate the irate canon. Heloise refused the offer with a long philosophical argument studded with citations from Holy Scripture, Saint Jerome, and Saint Augustine, as well as Seneca and Socrates. Her reasoning, basically, was that the married life was incompatible with the scholarly life: "What," Heloise asked, "could be in common between scholars and wet nurses, writing desks and cradles, books, writing tablets, and distaffs, styles, pens, and spindles? Or who is there who is bent on sacred or philosophical reflections who could bear the wailing of babies, the silly lullabies of nurses to quiet them, the noisy herd of servants, both male and female; who could endure the constant degrading defilement of infants?" (Though her tone was vastly different, another Frenchwoman, but of our century, Simone de Beauvoir, used the same argument to the philosopher Jean-Paul Sartre when he suggested marriage: "I saw," Beauvoir wrote in her autobiography, "what it was costing Sartre to say goodbye to travel and freedom and youth in order to become a provincial schoolmaster and finally and conclusively, an adult. Joining the ranks of the married would have been a further renunciation.")

Despite the intellectual resistance of Heloise, the two were married in Paris in the presence of the uncle and his friends. Fulbert made the news of the marriage public—something the couple did not want—and, as a consequence, Abelard persuaded Heloise to seek the security of a nearby convent. Abelard, betrayed by a servant, was ambushed by the cohorts of the indignant uncle who, as an act of fearful revenge for the seeming repudiation of his niece, assaulted and castrated him.

After this horrendous incident Heloise entered permanently into the monastic life of the convent. She finally settled in a religious house as its superior—a house Abelard had originally founded as a hostel for students. She remained as superior of this convent until her death. In her mature years Heloise wrote Abelard telling him of the sacrifice that life in the convent had brought her, frank confession that more than any other incident in their story created the later romantic legend about the couple. The letters between Heloise and Abelard reveal a bitterly human exchange of accusation ("Tell me if you can why after the two of us embraced the religious life—a decision which was yours alone—I had neither your presence to fortify me nor even a letter to console me in my loneliness?" asks Heloise), guilt ("Shall I remind you," asks Abelard, "of our early defilements, of the shameful licentiousness which preceded our marriage, the base treachery I inflicted on your uncle by so brazenly seducing you at a time when I was his guest and table companion?"), and unabashed lust ("The sensual delights which we enjoyed together were so dear to me that I cannot help loving the memory of them and am quite unable to erase them from my mind. . . . I ought to groan at the sins which I have perpetrated yet I sigh for those which I am unable to commit.").

Abelard's subsequent life was marked by restlessness and turmoil. After Heloise became a nun, he entered the famous Parisian monastery of Saint Denis, but left when the monks threatened him because of his suggestion—correct, as it turns out—that their patron saint was not the Saint Denis who wrote the famous mystical treatises so much revered in the medieval period. He founded the hostel of the Paraclete in 1125 after having been censured as a heretic by a cabal of his enemies at Soissons in 1121. From the Paraclete he went to Brittany, where he served as abbot of a monastery. His return to teaching brought him into conflict with the famous Saint Bernard of Clairvaux, who was responsible for Abelard's condemnation at the Council of Sens in 1141. Abelard, appealing the condemnation to the pope, found temporary refuge at the famous abbey of Cluny under the patronage of its abbot, Peter the Venerable. A year later Abelard died. In an exquisite gesture of friendship, Peter sent his body back to Heloise, who had it interred at the Paraclete. When she herself died at this religious center in 1164, the nuns wrote in their book of necrology that their late lamented foundress had been "renowned for her learning and piety, having given us the hope of her life. . . ."

Despite the high drama of their life, the story of Heloise and Abelard held few attractions for the people of the later Middle Ages. Jean de Meun did tell the story of the two lovers in *The Romance of the Rose,* an immensely popular 13th-century love poem, but his purpose was to use the story as an example of the dangers of marriage. Chaucer's wife of Bath makes a passing reference to Heloise in *The Canterbury Tales,* and Petrarch had a copy of their letters, but by and large their story was obscured as the Renaissance turned away from the happenings of the medieval world. It was inevitable that the more sophisticated world of the 18th-century Enlightenment would see Abelard as a champion of intellectual freedom and Heloise as a romantic lover as well as a victim of circumstance.

The story of Heloise and Abelard kindled an intense curiosity combined with a wave of sentimental enthusiasm for these now-famous lovers. The graves of the pair—still at the Paraclete in this period—became a tourist attraction of some repute in late-18th-century travels. In 1802 the remains of the lovers were transferred to Paris and housed in a rather strange "Museum of French Monuments" built to preserve cultural monuments threatened by the egalitarian zeal of the French Revolution. The monument to Heloise and Abelard, constructed by the founder of the museum, Alexander Lenoir, consisted of an elaborate tomb housed in a small chapel with a rather dramatic inscription carved in Greek over the chapel doors: "Forever United."

In 1815 the remains of the pair were again moved, this time to that most curious of European cemeteries, Père Lachaise in Paris. The burial chapel became a required pilgrimage spot for admirers and romantics of the 19th century, just as admirers go today to Père Lachaise to leave a rose at the grave of Jim Morrison of the rock group The Doors or the tomb of Edith Piaf the singer. The decidedly unromantic American humorist and novelist Mark Twain could write in *Innocents Abroad* (1869) that "Go when you will, you find somebody snuffling over that tomb. Go when you will, you find it furnished with those bouquets and *immortèles*."

The legend of Heloise and Abelard has been kept alive in this century through the agency of both novel and drama. George Moore's *Heloise and Abelard* (1921) was in keeping with the Celtic romanticism of the author himself. Moore depicted Abelard as a thinker, musician, lover, and victim—all characteristics the author attributed to himself. Heloise was depicted as a semipagan given to a wild capacity for love and nature, nurtured more on the classics than on the constrictive tradition of the medieval Church. Helen Waddell's *Peter Abelard* (1933) is a much more satisfactory novel. The author, an eminent medievalist, had a better grasp of the milieu of the Middle Ages. Her eye for detail gives the picture of an era which is more faithful to the original than Moore's. For all of that, the novel has been written not from the presuppositions of the 12th century, but against the background of two hundred years of a sentimental legend about the lovers as well as the Freudianism of our time. This novel has been influential in our perception of Abelard and Heloise. That Heloise should exalt a moment of passion that transcends the boundaries of time— that provides an "eternity"—is a sentiment about ecstasy with which the modern temper can identify; it is not a very convincing evocation of the medieval understanding of the nature of reality.

Further Reading

Gilson, Etienne. *Heloise and Abelard*. Translated by L. K. Shook. Ann Arbor: University of Michigan, 1961. A work that defends the authenticity of the couple's letters, it is also one of the classic studies of Heloise and Abelard.

Muckle, J. T. (trans.). *The Story of Abelard's Adversities*. Toronto: Pontifical Institute of Medieval Studies, 1954. A translation of Abelard's "autobiography" with an excellent introduction. The other letters of the couple are also to appear in this series. They are currently available in Muckle's edition in *Medieval Studies* (1950, 1953, 1955).

Pernoud, Regine. *Heloise and Abelard*. Translated by Peter Wiles. New York: Stein & Day, 1973. A very readable study of the couple written for a nonscholarly audience. There is a bibliography but the translator did not revise it for an English audience.

Robertson, D. W. *Abelard and Heloise*. New York: Dial, 1972. The best book on the pair from the humanistic perspective. Robertson traces their story from its origin down to the present age. Indispensable.

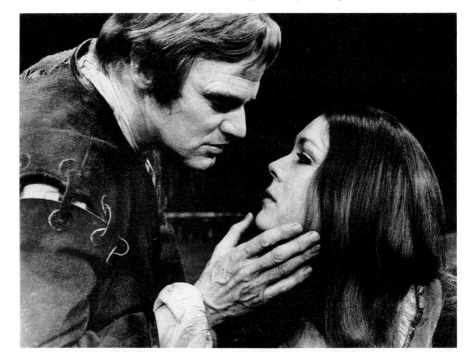

Diana Rigg as Heloise and Keith Mitchell as Abelard in Ronald Millar's stage adaptation of the novel by Helen Waddell. Los Angeles, 1971.

GENERAL EVENTS	LITERATURE & PHILOSOPHY	ART

13th cent. Dependence on Byzantine models in Italian painting

c. 1280–1290 Cimabue, *Madonna Enthroned; Crucifix*, Arezzo

1299 Ottoman Turk dynasty founded

1300 Pope Boniface VIII proclaims first Jubilee Year ("Holy Year")

c. 1300 New naturalism in Italian painting appears with work of Giotto

1303 Philip the Fair of France humiliates Pope Boniface VIII

c. 1303–1321 Dante, *Divine Comedy*

1305–1306 Giotto, Arena Chapel frescoes

c. 1308–1311 Duccio, *Maestà* altarpiece, Siena

1309

1309 "Babylonian Captivity" of the papacy at Avignon begins

c. 1310 G. Pisano completes Pisa Cathedral pulpit; Giotto, *Madonna Enthroned*

1326 Earliest known use of cannon

1333 Martini, *Annunciation*

1337–1453 "Hundred Years' War" between France and England

1338–1339 A. Lorenzetti, *Good Government* fresco, Siena

1346–1378 Reign of Charles IV, Holy Roman emperor

1346 English defeat French at Crécy

c. 1347–1360 Prague, as residence of Charles IV, becomes major art center

1348 Bubonic plague depopulates Europe

1348–1352 Boccaccio, *Decameron*, collection of tales

c. 1350–1360 Unknown Bohemian Master, *Death of the Virgin*

1356 English defeat French at Poitiers

after 1350 Petrarch compiles *Canzoniere*, collection of poems

1358 Revolt of lower classes (*Jacquerie*) in France

c. 1370 Saint Catherine of Siena urges end of "Babylonian Captivity"

1363–1404 Reign of Philip the Bold, duke of Burgundy

c. 1363 Court of dukes of Burgundy at Dijon becomes important center of International Style

1373 Petrarch, *Letter to Posterity*, autobiography

1376 Popes return to Rome from Avignon

1377

1377–1399 Reign of Richard II in England

c. 1377 Wycliff active in English church reform; translates Bible into English

c. 1377–1413 *Wilton Diptych*

1378 "Great Schism" begins

1381 Peasant riots ("Wat Tyler Rebellion") in England

c. 1385–1400 Chaucer, *The Canterbury Tales*, collection of tales

1395–1399 Broederlam, *Presentation in the Temple and Flight into Egypt*

1399–1413 Reign of Henry IV in England

1395–1406 Sluter, *Well of Moses*

1413 English defeat French at Agincourt

1413–1416 Limbourg Brothers, illustrations for *Très Riches Heures du Duc de Berry*

1417 Council of Constance ends "Great Schism" with election of Pope Martin V

LATE MIDDLE AGES / PROTO-RENAISSANCE

"Babylonian Captivity" of the Papacy

The Great Schism

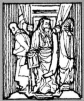

9

The 14th Century: A Time of Transition

1288–1309 Palazzo Pubblico, Siena

1295 Santa Croce, Florence, begun

1296 Florence Cathedral (Duomo) begun

1298 Palazzo Vecchio, Florence, begun

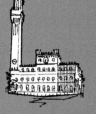

14th cent. Secular music flourishes

1325 Vitry, *Ars Nova Musicae*, treatise describing new system of musical notation

1332–1357 Gloucester Cathedral choir ("Perpendicular" style)

after 1337 Machaut, *Messe de Notre Dame*, polyphonic setting of the Ordinary of the Mass

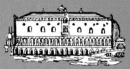

c. 1345–1438 Doge's Palace, Venice

c. 1350 Landini famous in Florence as performer and composer of madrigals and ballads

1386 Duomo of Milan begun

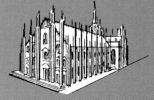

Calamity, Decay, and Violence

The 14th century (often called the *Trecento,* Italian for "thirteen hundred") is usually described by historians as the age that marks the end of the medieval period and the beginning of the Renaissance in Western Europe. If we accept this rather neat description of the period we should expect to see strong elements of the medieval sensibility as well as some stirrings of the "new birth" (*Renaissance*) of culture that was the hallmark of 15th-century European life. We must be cautious, however, about expecting the break between "medieval" and "Renaissance" to be clean and dramatic. History does not usually work with the precision employed by the historians. Nor should we expect to see cultural history moving upward in a straight line toward greater modernity or greater perfection. In fact, the 14th century was a period of unparalleled natural calamity, institutional decay, and cruel violence.

The Black Death

Midway through the century, in 1348, bubonic plague swept through Europe in a virulent epidemic that killed untold numbers of people and upset trade, culture, and daily life in ways hard for us to imagine.

It has been estimated that some cities in Italy lost as much as two-thirds of their population in that year.

One prominent figure who lived through that devastation was the Italian writer Giovanni Boccaccio (1313–1375). His great collection of stories, the *Decameron,* has a plague setting. A group of young men and women flee Florence to avoid the plague; during their ten days' sojourn in the country (*Decameron* is Greek for "ten days") they amuse each other by the telling of stories. Each of the ten young people tells a story on each of the ten days. The resulting one hundred stories constitute a brilliant collection of folk tales, *fabliaux* (ribald fables), *exempla* (moral stories), and romances Boccaccio culled from the oral and written traditions of Europe. Because of their romantic elements, earthiness, and somewhat shocking bawdiness the *Decameron* has often been called the "Human Comedy" to contrast it with the lofty moral tone of Dante's epic work of an earlier generation.

However delightful and pleasing those stories are to read, they stand in sharp contrast to the horrific picture Boccaccio draws of the plague in his introduction to the *Decameron.* Boccaccio's account has the ring of authenticity. He had been an eyewitness to the events he describes. His vivid prose gives some small sense of what the plague must have been like for a people who possessed only the most rudimentary knowledge of medicine and no knowledge at all about the source of illness and disease.

EAST MEETS WEST

The Crusades

It has been suggested that the plague that decimated Europe in 1348 was first introduced into Europe by Crusaders returning from the East who in the 1330s brought the disease into Constantinople, from whence it spread west. That theory is not accepted by all scholars, but the Crusades—the numerous military expeditions against the Muslims who controlled the Holy Places in Jerusalem—which began in the 12th century and took place intermittently until the end of the 13th century (with others encouraged as late as the 15th century) had an enormous impact on European culture. The purpose of the Crusader was to recapture the Holy Places from the Infidel (nonbeliever), while the purpose of the wars of the Muslims in the West was to spread the religion of Islam to those they also saw as infidels. Wars of religion sadly take on a peculiar ferocity because of the devotion they inspire in the warriors themselves.

Great port cities on the Mediterranean such as Venice flourished as a result of the crusading enterprise. They were not only enriched by servicing the crusade fleets but also became active links between the West and the East. The European taste for spices, silks, and other wares not only encouraged East–West trade but were a factor in encouraging exploration. (Remember that Columbus sailed from Spain to find a sure trade route to India.) The Crusades also forged, however unwittingly, another link with the culture of Islam so that the crusade routes also became a pathway for books, ideas, and artistic advances. This cross-fertilization of cultures was helped by the presence of Italian traders and merchants who had established themselves in Palestine, Lebanon, and Syria, where they remained even after the last formal crusades in the late 13th century.

The Crusades took a terrible toll on the vitality of the Byzantine Empire in the East. When Christian Constantinople fell to the Turks in the 15th century it had conquered an empire weakened by centuries of fighting. One paradoxical result of the Crusades, lasting to this day, was the Islamization of Constantinople (now Istanbul) and the export of Greek culture from that city to the West.

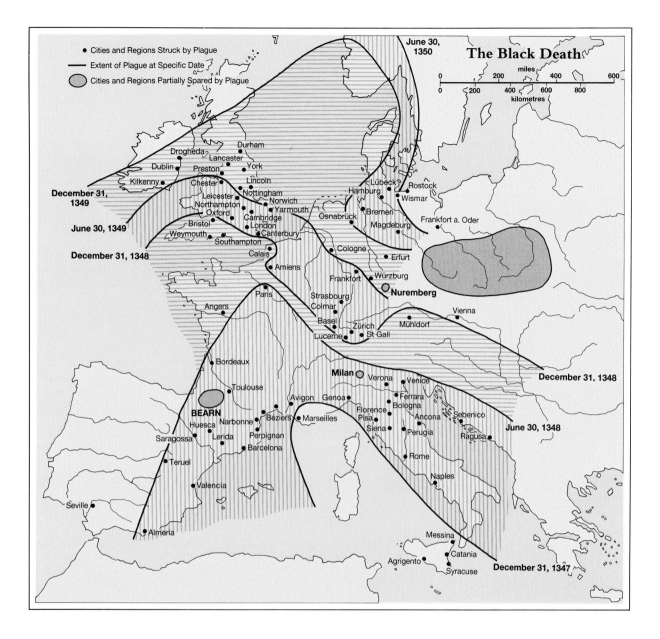

The following labels appear on the map:

The Black Death

- Cities and Regions Struck by Plague
- Extent of Plague at Specific Date
- Cities and Regions Partially Spared by Plague

miles
0 — 200 — 400 — 600

kilometres
0 — 200 — 400 — 600 — 800

June 30, 1350

December 31, 1349

June 30, 1349

December 31, 1348

December 31, 1348

June 30, 1348

December 31, 1347

Drogheda, Durham, Lancaster, Dublin, Preston, York, Kilkenny, Chester, Lincoln, Nottingham, Leicester, Norwich, Northampton, Oxford, Yarmouth, Cambridge, Bristol, London, Weymouth, Canterbury, Southampton, Calais, Amiens, Paris, Angers, Lübeck, Rostock, Hamburg, Wismar, Bremen, Osnabrück, Magdeburg, Frankfort a. Oder, Cologne, Erfurt, Würzburg, Frankfort, **Nuremberg**, Strasbourg, Colmar, Basel, Zürich, Mühldorf, Lucerne, St Gall, Vienna, Bordeaux, **Milan**, Verona, Venice, Toulouse, Ferrara, Avignon, Genoa, Bologna, **BEARN**, Florence, Ancona, Sebenico, Huesca, Narbonne, Béziers, Marseilles, Pisa, Siena, Perugia, Ragusa, Saragossa, Lerida, Perpignan, Rome, Teruel, Barcelona, Valencia, Naples, Seville, Almeria, Messina, Catania, Agrigento, Syracuse

The Great Schism

Nature was not the only scourge to affect the stability of Europe. The medieval Christian church, that most powerful and permanent large institution in medieval life, underwent convulsive changes in the 14th century, changes that were distant warning signals of the Reformation at the beginning of the 16th century.

A quick look at some dates indicates clearly the nature of these changes. In 1300 Pope Boniface VIII celebrated the great jubilee year at Rome that brought pilgrims and visitors from all over the Christian West to pay homage to the papacy and the church it represented and headed. This event was one of the final symbolic moments of papal supremacy over European life and culture. Within the next three years Philip the Fair of France imprisoned and abused the same pope at the papal palace of Anagni. The pope died as a result of his humiliating encounters with royal power; even Dante's implacable hatred of Boniface could not restrain his outrage at the humiliation of the office of the pope. By 1309 the papacy, under severe pressure from the French, had been removed to Avignon in southern France, where it was to remain for nearly 70 years. In 1378 the papacy was further weakened by the Great Schism, which

John Ball

Good people, things cannot go right in England and never will, until goods are held in common and there are no more villeins [peasants] and gentlefolk. . . . In what way are those whom we call lords greater masters than ourselves? How have they deserved it? If we all spring from a common mother and father, Adam and Eve, how can they claim or prove that they are lords more than us except by making us produce and grow the wealth which they spend?

They are clad in velvet and camlet lined with squirrel and ermine, while we go dressed in coarse cloth.

They have the wines, the spices, and the good bread; we have the rye, the husks, and the straw and we drink water.

They have shelters and ease in their fine manors and we have hardship and toil, the winds and the rains in the fields.

And from us must come, from our labor, the things which keep them in luxury.

We are called serfs and beaten if we are slow in service to them, yet we have no sovereign lord we can complain to; none to hear us and do us justice.

Let us go to the king—he is young—and show him how we are oppressed and tell him how we want things changed or else we will change them ourselves. If we go in good earnest and all together, very many people who are called serfs and are held in subjection will follow us to get their freedom.

When the king hears us he will remedy the evil, willingly or otherwise!

[Sermon of the priest John Ball, a leader in the English Peasant Revolt of 1381, recorded in *The Chronicles* of Froissart]

---

saw European Christianity divided into hostile camps, each of which pledged allegiance to a rival claimant to the papacy. Not until 1417 was this breach in church unity healed; a church council had to depose three papal pretenders to accomplish the reunification of the church.

The general disarray of the church in this period spawned ever more insistent demands for church reforms. Popular literature (as both Boccaccio and, in England, Geoffrey Chaucer, clearly demonstrate) unmercifully satirized the decadence of the church. Great saints like the mystic Catherine of Siena (1347–

EAST MEETS WEST

The Rise of the Ottoman Empire

The problems faced by church leaders in the 14th century were not limited to putting their own affairs in order. The preceding century had seen Western forces involved in the Crusades; in theory these "holy wars" were intended to capture Jerusalem for the West, although their principal practical result was to cause lasting damage to the Byzantine empire. By 1261 Byzantium, center of the Eastern church, was reduced to Constantinople and the land around it.

With the fall of Constantinople in 1291, the last Christian stronghold in the Holy Land, to Egyptian troops, the former Byzantine territories fell into the hands of a new force, that of the Ottoman Turks. The Ottoman dynasty was founded in 1299, and from the beginning the Ottoman sultans showed themselves equally good at winning wars and building a strong, effectively administered state. By the mid-14th century they had conquered most of western Asia Minor (modern Turkey) and had begun to form permanent settlements on the European side of the straits of the Bosporus. Neither Eastern nor Western Christians presented any resistance, and in 1365 the Turks established their capital on European soil at Adrianople.

Within a few years the Turks had driven to the borders of Hungary, and in alarm the pope declared a crusade. A large disorganized Christian army was routed at the battle of Nicopolis in 1396. The Turks might well have gone on to besiege Central Europe, but they themselves were attacked from the east by nomad Mongol troops. It took a generation for the Ottoman rulers to regain control and complete their capture of the Byzantine empire by taking Constantinople in 1453.

Thus in the course of the 14th century a powerful Islamic empire (the Turks had been converted to Islam around A.D. 1000) became established within all too easy reach of the European powers. Most of the connections between Europe and Turkey were to take the form of trade. Venice, in particular, soon developed strong economic ties with Constantinople. Cultural influences were mainly transmitted from West to East, since the Ottoman Turks were more interested in effective organization and in maintaining traditional religious modes than in philosophy, science, or the arts. Indeed, the most profound effect on the West of the Ottoman conquests was that the last generation of Byzantine scholars fled to Western Europe carrying with them their precious manuscripts of Greek texts, which did much to inspire the Renaissance of the 15th century.

1380) wrote impassioned letters to the popes at Avignon in their "Babylonian Captivity" demanding that they return to Rome free from the political ties of the French monarchy. In England, John Wyclif's cries against the immorality of the higher clergy and the corruption of the church fueled indignation at all levels. The famous Peasant Revolt of 1381 was greatly aided by the activism of people aroused by the ideas of Wyclif and his followers.

The 1381 revolt in England was only the last in a series of lower-class revolutions that occurred in the 14th century. The frequency and magnitude of these revolts (like that of the French peasants beginning in 1356) highlight the profound dissatisfactions with the church and the nobility in the period. It is not accidental that the story of Robin Hood, with its theme of violence toward the wealthy and care for the poor, began in the 14th century.

The Hundred Years' War

The terrible violence of the 14th century was caused not only by the alienation of the peasants but also by the Hundred Years' War between France and England. While the famous battles of the period—Poitiers, Crécy, Agincourt—now seem romantic and distant, it is undeniable that they brought unrelieved misery to France for long periods. Between battles, roaming bands of mercenaries pillaged the landscape to make up for their lack of pay. The various battles were terrible in themselves. One example must suffice. According to Jean Froissart's *Chronicles,* the English King Edward III sent a group of his men to examine the battlefield after the battle of Crécy (1346)—in which the English longbowmen slaughtered the more traditionally armed French and mercenary armies: "They passed the whole day upon the field and made a careful report of all they saw. According to their report it appeared that 80 banners, the bodies of 11 princes, 1200 knights, and 30,000 common men were found dead on the field." It is no wonder that Barbara Tuchman's splendid history of life in 14th-century France, *A Distant Mirror* (1978), should have been subtitled "The Calamitous Fourteenth Century."

Literature in Italy, England, and France

Amid the natural and institutional disasters of the 14th century there were signs of intense human creativity in all the arts, especially in literature. In Italy, Dante's literary eminence was secure at the time of his death (1321) and the reputation of Italian letters was further enhanced by two other outstanding Tuscan writers: Francesco Petrarch and Giovanni Boccaccio, famed for the *Decameron*. In England, one of the greatest authors in the history of English letters was active: Geoffrey Chaucer. His life spanned the second half of the 14th century; he died, almost symbolically, in 1400.

Petrarch

It is appropriate to begin a discussion of 14th-century culture with Petrarch. His life spanned the better part of the century (1304–1374) and in that life we can see the conflict between the medieval and early Renaissance ideals being played out.

Petrarch (Petrarca in Italian) was born in Arezzo, a small town in Tuscany south of Florence. As a young man, in obedience to parental wishes, he studied law for a year in France and for three years at the law faculty in Bologna. He abandoned his legal studies immediately after the death of his father to pursue a literary career. To support himself he accepted some minor church offices but was never ordained to the priesthood.

Petrarch made his home at Avignon (and later at a much more isolated spot near that papal city, Vaucluse), but for the greater part of his life he wandered from place to place. He never could settle down; his restlessness prevented him from accepting lucrative positions that would have made him a permanent resident of any one place. He received invitations to serve as secretary to various popes in Avignon and, through the intercession of his close friend Boccaccio, was offered a professorship in Florence. He took none of these positions.

Petrarch was insatiably curious. He fed his love for the ancient classics by searching out and copying ancient manuscripts that had remained hidden and unread in the various monasteries of Europe. It is said that at his death he had one of the finest private libraries in Europe. He wrote volumes of poetry and prose, carried on a vast correspondence, advised the rulers of the age, took a keen interest in horticulture, and kept a wide circle of literary and artistic friends. At his death we know that he possessed pictures by both Simone Martini and Giotto, two of the most influential artists of the time. In 1348 he was crowned poet laureate of Rome, the first artist so honored since the ancient days of Rome.

One true mark of the Renaissance sensibility was a keen interest in the self and an increased thirst for personal glory and fame. Petrarch surely is a 14th-century harbinger of that spirit. Dante's *Divine Comedy* was totally oriented to the next life; the apex of Dante's vision is that of the soul rapt in the vision of God in eternity. Petrarch, profoundly religious, never denied that such a vision was the ultimate goal of life. At the same time, his work exhibits a tension between that goal and his thirst for earthly success and fame. In his famous prose work *Secretum (My Secret),* written in 1343, the artist imagines himself in conversation with Saint Augustine. In a dialogue extraordinary for its sense of self-confession and self-scrutiny Petrarch discusses his moral and intellectual failings, his besetting sins, and his tendency to fall into fits of depression. He agrees with his great hero Augustine that he should be less concerned with his intellectual labors and the fame that derives from them and concern himself more with salvation and the spiritual perfection of his life. However, Petrarch's argument has a note of ambivalence: "I will be true to myself as far as it is possible. I will pull myself together and collect my scattered wits, and make a great endeavor to possess my soul in patience. But even while we speak, a crowd of important affairs, though only of this world, is waiting for my attention."

The inspiration for the *Secretum* was Augustine's *Confessions,* a book Petrarch loved so much that he carried it with him everywhere. It may well have been the model for Petrarch's *Letter to Posterity,* one of the few examples of autobiography we possess after the time of Augustine. That Petrarch would have written an autobiography is testimony to his strong interest in himself as a person. The *Letter* was probably composed in 1373, a year before his death. Petrarch reviews his life up until 1351, where the text abruptly breaks off. The unfinished work is clear testimony to Petrarch's thirst for learning, fame, and self-awareness. At the same time, it is noteworthy for omitting any mention of the Black Death of 1348, which carried off the woman he loved. The letter is an important primary document of the sensibility of the 14th-century "proto-Renaissance."

Petrarch regarded as his most important works the Latin writings over which he labored with devotion and in conscious imitation of his most admired classical masters: Ovid, Cicero, and Vergil. Today, however, only the literary specialist or the antiquarian is likely to read his long epic poem in Latin called *Africa* (written in imitation of Vergil's *Aeneid*), or his prose work in praise of the past masters of the world (*De Viris Illustris*), or his meditations on the benefits of contemplative life (*De Vita Solitaria*). What has assured the literary reputation of Petrarch is his incomparable vernacular poetry, which he considered somewhat trifling but collected carefully into his *Canzoniere (Songbook)*. The *Canzoniere* contains more than three hundred sonnets and 49 *canzoni* (songs) written in Italian during the span of his adult career.

The subject of a great deal of Petrarch's poetry is his love for Laura, a woman with whom he fell immediately in love in 1327 after seeing her at church in Avignon. Laura died in the plague of 1348. The poems in her honor are divided into those written in her lifetime and those mourning her untimely death. Petrarch poured out his love for Laura in over three hundred *sonnets,* fourteen-line poems he typically broke into an octave and a sestet. Although they were never actually lovers (Petrarch says in the *Secretum* that this was due more to her honor than to his; Laura was a married woman), his Laura was no mere literary abstraction. She was a flesh-and-blood woman whom Petrarch genuinely loved. One of the characteristics of his poetry, in fact, is the palpable reality of Laura as a person; she never becomes (as Beatrice does for Dante) a symbol without earthly reality.

The interest in Petrarch's sonnets did not end with his death. Petrarchism, by which is meant the Petrarchan form of the sonnet and particularly the poet's attitude to his subject matter—praise of a woman as the perfection of human beauty and the object of the highest expression of love—was introduced into other parts of Europe before the century was over. In England, Petrarch's sonnets were first imitated in form and subject by Sir Thomas Wyatt in the early 16th century. Although the Elizabethan poets eventually developed their own English form of the sonnet, the Renaissance English tradition of poetry owes a particularly large debt to Petrarch, as the poetry of Sir Philip Sidney (1554–1586), Edmund Spenser (1552–1599), and William Shakespeare (1564–1616) shows. Their sonnet sequences follow the example of Petrarch in linking together a series of sonnets in such a way as to indicate a development in the relationship of the poet to his love.

John Addington Symonds
PETRARCH'S SONNET 15

> Backwards at every weary step and slow
> These limbs I turn which with great pain I bear;
> Then take I comfort from the fragrant air
> That breathes from thee, and sighing onward
>   go.
> But when I think how joy is turned to woe,   5
> Remembering my short life and whence I fare,
> I stay my feet for anguish and despair,
> And cast my tearful eyes on earth below.
> At times amid the storm of misery
> This doubt assails me: how frail limbs and poor
> Can severed from their spirit hope to live.   11
> Then answers Love: Hast thou no memory
> How I to lovers this great guerdon give,
> Free from all human bondage to endure?

Chaucer

While it is possible to see the beginning of the Renaissance spirit in Petrarch and other Italian writers of the 14th century, the greatest English writer of the century, Geoffrey Chaucer (1340–1400), still reflects the culture of his immediate past. The new spirit of individualism discernible in Petrarch is missing in Chaucer. He is still very much a medieval man. Only in the later part of the 15th century, largely under the influence of Italian models, can we speak of the Renaissance in England. This underscores the valuable lesson about history that movements do not necessarily happen immediately and everywhere.

Scholars have been able to reconstruct Chaucer's life with only partial success. We know that his family had been fairly prosperous wine merchants and vintners and that he entered royal service early in his life, eventually becoming a squire to King Edward III. After 1373 he undertook various diplomatic tasks for the king, including at least two trips to Italy to negotiate commercial contracts. During these Italian journeys Chaucer came into contact with the writings of Dante, Petrarch, and Boccaccio. There has been some speculation that he actually met Petrarch, but the evidence is tenuous. Toward the end of his life Chaucer served as the customs agent for the port of London on the river Thames. He was thus never a leisured "man of letters"; his writing had to be done amid the hectic round of public affairs that engaged his attention as a highly placed civil servant.

Like many other successful writers of the late medieval period, Chaucer could claim a widespread acquaintance with the learning and culture of his time. This was still an age when it was possible to read most of the available books. Chaucer spoke and wrote French fluently, and his poems show the influence of many French allegories and "dream visions." That he also knew Italian literature is clear from his borrowings from Dante and Petrarch and from his use of stories and tales in Boccaccio's *Decameron* (although it is not clear that he knew that work directly). Chaucer also had a deep knowledge of Latin literature, both classical and ecclesiastical. Furthermore, his literary output was not limited to the composition of original works of poetry. He made a translation from Latin (with an eye on an earlier French version) of Boethius' *Consolation of Philosophy* as well as a translation from French of the 13th century allegorical erotic fantasy *The Romance of the Rose*. He also composed a short treatise on the astrolabe and its relationship to the study of astronomy and astrology (two disciplines not clearly distinguished at that time).

The impressive range of Chaucer's learning pales in comparison with his most memorable and noteworthy talents: his profound feeling for the role of the English language as a vehicle for literature; his efforts to extend the range of the language (the richness of Chaucer's vocabulary was not exceeded until Shakespeare); and his incomparable skill in the art of human observation. Chaucer's characters are so finely realized that they have become standard types in English literature: his pardoner is an unforgettable villain, his knight the essence of courtesy, his wife of Bath a paradigm of rollicking bawdiness.

These characters, and others, are from Chaucer's masterpiece, *The Canterbury Tales,* begun sometime after 1385. To unify this vast work, a collection of miscellaneous tales, Chaucer used a typical literary device: a narrative frame, in this case a journey during which people tell each other tales. As noted, Boccaccio had used a similar device in the *Decameron.*

Chaucer's plan was to have a group of thirty pilgrims travel from London to the shrine of Thomas à Becket at Canterbury and back. After a general introduction, each pilgrim would tell two tales on the way and two on the return trip in order to pass the long hours of travel more pleasantly. Between tales they might engage in perfunctory conversation or prologues of their own to cement the tales further into a unified whole.

Chaucer never finished this ambitious project; he died before half of it was complete. The version we possess has a General Prologue in which the narrator, Geoffrey Chaucer, describes the individual pilgrims, his meeting with them at the Tabard Inn in London, and the start of the journey. Only 23 of the 30 pilgrims tell their tales (none tells two tales) and the group has not yet reached Canterbury. There is even some internal evidence that the material we possess was not meant for publication in its present form.

Although *The Canterbury Tales* is only a draft of what was intended to be Chaucer's masterwork, it is of incomparable literary and social value. A close reading of the General Prologue, for instance—with its representative, although limited, cross-section of medieval society (no person lower in rank than a plowman or higher in rank than a knight appears)—affords an effortless entry into the complex world of late-medieval England. With quick, deft strokes Chaucer not only creates verbal portraits of people who at the same time seem both typical and uniquely real but also introduces us to a world of slowly dying knightly values, a world filled with such contrasts as clerical foibles, the desire for knowledge, the ribald taste of the lower social classes, and an appetite for philosophical conversation.

After the General Prologue, the various members of the pilgrim company begin to introduce themselves and proceed to tell their tales. Between the tales, they engage in small talk or indulge in lengthy prologues of their own. In the tales that he completed, we see that Chaucer drew on the vast treasury of literature, both written and oral, that was the common patrimony of medieval culture. The Knight's Tale is a courtly romance; the miller and reeve tell stories that spring from the ribald *fabliaux* tradition of the time; the pardoner tells an *exemplum* such as any medieval preacher might employ; the prioress draws from the legends of the saints; the nun's priest uses an animal fable, while the parson characteristically enough provides a somewhat tedious example of a medieval prose sermon.

Christine de Pisan

Christine de Pisan (1365–1428?) is an extraordinary figure in late medieval literature if for no other reason than her pioneering role as one of Europe's first woman professional writers to make her living with the power of her pen.

Born in Venice, Christine accompanied her father Thomas de Pizzano to the French court of Charles V when she was still a small child. Thomas was the king's physician, astrologer, and close adviser. He evidently gave his daughter a thorough education: she was able to write in both Italian and French and probably knew Latin well enough to read it. At 15 she married Eugene of Castel, a young nobleman from Picardy. That same year (1380) the king died and the family fell on hard times with the loss of royal patronage. Five years later her father and her husband were both dead, leaving Christine the sole support of her mother, niece, and three young children. To maintain this large family, Christine hit on an almost unheard-of solution for a woman of the time: she turned to writing and the patronage such writing could bring to earn a living.

Between 1399 and 1415 she composed 15 books—which, as one of her translators has noted, is a staggering record in an age which had neither typewriters nor word processors. In 1399 she entered a famous literary debate about the *Romance of the Rose*. The *Romance,* a long and rather tedious poem, had been written in the preceding century and was immensely popular (Chaucer did an incomplete English translation of it). In 1275 Jean de Meung had written an addition to it that was violently critical of women. Christine attacked this misogynistic addition in a treatise called *A Letter to the God of Love.* In 1404 she wrote her final word on this debate in a long work entitled *The Book of the City of Ladies.*

The Book of the City of Ladies is indebted in its structure to Augustine's *The City of God* and for its sources on a Latin treatise by Boccaccio entitled *De Claris Mulieribus.* Through use of stories of famous women (*clarae mulieres*) Christine demonstrates that they possessed virtues precisely opposite those vices imputed to women by Jean de Meung.

The following year (1405) Christine wrote *The Treasure of the City of Ladies,* a book of etiquette and advice to help women survive in society. What is extraordinarily interesting about this book (one of the few available in English translation) is its final section, in which Christine pens advice for every class of women from young brides and wives of shopkeepers to prostitutes and peasant women.

Around 1418 Christine retired to a convent in which her daughter was a nun, where she continued to write. Besides a treatise on arms and chivalry and a lament about the horrors of civil war, she also composed prayers and seven allegorial psalms. Of more enduring interest was *The Book of Peace,* a handbook of instruction for the Dauphin who was to become Charles VII and a short hymn in honor of the great Joan of Arc. Whether Christine lived to see the bitter end of Joan is uncertain, but her hymn is one of the few extant works written while Joan was alive.

Immensely popular in her own time (the Duc de Berry owned copies of every book she wrote), her reputation waned in the course of time, to be revived only in the last decade or so as scholars have tried to do justice to the forgotten heroines of our common history.

Art in Italy

Giorgio Vasari's *Lives of the Artists* (1550), the earliest account of the rebirth of Italian art in the Renaissance, treats first of all the great Florentine painter Giotto di Bondone (1266 or 1267–1337). In his *Life of Giotto* Vasari pays tribute to Giotto's work and also gives him credit for setting painting once again on to the right path, from which it had strayed.

Later generations have accepted Vasari's assessment and have seen Giotto as a revolutionary figure not for the 14th century alone but for the entire history of European art, marking a major break with the art of the Middle Ages. Like all revolutionary figures, Giotto was more intimately linked with his past than his contemporaries and immediate successors realized, and to understand the magnitude of his achievements we must first see something of their context.

The Italo-Byzantine Background

Throughout the later Middle Ages art in Italy showed little of the richness and inventiveness of the

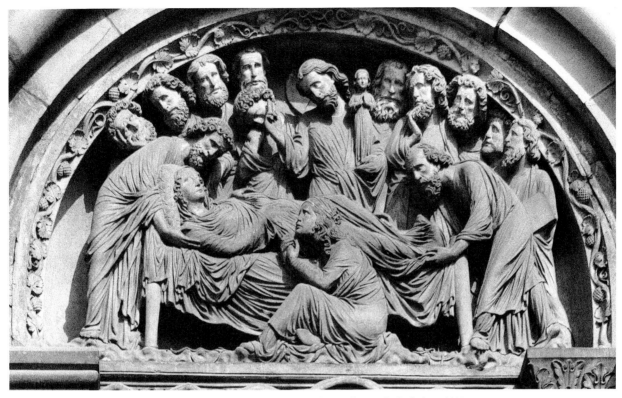

9.1 *The Death of the Virgin,* tympanum of the south transept portal, Strasbourg Cathedral. c. 1220. The expressive faces and elaborate drapery show the influence of classical sculpture.

great centers of northern Europe. Not only in France, where the University of Paris formed the intellectual capital of the Western world, but also in England and Germany, construction of the great Gothic cathedrals provided opportunities for artists to refine and develop their techniques. Sculptured decorations like *The Death of the Virgin* from Strasbourg Cathedral [9.1] are stylistically far more advanced than contemporary work in Italy. One of the reasons for this is that northern Gothic artists were beginning to return for inspiration not to their immediate predecessors but to classical art, with its realistic portrayal of the body and drapery. In Italy, however, artists were still rooted in the Byzantine tradition. Italian churches were generally decorated not with lifelike sculptural groups like the one from Strasbourg but with solemn and stylized frescoes and mosaics, a style called Italo-Byzantine.

There are notable exceptions to the generally conservative character of Italian art in the 13th century. Nicola Pisano (1220/1225–1284?) and his son Giovanni (1245/1250–1314) have been described as the creators of modern sculpture. Nicola's first major work was a marble pulpit for the Baptistery in Pisa completed in 1260, clearly influenced by the Roman sarcophagi the sculptor could see around him in Pisa.

By crowding in his figures and filling the scene with lively detail Nicola recaptured much of the vitality and realism of late Roman art while retaining the expressive qualities of Gothic sculpture. The work of his son Giovanni was less influenced by classical models than by his contemporaries in northern Europe—so much so that some scholars believe he must have spent some time in France. In his pulpit for the cathedral at Pisa, finished in 1310, the figures are more elegant and less crowded than those of his father, and show an intensity of feeling typical of northern late Gothic art [9.2, 9.3]. Both of these great sculptors foreshadowed major characteristics in the art of the Renaissance, Nicola by his emphasis on classical models and Giovanni by the naturalism and emotionalism of his figures and by his use of space.

While some Italian sculptors were responding to influences from outside, painting in Italy remained firmly grounded in the Byzantine tradition. Byzantine art was originally derived from classical art. Although its static and solemn characteristics seem a long way away from Greek or Roman styles, Byzantine painters and mosaicists inherited the late Hellenistic and Roman artists' ability to give their figures a three-dimensional quality and to represent foreshortening. With these techniques available to him, Giotto

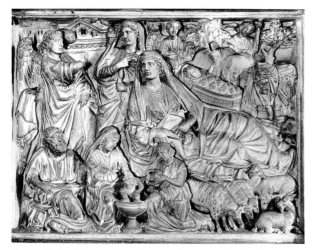

9.2 Nicola Pisano. *Annunciation and Nativity,* detail of pulpit. 1259–1260. Marble. Baptistery, Pisa. By crowding his figures together Nicola was able to combine the scene of the Nativity with the Annunciation and the shepherds in the fields.

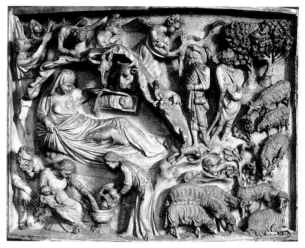

9.3 Giovanni Pisano. *Nativity and Annunciation to the Shepherds,* detail of pulpit. 1302–1310. Marble. Cathedral, Pisa. The slender figures and sense of space create an effect very different from that of the work of the artist's father.

was better able to break away from the stereotyped forms of Italo-Byzantine art and bring to painting the same naturalism and emotional power that appear in Giovanni Pisano's sculptures.

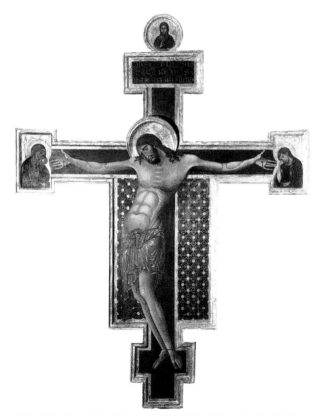

9.4 Cimabue. *Crucifixion.* c. 1268–1271. Painted and gilded wood, 10′11″ × 8′8⅛″ (3.36 × 2.67 m). San Domenico, Arezzo.

Giotto's predecessor as the leading painter in Florence, and perhaps also his teacher, was Cimabue (1240?–1302?). Not enough of his work has survived for us to have a clear impression of how much Giotto owed to Cimabue's influence, but the crucifix he painted for the church of San Domenico in Arezzo shows a remarkable realism and sophistication in the depiction of Christ's body [9.4]. Cimabue shows a genuine if incomplete understanding of the anatomy of the figure and, more important, uses it to enhance the emotional impact of his painting by emphasizing the sense of strain and weight. At the same time the draped loincloth is not merely painted as a decorative design but as naturalistically soft folds through which the limbs beneath are visible. If in other works, like the immense Santa Trinità *Madonna* [9.5], Cimabue is more directly in the Italo-Byzantine tradition, here at

TABLE 9.1 Siena in the Age of Duccio (1255/60–1318/19)

Population	20,000
Political Institutions	Council of the Nine, rotating Consistory (Magistracy)
Economy	Banking, wool manufacture, jewelry, and goldwork
Cultural Life	Painting (Duccio, Martini); Sculpture (Della Quercia); *Laudi,* or sacred songs (Bianco da Siena); Theology (St. Catherine)
Principal Buildings	Cathedral, Palazzo Pubblico (Town Hall)
Divine Protectress	The Virgin Mary, Queen of Siena

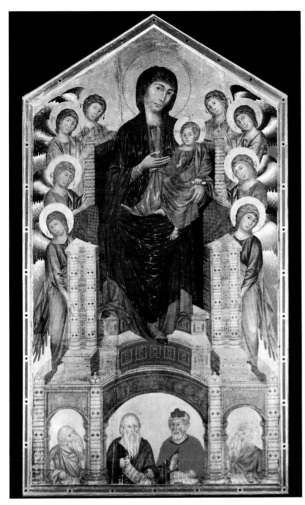

9.5 Cimabue. *Madonna Enthroned.* 1270–1285. Tempera on panel, 12′6″ × 7′4″ (3.81 × 2.24 m). Uffizi, Florence. Although much of the detail is Byzantine in inspiration, the scale of this painting has no Byzantine counterpart.

9.7 Duccio. *The Annunciation of the Death of the Virgin,* from the *Maestà* Altar. c. 1308–1311. Tempera on panel. Cathedral Museum, Siena. One of the episodes from the *Maestà* altarpiece, this scene demonstrates Duccio's ability to create a convincing architectural space around his figures.

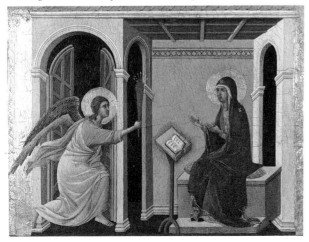

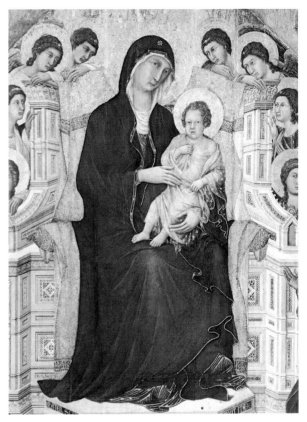

9.6 Duccio. *Madonna Enthroned,* detail of front panel of *Maestà* Altar. c. 1308–1311. Tempera on panel, height 6′10½″ (2.1 m). Cathedral Museum, Siena. Notice the greater gentleness of the faces and the softer, flowing robe of the Virgin here than in Cimabue's painting.

least he seems directly to prefigure the impact of Giotto's art.

The works of Cimabue's contemporary Duccio di Buoninsegna (1255/1260–1318/1319) are more directly Byzantine in inspiration, but here too the new spirit of the times can be felt [Table 9.1]. His greatest achievement was the huge *Maestà,* painted between 1308 and 1311, for the high altar of the cathedral of Siena, his native city. The majestic Madonna who gives the work its name faced the congregation [9.6], while both the front and back of the altarpiece were covered with small compartments filled with scenes from the lives of Christ and the Virgin. The episodes themselves are familiar from earlier painters, but the range of emotional expression is new and astonishing, as Duccio reveals to us not only the physical appearance of each of his subjects but their emotional states as well. In a number of the scenes the action takes place within an architectural setting that conveys a greater sense of space than we find in any earlier paintings, including those from the ancient world [9.7].

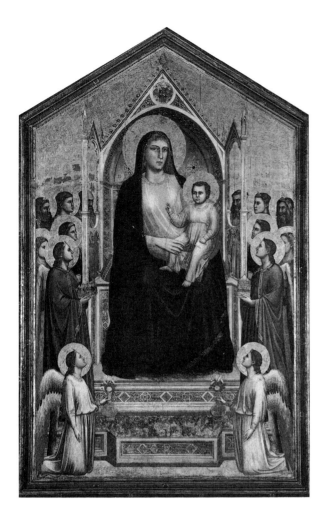

9.8 Giotto. *Madonna Enthroned.* c. 1310. Tempera on panel, 10′8″ × 6′8″ (3.25 × 2.03 m). Uffizi, Florence. Although contemporary with Duccio's Madonna from the *Maestà* altarpiece, Giotto's painting has a much greater sense of weight and volume.

Giotto's Break with the Past

Great as was Duccio's contribution to the development of painting, it was achieved without any decisive break with the tradition in which he worked. Even if we can now see the roots of some of Giotto's achievements in the works of Cimabue, the boldness of his vision, and the certainty with which he communicates it to us, represent one of the supreme achievements of Western art.

Giotto's preeminent characteristic was his realism. The Byzantine style had aimed for a rich, glowing surface, with elaborate linear designs. Now for the first time figures were painted with a sense of depth, their volume represented by a careful use of light and dark, so that they took on the same strength and presence as works of sculpture. Instead of being confronted with an image, spectators saw the living and breathing figures before them. In his great altarpiece of the Madonna enthroned, painted in 1310, Giotto brings us into the presence of the Virgin herself [9.8]. We see the majestic solidity of her form, an impression enhanced by the realistic throne on which she sits. This is achieved not only by the three-dimensional modeling of the figures but also by the sense of space that surrounds the Virgin and Child and separates them from the worshiping angels.

THE ARTS AND INVENTION: *Panel Painting*

The vast majority of paintings in the late medieval and early Renaissance periods were done on wooden panels. Preparation for the finished artwork required a series of steps that involved a considerable amount of physical work.

The artist (or, more typically, an assistant) would choose a piece of flat wood appropriate for the subject to be painted. The surface of the wood had to be flat, so the first task was to plane and sand the surface to a smooth surface. When that was done, a series of coats of chalky plaster of paris (*gesso*) was applied to the surface of the wood until there was a smooth buildup of the gesso surface. Each coat was sanded before the next application. Close examination of painted panels show that the gesso surface might be quite thick before the artist was satisfied that the surface was smooth enough for painting.

The picture was roughed out on the smooth gesso surface in pencil or colored chalk. Before the actual painting was done the colors had to be pulverized to a fine consistency and liquified with water. Since colors suspended in water would run, it was also necessary to add a fixative to the paint. Until the widespread use of oil paints, the most common fixative was egg white. Ground color in a water base with a fixative like egg white is called *tempera*. The gold backgrounds and/or highlights (such as a saint's halo) were achieved either by gold leaf or by gold tempera. Decorative indentations on the gold leaf would be made with a punch or a stylus.

Artist's bills of the period indicate that works containing rare colors or much gold were costly. Patrons often specified, for example, how much gold was to go onto a painting or whether they would pay for the semiprecious lapis lazuli that was ground to obtain brilliant blue.

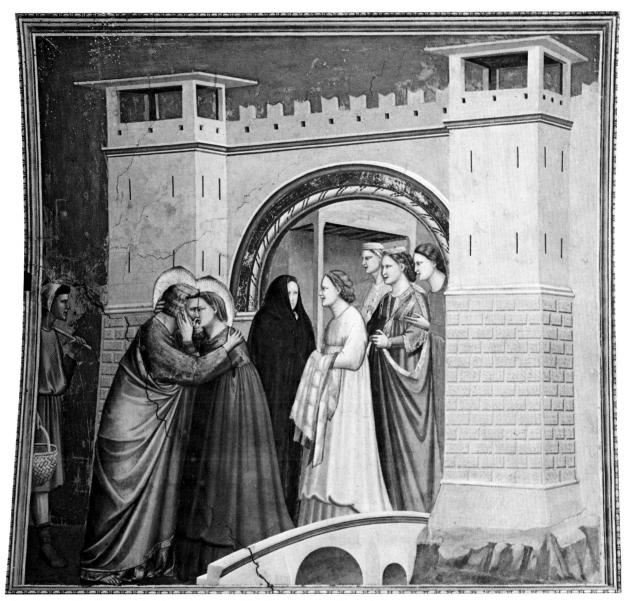

9.9 Giotto. *The Meeting of Joachim and Anna.* c. 1305. Fresco. Arena Chapel, Padua.

But Giotto's greatness lay not so much in his ability to create realistic images—to "imitate Nature," as his contemporaries called it—as in using these images for dramatic effect. Rather than confining himself to single subjects in individual panel paintings, like that of the Madonna enthroned, he preferred to work on a more complex and monumental scale. His chief claim to fame is the great cycle of frescoes that fills the walls of the Arena Chapel in Padua. In these panels, which illustrate the lives of the Virgin and of Christ, Giotto used the new naturalistic style he had developed to express an almost inexhaustible range of emotions and dramatic situations. In the scene depicting the meeting of Joachim and Anna, the parents of the Virgin, the couple's deep affection is communicated to us with simplicity and humanity [9.9]. The quiet restraint of this episode is in strong contrast to the cosmic drama of the lamentation over the dead body of Christ [9.10]. Angels wheel overhead, screaming in grief, while below Mary supports her dead son and stares fiercely into his face. Around her are the other mourners, each a fully characterized individual. If the disciple John is the most passionate in the expression of his sorrow, as he flings his arms out, no less moving are the silent hunched figures in the foreground.

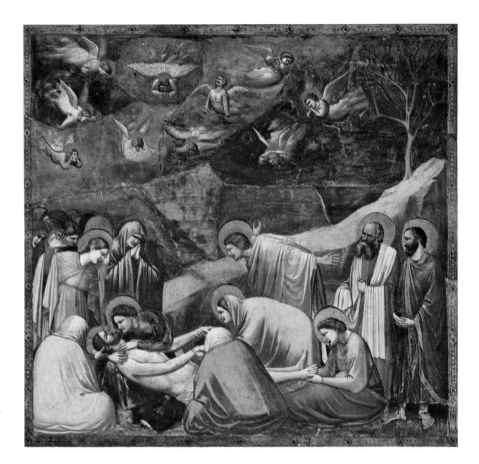

9.10 Giotto. *Pietà* (*Lamentation*). 1305–1306. Fresco, 7'7" × 7'9" (2.31 × 2.36 m). Arena Chapel, Padua.

Painting in Siena

Giotto's appeal was direct and immediate, and at Florence his pupils and followers continued to work under his influence for most of the rest of the 14th century, content to explore the implications of the master's ideas rather than devise new styles. As a result, the scene of the most interesting new developments in the generation after Giotto was Siena, where Duccio's influence (although considerable) was much less overpowering. Among Duccio's pupils was Simone Martini (c. 1285–1344), a close friend of Petrarch, who worked for a time at Naples for the French king Robert of Anjou and spent the last years of his life at the papal court of Avignon. In Martini's work we find the first signs of the last great development of Gothic art, the so-called International Style. The elegant courts of France and the French kingdoms of Italy had developed a taste for magnificent colors, fashionable costumes, and rich designs. Although Simone's Sienese background preserved him from the more extreme effects, his *Annunciation* has an insubstantial grace and sophistication that are in strong contrast to the solid realism of Giotto [9.11]. The resplendent robe and mantle of the angel Gabriel and the deep blue dress of the Virgin, edged in gold, produce an impression of great splendor, while their willowy figures approach the ideal of courtly elegance.

If Simone Martini was willing to sacrifice naturalism to surface brilliance, two of his contemporaries in Siena were more interested in applying Giotto's discoveries to their own work. Pietro Lorenzetti was born around 1280, his brother Ambrogio around 1285; both probably died in 1348, the year of the Black Death. The younger brother's best-known work is a huge fresco that decorates an entire wall in Siena's city hall, the Palazzo Pubblico; it was painted between 1338 and 1339 and illustrates the effects of good government on the city of Siena and the surrounding countryside [9.12]. The streets and buildings, filled with scenes of daily life, are painted with elaborate perspective. Richly dressed merchants with their wives, craftsmen at work, and graceful girls who dance in the street preserve for us a vivid picture of a lifestyle that was to be abruptly ended by the Black Death. The scenes in the country, on the other hand, show a world that survives even today in rural Tuscany: peasants at work on farms and in orchards and vineyards [9.13].

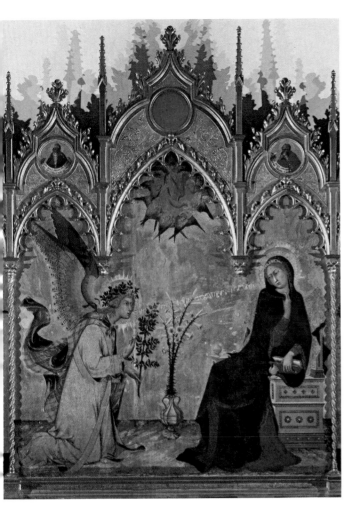

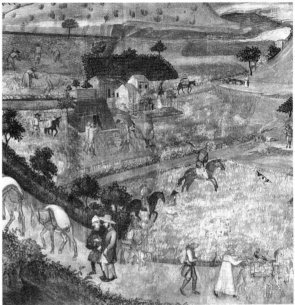

9.11 Simone Martini. *Annunciation.* 1333. Tempera on panel, 8'8" × 10' (2.64 × 3.05 m). Uffizi, Florence. The courtly elegance of the figures is in strong contrast to the massive realism of Giotto's Madonna.

9.13 Ambrogio Lorenzetti. *Effects of Good Government,* detail (scenes in the countryside). 1337–1339. Fresco. Sala dei Nove, Palazzo Pubblico, Siena.

9.12 Ambrogio Lorenzetti. *Effects of Good Government* (scenes in the city). 1337–1339. Fresco. Sala dei Nove, Palazzo Pubblico, Siena. Note the skillful use of perspective.

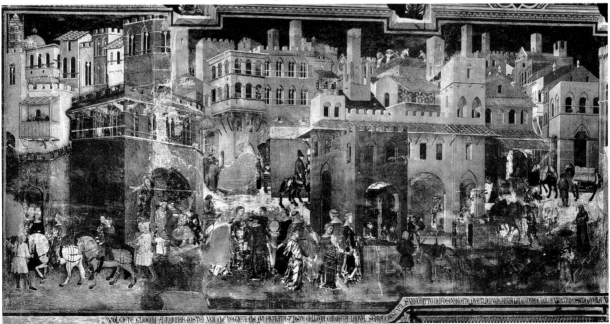

Art in Northern Europe

By the middle of the 14th century the gulf between artists in Italy and those north of the Alps had been reduced considerably. Painters like Simone Martini carried the latest developments in Sienese art to France, were in turn influenced by styles they found there, and subsequently brought them back to Italy. The growing tendency toward a unity of artistic language throughout Western Europe was further increased by political developments. When, for example, in 1347 the city of Prague became the residence of the Emperor Charles IV, it became a major art center rivaling even Paris in importance. Around 1360 an unknown Bohemian master working there painted a panel showing the death of the Virgin that combines the rich colors and careful architecture of Sienese painting with the strong emotional impact of northern Gothic art [9.14]. By the end of the century it was no longer possible to identify an artist's origins from the work. The *Wilton Diptych* was painted in England sometime after 1377 [9.15]. One of the two panels shows the young king Richard II accompanied by his patron saints, while on the other the Virgin and Child appear before the praying king, accompanied by eleven angels. They probably commemorate Richard's coronation in 1377, since he was eleven years old at the time. The wonderfully delicate yet rich colors and the careful use of shading have no parallel in English art of the period. The artist seems to have been familiar with the work of painters like Duccio and Simone Martini, but the elegance of the

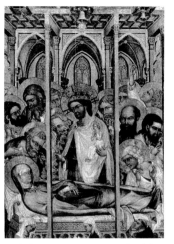

9.14 Unknown Bohemian Master. *Death of the Virgin.* 1325–1350. Tempera on panel, 39⅜ × 28″ (100 × 71 cm). Museum of Fine Arts, Boston (William Francis Warden Fund; Seth K. Sweetser Fund, The Henry C. and Martha B. Angell Collection, Juliana Cheney Edwards Collection, Gift of Martin Brimmer, and Gift of Reverend and Mrs. Frederick Frottingham, by exchange.)

paintings and technique are neither simply Italian nor French. The painter of the *Wilton Diptych* was working in a style that can only be called International.

One of the first great centers of the International Style was the court of the Duke of Burgundy at Dijon, where sculptors like the Dutchman Claus Sluter and painters like the Flemish Melchior Broederlam served Duke Philip the Bold, who ruled there from 1364 to 1404, and his brother John, Duke

9.15 French School. *Richard II Presented to the Virgin and Child by His Patron Saints* (*Wilton Diptych*). c. 1395. Oak panels, each 18 × 11½″ (46 × 29 cm). National Gallery, London (reproduced by courtesy of the Trustees).

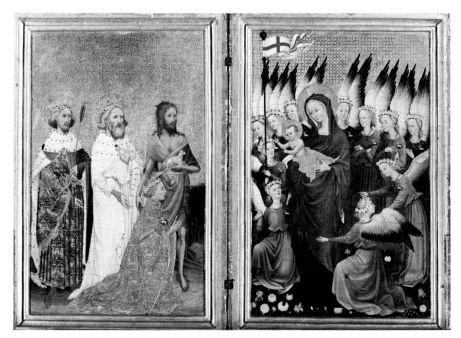

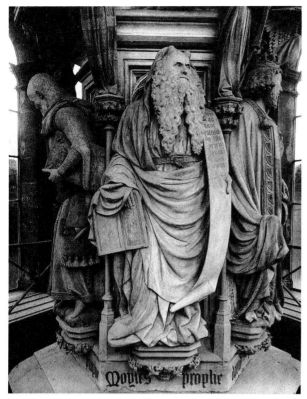

9.16 Claus Sluter. *The Well of Moses.* 1395–1406. Marble, height of figures about 6′ (1.83 m). Chartreuse de Champmol, Dijon. The horns represent rays of light (a usage based on a Bible mistranslation).

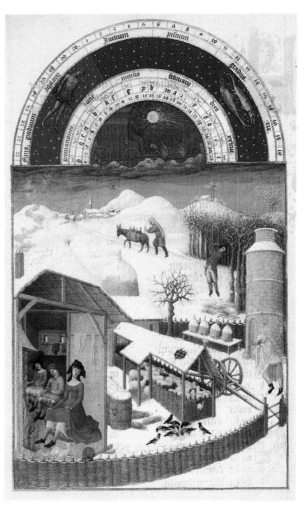

9.17 Limbourg Brothers. February page from the *Très Riches Heures du Duc de Berry.* 1416. Manuscript illumination, 8⅞ × 5⅜″ (22 × 14 cm), Musée Condé, Chantilly. The chart above the painting represents the signs of the zodiac for the month of February.

of Berry. Sluter (active about 1380–1406) was commissioned to provide sculpture for a monastery founded near Dijon by Duke Philip, the Chartreuse de Champmol. His most impressive work there is the so-called *Well of Moses,* designed for the monastery's cloister [9.16]. Not really a well at all, it consists of an elaborate base surrounded by statues of Moses and five other Old Testament prophets on which originally stood a crucifixion, now missing. At first glance the style of the figures is reminiscent of earlier Gothic statues, like those at Strasbourg, but a more careful look shows a host of carefully depicted details. In the figure of Moses the textures of the heavy drapery, the soft beard, and the wrinkled face are skillfully differentiated, and the expression has the vividness of a portrait. Equally realistic is the sense of weight and mass of the body beneath the drapery.

But for the most attractive details in all of late Gothic art we must turn to the *Très Riches Heures du Duc de Berry,* an illustrated prayerbook commissioned by Philip the Bold's brother and completed in 1416. It was painted by the Limbourg brothers—Pol, Hennequin, and Herman. They were Flemish in origin, may have spent some time in Italy, and finally settled in France. Twelve illuminated pages are included in the book, which illustrate the twelve months of the year. These paintings are filled with an almost inexhaustible range of details that combine to depict the changing seasons of the year with poetry and humanity. On the page representing February the farm workers warming themselves inside the cottage and the sheep huddling together outside attract our attention immediately, but the whole scene is filled with marvelously painted details, from the steamy breath of the girl on the far right, stumbling back through the snow toward a warm fireside, to the snow-laden roofs of the frozen village in the far distance [9.17]. In May we move from the world of

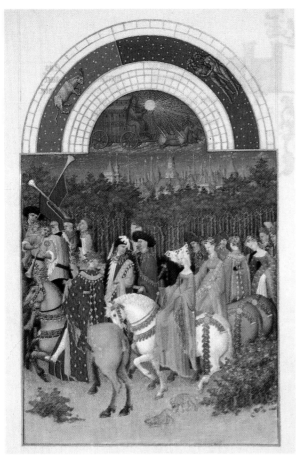

peasants to that of the aristocracy as a gorgeously dressed procession of lords and ladies rides out in the midst of the fresh greenery of springtime with the roof and turrets of a great castle in the background [9.18]. The sense of idleness and the delightful conceits of chivalry seem to evoke the world of Chaucer, while stylistically the sense of perspective and elegance of the figures is still another reminder of the influence of Sienese art.

Late Gothic Architecture

As in the case of painting and sculpture, the generally unified style of northern Gothic architecture never really crossed the Alps into Italy. Although some of the most important Italian buildings of the 14th century are generally labeled Gothic, their style is very different from their northern counterparts. Two of the century's greatest churches illustrate this, both begun at Florence at the end of the 13th century— Santa Croce around 1295 and the cathedral (better known by the Italian word for cathedral, *duomo*) in 1296. Neither has buttresses and in both most of the wall surface is solid rather than pierced with the typical Gothic windows. The Duomo's most outstanding feature does not even date to the 14th century: Its magnificent dome was built by the great early Renaissance architect Filippo Brunelleschi between 1420 and 1436 [9.19].

More self-consciously Gothic is the Duomo in Milan, begun in 1386, which perhaps makes one feel

9.18 Limbourg Brothers. May page from the *Très Riches Heures du Duc de Berry*. 1416. Manuscript illumination, 8⅞ × 5⅜″ (22 × 14 cm), Musée Condé, Chantilly. The hunters blow their horns, but the courtiers are more interested in the ladies.

9.19 Duomo, Florence. 1296–1436.

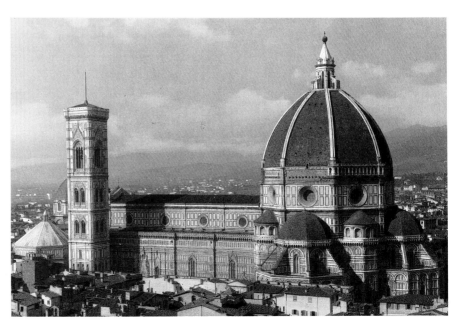

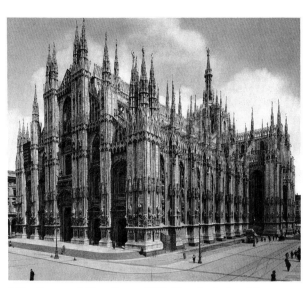

9.20 Duomo, Milan. Begun 1368. The classical moldings over the windows and doorways of the facade are a reminder that the Duomo was not completed until the Renaissance.

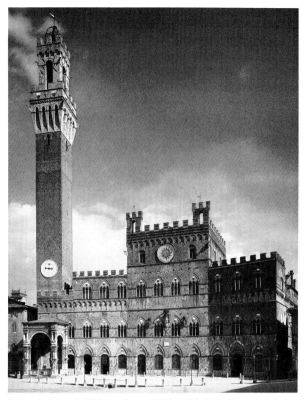

9.21 Palazzo Pubblico, Siena. 1288–1309. The slits around the base of the gallery at the top of the tower were used for firing through on attackers below.

9.22 Doge's Palace, Venice. 1345–1438. Unlike the heavily fortified Palazzo Pubblico at Siena, this palace of the rulers of Venice, with its light, open arches, reflects the stability and security of the Venetian Republic.

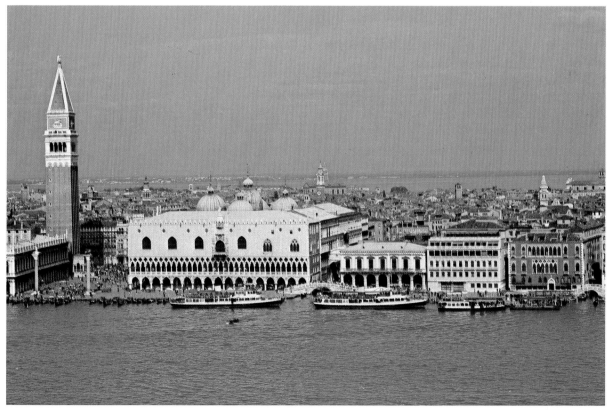

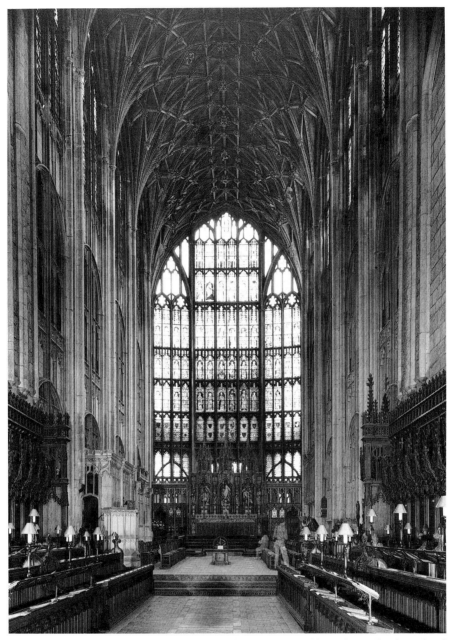

9.23 Choir, Gloucester Cathedral. 1332–1357. The strong vertical lines show why the style of such buildings is called Perpendicular.

relieved that Italian architects in general avoided the chief features of northern Gothic style. The immensely elaborate facade, bristling with spires, and the crowded piers of the sides seem to be stuck on rather than integrated into the design. The presence of classical elements in the decorations is a reminder that by the time the Milan Duomo was completed the Renaissance had dawned [9.20].

Far more attractive are the secular public buildings of the age. The town halls of Florence and Siena, the Palazzo Vecchio (begun 1298) and the Palazzo Publico (begun 1288), convey the sense of strong government and civic pride that characterized life in these cities during the Trecento [9.21]. The towers served the double purpose of providing a lookout over the city and surrounding countryside while they expressed the determination of the city rulers to resist attack. The most beautiful of all government centers is probably the Doge's Palace in Venice, a city where more than anywhere else Gothic architecture took on an almost magical quality of lightness and delicacy. The Doge's Palace (begun about 1345) is composed of a heavy upper story that seems to float on two arcades, the lower a short and sturdy colonnade and the upper composed of tall, slender columns. The effect is enhanced by the way in which the whole building seems suspended in space between sky and sea [9.22].

For a final look at the late Gothic architecture at its most typical we must turn to England, where the style of this period is generally known as Perpendicular. The choir of Gloucester Cathedral, built between 1332 and 1357, illustrates the reason for the label [9.23]. The vertical line is emphasized, and our eyes are carried up to the roof, where a complex web of ribs decorate the vault. Unlike the ribs in earlier buildings, these serve no structural purpose but have become purely decorative. Their delicacy seems an apt reflection in stone of the graceful precision of the *Wilton Diptych* and the *Très Riches Heures*.

Music: *Ars Nova*

While Giotto was laying the foundations of a new naturalistic style of painting and writers like Petrarch and Chaucer were breathing fresh life into literary forms, composers in France and Italy were changing the style of music. To some extent this was the result of social changes: musicians had begun to break away from their traditional role as servants of the church and to establish themselves as independent creative figures; most of the music that survives from the 14th century is secular. Much of it was written for singers and instrumentalists to perform at home for their own pleasure [9.24], or for the entertainment of aristocratic audiences like those depicted in the *Très Riches Heures*. The texts composers set to music were increasingly varied; ballads, love songs, even descriptions of contemporary events, in contrast to the religious settings of the preceding century.

As the number of people who enjoyed listening to music and performing it began to grow, so did the range of musical expression. The term generally used to describe the sophisticated musical style of the 14th

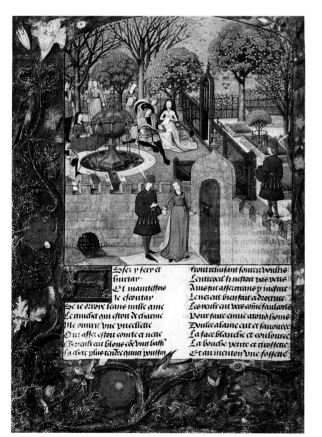

9.24 A knight playing and singing to a lady, manuscript illumination illustrating the *Romance of the Rose*. Flemish, 14 × 10″ (36 × 25 cm). British Library, London. The romantic interlude is enhanced by the idyllic surroundings; a walled garden with a fountain playing.

century is *Ars Nova,* derived from the title of a treatise written by the French composer Philippe de Vitry (1291–1361) around 1325. The work was written in Latin and called *Ars Nova Musicae (The New Art of Music).* Although it is really concerned only with one aspect of composition and describes a new system of rhythmic notation, the term *ars nova* has taken on a wider use and is applied to the new musical style that began to develop in France in the early 14th century and soon spread to Italy.

Its chief characteristic is a much greater richness and complexity of sound than before. This was partly achieved by the use of richer harmonies; thirds and sixths were increasingly employed and the austere sound of parallel fifths, unisons, and octaves was generally avoided. Elaborate rhythmic devices were also introduced, including the method of construction called *isorhythm* (from the Greek word *isos,* which means equal). Isorhythm consisted of allotting to one of the voices in a polyphonic composition a repeated single melody. The voice was also assigned a repeating rhythmical pattern. Since the rhythmical pattern was of a different length from the melody, different notes would be stressed on each repetition. The purpose of this device was twofold: it both created a richness and variety of texture and imparted an element of unity to the piece.

The most famous French composer of this period was Guillaume de Machaut (1304?–1377), whose career spanned the worlds of traditional music and of the *Ars Nova.* He was trained as a priest and took holy orders, but much of his time was spent traveling throughout Europe in the service of the kings of Bohemia, Navarre, and France. Toward the end of his life he retired to Rheims, where he spent his last years as a canon. His most famous composition, and the most famous piece of music from the 14th century, is the *Messe de Notre Dame.* A four-part setting of the Ordinary of the Mass, it is remarkable chiefly for the way in which Machaut gives unity to the five sections that make up the work by creating a similarity of mood and even using a single musical motive that recurs throughout:

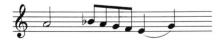

Machaut's *Messe de Notre Dame* is the first great example of the entire Ordinary of the Mass set to polyphonic music by a single composer. The Ordinary of the Mass refers to those parts of the Roman Catholic liturgy that do not change from day to day in contrast to the Propers (the readings from the Gospel or Epistle), which change daily. The parts of the Ordinary are:

1. The *Kyrie Eleison:* the repeated Greek phrases that mean "Lord have mercy on us!" and "Christ have mercy on us!"
2. The *Gloria:* a hymn of praise sung at all masses except funerals and masses during Lent and Advent.
3. The *Credo:* the Profession of Faith sung after the Gospel.
4. The *Sanctus* and *Benedictus:* a short hymn based on the angelic praise found in Isaiah 6, sung at the beginning of the eucharistic prayer.
5. The *Agnus Dei:* the prayer that begins "Lamb of God," sung before Communion.

Machaut's *Messe de Notre Dame,* then, stands at the head of a long tradition of musical composition in which composers use the Ordinary of the Mass to express in their own cultural idiom the timeless words of the liturgy. Machaut's Mass, in that sense, is the ancestor of the Renaissance compositions of Palestrina in the 16th century, the Baroque masses of Johann Sebastian Bach in the 18th century, and the frenetically eclectic contemporary *Mass* of Leonard Bernstein.

Machaut also contributed to another great musical tradition, that of secular song. With the increasing use of polyphony, composers began to turn their attentions to the old troubadour songs and write new settings that combined several different voices. Machaut's polyphonic secular songs took a number of forms. His *ballades* were written for two or three voices, the top voice carrying the melody while the others provided the accompaniment. These lower voices were probably sometimes played by instruments rather than sung. As in the ballades of earlier times the poems consisted of three stanzas, each of seven or eight lines, the last one or two lines being identical in all the stanzas to provide a refrain.

Many of these secular songs, both by Machaut and by other composers, deal with amorous topics, and often are addressed to the singer's beloved. The themes are predictable—the sorrow of parting, as in Machaut's *Au departir de vous*—reproaches for infidelity, protestations of love, and so on, but the freshness of the melodies and Machaut's constant inventiveness prevent them from seeming artificial.

The other important composer of the 14th century was the Italian Francesco Landini (1325–1397), who lived and worked in Florence. Blinded in his youth by smallpox, he was famous in his day as a virtuoso performer on the organ, lute, and flute. Among his

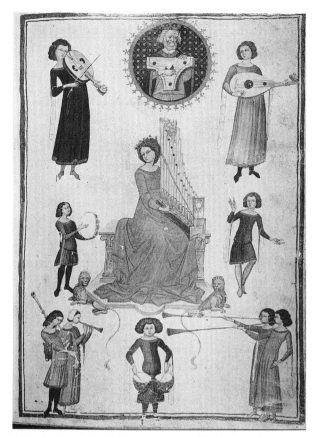

9.25 Music and musicians, manuscript illumination illustrating a treatise, *De Musica.* 14th century. Biblioteca Nazionale, Naples. Some of the instruments of the time are shown. The goddess Music is at center, playing a small organ. Grouped around her are musicians with stringed instruments, percussion, and wind instruments. The inset shows David, founder of church music, plucking a psaltery.

surviving works are a number of *madrigals,* a form of word settings involving two or three verses set to the same music and separated by a refrain set to different music. In addition, he wrote a large number of *ballate* (ballads) including many for solo voice and two accompanying instruments. The vocal lines are often elaborate, and Landini makes use of rich, sonorous harmonies. But in the case of these and other works of the period, there is no specification of the instruments intended, or, indeed, of the general performance style Landini would have expected [9.25]. We know from contemporary accounts that in some cases performers would have changed the written notes by sharpening or flattening them, following the convention of the day. This practice of making

sounds other than those on the page was called *musica ficta* (fictitious music), but no systematic description of the rules followed has been handed down to us. As a result, modern editors and performers often have only their own historical research and instincts to guide them. Although the *Ars Nova* of the 14th century marks a major development in the history of music, our knowledge of it is far from complete.

The 14th century was a time of stark contrast between the horrors of natural and social disasters and the flowering of artistic and cultural movements that were the harbingers of the 15th-century Renaissance in Italy. Chaucer, as we have seen, died in 1400, the year that may be taken as the close of the medieval period. By that time, some of the prime figures of the Italian Renaissance—Donatello, Fra Angelico, and Ghiberti—were already in their teens. The great outburst of cultural activity that was to mark Florence in the 15th century was near, even though it would not make a definite impact on England until the end of the century. The calamitous 14th century was a costly seedbed for rebirth and human renewal.

Summary

The 14th century marks the painful transition from the medieval period to the world of the Renaissance. Its beginning saw the construction of several major buildings in Italy, including Florence's Duomo and Siena's Palazzo Pubblico, seat of city government. Music flourished throughout the century, especially in France, where Machaut was the leading composer of his day. In the years shortly after 1300 the new naturalistic style of Giotto revolutionized the art of painting, while the works of the Pisano family proved equally important for the history of sculpture. Yet the age was fraught with disasters and racked by war: the Hundred Years' War between France and England (1337–1453) was barely under way when in 1348 Europe was devastated by bubonic plague—the Black Death. Among the works of literature to reflect the effects of the terrible plague is Boccaccio's *Decameron.*

As the century began, the church appeared to be at the height of its influence. In 1300 Pope Boniface VIII proclaimed the first holy year, and pilgrims flocked to Rome. Yet within a few years the French had forced the transfer of the papacy to Avignon in southern France. Among those who accompanied the papal court was the poet Petrarch, many of whose sonnets deal with his love for Laura, killed by the Black Death. The "Babylonian Captivity" lasted from 1309 to 1376, and the pope's return to Rome was embittered by the Great Scism, which saw the Western powers locked in a struggle to impose rival claimants.

One of the artistic consequences of the papal move from Rome was that Italian styles were carried north of the Alps. The resulting blend of Italian and Northern elements is called the International style, which quickly spread throughout Europe: two of its main centers were at Prague and at Dijon. The more cosmopolitan spirit of the age is also illustrated by the career of the greatest English writer of the time, Chaucer, who traveled to Italy and to France and may actually have met Petrarch.

In an age of such ferment the pressure for reform intensified. In England, John Wyclif's charges of church corruption heightened dissatisfaction among the lower classes, leading to peasant riots in 1381. Similar popular protests against both the church and the aristocracy occurred in France in 1356, while in 1378 the poor woollen workers of Florence revolted against the city authorities. These manifestations of general discontent brought no immediate radical changes in government, but they prepared the way for the social mobility of the Renaissance.

The greatest struggle of the century, the Hundred Years' War, was supposedly fought over the right of succession to the French throne. In fact, its underlying cause was the commercial rivalry between France and England and the attempts of both countries to gain control of the wool-manufacturing region of Flanders. The war's early stages were marked by a series of English victories, culminating in the battle of Poitiers of 1356. By 1380 the French had reversed the tide, and the last years of the century saw inconclusive skirmishes, with both sides resigned to a stalemate.

Thus a century in which political, economic, and religious strife and revolutionary artistic developments were accompanied by the disaster of plague produced deep changes in the fabric of European society and made possible the renewal of the Renaissance.

Pronounciation Guide

Arezzo: a-RET-so
Avignon: AV-een-yon
Boccaccio: Bo-KACH-i-owe
Chaucer: CHORE-ser
Cimabue: Chim-a-BOO-ay
Crecy: CRAY-see
Duccio: DO-chee-owe
Duomo: Do-OWE-mo
Froissart: Fr-WAS-are
Giotto: JOT-toe
Guillaume Machaut: Ghee-OHM Mash-OWE
Lorenzetti: Lo-ren-ZETT-i
Maesta: My-STAH
Palazzo Vecchio: Pa-LAT-so VEK-ee-owe
Petrarch: PET-rark
Pisano: Pee-ZAN-owe
Poitiers: PWAH-tee-ay
Santa Croce: SAN-ta CROW-chay

Scism: SISM
Trecento: Tray-CHEN-toe
Vasari: Vaz-ARE-ee

Exercises

1. Compare the literary achievements of Boccaccio and Petrarch. What light do they throw on the history of their times?
2. How does Chaucer characterize the participants in *The Canterbury Tales*? Select two and describe their chief features.
3. Describe Giotto's contribution to the history of painting and compare him to his predecessors.
4. What are the principal characteristics of northern European art in the 14th century? How does it differ from Italian art?
5. How did musical styles change in the 14th century? Discuss the contribution of Guillaume Machaut.

Further Reading

Gottfried, Robert S. *The Black Death: Natural and Human Disaster in Medieval Europe*. New York: Free Press, 1983. An important cultural study of the plague and its impact on late medieval culture.

Howard, Donald. *The Idea of Canterbury Tales*. Berkeley: University of California Press, 1977. An important study of the structure of Chaucer's greatest work.

Kane, George. *Chaucer*. New York: Oxford University Press, 1984. A brief, well-written study; part of the "Past Masters" series.

Lerner, Robert. *The Age of Adversity: The Fourteenth Century*. Ithaca, N.Y.: Cornell University Press, 1968. A brief but readable survey of the period covering both historical and cultural events of the century.

Martindale, Andrew. *The Complete Paintings of Giotto*. New York: Abrams, 1966. After a brief introduction the book consists of a fully illustrated catalogue of Giotto's paintings with some excellent detail photographs.

Meiss, Millard. *Painting in Florence and Siena after the Black Death*. New York: Harper, 1964. A brilliant work of scholarship that treats "The arts, religion and society in the mid-Fourteenth Century."

Pope-Hennessy, John. *Italian Gothic Sculpture*. London: Phaidon, 1972. An excellent illustrated survey. The comprehensive bibliography is especially valuable.

Stubblebine, James (ed.). *The Arena Chapel Frescoes*. New York: Norton, 1969. A collection of essays on Giotto's frescoes, illustrated.

Tuchman, Barbara. *A Distant Mirror: The Calamitous Fourteenth Century*. New York: Knopf, 1978. A brilliant work by one of our best popular writers on history. The book focuses almost exclusively on France and as a result lacks some balance. A joy to read and very revealing nevertheless.

White, John. *Art and Architecture in Italy 1250–1400*. Baltimore: Pelican, 1966. A useful single-volume survey, comprehensive yet detailed. Highly recommended.

Wilkins, Ernest H. *Life of Petrarch*. Chicago: University of Chicago Press, 1961. An exemplary biography valuable for its discussion of Italy in the 14th century and Petrarch's relationship with such figures as Boccaccio, Giotto, Simone Martini, and Chaucer.

Reading Selections

Giovanni Boccaccio, DECAMERON

Preface to the Ladies

This selection is the prologue to the hundred tales that make up the Decameron. *It reflects not only the experience of the writer who lived through the terrible plague year of 1348 but also his reflections on the effects of this terrible plague on both the minds of the population and the structures of society. Boccaccio senses the tendency of some to "let go" in the face of death by seizing whatever pleasures are available while others turn to God for mercy and relief from the scourge of sickness. Furthermore, he details how the very whisper of plague destroyed public order and familial bonds. In our own century the French writer Albert Camus would use a plague setting as a symbol of the Nazi occupation of France to depict the reactions of people faced with extreme social conditions—conditions that call forth both cowardice and heroism and much in between.*

How many times, most gracious ladies, have I considered in my innermost thoughts how full of pity you all are by nature. As often as I have thought this, I recognized that this present work will have in your judgment a depressing and unpleasant beginning. For it bears in its initial pages a disheartening remembrance of the past mortal pestilence, which was irksome and painful to all who saw it or otherwise knew it. But I do not wish that this should frighten you from going further, as if your reading will continuously carry you through sighs and tears. Let this horrid beginning be to you not otherwise than a rugged and steep mountain to travelers, next to which lies a lovely and delightful plain. The plain is all the more pleasing to them, in proportion to the great difficulties of climbing and descending. For just as sorrow dims out extreme happiness, so miseries are ended by supervening joy. To this brief unpleasantness (I say brief since it is contained in few words) there shall at once follow sweetness and delight. I have promised it

to you in advance; for it might not have been expected from such a beginning, if it hadn't been told you. In truth, if I could have in honesty led you where I want by a way other than a path as rough as this, I would willingly have done so. But without this recollection I could not have shown you the reason why the things took place, of which you soon will be reading. Thus even, strained, as if by necessity, I brought myself to write of them.

I say, then, that it was the year of the bountiful Incarnation of the Son of God, 1348. The mortal pestilence then arrived in the excellent city of Florence, which surpasses every other Italian city in nobility. Whether through the operations of the heavenly bodies, or sent upon us mortals through our wicked deeds by the just wrath of God for our correction, the plague had begun some years before in Eastern countries. It carried off uncounted numbers of inhabitants, and kept moving without cease from place to place. It spread in piteous fashion towards the West. No wisdom of human foresight worked against it. The city had been cleaned of much filth by officials delegated to the task. Sick persons were forbidden entrance, and many laws were passed for the safeguarding of health. Devout persons made to God not just modest supplications and not just once, but many, both in ordered processions and in other ways. Almost at the beginning of the spring of that year, the plague horribly began to reveal, in astounding fashion, its painful effects.

It did not work as it had in the East, where anyone who bled from the nose had a manifest sign of inevitable death. But in its early stages both men, and women too, acquired certain swellings either in the groin or under the armpits. Some of these swellings reached the size of a common apple, and others were as big as an egg, some more and some less. The common people called them plague-boils. From these two parts of the body, the deadly swellings began in a short time to appear and to reach indifferently every part of the body. Then, the appearance of the disease began to change into black or livid blotches, which showed up in many on the arms or thighs and in every other part of the body. On some they were large and few, on others small and numerous. And just as the swellings had been at first and still were an infallible indication of approaching death, so also were these blotches to whomever they touched. In the cure of these illnesses, neither the advice of a doctor nor the power of any medicine appeared to help and to do any good. Perhaps the nature of the malady did not allow it; perhaps the ignorance of the physicians (of whom, besides those trained, the number had grown very large both of women and of men who were completely without medical instruction) did not know whence it arose, and consequently did not take required action against it. Not only did very few recover, but almost everyone died within the third day from the appearance of these symptoms, some sooner and some later, and most without any fever or other complication. This plague was of greater virulence, because by contact with those sick from it, it infected the healthy, not otherwise than fire does, when it is brought very close to dry or oily material.

The evil was still greater than this. Not only conversation and contact with the sick carried the illness to the healthy and was cause of their common death. But even to handle the clothing or other things touched or used by the sick seemed to carry with it that same disease for those who came into contact with them. You will be amazed to hear what I now must tell you. If the eyes of many, including my own, had not seen it, I would hardly dare to believe it, much less to write it, even if I had heard it from a person worthy of faith. I say that the character of the pestilence we describe was of such virulence in spreading from one person to another, that not only did it go from man to man, but many times it also apparently did the following, which is even more remarkable. If an animal outside the human species contacted the belongings of a man sick or dead of this illness, it not only caught the disease, but within a brief time was killed by it. My own eyes, as I said a little while ago, saw one day (and other times besides) this occurrence. The rags of a poor man dead from this disease had been thrown in a public street. Two pigs came to them and they, in their accustomed manner, first rooted among them with their snouts, and then seized them with their teeth and tossed them about with their jaws. A short hour later, after some staggering, as if the poison was taking effect, both of them fell dead to earth upon the rags which they had unhappily dragged.

Such events and many others similar to them or even worse conjured up in those who remained healthy diverse fears and imaginings. Almost all were inclined to a very cruel purpose, that is, to shun and to flee the sick and their belongings. By so behaving, each believed that he would gain safety for himself. Some persons advised that a moderate manner of living, and the avoidance of all excesses, greatly strengthened resistance to this danger. Seeking out companions, such persons lived apart from other men. They closed and locked themselves in those houses where no sick person was found. To live better, they consumed in modest quantities the most delicate foods and the best wines, and avoided all sexual activity. They did not let themselves speak to anyone, nor did they wish to hear any news from the outside, concerning death or the sick. They lived amid music and those pleasures which they were able to obtain.

Others were of a contrary opinion. They affirmed that heavy drinking and enjoyment, making the rounds with singing and good cheer, the satisfaction of the appetite with everything one could and the laughing and joking which derived from this, were the most effective medicine for this great evil. As they recommended, so they put into practice, according to their ability. Night and day, they went now to that tavern and now to another, drinking without moderation or measure. They did even more in the houses of others; they had only to discern there things which were to their liking or pleasure. This they could easily do, since everyone, as if he was destined to live no more, had abandoned all care of his possessions and of himself. Thus, most houses had become open to all, and strangers used them as they happened upon them, as their proper owner might have done. With this inhuman intent, they continuously avoided the sick with all their power.

In this great affliction and misery of our city, the revered authority of both divine and human laws was left to fall and decay by those who administered and executed them. They too, just as other men, were all either dead or sick or so destitute of their families, that they were unable to fulfill any office. As a result everyone could do just as he pleased.

Many others held a middle course between the two mentioned above. Not restraining themselves in their diet as much as the first group, nor letting themselves go in drinking and other excesses as the second, they satisfied their appetites sufficiently. They did not go into seclusion but went about carrying flowers, fragrant herbs and various spices which they often held to their noses, believing a good to comfort the brain with such odors since the air was heavy with the stench of dead bodies, illness and pungent medicines. Others had harsher but perhaps safer ideas. They said that against plagues no medicine was better than or even equal to simple flight. Moved by this reasoning and giving heed to nothing but themselves, many men and women abandoned their own city, their houses and homes, their relatives and belongings in search of their own country places or those of others. Just as if the wrath of God, in order to punish the iniquity of men with the plague, could not pursue them, but would only oppress those within city walls! They were apparently convinced that no one should remain in the city, and that its last hour had struck.

Although these people of various opinions did not all die, neither did they all live. In fact many in each group and in every place became ill, but having given example to those who were still well, they in turn were abandoned and left to perish.

We have said enough of these facts: that one townsman shuns another; that almost no one cares for his neighbor; that relatives rarely or never exchange visits, and never do they get too close. The calamity had instilled such terror in the hearts of men and women that brother abandoned brother, uncle nephew, brother sister, and often wives left their husbands. Even more extraordinary, unbelievable even, fathers and mothers shunned their children, neither visiting them nor helping them, as though they were not their very own.

Consequently, for the enormous number of men and women who became ill, there was no aid except the charity of friends, who were few indeed, or the avarice of servants attracted by huge and exorbitant stipends. Even so, there weren't many servants, and those few men and women were of unrefined capabilities, doing little more than to hand the sick the articles they requested and to mark their death. Serving in such a capacity, many perished along with their earnings. From this abandonment of the sick by neighbors, relatives and friends and from the scarcity of servants arose an almost unheard-of custom. Once she became ill, no woman, however attractive, lovely or well-born, minded having as her servant a man, young or old. To him without any shame she exhibited any part of her body as sickness required, as if to another woman. This explains why those who were cured were less modest than formerly. A further consequence is that many died for want of help who might still be living. The fact that the ill could not avail themselves of services as well as the virulence of the plague account for the multitude who died in the city by day and by night. It was dreadful to hear tell of it, and likewise to see it. Out of necessity, therefore, there were born among the survivors customs contrary to the old ways of the townspeople.

It used to be the custom, as it is today, for the female relative and neighbors of the dead man to gather together with those close to him in order to mourn. Outside the house of the dead man his friends, neighbors and many others would assemble. Then, according to the status of the deceased, a priest would come with the funeral pomp of candles and chants, while the dead man was borne on the shoulders of his peers to the church chosen before death. As the ferocity of the plague increased, such customs ceased either totally or in part, and new ones took their place. Instead of dying amidst a crowd of women, many left this life without a single witness. Indeed, few were conceded the mournful wails and bitter tears of loved ones. Instead, quips and merry-making were common and even normally compassionate women had learned well such habits for the sake of their health. Few bodies had more than ten or twelve neighbors to accompany them to church, and even those were not upright citizens, but a species of vulture sprung from the lowly who called themselves "grave-diggers," and sold their services. They shouldered the bier and with hurried steps went not to the church designated by the deceased, but more often than not to the nearest church. Ahead were four or six clerics with little light or sometimes none, who with the help of the grave-diggers placed the dead in the nearest open grave without straining themselves with too long or solemn a service.

Much more wretched was the condition of the poor people and even perhaps of the middle class in large part. Because of hope or poverty, these people were confined to their houses. Thus keeping to their quarters, thousands fell ill daily and died without aid or help of any kind, almost without exception. Many perished on the public streets by day or by night, and many more ended their days at home, where the stench of their rotting bodies first notified their neighbors of their death. With these and others dying all about, the city was full of corpses. Now a general procedure was followed more out of fear of contagion than because of pity felt for the dead. Alone or with the help of whatever bearers they could find, they dragged the corpses from their houses and piled them in front so, particularly in the morning, anyone abroad could see countless bodies. Biers were sent for and when they were lacking, ordinary planks carried the bodies. It was not an isolated bier which carried two or three together. This happened not just once, but many biers could be counted which held in fact a wife and husband, two or three brothers, or father and son. Countless times, it happened that two priests going forth with a cross to bury someone were joined by three or four biers carried behind by bearers, so that whereas the priests thought they had one corpse to bury, they found themselves with six, eight or even more. Nor were these dead honored with tears, candles or mourners. It had come to such a pass that men who died were shown no more concern than dead goats today.

All of this clearly demonstrated that although the natural course of events with its small and occasional stings had failed to impress the wise to bear such trials with patience, the very magnitude of this now had forced even the simple people to become indifferent to them. Every hour of every day there was such a rush to carry the huge number of corpses that there was not enough blessed burial ground, especially with the usual custom of giving each body its own place. So when the ground was filled, they made huge trenches in every churchyard, in which they stacked hundreds of bodies in layers like goods stowed in the hold of a ship, covering them with a bit of earth until the bodies reached the very top.

And so I won't go on searching out every detail of our city's miseries, but while such hard times prevailed, the surrounding countryside was spared nothing. There, in the scattered villages (not to speak of the castles which were like miniature cities) and across the fields, the wretched and impoverished peasants and their families died without any medical aid or help from servants, not like men but like beasts, on the roads, on their farms, and about the houses by day and by night. For this reason, just like the townspeople, they became lax in their ways and neglected their chores as if they expected death that very day. They became positively ingenious, not in producing future yields of crops and beasts, but in ways of consuming what they already possessed. Thus, the oxen, the asses, sheep, goats, pigs and fowl and even the dogs so faithful to man, were driven from the houses, and roamed through the fields where the abandoned wheat grew uncut and unharvested. Almost as if they were rational, many animals having eaten well by day returned filled at night to their houses without any shepherding.

To leave the countryside and to return to the city, what more could be said? Such was heaven's cruelty (and perhaps also man's) that between March and the following July, the raging plague and the absence of help given the sick by the fearful healthy ones took from this life more than one hundred thousand human beings within the walls of Florence. Who would have thought before this deadly calamity that the city had held so many inhabitants? Oh, how many great palaces, how many lovely houses, how many rich mansions once filled with families of lords and ladies remained empty even to the lowliest servant! Alas! How many memorable families, how many ample heritages, how many famous fortunes remained without a lawful heir! What number of brave and beautiful ladies, lively youths, whom not only others, but Galen, Hippocrates, and Aesculapius themselves would have pronounced in the best of health, breakfasted in the morning with their relatives, companions and friends, only to dine that very night with their ancestors in the other world!

Geoffrey Chaucer, THE CANTERBURY TALES

Two extensive selections from the Canterbury Tales *appear here. The* General Prologue, *reprinted in its entirety, should be read both for the sheer poetry of Chaucer's characterizations and for its careful descriptions of the various individuals in medieval society who make up the pilgrimage groups. Pay particular attention to the economy with which Chaucer sketches a personality. One way to do that is to ask what particulars the author notices to give us an image of a person. For example, what physical charac-*

teristics of the Pardoner make us say, almost instinctively, that here is a person about whom the author holds very negative feelings?

The Nun Priest's Tale *combines a* fabliaux *(animal tale) and some typical clergyman's moralizing. The delight of the piece comes from the author's use of mock heroics, telling the story of the animals as if they were knight warriors and ladies in a story of courtly romances.*

General Prologue

Here begins the Book of the Tales of Canterbury

When April with his showers sweet with fruit
The drought of March has pierced unto the root
And bathed each vein with liquor that has power
To generate therein and sire the flower;
When Zephyr also has, with his sweet breath,
Quickened again, in every holt and heath,
The tender shoots and buds, and the young sun
Into the Ram one half his course has run,
And many little birds make melody
That sleep through all the night with open eye   10
(So Nature pricks them on to ramp and rage)
Then do folk long to go on pilgrimage,
And palmers to go seeking out strange strands,
To distant shrines well known in sundry lands.
And specially from every shire's end
Of England they to Canterbury wend,
The holy blessed martyr there to seek
Who helped them when they lay so ill and weak.

   Befall that, in that season, on a day
In Southwark, at the Tabard, as I lay   20
Ready to start upon my pilgrimage
To Canterbury, full of devout homage,
There came at nightfall to that hostelry
Some nine and twenty in a company
Of sundry persons who had chanced to fall
In fellowship, and pilgrims were they all
That toward Canterbury town would ride.
The rooms and stables spacious were and wide,
And well we there were eased, and of the best.
And briefly, when the sun had gone to rest,   30
So had I spoken with them, every one,
That I was of their fellowship anon,
And made agreement that we'd early rise
To take the road, as you I will apprise.

   But none the less, whilst I have time and space,
Before yet farther in this tale I pace,
It seems to me accordant with reason
To inform you of the state of every one
Of all of these, as it appeared to me,
And who they were, and what was their degree,   40
And even how arrayed there at the inn;
And with a knight thus will I first begin.

   A *knight* there was, and he a worthy man,
Who, from the moment that he first began

To ride about the world, loved chivalry,
Truth, honour, freedom and all courtesy.
Full worthy was he in his liege-lord's war,
And therein had he ridden (none more far)
As well in Christendom as heathenesse,
And honoured everywhere for worthiness.   50
    At Alexandria, he, when it was won;
Full oft the table's roster he'd begun
Above all nations' knights in Prussia.
In Latvia raided he, and Russia,
No christened man so oft of his degree.
In far Granada at the siege was he
Of Algeciras, and in Belmarie.
At Ayas was he and at Satalye
When they were won; and on the Middle Sea
At many a noble meeting chanced to be.   60
Of mortal battles he had fought fifteen,
And he'd fought for our faith at Tramissene
Three times in lists, and each time slain his foe.
This self-same worthy knight had been also
At one time with the lord of Palatye
Against another heathen in Turkey:
And always won he sovereign fame for prize.
Though so illustrious, he was very wise
And bore himself as meekly as a maid.
He never yet had any vileness said,   70
In all his life, to whatsoever wight.
He was a truly perfect, gentle knight.
But now, to tell you all of his array,
His steeds were good, but yet he was not gay.
Of simple fustian wore he a jupon
Sadly discoloured by his habergeon;
For he had lately come from his voyage
And now was going on this pilgrimage.
    With him there was his son, a youthful
        squire,
A lover and a lusty bachelor,   80
With locks well curled, as if they'd laid in press.
Some twenty years of age he was, I guess.
In stature he was of an average length,
Wondrously active, aye, and great of strength.
He'd ridden sometime with the cavalry
In Flanders, in Artois, and Picardy,
And borne him well within that little space
In hope to win thereby his lady's grace.
Prinked out he was, as if he were a mead,
All full of fresh-cut flowers white and red.   90
Singing he was, or fluting, all the day;
He was as fresh as is the month of May.
Short was his gown, with sleeves both long and
        wide.
Well could he sit on horse, and fairly ride.
He could make songs and words thereto indite,
Joust, and dance too, as well as sketch and write.
So hot he loved that, while night told her tale,
He slept no more than does a nightingale.

Courteous he, and humble, willing and able,
And carved before his father at the table.   100
    A *yeoman* had he, nor more servants, no,
At that time, for he chose to travel so;
And he was clad in coat and hood of green.
A sheaf of peacock arrows bright and keen
Under his belt he bore right carefully
(Well could he keep his tackle yeomanly:
His arrows had no draggled feathers low),
And in his hand he bore a mighty bow.
A cropped head had he and a sun-browned face.
Of woodcraft knew he all the useful ways.   110
Upon his arm he bore a bracer gay,
And at one side a sword and buckler, yea,
And at the other side a dagger bright,
Well sheathed and sharp as spear point in the light;
On breast a Christopher of silver sheen.
He bore a horn in baldric all of green;
A forester he truly was, I guess.
    There was also a nun, a *prioress,*
Who, in her smiling, modest was and coy;
Her greatest oath was but "By Saint Eloy!"   120
And she was known as Madam Eglantine.
Full well she sang the services divine,
Intoning through her nose, becomingly;
And fair she spoke her French, and fluently,
After the school of Stratford-at-the-Bow,
For French of Paris was not hers to know.
At table she had been well taught withal,
And never from her lips let morsels fall,
Nor dipped her fingers deep in sauce, but ate
With so much care the food upon her plate   130
That never driblet fell upon her breast.
In courtesy she had delight and zest.
Her upper lip was always wiped so clean
That in her cup was no iota seen
Of grease, when she had drunk her draught of
        wine.
Becomingly she reached for meat to dine.
And certainly delighting in good sport,
She was right pleasant, amiable—in short.
She was at pains to counterfeit the look
Of courtliness, and stately manners took,   140
And would be held worthy of reverence.
    But, to say something of her moral sense,
She was so charitable and piteous
That she would weep if she but saw a mouse
Caught in a trap, though it were dead or bled.
She had some little dogs, too, that she fed
On roasted flesh, or milk and fine white bread.
But sore she'd weep if one of them were dead,
Of if men smote it with a rod to smart:
For pity ruled her, and her tender heart.   150
Right decorous her pleated wimple was;
Her nose was fine; her eyes were blue as glass;
Her mouth was small and therewith soft and red;

But certainly she had a fair forehead;
It was almost a full span broad, I own,
For, truth to tell, she was not undergrown.
Neat was her cloak, and I was well aware.
Of coral small about her arm she'd bear
A string of beads and gauded all with green;
And therefrom hung a brooch of golden sheen   160
Whereon there was first written a crowned "A,"
And under, *Amor vincit omnia.*

    Another little *nun* with her had she,
Who was her chaplain; and of *priests* she'd three.

    A *monk* there was, one made for mastery,
An outrider, who loved his venery;
A manly man, to be an abbot able.
Full many a blooded horse had he in stable:
And when he rode men might his bridle hear
A-jingling in the whistling wind as clear,   170
Aye, and as loud as does the chapel bell
Where this brave monk was master of the cell.
The rule of Maurus or Saint Benedict,
By reason it was old and somewhat strict,
This said monk let such old things slowly pace
And followed new-world manners in their place.
He cared not for that text a clean-plucked hen
Which holds that hunters are not holy men;
Nor that a monk, when he is cloisterless,
Is like unto a fish that's waterless;   180
That is to say, a monk out of his cloister.
But this same text he held not worth an oyster;
And I said his opinion was right good.
What? Should he study as a madman would
Upon a book in cloister cell? Or yet
Go labour with his hands and swink and sweat,
As Austin bids? How shall the world be
       served?
Let Austin have his toil to him reserved.
Therefore he was a rider day and night;
Greyhounds he had, as swift as bird in flight.   190
Since riding and the hunting of the hare
Were all his love, for no cost would he spare.
I saw his sleeves were purfled at the hand
With fur of grey, the finest in the land;
Also, to fasten hood beneath his chin,
He had of good wrought gold a curious pin:
A love-knot in the larger end there was.
His head was bald and shone like any glass,
And smooth as one anointed was his face.
Fat was this lord, he stood in goodly case.   200
His bulging eyes he rolled about, and hot
They gleamed and red, like fire beneath a pot;
His boots were soft; his horse of great estate.
Now certainly he was a fine prelate:
He was not pale as some poor wasted ghost.
A fat swan loved he best of any roast.
His palfrey was as brown as is a berry.

    A *friar* there was, a wanton and a merry,

A limiter, a very festive man.
In all the Orders Four is none that can   210
Equal his gossip and his fair language.
He had arranged full many a marriage
Of women young, and this at his own cost.
Unto his order he was a noble post.
Well liked by all and intimate was he
With franklins everywhere in his country,
And with the worthy women of the town:
For at confessing he'd more power in gown
(As he himself said) than a good curate,
For of his order he was licentiate.   220
He heard confession gently, it was said,
Gently absolved too, leaving naught of dread.
He was an easy man to give penance
When knowing he should gain a good pittance;
For to a begging friar, money given
Is sign that any man has been well shriven.
For if one gave (he dared to boast of this),
He took the man's repentance not amiss.
For many a man there is so hard of heart
He cannot weep however pains may smart.   230
Therefore, instead of weeping and of prayer,
Men should give silver to poor friars all bare.
His tippet was stuck always full of knives
And pins, to give to young and pleasing wives.
And certainly he kept a merry note:
Well could he sing and play upon the rote.
At balladry he bore the prize away.
His throat was white as lily of the May;
Yet strong he was as ever champion.
In towns he knew the taverns, every one,   240
And every good host and each barmaid too—
Better than begging lepers, these he knew.
For unto no such solid man as he
Accorded it, as far as he could see,
To have sick lepers for acquaintances.
There is no honest advantageousness
In dealing with such poverty-stricken curs;
It's with the rich and with big victuallers.
And so, wherever profit might arise,
Courteous he was and humble in men's eyes.   250
There was no other man so virtuous.
He was the finest beggar of his house;
A certain district being farmed to him,
None of his brethren dared approach its rim;
For though a widow had no shoes to show,
So pleasant was his *In principio,*
He always got a farthing ere he went.
He lived by pickings, it is evident.
And he could romp as well as any whelp.
On love days could he be of mickle help.   260
For there he was not like a cloisterer,
With threadbare cope as is the poor scholar,
But he was like a lord or like a pope.
Of double worsted was his semi-cope,

That rounded like a bell, as you may guess.
He lisped a little, out of wantonness,
To make his English soft upon his tongue;
And in his harping, after he had sung,
His two eyes twinkled in his head as bright
As do the stars within the frosty night. 270
This worthy limiter was named Hubert.
    There was a *merchant* with forked beard, and girt
In motley gown, and high on horse he sat,
Upon his head a Flemish beaver hat;
His boots were fastened rather elegantly.
He spoke his notions out right pompously,
Stressing the times when he had won, not lost.
He would the sea were held at any cost
Across from Middleburgh to Orwell town.
At money-changing he could make a crown. 280
This worthy man kept all his wits well set;
There was no one could say he was in debt,
So well he governed all his trade affairs
With bargains and with borrowings and with shares.
Indeed, he was a worthy man withal,
But, sooth to say, his name I can't recall.
    A *clerk* from Oxford was with us also,
Who'd turned to getting knowledge, long ago.
As meagre was his horse as is a rake,
Nor he himself too fat, I'll undertake, 290
But he looked hollow and went soberly.
Right threadbare was his overcoat; for he
Had got him yet no churchly benefice,
Nor was so worldly as to gain office.
For he would rather have at his bed's head
Some twenty books, all bound in black and red,
Of Aristotle and his philosophy
Than rich robes, fiddle, or gay psaltery.
Yet, and for all he was philosopher,
He had but little gold within his coffer; 300
But all that he might borrow from a friend
On books and learning he would swiftly spend,
And then he'd pray right busily for the souls
Of those who gave him wherewithal for schools.
Of study took he utmost care and heed.
Not one word spoke he more than was his need;
And that was said in fullest reverence
And short and quick and full of high good sense.
Pregnant of moral virtue was his speech;
And gladly would he learn and gladly teach. 310
    A *sergeant of the law,* wary and wise,
Who'd often gone to Paul's walk to advise,
There was also, compact of excellence.
Discreet he was, and of great reverence;
At least he seemed so, his words were so wise.

Often he sat as justice in assize,
By patent or commission from the crown;
Because of learning and his high renown,
He took large fees and many robes could own.
So great a purchaser was never known. 320
All was fee simple to him, in effect,
Wherefore his claims could never be suspect.
Nowhere a man so busy of his class,
And yet he seemed much busier than he was.
All cases and all judgments could he cite
That from King William's time were apposite.
And he could draw a contract so explicit
Not any man could fault therefrom elicit;
And every statute he'd verbatim quote.
He rode but badly in a medley coat, 330
Belted in a silken sash, with little bars,
But of his dress no more particulars.
    There was a *franklin* in his company;
White was his beard as is the white daisy.
Of sanguine temperament by every sign,
He loved right well his morning sop in wine.
Delightful living was the goal he'd won,
For he was Epicurus' very son,
That held opinion that a full delight
Was true felicity, perfect and right. 340
A householder, and that a great, was he;
Saint Julian he was in his own country.
His bread and ale were always right well done;
A man with better cellars there was none.
Baked meat was never wanting in his house,
Of fish and flesh, and that so plenteous
It seemed to snow therein both food and drink
Of every dainty that a man could think.
According to the season of the year
He changed his diet and his means of cheer. 350
Full many a fattened partridge did he mew,
And many a bream and pike in fish-pond too.
Woe to his cook, except the sauces were
Poignant and sharp, and ready all his gear.
His table, waiting in his hall alway,
Stood ready covered through the livelong day.
At county sessions was he lord and sire,
And often acted as a knight of shire.
A dagger and a trinket-bag of silk
Hung from his girdle, white as morning milk. 360
He had been sheriff and been auditor;
And nowhere was a worthier vavasor.
    A *haberdasher* and a *carpenter,*
An *arras-maker, dyer,* and *weaver*
Were with us, clothed in similar livery.
All of one sober, great fraternity.
Their gear was new and well adorned it was;
Their weapons were not cheaply trimmed with brass,
But all with silver; chastely made and well.
Their girdles and their pouches too, I tell. 370

Each man of them appeared a proper burgess
To sit in guildhall on a high dais.
And each of them, for wisdom he could span,
Was fitted to have been an alderman;
For chattels they'd enough, and, too, of rent;
To which their goodwives gave a free assent,
Or else for certain they had been to blame.
It's good to hear "Madam" before one's name,
And go to church when all the world may see,
Having one's mantle borne right royally.   380
    A *cook* they had with them, just for the
      nonce,
To boil the chickens with the marrow-bones,
And flavour tartly and with galingale.
Well could he tell a draught of London ale.
And he could roast and seethe and broil and fry,
And make a good thick soup, and bake a pie.
But very ill it was, it seemed to me,
That on his shin a deadly sore had he;
For sweet blanc-mange, he made it with the
    best.
    There was a *sailor,* living far out west;   390
For aught I know, he was of Dartmouth town.
He sadly rode a hackney, in a gown,
Of thick rough cloth falling to the knee.
A dagger hanging on a cord had he
About his neck, and under arm, and down.
The summer's heat had burned his visage
    brown;
And certainly he was a good fellow.
Full many a draught of wine he'd drawn, I
    trow,
Of Bordeaux vintage, while the trader slept.
Nice conscience was a thing he never kept.   400
If that he fought and got the upper hand,
By water he sent them home to every land.
But as for craft, to reckon well his tides,
His currents and the dangerous watersides,
His harbours, and his moon, his pilotage,
There was none such from Hull to far Carthage.
Hardy, and wise in all things undertaken,
By many a tempest had his beard been shaken.
He knew well all the havens, as they were,
From Gottland to the Cape of Finisterre,   410
And every creek in Brittany and Spain;
His vessel had been christened *Madeleine.*
    With us there was a *doctor of physic;*
In all this world was none like him to pick
For talk of medicine and surgery;
For he was grounded in astronomy.
He often kept a patient from the pall
By horoscopes and magic natural.
Well could he tell the fortune ascendent
Within the houses for his sick patient.   420
He knew the cause of every malady,
Were it of hot or cold, of moist or dry,

And where engendered, and of what humour;
He was a very good practitioner.
The cause being known, down to the deepest
    root,
Anon he gave to the sick man his boot.
Ready he was, with his apothecaries,
To send him drugs and all electuaries;
By mutual aid much gold they'd always won—
Their friendship was a thing not new begun.   430
Well read was he in Esculapius,
And Deiscorides, and in Rufus,
Hippocrates, and Hali, and Galen,
Serapion, Rhazes, and Avicen,
Averrhoës, Gilbert, and Constantine,
Bernard, and Gatisden, and John Damascene.
In diet he was measured as could be,
Including naught of superfluity,
But nourishing and easy. It's no libel
To say he read but little in the Bible.   440
In blue and scarlet he went clad, withal,
Lined with a taffeta and with sendal;
And yet he was right chary of expense;
He kept the gold he gained from pestilence.
For gold in physic is a fine cordial,
And therefore loved he gold exceeding all.
    There was a *housewife* come from *Bath,* or
      near,
Who—sad to say—was deaf in either ear.
At making cloth she had so great a bent
She bettered those of Ypres and even of Ghent.   450
In all the parish there was no goodwife
Should offering make before her, on my life;
And if one did, indeed, so wroth was she
It put her out of all her charity.
Her kerchiefs were of finest weave and ground;
I dare swear that they weighed a full ten pound
Which, of a Sunday, she wore on her head.
Her hose were of the choicest scarlet red,
Close gartered, and her shoes were soft and new.
Bold was her face, and fair, and red of hue.   460
She'd been respectable throughout her life,
With five churched husbands bringing joy and
    strife,
Not counting other company in youth;
But thereof there's no need to speak, in truth.
Three times she'd journeyed to Jerusalem;
And many a foreign stream she'd had to stem;
At Rome she'd been, and she'd been in
    Boulogne,
In Spain at Santiago, and at Cologne.
She could tell much of wandering by the way:
Gap-toothed was she, it is no lie to say.   470
Upon an ambler easily she sat,
Well wimpled, aye, and over all a hat
As broad as is a buckler or a targe;
A rug was tucked around her buttocks large,

And on her feet a pair of sharpened spurs.
In company well could she laugh her slurs.
The remedies of love she knew, perchance,
For of that art she'd learned the old, old dance.
　There was a good man of religion, too,
A country *parson*, poor, I warrant you;　　480
But rich he was in holy thought and work.
He was a learned man also, a clerk,
Who Christ's own gospel truly sought to
　　preach;
Devoutly his parishioners would he teach.
Benign he was and wondrous diligent,
Patient in adverse times and well content,
As he was ofttimes proven; always blithe,
He was right loath to curse to get a tithe,
But rather would he give, in case of doubt,
Unto those poor parishioners about,　　490
Part of his income, even of his goods.
Enough with little, coloured all his moods.
Wide was his parish, houses far asunder,
But never did he fail, for rain or thunder,
In sickness, or in sin, or any state,
To visit to the farthest, small and great,
Going afoot, and in his hand a stave.
This fine example to his flock he gave,
That first he wrought and afterwards he taught;
Out of the gospel then that text he caught,　　500
And this figure he added thereunto—
That, if gold rust, what shall poor iron do?
For if the priest be foul, in whom we trust,
What wonder if a layman yield to lust?
And shame it is, if priest take thought for keep,
A shitty shepherd, shepherding clean sheep.
Well ought a priest example good to give,
By his own cleanness, how his flock should
　　live.
He never let his benefice for hire,
Leaving his flock to flounder in the mire,　　510
And ran to London, up to old Saint Paul's
To get himself a chantry there for souls,
Nor in some brotherhood did he withhold;
But dwelt at home and kept so well the fold
That never wolf could make his plans miscarry;
He was a shepherd and not mercenary.
And holy though he was, and virtuous,
To sinners he was not impiteous,
Nor haughty in his speech, nor too divine,
But in all teaching prudent and benign.　　520
To lead folk into Heaven but by stress
Of good example was his busyness.
But if some sinful one proved obstinate,
Be who it might, of high or low estate,
Him he reproved, and sharply, as I know.
There is nowhere a better priest, I trow.
He had no thirst for pomp or reverence,
Nor made himself a special, spiced conscience,

But Christ's own lore, and His apostles' twelve
He taught, but first he followed it himselve.　　530
　　With him there was a *plowman*, was his
　　　brother,
That many a load of dung, and many another
Had scattered, for a good true toiler, he,
Living in peace and perfect charity.
He loved God most, and that with his whole
　　heart,
At all times, though he played or plied his art,
And next, his neighbour, even as himself.
He'd thresh and dig, with never thought of pelf,
For Christ's own sake, for every poor wight,
All without pay, if it lay in his might.　　540
He paid his taxes, fully, fairly, well,
Both by his own toil and by stuff he'd sell.
In a tabard he rode upon a mare.
　　There were also a *reeve* and *miller* there;
A *summoner, manciple* and *pardoner*,
And these, beside myself, made all there were.
　　The *miller* was a stout churl, be it known,
Hardy and big of brawn and big of bone;
Which was well proved, for when he went on
　　lam
At wrestling, never failed he of the ram.　　550
He was a chunky fellow, broad of build;
He'd heave a door from hinges if he willed,
Or break it through, by running, with his head.
His beard, as any sow or fox, was red.
And broad it was as if it were a spade.
Upon the coping of his nose he had
A wart, and thereon stood a tuft of hairs,
Red as the bristles in an old sow's ears;
His nostrils they were black and very wide.
A sword and buckler bore he by his side.　　560
His mouth was like a furnace door for size.
He was a jester and could poetize,
But mostly all of sin and ribaldries.
He could steal corn and full thrice charge his
　　fees;
And yet he had a thumb of gold, begad.
A white coat and blue hood he wore, this lad.
A bagpipe he could blow well, be it known,
And with that same he brought us out of town.
　　There was a *manciple* from an inn of court,
To whom all buyers might quite well resort　　570
To learn the art of buying food and drink;
For whether he paid cash or not, I think
That he so knew the markets, when to buy,
He never found himself left high and dry.
Now is it not of God a full fair grace
That such a vulgar man has wit to pace
The wisdom of a crowd of learned men?
Of masters had he more than three times ten,
Who were in law expert and curious;
Whereof there were a dozen in that house　　580

Fit to be stewards of both rent and land
Of any lord in England who would stand
Upon his own and live in manner good,
In honour, debtless (save his head were wood)
Or live as frugally as he might desire;
These men were able to have helped a shire
In any case that ever might befall;
And yet this manciple outguessed them all.
    The *reeve* he was a slender, choleric man,
Who shaved his beard as close as razor can.   590
His hair was cut round even with his ears;
His top was tonsured like a pulpiteer's.
Long were his legs, and they were very lean,
And like a staff, with no calf to be seen.
Well could he manage granary and bin;
No auditor could ever on him win.
He could foretell, by drought and by the rain,
The yielding of his seed and of his grain.
His lord's sheep and his oxen and his dairy,
His swine and horses, all his stores, his poultry, 600
Were wholly in this steward's managing;
And, by agreement, he'd made reckoning
Since his young lord of age was twenty years;
Yet no man ever found him in arrears.
There was no agent, hind, or herd who'd cheat
But he knew well his cunning and deceit;
They were afraid of him as of the death.
His cottage was a good one, on a heath;
By green trees shaded with this dwelling-place.
Much better than his lord could he purchase.   610
Right rich he was in his own private right,
Seeing he'd pleased his lord, by day and night,
By giving him, or lending, of his goods,
And so got thanked—but yet got coats and
    hoods.
In youth he'd learned a good trade, and had been
A carpenter, as fine as could be seen.
This steward sat a horse that well could trot,
And was all dapple-grey, and was named Scot.
A long surcoat of blue did he parade,
And at his side he bore a rusty blade.   620
Of Norfolk was this reeve of whom I tell,
From near a town that men call Badeswell.
Bundled he was like friar from chin to croup,
And ever he rode hindmost of our troop.
    A *summoner* was with us in that place,
Who had a fiery-red, cherubic face,
For eczema he had; his eyes were narrow.
As hot he was, and lecherous, as a sparrow;
With black and scabby brows and scanty beard;
He had a face that little children feared.   630
There was no mercury, sulphur, or litharge,
No borax, ceruse, tartar, could discharge,
Nor ointment that could cleanse enough, or
    bite,
To free him of his boils and pimples white,

Nor of the bosses resting on his cheeks.
Well loved he garlic, onions, aye and leeks,
And drinking of strong wine as red as blood.
Then would he talk and shout as madman
    would.
And when a deal of wine he'd poured within,
Then would he utter no word save Latin.   640
Some phrases had he learned, say two or three,
Which he had garnered out of some decree;
No wonder, for he'd heard it all the day;
And all you know right well that even a jay
Can call out "Wat" as well as can the pope.
But when, for aught else, into him you'd grope,
'Twas found he'd spent his whole philosophy;
Just *"Questio quid juris"* would he cry.
He was a noble rascal, and a kind;
A better comrade 'twould be hard to find.   650
Why, he would suffer, for a quart of wine,
Some good fellow to have his concubine
A twelve-month, and excuse him to the full
(Between ourselves, though, he could pluck a
    gull)
And if he chanced upon a good fellow,
He would instruct him never to have awe,
In such a case, of the archdeacon's curse,
Except a man's soul lie within his purse;
For in his purse the man should punished be.
"The purse is the archdeacon's Hell," said he.   660
But well I know he lied in what he said;
A curse ought every guilty man to dread
(For curse can kill, as absolution save),
And 'ware *significavit* to the grave.
In his own power had he, and at ease,
The boys and girls of all the diocese,
And knew their secrets, and by counsel led.
A garland had he set upon his head,
Large as a tavern's wine-bush on a stake;
A buckler had he made of bread they bake.   670
    With him there rode a gentle *pardoner*
Of Rouncival, his friend and his compeer;
Straight from the court of Rome had journeyed
    he.
Loudly he sang "Come hither, love, to me,"
The summoner joining with a burden round;
Was never horn of half so great a sound.
This pardoner had hair as yellow as wax,
But lank it hung as does a strike of flax;
In wisps hung down such locks as he'd on head,
And with them he his shoulders overspread;   680
But thin they dropped, and stringy, one by one.
But as to hood, for sport of it, he'd none,
Though it was packed in wallet all the while
It seemed to him he went in latest style,
Dishevelled, save for cap, his head all bare.
As shiny eyes he had as has a hare.
He had a fine veronica sewed to cap.

His wallet lay before him in his lap,
Stuffed full of pardons brought from Rome all
    hot.
A voice he had that bleated like a goat. 690
No beard had he, nor ever should he have,
For smooth his face as he'd just had a shave;
I think he was a gelding or a mare.
But in his craft, from Berwick unto Ware,
Was no such pardoner in any place.
For in his bag he had a pillowcase
The which, he said, was Our True Lady's veil:
He said he had a piece of the very sail
That good Saint Peter had, what time he went
Upon the sea, till Jesus changed his bent. 700
He had a latten cross set full of stones,
And in a bottle had he some pig's bones.
But with these relics, when he came upon
Some simple parson, then this paragon
In that one day more money stood to gain
Than the poor dupe in two months could attain.
And thus, with flattery and suchlike japes,
He made the parson and the rest his apes.
But yet, to tell the whole truth at the last,
He was, in church, a fine ecclesiast. 710
Well could he read a lesson or a story,
But best of all he sang an offertory;
For well he knew that when that song was
    sung,
Then might he preach, and all with polished
    tongue,
To win some silver, as he right well could;
Therefore he sang so merrily and so loud.
    Now have I told you briefly, in a clause,
The state, the array, the number, and the cause
Of the assembling of this company
In Southwark, at this noble hostelry 720
Known as the Tabard Inn, hard by the Bell.
But now the time is come wherein to tell
How all we bore ourselves that very night
When at the hostelry we did alight.
And afterward the story I engage
To tell you of our common pilgrimage.
But first, I pray you, of your courtesy,
You'll not ascribe it to vulgarity
Though I speak plainly of this matter here,
Retailing you their words and means of cheer; 730
Nor though I use their very terms, nor lie.
For this thing do you know as well as I:
When one repeats a tale told by a man,
He must report, as nearly as he can,
Every least word, if he remember it.
However rude it be, or how unfit;
Or else he may be telling what's untrue,
Embellishing and fictionizing too.
He may not spare, although it were his brother;
He must as well say one word as another. 740

Christ spoke right broadly out, in holy writ,
And, you know well, there's nothing low in it.
And Plato says, to those able to read:
"The word should be the cousin to the deed."
Also, I pray that you'll forgive it me
If I have not set folk, in their degree
Here in this tale, by rank as they should stand.
My wits are not the best, you'll understand.

    Great cheer our host gave to us, every one,
And to the supper set us all anon; 750
And served us then with victuals of the best.
Strong was the wine and pleasant to each guest.
A seemly man our good host was, withal,
Fit to have been a marshal in some hall;
He was a large man, with protruding eyes,
As fine a burgher as in Cheapside lies;
Bold in his speech, and wise, and right well
    taught,
And as to manhood, lacking there in naught.
Also, he was a very merry man,
And after meat, at playing he began, 760
Speaking of mirth among some other things,
When all of us had paid our reckonings;
And saying thus: "Now masters, verily
You are all welcome here, and heartily:
For by my truth, and telling you no lie,
I have not seen, this year, a company
Here in this inn, fitter for sport than now.
Fain would I make you happy, knew I how.
And of a game have I this moment thought
To give you joy, and it shall cost you naught. 770
    "You go to Canterbury; may God speed
And the blest martyr soon requite your meed.
And well I know, as you go on your way,
You'll tell good tales and shape yourselves to
    play;
For truly there's no mirth nor comfort, none,
Riding the roads as dumb as is a stone;
And therefore will I furnish you a sport,
As I just said, to give you some comfort.
And if you like it, all, by one assent,
And will be ruled by me, of my judgment, 780
And will so do as I'll proceed to say,
Tomorrow, when you ride upon your way,
Then, by my father's spirit, who is dead,
If you're not gay, I'll give you up my head.
Hold up your hands, nor more about it speak."
    Our full assenting was not far to seek;
We thought there was no reason to think twice,
And granted him his way without advice,
And bade him tell his verdict just and wise,
    "Masters," quoth he, "here now is my
      advice; 790
But take it not, I pray you, in disdain;
This is the point, to put it short and plain,

That each of you, beguiling the long day,
Shall tell two stories as you wend your way
To Canterbury town; and each of you
On coming home, shall tell another two,
All of adventures he has known befall.
And he who plays his part the best of all,
That is to say, who tells upon the road
Tales of best sense, in most amusing mode,   800
Shall have a supper at the others' cost
Here in this room and sitting by this post,
When we come back again from Canterbury.
And now, the more to warrant you'll be merry,
I will myself, and gladly, with you ride
At my own cost, and I will be your guide.
But whosoever shall my rule gainsay
Shall pay for all that's bought along the way.
And if you are agreed that it be so,
Tell me at once, or if not, tell me no,   810
And I will act accordingly. No more."
    This thing was granted, and our oaths we
        swore,
With right glad hearts, and prayed of him, also,
That he would take the office, nor forgo
The place of governor of all of us,
Judging our tales; and by his wisdom thus
Arrange that supper at a certain price,
We to be ruled, each one, by his advice
In things both great and small; by one assent,
We stood committed to his government.   820
And thereupon, the wine was fetched anon;
We drank, and then to rest went every one,
And that without a longer tarrying.
    Next morning, when the day began to spring,
Up rose our host, and acting as our cock,
He gathered us together in a flock,
And forth we rode, a jog-trot being the pace,
Until we reached Saint Thomas' watering-place.
And there our host pulled horse up to a walk,
And said: "Now, masters, listen while I talk.   830
You know what you agreed at set of sun.
If even-song and morning-song are one,
Let's here decide who first shall tell a tale.
And as I hope to drink more wine and ale,
Whoso proves rebel to my government
Shall pay for all that by the way is spent.
Come now, draw cuts, before we farther win,
And he that draws the shortest shall begin.
Sir knight," said he, "my master and my lord,
You shall draw first as you have pledged your
        word.   840
Come near," quoth he, "my lady prioress:
And you, sir clerk, put by your bashfulness,
Nor ponder more; out hands, now, every
        man!"
    At once to draw a cut each one began,
And, to make short the matter, as it was,

Whether by chance or whatsoever cause,
The truth is, that the cut fell to the knight,
At which right happy then was every wight.
Thus that his story first of all he'd tell.
According to the compact, it befell,   850
As you have heard. Why argue to and fro?
And when this good man saw that it was so,
Being a wise man and obedient
To plighted word, given by free assent,
He said: "Since I must then begin the game,
Why, welcome be the cut, and in God's name!
Now let us ride, and hearken what I say."
    And at that word we rode forth on our way;
And he began to speak, with right good cheer,
His tale anon, as it is written here.   900

HERE ENDS THE PROLOGUE OF THIS BOOK.

The Nun's Priest's Tale

Once, long ago, there dwelt a poor old widow
In a small cottage, by a little meadow
Beside a grove and standing in a dale.
This widow-woman of whom I tell my tale
Since the sad day when last she was a wife   5
Had led a very patient, simple life.
Little she had in capital or rent,
But still, by making do with what God sent,
She kept herself and her two daughters going.
Three hefty sows—no more—   10
        were all her showing,
Three cows as well; there was a sheep called
        Molly.
Sooty her hall, her kitchen melancholy,
And there she ate full many a slender meal;
There was no *sauce piquante* to spice her veal,   15
No dainty morsel ever passed her throat,
According to her cloth she cut her coat.
Repletion never left her in disquiet
And all her physic was a temperate diet,
Hard work for exercise and heart's content.   20
And rich man's gout did nothing to prevent
Her dancing, apoplexy struck her not;
She drank no wine, nor white, nor red had got.
Her board was mostly served with white and
        black,
Milk and brown bread, in which she found no
        lack;   25
Broiled bacon or an egg or two were common,
She was in fact a sort of dairy-woman.
    She had a yard that was enclosed about
By a stockade and a dry ditch without,
In which she kept a cock called Chanticleer.   30
In all the land for crowing he'd no peer;
His voice was jollier than the organ blowing
In church on Sundays, he was great at crowing.
Far, far more regular than any clock

Or abbey bell the crowing of this cock. 35
The equinoctial wheel and its position
At each ascent he knew by intuition;
At every hour—fifteen degrees of movement—
He crowed so well there could be no
    improvement.
His comb was redder than fine coral, tall 40
And battlemented like a castle wall,
His bill was black and shone as bright as jet,
Like azure were his legs and they were set
On azure toes with nails of lily white,
Like burnished gold his feathers, flaming
    bright. 45
  This gentlecock was master in some measure
Of seven hens, all there to do his pleasure.
They were his sisters and his paramours,
Coloured like him in all particulars;
She with the loveliest dyes upon her throat 50
Was known as gracious Lady Pertelote.
Courteous she was, discreet and debonair,
Companionable too, and took such care
In her deportment, since she was seven days old
She held the heart of Chanticleer controlled, 55
Locked up securely in her every limb;
O what a happiness his love to him!
And such a joy it was to hear them sing,
As when the glorious sun began to spring,
In sweet accord, *My Love is far from land* 60
—For in those far off days I understand
All birds and animals could speak and sing.
  Now it befell, as dawn began to spring,
When Chanticleer and Pertelote and all
His wives were perched in this poor widow's
    hall 65
(Fair Pertelote was next him on the perch),
This Chanticleer began to groan and lurch
Like someone sorely troubled by a dream,
And Pertelote who heard him roar and scream
Was quite aghast and said, 'O dearest heart, 70
What's ailing you? Why do you groan and start?
Fie, what a sleeper! What a noise to make!'
'Madam,' he said, 'I beg you not to take
Offence, but by the Lord I had a dream
So terrible just now I had to scream; 75
I still can feel my heart racing from fear.
God turn my dream to good and guard all here,
And keep my body out of durance vile!
I dreamt that roaming up and down a while
Within our yard I saw a kind of beast, 80
A sort of hound that tried or seemed at least
To try and seize me . . . would have killed me dead!
His colour was a blend of yellow and red,
His ears and tail were tipped with sable fur
Unlike the rest; he was a russet cur. 85
Small was his snout, his eyes were glowing bright.
It was enough to make one die of fright.

That was no doubt what made me groan and
    swoon.'
  'For shame,' she said, 'you timorous poltroon!
Alas, what cowardice! By God above, 90
You've forfeited my heart and lost my love.
I cannot love a coward, come what may.
For certainly, whatever we may say,
All women long—and O that it might be!—
For husbands tough, dependable and free, 95
Secret, discreet, no niggard, not a fool
That boasts and then will find his courage cool
At every trifling thing. By God above,
How dare you say for shame, and to your love,
That there was anything at all you feared? 100
Have you no manly heart to match your beard?
And can a dream reduce you to such terror?
Dreams are a vanity, God knows, pure error.
Dreams are engendered in the too-replete
From vapours in the belly, which compete 105
With others, too abundant, swollen tight.
  'No doubt the redness in your dream to-night
Comes from the superfluity and force
Of the red choler in your blood. Of course.
That is what puts a dreamer in the dread 110
Of crimsoned arrows, fires flaming red,
Of great red monsters making as to fight him,
And big red whelps and little ones to bite him;
Just so the black and melancholy vapours
Will set a sleeper shrieking, cutting capers 115
And swearing that black bears, black bulls as well,
Or blackest fiends are haling him to Hell.
And there are other vapours that I know
That on a sleeping man will work their woe,
But I'll pass on as lightly as I can. 120
  'Take Cato now, that was so wise a man,
Did he not say, "Take no account of dreams"?
Now, sir,' she said, 'on flying from these beams,
For love of God do take some laxative;
Upon my soul that's the advice to give 125
For melancholy choler; let me urge
You free yourself from vapours with a purge.
And that you may have no excuse to tarry
By saying this town has no apothecary,
I shall myself instruct you and prescribe 130
Herbs that will cure all vapours of that tribe,
Herbs from our very farmyard! You will find
Their natural property is to unbind
And purge you well beneath and well above.
Now don't forget it, dear, for God's own love! 135
Your face is choleric and shows distension;
Be careful lest the sun in his ascension
Should catch you full of humours, hot and many.
And if he does, my dear, I'll lay a penny
It means a bout of fever or a breath 140
Of tertian ague. You may catch your death.
  'Worms for a day or two I'll have to give

As a digestive, then your laxative.
Centaury, fumitory, caper-spurge
And hellebore will make a splendid purge;   145
And then there's laurel or the blackthorn berry,
Ground-ivy too that makes our yard so merry;
Peck them right up, my dear, and swallow whole.
Be happy, husband, by your father's soul!
Don't be afraid of dreams. I'll say no more.'   150
   'Madam,' he said, 'I thank you for your lore,
But with regard to Cato all the same,
His wisdom has, no doubt, a certain fame,
But though he said that we should take no heed
Of dreams, by God, in ancient books I read   155
Of many a man of more authority
Than ever Cato was, believe you me,
Who say the very opposite is true
And prove their theories by experience too.
Dreams have quite often been significations   160
As well of triumphs as of tribulations
That people undergo in this our life.
This needs no argument at all, dear wife,
The proof is all too manifest indeed.
   'One of the greatest authors one can read   165
Says thus: there were two comrades once who
    went
On pilgrimage, sincere in their intent.
And as it happened they had reached a town
Where such a throng was milling up and down
And yet so scanty the accommodation,   170
They could not find themselves a habitation,
No, not a cottage that could lodge them both.
And so they separated, very loth,
Under constraint of this necessity
And each went off to find some hostelry,   175
And lodge whatever way his luck might fall.
   'The first of them found refuge in a stall
Down in a yard with oxen and a plough.
His friend found lodging for himself somehow
Elsewhere, by accident or destiny,   180
Which governs all of us and equally.
   'Now it so happened, long ere it was day,
This fellow had a dream, and as he lay
In bed it seemed he heard his comrade call,
"Help! I am lying in an ox's stall   185
And shall tonight be murdered as I lie.
Help me, dear brother, help or I shall die!
Come in all haste!" Such were the words he spoke;
The dreamer, lost in terror, then awoke.
But, once awake, he paid it no attention,   190
Turned over and dismissed it as invention,
It was a dream, he thought, a fantasy.
And twice he dreamt this dream successively.
   'Yet a third time his comrade came again,
Or seemed to come, and said, "I have been
    slain!   195

Look, look! my wounds are bleeding wide and
    deep.
Rise early in the morning, break your sleep
And go to the west gate. You there shall see
A cart all loaded up with dung," said he,
"And in that dung my body has been hidden.   200
Boldly arrest that cart as you are bidden.
It was my money that they killed me for."
   'He told him every detail, sighing sore,
And pitiful in feature, pale of hue.
This dream, believe me, Madam, turned out
    true;   205
For in the dawn, as soon as it was light,
He went to where his friend had spent the night
And when he came upon the cattle-stall
He looked about him and began to call.
   'The innkeeper, appearing thereupon,   210
Quickly gave answer, "Sir, your friend has gone.
He left the town a little after dawn."
The man began to feel suspicious, drawn
By memories of his dream—the western gate,
The dung-cart—off he went, he would not
    wait,   215
Towards the western entry. There he found,
Seemingly on its way to dung some ground,
A dung-cart loaded on the very plan
Described so closely by the murdered man.
So he began to shout courageously   220
For right and vengeance on the felony,
"My friend's been killed! There's been a foul
    attack,
He's in that cart and gaping on his back!
Fetch the authorities, get the sheriff down
—Whosever job it is to run the town—   225
Help! My companion's murdered, sent to glory!"
   'What need I add to finish off the story?
People ran out and cast the cart to ground,
And in the middle of the dung they found
The murdered man. The corpse was fresh and
    new.   230
   'O blessed God, that art so just and true,
Thus thou revealest murder! As we say,
"Murder will out." We see it day by day.
Murder's a foul, abominable treason,
So loathsome to God's justice, to God's
    reason,   235
He will not suffer its concealment. True,
Things may lie hidden for a year or two,
But still "Murder will out", that's my conclusion.
   'All the town officers in great confusion
Seized on the carter and they gave him hell,   240
And then they racked the innkeeper as well,
And both confessed. And then they took the
    wrecks
And there and then they hanged them by their necks.

'By this we see that dreams are to be dreaded.
And in the self-same book I find embedded,   245
Right in the very chapter after this
(I'm not inventing, as I hope for bliss)
The story of two men who started out
To cross the sea—for merchandise no doubt—
But as the winds were contrary they waited.   250
It was a pleasant town, I should have stated,
Merrily grouped about the haven-side.
A few days later with the evening tide
The wind veered round so as to suit them best;
They were delighted and they went to rest   255
Meaning to sail next morning early. Well,
To one of them a miracle befell.

'This man as he lay sleeping, it would seem,
Just before dawn had an astounding dream.
He thought a man was standing by his bed   260
Commanding him to wait, and thus he said:
"If you set sail to-morrow, as you intend,
You will be drowned. My tale is at an end."

'He woke and told his friend what had occurred
And begged him that the journey be deferred   265
At least a day, implored him not to start.
But his companion, lying there apart,
Began to laugh and treat him to derision.
"I'm not afraid," he said, "of any vision,
To let it interfere with my affairs;   270
A straw for all your dreamings and your scares.
Dreams are just empty nonsense, merest japes;
Why, people dream all day of owls and apes,
All sorts of trash that can't be understood,
Things that have never happened and never
     could.   275
But as I see you mean to stay behind
And miss the tide for wilful sloth of mind
God knows I'm sorry for it, but good day!"
And so he took his leave and went his way.

'And yet, before they'd covered half the
     trip   280
—I don't know what went wrong—
     there was a rip
And by some accident the ship went down,
Her bottom rent, all hands aboard to drown
In sight of all the vessels at her side,
That had put out upon the self-same tide.   285

'So, my dear Pertelote, if you discern
The force of these examples, you may learn
One never should be careless about dreams,
For, undeniably, I say it seems
That many are a sign of trouble breeding.   290

'Now, take St Kenelm's life which I've been
     reading;
He was Kenulphus' son, the noble King
Of Mercia. Now, St Kenelm dreamt a thing
Shortly before they murdered him one day.

He saw his murder in a dream, I say.   295
His nurse expounded it and gave her reasons
On every point and warned him against treasons
But as the saint was only seven years old
All that she said about it left him cold.
He was so holy how could visions hurt?   300

'By God, I willingly would give my shirt
To have you read his legend as I've read it;
And, Madam Pertelote, upon my credit,
Macrobius wrote of dreams and can explain us
The vision of young Scipio Africanus,   305
And he affirms that dreams can give a due
Warning of things that later on come true.

'And then there's the Old Testament—a manual
Well worth your study; see the *Book of Daniel*.
Did Daniel think a dream was vanity?   310
Read about Joseph too and you will see
That many dreams—I do not say that all—
Give cognizance of what is to befall.

'Look at Lord Pharaoh, king of Egypt! Look
At what befell his butler and his cook.   315
Did not their visions have a certain force?
But those who study history of course
Meet many dreams that set them wondering.

'What about Croesus too, the Lydian king,
Who dreamt that he was sitting in a tree,   320
Meaning he would be hanged? It had to be.

'Or take Andromache, great Hector's wife;
The day on which he was to lose his life
She dreamt about, the very night before,
And realized that if Hector went to war   325
He would be lost that very day in battle.
She warned him; he dismissed it all as prattle
And sallied forth to fight, being self-willed,
And there he met Achilles and was killed.
The tale is long and somewhat overdrawn,   330
And anyhow it's very nearly dawn,
So let me say in very brief conclusion
My dream undoubtedly foretells confusion,
It bodes me ill, I say. And, furthermore,
Upon your laxatives I set no store,   335
For they are venomous. I've suffered by them
Often enough before, and I defy them.

'And now, let's talk of fun and stop all this.
Dear Madam, as I hope for Heaven's bliss,
Of one thing God has sent me plenteous
     grace,   340
For when I see the beauty of your face,
That scarlet loveliness about your eyes,
All thought of terror and confusion dies.
For it's as certain as the Creed, I know,
Mulier est hominis confusio   345
(A Latin tag, dear Madam, meaning this:
"Woman is man's delight and all his bliss"),
For when at night I feel your feathery side,

Although perforce I cannot take a ride
Because, alas, our perch was made too narrow, 350
Delight and solace fill me to the marrow
And I defy all visions and all dreams!'
    And with that word he flew down from the
      beams,
For it was day, and down his hens flew all,
And with a chuck he gave the troupe a call 355
For he had found a seed upon the floor.
Royal he was, he was afraid no more.
He feathered Pertelote in wanton play
And trod her twenty times ere prime of day.
Grim as a lion's was his manly frown 360
As on his toes he sauntered up and down;
He scarcely deigned to set his foot to ground
And every time a seed of corn was found
He gave a chuck, and up his wives ran all.
Thus royal as a prince who strides his hall 365
Leave we this Chanticleer engaged on feeding
And pass to the adventure that was breeding.
    Now when the month in which the world
      began,
March, the first month, when God created man,
Was over, and the thirty-second day 370
Thereafter ended, on the third of May
It happened that Chanticleer in all his pride,
His seven wives attendant at his side,
Cast his eyes upward to the blazing sun,
Which in the sign of *Taurus* then had run 375
His twenty-one degrees and somewhat more,
And knew by nature and no other lore
That it was nine o'clock. With blissful voice
He crew triumphantly and said, 'Rejoice,
Behold the sun! The sun is up, my seven. 380
Look, it has climbed forty degrees in heaven,
Forty degrees and one in fact, by this.
Dear Madam Pertelote, my earthly bliss,
Hark to those blissful birds and how they sing!
Look at those pretty flowers, how they spring! 385
Solace and revel fill my heart!' He laughed.
    But in that moment Fate let fly her shaft;
Ever the latter end of joy is woe,
God knows that worldly joy is swift to go.
A rhetorician with a flair for style 390
Could chronicle this maxim in his file
Of Notable Remarks with safe conviction.
Then let the wise give ear; this is no fiction.
My story is as true, I undertake,
As that of good Sir Lancelot du Lake 395
Who held all women in such high esteem.
Let me return full circle to my theme.
    A coal-tipped fox of sly iniquity
That had been lurking round the grove for three
Long years, that very night burst through and
      passed 400

Stockade and hedge, as Providence forecast,
Into the yard where Chanticleer the Fair
Was wont, with all his ladies, to repair.
Still, in a bed of cabbages, he lay
Until about the middle of the day 405
Watching the cock and waiting for his cue,
As all these homicides so gladly do
That lie about in wait to murder men.
O false assassin, lurking in thy den!
O new Iscariot, new Ganelon! 410
And O Greek Sinon, thou whose treachery won
Troy town and brought it utterly to sorrow!
O Chanticleer, accursed be that morrow
That brought thee to the yard from thy high
      beams!
Thou hadst been warned, and truly, by thy
      dreams 415
That this would be a perilous day for thee.
    But that which God's foreknowledge can foresee
Must needs occur, as certain men of learning
Have said. Ask any scholar of discerning;
He'll say the Schools are filled with altercation 420
On this vexed matter of predestination
Long bandied by a hundred thousand men.
How can I sift it to the bottom then?
The Holy Doctor St Augustine shines
In this, and there is Bishop Bradwardine's 425
Authority, Boethius too, decreeing
Whether the fact of God's divine foreseeing
Constrains me to perform a certain act
—And by 'constraint' I mean the simple fact
Of mere compulsion by necessity— 430
Or whether a free choice is granted me
To do a given act or not to do it
Though, ere it was accomplished, God
      foreknew it,
Or whether Providence is not so stringent
And merely makes necessity contingent. 435
    But I decline discussion of the matter;
My tale is of a cock and of the clatter
That came of following his wife's advice
To walk about his yard on the precise
Morning after the dream of which I told. 440
    O woman's counsel is so often cold!
A woman's counsel brought us first to woe,
Made Adam out of Paradise to go
Where he had been so merry, so well at ease.
But, for I know not whom it may displease 445
If I suggest that women are to blame,
Pass over that; I only speak in game.
Read the authorities to know about
What has been said of women; you'll find out.
These are the cock's words, and not mine,
      I'm giving; 450
I think no harm of any woman living.

Merrily in her dust-bath in the sand
Lay Pertelote. Her sisters were at hand
Basking in sunlight. Chanticleer sang free,
More merrily than a mermaid in the sea   455
(For *Physiologus* reports the thing
And says how well and merrily they sing).
And so it happened as he cast his eye
Towards the cabbage at a butterfly
It fell upon the fox there, lying low.   460
Gone was all inclination then to crow.
'Cok cok,' he cried, giving a sudden start,
As one who feels a terror at his heart,
For natural instinct teaches beasts to flee
The moment they perceive an enemy,   465
Though they had never met with it before.
  This Chanticleer was shaken to the core
And would have fled. The fox was quick to say
However, 'Sir! Whither so fast away?
Are you afraid of me, that am your friend?   470
A fiend, or worse, I should be, to intend
You harm, or practise villainy upon you;
Dear sir, I was not even spying on you!
Truly I came to do no other thing
Than just to lie and listen to you sing.   475
You have as merry a voice as God has given
To any angel in the courts of Heaven;
To that you add a musical sense as strong
As had Boethius who was skilled in song.
My Lord your Father (God receive his soul!),   480
Your mother too—how courtly, what control!—
Have honoured my poor house, to my great ease;
And you, sir, too, I should be glad to please.
For, when it comes to singing, I'll say this
(Else may these eyes of mine be barred from
    bliss),   485
There never was a singer I would rather
Have heard at dawn than your respected father.
All that he sang came welling from his soul
And how he put his voice under control!
The pains he took to keep his eyes tight shut   490
In concentration—then the tip-toe strut,
The slender neck stretched out, the delicate beak!
No singer could approach him in technique
Or rival him in song, still less surpass.
I've read the story in *Burnel the Ass,*   495
Among some other verses, of a cock
Whose leg in youth was broken by a knock
A clergyman's son had given him, and for this
He made the father lose his benefice.
But certainly there's no comparison   500
Between the subtlety of such a one
And the discretion of your father's art
And wisdom. Oh, for charity of heart,
Can you not emulate your sire and sing?'
  This Chanticleer began to beat a wing   505

As one incapable of smelling treason,
So wholly had this flattery ravished reason.
Alas, my lords! there's many a sycophant
And flatterer that fill your courts with cant
And give more pleasure with their zeal
    forsooth   510
Than he who speaks in soberness and truth.
Read what *Ecclesiasticus* records
Of flatterers. 'Ware treachery, my lords!
  This Chanticleer stood high upon his toes,
He stretched his neck, his eyes began to close,   515
His beak to open; with his eyes shut tight
He then began to sing with all his might.
  Sir Russel Fox leapt in to the attack,
Grabbing his gorge he flung him o'er his back
And off he bore him to the woods, the brute,   520
And for the moment there was no pursuit.
  O Destiny that may not be evaded!
Alas that Chanticleer had so paraded!
Alas that he had flown down from the beams!
O that his wife took no account of dreams!   525
And on a Friday too to risk their necks!
O Venus, goddess of the joys of sex,
Since Chanticleer thy mysteries professed
And in thy service always did his best,
And more for pleasure than to multiply   530
His kind, on thine own day, is he to die?
  O Geoffrey, thou my dear and sovereign master
Who, when they brought King Richard to disaster
And shot him dead, lamented so his death,
Would that I had thy skill, thy gracious
    breath,   535
To chide a Friday half so well as you!
(For he was killed upon a Friday too.)
Then I could fashion you a rhapsody
For Chanticleer in dread and agony.
  Sure never such a cry or lamentation   540
Was made by ladies of high Trojan station,
When Ilium fell and Pyrrhus with his sword
Grabbed Priam by the beard, their king and lord,
And slew him there as the *Aeneid* tells,
As what was uttered by those hens. Their
    yells   545
Surpassed them all in palpitating fear
When they beheld the rape of Chanticleer.
Dame Pertelote emitted sovereign shrieks
That echoed up in anguish to the peaks
Louder than those extorted from the wife   550
Of Hasdrubal, when he had lost his life
And Carthage all in flame and ashes lay.
She was so full of torment and dismay
That in the very flames she chose her part
And burnt to ashes with a steadfast heart.   555
O woeful hens, louder your shrieks and higher
Than those of Roman matrons when the fire

Consumed their husbands, senators of Rome,
When Nero burnt their city and their home;
Beyond a doubt that Nero was their bale!   560
  Now let me turn again to tell my tale;
This blessed widow and her daughters two
Heard all these hens in clamour and halloo
And, rushing to the door at all this shrieking,
They saw the fox towards the covert streaking   565
And, on his shoulder, Chanticleer stretched flat.
'Look, look!' they cried, 'O mercy, look at that!
Ha! Ha! the fox!' and after him they ran,
And stick in hand ran many a serving man,
Ran Coll our dog, ran Talbot, Bran and
    Shaggy,   570
And with a distaff in her hand ran Maggie,
Ran cow and calf and ran the very hogs
In terror at the barking of the dogs;
The men and women shouted, ran and cursed,
They ran so hard they thought their hearts
    would burst,   575
They yelled like fiends in Hell, ducks left the water
Quacking and flapping as on point of slaughter,
Up flew the geese in terror over the trees,
Out of the hive came forth the swarm of bees;
So hideous was the noise—God bless us all,   580
Jack Straw and all his followers in their brawl
Were never half so shrill, for all their noise,
When they were murdering those Flemish boys,
As that day's hue and cry upon the fox.
They grabbed up trumpets made of brass and
    box,   585
Of horn and bone, on which they blew and pooped,
And therewithal they shouted and they whooped
So that it seemed the very heavens would fall.
  And now, good people, pay attention all.
See how Dame Fortune quickly changes side   590
And robs her enemy of hope and pride!
This cock that lay upon the fox's back
In all his dread contrived to give a quack
And said, 'Sir Fox, if I were you, as God's
My witness, I would round upon these clods   595
And shout, "Turn back, you saucy bumpkins all!
A very pestilence upon you fall!
Now that I have in safety reached the wood
Do what you like, the cock is mine for good;
I'll eat him there in spite of every one."'   600
  The fox replying, 'Faith, it shall be done!'
Opened his mouth and spoke. The nimble bird,
Breaking away upon the uttered word,
Flew high into the tree-tops on the spot.
And when the fox perceived where he had
    got,   605
'Alas,' he cried, 'alas, my Chanticleer,
I've done you grievous wrong, indeed I fear
I must have frightened you; I grabbed too hard
When I caught hold and took you from the yard.

But, sir, I meant no harm, don't be offended,   610
Come down and I'll explain what I intended;
So help me God I'll tell the truth—on oath!'
'No,' said the cock, 'and curses on us both,
And first on me if I were such a dunce
As let you fool me oftener than once.   615
Never again, for all your flattering lies,
You'll coax a song to make me blink my eyes;
And as for those who blink when they should look,
God blot them from his everlasting Book!'
'Nay, rather,' said the fox, 'his plagues be
    flung   620
On all who chatter that should hold their tongue.'
  Lo, such it is not to be on your guard
Against the flatterers of the world, or yard,
And if you think my story is absurd,
A foolish trifle of a beast and bird,   625
A fable of a fox, a cock, a hen,
Take hold upon the moral, gentlemen.
  St Paul himself, a saint of great discerning,
Says that all things are written for our learning;
So take the grain and let the chaff be still.   630
And, gracious Father, if it be thy will
As saith my Saviour, make us all good men,
And bring us to his heavenly bliss.
                        Amen.

Christine de Pisan
Book of the City of Ladies

This work (its title is a play on Augustine's City of God *) is an elaborate allegory describing the building of a city with women's accomplishments. It is an argument against the antifeminist writers of the day who condemned women as the snare of Satan and as inferior to men. This selection deals with some notable women: Sappho; the goddess Minerva; and notable educated women of the Middle Ages.*

30. HERE SHE SPEAKS OF SAPPHO, THAT MOST SUBTLE WOMAN, POET, AND PHILOSOPHER.

"The wise Sappho, who was from the city of Mytilene, was no less learned than Proba. This Sappho had a beautiful body and face and was agreeable and pleasant in appearance, conduct, and speech. But the charm of her profound understanding surpassed all the other charms with which she was endowed, for she was expert and learned in several arts and sciences, and she was not only well-educated in the works and writings composed by others but also discovered many new things herself and wrote many books and poems. Concerning her, Boccaccio has offered these fair words couched in the sweetness of poetic language: 'Sappho, possessed of sharp wit and burning desire for constant study in the midst of bestial and ignorant men, frequented the heights of Mount Parnassus, that is, of perfect study. Thanks to her fortunate boldness and daring, she kept company with the Muses, that is, the arts and sciences, without being turned away. She entered the forest of laurel trees filled with may boughs, greenery, and different colored flowers, soft fragrances and various aromatic spices, where Grammar, Logic, noble Rhetoric, Geometry, and Arithmetic live and take their leisure. She went on her way until she came to the deep grotto of Apollo, god of learning, and found the brook and conduit of the fountain of Castalia, and took up the plectrum and quill of the harp and played sweet melodies, with the nymphs all the while leading the dance, that is, following the rules of harmony and musical accord.' From what Boccaccio says about her, it should be inferred that the profundity of both her understanding and of her learned books can only be known and understood by men of great perception and learning, according to the testimony of the ancients. Her writings and poems have survived to this day, most remarkably constructed and composed, and they serve as illumination and models of consummate poetic craft and composition to those who have come afterward. She invented different genres of lyric and poetry, short narratives, tearful laments and strange lamentations about love and other emotions, and these were so well made and so well ordered that they were named 'Sapphic' after her. Horace recounts, concerning her poems, that when Plato, the great philosopher who was Aristotle's teacher, died, a book of Sappho's poems was found under his pillow.

"In brief this lady was so outstanding in learning that in the city where she resided a statue of bronze in her image was dedicated in her name and erected in a prominent place so that she would be honored by all and be remembered forever. This lady was placed and counted among the greatest and most famous poets, and, according to Boccaccio, the honors of the diadems and crowns of kings and the miters of bishops are not any greater, nor are the crowns of laurel and victor's palm.

"I could tell you a great deal about women of great learning. Leontium was a Greek woman and also such a great philosopher that she dared, for impartial and serious reasons, to correct and attack the philosopher Theophrastus, who was quite famous in her time."

34. HERE SHE SPEAKS OF MINERVA, WHO INVENTED MANY SCIENCES AND THE TECHNIQUE OF MAKING ARMOR FROM IRON AND STEEL.

"Minerva, just as you have written elsewhere, was a maiden of Greece and surnamed Pallas. This maiden was of such excellence of mind that the foolish people of that time, because they did not know who her parents were and saw her doing things which had never been done before, said she was a goddess descended from Heaven; for the less they knew about her ancestry, the more marvelous her great knowledge seemed to them, when compared to that of the women of her time. She had a subtle mind, of profound understanding, not only in one subject but also generally, in every subject. Through her ingenuity she invented a shorthand Greek script in which a long written narrative could be transcribed with far fewer letters, and which is still used by the Greeks today, a fine invention whose discovery demanded great subtlety. She invented numbers and a means of quickly counting and adding sums. Her mind was so enlightened with general knowledge that she devised various skills and designs which had never before been discovered. She developed the entire technique of gathering wool and making cloth and was the first who ever thought to shear sheep of their wool and then to pick, comb, and card it with iron spindles and finally to spin it with a distaff, and then she invented the tools needed to make the cloth and also the method by which the wool should finally be woven.

"Similarly she initiated the custom of extracting oil from different fruits of the earth, also from olives, and of squeezing and pressing juice from other fruits. At the same time she discovered how to make wagons and carts to transport things easily from one place to another.

"This lady, in a similar manner, did even more, and it seems all the more remarkable because it is far removed from a woman's nature to conceive of such things; for she invented the art and technique of making harnesses and armor from iron and steel, which knights and armed soldiers employ in battle and with which they cover their bodies, and which she first gave to the Athenians whom she taught how to deploy an army and battalions and how to fight in organized ranks.

"Similarly she was the first to invent flutes and fifes, trumpets and wind instruments. With her considerable force of mind, this lady remained a virgin her entire life. Because of her outstanding chastity, the poets claimed in their fictions that Vulcan, the god of fire, wrestled with her for a long time and that finally she won and overcame him, which is to say that she overcame the ardor and lusts of the flesh which so strongly assail the young. The Athenians held this maiden in such high reverence that they worshiped her as a goddess and called her the goddess of arms and chivalry because she was the first to devise their use, and they also called her the goddess of knowledge because of her learnedness.

"After her death they erected a temple in Athens dedicated to her, and there they placed a statue of her, portraying a maiden, as a representation of wisdom and chivalry. This statue had terrible and cruel eyes because chivalry has been instituted to carry out rigorous justice; they also signified that one seldom knows toward what end the meditation of the wise man tends. She wore a helmet on her head which signified that a knight must have strength, endurance, and constant courage in the deeds of arms, and further signified that the counsels of the wise are concealed, secret, and hidden. She was dressed in a coat of mail which stood for the power of the estate of chivalry and also taught that the wise man is always armed against the whims of Fortune, whether good or bad. She held some kind of spear or very long lance, which meant that the knight must be the rod of justice and also signified that the wise man casts his spears from great distances. A buckler or shield of crystal hung at her neck, which meant that the knight must always be alert and oversee everywhere the defense of his country and people and further signified that things are open and evident to the wise man. She had portrayed in the middle of this shield the head of a serpent called Gorgon, which teaches that the knight must always be wary and watchful over his enemies like the serpent, and furthermore, that the wise man is aware of all the malice which can hurt him. Next to this image they also placed a bird that flies by night, named the owl, as if to watch over her, which signified that the knight must be ready by night as well as by day for civil defense, when necessary, and also that the wise man should take care at all times to do what is profitable and fitting for him. For a long time this lady was held in such high regard and her great fame spread so far that in many places temples were founded to praise her. Even long afterward, when the Romans were at the height of their power, they included her image among their gods."

36. AGAINST THOSE MEN WHO CLAIM IT IS NOT GOOD FOR WOMEN TO BE EDUCATED.

Following these remarks, I, Christine, spoke, "My lady, I realize that women have accomplished many good things and that even if evil women have done evil, it seems to me, nevertheless, that the benefits accrued and still accruing because of good women—particularly the wise and literary ones and those educated in the natural sciences whom I mentioned above—outweigh the evil. Therefore, I am amazed by the opinion of some men who claim that they do not want their daughters, wives, or kinswomen to be educated because their mores would be ruined as a result."

She responded, "Here you can clearly see that not all opinions of men are based on reason and that these men are wrong. For it must not be presumed that mores necessarily grow worse from knowing the moral sciences, which teach the virtues, indeed, there is not the slightest doubt that moral education amends and ennobles them. How could anyone think or believe that whoever follows good teaching or doctrine is the worse for it? Such an opinion cannot be expressed or maintained. I do not mean that it would be good for a man or a woman to study the art of divination or those fields of learning which are forbidden—for the holy Church did not remove them from common use without good reason—but it should not be believed that women are the worse for knowing what is good.

"Quintus Hortensius, a great rhetorician and consumately skilled orator in Rome, did not share this opinion. He had a daughter, named Hortensia, whom he greatly loved for the subtlety of her wit. He had her learn letters and study the science of rhetoric, which she mastered so thoroughly that she resembled her father Hortensius not only in wit and lively memory but also in her excellent delivery and order of speech—in fact, he surpassed her in nothing. As for the subject discussed above, concerning the good which comes about through women, the benefits realized by this woman and her learning were, among others, exceptionally remarkable. That is, during the time when Rome was governed by three men, this Hortensia began to support the cause of women and to undertake what no man dared to undertake. There was a question whether certain taxes should be levied on women and on their jewelry during a needy period in Rome. This woman's eloquence was so compelling that she was listened to, no less readily than her father would have been, and she won her case.

"Similarly, to speak of more recent times, without searching for examples in ancient history, Giovanni Andrea, a solemn law professor in Bologna not quite sixty years ago, was not of the opinion that it was bad for women to be educated. He had a fair and good daughter, named Novella, who was educated in the law to such an advanced degree that when he was occupied by some task and not at leisure to present his lectures to his students, he would send Novella, his daughter, in his place to lecture to the students from his chair. And to prevent her beauty from distracting the concentration of her audience, she had a little curtain drawn in front of her. In this manner she could on occasion supplement and lighten her father's occupation. He loved her so much that, to commemorate her name, he wrote a book of remarkable lectures on the law which he entitled *Novella super Decretalium,* after his daughter's name.

"Thus, not all men (and especially the wisest)

share the opinion that it is bad for women to be educated. But it is very true that many foolish men have claimed this because it displeased them that women knew more than they did. Your father, who was a great scientist and philosopher, did not believe that women were worth less by knowing science; rather, as you know, he took great pleasure from seeing your inclination to learning. The feminine opinion of your mother, however, who wished to keep you busy with spinning and silly girlishness, following the common custom of women, was the major obstacle to your being more involved in the sciences.

But just as the proverb already mentioned above says, 'No one can take away what Nature has given,' your mother could not hinder in you the feeling for the sciences which you, through natural inclination, had nevertheless gathered together in little droplets. I am sure that, on account of these things, you do not think you are worth less but rather that you consider it a great treasure for yourself; and you doubtless have reason to."

And I, Christine, replied to all of this, "Indeed, my lady, what you say is as true as the Lord's Prayer."

Glossary

Terms *italicized* within the definitions are themselves defined within the glossary.

a capella Music sung without instrumental accompaniment.

abacus (1) The slab that forms the upper part of a *capital*. (2) A computing device using movable counters.

Academy Derived from *Akademeia,* the name of the garden where Plato taught his students, the term came to be applied to official (generally conservative) teaching establishments.

accompaniment The musical background to a melody.

acoustics The science of the nature and character of sound.

Acropolis Literally, the high point of a Greek city, frequently serving as refuge in time of war. The best-known is the Acropolis of Athens.

aesthetic Pertaining to the pleasure derived from a work of art, as opposed to any practical or informative value it might have. In philosophy, aesthetics is the study of the nature of art and its relation to human experience.

agora In ancient Greek cities, the open market place, often used for public meetings.

aisle In church *architecture,* the long open spaces parallel to the *nave.*

allegory A dramatic or artistic device in which the superficial sense is accompanied by a deeper or more profound meaning.

altar In ancient religion, a table at which offerings were made or victims sacrificed. In Christian churches, a raised structure at which the sacrament of the Eucharist is consecrated, forming the center of the ritual.

altarpiece A painted or sculptured *panel* placed above and behind an altar to inspire religious devotion.

alto The lowest range of the female voice, also called contralto.

ambulatory Covered walkway around the *apse* of a church.

amphora Greek wine jar.

anthropomorphism The endowing of nonhuman objects or forces with human characteristics.

antiphony Music in which two or more *voices* alternate with one another.

apse Eastern end of a church, generally semicircular, in which the *altar* is housed.

architecture The art and science of designing and constructing buildings for human use.

architrave The lowest division of an *entablature.*

archivault The molding that frames an arch.

Ars Nova Latin for "the New Art." Describes the more complex new music of the 14th century, marked by richer harmonies and elaborate rhythmic devices.

atelier Workshop.

atrium An open court in a Roman house or in front of a church.

aulos Greek wind instrument, similar to an oboe but consisting of two pipes.

axis Imaginary line around which the elements of a painting, sculpture, or building are organized; the direction and focus of these elements establishes the axis.

ballad Narrative poem or song with simple stanzas and a refrain that is usually repeated at the end of each stanza.

basilica Originally a large hall used in Roman times for public meetings, law courts, and the like; later applied to a specific type of early Christian church.

bas-relief Low relief; see *relief.*

bass The lowest range of the male voice.

black figure A technique used in Greek vase painting that involved painting figures in black paint in silhouette and incising details with a sharp point. It was used throughout the Archaic period. Compare *red figure.*

Bronze Age The period during which bronze (an alloy of copper and tin) was the chief material for tools and weapons. It began in Europe around 3000 B.C. and ended around 1000 B.C. with the introduction of iron.

buttress An exterior architectural support.

caliph An Arabic term for leader or ruler.

campanile In Italy the belltower of a church, often standing next to but separate from the church building.

canon From the Greek meaning "rule" or "standard." In *architecture* it is a standard of proportion. In literature it is the authentic list of an author's works. In music it is the melodic line sung by overlapping voices. In religious terms it represents the authentic books in the Bible or the authoritative prayer of the Eucharist in the Mass or the authoritative law of the church promulgated by ecclesiastical authority.

cantata Italian word for a piece of music that is sung rather than played; an instrumental piece is known as a *sonata.*

cantus firmus Latin for "fixed song," a system of structuring a *polyphonic* composition around a preselected melody by adding new melodies above and/or below. The technique was used by medieval and Renaissance composers.

canzoniere The Italian word for songbook.

capital The head, or crowning part, of a column, taking the weight of the *entablature.*

capitulary A collection of rules or regulations sent out by a legislative body.

caryatid A sculptured female figure that serves the function of a column.

cast A molded replica made by a process whereby plaster, wax, clay, or metal is poured in liquid form into a mold. When the material had hardened the mold is removed, leaving a replica of the original from which the mold was taken.

catharsis Literally "purgation" in Greek. Technical term used by Aristotle to describe the emotional effect upon the spectator of a tragic drama.

cathedra The bishop's throne. From that word comes the word cathedral—a church where a bishop officiates.

cella Inner shrine of a Greek or Roman temple.

ceramics Objects made of baked clay, such as vases and other forms of pottery, tiles, and small sculptures.

chancel The part of a church east of the *nave;* includes choir and *sanctuary.*

chanson de geste Song of heroic deeds; epic poems and tales disseminated by poets and *jongleurs.*

chant A single line of unaccompanied melody in free rhythm. The term is most frequently used for liturgical music such as Gregorian or Ambrosian chant.

chapel A small space within a church or a secular building such as a palace or castle, containing an *altar* consecrated for ritual use.

chapter The body of priests who advise a bishop and conduct services at the cathedral.

chevet The eastern (altar) end of a church.

choir The part of a church *chancel* between *nave* and *sanctuary* where the monks sang the office; a group of singers.

chord Any combination of three or more notes sounded together.

chorus In ancient Greek drama, a group of performers who comment collectively on the main action. The term came to be used, like *choir,* for a group of singers.

cithara An elaborate seven-string *lyre* used in Greek and Roman music.

Classical Generally applied to the civilizations of Greece and Rome, more specifically to Greek art and culture in the 5th and 4th centuries B.C. Later imitations of classical styles are called neoclassical. Classical is also often used as a broad definition of excellence: a "classic" can date to any period.

clef French for "key." In written music the term denotes the sign placed at the beginning of the *staff* to indicate the range of notes it contains.

clerestory A row of windows in a wall above an adjoining roof.

cloister The enclosed garden of a monastery, surrounded by a covered walkway; by extension the monastery itself. Also, a covered walkway alone.

codex A manuscript volume.

coffer In *architecture,* a recessed panel in a ceiling.

colonnade A row of columns.

comedy An amusing and light-hearted play intended to provoke laughter on the part of the spectator.

composer The writer of a piece of music.

composition Generally, the arrangement or organization of the elements that make up a work of art. Particularly, a piece of music.

consul One of two Roman officials elected annually to serve as the highest state magistrates in the Republic.

contralto See *alto.*

Corinthian An order of *architecture* that was popular at Rome, marked by elaborately decorated *capitals* bearing acanthus leaves. Compare *Doric, Ionic.*

cornice The upper part of an *entablature.*

counterpoint Two or more distinct melodic lines sung or played simultaneously in a single unified composition.

cruciform Arranged or shaped like a cross.

crypt A *vaulted* chamber, completely or partially underground, which usually contains a *chapel.* Found in a church under the *choir.*

cult A system of religious belief and its followers.

cuneiform A system of writing, common in the ancient Near East, using characters made up of wedge shapes. Compare *hieroglyphics.*

design The overall conception or scheme of a work of art. In the visual arts, the organization of a work's *composition* based on the arrangement of lines or contrast between light and dark.

dialectics A logical process of arriving at the truth by putting in juxtaposition contrary propositions; a term often used in medieval philosophy and theology.

diatonic The seven notes of a major or minor *scale,* corresponding to the piano's white *keys* in an *octave.*

dithyramb Choral hymn, often wild and violent, to the Greek god Dionysus. Later, any violent song, speech, or writing. Compare *paean.*

dome A hemispherical *vault.*

dominant The fifth note of a *diatonic scale.*

Doric One of the Greek orders of *architecture,* simple and austere in style. Compare *Corinthian, Ionic.*

dramatis personae The characters in a play.

dynamics In music, the various levels of loudness and softness of sound, together with their increase and decrease.

echinus The lower part of a capital.

elevation In *architecture,* a drawing of the side of a building which does not show perspective.

encaustic A painting technique using molten wax colored by pigments.

entablature The part of a Greek or Roman temple above the columns, normally consisting of *architrave, frieze,* and *cornice.*

entasis The characteristic swelling of a Greek column at a point about a third above its base.

epic A long narrative poem celebrating the exploits of a heroic character.

Epicurean A follower of the Greek philosopher Epicurus, who held that pleasure was the chief aim in life.

epithet Adjective used to describe the special characteristics of a person or object.

ethos Greek word meaning "character." In general, that which distinguishes a particular work of art and gives it character. More specifically, a term used by the Greeks to describe the moral and ethical character they ascribed to music.

Evangelist One of the authors of the four *gospels* in the Bible: Matthew, Mark, Luke, and John.

façade The front of a building.

flat A symbol (♭) used in music to signify that the note it precedes should be lowered by one half step.

flute Architectural term for the vertical grooves on Greek (and later) columns.

foreshortening The artistic technique whereby a sense of depth and three-dimensionality is obtained by the use of receding lines.

form The arrangement of the general structure of a work of art.

fresco A painting technique that employs the use of pigments on wet plaster.

friar A member of one of the religious orders of begging brothers founded in the Middle Ages.

frieze The middle section of an *entablature*. A band of painted or carved decoration often running around the outside of a Greek or Roman temple.

gallery A long, narrow room or corridor such as the spaces above the *aisles* of a church.

genre A type or category of art. In the visual arts, the depiction of scenes from everyday life.

glaze In oil painting, a transparent layer of paint laid over a dried painted canvas. In *ceramics,* a thin coating of clay fused to the piece by firing in a kiln.

gospels The four biblical accounts of the life of Jesus, ascribed to Matthew, Mark, Luke, and John. Compare *Evangelists.*

graphic Pertaining to description and demonstration by visual means.

Greek cross A cross with arms of equal length.

Gregorian chant *Monophonic* religious music usually sung without accompaniment. Called plainsong. Compare *melisma, neum, trope.*

ground Coating applied to a surface to prepare it for painting.

guilloche A decorative band made up of interlocking lines of design.

hamartia Literally, "failure" or "error." Term used by Aristotle to describe the character flaw which would cause the tragic end of an otherwise noble hero.

harmony The *chords* or vertical structure of a piece of music; the relationships existing between simultaneously sounding notes and *chord* progressions.

hedonism The philosophical theory that material pleasure is the principal good in life.

hierarchy A system of ordering people or things that places them in higher and lower ranks.

hieroglyphics A system of writing in which the characters consist of realistic or stylized pictures of actual objects, animals, or human beings (whole or part). The Egyptian hieroglyphic script is the best known, but by no means the only one. Compare *cuneiform.*

high relief See *relief.*

hippodrome A race course for horses and chariots. Compare *spina.*

homophony Music in which a single melody is supported by a harmonious accompaniment. Compare *monophonic.*

hubris The Greek word for "insolence" or "excessive pride."

hymn A religious song of praise and adoration.

icon Greek word for "image." Panel paintings used in the Orthodox church as representations of divine realities.

iconography The set of symbols and allusions that gives meaning to a complex work of art.

ideal The depiction of people, objects, and scenes according to an idealized, preconceived model.

idol An image of a deity that serves as the object of worship.

image The representation of a human or nonhuman subject or an event.

imitation In music, the restatement of a melodic idea in different voice parts of a *contrapuntal* composition.

impasto Paint laid on in thick textures.

improvisation In musical performance, the spontaneous invention of music for voice or instrument.

incising Cutting into a surface with a sharp instrument.

intercolumniation The horizontal distance between the central points of adjacent columns in a Greek or Roman temple.

interval Musical term for the difference in pitch between two musical notes.

Ionic One of the Greek orders of *architecture;* elaborate and graceful in style. Compare *Doric, Corinthian.*

Iron Age The period beginning in Europe around 1000 B.C. during which iron was the chief material used for tools and weapons.

isorhythmic *Polyphonic* music in which the various sections are unified by repeated rhythmic patterns but the melodies are varied.

jamb Upright piece of a window or door frame, often decorated in medieval churches.

jongleur Wandering minstrel. A professional musician, actor, or mime who went from place to place offering entertainment.

key (1) The tonal center around which a composer bases a musical work. (2) The mechanism by which a keyboard instrument (piano, organ, etc.) or wind instrument (clarinet, bassoon, etc.) is made to sound.

keystone Central stone of an arch.

kore Type of standing female statue produced in Greece in the Archaic period.

kouros Type of standing male statue, generally nude, produced in Greece in the Archaic period.

lancet A pointed window frame of a medieval Gothic cathedral.

landscape In the visual arts, the depiction of scenery in nature.

Latin cross A cross with a vertical arm longer than the horizontal arm.

lekythos Small Greek vase for oil or perfume, often used during funeral ceremonies.

lintel The piece that spans two upright posts.

liturgy Rites used in public and official religious worship.

loggia A gallery open on one or more sides, often with arches.

low relief See *relief.*

lunette Semicircular space in wall for window or decoration.

lyre Small stringed instrument used in Greek and Roman music. Compare *cithara.*

lyric (1) Words or verses written to be set to music. (2) Descriptive of a work of art that is poetic, personal, even ecstatic in spirit.

madonna Italian for "my Lady." Used of the Virgin Mary.

madrigal *Polyphonic* song for three or more voices, with verses set to the same music and a refrain set to different music.

mandorla Almond-shaped light area surrounding a sacred personage in a work of art.

Mass The most sacred rite of the Catholic *liturgy.*

matroneum Gallery for women in

churches, especially those in the Byzantine tradition.

mausoleum Burial chapel or shrine.

meander Decorative pattern in the form of a maze, commonly found in Greek Geometric art.

melisma In *Gregorian chant,* singing an intricate chain of notes on one syllable. Compare *trope.*

metopes Square slabs often decorated with sculpture that alternated with *triglyphs* to form the *frieze* of a *Doric* temple.

Minnesingers German medieval musicians of the aristocratic class who composed songs of love and chivalry. Compare *troubadors.*

mode (1) In ancient and medieval music an arrangement of notes forming a scale that, by the character of intervals, determines the nature of the composition. Compare *tetrachord.* (2) In modern music one of the two classes, major or minor, into which musical scales are divided.

modulation In music, movement from one *key* to another.

monastery A place where monks live in communal style for spiritual purposes.

monochrome A single color or variations on a single color.

monophonic From the Greek meaning "one voice." Describes music that consists of a single melodic line. Compare *polyphonic.*

mosaic Floor or wall decoration consisting of small pieces of stone, ceramic, shell, or glass set into plaster or cement.

motet (1) Musical composition, developed in the 13th century, in which words (French *mots*) were added to fragments of *Gregorian chant.* (2) In 16th-century composition, four- or five-voiced sacred work, generally based on a Latin text.

mullions The lines dividing windows into separate units.

mural Wall painting or mosaics attached to a wall.

myth Story or legend whose origin is unknown; myths often help explain a cultural tradition or cast light on a historical event.

narthex The porch or vestibule of a church.

natural In music, the sign (♮) that cancels any previously indicated *sharp* or *flat.*

nave From the Latin for "ship." The central space of a church.

Neanderthal Early stage in the development of the human species, lasting from before 100,000 B.C. to around 35,000 B.C.

Neolithic Last part of the Stone Age, when agricultural skills had been developed but stone was still the principal material for tools and weapons. It began in the Near East around 8000 B.C. and in Europe around 6000 B.C.

neum The basic symbol used in the notation of *Gregorian chant.*

niche A hollow recess or indentation in a wall to hold a statue or other object.

notation The system of writing in symbols music that can be reproduced in performance.

obelisk A rectangular shaft of stone that tapers to a pyramidal point.

octave The *interval* from one note to the next with the same pitch as from C to the C above or below.

oculus A circular, eyelike window or opening.

oil painting Painting in a medium made up of powdered colors bound together with oil, generally linseed.

opus Latin for "work." Used for chronological lists of composers' works.

Opus Dei Latin for "work of God." Used to describe the choral offices of monks sung during the hours of the day.

oral composition The composition and transmission of works of literature by word of mouth, as in the case of the Homeric epics.

Orchestra (1) In Greek theaters, the circular space in front of the stage in which the *chorus* moves. (2) A group of instrumentalists who come together to perform musical *compositions.*

Order (1) In *classical architecture,* a specific form of column and *entablature;* see *Doric, Ionic,* and *Corinthian.* (2) More generally, the arrangement imposed on the various elements in a work of art.

organum An early form of *polyphonic* music in which one or more melody lines were sung along with

the song line of plainsong. Compare *Gregorian chant.*

Orientalizing Term used to describe Greek art of the 7th century B.C. that was influenced by Eastern artistic styles.

paean A Greek hymn to Apollo and other gods, either praying for help or giving thanks for help already received. Later generally applied to any song of praise or triumph. Compare *dithyramb.*

Paleolithic The Old Stone Age, during which human beings appeared and manufactured tools for the first time. It began around two and a half million years ago.

palette (1) The tray on which a painter mixes colors. (2) The range and combination of colors typical of a particular painter.

panel A rigid, flat support, generally square or rectangular, usually of wood, for a painting.

pantheon The collected gods. By extension, a temple to them. In modern usage a public building containing the tombs or memorials of famous people.

Pantocrator From the Greek meaning "one who rules or dominates all." Used for those figures of God and/or Christ found in the *apses* of Byzantine churches.

parallelism A literary device, common in the psalms, of either repeating or imaging one line of poetry with another which uses different words but expresses the same thought.

pathos That aspect of a work of art which evokes sympathy or pity.

pediment The triangular space formed by the roof *cornices* on a Greek or Roman temple.

pendentives Triangular architectural devices used to support a dome of a structure; the dome may rest directly on the pendentives. Compare *squinches.*

peripatetic Greek for "walking around." Specifically applied to followers of the philosopher Aristotle.

peristyle An arcade (usually of columns) around the outside of a building. The term is often applied to temple *architecture.*

perspective A technique in the visual arts for producing on a flat or shallow surface the effect of three dimensions and deep space.

pietà An image of the Virgin with the dead Christ.

pilaster In *architecture,* a pillar in *relief.*

pitch In music the relative highness or lowness of a note as established by the frequency of vibrations occurring per second within it.

plainsong See *Gregorian chant.*

plan An architectural drawing showing in two dimensions the arrangement of space in a building.

podium A base, platform, or pedestal for a building, statue, or monument.

polis The Greek word for "city," used to designate the independent city-states of ancient Greece.

polychrome Several colors. Compare *monochrome.*

polyphonic From the Greek meaning "many voices." Describes a musical composition built from the simultaneous interweaving of different melodic lines into a single whole. Compare *monophonic.*

portal A door, usually of a church or cathedral.

portico A porch with a roof supported by columns.

presocratic Collective term for all Greek philosophers before the time of Socrates.

prophet From the Greek meaning "one who speaks for another." In the Hebrew and Christian tradition, one who speaks with the authority of God. In a secondary meaning, one who speaks about the future with authority.

proportion The relation of one part to another, and each part to the whole, in respect of size, whether of height, width, length, or depth.

prosody The art of setting words to music.

prototype An original model or form on which later works are based.

Psalter Another name for the book of Psalms from the Bible.

red figure technique used in Greek vase painting that involved painting red figures on a black background and adding details with a brush. Compare *black figure.*

relief Sculptural technique whereby figures are carved out of a block of stone, part of which is left behind to form a background. Depending on the degree to which the figures project, the relief is described as either high or low.

reliquary A small casket or shrine in which sacred relics are kept.

requiem A *Mass* for the dead.

sanctuary In religion, a sacred place. The part of a church where the altar is placed.

sarcophagus From the Greek meaning "flesh-eater." A stone (usually limestone) coffin.

satire An amusing exposure of folly and vice that aims to produce moral reform.

satyr Greek mythological figure usually shown with an animal's ears and tail.

scale (1) In music, a succession of notes arranged in ascending or descending order. (2) More generally, the relative or proportional size of an object or image.

score The written form of a piece of music in which all the parts are shown.

scriptorium That room in a medieval *monastery* in which manuscripts were copied and illuminated.

section An architectural drawing showing the side of a building.

secular Not sacred; relating to the worldly.

sequence In music, the repetition of a melodic phrase at different pitches.

sharp In music, a sign (♯) which raises the note it precedes by one half step.

silhouette The definition of a form by its outline.

skolion Greek drinking song, generally sung at banquets.

sonnet A fourteen-line poem, either eight lines (octave) and six lines (sestet) or three quatrains of four lines with an ending couplet. Often attributed to Petrarch, the form—keeping the basic fourteen lines—was modified by such poets as Spenser, Shakespeare, and Milton.

soprano The highest register of the female voice.

spina A monument at the center of a stadium or *hippodrome,* usually in the form of a triangular *obelisk.*

squinches Either columns or *lintels* used in corners of a room to carry the weight of a superimposed mass.

Their use resembles that of *pendentives.*

staff The five horizontal lines, with four spaces between, on which musical notation is written.

stele Upright stone slab decorated with relief carvings, frequently used as a grave marker.

still life A painting of objects such as fruit, flowers, dishes, and the like arranged to form a pleasing composition.

stoa A roofed *colonnade,* generally found in ancient Greek open markets, that provides space for shops and shelter.

Stoic Pertaining to a school of Greek philosophy, later popular at Rome, which taught that the universe is governed by Reason and that Virtue is the only good in life.

stretcher A wooden or metal frame on which a painter's canvas is stretched.

stylobate The upper step on which the columns of a Greek temple stand.

summa The summation of a body of learning, particularly in the fields of philosophy and theology.

symmetry An arrangement in which various elements are so arranged as to parallel one another on either side of an *axis.*

tabernacle A container for a sacred object; a receptacle on the altar of a Catholic church that contains the Eucharist.

tempera A painting technique using coloring mixed with egg yolk, glue, or casein.

tempo In music, the speed at which the notes are performed.

tenor The highest range of the male voice. In medieval *organum,* the voice that holds the melody of the plainsong.

terra cotta Italian meaning "baked earth." Baked clay used for *ceramics.* Sometimes refers to the reddish-brown color of baked clay.

tesserae The small pieces of colored stone used for the creation of a *mosaic.*

tetrachord Musical term for a series of four notes. Two tetrachords formed a *mode.*

theme In music, a short melody or a self-contained musical phrase.

tholos Term in Greek *architecture* for a round building.

timbre The particular quality of sound produced by a voice or instrument.

toga Flowing woollen garment worn by Roman citizens.

tonic The first and principal note of a *key,* serving as a point of departure and return.

tragedy A serious drama in which the principal character is often brought to disaster by his/her *hamartia* or tragic flaw.

transept In a cruciform church, the entire part set at right angles to the *nave.*

treble In music, the higher voices, whose music is written on a *staff* marked by a treble *clef.*

triglyphs Rectangular slabs divided by two vertical grooves into three vertical bands; these alternate with *metopes* to form the *frieze* of a *Doric* temple.

triptych A painting consisting of three panels. A painting with two panels is called a diptych; one with several panels is a polyptych.

trompe l'oeil From the French meaning "to fool the eye." A painting technique by which the viewer seems to see real subjects or objects instead of their artistic representation.

trope In *Gregorian chant,* words added to a long *melisma.*

troubadors Aristocratic southern French musicians of the Middle Ages who composed *secular* songs with themes of love and chivalry; called trouvères in northern France. Compare *Minnesingers.*

trumeau A supporting pillar for a church *portal,* common in medieval churches.

tympanum The space, usually decorated, above a *portal,* between a *lintel* and an arch.

unison The sound that occurs when two or more voices or instruments simultaneously produce the same note or melody at the same *pitch.*

vault A roof composed of arches of masonry or cement construction.

volutes Spirals that form an *Ionic capital.*

votive An offering made to a deity either in support of a request or in gratitude for the fulfillment of an earlier prayer.

voussoirs Wedge-shaped blocks in an arch.

ziggurat An Assyrian or Babylonian stepped pyramid.

Index

References are to page numbers. **Boldface** numbers indicate illustrations and literary selections. Works are listed under the names of their creators, when known; otherwise under their titles. Architectural works and the art associated with them are listed under the cities in which they are located. Unless re-peated in the text, events cited in the chapter-opening chronologies are not indexed. Many technical terms are included in the Index, with references to their text definitions. For a more complete list of terms, consult the Glossary.

Literary Acknowledgments

Photographic Credits

The authors and publisher wish to thank the custodians of the works of art for supplying photographs and granting permission to use them. Photographs have been obtained from sources noted in the captions, unless listed below.

A/AR: Alinari/Art Resource, New York
AF: Alison Frantz, Princeton, New Jersey
AM: Ann Munchow, Aachen, West Germany
B/AR: Borromeo/Art Resource, New York
BAM/AR: Bildarchiv Marburg/Art Resource, New York
BPK: Bildarchiv Preuissicher Kulturbesitz, West Berlin
Br/AR: Bridgeman/Art Resource, New York
CNMHS: Caisse Nationale des Monuments Historiques et des Sites, Paris
DAI: Deutsches Archaeologisches Institut, Athens
FU: Fototeca Unione at the American Academy, Rome
G/AR: Giraudon/Art Resource, New York
H: Hirmer, Munich
NYPL: New York Public Library, Astor, Lenox and Tilden Foundations
PR: Photo Researchers, New York
RMN: Service de Documentation Photographique de la Reunion des Musees Nationaux, Paris
RS: Ronald Sheridan Photo Library/Ancient Art and Architecture Collection, London
S/AR: Scala/Art Resource, New York

References are to figure numbers (**boldface**).
Cover: S/AR.
Chapter 1 **1.1:** Colorphoto Hans Hinz, Allschwil-Basel. **1.2, 1.3:** H. **1.4:** Hamilton Wright, Inc., New York. **1.5, 1.6:** H. **1.7:** BPK/Margarete Busing. **1.8:** BPK. **1.9:** Photography by the Egyptian Expedition, The Metropolitan Museum of Art, New York. **1.10:** George Holton/PR. **1.11:** Top—Ashmolean Museum, Oxford; bottom—H. **1.12, 1.13, 1.14, 1.15, 1.16:** H. **1.17:** G/AR. **1.21:** B/AR. **1.22:** After S. Marinatos, *Kreta und das Mykenische Hellas,* Hirmer Verlag, Munchen, 1959, fig. 4/NYPL. **1.23:** J. Edwards/Robert Harding Picture Library. **1.24:** H. **1.25:** RS: **1.26, 1.27:** H. **1.28:** Painting and photo by Alton S. Tobey, Larchmont, New York.
Chapter 2 **2.1:** S/AR. **2.3, 2.4:** DAI. **2.5, 2.6, 2.7:** H. **2.8:** DAI. **2.10, 2.11, 2.12:** H. **2.13:** A/AR. **2.14, 2.15, 2.16:** H. **2.18:** John Lewis Stage/Image Bank. **2.21:** H. **2.22:** DAI.
Chapter 3 **3.1:** Paul Warchol, New York. **3.2:** A/AR. **3.3:** RS. **3.5:** David Seymour/Magnum Photos, New York. **3.6:** AR. **3.7:** S/AR. **3.9, 3.10:** H. **3.11:** Reconstruction drawing: from Helmut Berve and Gottfried Gruben, *Griechische Tempel und Heiligtumer,* Hirmer Verlag, Munchen, 1964, fig. 10/NYPL. **3.12:** AF. **3.14:** Photo: H; plan:—After Isobel Grinnell. *Greek Temples,* Metropolitan Museum of Art, 1943, p. 34/NYPL. **3.15, 3.16, 3.17, 3.18:** H. **3.19:** S/AR. **3.20:** Courtesy Professor Manolis Andronikos. **3.21:** S/AR.

3.22: A/AR. **3.23:** Barbara Malter/Capitoline Museums, Rome. **3.25:** After *Milet, Ergebnisse d. Ausgrabungen,* II, 3 (1935). From J.B. Ward-Perkins, *Cities of Ancient Greece and Italy: Planning in Classical Antiquity,* BrazIller, New York, 1974, fig. 7/NYPL **3.26:** S/AR. **3.27:** H. **3.28:** From Hermann Thiersch, *Pharos Antike, Islam und Occident,* B.G. Teubner, Leipzig, 1909, opp. title page/NYPL. **3.31:** S/AR.
Chapter 4 **4.2:** A/AR. **4.3:** German Archaeological Institute, Rome. **4.4:** Estate of Leonard von Matt, Stansstad, Switzerland. **4.5:** A/AR. **4.6:** Graziano Paiella, Rome. **4.7:** S/AR. **4.8:** After H. Kahler, "Das Fortunaheiligtum von Palestrina Praeneste," in *Annales Universitatis Saraviensis,* vol. VII, Saarbruken, 1958, page 198/NYPL. **4.9:** RMN. **4.10:** S/AR. **4.11:** A/AR. **4.12:** FU. **4.13:** A/AR. **4.14:** FU. **4.15:** A/AR. **4.16:** A/AR. **4.17, 4.18:** S/AR. **4.19:** FU. **4.20:** A/AR. **4.22:** © Jan Halaska 1985/PR. **4.24, 4.25, 4.26:** FU. **4.27:** S/AR. **4.28, 4.29, 4.30:** A/AR. **Interlude p. 168:** Culver Pictures, New York. **p. 170:** Angus McBean Photograph/Harvard Theatre Collection.
Chapter 5 **5.1:** Lee C. Ellenberger for The American Schools of Oriental Research, Philadelphia. **5.2:** A/AR. **5.3:** Andre Held, Ecublens. **5.5:** A/AR. **5.6:** Robert Harding Picture Library, London. **5.7:** Zev Radovan, Jerusalem. **5.10:** From Kenneth John Conant, *Early Medieval Church Architecture,* The Johns Hopkins Press, Baltimore, 1942, Plate VIb/NYPL.
Chapter 6 **6.2:** Ara Guler, Istanbul. **6.3:** Wim

Swaan, New York. **6.4:** H. **6.5:** S/AR. **6.6:** A/AR. **6.7:** S/AR. **6.9, 6.10:** Estate of Leonard von Matt, Stansstad, Switzerland. **6.11:** H. **6.12:** RS. **6.13:** A/AR. **6.14, 6.15:** Fotocielo, Rome. **6.16:** S/AR. **6.17, 6.18:** A/AR. **6.19:** Estate of Leonard von Matt, Stansstad, Switzerland. **6.20:** H. **6.21:** Reproduced through the courtesy of the Michigan-Princeton-Alexandria Expedition to Mount Sinai. **6.22:** RS.

Chapter 7 **7.2:** From *The Dramas of Hrotsvit of Gandersheim,* trans. with introd. by Katharina M. Wilson. Matrologia Latina, Peregrina Publishing Company, 1985/Special Collections, Ellis Library, University of Missouri-Columbia. **7.3, 7.4, 7.6:** AM. **7.8:** G/AR. **7.10:** AM. **7.11:** After Walter Horn and Ernest Born, *The Plan of St. Gall,* University of California Press, 1979, vol. II, p. xii © 1979 Walter Horn and Ernest Born/Univ. of Cal. Press. **7.12:** After Kenneth J. Conant, *Carolingian and Romanesques Architecture,* The Pelican History of Art, second integrated editions revised, 1978, p. 159, fig. 113/4. copyright © Kenneth John Conant 1978/NYPL. **7.13:** H. Roger Viollet, Paris. **7.14:** BAM/AR. **7.16:** CNMHS. **7.17:** J.E. Bulloz, Paris.

Chapter 8 **8.1:** top—After Professor Sumner McK. Crosby, Yale University: bottom—BAM/AR. **8.2:** Mikael Audrain/Editions Arthaud, Paris/fapc. **8.3:** From: Banister Fletcher, *A History of Architecture,* 18th edition, p. 584; Copyright Royal Institute of British Architects, University of London, permission granted by Athalone Press, London. **8.4:** A. F. Kersting, London. **8.5:** Wim Swaan, New York. **8.6:** CNMHS. **8.7:** A/AR. **8.8:** A.F. Kersting, London. **8.9:** G/AR. **8.11:** James Austin, Cambridge, England. **8.12:** BPK. **8.13:** A/AR. **8.14:** Colorphoto Hans Hinz, Allschwil-Basel. **8.15:** S/AR. **8.16:** A/AR. **Interlude p. 347:** Theatre World Collection, New York.

Chapter 9 **9.1:** CNMHS **9.2, 9.3, 9.4:** A/AR. **9.5, 9.6:** S/AR. **9.7** A/AR. **9.8:** Soprintendenza alle Gallerie, Florence. **9.9, 9.10, 9.11:** S/AR. **9.12, 9.13:** A/AR. **9.15:** Br/AR. **9.16:** CNMHS. **9.17. 9.18:** Photographie Giraudon, Paris. **9.19, 9.20, 9.21:** A/AR. **9.22:** G. Barone, Shostal. **9.23:** A.F. Kersting, London. **9.24:** (Ms. Harl. 4425 fol. 12 v.).

Figs. 7.15, 7.16, 8.6, 9.1, 9.16: Copyright 1990 ARS N.Y./ARCH. PHOT. PARIS.